Apologia Pro Vita Sua and Six Sermons

JOHN HENRY CARDINAL NEWMAN

Apologia Pro Vita Sua and Six Sermons

Edited, annotated, and with an
Introduction by Frank M. Turner

Yale University Press
New Haven &
London

Copyright © 2008 by Yale University.
All rights reserved.
This book may not be reproduced, in whole or in part, including illustrations, in any form (beyond that copying permitted by Sections 107 and 108 of the U.S. Copyright Law and except by reviewers for the public press), without written permission from the publishers.

Set in Sabon type by Keystone Typesetting, Inc.
Printed in the United States of America.

Library of Congress Control Number: 2007938703
ISBN 978-0-300-11507-9
ISBN 978-0-300-17786-2 (pbk.)

A catalogue record for this book is available from the British Library.

10 9 8 7 6 5 4 3 2 1

Contents

Editor's Preface *vii*
Editor's Introduction: The Newman of the *Apologia* and
    the Newman of History *1*

Apologia Pro Vita Sua: Being a History of His Religious Opinions
    Preface *119*
        Chapter I. History of My Religious Opinions to the Year 1833 *131*
        Chapter II. History of My Religious Opinions from 1833 to 1839 *163*
        Chapter III. History of My Religious Opinions from 1839 to 1841 *208*
        Chapter IV. History of My Religious Opinions from 1841 to 1845 *252*
        Chapter V. Position of My Mind since 1845 *320*

Editor's Preface to Newman's Notes *354*
Note A. On page 144. Liberalism *359*
Note B. On page 152. Ecclesiastical Miracles *370*
Note C. On page 257. Sermon on Wisdom and Innocence *379*
Note D. On page 301. Series of Saints' Lives of 1843–4 *389*
Note E. On page 312. The Anglican Church *408*
Note F. On page 343. The Economy *412*
Note G. On page 350. Lying and Equivocation *416*

Editor's Preface to Newman's Supplemental Matter 427
Supplemental Matter 429
    I. Letters and Papers of the Author Used in the Course of This Work 429
    II. List of the Author's Publications 431
    III. Letter of Approbation and Encouragement from the Bishop of the Diocese of Birmingham, Dr. Ullathorne 433
    IV. Letters of Approbation and Encouragement from Clergy and Laity 436

Editor's Appendix: Six Sermons by John Henry Newman 445
    Obedience to God the Way to Faith in Christ 448
    Religious Emotion 457
    The Religious Use of Excited Feelings 464
    Sudden Conversions 471
    Wisdom and Innocence 478
    The Parting of Friends 487

Index 497

Editor's Introduction
The Newman of the *Apologia* and the Newman of History

Sometimes a life provides the makings for successful autobiography; in other instances an autobiography itself embeds a life in history and cultural memory. The latter is the case with John Henry Newman's *Apologia Pro Vita Sua: Being a History of His Religious Opinions,* first published in 1864 as a series of pamphlets and then with extensive revisions in 1865 as a book. Without the *Apologia,* his apology in the sense of a self-defense of the religious journey embodied in his life, Newman, who a generation earlier had dominated Victorian religious life, might well have ended his days in the relative obscurity of the Roman Catholic Birmingham Oratory with his former Anglican life encased in perplexing mystery and his writings languishing as curiosities on used bookshop shelves. Instead, the *Apologia* transformed Newman into a religious, literary, and cultural icon world-renowned for his spiritual journey from evangelical Protestantism to Roman Catholicism, honored in 1879 by Pope Leo XIII as a cardinal, and, in the late twentieth century, set on the path to possible sainthood. Because of the *Apologia* Newman stands as the only Victorian author of Christian theological prose to enjoy a substantial, engaged transatlantic readership in 2000 as well as 1900.

Newman had led a controversial ecclesiastical life in both the Church of England and the Roman Catholic Church and by 1864 bore a tarnished reputation in each communion. But the *Apologia,* which Newman composed in a furiously energized response to Charles Kingsley's charge that he and other Roman Catholic clergy did not value truth for its own sake, almost overnight rehabilitated Newman throughout the English-speaking religious world. Indeed, from 1864 onward Newman's reputation rode the wave of the favorable response to the *Apologia*. The reception of the *Apologia* and consequent restoration of Newman's reputation in turn led to the republication of numerous of his Anglican and previous Roman Catholic writings from that time to the present.

The *Apologia* furthermore immediately achieved a privileged place among English autobiographies, with many readers and commentators assuming that it provided the last word on Newman's years in the Anglican Church.[1] The narrative thus constituted the single most important framework for most future considerations not only of Newman's life but also of the Tractarian Movement (also frequently termed the Oxford Movement), which he had led between 1833 and 1845 and for which in 1864 there as yet existed no published history. All later Victorian biographers of Newman and historians of the Tractarian era as well as the early editors of his correspondence from his Anglican years used the *Apologia* as their point of interpretive departure and only rarely turned to the vast body of other contemporary printed and manuscript sources. This scholarly lassitude continued throughout the twentieth century, with historians and biographers more often than not refraining from significant exploration of other easily available historical documentation that challenged Newman's self-portrait, supplied additional important information, and provided alternative viewpoints regarding both Newman and the Tractarians.[2] The as-

---

1. The most probing, skeptical Victorian treatment of the *Apologia* appeared in Edwin A. Abbott, *The Anglican Career of Cardinal Newman* (London: Macmillan, 1892), 2 vols. As early as 1864, however, at least one commentator noticed how little attention reviewers paid to the theological substance of Newman's book as opposed to his refutation of Kingsley. W. J. Irons, a high church Anglican clergyman, complaining that some readers regarded the thoughts and expressions found in Newman's pages as "spiritual fossils," deplored what he saw as "the apparent shrinking [from comment on the content of the *Apologia*] of those who would pretend to close the oratory door where a Newman has taken refuge, — much as the friends of some shattered genius might forbid intrusion into the asylum which shielded an intellectual ruin." William Joseph Irons, "*Apologia Pro Vitâ*" *Ecclesiae Anglicanae. In Reply to John Henry Newman, D.D.* (Oxford and London: J. H. and Jas. Parker, n.d. [1864]), 4–5.

2. Curiously, just as Newman was writing Frederick Oakeley, another Tractarian convert, who will appear later in this introduction, contributed a series of brief articles on the history of the Tractarian Movement to the *Dublin Review*, later published as Frederick Oakeley, *Historical Notes on the Tractarian Movement, A.D. 1833–1845* (London:

Editor's Preface

This version of John Henry Cardinal Newman's *Apologia Pro Vita Sua: Being a History of His Religious Opinions* is a historian's edition of the work. Previously, scholars trained primarily in literary or theological disciplines have edited Newman's masterpiece. The present volume is intended for readers interested in the connection and relationship of this remarkable Victorian autobiographical narrative to the life of its author and to the religious crosscurrents of the two great Christian communions within which he dwelled.

The text for this edition of the *Apologia Pro Vita Sua* is that of 1865 published by Longman. This text represents Newman's first revision of the book that had originally appeared as a series of pamphlets in the spring of 1864 as his response to an unprovoked attack on his honesty by Charles Kingsley. I have chosen not to reprint Newman's initial response in 1864 to Kingsley, *Mr. Kingsley and Dr. Newman: A Correspondence on the Question Whether Dr. Newman Teaches That Truth Is No Virtue*, nor Kingsley's pamphlet, *"What, Then, Does Dr. Newman Mean?" A Reply to a Pamphlet Lately Published by Dr. Newman*, which elicited the writing of the *Apologia*. Both of these are available in other editions of the work as well as online. Instead, I have chosen to include in an editor's appendix six of Newman's Anglican sermons. The most significant of these in regard to the publication of the *Apologia* is "Wisdom and Innocence" of 1843. It was this sermon upon which

Kingsley in part based his assault on Newman. The latter, on advice of a lawyer friend, determined not to publish it during the initial pamphlet response to Kingsley or later with the *Apologia*. "The Parting of Friends" is Newman's final sermon preached while still a priest in the Church of England. The other four sermons appeared earlier in Newman's Anglican career although they continued to be reprinted throughout his life in the English Church and then later. They illustrate his powerful practical and theological critique of the evangelical religion of his day.

In addition to the annotated text of the *Apologia*, this edition includes an extensive historical introduction that explains the origins of the book in 1864 and 1865. It also explores through sources well beyond those contained in Newman's own narrative the character and events of Newman's life, thought, and work in the Church of England; his relationship to members of his family; his rivalries in the Oriel College fellowship; the tensions surrounding his position in the English Roman Catholic Church at the time of his composing his response to Kingsley; and the relationship of his life and autobiography to the broader religious and spiritual crosscurrents of the Victorian age.

As editor, I assume both that Newman's *Apologia* is one of the most significant spiritual autobiographies of the nineteenth century and that his book does not fully relate or account for the personal, intellectual, religious, or spiritual history of its protagonist. In that respect, the *Apologia* constitutes only one of numerous sources for the history of Newman's life and not necessarily even a privileged one. Admiration for Newman's narrative and skepticism regarding its historical adequacy need not stand apart or in antagonism. I hope the readers of this edition will find themselves led to adopt a similar outlook.

Much of the research informing the introduction and notes to the text is new while much is also drawn from my book *John Henry Newman: The Challenge to Evangelical Religion,* published by Yale University Press in 2002. I wish to thank Yale University Press for permission to draw from passages of that work. In completing the annotations I have benefited from and also drawn upon the scholarship of previous editors of the *Apologia,* most particularly A. Dwight Culler and Martin J. Svaglic, who published editions of the work respectively with Houghton Mifflin Company in 1956 and with Oxford University Press in 1967, as well as the French translation edited with an introduction and notes by Maurice Nédoncelle and published in 1939 in Paris by Bloud et Gay. Like all scholars of Newman, I am indebted to the editors of *The Letters and Diaries of John Henry Newman* (Vols. 11–31, London: T. Nelson, 1961–1972; Vols. 1–10, Oxford: Clarendon Press, 1978–2006).

I wish to thank Jonathan Brent of Yale University Press for his encouraging support and characteristically helpful ideas throughout this project. The two anonymous readers for Yale University Press as well as Dr. Patricia Willis, Dr. Braxton McKee, and Rev. Roger White made thoughtful suggestions for the introduction. Rev. Benjamin King provided helpful advice on an important question. Jessie Dolch, as copy editor, and Margaret Otzel, as production editor, contributed numerous welcome improvements to the text of the introduction and notes. I also wish to thank my wife Ellen L. Tillotson for her comments, criticisms, and good humor throughout the process of editing this volume.

sumption seemed to be that since Kingsley had been unfair, other critics by definition would be so as well. Lytton Strachey pilloried Thomas Arnold and Henry Edward Cardinal Manning in his *Eminent Victorians* (1918) but dared not touch Newman. Furthermore, in 1961 when editors based at the Birmingham Oratory undertook publication of *The Letters and Diaries of John Henry Newman,* they commenced at Volume 11 with the letters composed on the day of his reception into the Roman Catholic Church and completed the series through Volume 31 before turning to the materials of his Anglican life. The final volume of his Anglican years appeared only in late 2006 — forty-five years after the appearance of the first volume in the project.

Consequently, for almost a century and a half the *Apologia* has been left largely to explicate itself and to determine the manner in which much of the history of Newman and the Tractarian Movement would be written. No comparable situation exists in Victorian autobiography or Victorian intellectual and religious history. For people devoted to Newman as a religious thinker, a model for conversion and personal piety, and a potential saint, the stakes in defending the historical adequacy of the *Apologia* have become cumulatively greater decade by decade, as it has for those historians and biographers who chose not to conduct deep research in the extensive array of additional contemporary evidence. Shake the historical adequacy of the *Apologia* and other structures of historical understanding and religious devotion based on that

---

Longman, Green, Longman, Roberts, and Green, 1865). Recent biographers and Tractarian scholars who have not deeply explored contemporary printed sources in both the Victorian religious and secular press as well as in the vast pamphlet literature surrounding the Tractarian Movement include Ian Ker, *John Henry Newman: A Biography* (Oxford: Clarendon Press, 1988); Sheridan Gilley, *Newman and His Age* (Westminster, Md.: Christian Classics, 1990); Vincent Ferrer Blehl, *Pilgrim Journey: John Henry Newman, 1801–1845* (New York: Paulist Press, 2001); and C. Brad Faught, *The Oxford Movement: A Thematic History of the Tractarians and Their Times* (University Park: Pennsylvania State Univ. Press, 2003). Ker and Anthony Kenny have even complained of the inclusion of otherwise hard-to-find manuscript materials in the final two volumes of the Anglican years of *The Letters and Diaries of John Henry Newman* [*Times Literary Supplement,* October 27, 2006, p. 30; December 15, 2006, p. 13]. By contrast with these writers Peter B. Nockles, *The Oxford Movement in Context: Anglican High Churchmanship 1760–1857* (Cambridge: Cambridge Univ. Press, 1994), and S. A. Skinner, *Tractarians and the "Condition of England": The Social and Political Thought of the Oxford Movement* (New York: Oxford Univ. Press, 2004), are deeply grounded in the whole spectrum of contemporary source materials. For an exploration of some of the difficulties surrounding the original Tractarian historiography, see Owen Chadwick, *The Spirit of the Oxford Movement: Tractarian Essays* (Cambridge: Cambridge Univ. Press, 1990), pp. 135–197.

foundation might collapse. Some years ago the late Professor Josef L. Altholz bluntly summed up the problem confronting the pursuit of professional, critical Newman scholarship in face of the ongoing hagiographic legacy: "The Newman industry has built up a literature so vast and dense that it is unmanageable and in the end overwhelms the facts. The only way to deal with this literature is to dispense with it altogether."[3]

Even historians and religious commentators otherwise capable of writing serious, critical scholarship defend the worthiness of hagiography when it comes to the life of John Henry Newman. One historian, after presenting the most searing criticism of the veracity of Newman's historical account of certain events in the *Apologia*, nonetheless followed that critique with pages of apology for Newman and praise for his "towering moral strength."[4] The authority of the *Apologia* and the determination of its admirers to defend its narrative have caused readers and scholars repeatedly to avoid or to divert their eyes from contrary evidence or displeasing information about its protagonist. As a result, enormous historical misunderstanding and ignorance have continued to enshroud both Newman's Anglican life and the character of the Tractarian Movement.

Another persisting factor in the hagiographic legacy is that to this day many commentators on Newman insist that Providence be invoked when examining his life. Historians are rarely equipped to discern in the past or in the lives of individuals the workings of Providence, the patterns of which most often appear only in hindsight to protagonists and external observers alike. Moreover, just as engaged commentators from the Church of England or the Roman Catholic Church discern the action of Providence in the life of John Henry Newman, others with faith commitments outside those communions may with equal sincerity and fervor discern Providence at work in the lives of religious figures such as Thomas Chalmers, Alexander Campbell, John Nelson Darby, Joseph Smith, or Mary Baker Eddy. As George Levine once so trenchantly commented, "As an isolated saintly figure," Newman "is one sort of writer; as a characteristic Victorian man doing characteristic Victorian things,

---

3. Josef L. Altholz, "The Tractarian Movement: The Incidental Origins of the Oxford Movement," *Albion* 26 (1994): 273.

4. Peter Nockles, "Oxford, Tract 90 and the Bishops," in *John Henry Newman: Reason, Rhetoric and Romanticism,* ed. David Nicholls and Fergus Kerr (Carbondale and Edwardsville: Southern Illinois Univ. Press, 1991), p. 73. For an example of commendation of Newman hagiography, see Geoffrey Rowell's review of Blehl, *Pilgrim Journey* in *Times Literary Supplement,* May 2, 2003, p. 27.

he is another."⁵ Only in taking that judgment into account, eschewing the resort to Providence and setting aside the hagiographic legacy, can a reader of the early twenty-first century understand Newman's *Apologia*.

Magnificent, memorable, and persuasive as it is, the *Apologia* remains neither a wholly trustworthy nor an undistorted source of historical documentation and analysis for Newman's Anglican years and the various ecclesiastical and university conflicts in which he participated. More than half a century ago in a deeply sympathetic book, Sean O'Faolain observed that Newman's "postcogitative memory is not always to be trusted" and that "to follow the course of his adventure by his own map of it is dangerous." Josef Altholz many years later commented, "In the refractive prism of Newman's mind, events are elevated by his genius to a transcendence which leaves behind their primitive factual simplicity and to a coherence which belies the original confusion." As early as 1843 Newman himself told a correspondent that he did not have "a sufficiently vivid memory of the contents of the Tracts for the Times, to be able to say whether this or that *proposition* is to be found in them or can be deduced from them."⁶ In at least one key passage in the *Apologia* itself he noted the problem of memory (252). There is no reason to doubt that similar failures of memory, selective use of memory and other sources, consciously chosen areas of silence, and immediate polemical intentions shaped the contours of the *Apologia* in 1864 and 1865. Newman drew from and assigned to his public and private writings different meanings at different moments of his life. In this sense he was no different, no worse, and no better than any other person engaged in the autobiographical enterprise. After all, the authors of autobiography know how their stories end while the protagonists in the process of living those recounted lives do not. Those who write autobiographies must make sense of the ending; they also necessarily use the ending to give shape and purpose to the years before.

In point of fact, there exists a Newman of the *Apologia* and a Newman of

---

5. George Levine, *The Boundaries of Fiction: Carlyle, Macaulay, Newman* (Princeton, N.J.: Princeton Univ. Press, 1968), p. 166. Levine's discussion continues to be the single most probing and enlightening exploration of Newman and the *Apologia*.
6. Sean O'Faolain, *Newman's Way: The Odyssey of John Henry Newman* (New York: The Devin-Adair Co., 1952), p. 259; Altholz, "The Tractarian Movement," 273; John Henry Newman (hereafter cited as JHN) to an Unknown Correspondent, March 4, 1843, *The Letters and Diaries of John Henry Newman*, Vols. 1–10, ed. Ian Ker, Thomas Gornall, Gerard Tracey, and Francis J. McGrath (Oxford: Clarendon Press, 1978–2006), Vols. 11–31, ed. Charles Stephen Dessain, Edward E. Kelly, and Thomas Gornall (London: Thomas Nelson and Sons, 1961–1972) (hereafter cited as *L&D*) 9: 265.

history; sometimes, but by no means always, are they one and the same person. Newman's autobiography reveals only a portion of the historical figure and even that portion only through a particular lens. George Grote, the great nineteenth-century historian of ancient Greece, described the Greek myths as recounting a "past which never was present."[7] Newman's history of his religious opinions portrayed and evoked a past that had *only partly* been present. Those writers who have drawn uncritically upon Newman's partial account have themselves sometimes moved close to the realm Grote described. It is the purpose of this introduction to explore aspects of Newman's life and thought and other features of the era through which he lived that he chose not to record or to record only partially in the *Apologia*. Such is the task, even the duty, of the historian so that the past does not by default determine its own interpretation and in doing so leave its fuller, critical truth obscured.

Newman before the Apologia

John Henry Newman was received into the Roman Catholic Church in early October 1845. He had been born in 1801 to moderate Anglican parents. His father had been a banker and businessman who twice experienced financial failure. In 1816 while a student at Ealing School the younger Newman experienced a powerful, personal religious experience or conversion under the tutelage of Walter Mayers, an evangelical cleric and instructor at the school. The same year Newman entered Trinity College Oxford, graduating in 1821 after poor performance on his examinations. The next year, upon successful completion of a separate fellowship examination, he became a fellow of Oriel College and remained one until a few days before his reception as a Roman Catholic. From 1826 to 1832 Newman provided tutorial instruction in Oriel College, after which, under difficult circumstances, his formal college instructional duties concluded. Beginning in 1828 he served for fifteen years as vicar of St. Mary the Virgin, the unofficial university church in Oxford, where his sermons, often preached at Evensong, drew considerable numbers of students and when later published, a significant readership.

Newman's sermons proclaimed a rigorous call to Christian obedience and personal self-denial. For example, on November 4, 1832, he declared to his congregation: "Praise to the obedient, punishment on the transgressor, is the revealed rule of God's government from the beginning to the consummation of all things. The fall of Adam did not abolish, nor do the provisions of Gospel-

---

7. George Grote, *A History of Greece,* new ed. (London: John Murray, 1869), 1: 43.

mercy supersede it."[8] This message, enunciated in one sermon after another, contrasted starkly with the prevalent contemporary evangelical message of God's mercy and grace made available and freely given through faith in the atonement of Jesus Christ. Newman regarded the latter as easy religion constituting only a portion of the Christian message. He also deeply distrusted and firmly denounced the contemporary evangelical emphasis on subjective religious feeling and the necessity of a conversion experience as validating one's sense of having attained personal salvation.

Newman's first decade in Oriel and his years establishing his voice at St. Mary's had been tumultuous for the Church of England. The period from 1827 through 1834 saw the end of a denominational definition of full English citizenship and the collapse of the English confessional state through parliamentary repeal of civil disabilities against Protestant Dissenters, enactment of Catholic Emancipation, passage of the Irish Temporalities Act, and establishment of the Ecclesiastical Commission to reform the finances and administration of the English Church. Each measure, as well as the more general climate of reform and its accompanying legislation in numerous areas of English life, diminished the political privileges associated with membership in the Church of England and the Church of Ireland and held those established churches to new public accountability. This body of profoundly controversial and transforming legislation marked the culmination of decades of internal and external criticism of the Anglican ecclesiastical establishments and closed the era when the English and Irish political nations were defined by membership in an exclusive Protestant establishment.[9]

The bishops, clergy, and active laity of the Church of England had to accommodate themselves to a vastly altered political landscape and religious marketplace. The established church found itself having to compete for institutional and spiritual loyalty with evangelically energized Dissenting denominations

---

8. John Henry Newman, *Fifteen Sermons Preached before the University of Oxford, between A.D. 1826 and 1843*, new ed. (London: Rivingtons, 1880), p. 137.

9. Olive Brose, *Church and Parliament: The Reshaping of the Church of England, 1828–1860* (Stanford: Stanford Univ. Press, 1959); G. F. A. Best, *Temporal Pillars: Queen Anne's Bounty, the Ecclesiastical Commissioners, and the Church of England* (Cambridge: Cambridge Univ. Press, 1964); G. I. T. Machin, *Politics and the Churches in Great Britain, 1832 to 1868* (Oxford: Clarendon Press, 1977); Stewart J. Brown, *The National Churches of England, Ireland and Scotland 1801–1846* (Oxford: Oxford Univ. Press, 2001); Arthur Burns, "English 'Church Reform' Revisited, 1780-1840," in *Rethinking the Age of Reform: Britain 1780–1850*, ed. Arthur Burns and Joanna Innes (Cambridge: Cambridge Univ. Press, 2003), pp. 136–162.

but suddenly without the benefit of political privileges previously accruing to Anglican membership. The situation fostered enormous internal debate and rancor within the church as well as intense rivalry between the English Church and Dissenters. Many spokesmen believed it in the interest of the established church to embrace structural reform that would remove the most glaring financial and administrative abuses. Others believed the church and closely associated foundations, such as Oxford and Cambridge, should make timely accommodations to the demands of Dissenters and to a lesser extent Roman Catholics so as to become in reality more nearly national institutions. Evangelical clergy within the English Church thought it could best compete in the new religious marketplace by emphasizing a preaching ministry that mimicked the success of contemporary evangelical Dissent, which by then included the large body of Methodist churches. Traditional high churchmen, understanding that the Church of England still retained numerous legal privileges, believed they could make a case for the mutual benefit flowing to the nation and the church from ecclesiastical establishment even if significantly modified from that of the previous century.

In late 1833 Newman, along with John Keble, Richard Hurrell Froude, and others, who were later most importantly joined by E. B. Pusey, began publication of *Tracts for the Times* (1833–1841), on the basis of which they became known as the *Tractarians*.[10] This loosely knit group, always driven primarily by Newman's energy and leadership, introduced into the already corrosive contemporary ecclesiastical debate a new radical high church alternative that sharply contrasted with other Anglican political positions. The Tractarians rejected even modest structural reform, questioned the Christian faithfulness of proponents of compromise with Dissenters, and denounced internal Anglican evangelical initiatives as leading to Socinianism, a protean polemical term by which they denoted lack of Trinitarian orthodoxy. They saw traditional high churchmen as timorous and staking their claims for the value of the

---

10. Consult Marvin O'Connell, *The Oxford Conspirators: A History of the Oxford Movement, 1833–1845* (New York: Macmillan, 1969), for an excellent and well-grounded narrative of the Tractarian Movement. Much of the first volume of Owen Chadwick, *The Victorian Church* (New York: Oxford Univ. Press, 1966, 1970), 2 vols., is devoted to a narrative of the Tractarian Movement. It should be noted that the Tractarian Movement was also known as the Oxford Movement after the university of its origins, and as the Puseyite Movement. The latter term originated from Anglican evangelical critics in the *Record* newspaper who associated the entire movement with E. B. Pusey's controversial views on baptism. See *Record*, September 18, 1837, and E. B. Pusey to H. A. Woodgate, September 14, 1843, H. A. Woodgate Letters, Lambeth Palace Library, London, Ms. 3535, f. 22.

Church of England on utilitarian rather than distinctly religious grounds. In this fashion the Tractarians consciously set out to disrupt current internal Anglican discourse, taking no prisoners and brooking no compromise.

Publicly and privately the Tractarians presented the Church of England and more particularly its clergy as in danger of loss of property and social standing through any projected parliamentary accommodation to the Dissenters. The Tractarians demanded that their fellow clergy consider how they would henceforth command deference from their congregations now that they competed with Dissenters while lacking so many of their former political privileges associated with establishment. The Tractarians self-consciously voiced an extreme message for what they regarded as extreme times. Even many of their friends believed they overstated the situation confronting the English Church. Indeed, the Tractarians adopted a near apocalyptic vision of the situation of the Church of England.

As their solution to their projected plight of Church of England clergy, the Tractarians, in contrast to many other high churchmen, urged their fellow clergy to embrace the authority of a sacramental clericalism that claimed spiritual validity only for sacraments performed by priests ordained by bishops enjoying apostolic succession.[11] Whereas evangelicals believed grace came to an individual through a subjective conversion experience provoked by preaching, the Tractarians urged that grace could be communicated only through sacraments validly administered by episcopally ordained priests. Evangelicals inside and outside the English Church argued that people might endanger their salvation without a conversion experience; the Tractarians raised the same specter for people lacking access to valid sacraments.

The Tractarians, like other high churchmen before them, held very high views of the sacraments in relation to Christian regeneration and devotion.

---

11. A. P. Perceval stated the most extreme version of this view in *Tract 35:* "A person not commissioned from the bishop, may use the words of Baptism, and sprinkle or bathe with the water *on earth,* but there is no promise from CHRIST, that such a man shall admit souls to the *Kingdom of Heaven.* A person not commissioned may break bread, and pour out wine, and pretend to give the LORD's Supper, but it can afford no comfort to any to receive it at his hands, because there is no warrant from CHRIST to lead communicants to suppose that while he does so here *on earth,* they will be partakers in the SAVIOUR's *heavenly* Body and Blood" (*Tract 35:* 3) Although each author was responsible for the contents of his own tract, Newman neither as editor nor as contributor disassociated himself from Perceval's statement. Unless otherwise noted, all quotations from the tracts are taken from *Tracts for the Times by Members of the University of Oxford,* new ed. (London: J. G. F. & J. Rivington, 1840), 5 vols. Volume 3 as published in 1840 carries the words "New Edition" on the title page.

Episcopally ordained priests were the lynchpin in the system. Tractarian clericalism supported the claims that the Church of England was the only branch of the Holy Catholic and Apostolic Church in the land and that its clergy, by virtue of ordination by bishops who were successors to the apostles, were the exclusive source of efficacious grace through the Christian sacraments. At their mildest the Tractarians had urged "adherence to Episcopal ordination" as "the *safest course* for the security of the validity of the sacraments and of the existence of Church fellowship." In regard to baptism Newman further explained that the tracts had taught that "no other *appointed* means but Baptism is *revealed in Scripture* for regeneration." Although traditionally, Christian churches had held that technically any Christian could perform a valid baptism, Newman privately communicated his doubt as to the validity of baptism performed by Dissenting clergy. He explained to one correspondent: "I do not think that the Bishops of the Church of England have so clearly given their sanction to Dissenting Baptism, as to hinder me advising a Dissenter conforming to the Church, to be baptized conditionally, which I certainly would do. By 'conditionally,' I mean under the form, 'If thou hast not been baptized etc.' "[12] He had personally performed such a conditional baptism of the wife of E. B. Pusey, who had originally been baptized by a Dissenting minister.

The Tractarians held a similarly high view of the Eucharist. Early in the movement, in *Tract 10,* Newman contended that only clergy of the English Church had the power of transforming the elements of the Eucharist into the body and blood of Christ though in a later edition of the tract he modified that position, regarded as Romanish, without noting that the revision had taken place. These Tractarian clerical claims were not entirely new, but they were asserted with a novel instrumental urgency and lack of compromise that, as Newman indicates in the *Apologia,* were not entirely welcomed by more traditional high churchmen.[13]

---

12. JHN to an Unknown Correspondent, March 4, 1843, *L&D* 9: 266,267. This is an important letter in which Newman provides a summary of what he then recollected as the basic doctrines taught by the *Tracts for the Times.* In some parts of this letter, however, he understates the harshness and exaggeration of the Tractarian rhetoric as it appeared in the tracts themselves. JHN to Miss M. R. Giberne, August 12, 1842, *L&D* 9: 65. See also JHN to Simeon Wilberforce O'Neill, August 11, 1865, *L&D* 22: 28–31, for further of Newman's musings on the complexities he associated with baptism as a Roman Catholic. The particular Tractarian emphasis on and interpretation of baptismal regeneration set them in direct opposition to evangelicals within the Church of England and to the Lutheran and Reformed communions on the continent. See J. B. Mozley, *A Review of the Baptismal Controversy,* 2nd ed. (London: Rivingtons, 1893).

13. See Alf Hardelin, *The Tractarian Understanding of the Eucharist* (Uppsala and

The point of Tractarian sacramental clericalism was to assign an exclusive spiritual power and authority to Church of England clergy and by the same arguments to deny such authority to Dissenting clergy. Later in the century Thomas Arnold Jr., an Anglican convert to Roman Catholicism, explained the ecclesiastical implications of the Tractarian position: "Hundreds of the Anglican clergy, soon to become thousands, were not difficult to convince that they and they alone were in England the legitimate representatives of the Apostles, enjoying, by succession to them, the exclusive right of teaching with authority the gospel of Christ. This doctrine, once generally accepted, put the Dissenting minister nowhere; the ground was cut from under his feet; however personally devout, he had no commission, and was intruding into an office to which he had not been called."[14] By thus asserting the absence of sacramental authority to Dissenting clergy, the Tractarians hoped to draw or drive the laity to the ministry of the Church of England.

Newman in *Tract 15* had been equally forthright about the Tractarian understanding of the authority of Church of England clergy over not only Dissenters but also the laity in the English Church. There he declared, "that the Clergy [of the Church of England] have a commission from GOD ALMIGHTY through regular succession from the Apostles, to preach the Gospel, administer the Sacraments, and guide the Church; and, again, that in consequence the people are bound to hear them with attention, receive the Sacrament from their hands, and pay them all dutiful obedience." Thus much of the thrust of the *Tracts for the Times* vigorously asserted the social position of Church of

---

Stockholm: Almquist and Wiksell, 1965). For a general summary of the contents of the early *Tracts for the Times*, see Frank M. Turner, *John Henry Newman: The Challenge to Evangelical Religion* (New Haven, Conn.: Yale Univ. Press, 2002), pp. 162–206, and for an account of the varying editions, see Rune Imberg, *Tracts for the Times: A Complete Survey of All the Editions* (Lund, Sweden: Lund Univ. Press, 1987) and *In Quest of Authority: The "Tracts for the Times" and the Development of the Tractarian Leaders, 1833–1841* (Lund, Sweden: Lund Univ. Press, 1987). For the background of Tractarian ideas among the previous generation of high churchmen, see Nockles, *The Oxford Movement in Context*.

14. Thomas Arnold Jr., Unpublished review of *Letters and Correspondence of John Henry Newman during His Life in the English Church*, Anne Mozley, ed. (London: Rivingtons, 1890), 2 vols., Beinecke Rare Book and Manuscript Library, Yale University, Uncat Mss 552 20031002-a. See also Richard Whately, ed., *Cautions for the Times: Addressed to the Parishioners of a Parish in England by Their Former Rector* (London: John W. Parker and Son, 1853), pp. 336–342. Whately's volume contains some of the most interesting critical, contemporary comments on the Tractarian Movement offered several years after its collapse.

England clergy by substituting clerical spiritual authority for the political advantages that the church and its clergy had lost in recent years. As R. H. Hutton, a sympathetic late-century observer, commented, "Now Tractarianism was clerical to the core — more clerical . . . in some real sense than the Church of Rome itself."[15]

Tractarian sacramental clericalism assaulted not only the ecclesiology of Dissent but also the evangelical theology, devotional impulses, and reform vision that by the 1830s informed the preponderant body of Dissent as well as a significant group of evangelical clergy in the English Church itself.[16] Proponents of evangelical religion among both Dissenters and Anglicans distinguished between nominal and vital religion, defined the true church as the "invisible church" of the Christian saints through the ages, looked to scripture alone for authority in matters of faith, regarded a personal conversion experience rather than baptism as essential to Christian regeneration, preached the doctrine of the atonement to the near exclusion of other major Christian doctrines, and undertook a broad array of socially reformist activities as well as others relating to Christian outreach such as the British and Foreign Bible Society. Evangelicals within the Church of England were to greater and lesser degrees sympathetic to ecumenical cooperation through these various societies. In that respect, whatever their distinct political affiliation, evangelicals

---

15. *Tract 15:* 1; Richard H. Hutton, *Cardinal Newman* (London: Methuen, 1891), p. 47.

16. Grayson Carter, *Anglican Evangelicals: Protestant Secessions from the Via Media, 1800–1850* (Oxford: Oxford Univ. Press, 2001); Michael Watts, *The Dissenters: The Expansion of Evangelical Nonconformity 1791–1859* (Oxford: Clarendon Press, 1995); D. Bruce Hindmarsh, *John Newton and the English Evangelical Tradition between the Conversions of Wesley and Wilberforce* (Oxford: Clarendon Press, 1996), pp. 119–168; Alan C. Clifford, *Atonement and Justification: English Evangelical Theology, 1640–1790* (Oxford: Oxford Univ. Press, 1990); Boyd Hilton, *The Age of Atonement: The Influence of Evangelicalism on Social and Economic Thought, 1795–1865* (Oxford: Clarendon Press, 1988); Roger H. Martin, *Evangelicals United: Ecumenical Stirrings in Pre-Victorian Britain, 1794–1840* (Metuchen, N.J.: The Scarecrow Press, 1983); Bernard Semmel, *The Methodist Revolution* (New York: Basic Books, 1973). Evangelical impulses had deeply informed English religious life within and without the English Church since the onset of the Methodist revival in the late 1730s. The late eighteenth-century Methodist schism both significantly enlarged the ranks of historic Dissent and furthermore energized the evangelical energies already at work in those congregations. The Tractarians often presented Dissent as leading to Unitarianism, whereas in reality the direction of the previous half-century of developments in Dissent had been toward increasingly fervent evangelical religion.

across the denominational boundaries were culturally at one with the currents of reform. Such was particularly the case with Dissenters, who were still subject to various civil disabilities. It should also be noted that during the 1820s and early 1830s evangelicals across the ecclesiastical spectrum had become more theologically radical in regard to the literal reading of scripture and the premillennialist interpretation of prophecy as a result of religious developments in Scotland and Ireland that impinged on England.

The Tractarians' championing of the authority of the visible church, apostolic succession, and clerical sacramentalism; their criticism of the free preaching of the atonement and of emotional religiosity; their rejection of private judgment in the reading of scripture; and their demand for Christian discipline and personal self-denial challenged point by point evangelical religion within and without the English Church. In the words of *Tract 41* the Tractarians demanded a "SECOND REFORMATION" that would remove the Protestant excesses of the past century. As Newman commented privately in the spring of 1836, "The truth is this—the Ultra Protestants have had every thing their own way for about a Century, and now when things are coming to a crisis, God's good Providence is lifting up a Standard against them."[17] Over the course of the 1830s the focus of Newman's challenge expanded from an assault on Dissent to a vigorous critique of one aspect after another of evangelicalism in the English Church to a more generally critical conflation of what he most despised in evangelical religion with the main ideas of historic Protestantism.

Beyond his sermons, which he began publishing in 1833 and then continued to republish, Newman's attack on evangelical Protestantism appeared in books, tracts, and articles first in the *British Magazine* and later in the *British Critic,* which the Tractarians controlled and made their party organ from 1838 to 1843. In *Lectures on the Prophetical Office of the Church, Viewed Relatively to Romanism and Popular Protestantism* (1837), Newman criticized evangelical ecclesiology and Protestant assertions of the right of private judgment. In *Lectures on Justification* (1838), arguably Newman's most powerful theological treatise, he dissected the Protestant doctrine of justification by faith without recourse to the sacraments, which he later described as "the essence of sectarian and (modern) heretical doctrine." In *Tract 85* (1838), titled *Lectures on the Scripture Proof of the Doctrines of the Church,* he attacked the Protestant doctrine of *sola scriptura* in so trenchant a manner that T. H. Huxley later wrote that an unbeliever could not improve upon Newman's critique of biblical authority. In various articles in the *British Critic*

---

17. *Tract 41*: 12; JHN to Miss M. R. Giberne, March 20, 1836, *L&D* 5: 262–263.

and in *The Church of the Fathers* (1840), Newman pilloried and denigrated the social manifestations of evangelical religion.[18] Taken as a whole, this extensive outpouring of social, religious, and theological polemic constitutes the most destructively probing Victorian critique of evangelical religion, with much of the criticism as applicable to evangelical religion in the early twenty-first century as in the early nineteenth.

In the *Apologia* Newman discussed in detail very few of these remarkable anti-evangelical publications. He wrote virtually nothing about the harsh controversy provoked by anti-evangelical and anti-Protestant articles in the *British Critic* under his and later Thomas Mozley's editorship.[19] Newman thus remained largely silent about the fact that the sheer quantity of his prose devoted to formulating an Anglican via media, or "middle way" between Roman Catholicism and popular Protestantism, stood dwarfed, indeed overwhelmed, by his critique of evangelical and finally historic Protestantism. In the *Apologia* Newman seems to have been determined to deflect his readers from grasping this fundamental aspect of his Anglican career. In the body of the *Apologia* he described the English Church as being "tyrannized over by a mere party" (210), but in Note A, "Liberalism," he wrote, "the party called Evangelical never has been able to breathe freely in the atmosphere of Oxford, and at no time has been conspicuous, as a party, for talent or learning" (362). Although evangelicals did not intellectually dominate Oxford, they nonetheless exerted a broad pervasive influence over the wider culture as well as the internal life of the Church of England, an influence that Newman deplored and regarded as growing in a dangerous manner, as witnessed by private correspondence and public writings of both his Anglican and Roman Catholic years. It is quite simply a fact that the Anglican Newman of history spent the preponderance of his polemical energy attacking the doctrines, mores, institutions, and ecclesiastical influence of evangelical Protestants. During his last

---

18. JHN to an Unknown Correspondent, March 4, 1843, *L&D* 9: 267; Bernard Lightman, *The Origins of Agnosticism: Victorian Unbelief and the Limits of Knowledge* (Baltimore: Johns Hopkins Univ. Press, 1987), pp. 114–115; see [John Henry Newman], "Exeter Hall," *British Critic* 24 (1838): 190–210.

19. Throughout the *Apologia* Newman markedly concealed the role and importance of the *British Critic,* which sparked enormous criticism and notoriety, as a self-conscious party vehicle for spreading many of the most controversial elements of Tractarian opinion. Through this concealment Newman downplayed his vigorous role as a party leader within the Church of England and disassociated himself from the most extreme statements of Tractarian anti-Protestantism. See S. A. Skinner, "Newman, the Tractarians and the *British Critic,*" *Journal of Ecclesiastical History* 50 (1999): 716–759, and Skinner, *Tractarians and the "Condition of England,"* pp. 33–64.

four years in the Church of England he was nothing less than obsessed with even the slightest indication of evangelical sway within the church, which he often termed "heresy," and of episcopal sympathy for evangelicals.

Although most Newman scholars have ignored Newman's brilliant, expansive campaign against evangelicalism, his contemporaries observed and commented upon it. Evangelical publications such as the moderate *Christian Observer* and the more strident *Record* saw Newman personally and the Tractarians in general as boring away at their doctrines and influence. In late 1839 John Stuart Mill, commenting upon the Tractarians, noted as "the principle peculiarity of this school" their "hostility to what they call ultra-Protestantism." Mill further remarked:

> They reprobate the "right of private judgment" & consider *learning* rather than original thinking the proper attribut[ion] of a divine. They discourage the Methodistical view of religion which makes devotional feeling a state of strong *excitement*, & inculcate rather a spirit of humility & self-mortification. . . . It is one of the forms, & the best form hitherto, of the *reaction* of Anglicanism against Methodism, incredulity, & rationalism . . . their doctrine, which is spreading fast among the younger clergy, is giving great offence to the evangelical part of the Church . . . which had previously been increasing very much in numbers & influence.

In 1856 the Unitarian theologian James Martineau recalled the Anglican Newman as having "assailed the Evangelical party with every weapon of antipathy which could be drawn from the armory of imagination or logic, Scripture or history."[20]

Contemporaneous with the launching of *Tracts for the Times* in 1833 and his ongoing assault on evangelical religion, Newman had also set upon a radical religious and theological experiment. Like those involved in many such radical religious movements across history, he and other Tractarians presented themselves as the restorers of a lost, more nearly pristine or primitive past. They called themselves "Catholics" and their religion "Catholicism," but they distinguished it from Roman Catholicism. They believed the latter to be insufficiently rigorous in its moral demands and to have permitted its devotional practices to suffer corruption. Newman and his companions sought to reclaim for their own elements of pre-Reformation Catholic worship, theology, prayers, and monastic life that most of their Victorian contemporaries, including more

---

20. J. S. Mill to Gustave D'Eichthal, December 27, 1839, in *The Earlier Letters of John Stuart Mill 1812–1848*, ed. Francis E. Mineke (Toronto: Univ. of Toronto Press, 1963), pp. 415–416; James Martineau, *Essays, Reviews, and Addresses* (London: Longmans, Green, 1890), 1: 223.

moderate high churchmen, regarded as "papist" or "Romanish." This process of Tractarian devotional reclamation was eclectic and never systematic.

To counter those charges of Romanish sympathy and to deflect attention from his very real attraction to pre-Reformation modes of devotion, Newman undertook in certain of the tracts and in *The Prophetical Office of the Church* severe criticisms of Roman Catholicism, many of which he publicly retracted in early 1843. As he once explained the situation he had faced in the mid-1830s to Catherine Froude: "If Catholic doctrines were to be inculcated, it was an act of treachery to our church, not to accompany the teaching with such safeguards against Romanizing which would be their infallible effect on the mind, if they were left to work freely. One could not give our church the benefit of Catholicism, without opening upon it the danger of Romanism. To throw up bulwarks then against the Church of Rome was necessary for our position."[21] In the *Apologia* Newman necessarily paid considerable attention to those anti-Roman statements, but they had at best composed only a modest portion of his prose output. Furthermore, his Anglican critique of Roman Catholicism embraced high church views of the corruption of Roman Catholicism, particularly its departures from antiquity, rather than the standard fare of popular anti-Catholicism. Newman, however, departed from traditional high church anti-Catholicism because he wrote in sadness rather than anger of Roman Catholicism as requiring reform not repudiation.

These were nonetheless the anti–Roman Catholic positions along with residual evangelical anti-Roman outlooks from which Newman had to liberate his mind and spirit as he moved toward the conviction that the Roman Catholic Church was the one true church. To both his Roman Catholic and Protestant audiences of the 1860s, these anti–Roman Catholic passages from his Anglican years were the statements that as a convert he had to provide an account, not his more aggressive and extensive program of challenging evangelicalism, about which he felt few if any regrets. Consequently, those anti–Roman Catholic statements as presented so prominently in the *Apologia* give

---

21. JHN to Catherine Froude, December 9, 1843, *L&D* 10: 52. For Newman's retractions see *L&D* 9: 167–172. In 1850 Newman, commenting upon these years, had written: "It must be observed, then, that they [the Tractarians] were accustomed to regard theology generally, much more upon its anti-Protestant side than upon its anti-Roman; and, from the circumstances in which they found themselves, were far more solicitous to refute Luther and Calvin than Suarez or Bellarmine. Protestantism was a present foe; Catholicism, or Romanism as they called it, was but a possible adversary." John Henry Newman, *Certain Difficulties Felt by Anglicans in Catholic Teaching Considered: In Twelve Lectures Addressed in 1850 to the Party of the Religious Movement of 1833* (London: Longmans, Green, 1918), 1: 143.

a distorted picture of the spectrum and relative content of Newman's intellectual and theological preoccupations while in the English Church.

What most struck contemporaries about Newman's Catholic religious experiment of the 1830s and early 1840s was not his occasional, fierce anti-Roman statements, but his drive toward an expansive, experimental devotional life. In his pursuit of the Catholic, Newman articulated and embraced what he termed a "prophetical tradition" that extended beyond the formal episcopal tradition grounded in the Bible and the creeds handed down from bishop to bishop over the centuries. This largely indeterminate prophetical tradition according to Newman constituted

> a vast system, not to be comprised in a few sentences, not to be embodied in one code or treatise, but consisting of a certain body of Truth, permeating the Church like an atmosphere, irregular in its shape from its very profusion and exuberance; at times separable only in idea from Episcopal Tradition, yet at times melting away into legend and fable; partly written, partly unwritten, partly the interpretation, partly the supplement of Scripture, partly preserved in intellectual expressions, partly latent in the spirit and temper of Christians; poured to and fro in closets and upon the housetops, in liturgies, in controversial works, in obscure fragments, in sermons.[22]

This eclectic, ill-defined, and nondogmatic tradition preserved in the writings of the Church Fathers and other documents, legends, and stories of the Christian Church provided for Newman and other Tractarians a plentiful storehouse of Christian practices that might enliven and enrich the faith, devotion, and liturgy of the early nineteenth-century Church of England. The concept of the prophetical tradition offended evangelicals because of its lack of a scriptural foundation and high churchmen because of its extending beyond their boundaries for the authority of antiquity, which ended around the fifth century.

Throughout the Tractarian years as he explored this prophetical tradition, Newman worked under the assumption that the Church of England did not actually possess a real theology. As Newman recounted in the *Apologia*, "I

---

22. John Henry Newman, *Lectures on the Prophetical Office of the Church, Viewed Relatively to Romanism and Popular Protestantism* (London: J. G. & F. Rivington, 1837), p. 298. Newman had first formulated this idea in an exchange with a French Roman Catholic priest in 1834. See Louis Allen, ed., *John Henry Newman and the Abbé Jager: A Controversy on Scripture and Tradition (1834–1836)* (London: Oxford Univ. Press, 1975), pp. 94–95. Allen's entire introduction is relevant to an understanding of the emergence of Newman's views on prophetical tradition. On the issue of antiquity in regard to both traditional high churchmen and Tractarians, see Nockles, *The Oxford Movement in Context*, pp. 104–145.

wished to build up an Anglican theology" (187). That aspiration grew out of his peculiar religious biography. In a particularly penetrating comment regarding Newman's relationship to Anglican tradition in contrast to that of other Tractarians, Archbishop Michael Ramsey once noted, "In a sense he was not quite of it; that is, he had not quite got historic Anglicanism into his bones in the way that the others had, and he came to it rather as one who is fulfilling deep personal needs of his own."[23] Newman's initial theological education under Walter Mayers had involved deep reading of recent evangelical writers and of scripture according to evangelical systems of interpretation. Newman became acquainted with the major figures of Anglican tradition, especially the seventeenth-century Caroline divines, only later as a young adult in the Oriel fellowship after his intense adolescent religious and emotional yearnings had first been addressed by largely systematic Calvinistic evangelical writings and a fundamentally Bible-based Christianity.

Rather than a disinterested academic pursuit, Newman's study of both the Anglican divines and the early Church Fathers constituted a continuation of his addressing deep personal religious needs and aspirations previously addressed by evangelical writers. Neither the Anglican divines nor the Fathers presented the same kind of relatively closed, systematic theology Newman had first encountered among generally moderate Calvinist evangelicals, an experience that had conditioned his expectation that a religious tradition presupposed or required a systematic theology. As a result, in the writings of Newman's Tractarian era, the term *Anglican Theology* indicated his own particular, self-constructed, utopian understanding and aspiration of what the character of the English Church should be or should become as drawn from his own highly selective reading of Anglican divines, the Church Fathers, and other Christian writers as well as the Bible. As he explained in the *Apologia* (192), neither he nor others in the movement knew exactly where their principles would lead them. One reason for the constant state of movement in their thought was the desire to impose a system upon a body of patristic and Anglican materials that were inherently unsystematic.

The via media as a concept of the theological path Newman had pursued in the 1830s was largely a retrospective construct as Newman in 1864 and beyond sought to explain to himself as well as to others what he had sought to accomplish almost three decades before. The titles assigned to one of his books illustrate the process. As already noted, Newman in 1837 published *Lectures on the Prophetical Office of the Church, Viewed Relatively to Romanism and*

---

23. Michael Ramsey, *The Anglican Spirit,* ed. Dale D. Coleman (New York: Church Publishing, 2004), p. 48.

Popular Protestantism. Within high church and Tractarian circles the book, despite its powerful critique of popular Protestantism, soon became known as *Against Romanism* in an effort by high churchmen to refute accusations of Tractarian sympathy for Roman Catholicism. In the *Apologia* Newman portrayed himself as having attempted in this book, as well as in other works of the period, to construct an ecclesiastical via media in which he later lost faith. Thirteen years later in 1877 Newman republished *Lectures on the Prophetical Office of the Church,* with an important new introduction as well as a miscellaneous series of pamphlets mostly surrounding *Tract 90,* in a two-volume collection titled *The Via Media of the Anglican Church. Illustrated in Lectures, Letters, and Tracts Written between 1830 and 1841*. His extensive commentary from a Roman Catholic standpoint on this eclectic collection of Anglican writings imposed the appearance of far more system than they had possessed at the time.

This transformation of ad hoc Tractarian publications into a supposedly systematic articulation of a via media continued during the late twentieth century. In 1990 a critical scholarly edition of *Lectures on the Prophetical Office of the Church* appeared without any of the other Tractarian-era materials of the 1877 edition under the title *The Via Media of the Anglican Church,* with the editor devoting more space to the discussion of Newman's preface of 1877 than to consideration of the lectures themselves.[24] The editor said virtually nothing about Newman's assault of 1837 on popular Protestantism though it still appears in the pages of the critical edition. These ongoing modifications in title and content reflect the shifting atmospheres in which Newman's lectures were delivered, published, read, interpreted, and reinterpreted as well as the manner in which the original polemic against popular Protestantism became deliberately obscured and ignored and then eventually forgotten.

Very few early Victorian clergy or laity ever actually subscribed to Newman's via media because his vision was in a perpetual process of becoming, or what he would later term "development." At most, it represented an ethos of expansive Christian devotion. As William Gladstone once wrote in near despair to Henry Manning, "The Newman of 1843 is not the Newman of 1842, nor is he of 1842 the same with him of 1841." Consequently, the ideas and experiences that, as recorded in the *Apologia,* caused Newman to lose faith in his via media influenced very few other people because so few had embraced that via media or even really understood what he meant by it. Moreover, as will be seen later in this introduction, it was less that he lost faith in the via

---

24. John Henry Newman, *The Via Media of the Anglican Church,* ed. H. D. Weidner (Oxford: Clarendon Press, 1990).

media than that a set of contingent events made it impossible for him to maintain his devotional ethos within the confines of the Church of England. The set of theological and ecclesiastical ideas that Newman abandoned, which amounted almost to a private religion, had never been a stable construct even in his own mind. As William Ralph Inge once commented, "The ideal which is presented [in Newman's idealization of the past] as a return or a revival is nothing of the kind, but a creation of our own time, projected by the imagination into the past, from which it comes back with a halo of authority."[25]

Over the years that Newman pursued his indeterminate via media, his constituency of followers changed dramatically. Initially, the Tractarians had attracted clergy across the theological spectrum fearful of what Parliament might do in the wake of the Reform Act and most particularly high churchmen who saw the Tractarian championing of church principles as blocking the advance of evangelicalism within the church and of Dissent outside. By 1836, however, the alarm caused by the Reform Act and the advance of church reform had subsided. It was clear that the Church of England was institutionally safe from undue parliamentary intrusion. Thereafter, generally younger men more attracted to Catholic principles and the assault on evangelical religion and historic Protestantism supplanted the original Tractarian sympathizers, who had been attracted by resistance to possible parliamentary intrusions on the life of the church. The later 1830s were the years of Newmania in Oxford. The man whose head of college would no longer send him students for instruction had generated the most extensive student following in the university. These new, generally younger Oxford men listened to Newman's sermons, frequented his breakfasts, engaged in endless conversation with him, had him occasionally hear their confessions, and spent much time with each other. Newman spoke to them in private without the reticence of his careful public statements.

During these same years Newman experienced an increasing affection for Roman Catholic modes of devotion. He became fascinated with the Roman Catholic breviary, publishing portions of it as a tract. In 1839 Newman complained to Henry Manning that the English Church lacked "the provisions and methods by which Catholic feelings are to be detained, secured, sobered, and trained heavenwards." Catholics must say to Protestants in the Church of England: "Give us more services — more vestments and decorations in worship

---

25. W. E. Gladstone to H. Manning, October 24, 1843, in *Correspondence on Church and Religion of William Ewart Gladstone*, ed. D. C. Lathbury (New York: Macmillan, 1910), 1: 281; William Ralph Inge, *Outspoken Essays* (London: Longmans, Green, 1920), p. 184.

—give us monasteries—give us the 'signs of an Apostle'—the pledges that the Spouse of Christ is among us."[26] By 1840 Newman began to contemplate a formal revival of monastic life in the English Church. These yearnings made both Newman and his close followers increasingly restless and impatient in a church that they saw as overwhelmingly defining itself by Protestantism and hostility to Rome and as becoming ever more subject to peculiar evangelical influences.

During the summer of 1839, Newman encountered what in the *Apologia* he recounts as his first doubts about the validity of his concept of the Church Catholic within the Church of England as well as the catholicity of the English Church in general. In reading an article by Nicholas Wiseman in the Roman Catholic *Dublin Review*, Newman recalls having first seen what he regarded as a parallel between his version of the Church of England and ancient heresies. Most important of these was the analogy he perceived between his modern Church Catholic residing in the Church of England and the Monophysite heresy. The key to the parallel for Newman was not the Monophysite Christological heresy of regarding the human and the divine as constituting a single entity in Christ, but the fact that the Monophysites had not been in communion with Rome.

Newman had long satisfied himself that the Church of England through apostolic succession possessed the apostolicity required to make it constitute one of the legitimate branches of the Holy Catholic and Apostolic Church. He had also believed the Church of England possessed catholicity, that is, could understand itself as part of the Holy Catholic and Apostolic Church on the grounds that at the time of the Reformation the Church of Rome has passed into schism from the true Catholic Church residing in England. Newman's key disturbing insight regarding the Monophysites was that it might be impossible for a church, whether the Church of England or his Catholic coterie, to possess catholicity apart from communion with Rome. The persuasive power of this perceived historical parallel would grow in Newman's mind over the next five years and would in two pre-*Apologia* Roman Catholic publications and the *Apologia* itself constitute the basis for his account of his eventual loss of faith in the via media and his conversion to Rome. In the autumn of 1839, the insight had not yet produced that revolution in his mind. It is uncertain whether that

---

26. JHN to Henry Manning, September 1, 1839, *L&D* 7: 133; see also, JHN to H. A. Woodgate, October 20, 1839, *L&D* 7: 169. Also consult Donald A. Withey, *John Henry Newman: The Liturgy and the Breviary, Their Influence on His Life as an Anglican* (London: Sheed and Ward, 1992).

revolution would have occurred or would have produced consequent action had not subsequent events transpired.[27] He would appeal to the Monophysite parallel as a possible pretense or explanation for action only after those subsequent events transformed his situation in both Oxford and the English Church.

Between 1837 and 1841 three Tractarian publications cumulatively produced a momentous, new outpouring of Protestant and more general public hostility toward the movement and toward Newman himself and caused their eventual repudiation by former high church supporters.[28] It was the latter development that would leave Newman and his late Tractarian followers largely isolated, with few defenders or sympathizers in the English Church. In the *Apologia* Newman devotes substantial attention to only one of these crucial publications.

First, in 1837 Isaac Williams published his initial tract *On Reserve in Communicating Religious Knowledge.* There he urged withholding the open preaching of the atonement until a church member demonstrated personal discipline and virtuous living. Williams composed his tract self-consciously as a direct assault on evangelical religion, but it also became read as an injunction to secret, esoteric religious teaching.[29] Churchmen across the theological spectrum of the English Church rejected the premises of Williams's argument and saw it as a Tractarian assault on the proper teaching and propagation of the Christian faith.

Second, in 1838 and 1839 there appeared the four-volume collection of *Remains of the Late Reverend Richard Hurrell Froude* edited by Newman and Keble. It contained among other things a personal diary recounting a life of intense introspective religious struggle accompanied by asceticism as well as various remarks deeply hostile to the English Reformation, the English reformers, and the Church of England defined as a Protestant communion.[30] The publication of Froude's *Remains* came to mark in the minds of many a

---

27. See Stephen Thomas, *Newman and Heresy: The Anglican Years* (Cambridge: Cambridge Univ. Press, 1991), pp. 203–224.

28. On these publications and Newman's silence in the *Apologia,* see O'Faolain, *Newman's Way,* pp. 259–266.

29. Isaac Williams, *The Autobiography of Isaac Williams,* ed. George Prevost (London: Longmans, Green, 1892), pp. 91, 92. Newman had also objected to the frequent preaching of the atonement. See JHN to James Stephen, March 16, 1835, *L&D* 5: 44–48.

30. See William J. Baker, "Hurrell Froude and the Reformers," *Journal of Ecclesiastical History* 21 (1970): 243–259; Piers Brendon, "Newman, Keble, and Froude's *Remains,*" *English Historical Review* 88 (1972): 697–716; Piers Brendon, *Hurrell Froude and the Oxford Movement* (London: Paul Elek, 1974), pp. 180–197.

distinct turning point in the Tractarian Movement where a yearning for things Catholic and deep animus toward the English Reformation displaced the earlier concern for the position of the Church of England in the religious marketplace. Froude's *Remains* provoked the first major attacks on the Tractarians from high churchmen, who for all their understanding of the English Church as a branch of the Holy Catholic and Apostolic Church also regarded it as a fundamentally Protestant institution. Evangelical critics thought that in the publication of Froude's *Remains* the Tractarians had at last revealed their true, and long concealed, Romanish sentiments and intentions to the world.

The doubts roused by Froude's posthumous volumes received radical confirmation in early 1841 with the publication of Newman's *Tract 90*, titled *Remarks on Certain Passages in the Thirty-Nine Articles*. There, as Newman stated in the *Apologia*, "I wanted to ascertain what was the limit of that elasticity [of the Articles] in the direction of Roman dogma"; "to institute an inquiry how far, in critical fairness, the text *could* be opened"; and to ascertain "what a man who subscribed it might hold than what he must" (198). His purpose in 1841 had been to assure the restless Catholic followers who surrounded him that at the time of ordination they could subscribe to the articles before their bishop without denying what they and Newman regarded as Catholic truth. In the words of the tract, Newman had declared, "that, while our Prayer Book is acknowledged on all hands to be of Catholic origin, our Articles also, the offspring of an uncatholic age, are through GOD's good providence, to say the least, not uncatholic, and may be subscribed by those who aim at being catholic in heart and doctrine." Newman further argued that the Thirty-Nine Articles were to be interpreted not according to the intent of their framers but according to the voice of the Church Catholic. In this regard, toward the close of the tract he urged, "It is a *duty* which we owe both to the Catholic Church and to our own, to take our reformed confessions in the most Catholic sense they will admit; we have no duties towards their framers."[31] In

---

31. John Henry Newman, *Tract Ninety, or Remarks on Certain Passages in the Thirty-Nine Articles*, ed. A. W. Evans (London: Constable, 1933), pp. 1, 100 [hereafter cited as *Tract 90*]. This is a reprint of the extremely rare first edition of *Tract 90*. Archbishop Whatley wrote: "Tract 90 was elicited from Newman by the solicitations of a great body of his followers, who insisted on having, if they were not to join the Roman Church, some scheme of interpretation laid before them by which they could professedly adhere to the Articles. And they accordingly obtained one which would have taught them, if need were, to subscribe to the Koran." Whatley quoted in David Newsome, *The Convert Cardinals: John Henry Newman and Henry Edward Manning* (London: John Murray, 1993), p. 142. For a general discussion of the events surrounding *Tract 90*, see Turner, *John Henry Newman*, pp. 351–389.

this fashion Newman disconnected the meaning to be ascribed to the articles from the intent of their authors, from the Reformation context of their composition, and from the institutional authority of the contemporary Church of England and its bishops. Newman had furthermore also presented highly tendentious Catholic interpretations of individual articles, none of the more offensive of which did he quote in the *Apologia*.

Yngve Brilioth, an otherwise generally sympathetic early twentieth-century scholar of Newman, commented: "Tract 90 is and remains a very melancholy document. It shows how a really great man can become little in a false and ambiguous position. It is hard not to affirm a certain double-dealing when one compares Newman's later presentation of the matter with the contents of the disputed document." But Newman's mode of reasoning in *Tract 90* had roused immediate criticism at the time of its publication even from his close friends, a fact about which Newman remained silent in the *Apologia*. J. W. Bowden complained, "One thing, (candidly) I do *not* like in the tract is its vagueness — it does not clearly tell us what you *do* mean — what you really wish to say, and *what not*." Pusey, writing to a Tractarian-minded friend, anticipated "a lasting impression of our Jesuitism" flowing from the tract. Pusey had also earlier told Newman as much in a letter that Newman withheld from public knowledge during the nineteenth century.[32]

On March 15 the Heads of Houses at Oxford issued a statement denouncing the "modes of interpretation" advanced by *Tract 90* "as evading rather than explaining the sense of the Thirty-nine Articles"; as "reconciling subscription to them with the adoption of errors, which they were designed to counteract"; and as defeating "the object" and being "inconsistent with the due observance" of the university statutes. Shortly after receiving this condemnation, Newman defended the tract on the grounds that it had been "addressed to one set of persons" but "used and commented on by another,"[33] thus confirming the conviction that the Tractarians were engaged in a secret teaching of Roman Catholic doctrine.

32. Yngve Brilioth, *The Anglican Revival: Studies in the Oxford Movement* (London: Longmans, Green, 1925), p. 155; J. W. Bowden to JHN, March 15, 1841; E. B. Pusey to J. R. Hope, April 18, 1841; E. B. Pusey to JHN, March 8, 1841, *L&D* 8: 71, 178, 62. See also R. W. Church to F. Rogers, March 14, 1841, *L&D* 8: 108–111, which reports Pusey's unhappiness with *Tract 90* as well as other contemporary reactions to the tract.

33. Condemnation by Heads of Houses; J. H. Newman, "Postscript," *A Letter Addressed to the Rev. R. W. Jelf, D.D., Canon of Christ Church, In Explanation of the Ninetieth Tract in the Series Called the Tracts for the Times,* reprinted in John Henry Newman, *The Via Media of the Anglican Church. Illustrated in Lectures, Letters, and Tracts Written between 1830 and 1841* (London: Longmans, Green, 1899), 2: 362, 390.

Shortly thereafter the archbishop of Canterbury demanded that the publication of the *Tracts for the Times* cease. For him and other bishops *Tract 90* had proved particularly inflammatory because of its implicit challenge to episcopal authority. The bishops, as well as other contemporary religious and secular commentators, clearly understood Newman to have contended that ordinands might subscribe to the articles according to their own private interpretation not necessarily shared with the bishop before whom they were making the subscription. During the next four years English bishops as well as other religious and secular commentators unleashed relentless accusations of Newman's harboring secret Roman Catholic sympathies and of promoting an insincere, evasive, dishonest subscription to the Thirty-Nine Articles. Only as those episcopal attacks—often linked to criticism of Williams's tract on reserve, Froude's *Remains,* and the *British Critic*—continued to explode did Newman begin to write extensively in private about the impact upon him in 1839 of the Monophysite parallel and his concerns regarding the catholicity of the English Church. In May 1843, Newman candidly stated to Keble, "For surely I should feel no anxiety at all about treachery to the Church, if they, as organs of prevailing opinion as well as Bishops, had one and all *approved* and *recommended* No. 90, instead of censuring it."[34]

By the end of 1841, as the controversy over *Tract 90* swept the Church of England and the nation, Newman had begun to withdraw from Oxford to live at nearby Littlemore where he established a retreat house for himself, friends, and sympathizers and where for the next four years he pursued a private, deeply ascetic monastic experiment. In a letter of late 1841 quoted in the *Apologia,* Newman called Littlemore the "refuge for the destitute" (262). He presided over the self-selected Littlemore group very much as a head of an Oxford college, guiding their reading, devotional life, diet, and table conversations. He now self-consciously understood himself to have undertaken a prophetic ministry. One contemporary newspaper described Newman and his late Tractarian coterie as in "a state of schism with the whole Christian world."[35]

In sermons and letters of the time as well as in the *Apologia* Newman described his religious role at Littlemore as resembling the prophet Elijah, who, having overturned the idols, still did not worship in the temple in Jerusalem. Newman and his followers regarded themselves as an enclave or gathered conventicle of the Church Catholic waiting for either the Church of England or the Roman Catholic Church to undertake a program of reform. In the *Apologia* Newman described Littlemore as his Torres Vedras where he, like

---

34. JHN to J. Keble, May 18, 1843, *L&D* 9: 348.

35. JHN to Richard Church, December 24, 1841, *L&D* 8: 384; *Morning Herald,* March 26, 1841, p. 4.

the Duke of Wellington in the Peninsular War, retreated, waiting to fight another day. He also began to admit to himself and others the eccentricity of his understanding of the Anglican faith. In March 1843 Newman confessed to Keble that his particular interpretation of the Thirty-Nine Articles had actually "never been drawn out, to say the least, before," even by Catholic-minded divines.[36]

In September 1843, after William Lockhardt, one of his Littlemore followers, suddenly converted to Roman Catholicism, Newman resigned his living at St. Mary's while retaining his Oriel fellowship and its income. In "The Parting of Friends," his final sermon delivered as a priest of the Church of England, he bemoaned the incapacity of the Church of England and particularly its high churchmen to make use of its Catholic sons. In the early autumn of 1843 Newman felt special animus toward the latter group, who had once supported him but were now overwhelmingly turning on him and the movement he had led.

Those months had witnessed first the publication of an article by William Gladstone sharply criticizing the direction of the Tractarian Movement since the publication of Froude's *Remains*. At approximately the same moment William Palmer, the early conservative high church supporter of the Tractarian Movement to whom Newman devotes considerable attention in the *Apologia*, published *A Narrative of Events Connected with the Publication of the Tracts for the Times, with Reflections on Existing Tendencies to Romanism, and on the Present Duties and Prospects of Members of the Church*.[37] This long pamphlet, about the publication of which Newman had been warned for weeks, denounced the Romanizing tendencies of the Tractarians, again dating the shift from the publication of Froude's *Remains*. Shortly thereafter Palmer persuaded the Rivington publishing firm to cease publication of the *British Critic*, which by then Newman's brother-in-law Thomas Mozley edited with increasing deference to radical late Tractarian authors. Newman omits from

---

36. JHN to John Keble, March 14, 1843, *L&D* 9: 280.

37. W. E. Gladstone, "Present Aspect of the Church," *Foreign and Colonial Review* 2 (1843): 554; William Palmer, *A Narrative of Events Connected with the Publication of the Tracts for the Times, with Reflections on Existing Tendencies to Romanism, and on the Present Duties and Prospects of Members of the Church* (Oxford: John Henry Parker, 1843). Both Gladstone and Palmer despite private misgivings had long been publicly considered sympathetic to the Tractarians. Their publications of the autumn of 1843 represented efforts on their respective parts to protect Gladstone's political career and Palmer's ecclesiastical reputation from the rapidly growing high church hostility to Tractarian radicalism. The former succeeded, the latter did not. On this high church assault on Newman and the Tractarians, see Turner, *John Henry Newman*, pp. 465–473.

the *Apologia* all these details of high church attacks and relentless Tractarian radicalism in the *British Critic,* as well as other events to be examined later surrounding his last years in the Church of England.

Also in 1843, in hope of giving his restless group something to do to subsume their Catholic devotion, Newman had launched a series on *Lives of the English Saints.* As soon as the first manuscripts were circulated, high churchmen stood aghast at the Romanish sympathies appearing therein and urged Newman to desist. To one of them, J. R. Hope, he responded: "Now Church History is made up of these three elements — miracles, monkery, Popery. If any sympathetic feeling is expressed on behalf of the persons and events of Church History, it is a feeling in favor of miracles, or monkery, or Popery, one or all." The series — with numerous examples of credulity toward medieval miracles, admiration for monastic celibacy, and sympathy for the medieval papacy — continued, but by early December 1843 Newman resigned quite angrily as editor. At that time he told Hope, "I assure you, to find that the English Church cannot bear the lives of her Saints . . . does not tend to increase my faith and confidence in her."[38] Two decades later Charles Kingsley would cite these saints' lives as ammunition in his hapless attack on Newman. For Kingsley and others the *Lives of the English Saints* embodied not only credulity but also distasteful interest in saintly virginity and celibacy, both of which they regarded as attacks on the institution of the Victorian family.

Hostility directed toward Newman exacerbated in both the English Church and Oxford as other late Tractarians, most importantly W. G. Ward and Frederick Oakeley, published their own more radical interpretations of *Tract 90.* In the *Apologia* Newman would sharply criticize both men but name only Ward. There, Newman described his radical Catholic followers of the late 1830s and early 1840s as "younger men, and of a cast of mind in no small degree uncongenial to my own" who represented "a new school of thought . . . sweeping the original party of the Movement aside, and . . . taking its place" (255–266). According to this view in 1864, "These men cut into the original Movement at an angle, fell across its lines of thought, and then set about turning that line in its own direction" (266). Newman complained of their needing "to be kept in order," a task he undertook because of their "great zeal" for him (267, 266). But in fact during 1841 and for some time thereafter Newman treated the brilliantly brash Ward as an intimate theological confidant and repeatedly urged the inclusion of his articles in the *British Critic.* Although Newman later claimed that he had not intended to make the Thirty-Nine Articles compatible with Rome, throughout 1841 there is no evidence

38. JHN to J. R. Hope, November 6 and December 11, 1843, *L&D* 10: 12, 55.

that he sought to dissuade or silence Ward, but rather he privately defended Ward steadily against his detractors. Indeed, Newman urged Mozley to be particularly solicitous of Ward in relation to the *British Critic*, telling him in late August 1841: "Ward is *full* of ideas of writing—and it would be a great point to *expand* him. He is most desirous to be moderate."[39]

Thereafter, over the next three years, Ward became only more radical. In *The Ideal of a Christian Church* (1844), he declared in regard to one of the Thirty-Nine Articles, "of course I think its natural meaning may be explained away, for I subscribe it myself in a non-natural sense." Furthermore, along with Frederick Oakeley he argued that the articles were compatible with all Roman doctrine. Newman had not made that argument, but he did not publicly refute it during his Tractarian years. Early in 1845 Oxford Convocation, the university governing body composed of those graduates holding master of arts degrees, urged on by evangelicals and disillusioned high churchmen, would condemn Ward's *Ideal of a Christian Church* and rescind his degrees.[40]

On October 9, 1845, two years after the opening of this high church onslaught, Newman entered the Roman Catholic Church, publishing *An Essay on the Development of Christian Doctrine* (1845) shortly thereafter. This remarkable book had little effect at the time among either Anglicans or Roman Catholics. Newman's entry into the Roman Catholic Church essentially removed Newman for many years from general public notice. By 1857 he would write his closest friend, "To the rising generation itself, to the sons of those who knew or read me 15 or 20 years ago, I am a character of history—they know nothing of me; they have heard my name, and nothing more—they have no associations with it."[41]

In 1848, after studying in Rome and having been ordained a Roman Catholic priest the previous year, Newman founded an English Oratory of St. Philip

---

39. JHN to Thomas Mozley, August 23, 1841, *L&D* 8: 252.

40. W. G. Ward, *The Ideal of a Christian Church Considered in Comparison with Existing Practice, Containing a Defence of Certain Articles in the British Critic in Reply to Remarks on Them in Mr. Palmer's "Narrative."* (London: J. Toovey, 1844), p. 479; see also pp. 474–481, 567–568. Wilfrid Philip Ward, *William George Ward and the Oxford Movement* (London: Macmillan, 1890), p. 173. Nockles, "Oxford, Tract 90 and the Bishops," p. 54, suggested that Newman himself bordered on a nonnatural interpretation. Oxford Convocation played an important role in the history of the Tractarian Movement. When Convocation met, large numbers of graduates from around the country would attend if the issues were controversial. During the Tractarian era the majority in the Convocation shifted first against any hint of government-instigated reform at Oxford and then within a few years against any hint of Romanish influences arising from the Tractarians.

41. JHN to A. St. John, July 15, 1857, *L&D* 18: 94.

Neri, which located itself the next year in Birmingham, with a second branch later being established in London under the leadership of Father Frederick Faber. In 1850 Newman intruded himself into the internal conflicts of the Church of England occasioned by the Gorham Judgment, whereby the Judicial Committee of the Privy Council, a civil court, had endorsed a low church or evangelical interpretation of the sacrament of baptism as standing within the teaching of the Church of England. This judgment, whereby the English state decided a matter of internal Church of England doctrine, spurred a number of Anglicans, including Henry (later Cardinal) Manning, to convert to Roman Catholicism. In the wake of the Gorham Judgment Newman published *Certain Difficulties Felt by Anglicans in Catholic Teaching Considered*. In it, he presented his first extensive interpretation of the Tractarian Movement, which he termed "The Religious Movement of 1833," as initially targeting Erastianism but no less importantly seeing as "their great and deadly foe, their scorn, and their laughing-stock, . . . that imbecile, inconsistent thing called Protestantism."[42] Contending the inevitable outcome of the movement was toward Roman Catholicism, Newman called his former colleagues to convert to Rome in the wake of the Gorham Judgment, which demonstrated the power of the Protestant culture of the nation over the English state and thereby over the Church of England, thus dooming the effectiveness of Catholics in that communion. It was in this book that Newman first extensively explored for a Protestant audience the Monophysite parallel that he would make the core of his *Apologia* conversion narrative.

In 1851 Newman delivered the series of addresses later published as *Lectures on the Present Position of Catholics in England*. There he harshly criticized G. G. Achilli, an Italian monk who had renounced his orders and taken up anti–Roman Catholic lecturing. A criminal libel suit was brought against Newman, who in 1853 was condemned to a relatively modest fine and high

---

42. Newman, *Certain Difficulties*, 1: 145. The entire subject of the Tractarian view of the relationship between church and state is a difficult one. Anti-Erastianism was less fundamental in 1833 and the immediate years thereafter than Newman claimed in both *Certain Difficulties* and the *Apologia*. The Gorham Judgment and the judicial rulings regarding the publication of *Essays and Reviews* provided the immediate background for Newman's emphasis first in 1850 and again in 1864 on the anti-Erastianism of the Tractarian Movement. For a brilliant, subtle discussion of the numerous ambiguities surrounding this subject, consult Skinner, *Tractarians and the "Condition of England,"* pp. 87–138, as well as the discussion of the Gorham case and Newman's reaction in Chadwick, *The Victorian Church*, 1: 250–271, 288–289. See also John Henry Newman, *Discourses Addressed to Mixed Congregations,* 2nd ed. (London: Longman, Brown, Green, and Longmans, 1850), p. vi, where Newman, in dedicating the volume in 1849 to Bishop Wiseman, recalled the effect of having read his article of 1839.

court costs paid by his Roman Catholic supporters.[43] Newman believed the case might have been decided otherwise had Cardinal Nicholas Wiseman provided more support. Further disappointment and disillusionment with the English Roman Catholic hierarchy would follow later in the decade.

In 1851 Archbishop Paul Cullen invited Newman to preside over the establishment of a Roman Catholic University in Dublin. Newman accepted the invitation. One result of his academic work in Ireland was his composing the lectures that became *The Idea of a University* (1852). Newman left the Catholic University in 1858 and returned to Birmingham, his Irish experience and his relationship with Irish Roman Catholic authorities having been anything but a success. Thereafter, Newman's life continued within the subculture of the mid-century English Catholic community, where by this time he had become only one of many Anglican converts. Over the course of this decade he quarreled seriously with almost all of the converts to Roman Catholicism who had once formed the core of his most fervent late Tractarian Anglican admirers, most particularly Frederick Faber, J. B. Dalgairns, and W. G. Ward. In the middle of the decade the Birmingham and London oratories split after considerable friction and ill will.[44]

Toward the close of the 1850s Newman became deeply involved with a group of liberal Roman Catholics who published the *Rambler,* which he himself briefly edited. His work on the *Rambler* included his important article of 1859 "On Consulting the Faithful in Matters of Doctrine." In that highly controversial article, which was not fully reprinted in his lifetime, Newman reverted to an expansive understanding of doctrinal development occurring outside established ecclesiastical authority that very much resembled his previously articulated Tractarian view of a prophetical tradition. In this crucial article of 1859 he wrote:

> I think I am right in saying that the tradition of the Apostles, committed to the whole Church in its various constituents and functions *per modum unius,*

---

43. This case is addressed, though often only briefly, in all the Newman biographies. For a reconsideration of this historiography, see F. B. Smith, *The Queen, On the Prosecution of Giovanni Giacinto Achilli v John Henry Newman. For Criminal Libel, Court of Queen's Bench Westminster 1851–1853* (Canberra: privately printed, F. B. Smith, History Program, Research School of Social Sciences, Australian National Univ., 2000).

44. The best historical analysis of Newman's career in Ireland is Colin Barr, *Paul Cullen, John Henry Newman, and the Catholic University of Ireland, 1845–1865* (Notre Dame, Ind.: Univ. of Notre Dame Press, 2003). A. Dwight Culler, *The Imperial Intellect: A Study of Newman's Educational Ideal* (New Haven, Conn.: Yale Univ. Press, 1955) remains the classic study of Newman's educational ideal. For a clear, succinct discussion of Newman's situation within the English Roman Catholic Church from 1850 to the publication of the *Apologia,* see Newsome, *The Convert Cardinals,* pp. 185–234.

manifests itself variously at various times: sometimes by the mouth of the episcopacy, sometimes by the doctors, sometimes by the people, sometimes by liturgies, rites, ceremonies, and customs, by events, disputes, movements, and all those other phenomena which are comprised under the name of history. It follows that none of these channels of tradition may be treated with disrespect; granting at the same time fully, that the gift of discerning, discriminating, defining, promulgating, and enforcing any portion of that tradition resides solely in the *Ecclesia docens*.[45]

These and other views enunciated in the article roused suspicions about Newman's loyalty to Roman Catholic authorities among ultramontane English Roman Catholics who championed centralizing ecclesiastical and doctrinal authority in the papacy.

As John Coulson commented, Newman's publication of "On Consulting the Faithful in Matters of Doctrine" constituted "an act of political suicide from which his career within the Church was never fully to recover; at one stroke, he, whose reputation as the one honest broker between the extremes of English catholic opinion had hitherto stood untarnished, gained the Pope's personal displeasure, the reputation at Rome of being the most dangerous man in England, and a formal accusation of heresy preferred against him by the Bishop of Newport."[46] Newman communicated to Cardinal Wiseman his willingness to obey the Roman authorities, but Wiseman failed to deliver the message. Through various missteps Newman mistakenly came to believe the matter had been settled; the Roman authorities for their part thought he had ignored them. Once again, doubt swirled around Newman. Thereafter, rumors circulated in both the Roman Catholic and English Church communions that Newman might return to the English Church.

In 1862 Newman formally repudiated those rumors in a public letter that concluded, "I do hereby profess *ex animo*, with an absolute internal assent and consent, that Protestantism is the dreariest of possible religions; that the thought of the Anglican service makes me shiver, and the thought of the Thirty-nine Articles makes me shudder." On this occasion the *Saturday Review* commented that "the old lion" had "since his change of religion, hardly sustained his old reputation or fulfilled the expectations of his new allies."

45. John H. Newman, *On Consulting the Faithful in Matters of Doctrine*, ed. John Coulson (New York: Sheed and Ward, 1961), p. 63. This essay originally appeared in the *Rambler* in July 1859.

46. John Coulson, "Introduction," ibid., p. 2. The entire introduction is a good discussion of this important incident in Newman's life. See also Josef L. Altholz, *The Liberal Catholic Movement in England: the "Rambler" and Its Contributors, 1848–1864* (London: Burns and Oates, 1862); Hugh A. MacDougall, *The Acton-Newman Relations: The Dilemma of Christian Liberalism* (New York: Fordham Univ., 1962).

Two years later the *Christian Remembrancer* would similarly observe: "For some reason or other Dr. Newman is to all appearance stranded where he is. The Church of his adoption does not seem to appreciate him, or is afraid of him. It gives him no work commensurate with his powers. To us outsiders he seems condemned to an aimless inactivity."[47]

Newman's personal self-assessment was not much different as he noted on January 21, 1863, in his private journal: "O how forlorn & dreary has been my course since I have been a Catholic! Here has been the contrast — as a Protestant, I felt my religion dreary, but not my life — but, as a Catholic, my life dreary, not my religion. . . . since I have been a Catholic, I seem to myself to have had nothing but failure, personally."[48] Newman at this point saw his life as having been a series of failures in both the Anglican and the Roman Catholic churches.

At the very close of 1863, however, a potentially obscure event transformed Newman's situation, drew him from religious isolation and intellectual underemployment, and spurred the production of a masterpiece of English prose and religious autobiography. From the Newman of history there emerged the Newman of the *Apologia Pro Vita Sua*.

The Dispute with Kingsley

In late December 1863 an anonymous correspondent sent Newman a copy of *Macmillan's Magazine* for the next month. The journal included an unsigned article by the well-known Church of England clergyman, novelist, and social activist Charles Kingsley in which he asserted: "Truth, for its own sake, had never been a virtue with the Roman Clergy. Father Newman informs us that it need not, and on the whole ought not to be."[49]

Receipt of the offensive article, like Charles Darwin's receiving the letter

---

47. JHN to the Editor of the *Globe,* June 28, 1862, *L&D* 20: 216. He sent the same letter to other papers as well. See *L&D* 20: 216–220. In a private memorandum on this letter Newman wrote in regard to the Church of England: "I do not say that no one is saved *in* it; I only say that no one is saved *by* it. . . . I account it to be a breakwater against infidelity, and do not wish it destroyed. Catholics in England could not take its place at this time." *L&D* 20: 221. These latter sentiments would reappear in the *Apologia,* especially in Note E, "The Anglican Church." "Dr. Newman," *Saturday Review* 14 (1862): 12; "Dr. Newman's Apology," *Christian Remembrancer* 48 (1864): 164.

48. John Henry Newman, *Autobiographical Writings,* ed. Henry Tristram (New York: Sheed and Ward, 1957), pp. 254–255.

49. *Mr. Kingsley and Dr. Newman: A Correspondence on the Question "Whether Dr. Newman Teaches That Truth Is No Virtue?"* as reprinted in Wilfrid Ward, ed., *Newman's Apologia Pro Vita Sua: The Two Versions of 1864 & 1865, Preceded by Newman's and Kingsley's Pamphlets* (London: Oxford Univ. Press, 1913), p. 6.

from Alfred Wallace containing his own unpublished theory of evolution by natural selection, moved Newman from depressed lethargy to inspired action. On December 30, 1863, Newman protested to Alexander Macmillan that the then still anonymous article contained "no reference at the bottom of the page to any words of mine, much less any quotation from my writings, in justification of this statement." On January 6, Kingsley replied to Newman, "That my words were just, I believed from many passages in your writings; but the document to which I expressly referred was one of your Sermons on 'Subjects of the Day,' No. XX, in the Volume published in 1844, and entitled 'Wisdom and Innocence.'" Two days later Newman expressed surprise to Macmillan that Kingsley, with whom he had clashed previously, was the offending author and stated that he would "account public property" any further correspondence that might ensue between him and Kingsley.[50] After receiving two drafts of unsatisfactory proffered apologies, Newman on January 31, 1864, completed a pamphlet titled *Mr. Kingsley and Dr. Newman: A Correspondence on the Question 'Whether Dr. Newman Teaches That Truth Is No Virtue?'* It contained the previous correspondence and a sharp complaint that Kingsley had been unjust and ungentlemanly. Newman's pamphlet appeared on February 12.

On March 20, in one of the most momentous rhetorical and polemical failures of the Victorian age, Kingsley defended himself in *"What, Then, Does Dr. Newman Mean?" A Reply to a Pamphlet Lately Published by Dr. Newman.* There returning to the subject of the sermon "Wisdom and Innocence," Kingsley declared his "right, in self-justification, to put before the public so much of that sermon, and the rest of Dr. Newman's writings, as will show why I formed so harsh an opinion of them and him, and why I still consider that sermon (whatever may be its meaning) as most dangerous and misleading." Evoking all the long-simmering suspicions of Newman's Roman Catholic allegiance while in the English Church, Kingsley contended that the sermon of 1843 was not "a Protestant" but rather "a Romish sermon" because Newman had written of monks and nuns as "the only perfect Christians" and had given to the terms "'wisdom,' 'prudence,' 'silence,' the meaning which they would have in the mouth of a Romish teacher — St. Alfonso de Liguori, for instance." Consequently, Newman had only himself to blame, Kingsley claimed, if Kingsley had read the sermon as not making a virtue of truthfulness. Kingsley then pro-

---

50. JHN to Messrs. Macmillan and Co., December 30, 1863, *L&D* 20: 571; Charles Kingsley to JHN, January 6, 1864, JHN to Alexander Macmillan, January 8, 1864, *L&D* 21: 10, 15. Kingsley's name had appeared on the cover of the relevant issue of *Macmillan's Magazine,* but Newman may not have been sent the cover.

nounced, "No one would have suspected" Newman "to be a dishonest man, if he had not perversely chosen to assume a style which (as he himself confesses) the world always associates with dishonesty."[51]

Kingsley also harshly criticized other of Newman's writings drawn from both his Anglican and Roman Catholic years. He cited the examples of Newman's credulity in the historical reality of medieval miracles manifested in the *Lives of the English Saints* and of modern miracles in *Certain Difficulties Felt by Anglicans* and *Lectures on the Present Position of Catholics* as evidence of intellectual dishonesty. He further accused Newman of repeatedly employing an economy of truth and writing in such a manner that a reasonable reader might conclude he was a dishonest man. Again associating Newman with St. Alfonso de Liguori on economy, Kingsley concluded:

> Yes — I am afraid that I must say it once more — Truth is not honoured among these men for its own sake. There are, doubtless, pure and noble souls among them, superior, through the grace of God, to the morality of their class: but in their official writings, and in too much of their official conduct, the great majority of them seem never, for centuries past to have perceived that truth is the capital virtue, the virtue of all virtues, without which all others are hollow and rotten; and with which there is hope for a man's repentance and conversion, in spite of every vice, if only he remains honest.

Kingsley venomously closed the pamphlet, "And so I leave Dr. Newman, only expressing my fear, that if he continues to 'economize' and 'divide' the words of his adversaries as he has done mine, he will run great danger of forfeiting once more his reputation for honesty."[52]

As commentators have long noted, the vitriolic animosity of Kingsley's pamphlet as well as the contempt for Newman residing behind his original comment had deep personal roots.[53] Kingsley identified Newman's influence

---

51. Charles Kingsley, *"What, Then, Does Dr. Newman Mean?" A Reply to a Pamphlet Lately Published by Dr. Newman* in Ward, ed., *Newman's Apologia Pro Vita Sua*, pp. 17–19, 36.

52. Ibid., pp. 60–61, 62. For the chaotic conditions under which Kingsley composed his pamphlet, his difficulty in locating copies of Newman's relevant publications, and the manner that his dispute with Newman split the liberal Victorian religious publishing community, see Alan Hertz, "The Broad Church Militant and Newman's Humiliation of Charles Kingsley," *Victorian Periodicals Review* 19 (1986): 141–149.

53. The standard biographies of Kingsley are Robert Bernard Martin, *The Dust of Combat: A Life of Charles Kingsley* (London: Faber, 1959); Susan Chitty, *The Beast and the Monk: A Life of Charles Kingsley* (New York: Mason/Charter, 1975). See also Michael Wheeler, *The Old Enemies: Catholic and Protestant in Nineteenth-Century English Culture* (Cambridge: Cambridge Univ. Press, 2006), pp. 67–76; Oliver S. Buckton, *Secret*

in the Church of England not only with the revival of Roman Catholic sympathies, but also and more important with the championing of a revival of clerical celibacy, monasticism, and hatred of sexuality and marriage, both of which Kingsley strongly approved. Kingsley's future wife had considered entering a religious order as a young woman. Kingsley himself had considered practicing celibacy. All of his personal animus as well as his strong, heartfelt anti–Roman Catholicism burst forth in his pamphlet as it had in his novel *Hypatia; or, New Foes with an Old Face* (1852–1853), which related the story of an ancient female philosopher killed by a group of fanatical monks. On that occasion Newman had responded with his own novel of early Christianity titled *Callista: A Sketch of the Third Century* (1855). Hence the hostility between Kingsley and Newman had extended for more than a decade. Kingsley, who had written other novels attacking Roman Catholicism, embodied the face and voice of a respectable mode of English Protestant anti–Roman Catholicism. His stature made him a figure to whom a response, if properly gauged, would gain attention. For Newman that attention could serve a number of immediate purposes.

Kingsley's ill-conceived pamphlet of 1864 provided Newman with the occasion to address both long-standing Protestant and more recent Roman Catholic challenges to his reputation. The latter was important since Kingsley's attack coincided with an ultimately unsuccessful effort on Newman's part to return to Oxford as head of a Roman Catholic college or house. To members of the Roman Catholic Church Newman would demonstrate firm zeal for dogmatic religion in the face of ultramontane doubts and establish distance from his former liberal Roman Catholic associates, thus justifying his undertaking a new Roman Catholic mission. To Protestants he would present himself as an honest Englishman and Roman Catholicism as a religion that Protestant Englishmen could respect and not fear its dwelling in the midst of their nation and perhaps in one of their ancient universities.

Kingsley's pamphlet thus provided Newman with the opportunity to redefine and reinterpret on his own terms his Anglican career and his Roman

---

Selves: Confession and Same-Sex Desire in Victorian Autobiography (Chapel Hill: Univ. of North Carolina Press, 1998), pp. 21–59; David Hilliard, "Unenglish and Unmanly: Anglo-Catholicism and Homosexuality," *Victorian Studies* 25 (1982): 181–219; Susan Dorman, "Hypatia and Callista: The Initial Skirmish between Kingsley and Newman," *Nineteenth-Century Fiction* 34, No. 2 (September 1979): 173–193; Frank M. Turner, "Christians and Pagans in Victorian Novels," in *Roman Presences: Receptions of Rome in European Culture, 1789–1945,* ed. Catharine Edwards (Cambridge: Cambridge Univ. Press, 1999), pp. 173–188.

Catholic aspirations. This goal had energized Newman's mind as he awaited Kingsley's pamphlet. During that interval Newman told his sister Jemima, "I have never defended myself—and I have let others speak for me whose aims were not mine, though they were most kind in doing it." And defend himself Newman did. Kingsley had so meanly and crudely exaggerated his accusations that Newman could elicit immediate sympathy from his own readers. Denouncing Kingsley's anticipatory accusations of dishonesty in his opening salvo titled "Mr. Kingsley's Method of Disputation," Newman announced with enormous polemical energy: "What I insist upon here is this unmanly attempt of his, in his concluding pages, to cut the ground from under my feet;—to poison by anticipation the public mind against me, John Henry Newman, and to infuse into the imaginations of my readers, suspicion and mistrust of everything that I may say in reply to him. This I call *poisoning the wells.*"[54] Exposing Kingsley's blatant unfairness in all its cheapness, Newman declared that he would defend himself against "the impression of twenty years ago and the impression now" that "I was for years where I had no right to be; that I was a 'Romanist' in Protestant livery and service; that I was doing the work of a hostile Church in the bosom of the English Establishment, and knew it, or ought to have known it" (125). The vehicle of his defense would be autobiography. To "break through this barrier of prejudice against me" Newman explained that he would present the history of his religious opinions, explore his most private thoughts, and set "nothing down . . . as certain, of which I have not a clear memory, or some written memorial, or the corroboration of some friend" (127, 129). All this vast effort he would undertake because "I do not like to be called to my face a liar and a knave" (130).

To refute Kingsley's charges and to dissolve those prejudices, Newman published two distinct versions of the *Apologia Pro Vita Sua*, that of 1864 and that of 1865. The first consisted of a series of seven consecutively numbered pamphlets published on Thursdays between April 21 and June 2, 1864, supplemented by an extensive, fiercely antagonistic appendix. Four of these pamphlets bore Kingsley's name in the title. The publishing house of Longman in June 1864 issued these pamphlets and the appendix as a book that constitutes the first edition with the full title of *Apologia Pro Vita Sua: Being a Reply to a Pamphlet Entitled "What, Then, Does Dr. Newman Mean?"*[55] Of this mate-

---

54. JHN to Jemima Mozley, March 4, 1864, *L&D* 21: 70; Ward, ed., *Newman's Apologia Pro Vita Sua*, p. 81.

55. The original pamphlets of 1864 were titled: Part I: *Mr. Kingsley's Method of Disputation*, pp. 1–25; Part II: *True Mode of Meeting Mr. Kingsley*, pp. 29–51; Part III:

rial Newman omitted almost one hundred pages as well as most of the direct references to Kingsley in the revised narrative published in June 1865; it had a preface dated May 2, followed by certain paragraphs from his original opening pamphlet of 1864 that set the stage for his defense of his reputation. He titled the second edition *History of My Religious Opinions*. There he relegated much of the Kingsley-related materials to a series of important notes following the narrative—notes that have received curiously little subsequent analysis. This second version is the book that became the classic and that is presented in this volume.[56] In 1873 Newman returned to his original title *Apologia Pro Vita Sua* with the subtitle *Being a History of His Religious Opinions*. Thereafter, the title and text remained largely set through frequent reprintings, into which Newman introduced usually minor verbal changes.

A text originating in a bombastic polemic and not wholly edifying exchange on both sides had been transformed into a classic of the language. The *Apologia* became a classic not because of Newman's extraordinary prose, which had marked his other postconversion books and articles. Rather it became a classic because Newman persuaded his audience that he could be both a Roman Catholic convert and a good Englishman. Such had not been obvious to most of Newman's Protestant contemporaries. His convincing Protestants redounded powerfully to his credit among most, though not all, Roman Catholics. The *Apologia* also became a classic for many Roman Catholics because of the courage Newman had demonstrated against a prejudiced detractor and because of the intellectual and theological freedom he asserted for Roman Catholics within their own church. As Newman confided in his journal in February 22, 1865: "in the last year a most wonderful deliverance has been wrought in my favour, by the controversy, of which the upshot was my Apolo-

---

History of My Religious Opinions, pp. 55–100; *Part IV: History of My Religious Opinions*, pp. 103–175; *Part V: History of My Religious Opinions*, pp. 179–253; *Part VI: History of My Religious Opinions*, pp. 257–369; *Part VII: General Answer to Mr. Kingsley*, pp. 373–430; *Appendix: Answer in Detail to Mr. Kingsley's Accusations*, pp. 3–127.

56. This pattern of a series of energized pamphlets giving way to a more stolid book had a long history in English autobiography. See James Treadwell, *Autobiographical Writing and British Literature, 1783–1834* (Oxford: Oxford Univ. Press, 2005), pp. 3–31, 59–123. On Newman's text see Martin J. Svaglic, "Editor's Introduction," John Henry Cardinal Newman, *Apologia Pro Vita Sua: Being a History of His Religious Opinions* (Oxford: Clarendon Press, 1967), pp. lii–lv. This volume is the major critical edition of the text and surrounding pamphlet exchanges. See also Ward, ed., *Newman's Apologia Pro Vita Sua*. The latter version is also available at http://www.newmanreader.org/works/apologia/index.html.

gia. It has been marvelously blest, for, while I have regarnered, or rather gained, the favour of Protestants, I have received the approbation, in formal addresses, of a good part of the English [Roman Catholic] clerical body."[57]

Truth and Concealment in Newman and Kingsley

Kingsley's charges and Newman's response evoked such a broad contemporary response because the issue of personal truthfulness was a culturally charged matter in mid-Victorian Britain. From the leading writers of the late eighteenth-century evangelical revival such as Henry Venn and Henry Thornton through Thomas Arnold, Thomas Carlyle, John Ruskin, and Samuel Smiles, the English public encountered denunciations of lying and ringing calls for truthfulness and for what would today be termed *transparency*. For evangelical moralists, sincere, personal truthfulness indicated a life of holiness and the presence of vital as opposed to nominal religion. One Victorian writer declared, "Irreligion implies to a greater or lesser extent *belief in what is not true*. Its roots are struck into a soil of falsehood. It draws its nourishment from the belief in lies."[58] Not only was truthfulness a quality associated with sincere, vital Protestant religion but also with the best values of middle-class commercial life and with English self-identity.

Contemporaneously, the issue of truthfulness had become an especially significant matter in the Victorian courtroom where for much of the century

---

57. Newman, *Autobiographical Writings*, p. 260. Newman also refrained from major revisions after 1865 because as he explained to a friend almost twenty years later, "at present my Apologia sells very fairly." JHN to P. W. Bunting, May 14, 1883, *L&D* 30: 218. For further comment on this process of the domestication of Victorian polemics, see Frank M. Turner, *Contesting Cultural Authority: Essays in Victorian Intellectual Life* (Cambridge: Cambridge Univ. Press, 1993), pp. 38–43.

58. William Landels, *True Manhood* (London: Nisbet, 1861), n.p., as quoted in Wendie Ellen Schneider, "The Liar's Cloth: Producing Veracity in the Victorian Courtroom" (Ph.D. diss., Yale Univ., 2006), p. 20. In Newman's famous discussion of the Gentleman in Discourse VIII of *The Idea of a University*, the qualities of concern for principle, honesty, or keeping of one's word do not appear. For evangelical moralists on this subject, consult Henry Venn, *The Complete Duty of Man; or, A System of Doctrinal and Practical Christianity, Designed for the Use of Families*, A New Edition Carefully Revised and Corrected by Rev. H. Venn. B.D. (New York: American Tract Society, n.d.), and Thomas Gisborne, *An Enquiry into the Duties of Men in the Higher and Middle Classes of Society in Great Britain, Resulting from Their Respective Stations, Professions, and Employments*, 4th ed., corrected (London: B. and J. White and Cadell and Davies, 1797), 2 vols. See also Margot Finn, *Character of Credit: Personal Debt in English Culture, 1740–1914* (Cambridge: Cambridge Univ. Press, 2003); Geoffrey Searle, *Morality and the Market in Victorian Britain* (Oxford: Clarendon Press, 1998).

judges and lawyers simply assumed that many witnesses and plaintiffs would lie. During the first half of the century the effort to attain truthfulness in the courtroom led to numerous persecutions for perjury. From midcentury onward the judicial device to assure truthful testimony was the emergence of elaborate cross-examination of witnesses.[59] Consequently, in numerous areas of Victorian public and civic life there was concern about the willingness of people to be voluntarily truthful linked to a lingering apprehension that they might not be.

Furthermore, since the sixteenth century anti-Catholic writers in Protestant Britain had charged that Roman Catholics might lie, dissimulate, or equivocate. During the early nineteenth century English anti-Catholic writers had pointed to the moral theology of Alfonso Maria de Liguori (1696–1787) and its official approval by Roman Catholic authorities as permitting Roman Catholic clergy to lie or equivocate. This moral theologian and founder of the Redemptionist order, who had been declared a saint in 1839, had in his instruction for priestly confession taught that penitents might be absolved even if they had in certain ways equivocated. He had also given approval to certain forms of mental reservation. Although Liguori appears to have had little or no following among Roman Catholic priests in Britain, during the 1840s and 1850s anti–Roman Catholic writers made much of this now-obscure theologian, attempting to thrust the most low-minded interpretation of his writings upon all Roman Catholic priests. The Liguori problem had been discussed and debated during the 1850s in English Roman Catholic publications, such as the *Dublin Review* and the *Rambler*. The general view that emerged was that whatever the exact details of Liguori's position or the approval his theology had received from the Roman Catholic Church, his thinking was not binding on Roman Catholic priests or clergy. In 1862 Newman himself had told a correspondent that he was not familiar with Liguori and did not think himself bound by his opinions.[60]

Nonetheless, even liberal English Protestants who should have known better assumed that Roman Catholic clergy might not follow dictates of personal truthfulness. When Newman initially complained to Alexander Macmillan about Kingsley's original charge, the publisher had replied: "I have read the

---

59. Consult Schneider, "The Liar's Cloth"; P. S. Atiyah, *The Rise and Fall of Freedom of Contract* (Oxford: Clarendon Press, 1979).

60. Perez Zagorin, *Ways of Lying* (Cambridge, Mass.: Harvard Univ. Press, 1990); Josef L. Altholz, "Truth and Equivocation: Liguori's Moral Theology and Newman's *Apologia*," *Church History* 44 (1975): 73–84; JHN to W. J. O'Neill Daunt, October 21, 1862, *L&D* 20: 316–318.

passage, and I will confess to you plainly that I did not even think at the time that you or any of your communion would think it unjust. It is many years since I had intercourse with members of the Church that holds us heretics. My intercourse then was mainly with young men—some of them as noble and good as I have ever known. On the point alluded to in Mr. Kingsley's article... I received an impression that it was generally true that their Catholic way of looking at these matters was what Mr. Kingsley says it is."[61] Macmillan's powerful anti–Roman Catholic animus must have determined much of Newman's reaction to Kingsley's subsequent correspondence with its only tepid nod toward full apology. It would also explain why Newman saw himself as bearing a responsibility for the entire Roman Catholic priesthood.

Kingsley's resort to the Liguori card required Newman to address formally the issue of Roman Catholic truthfulness in Chapter V of the *Apologia* and in Note G on "Lying and Equivocation." Some reviewers, considering Liguori irrelevant, refused to assume that any individual Roman Catholic priest or layperson actually felt bound by the thought of every writer commended by church authorities. The *Athenaeum* quipped: "All generals do not include all particulars; and one particular does not necessarily imply another particular. Liguori . . . does not include Newman, much less absorb him as an individual."[62] Nonetheless, Newman could not ignore Liguori. Contemporary commentators by no means agreed with Newman's interpretation of Liguori, but what allowed Newman to carry the day was his demand that the truthfulness, veracity, and character of English Roman Catholic clergy be judged from their own actions rather than from the content of even authoritative continental Roman Catholic writings.

Beginning with the Liguori matter, Newman moved through the issues of his own personal and general Roman Catholic honesty, including economy in presenting religious truth, lying, and equivocation. In each instance he demonstrated that either widely admired English Protestant writers or practices of everyday English life differed little or not at all from statements and practices of Roman Catholics. In Chapter V of the *Apologia* he provided examples of English Protestant moralists who had condoned lying under certain conditions. Since Protestants did not conclude that those authors had advocated lying at will, the same fairness should be extended to St. Alfonso. In regard to

---

61. Alexander Macmillan to JHN, January 8, 1864, *L&D* 21: 12n.

62. Newman also received encouragement from Lord Acton to do so. The latter believed the early parts of the *Apologia* had vindicated Newman but not the Roman Catholic priesthood. See MacDougall, *The Acton-Newman Relations,* pp. 91–93. *Athenaeum* 37 (1864): 502.

practicing certain economy in communicating religious doctrines, Newman declared, as would any other Englishman, "When we would persuade others, we do not begin by treading on their toes" (415). But then he urged, in language worthy of an evangelical, his conviction that for Roman Catholics communicating their faith, "the truest expedience is to answer right out, when you are asked; ... the wisest economy is to have no management; ... the best prudence is not to be a coward; ... the most damaging folly is to be found out shuffling; and ... the first of virtues is to 'tell truth, and shame the devil.'" (415).

In Note G on "Lying and Equivocation" Newman explored those circumstances that some Roman Catholic moralists regarded as "those special and rare exigencies or emergencies, which constitute the *justa causa* of dissembling or misleading" (421). Under such conditions four possible actions were permitted: a material but not formal lie, an equivocation, evasion, and silence. Quickly again domesticating evasion into a familiar English setting that would evoke an immediate sympathetic response from his readers, Newman declared: "The greatest school of evasion, I speak seriously, is the House of Commons; and necessarily so, from the nature of the case. And the hustings is another" (422).

But more important than associating commonsensical John Bull Englishmen with views of economy, lying, and evasion permitted by some Roman Catholic moralists, Newman also asserted that Roman Catholics could exercise considerable choice among differing Roman Catholic moralists. Personally distancing himself from Liguori, as he had done privately in 1862, he wrote, "I plainly and positively state, and without any reserve, that I do not at all follow this holy and charitable man in this portion of his teaching"[63] (350). Furthermore, after examining a variety of Roman Catholic opinions on lying and equivocation, some quite strict, others more flexible, Newman contended that "a given individual, such as I am, *cannot* agree with all of them, and has a full right to follow which of them he will" (419). He then added: "The freedom of the Schools, indeed, is one of those rights of reason, which the Church is too wise really to interfere with. And this applies not to moral questions only, but to dogmatic also" (419). Even if some Roman Catholic moralists thought equivocation permissible under certain circumstances, Newman commented, "For myself, I can fancy myself thinking it was allowable in extreme cases for me to lie, but never to equivocate" (424).

In the seventh of his original pamphlets, which became Chapter V of the

---

63. Moreover, Newman contended, Protestants must understand the nature of Roman Catholic confessional manuals: "They are intended for the Confessor, and Protestants view them as intended for the Preacher" (350).

revised *Apologia,* Newman undertook a quite forthright though subtle defense of liberty of thought and devotion for English Roman Catholics. He was seizing the opportunity of the favorable reception of the earlier pamphlets to articulate views that would aid the position of liberal English Roman Catholics whose journal the *Home and Foreign Review,* the successor to the *Rambler,* had concluded publication under duress in April 1864. Newman defended the presence and infallibility of the Roman Catholic Church in the world as God's response to "the wild living intellect of man" (325). The Roman Catholic Church through the ages had been "a suitable antagonist" lodging "an emphatic protest against the existing state of mankind" (326). Having ascribed divine purpose and enormous authority to the Roman Catholic Church, Newman, however, refused to say "any thing about the essential seat of that power" or "the direct subject-matter, over which that power of Infallibility has jurisdiction, beyond religious opinion" (329). Rather, he claimed that contrary to Protestant assumptions there had existed within the church throughout history a struggle between authority and private judgment as the exercise of infallibility had inevitably and properly called forth the exercise of reason. Newman insisted, "It is necessary for the very life of religion, viewed in its large operations and its history, that the warfare should be incessantly carried on" (330). Consequently, according to Newman, the history of "Catholic Christendom is no simple exhibition of religious absolutism, but presents a continuous picture of Authority and Private Judgment alternately advancing and retreating as the ebb and flow of the tide" (331). Here what Newman ascribed to the history of the Roman Catholic Church constituted his prescriptive agenda for the life of the mind and criticism within the contemporary church and beyond.

Newman further asserted that even though the Roman Catholic Church as a whole possessed "a gift of infallibility," it did not necessarily follow "that the parties who are in possession of it are in all their proceedings infallible" (334). With his ultramontane contemporaries in mind he also warned of the price in the opinion of posterity that might be paid for the exercise of ecclesiastical authority when "the said authority may be accidentally supported by a violent party, which exalts opinions into dogmas, and has it principally at heart to destroy every school of thought but its own" (336). Moreover, Newman contended that the authority, infallibility, and catholicity of the Roman Church did not mean that there must exist a rigorous devotional uniformity. Reacting against Italianate devotions popular among some English Roman Catholics, Newman urged that each national Roman Catholic communion might display devotional life appropriate to its own culture. In this regard, Newman praised Pope Pius IX for having formally restored the English Roman Catholic Church in 1850 and having thus "prepared the way for our own habits of mind, our own manner of reasoning, our own tastes, and our own virtues, finding a place and thereby a sanctification, in the Catholic Church" (343).

In all these statements Newman flouted the prejudices that informed Protestant accusations of Roman Catholic dishonesty and simultaneously asserted a broad circle of free opinion within the Roman Catholic Church as he understood it. In these passages he addressed an audience internal to the English Roman Catholic Church as much as the broader Protestant public. Newman further sought to counter the ultramontane opinion flowing from figures such as Manning, George Talbot, and Ward, as well as Herbert Vaughn, associated with the *Dublin Review,* who had for years spread doubt about Newman's loyalty to the Roman Catholic Church in Rome and who now opposed his opening a Roman Catholic house at Oxford.[64] By asserting intellectual, moral, devotional, and theological freedom for English Roman Catholics as part of his strategy for defending Roman Catholic honesty to the Protestant world, he made more difficult any authoritative ultramontane dissent from his position. Should his Roman Catholic enemies attack his views of Roman Catholic ecclesiastical authority, they would only seem to confirm the Protestant prejudices that Newman had so brilliantly disarmed. The more successfully he defended Roman Catholicism in English culture and its capacity for achieving a distinctly English character, the wider the space of safety he established for himself and others like him in the Roman Catholic faith.

In 1865 Newman further shored himself up against the ultramontanes by reprinting as "Supplemental Matter" to his personal narrative various letters of approbation and encouragement that he had received from English Roman Catholic priests and laity and most importantly from Bishop William Bernard Ullathorne of Birmingham in response to the first edition of the *Apologia.* Those letters of approval, from people who were often Old Catholics rather than recent converts and from his own bishop, became and remained an integral part of the *Apologia.* The letters, published in edition after edition, served the important polemical purpose of demonstrating that Newman's was not an isolated, eccentric, or disloyal voice in the English Roman Catholic Church. They served as an imprimatur for his enunciation of freedom of theological opinion within the Roman Catholic communion and also served to dissolve the aura of doubt that had for many years surrounded him. In this manner

---

64. Edward Kelly, "The *Apologia* and the Ultramontanes," in *Newman's* Apologia: *A Classic Reconsidered,* ed. Vincent Ferrer Blehl and Francis X. Connolly (New York: Harcourt, Brace & World, 1964), pp. 26–46; Newsome, *The Convert Cardinals,* pp. 235–284; Ker, *John Henry Newman,* pp. 533–617; Meriol Trevor, *Newman: Light in Winter* (London: Macmillan & Co. 1962), pp. 346–417.

Newman brought other faithful English Roman Catholics to bear witness to his own faithfulness against the machinations of the ultramontane coteries of London and Rome.

Newman's demand that he be judged as an Englishman was a demand that he not be judged by the stereotypical prejudices daily exerted over the Roman Catholic minority. Newman invoked English middle-class, essentially evangelical, earnestness to cut through anti–Roman Catholic prejudice so as to be heard on his own terms. Throughout all the difficult prose in the *Apologia* about truthfulness, authority, infallibility, variety of devotion, and Roman Catholic belief in miracles and miraculous doctrines such as the immaculate conception, Newman's is the voice of a despised Roman Catholic minority in England. In these passages he was seeking to demonstrate that however profound the religious differences between this minority and the Protestant (and overwhelmingly evangelical Protestant) majority in England, there existed no real cultural divide in terms of values of shared social intercourse or identity with the English nation.[65] In this respect Newman's book stands as a major example of autobiography emerging from a minority culture defending itself to the majority and asserting its inherent right to respect, if not necessarily approval, from that culture.

The consequences of Newman's efforts were quite remarkable and lasting. As R. H. Hutton wrote, Newman's *Apologia* "has done more to break down the English distrust of Roman Catholics, and to bring about a hearty good fellowship between them and the members of other Churches, than all the rest of the religious literature of our time put together."[66] For many readers the *Apologia* has continued to serve that function.

At the same time, as his contemporary ultramontane critics perceived and disapproved, Newman had also concealed in the pages of the *Apologia* another minority position, that of a liberal within the English Roman Catholic Church. Suspicious of him ever since his association with the *Rambler* and his hesitancy to support the temporal power of the papacy, these critics saw the *Apologia* and subsequently Newman's *Letter Addressed to the Rev. E. B.*

---

65. The *Athenaeum* easily distinguished between Newman's belief in miracles and his personal honesty, simply asking, "But does it follow that because Dr. Newman is credulous, he is also dishonest in his use of words?" *Athenaeum* 37 (1864): 432. Regarding autobiography written from the standpoint of a cultural minority, see Louis A. Renza, "A Theory of Autobiography," in *Autobiography: Essays, Theoretical and Critical,* ed. James Olney (Princeton, N.J.: Princeton Univ. Press, 1980), p. 291.

66. Hutton, *Cardinal Newman,* p. 230. See Erik Sidenvall, *After Anti-Catholicism? John Henry Newman and Protestant Britain, 1845–c. 1890* (London: T&T Clark International, 2005).

Pusey, D.D. on Occasion of his Eirenicon (completed in December 1865 and published January 31, 1866) as vehicles for creating an intellectual school of English Roman Catholic thought and opinion outside the control of the hierarchy, which in June 1865 came under Manning's authority as archbishop of Westminster. In 1864 Ward had commissioned a review of the *Apologia* for the *Dublin Review* that made no mention of Newman's having cast himself as a lifelong opponent of liberals and liberalism and thus as one in tune with Pope Pius IX's long campaign against liberalism. Ward's intractability regarding any further significant notice of Newman's book or any effort to counter what some on his staff regarded as unfair Protestant reviews led to considerable turmoil at the *Dublin*.[67]

Ultramontane hostility to Newman continued in the years after the initial publication of the *Apologia*. In the summer of 1865 Herbert Vaughn, later Manning's successor to the see of Westminster, wrote Mrs. W. G. Ward that he found views put forward in the *Apologia* "which I abhor, and which fill me with pain and suspicion." Ultramontanes particularly criticized Newman for his remarkable achievement in both the *Apologia* and the *Letter to Pusey* of persuading Protestant readers that one might be both a good Roman Catholic and a good Englishman. In February 1866, Monsignor George Talbot, who had long distrusted Newman and spread evil reports throughout Rome, wrote Manning: "You will have battles to fight, because every Englishman is naturally anti-Roman. To be Roman is to an Englishman an effort. Dr. Newman is more English than the English. His spirit must be crushed." Manning replied in what to most English Protestant readers would have been an incomprehensible judgment:

67. See Newman, *Certain Difficulties*, 2: 1–170. Newman had regarded Pusey's *An Eirenicon, In a Letter to the Author of "The Christian Year"* as a deeply unfair Anglican attack on Roman Catholicism and as an example of the equation of all Roman Catholic opinion with that of the ultramontanes. Newman used his response to Pusey, as he had his response to Kingsley, as an opportunity to present another public version of his own understanding of Roman Catholicism, which, as in the *Apologia*, differed markedly from that of the ultramontanes. (See JHN to J. R. Bloxam, November 6, 1865, and JHN to E. B. Pusey, November 17, 1865, *L&D* 22: 98, 103.) At the *Dublin Review* W. G. Ward refused to permit publication of a major article on the early reviews of the *Apologia*, with the result that Edward Healy Thompson and Henry James Coleridge left the journal. See Edward Healy Thompson to W. G. Ward, December 8, 1864; Henry James Coleridge to W. G. Ward, December 8, 1864; and Edward Healy Thompson to Henry Edward Manning, December 10, 1864, Catholic Record Society Archives, Archbishop's House, Westminster, London. These letters reveal the determination of Ward to allow the *Apologia* as little press as he could given the generally warm welcome the book had received among the community of Old English Roman Catholics.

What you write about Dr. Newman is true. Whether he knows it or not, he has become the centre of those who hold low views about the Holy See, are anti-Roman, cold and silent, to say no more, about the Temporal Power, national, English, critical of Catholic devotions, and always on a lower side . . . I see much danger of an English Catholicism, of which Newman is the highest type. It is the old Anglican, patristic, literary, Oxford tone transplanted into the Church. It takes the line of deprecating exaggerations, foreign devotions, Ultramontanism, anti-national sympathies. In one word, it is worldly Catholicism, and it will have the worldly on its side, and will deceive many.

Manning in effect treated Newman with much the same scorn that three decades earlier Newman had treated more moderate Anglicans. For Manning the chief point and danger arising from Newman was the possibility that there might arise around Newman a coterie of liberal English Roman Catholic clergy and laity who for the sake of cultural accommodation would dilute the distinctiveness of a papal-centered Roman Catholic faith, doctrine, and devotion. He saw Newman as domesticating the Roman Catholic faith into a comfortable, polite, nonaggressive, nonproselytizing religion identified with the English Roman Catholic literary and gentry classes who wanted their sons educated at Oxford. Such he termed "the watered, literary, worldly Catholicism of certain Englishmen."[68] Manning's counterbalance to those developments among the English Roman Catholic social elite was a strong ultramontane English Roman Catholicism supported by the growing numbers of Irish Roman Catholics who filled the English cities as well as those who remained in Ireland.

For Newman the burden and complexity of articulating a minority position within a religious communion and the consequent possible necessity of concealing personal religious opinion had long predated his conversion to Rome. During almost all of his Anglican life, whether as an evangelical undergraduate and young Oriel fellow or later as an advanced radical Tractarian Catholic in the English Church, Newman found himself having to articulate the religious and ecclesiastical position of the odd man out in his surrounding community. As a result of dwelling in these situations in which he could rarely openly or fully speak his mind, Newman had devised various strategies of concealment. He kept much of his thought to himself, allowed his ideas to be expressed only in response to questions of his followers, spoke his views only

---

68. Vaughan quoted in J. G. Snead-Cox, *The Life of Cardinal Vaughan* (London: Herbert & Daniel, 1912), 1: 215. Msgr. Talbot to H. E. Manning, February 20, 1866; H. E. Manning to Msgr. Talbot, February 25, 1866, Edmund Sheridan Purcell, *The Life of Cardinal Manning, Archbishop of Westminster* (London: Macmillan, 1895), 2: 323n, 322–323, 324.

to his closest friends, communicated them by private letters, or avoided subjects that might compel him to speak his whole mind. He published controversial books, pamphlets, and articles in which he sought to inject ideas that might invite disapproval and then claimed their acceptance if they were not formally condemned.

As an Anglican, Newman wished to believe certain things and pursue certain devotions deeply disapproved by most of his contemporaries and the bishops in the English Church. From 1833 to 1845 what he concealed (and not very well) was his aspiration for the Church of England to embrace within the spectrum of approved faith and practice ideas, liturgy, prayers, devotions, and the possibility of monastic community redolent of things Roman Catholic *as vehicles for reforming the English Church* of both relatively recent evangelical excesses and earlier flaws originating in the Reformation itself. As he wrote in a private letter of 1836, which he later feared would become public, "I have a great dislike of the superciliousness of present Protestantism — We think ourselves perfection and look down on the Romanists. Now *supposing* a man thinks that, greatly as the Romanists have sinned, we have sinned too, supposing he has suspicions that perchance judgments are upon the Anglican Church in consequence, he cannot allow himself to proclaim the existing system of things perfect."[69] What the Anglican Newman had concealed was first his growing conviction that neither the Church of England nor the Roman Catholic Church was free from serious faults and second that during the Reformation the English Church had abandoned devotional practices that it need not have abandoned, including ascetic modes of devotion, clerical celibacy, use of the breviary, and monasticism. Newman did not conceal a secret Roman Catholicism but rather a secret determination to carry out a religious experiment embodying devotional and moral rigor through the restoration of practices rooted in Christian experience dating from later than antiquity and earlier than the Reformation.

The rub came because Newman and his shifting group of Tractarian followers pursued these goals without leaving the English Church and while continuing to receive income from their positions in the church or Oxford University. Unlike the Scottish clergy, who separated from the Church of Scotland in the Great Disruption of 1843, the late Tractarians had been determined to be recognized as a tolerated minority within the Anglican establishment. *Tract 90* had been a device to permit men desirous of embracing rigorous Catholic

---

69. JHN to H. J. Rose, May 11, 1836, *L&D* 5: 295. On Newman's concern about this and other similar letters to Rose becoming public, see JHN to E. B. Pusey, January 19, 1840, *L&D* 7: 219–220.

devotional life while at the same time seeking ordination to achieve the latter without rejecting the former. All of Newman's negotiations with Oxford Bishop Richard Bagot at the time of *Tract 90* were intended to secure as much ground as possible for the Tractarian Catholic experiment, not to conform to episcopal obedience. On April 1, 1841, while relating his various interchanges with Bagot, Newman told Keble: "I am not at all sure but our game, if I may use the word, is to let the matter drop at present. We have got the *principle* of our interpretation admitted in that it has not been condemned—Do not let us provoke opposition—Numbers will be taking advantage silently and quietly of the admission for their own benefit. It will soon be *assumed* as a matter of course." Newman had no intention of retreating from his fundamental goal of achieving a safe space for Catholicism in the Church of England. As he told his brother-in-law Thomas Mozley, by then editor of the *British Critic,* in June 1841, "*Drop* the subject of Number 90, but *use* it."[70]

Newman in effect said the same thing to liberal Roman Catholics about the liberal positions he had set forth so vigorously in the *Apologia.* In late October 1865 William Lockhardt, whose precipitous conversion to Roman Catholicism in 1843 had occasioned Newman's resignation from St. Mary's, urged Newman to become more outspoken in his opposition to Ward, Manning, and others associated with the *Dublin Review.* Newman declined, stating to Lockhardt in a letter of October 26, 1865: "I *have* spoken *already* in my Apologia—there is no reason why I should speak again. Our Bishop as soon as he read my 7th Portion (ch. 5 of second edition) wrote to me, to endorse the doctrine of it. Afterwards an attempt was made at Rome to criticize it—but the Jesuits (I understand) took it up and defended its correctness in all points. Since then, our Bishop has a second time given it his imprimatur [i.e., presumably for the second edition of 1865]. Were I to write something anew, I could not say more than I said last year." Having received the private and public endorsement of Bishop Ullathorne for the ecclesiastically most controversial portion of the *Apologia,* Newman would not endanger that commendation by a more direct assault on the ultramontanes and most particularly on Ward. Newman explained to Lockhardt that Roman Catholics of their outlook had lost their position of influence with the closing the previous year of the liberal *Home and Foreign Review* and before that the *Rambler* because of their offenses to ecclesiastical authorities. Newman declared, "We have lost our position . . . and why? Because we have been very extravagant, very high and mighty, very

---

70. JHN to J. Keble, April 1, 1841 (II); JHN to Thomas Mozley, June 18, 1841, *L&D* 8: 149, 207.

dictatorial, very provoking; and now we must patiently suffer the consequences.... We do not mend matters by new imprudences, we have sowed the wind, and must reap the whirlwind."[71] Newman no doubt recalled that more than two decades earlier in late 1844 it had been Ward's own unstoppable determination to press for a more radical interpretation of *Tract 90* that had eventually precipitated the collapse of the Tractarian Catholic experiment in the Church of England. Newman in late 1865 in the midst of the current climate of the English Roman Catholic Church was not about to make a similar mistake by endangering the modest episcopal protection he had obtained for his liberal stance.

Indeed, in the years after the early denunciations of *Tract 90,* Newman himself, in contrast to Ward, had pursued a strategy of concealment rather than of defiance. Although silently condoning radical interpretations of the tract, Newman in sermons of December 1841 had urged his followers to remain in the Church of England while holding their minority opinions. By early 1843, as still further pressures came upon him from followers increasingly eager to move to Rome, Newman preached, and then published later in the year, his sermon on "Wisdom and Innocence" wherein he provided a more

---

71. JHN to William Lockhardt, October 26, 1865, *L&D* 22: 84, 85. In addition to the public letter of June 2, 1864, from Bishop W. B. Ullathorne approving the *Apologia,* Newman had received a private letter from his bishop written on the same date also warmly approving the final section of the *Apologia.* [John Henry Newman Papers Microfilm, Yale University Library, Reel 73, Batch 79 (hereafter cited as Newman Microfilms).] Nonetheless, Newman remained subject to ultramontane attacks on his Roman Catholic orthodoxy during 1865 and 1866 as part of the effort to stymie his possibly opening a Roman Catholic house in Oxford. On April 4, 1866, in a letter to the *Tablet* (April 7, 1866, p. 219), Ullathorne again strongly defended Newman's orthodoxy against ultramontane disparagement, this time in regard to his views on devotion to the Virgin Mary. Ullathorne specifically commended Newman's explication of the Immaculate Conception in particular and Marian devotion in general in his *Letter to the Rev. E. B. Pusey, D.D. on his Recent Eirenicon* (December 1865). By this point Ullathorne, quite perturbed with criticisms of Newman emanating from the *Dublin Review,* demanded, "Is petty caviling from Catholics without authority to be the present reward for a masterly exposition of the subject most difficult for a Protestant to comprehend, and which has made that subject classical in the English tongue?" He assured fellow English Roman Catholics that the Birmingham Oratory "is Roman in its devotions because it is Roman in the faith which its fathers believe and teach." *L&D* 22: 343, 344. See also *L&D* 22: 182, 187, 189–191, regarding public support for Newman from William Clifford, bishop of Clifton; private support from David Moriarty, bishop of Kerry; and Newman's private memorandum of March 16, 1866, on the recent attacks.

fully articulated strategy for concealment of opinion on the part of the persecuted Tractarian minority. This was the sermon that Kingsley in 1864 had so vigorously denounced.

The experience of persecution, Newman contended in "Wisdom and Innocence," denoted and confirmed the presence of the true church that possessed the right to self-defense through weapons of the powerless. Invoking Christ's injunction that his followers be wise as serpents, Newman argued that it was as if Christ had appealed "to the whole world of sin, and to the bad arts by which the feeble gain advantages here over the strong," and as if he had thus "set before us the craft, the treachery, the perfidy of the captive and the slave, and bade us extract a lesson even from so great an evil." Persecuted Christians who from the time of St. Paul had followed Christ's urging had been reproached for resorting to fraud, cunning, and priestcraft, "partly, nay, for the most part, not truly, but slanderously, and merely because the world called their wisdom craft, when it was found to be a match for its own numbers and power." As these Christians obeyed authorities in all things outward and not sinful, their conformity caused a confused world to believe they had "renounced their opinions as well as submitted their actions." The world, then surprised to learn "that their opinions remain," interpreted that situation as manifesting "an inconsistency, or a duplicity." Indeed, according to Newman, when Christians obey outwardly but refuse to assent inwardly, they "are called deceitful and double-dealing, because they do as much as they can, and not more than they may." Newman then declared, "The truest wisdom is to stand still and trust in God, and to the world it is also the strongest evidence of craft."[72]

"Wisdom and Innocence" represented Newman's prescriptive strategy of concealment so his persecuted followers might survive while waiting for better times in a reformed English Church. Newman in 1864 clearly realized the ambiguity of what he had preached and written two decades earlier. Thinking he should refrain from republishing the sermon as part of his response to Kingsley, he posed the issue to Edward Badeley:

> When I first thought of publishing, I said, "I will *reprint* the Sermon on 'Wisdom and Innocence.'" Then I said to myself decidedly, "No. That it would damage Mr. Kingsley is certain; but then, would it not *practically* damage me too? Let well alone—I have a strong case against him—but, if I reprint the Sermon, I am putting weapons into people's hands against me—I

---

72. John Henry Newman, *Sermons, Bearing on Subjects of the Day* (London: J. G. F. & J. Rivington, 1843), pp. 332, 333, 333–334, 334, 335, 334, 335, 337, 339, 340, 341, 342.

have plenty of ill wishers, and, if I re-print the Sermon at the end of the Pamphlet, they may say 'We can't defend Mr. K — but still he has something to say for himself. There is an unpleasant, suspicious tone, about the Sermon etc etc.' . . . No one, indeed, who knows me would fancy I had said what Mr. K imputes to me, but a man *might* think 'Well, I don't like the drift of his sermon, and, without even meaning it, the Author certainly has suggested what he should on the contrary have guarded against.'"

Newman ultimately decided to omit the sermon from the pamphlet "because it would be putting myself on the defensive."[73] He would discuss the sermon and devote Note C to it, but he would not reprint it as part of his contest with Kingsley.

Beyond his own reasoning Newman had received confirmatory advice from Badeley, a London attorney friend of long standing, urging him in the strongest terms to refrain from publishing the sermon. On February 4 Badeley advised Newman "there are some things in the Sermon, in its drift & bearing, which are capable, in the hands of an adversary, of some unfavorable misperceptions." Badeley did "not think that the publication" of the sermon "so imperatively called for" as to risk inviting such "criticism." Badeley told Newman that "without dragging the Sermon bodily before the Public, which you are not required to do [the published sermon being still available to readers], you have a full opportunity of damaging Mr. Kingsley as much as you need to do by the correspondence which you will publish."[74] Thus Newman did not publish "Wisdom and Innocence" in either his first reply to Kingsley or the *Apologia*. Here, the sermon appears in the editor's appendix and thus for the first time in the same volume with the *Apologia*.

The problem of concealment of opinion on Newman's part as an Anglican and as a Roman Catholic was by no means unique to him or his position in Victorian culture. It has seemed so only because Newman has been most frequently studied in isolation from other Victorian intellectuals.

Concealment of religious thinking or of ideas that might have heterodox religious implications was a way of life throughout the century for nearly all Victorian intellectuals, who found themselves profoundly stifled by the culture of evangelical Protestantism and the world of rancorous religious polemic within which they lived. Radical, secularist journalists, such as Richard Carlisle, suffered imprisonment. Philosophic radicals, such as Jeremy Bentham and George Grote, published their religious opinions only anony-

---

73. JHN to Edward Badeley, February 3 and 8, 1864, *L&D* 21: 35–36, 44.
74. Edward Badeley to JHN, February 4, 1864, Newman Microfilms, Reel 100, Letter 27. See also *L&D* 21: 36n.

mously. Charles Lyell had to equivocate on the biblical implications of his views on geology for fear of offending religious authorities. Charles Darwin delayed making public his theory of evolution by natural selection for almost twenty years for fear of public disapproval. James Frazer for similar reasons later in the century refused to draw out the implications of his anthropological theories for Christian theology. The list could go on. All of these secular writers—as well as religiously liberal theologians in the Church of England, such as the authors of *Essays and Reviews* and Bishop John William Colenso, and in the Free Church of Scotland, such as Robertson Smith—suffered the same kind of potential or actual persecution. These persecuted liberal theologians received much the same treatment as the Anglican Newman aspiring toward modes of Catholic devotion in the Church of England and as the liberal Roman Catholic Newman subject to attacks from ultramontanes.

No one, of course, so eloquently probed this situation of cultural repression of the free expression of opinion as John Stuart Mill in *On Liberty* (1859). As recent commentators have emphasized, Mill himself carefully concealed his own religious opinions. Two years before Newman preached "Wisdom and Innocence" Mill wrote to Auguste Comte about the necessity of concealing opinion, especially in regard to religion in English society: "You are doubtless aware that here an author who should openly admit to antireligious or even antichristian opinions, would compromise not only his social position . . . but also, and this would be more serious, his chance of being read. I am already assuming great risks when, from the start, I carefully put aside the religious perspective and abstained from rhetorical eulogies of the wisdom of Providence, customarily made even by unbelievers among the philosophers of my country."[75] Mill would have perfectly understood Newman's advice to his followers in "Wisdom and Innocence."

After publishing *Tract 90* with its expressed sympathy for Roman Catholic religious and theological positions, Newman had encountered exactly the social and intellectual isolation that Mill predicted for those who produced anti-Christian books or articles. Moreover, the grounds for evasion that Newman explored and suggested in "Wisdom and Innocence" as well as in the *Apologia* and its notes are almost exactly those that Mill pursued throughout his own

---

75. J. S. Mill to A. Comte, December 18, 1841, *Correspondence of John Stuart Mill and Auguste Comte* (New Brunswick, N.J.: Transaction Publishers, 1995), p. 42. On Mill and concealment, see Joseph Hamburger, *John Stuart Mill on Liberty and Control* (Princeton, N.J.: Princeton Univ. Press, 1999), pp. 55–85. See also Linda Raeder, *John Stuart Mill and the Religion of Humanity* (Columbia: Univ. of Missouri Press, 2002); Robert Devigne, *Reforming Liberalism: J. S. Mill's Use of Ancient, Religious, Liberal and Romantic Moralities* (New Haven, Conn.: Yale Univ. Press, 2006).

life, leading him to publish many of his opinions on religion posthumously. Both men in very different ways were religious radicals whose thought flew in the face of the surrounding evangelical culture. Mill rejected the reformed religion flowing from the Enlightenment; Newman as an Anglican rejected the reformed Protestantism flowing from the evangelical revival and as a Roman Catholic, the ultramontanism flowing from the midcentury Roman Catholic revival. Each writer in his own way was a religious utopian.

In 1864, however, Kingsley himself pursued an important line of personal concealment in his dispute with Newman, one that actually worked to the latter's benefit. In *"What, Then, Does Dr. Newman Mean?"* Kingsley refrained from criticizing the single publication that had most devastated Newman's reputation for honesty — *Tract 90*.

Why did Kingsley not pursue *Tract 90*, which he quite correctly observed had "made all the rest of England believe" Newman "a dishonest man"? Why did Kingsley not play his strongest card? He said in 1864 that the tract had not really persuaded him of Newman's conscious dishonesty in 1841. However, Kingsley in 1864 had his own problem of concealment. In 1841 Newman had published *Tract 90* in the hope that he might provide grounds for an elastic interpretation of the Thirty-Nine Articles in a Catholic direction. Contemporaneously, liberals within the Church of England sought their own elastic interpretation of the articles, with the young Arthur Stanley warning a friend opposed to *Tract 90,* "do not draw these Articles too tight, or they will strangle more parties than one." In 1841 traditional high churchmen as well as the archbishop of Canterbury worked to prevent Oxford Convocation from passing a sweeping condemnation of *Tract 90* that would confirm the judgment of high churchman Joshua Watson "that this Tract will be *a great triumph* to the Low Church party."[76] In 1841 Catholics, liberals, and many high churchmen feared a successful evangelical assault on *Tract 90* that would result in a narrow, ultra-Protestant interpretation of the Thirty-Nine Articles with which none of them could live.

When Kingsley and Newman clashed twenty-three years later, Parliament was about to receive a report from a commission on clerical subscription that would result the next year in legislation relieving Church of England clergy from the requirement of a narrow subscription to the Thirty-Nine Articles but requiring instead a more general assent to them. Kingsley had no desire to play into the hands of conservative opponents of that measure. Once rigid sub-

---

76. Kingsley, *"What, Then, Does Dr. Newman Mean?"* p. 38; A. P. Stanley to A. C. Tait, March 30, 1841, Tait Papers, Lambeth Palace Library, London, 77, f. 29; Joshua Watson as quoted in R. W. Jelf to JHN, March 18, 1841, *L&D* 8: 90.

scription to the articles was removed, a genuine, pluralistic broad church would be possible. In 1864 Kingsley declared of the articles, "The fullest licence of interpretation should be given to every man who is bound by the letter of a document."[77] Newman had for his own Catholic aspirations argued the same position in *Tract 90*. Kingsley gave Newman a pass on having to confront the issue of his honesty over *Tract 90* because going down that road would open the same issue for Kingsley and other Anglican liberals of the 1860s. Much as Kingsley wanted to attack Roman Catholicism, he had no desire to open the issue of subscription to the Thirty-Nine Articles.

Kingsley's general silence on this matter not only allowed Newman to define his own field of argument regarding *Tract 90,* but also permitted him to construct his own overarching interpretation of his life as a battle against liberalism when in fact in 1841 he, like the liberals of the day, wanted to stretch the articles and challenge what had become their narrow, traditional Protestant interpretation.

The Issue of Liberalism

Newman's *Apologia* is part spiritual autobiography, part bildungsroman, part historical narrative, part theological exposition, but throughout a purposeful polemic. On no subject is this judgment so true as that of Newman's portrayal of his life in the Church of England and beyond as a struggle against "liberals" and "liberalism." Arthur Lovejoy once quipped that "isms" are "trouble-breeding and usually thought-obscuring terms."[78] Certainly this is the case with Newman's appropriation of the term *liberalism* and his use of it to address both issues of his Anglican past and concerns of his Roman Catholic present.

A letter from Richard Holt Hutton, the Unitarian editor of the *Spectator,* appears to have occasioned Newman's use of this conceptual organizing template. On February 28, 1864, Hutton, reacting to the press coverage of Newman's first response to Kingsley, wrote, "It grieves me . . . to see the unfair-

---

77. Kingsley, *"What, Then, Does Dr. Newman Mean?"* p. 37. On the legislation reforming clerical subscription, see Chadwick, *The Victorian Church,* 2: 132–135. On the issue of subscription reform influencing English university life, see Christopher Harvie, *Lights of Liberalism: University Liberals and the Challenge of Democracy, 1860–1886* (London: Allen Lane, 1976), and Bart Schultz, *Henry Sidgwick, Eye of the Universe: An Intellectual Biography* (Cambridge: Cambridge Univ. Press, 2004), pp. 61–136.

78. Arthur O. Lovejoy, *The Great Chain of Being: A Study of the History of an Idea* (New York: Harper Torchbooks, 1963), p. 6.

ness with which you are treated by those whose profession is 'liberalism.' "[79] That group included Charles Kingsley, Alexander Macmillan, and other liberal Protestants who called for fairness in contemporary debates within the Church of England and between the Church of England and Protestant Dissenters, but who then denied exactly that basic fairness to Newman. Until Hutton's letter, there is no indication that Newman considered framing his life as a battle against liberalism.

By casting himself as a protagonist against liberals and liberalism, Newman could and did emerge from two decades of obscurity as a figure immediately relevant to both contemporary Anglican and Roman Catholic religious conflicts. Within Church of England circles this self-portrayal appealed to all groups still furious over the publication of *Essays and Reviews* in 1860, the exoneration of its authors by the Judicial Committee of the Privy Council in February 1864, and other contemporary efforts to liberalize the English Church.[80] Among Roman Catholics, presenting himself as a lifelong opponent of liberalism and champion of dogma rhetorically distanced Newman from his previous, compromising associations with outspoken liberal English Catholics while simultaneously providing protective cover for his assertions of broad theological freedoms available to his co-religionists. Moreover, as already noted, while writing the *Apologia,* Newman was also negotiating with Roman Catholic bishops to return to Oxford as head of a Catholic house. He undoubtedly believed projecting himself as a longtime advocate of dogma would shore up his widely questioned credentials as a priest deferential to Roman Catholic authorities while at the same time helping him find a possible welcome among former high church Anglican colleagues in Oxford.

Newman's strategy required that a great deal of the turmoil and animosity surrounding Tractarianism and his role therein during the 1830s and 1840s be forgotten, ignored, or left to history. To that end he pursued a stance of nostalgic affection for and respect toward the Anglican Church that had been

---

79. R. H. Hutton to JHN, February 28, 1864, *L&D* 21: 68; see also Hertz, "The Broad Church Militant," for the manner in which Hutton's steady defense of Newman infuriated his fellow religious liberals. F. D. Maurice joined Hutton in this defense. See F. D. Maurice, "Dr. Newman and Mr. Kingsley," *Spectator* 37 (1864): 420.

80. Victor Shea and William Whitla, "An Epoch in the History of Opinion," in *Essays and Reviews: The 1860 Text and Its Reading,* ed. Victor Shea and William Whitla (Charlottesville: Univ. Press of Virginia, 2000), pp. 3–130; Josef L. Altholz, *Anatomy of a Controversy: The Debate over Essays and Reviews (1860–1864)* (Aldershot: Scholar Press, 1994); Ieuan Ellis, *Seven Against Christ: A Study of "Essays and Reviews"* (Leiden: Brill, 1990).

missing in both *Certain Difficulties Felt by Anglicans* of 1850 and his harsh public comments on the Church of England of the early 1860s. That most of the principal actors of the earlier Tractarian decades and his most important opponents were dead, incapacitated, distracted, or more deeply concerned with recent rather than past ecclesiastical controversy also helped Newman. Even when opposing him, his earlier Anglican detractors had been fascinated and often puzzled by his behavior in the Church of England; now he revealed private and personal details in regard to himself and his fellow Tractarians about which both critics and friends beyond Oxford knew almost nothing beyond rumor and hearsay.

Other changes in English religious life aided the reception of the antiliberal framework of the *Apologia*. The Gorham Case of 1850 regarding baptism and the more recent case of the authors of *Essays and Reviews* expanding freedom of biblical interpretation as decided by the Judicial Committee of the Privy Council exemplified a civil court making irrevocable decisions regarding questions of doctrine in the Church of England. The very kind of state interference with doctrinal matters about which the Tractarians had warned in the mid-1830s, but which had not occurred then, had now taken place. Furthermore, English Dissent, which was still deeply evangelical, had become far more politically radical since 1845. The Liberal Party supported by Dissenters, now vigorously demanding disestablishment of the Church of England, had succeeded the Whigs. Anglican ecclesiastical liberals of the 1830s, who advocated modest accommodation with Dissent, had given way to theological liberals urging critical, historical reading of the Bible and the abolition of clerical subscription and religious tests for university dons. The early Victorian pursuit of science within the context of natural theology and reverence for scripture had given way to scientific naturalism associated with Darwinian evolution. By the close of the decade Matthew Arnold would group all of these forces under the term "Anarchy." Consequently, to readers of the 1860s Newman's account of what he and other Tractarians had believed to have threatened the English Church in the 1830s now really did seem to endanger it.

Yet throughout the *Apologia* Newman had great difficulty establishing a substantial link other than the term itself between what he designated as liberalism in the 1830s and 1840s and that of the 1860s. In the *Apologia* Newman might declare, "my battle was with liberalism; by liberalism I mean the anti-dogmatic principle and its developments" (173). Yet by the close of both the original 1864 edition and the 1865 edition of the *Apologia* Newman had established very little conceptual coherence regarding what he meant by liberalism, a fact recognized by contemporary reviewers. As previously noted, the ultramontane *Dublin Review* did not even mention the term or Newman's claims regarding it in its essay on the *Apologia*.[81] W. G. Ward as editor had no intention of legitimizing Newman's antiliberal claims within Roman Catholic circles by either quoting or contesting them.

More recent commentators who have acknowledged Newman's claims have found themselves deeply frustrated in making sense of what Newman meant by liberalism in the *Apologia*. Owen Chadwick simply confessed, "The fact is, what Newman denounced as liberalism, no one else regarded as liberalism." Avery Cardinal Dulles has contended that for Newman the term "meant approximately what many today would describe as the privatization of religion and its reduction to private sentiment." Terrence Merrigan has observed, "Liberalism, for Newman, is essentially a form of solipsism, a conviction that truth, especially in matters of religion, is ultimately a private affair."[82] While pointing to important elements in Newman's concept, none of these well-informed commentators has been able to assign the concept substantial historical content or meaning because they have left it alienated from the historical and religious contexts in which Newman wrote and recalled personalities and events of the Tractarian era.

Politically, Newman's comments on liberalism are confusing and even contradictory. He certainly did not see it as the preserve of any one party. He had regarded the Tory Duke of Wellington's embrace of Catholic Emancipation after long resistance as "dictated by liberalism" (145). While in Italy, hearing of the proposed Whig Irish Church legislation, Newman recalled, "I had fierce thoughts against the Liberals." He further stated: "It was the success of the Liberal cause which fretted me inwardly. I became fierce against its instruments and its manifestations" (160) — not even looking at the French tricolor in the Algiers harbor. In Newman's letters of these years, however, the term *liberal*, then itself a novelty, rarely appeared. Rather, he vented his anger at the *Whigs* as a party supported by Dissenters and Irish Roman Catholics, whom he saw threatening the privileges, property, and possibly the liturgy of the English Church. Later, he linked the Roman Catholic Church itself with liberalism because of its association with Daniel O'Connell in Ireland. In his great essays of 1841 on the Tamworth Reading Room, Newman's dual targets were both the liberal Lord Henry Brougham and the conservative Sir Robert Peel, but the term *liberalism* itself does not figure in this work.

---

81. Fitzjames Stephen, "Dr. Newman and Liberalism," *Saturday Review* 19 (1865): 768; "Newman's Apologia Pro Vita Sua," *Dublin Review* 55 (1864): 156–180.

82. Owen Chadwick, *Newman* (Oxford: Oxford Univ. Press, 1983), p. 74; Avery Robert Cardinal Dulles, *Newman* (New York: Continuum, 2002), p. 14; Terrence Merrigan, "Newman and Theological Liberalism," *Theological Liberalism* 66 (2005): 608.

Newman recalled that for Froude, "Erastianism, — that is, the union (so he viewed it) of Church and State, was the parent, or if not the parent, the serviceable and sufficient tool, of liberalism" (165). The future Tractarians had not complained during the 1820s when Parliament invested more public funds in the English Church than in more than a century. Erastianism emerged as a problem in their eyes only as *the political influence of other non-Anglican Christian groups,* not that of Utilitarians or other secular forces, produced the collapse of the exclusive Anglican confessional state, thereafter requiring them to compete in a radically transformed religious marketplace. Of those non-Anglican Christian forces, it was the Dissenters (and their Anglican evangelical sympathizers) who became the particular objects of Tractarian scorn and denigration.

What Newman and the other Tractarians so hated was the deeply Protestant character of the English nation long displaying itself in the actions of the English state. As Newman brilliantly articulated in *Certain Difficulties Felt by Anglicans,* this Protestant culture had since the Reformation exercised hostility against Catholic religion and Catholic spiritual aspirations within the established church through the state. Newman and many high church Anglicans saw the culmination of that Protestant-determined Erastian policy in the imposition on the English Church by the secular courts of the low church, evangelical understanding of baptism manifested in the Gorham Judgment. It was that action that Newman had denoted as "the liberalism of the day" in the opening sentence of *Certain Difficulties Felt by Anglicans.* High churchmen to whom Newman was appealing in that book had long regarded Anglican evangelicals, who approved the Gorham decision, as little more than a body of Dissenters residing in the Church of England. Thus the triumph of the formal accommodation of their theology of baptism represented in the mind of Newman and contemporary high churchmen the triumph of Dissenting theology in the establishment through the Erastian authority of the state. As already noted, contemporary readers of the *Apologia* would also have associated the liberalism of Erastianism with the ruling of the Judicial Committee of the Privy Council in favor of two authors of *Essays and Reviews* in February 1864.[83]

However, two substantial pre-Tractarian comments on Newman's part provide a different understanding of what the Tractarian Newman meant by

---

83. Chadwick, *The Victorian Church,* 1: 250–271. Manning had drawn these comparisons in his pamphlet *The Crown in Council on the Essays and Reviews* (1864), reprinted in Henry Edward Manning, *England and Christendom* (London: Longmans, Green, 1867), pp. 3–32.

liberalism. They point to his equation of liberalism in the 1830s with evangelicalism. Moreover, a reading of Newman's works of that decade demonstrates that the rhetoric he used to attack what he termed liberalism in the 1860s and 1870s he had first devised in the 1830s to characterize and denounce contemporary evangelical Protestant religion. He later simply transferred that language to his critique of mid- and late-Victorian religious and cultural targets.

Newman's most extensive pre-Tractarian statement occurred in a letter of August 15, 1830, to Simeon Lloyd Pope explaining his resignation from the British and Foreign Bible Society, the ecumenical evangelical organization that distributed Bibles containing no commentary on the text. He told Pope: "The tendency of the age is towards *liberalism* — i.e. a thinking established notions worth nothing — in this system of opinions a disregard of religion is included. No religion will stand if deprived of its forms." With his dislike for the congregational ecclesiology of Dissenters in mind, he then contended that "a system of Church government was *actually established* by the Apostles, and is thus the *legitimate* enforcement of Christian truth." He claimed: "The liberals know this — and are in every possible manner trying to break it up — and I think the B[ible]. S[ociety]. (unconsciously) is a means of aiding their object.... Hence it is joined by liberals.... *as a fact,* I do believe IT MAKES CHURCHMEN LIBERALS — it makes them undervalue the guilt of schism — it makes them feel a wish to conciliate Dissenters at the expence of truth. I think it is preparing the downfall of the Church."[84] Here his entire discussion of liberals, who would have included some, though by no means all, Anglican evangelicals, involves those who would in some manner countenance or make concessions to or cooperate with Protestant Dissenters by assuming the possibility of true Christian worship and ecclesiology outside the established church. Newman expressed these same views in sermons of the same period that attacked the idea and practice of toleration.

In his portrayal of the Tractarian Movement in the *Apologia* Newman again directly associated the liberalism of the 1830s with sympathy for Dissent, which in and of itself represented for him an abandonment of dogma. There he described R. D. Hampden's politically opportunistic advocacy of admitting

---

84. JHN to Simeon Lloyd Pope, August 15, 1830, *L&D* 2: 264-265. On the Bible Society, see Leslie Howsam, *Cheap Bibles: Nineteenth-Century Publishing and the British and Foreign Bible Society* (Cambridge: Cambridge Univ. Press, 1991). For Newman's critique of tolerance, see John Henry Newman, "Tolerance of Religious Error," in John Henry Newman, *Parochial and Plain Sermons*, new ed. (London: Longmans, Green, 1891), 2: 274-290.

Dissenters to Oxford in 1834, which will be discussed more fully later, as "that onset of Liberal principles, of which we were all in immediate anticipation, whether in the Church or in the University" (180) and as "the commencement of the assault of Liberalism upon the old orthodoxy of Oxford" (181). At the time, however, Newman and others had not accused Hampden of *liberalism* but rather of potential sympathy for *Socinianism*. In 1836 when Hampden was appointed regius professor of divinity, the Tractarian charge was that of "Rationalism," again with no mention of liberalism.

Newman's second major pre-Tractarian comment on the subject occurred in a poem titled "Liberalism," which he wrote in 1833 while in Palermo and published first in the *British Magazine* in 1834 and later in the *Lyra Apostolica* collection of poetry published in 1836 and republished throughout the next decade. Although in 1833 Newman had recently witnessed the extensive destruction of Italian Roman Catholic Church property as a result of the Napoleonic Wars, the object of Newman's condemnation throughout the poem was not the secular, political assault on the church, but rather the fact of evangelical religion requiring insufficient moral rigor from Christians.

> YE cannot halve the Gospel of God's grace;
>   Men of presumptuous heart! I know you well.
>   Ye are of those who plan that we should dwell,
> Each in his tranquil home and holy place;
> Seeing the Word refines all natures rude,
> And tames the stirrings of the multitude.
>
> And ye have caught some echoes of its lore,
>   As heralded amid the joyous choirs;
>   Ye marked it spoke of peace, chastised desires,
> Good-will and mercy, — and ye heard no more;
> But, as for zeal and quick-eyed sanctity,
> And the dread depths of grace, ye passed them by.
>
> And so ye halve the Truth; for ye in heart,
>   At best, are doubters whether it be true,
>   The theme discarding, as unmeet for you,
> Statesmen or Sages. O new-encompassed art
> Of the ancient Foe! — but what, if it extends
> O'er our own camp, and rules amid our friends?[85]

In this poem, which appeared in a section of *Lyra Apostolica* titled "Religious States," Newman criticized evangelical Protestants as "Men of presumptuous

---

85. *Lyra Apostolica* (Derby: Henry Mozley and Sons; London: J. G. & F. Rivington, 1836), pp. 131–132.

heart" because they taught the gospel of justification through faith in the atonement without teaching the necessity of sanctification. Proclaiming the gospel without the law, they emphasized "the Word" as capable of refining "all natures rude" rather than the necessity of instruction in holy living. They had passed by those portions of Christian teaching that inculcated "zeal and quick-eyed sanctity, / And the dread depths of grace." They had thereby halved Christian truth, casting doubt on the necessity for disciplined, virtuous Christian living.

In other contemporary comments Newman strenuously attacked the evangelical theology of ready access to divine grace that he equated with liberalism in his poem of 1833. On October 31, 1830, he preached "Obedience to God the Way to Faith in Christ" in which he directly criticized evangelical preaching of free grace. In private letters of 1835 to Samuel Wilberforce directly criticizing evangelical preaching, Newman defended his emphasis on sanctification over justification as arising from his conviction that the age required "*the Law* not the Gospel," "the claims of duty and the details of obedience," and the preaching of "a continual Ashwednesday." During these years, whatever else liberalism connoted in Newman's mind, it powerfully encompassed both the theology and ecclesiology of evangelical religion, whether in the realm of Dissent or the English Church. With those groups the Tractarian Newman consistently battled. Voicing his determined hostility to Anglican evangelicals, he wrote to Miss Maria R. Giberne in 1836: "The (so called) Evangelicals have thought to ride into the Church in this her hour of peril, to make certain reforms, to alter her liturgy in some matters, to fill her dignities with their own people . . . and behold they are suddenly encountered, Goliaths as they are . . . by one or two Davids . . . are called to controversy, and they find to their great indignation that these upstarts affect to be stricter than they, and call them carnal, and gallantly attack them . . . we will show these Midianites what Gideon can do."[86]

Beyond the evangelical enemy, liberalism, for the Tractarian Newman, also

---

86. John Henry Newman, "Obedience to God the Way to Faith in Christ," in Newman, *Parochial and Plain Sermons*, 8: 201–216. This sermon is reprinted in the editor's appendix of this volume. JHN to Samuel Wilberforce, February 4 and March 10, 1835; JHN to Miss M. R. Giberne, March 20, 1836, *L&D* 5: 22, 40, 263. See also Henry Chadwick, "The *Lectures on Justification*," in *Newman after a Hundred Years*, ed. Ian Ker and Alan G. Hill (Oxford: Clarendon Press, 1990), pp. 287–308; Thomas L. Sheridan, *Newman on Justification: A Theological Biography* (New York: Alba House, 1967); Peter Toon, *Evangelical Theology, 1833–1856: A Response to Tractarianism* (London: Marshal, Morgan and Scott, 1979), pp. 141–170; David Newsome, "Justification and Sanctification: Newman and the Evangelicals," *Journal of Theological Studies* n.s. 15 (1964): 32–53.

manifested itself in a Christian's simply asking or inquiring why his own particular church could regard itself as correct. In *Tract 71*, in one of the few appearances of the term in the tracts, Newman observed: "A certain liberalism is commonly the fruit of this perplexity. Men are led on to gratify the pride of human nature, by standing aloof from all systems, forming a truth for themselves and countenancing this or that denomination of Christians according as each maintains portions of that which they have already assumed to be the truth." Here and elsewhere Newman linked liberalism with the exercise of private judgment historically and culturally associated with Protestantism. On December 11, 1831, Newman preached a sermon in which he had declared, "The usurpations of the Reason may be dated from the Reformation."[87] Repeating that argument, Newman in the *Apologia* quoted a letter of September 12, 1841, in which he had written, "The spirit of lawlessness came in with the Reformation, and Liberalism is its offspring" (286).

In his sweeping denunciation of evangelical religion in the *Prophetical Office of the Church* of 1837 Newman applied to evangelical religion or popular Protestantism exactly the terms he had used to describe liberalism in *Tract 71*. In the *Prophetical Office of the Church* he argued that popular Protestantism constituted "that generalized idea of *religion,* now in repute, which merges all differences of faith and principle between Protestants as minor matters, as if the larger denominations among us agreed with us in essentials, and differed only in the accidents of form, ritual, government, or usage." Such doctrinally diffuse, ecumenical activity, seen in the cooperation of Dissenting and Church of England clergy within evangelical societies, displayed the English proclivity to "exult in what we think our indefeasible right and glorious privilege to choose and settle our religion for ourselves" and to stigmatize "as a bondage ... what the wise, good, and many have gone over and determined

---

87. *Tract 71*: 27; John Henry Newman, *Fifteen Sermons Preached before the University of Oxford,* new ed. (London: Rivingtons, 1880), p. 69. The full passage states: "The usurpations of the Reason may be dated from the Reformation. Then, together with the tyranny, the legitimate authority of the ecclesiastical power was more or less overthrown; and in some places its ultimate basis also, the moral sense. One school of men resisted the Church; another went farther, and rejected the supreme authority of the law of Conscience. Accordingly, Revealed Religion was in a great measure stripped of its proof; for the existence of the Church had been its external evidence, and its internal had been supplied by the moral sense. Reason now undertook to repair the demolition it had made, and to render the proof of Christianity independent both of the Church and of the law of nature. From that time (if we take a general view of its operations) it has been engaged first in making difficulties by the mouth of unbelievers, and then claiming power in the Church as a reward for having, by the mouth of apologists, partially removed them."

long before, or to submit to what almighty God has revealed."[88] Newman further associated this mode of religion with the use of private judgment in reading the Bible, which he saw resulting in heresy and Methodism.

The language that the Tractarian Newman had directed against evangelical religion in one publication after another reappeared in his 1879 Bilietto Speech, delivered in Rome at the time of his consecration as cardinal. On that occasion he stated, "For thirty, forty, fifty years I have resisted to the best of my powers the spirit of Liberalism in religion." He then offered this definition of that long-standing enemy: "Liberalism in religion is the doctrine that there is no positive truth in religion, but that one creed is as good as another, and this is the teaching which is gaining substance and force daily. It is inconsistent with any recognition of any religion, as *true*. It teaches that all are to be tolerated, for all are matters of opinion. Revealed religion is not a truth, but a sentiment and a taste; not an objective fact, not miraculous; and it is the right of each individual to make it say just what strikes his fancy."[89] These words repeat almost exactly the charges that he had made against popular Protestantism forty-two years earlier. Liberalism in religion was evangelical Protestantism with its emphasis on personal feeling, private judgment, and faith in an invisible church of true Christians spread across the ages and across competing denominations.

By subsuming evangelical Protestantism under the broader conceptual umbrella of liberalism, the Newman of the *Apologia* retreated from the profound criticisms of such religion, as manifested among Dissenters and within the English Church, voiced by the Newman of history. An exploration in 1864 of those earlier polemics would have been directly incompatible with his demand to be judged as an Englishman. Newman could present neither his earlier nor his present self as an enemy of evangelicalism because he was determined to demonstrate that Roman Catholics could be honest, active participants in the broader English culture that he had long understood to be dominated by such Protestantism. He was prepared to defend his religious apostasy from the Church of England; he was not prepared to defend that wider cultural apostasy that during his Anglican career had marked his challenge to evangelical Protestant religion and its influences pervading English culture. Hence in the

88. Newman, *Lectures on the Prophetical Office of the Church*, pp. v, 2, 3. For John Henry Newman this mode of evangelical religion and its associated behavior, which he had experienced directly in the life of his brother Francis and among the radical Oxford evangelical clergy, resulted necessarily in unsettled opinions among both those seeking personal religious truth and those living around them.

89. Wilfrid Ward, *The Life of John Henry, Cardinal Newman, Based on His Private Journals and Correspondence* (London: Longmans, Green, 1927), 2: 460.

Apologia Newman transformed his enemy of the 1830s and 1840s from evangelical Protestantism into the specter of an ill-defined liberalism. Furthermore, in 1864 the Roman Catholic Newman seeking accommodation for his co-religionists in the wider culture had no desire to indicate how far removed from the values of that culture he had been as an Anglican.

To that end, in 1864 Newman largely removed manifestations of what he defined as liberalism from the world of denominational religious conflict within which a quarter-century earlier he had been an engaged, noncompromising combatant. At one point in the *Apologia* Newman wrote: "The Liberalism which gives a colour to society now, is very different from that character of thought which bore the name thirty or forty years ago. Now it is scarcely a party; it is the educated lay world. . . . At present it is nothing else than that deep, plausible skepticism . . . as being the development of human reason, as practically exercised by the natural man" (337). Under this definition, presenting himself as an opponent of liberalism and upholder of dogmatic principles, Newman refocused his career from that of a religious and theological polemicist into that of an opponent of the march of mind, the spirit of improvement, and what Matthew Arnold would later describe as "Doing as One Likes." In this definition, he removed liberalism from the Victorian religious world and assigned it to a wider secular lay culture.[90] As a critic of the latter, Newman evoked considerable response and sympathy across the spectrum of mid-Victorian English religious denominations.

Contemporary reviewers of the *Apologia*, like the more recent scholars quoted previously, were also perplexed by what Newman meant by liberalism and assigned their own definitions to it. Richard Church, Newman's friend

---

90. Newman made a similar transformation of his own prose in 1872 when he republished his original *Sermons, Chiefly on the Theory of Religious Belief* of 1843 as *Fifteen Sermons Preached before the University of Oxford*. In the new volume he added a preface and notes that indicated that he was criticizing "secular" reason; these changes reframed his earlier volume into the template established by his *Apologia* narrative. See Newman, *Fifteen Sermons,* pp. ix–xvii, 68n. Here, Newman may have been building upon Matthew Arnold's both incorrect and anachronistic comments in *Culture and Anarchy* (1869) regarding Newman's concept of liberalism: "But what was it, this Liberalism, as Dr. Newman saw it, and as it really broke the Oxford Movement? It was the great middle-class Liberalism, which had for the cardinal points of its belief the Reform Bill of 1832, and local self-government, in politics; in the social sphere, free-trade, unrestricted competition, and the making of large industrial fortunes; in the religious sphere, the Dissidence of Dissent and the Protestantism of the Protestant religion." Matthew Arnold, *Culture and Anarchy,* ed. J. Dover Wilson (Cambridge: Cambridge Univ. Press, 1971), p. 62.

from Tractarian days and in 1864 a supporter against Kingsley, wrote in the *Guardian,* "The *Apologia* is the history of a great battle against Liberalism, understanding by Liberalism the tendencies of modern thought to destroy the basis of revealed religion, and ultimately of all that can be called religion at all."[91] This definition of liberalism had not appeared in the *Apologia* itself and bore almost no relation to the events and ideas of the Tractarian era. Nor could Church attach names from the 1830s and 1840s to this supposed liberal outlook.

In the 1860s Church's term "tendencies of modern thought" suggested critical historical rationalism and naturalism as manifested in contemporary science and biblical criticism. In the 1830s and early 1840s, however, the tendencies in contemporary thought against which Newman polemicized as undermining dogmatic religion had been evangelical theology and its associated religious sensibilities. For example, in 1838 in *Tract 83,* titled *Advent Sermons on Antichrist,* he had decried a vast contemporary "effort to do without religion" that involved "an attempt to supersede religion altogether, as far as it is external or objective, as far as it is displayed in ordinances, or can be expressed by written words,—to confine it to our inward feelings, and thus, considering how transient, how variable, how evanescent our feelings are, an attempt in fact, to destroy religion."[92] Throughout the 1830s Newman had advocated dogmatic principles not against an entity termed liberalism but against evangelical religion with its emphasis on feeling as giving validity to conversion, spirituality, and other religious experience, which he often termed "the religion of the day." His comments during those years against liberals, such as Thomas Arnold and even R. D. Hampden, however harsh, were brief and coincidental in comparison with the volume and centrality of his assault against popular Protestantism.

Furthermore, neither Newman nor later Church could in 1864 name opponents of revealed religion from the 1830s quite simply because none of Newman's chosen or provoked opponents of that era had questioned Christianity as a revealed religion. Rather, their quarrels had been over whether Christian revelation occurred over time through tradition or once through scripture.

91. R. W. Church, *Occasional Papers* (London: Macmillan, 1897), 2: 386.
92. *Tract 83:* 12. Newman had made similar assaults on the subjective character of evangelical religion in powerful sermons such as "Religious Emotion" of March 27, 1831, and "The Religious Use of Excited Feelings" of June 3, 1831, Newman, *Parochial and Plain Sermons,* 1: 177–189, 112–123. These sermons are reprinted in the editor's appendix of this volume. See also Francis Joseph Butler, *John Henry Newman's* Parochial and Plain Sermons *Viewed as a Critique of Religious Evangelicalism* (Ph.D. diss., Catholic Univ. of America, 1972).

Newman himself had memorably explained those differing outlooks in an important *British Critic* article of 1841. There he asserted that divine revelation had not been limited to the historical moment of the lives of the Old Testament patriarchs and prophets and of Jesus and the apostles, as evangelicals held, or the later age of the Church Fathers, as high churchmen believed. Rather, Newman urged the necessity of grasping that "the Moral Governor of the world" had "scattered the seeds of truth far and wide over its extent," which had taken root and grown as "wild plants indeed but living." Just as animals inferior to man "have tokens of an immaterial principle in them yet have not souls so the philosophies and religions of men have their life in certain true ideas, though they are not divine." The Church Catholic had ever actively functioned as "a treasure house, giving forth things old and new, casting the gold of fresh tributaries into her refiner's fire, or stamping upon her own, as time required it, a deeper impress of her Master's image." Tractarian Catholics such as Newman in 1841 were able to "conceive that the church, like Aaron's rod, devours the serpents of the magicians" while Protestants remained "ever hunting for a fabulous primitive simplicity." Whereas Protestants "are driven to maintain . . . that the church's doctrine was never pure," Catholics "readily grant . . . that it can never be corrupt."[93] Thus in the name of expansive, latitudinarian Catholicism the Tractarian Newman enthusiastically embraced a doctrinal indeterminacy lacking guides, boundaries, or definitions.

In terms of the critical reading of the Bible, and most particularly of the Old Testament, Newman's views from the 1830s through his career in the Roman Catholic Church actually closely paralleled the advanced biblical scholars whom so many Protestant writers attacked. In *Tract 85* Newman had pointed to the inadequacy of the Bible as the sole authority for Christianity, to the historical circumstances of its composition, to its inconsistencies, and to the multiple authorship of its books. Contemporary reviewers of Newman's *Essay on the Development of Christian Doctrine* (1845) observed similarities between its arguments and those of advanced German biblical critics such as David Friedrich Strauss. In late 1862 Newman wrote William Wilberforce that Bishop J. W. Colenso's *The Pentateuch and Book of Joshua Critically Examined* did not personally disturb him, but nonetheless "the extent of mischief" Colenso would create in the nation at large would be "fearful" because "in this country revealed religion is identified with the text of the whole Bible." In late January 1865, Newman wrote George William Cox that for forty years

---

93. [J. H. Newman], "Milman's History of Christianity," *British Critic* 29 (1841): 101, 102, 103.

he had believed Genesis to be the work of various authors. Several months later when A. P. Stanley visited Newman in Birmingham, he told Stanley that he saw great historical problems with the Old Testament, but hoped they might be averted in regard to the New Testament.[94] These views were no less advanced than those of contemporary biblical scholars who were condemned for their liberalism and not unlike the modestly critical views of scripture enunciated a generation before by Thomas Arnold and Connop Thirlwall.

When Newman published the *Apologia* as a book in the spring of 1865 he added, partly in response to reviewers, but also for other personal reasons, his important Note A on "Liberalism," which has ever since remained an integral part of the work. The note consisted of a historical review of liberalism at Oxford and eighteen propositions that Newman associated with the liberalism the Tractarians had opposed. Clarifying his own usage of the term while a Protestant, he associated "the rudiments of the Liberal party" with the reformers within Oxford University. He further explained: "Now by Liberalism I mean false liberty of thought, or the exercise of thought upon matters, in which, from the constitution of the human mind, thought cannot be brought to any successful issue, and therefore is out of place ... Liberalism then is the mistake of subjecting to human judgment those revealed doctrines which are in their nature beyond and independent of it, and claiming to determine on intrinsic grounds the truth and value of propositions which rest for their

---

94. R. A. Willmott [probable author], "Mr. Newman: His Theories and Character," *Fraser's Magazine* 33 (1846): 265, 256; H. H. Milman, "Newman on the Development of Christian Doctrine," *Quarterly Review* 77 (1846): 437–438; *British Magazine* 31 (1847): 578. JHN to William Wilberforce, December 4, 1862, *L&D* 20: 362; JHN to George William Cox, January 28, 1865, *L&D* 21:394–396; see also same to same, February 4, 1865, *L&D* 21: 402–403. On October 30, 1864, A. P. Stanley visited Newman in Birmingham and engaged in a wide-ranging conversation on biblical criticism that Stanley found largely disappointing. See Rowland E. Prothero, *The Life and Correspondence of Arthur Penrhyn Stanley, Late Dean of Westminster* (New York: Charles Scribner's Sons, 1894), 2: 340–342. A few months later Newman wrote R. H. Hutton: "Why do you take for granted that I admit no historical errors in the Bible? This is a question of fact—fact is fact, and can be proved." JHN to R. H. Hutton, June 3, 1865, *L&D* 21: 482–483. See also JHN to an Unknown Correspondent, March 19, 1865, *L&D* 21: 432–433, in which Newman urges the use of both private judgment and contemporary scholarship for the interpretation of passages of scripture for which the church has not formally provided interpretations. In addition, consult Jaak Seynaeve, *Cardinal Newman's Doctrine of Holy Scripture* (Louvain: Publications Universitaires de Louvain, 1953), a prolix but important work demonstrating the complexity of Newman's thought on the subject and the difficulties it posed to early twentieth-century Roman Catholic interpreters in the wake of the papal condemnation of Roman Catholic Modernism.

reception simply on the external authority of the Divine Word" (361–362). He continued that the party of Oxford reformers "were of a character of mind out of which Liberalism might easily grow up, as in fact it did" (362). That group, whom he associated with Thomas Arnold and his pupils, had "unconsciously encouraged and successfully introduced into Oxford a licence of opinion which went far beyond them" (362).

In this passage Newman directly echoed statements he had made in 1836 in *Tract 73* titled *On the Introduction of Rationalistic Principles into Religion*. There he had asserted, "To Rationalize is to ask for *reasons* out of place; to ask improperly how we are to *account* for certain things, to be unwilling to believe them unless they can be accounted for, i.e. referred to something else as a cause, to some existing system as harmonizing with them or taking them up into itself." As he then explored the manifestations of rationalism, he had associated it with biblical figures such as the rich Samaritan lord, who asked how Elisha's prophecy would be fulfilled; Naaman, who resisted bathing in the Jordan; Nicodemus, who objected to the doctrine of regeneration; and St. Thomas, who questioned Christ's resurrection. The protagonist in each biblical account illustrated the "desire of judging for oneself" or of judging on the basis of one's personal experience in matters of religion.[95]

In the modern world Newman argued that those practicing rationalism in religion linked religious truth to subjective experience rather than to a body of objective religious truth existing irrespective of subjectivity. Then, linking rationalism as manifested in contemporary religion to evangelicalism, Newman directly contrasted the objective Catholic faith to the subjectivity of what he termed "the popular theology of the day," which taught the atonement as "the chief doctrine of the Gospel" and emphasized not "its relation to the attributes of GOD and the unseen world, but . . . its experienced effects on our minds, in the change it effects where it is believed." Further relating rationalism to evangelical religion, Newman urged: "There is a widely spread, though various admitted School of doctrines among us, within and without the Church, which intends and professes peculiar piety, as directing its attention to the *heart itself*, not to any thing external to us, whether creed, actions, or ritual. I do not hesitate to assert that this doctrine is based upon error, that it is really a specious form of trusting man rather than God, that it is in its nature Ra-

---

95. [J. H. Newman], *On the Introduction of Rationalistic Principles into Religion* as printed in *Tracts for the Times by Members of the University of Oxford*, Volume III for 1835–36, new ed. (London: J. G. & F. Rivington; Oxford: J. H. Parker, 1839), *Tract 73*, p. 2.

tionalistic, and that it tends to Socinianism."[96] Newman in 1865 assigned the same outlooks to liberalism that he had assigned to rationalism in 1836. He had developed his understanding first of rationalism and then of liberalism through his articulation of a deep critique of evangelical theology with its emphasis on subjective religious experience. By 1864 and 1865 he had transformed his critique of the impulses informing evangelical religion of the heart into a critique of the broader cultural impulses informing mid-Victorian liberal society, politics, and religion.

Yet in fact during the Tractarian era no group in Oxford had exercised broader liberty of thought on religious issues, more vigorously exercised their private judgments in matters theological and ecclesiastical, and spawned more ecclesiastical skepticism than Newman and his friends. Recalling in 1864 the elasticity in regard to the Thirty-Nine Articles that the Anglican Newman in *Tract 90* and other writings had demanded for Catholics in the English Church, Theodore Walrond observed that "by a strange meeting of extremes, the champion of dogma and of definite Church teaching struck a fatal blow at the dogmatism of his Church, and enunciated a principle which has proved of the greatest importance in forwarding the development of liberal views." Walrond was exactly correct. James Anthony Froude would write many years later that Newman in *Tract 90* "had broken the back of the Articles."[97]

During the 1830s and 1840s commentators from both the Church of England and the Roman Catholic Church had seen Newman and the Tractarians as radically exercising private judgment as to what they would consider dogma. In 1836 R. D. Hampden commented privately to Richard Whately: "Holding themselves as the proper maintainers of the divine apostolical tradition . . . they feel themselves far above the condition of mere teachers and persuaders of men. . . . It is no wonder that persons actuated by such a spirit should be despisers of all authority except that which founds itself on views such as their own, and while they profess the highest reverence for Church authority in the abstract . . . treat with disrespect any existing authority, or an actual minister of religion not of their party."[98] Whatever their presumed Roman Catholic sympathies, the Tractarians with Newman in the lead were not Roman Catholics, but clergy of the English Church rejecting the faith and

---

96. Ibid., pp. 13, 53.

97. Theodore Walrond, "J. H. Newman's *Apologia*," *North British Review* 41 (1864): 94; James Anthony Froude, "The Oxford Counter-Reformation" (1881), in *Short Studies in Great Subjects* (London: Longmans, Green, 1898), p. 308.

98. R. D. Hampden to R. Whately, undated, 1836, Henrietta Hampden, *Some Memorials of Renn Dickson Hampden, Bishop of Hereford* (London: Longmans, Green, 1871), pp. 90–99; see also same to same, undated, 1836, p. 88.

practice of historic Protestantism for a religion of their own personally self-willed devising. In this regard, they were acting in the cultural mode of radical Protestants. They were in effect exercising the very kind of liberalism that Newman had attacked in *Tract 71* by seeking to determine whether their own was a true or correct church.

Ironically, in 1845 the Roman Catholic *Tablet* very nearly approximated Hampden's judgment of a decade earlier. The journal noted that despite the Tractarians' vigorous contention "for the necessity of an external Church authority, to repress the excesses of undisciplined zeal and of straggling imaginations," they had transformed themselves into "the followers of a man" and "his followers not in any special discipline or rule of life and manners, but in the choice of a Church!" Moreover, "Professing the utmost abhorrence of Protestantism and of all private choice in matter of religion, they were yet by virtue of their position the most ultra-Protestants in existence." Although calling themselves Catholics, the Tractarians, as the *Tablet* so incisively perceived, behaved as an ultra-Protestant offspring of the dominant early Victorian Protestant culture and as a self-referential ultra-Protestant conventicle within a larger Protestant body.[99]

Beyond suggesting doubt about Newman's actual deference to dogma or authority while an Anglican, questions can also be raised about the historical accuracy of his claim in the *Apologia*, "The men who had driven me from Oxford were distinctly the Liberals; it was they who had opened the attack upon Tract 90, and it was they who would gain a second benefit, if I went on to abandon the Anglican Church" (294–295), and his further assertion, "Excepting the Liberal, no other party, as a party, acted against me" (365). In reality, the chief Oxford critics of *Tract 90* had been high churchmen among the Heads of Houses as well as evangelicals throughout the university and wider church. A similar coalition in late 1844 and early 1845 proposed a New Test

99. *Tablet*, October 25, 1845, p. 673, as reprinted in *L&D* 10: 905, where the entire editorial appears on pp. 905–908. *The English Churchman* had immediately republished the *Tablet* editorial in its edition of October 30, 1845, p. 694. See also *Tablet*, September 20, 1845, p. 593, for previous comments on the Tractarian exercise of private judgment. Archbishop Whately once condemned the Tractarians' "resolute contempt of all Episcopal authority when used even in the slightest and most trivial matter against themselves." He continued, "The operations of the party were, in this respect, . . . disguised *Presbyterianism*." Furthermore, they had set about "to dictate to and oppose and insult the government of the Church they chuse [sic] to belong to; and this, while all the time, they are professing, not only to be devoted members of an Episcopal Church, but also to condemn and utterly disallow all forms of Church-government but the Episcopal." Whatley, *Cautions for the Times*, p. 329.

of orthodox loyalty to the Thirty-Nine Articles and a subsequent proposal to condemn *Tract 90* before Oxford Convocation. The first was withdrawn and the latter rejected. In both 1841 and 1845 many Oxford liberals opposed a condemnation of *Tract 90* not from sympathy for Newman but from the fear that similar restrictive measures might be turned against themselves.

Contemporary reviewers pointed to Newman's historical inaccuracy. In 1865 in the *North British Review* Theodore Walrond declared: "It is certain that the liberals had no share in the measures which ultimately drove from Oxford one whom they regarded with distrust indeed, but with unfeigned admiration and interest.... Dr. Newman ought to know well ... that the real force against which he had to contend, — the stream which ultimately swept him from his position, — was that turbid stream of mingled 'two-bottle orthodoxy' and narrow Puritanism." A. P. Stanley made the same comment privately to Newman. G. W. Cox in the *Westminster Review,* recalling the condemnation of *Tract 90* in 1841, stated: "the Liberals did not then exist as a party. The Heads of Houses who censured the tract were of the old high and dry and Evangelical schools. Arnold's pupils were as yet quite young, hardly out of undergradship." More recently in an article agreeing with these contemporary observations and eviscerating Newman's claims, Peter Nockles concluded, "The critique of Tract 90 was largely a High Church alarm at apparent disloyalty to the Anglican formularies that for some seemed suspiciously akin to the latitudinarian evasiveness that seemed to characterize the old Low Churchmanship." Nockles further commented, "In truth, it cannot fairly be maintained that Newman was driven out of the Church of England."[100]

Following the problematic historical comments in Note A on "Liberalism," Newman provided a list of eighteen propositions that he associated with his concept of the term in the 1830s. Those eighteen propositions completely perplexed contemporary reviewers and have received at best modest attention from later historians. These puzzling theses are directly related to an important external event that occurred between the first and second editions of the *Apologia* and deeply affected Newman and his fellow liberal English Roman Catholics as well as the wider Roman Catholic communion.

On December 8, 1864, Pope Pius IX had issued the Syllabus of Errors and the encyclical *Quanta Cura,* exceedingly controversial documents that

---

100. Theodore Walrond, "J. H. Newman's *Apologia,*" *North British Review* 41 (1864): 95. See *L&D* 21: 449n5 regarding A. P. Stanley's request that Newman in his revised edition alter his claim that the liberals had driven him from Oxford. G. W. Cox, *Westminster Review* 84 (1865): 231; Nockles, "Oxford, Tract 90 and the Bishops," pp. 60, 66.

experienced a hostile reception in England among Protestants and many Roman Catholics. Ward, Manning, and the *Dublin Review* circle welcomed the encyclical and the syllabus as infallible statements of the pope and of the church. Newman deeply feared the effect on general English public opinion and upon the thought and spirit of recent converts to Roman Catholicism arising from extravagant ultramontane interpretations of the papal statements and the positions they censured. Newman immediately sought to produce what at the time and since appears to be a minimizing interpretation. On January 12, 1865, Newman told William Monsell, "when we come to the *matter* of the propositions condemned, at first sight I see little which would not be condemned by Archdeacon Denison, or by Keble, or the great body of the Anglican Church thirty years ago." To another correspondent, Newman wrote on January 25, 1865: "And this seems to me clear, that it condemns little which would not have been condemned by all Anglican High Church men thirty years ago. Therefore it is no trouble to me to acquiesce in its denunciations." Nonetheless, he found the syllabus "a great disadvantage and discouragement to us English Catholics" and wished "it had never been issued." He also predicted in the spirit of the closing section of the *Apologia*, "whether in my time or not ... on certain parts a re-action in the Church, as there has been so often in the course of its history."[101] Throughout the rest of 1865 Newman voiced private reservations about the effect of the papal statements and even more about Ward's extreme interpretation of them in the *Dublin Review*.

In Note A on "Liberalism" Newman described his list of eighteen propositions as those liberal views that as a member of the Tractarian party "and together with the High Church, I earnestly denounced and abjured" (366). Newman's set of propositions, thus associated with the 1830s, as written and published in the spring of 1865 actually related directly and intimately to the contemporary Syllabus of Errors and the recent encyclical. Many of the propositions condemned by the syllabus are echoed quite closely in Newman's own set of theses he claims to have condemned three decades earlier. The following examples will suffice to demonstrate the strong parallels.

101. Ward, *The Life of John Henry, Cardinal Newman*, 2: 82–85; JHN to Henry Bittleston, July 29 and August 4, 1865; JHN to E. B. Pusey, September 5 and November 17, 1865; JHN to William Lockhardt, October 26, 1865, *L&D* 22: 19, 29–30, 44, 84–85, 103. For Ward's comments, see W. G. Ward, "Extent of the Church's Infallibility: The Encyclical" and "The Encyclical and Syllabus," *Dublin Review* 4 (n.s.) (1865): 41–69, 441–499; the same volume of the *Dublin Review* published a translation of both documents on pp. 500–529. JHN to William Monsell, January 12, 1865; JHN to Henry Nutcombe Oxenham, January 25, 1865, *L&D* 21: 386, 391–392.

PIUS IX 4: All the truths of religion proceed from the innate strength of human reason; hence reason is the ultimate standard by which man can and ought to arrive at the knowledge of all truths of every kind.[102]

NEWMAN 1: No religious tenet is important, unless reason shows it to be so.

PIUS IX 5: Divine revelation is imperfect, and therefore subject to a continual and indefinite progress, corresponding with the advancement of human reason.

NEWMAN 7: Christianity is necessarily modified by the growth of civilization, and the exigencies of times.

PIUS IX 9: All the dogmas of the Christian religion are indiscriminately the object of natural science or philosophy, and human reason, enlightened solely in an historical way, is able, by its own natural strength and principles, to attain to the true science of even the most abstruse dogmas; provided only that such dogmas be proposed to reason itself as its object.

NEWMAN 6: No revealed doctrines or precepts may reasonably stand in the way of scientific conclusions.

PIUS IX 63: It is lawful to refuse obedience to legitimate princes, and even to rebel against them.

NEWMAN 16: It is lawful to rise in arms against legitimate princes.

PIUS IX 79: Moreover, it is false that the civil liberty of every form of worship, and the full power, given to all, of overtly and publicly manifesting any opinions whatsoever and thoughts, conduce more easily to corrupt the morals and minds of the people, and to propagate the pest of indifferentism.

NEWMAN 12: The civil power has no positive duty, in a normal state of things, to maintain religious truth.

PIUS IX 3: Human reason, without any reference whatsoever to God, is the sole arbiter of truth and falsehood, and of good and evil; it is law to itself, and suffices, by its natural force, to secure the welfare of men and of nations.

NEWMAN 18: Virtue is the child of knowledge, and vice of ignorance.

Furthermore, Newman's propositions 9 and 10 state the manner whereby liberalism improperly asserts "a right of Private Judgment" and of conscience. In *Quanta Cura* Pius IX had similarly condemned "that erroneous opinion, most fatal in its effects on the Catholic Church and the salvation of souls,

---

102. Consult http://www.papalencyclicals.net/Pius09/p9syll.htm and http://www.papalencyclicals.net/Pius09/p9quanta.htm for the Syllabus of Errors and *Quanta Cura*, respectively. They also appear in Claudia Carlen, ed., *The Papal Encyclicals 1740–1878* (Ann Arbor, Mich.: Pierian Press, 1990). For the background of the issuance of the papal statements, see Don O'Leary, *Roman Catholicism and Modern Science: A History* (New York: Continuum, 2006), pp. 45–54; Owen Chadwick, *A History of the Popes, 1830–1914* (Oxford: Clarendon Press, 1998), pp. 168–181.

called by Our Predecessor, Gregory XVI, an 'insanity,' viz., that 'liberty of conscience and worship is each man's personal right, which ought to be legally proclaimed and asserted in every rightly constituted society; and that a right resides in the citizens to an absolute liberty, which should be restrained by no authority whether ecclesiastical or civil, whereby they may be able openly and publicly to manifest and declare any of their ideas whatever, either by word of mouth, by the press, or in any other way.'"

These parallels between the propositions that Newman claimed to have rejected as a Tractarian and those condemned by Pius IX constituted a public statement that sought to substantiate his private assertions that the pope had condemned nothing that Anglican Tractarians and high churchmen had not condemned long ago. Importantly, however, Newman did not cite quotations from his or other high church publications of the Tractarian era to corroborate his claims. Considering how often he did produce citations from those earlier works, their absence here is quite significant.

Contemporary reviewers seeking either an historical or contemporary relevance for Newman's note immediately found themselves perplexed by his set of theses. One, looking to the Tractarian past, stated, "The propositions which Dr. Newman enumerates ... as familiar to him among the tenets of Liberalism thirty years ago, were certainly not professed by any persons who influenced the proceedings against No. 90 in 1841." Fitzjames Stephen, writing in the *Saturday Review* and seeking some contemporary application of Newman's ideas, declared that Newman's comments proved "that he not only utterly misunderstands it [liberalism], but misunderstands it so completely as to fall into the double error of ascribing to Liberals principles which hardly any of them hold, and of drawing from those principles inferences which have nothing to do with them."[103]

The difficulty and frustration both contemporary and later commentators encountered understanding and interpreting Newman's eighteen propositions arose because Newman had directed them not toward a historical problem nor toward the general contemporary religious situation but rather toward the immediate problem that he and other liberal English Roman Catholics confronted over the recent papal decrees. On one hand Newman aligned himself with Pius IX's statements by presenting himself as a lifelong opponent of liberalism, defining that liberalism in the very terms enunciated by the pope. In this respect, Newman was seeking to set himself politically aright with Rome and also possibly to reposition himself for another attempt to open a house in Oxford. As he wrote John Walker, a fellow Roman Catholic priest, after

---

103. G. W. Cox, "Contemporary Literature: Theology and Philosophy," *Westminster Review* 84 (1865): 231; Stephen, "Dr. Newman and Liberalism," p. 769.

reading Fitzjames Stephen's sharp review: "I was amused at having at length caught it from the Saturday [Review]. Of course it must have come sooner or later. I wonder whether the wounds I have received will do me any good with the people in London who go about saying I am a liberal. As they have said this up to now, in spite of my Apologia, I suppose the testimony of the Saturday in my favour may go for nothing—still it ought to tell."[104] Any criticism he received might redound to his credit in Roman Catholic circles as an opponent of liberalism and protect him from what he knew to be continuing efforts by the ultramontanes to cast further suspicion on his reputation.

On the other hand, by asserting that Pius IX had said little that went beyond Anglican high churchmen, Newman interpreted the papal documents in a minimalist fashion that played down their novelty and blunted their extreme character. He would repeat those claims more forthrightly and with much eloquence many years later in his *Letter to the Duke of Norfolk* (1874).[105] In this manner, Newman sought to domesticate the unwelcome papal documents for English Roman Catholics and most especially for recent converts from the English Church, by making the syllabus and encyclical resemble the views of a familiar, if minority, party within the Church of England. In this fashion he made peace with the papal pronouncements on his own terms.

Newman remained very careful in his remarks about these propositions. In early June 1865 he replied rather incoherently to private criticisms of R. H. Hutton, "As to the deductions which I have set down in the shape of propositions, I did not mean them to be strictly logical, but propositions which the Tracts etc opposed." Later that month Newman told Frederic Rogers: "It is likely that a note I have written upon Liberalism in my 2nd Edition of the Apologia will bring criticism on me, which I ought to answer. Now I am so desperately lazy that I shall not be able to get myself to do so." But four years later in a curious statement inserted in the 1869 edition of the *Apologia* as a conclusion to the note on "Liberalism," Newman wrote, "How far the Liberal party of 1830–40 really held the above eighteen Theses, which I attributed to them, and how far and in what sense I should oppose those Theses now, could scarcely be explained without a separate Dissertation."[106] This statement was anything but clear about the past or the present, and the separate dissertation never materialized.

---

104. JHN to J. Walker of Scarborough, July 2, 1865, *L&D* 22: 4–5.
105. See John Henry Newman, *A Letter Addressed to His Grace the Duke of Norfolk on Occasion of Mr. Gladstone's Recent Expostulation* (1875) in Newman, *Certain Difficulties*, 2: 262–298.
106. JHN to Richard Holt Hutton, June 3, 1865; JHN to Frederic Rogers, June 25, 1865, *L&D* 21: 482, 502. Svaglic, ed., *Apologia Pro Vita Sua*, p. 262.

Newman's reticence about adding further explanations replicated a longstanding polemical tactic on his part. As an Anglican, Newman had regarded tendentious statements as standing approved if an authority did not formally and specifically repudiate them. Such again was his tactic in the note on "Liberalism." It amounted to his version of *Tract 90* in regard to the meaning of Pope Pius's syllabus and encyclical. In *Tract 90* Newman had interpreted the Thirty-Nine Articles to conform with his own self-constructed, expansive Catholicism of the 1830s, to oppose the narrow evangelical Protestant interpretation of the articles, and to permit his followers to remain in the Church of England. In the note on "Liberalism" Newman interpreted the Syllabus of Errors and *Quanta Cura* to conform to his liberal Roman Catholicism of the 1860s; to oppose the narrow interpretation applied to them by Ward, Manning, and the *Dublin Review*; and to encourage wavering converts to remain in the Roman Catholic Church. As Newman wrote to Frederic Rogers in January 1866: "We are in a strange time. I have not a shadow of a misgiving that the Catholic Church and its doctrine are directly from God—but then I know well that there is in particular quarters a narrowness which is not of God." As both an Anglican and a Roman Catholic, Newman had opposed such partisan narrowness. Whatever his proclivity in each communion to champion ecclesiastical exclusivity, in his own way he also eschewed theological and devotional rigidity in each. He had written *Tract 90* to keep people in the English Church; he pursued his minimalist interpretation of the syllabus and encyclical to keep people of liberal sentiment in the Roman Catholic Church.[107] He sought to protect the position of a theological minority in each institution. In 1864 and 1865 Newman's presentation of himself as an enemy of liberalism while an Anglican served as a device to protect his own pursuit of liberalism in the Roman Catholic Church and that of others as well.

Newman and the Oriel Fellowship

In the *Apologia* Newman related his struggle with liberalism as a battle with larger religious, political, and cultural forces of the day. A careful study of his life and intellectual development, however, reveals the fact that the actual landscape on which the history of his religious opinions emerged, including the conflict with what he termed liberalism, was that of Oriel College and his own family.

107. JHN to Frederic Rogers, January 18, 1866, *L&D* 22: 130; JHN to Henry Bittleston, July 29, 1865, *L&D* 22: 19. Newman feared Ward's extravagant view of the syllabus and encyclical as infallible utterances would drive people from the Roman Catholic Church. Such had already been the case with Thomas Arnold Jr. See also Bernard Bergonzi, *A Victorian Wanderer: The Life of Thomas Arnold the Younger* (New York: Oxford Univ. Press, 2003).

Except for his conversion at the age of fifteen and the difficulties his family faced through his father's two business failures, the most momentous event in Newman's early life was his election to the Oriel College fellowship in 1822 despite his poor performance on the undergraduate university examinations. At the time, in good evangelical fashion, he interpreted the election, which followed not long after his father's formal bankruptcy, providentially as "God's gift."[108] It had not been entirely a gift because he had been required to pass a separate set of Oriel examinations as part of the election process.

The Oriel College Common Room with its eighteen fellows and presiding provost introduced Newman, still shaken by his family's financial and social humiliation as well as his own weak completion of his undergraduate career, to a collection of remarkably bright clergy, to avenues of social mobility and income, and to a broad spectrum of Anglican theological and ecclesiastical opinion. In his autobiographical memoir Newman recalled that the Oriel fellowship stood as "neither high Church nor low Church," but as "a new school" marked by "its spirit of moderation and comprehension." Their enemies, according to Newman, were "the old unspiritual high-and-dry, then in possession of the high places of Oxford" and the residents of lesser colleges who "felt both envy at their reputation and took offence at the strictness of their lives." Newman then significantly stated, "Their friends ... as far as they had exactly friends, were of the Evangelical party."[109] The Oriel fellowship was also one of the more devout groups at Oxford, with fellows normally worshipping in chapel together after dinner.

In the pages of the *Apologia,* in contrast to Newman's autobiographical memoir, as well as in most subsequent Tractarian and Oxford University histories, the Oriel College Common Room has been associated with logic-chopping conversation generated by a group known as the "Noetics." Their number included Edward Copleston, John Davison, Richard Whately, Edward Hawkins, R. D. Hampden, Thomas Arnold, Baden Powell, J. B. White, and Samuel Hinds. These clerics, who were never all in residence at the same time, functioned as no more than a group of friends, each of whom was quite capable of criticizing the others. Once they assumed clerical positions outside the university—such as Copleston as bishop of Llandaff, Whately as archbishop of Dublin, and Arnold as headmaster of Rugby—they only occasionally interacted with former Oriel colleagues. The outlooks most deeply characterizing them were their general championing of ecclesiastical moderation, their looking to the Bible as the foundation of faith, their rejection of Calvinist

---

108. Journal, July 12, 1822, in Newman, *Autobiographical Writings,* pp. 186–187.

109. Newman, "Autobiographical Memoir," in Newman, *Autobiographical Writings,* p. 73.

theology, and their suspicion of both narrow evangelical ecclesiology and exclusive high church clericalism. They firmly believed that revelation and miracles had ended with the age of the apostles and regarded Roman Catholicism as a corrupt form of Christianity. As H. C. G. Matthew importantly and correctly emphasized, in the writing of the Noetics "nothing is more striking . . . than the fervour of their faith," and nothing could be "more misleading than to present them as incipient secularists, as is shown by their eagerness to refute both utilitarianism and Unitarianism."[110] These points are important because the various Noetics were the Oxford figures whom Newman in the *Apologia* was most likely to associate with liberalism.

Newman's movement in religious opinion between 1822 and 1828 from Calvinistic evangelicalism to moderate high churchmanship reflected the influence of changing Oriel friendships. For much of his Anglican life such shifting friendships determined Newman's movement in theological outlooks. With the marriage in 1824 of Walter Mayers, his evangelical mentor from Ealing School who had continued as a mentoring presence during his undergraduate years, Newman came under the influence of Edward Hawkins, who steadily drew the younger man away from evangelical bibliolatry toward a deeper appreciation of the sacrament of baptism and of the role of tradition in Christian teaching and ministry. Thereafter, Richard Whately offered him friendship, employment, and instruction on the importance of the institutional independence of the church. By 1826 Newman had become an Oriel tutor, a position that provided substantial income beyond his fellowship. Upon Hawkins's election to the Oriel provostship in 1828, Newman was appointed vicar of the Church of St. Mary the Virgin, a position that brought him still additional income. The former shy, evangelical undergraduate now commanded a circle of socially well-connected friends, a significant income, and the pulpit of the unofficial university church.

That same year Newman's beloved sister Mary died suddenly, as did Walter Mayers. E. B. Pusey, another Oriel fellow who had become a close friend, received the regius professorship of Hebrew, leaving Oriel for Christchurch. Both Pusey and Hawkins also married in that year. Such marriages of close male companions, including later Tractarian colleagues, usually proved difficult for Newman and led to prolonged periods of resentment, disruption in friendships, and a sense of personal loss. As these earlier Oriel friendships underwent stress, a new friendship with Richard Hurrell Froude began to blossom in 1828, as did Newman's appreciation for John Keble's sacramental

---

110. H. C. G. Matthew, "Noetics, Tractarians, and the Reform of the University of Oxford in the Nineteenth Century," *History of Universities* 9 (1990): 212.

poetry. Both Froude and Keble held quite conservative political and ecclesiastical opinions. Both men were also unmarried, with Froude being deeply enamored of the ideal of clerical celibacy. During 1828 Newman commenced his study of the early Church Fathers.

As 1828 gave way to 1829 Newman's behavior within Oriel and the wider university underwent considerable transformation, undoubtedly as a result of the events of the previous months. Although he had personally favored Catholic Emancipation, Newman in 1829 joined other younger and generally deeply conservative dons to oppose the reelection of Sir Robert Peel to his Oxford seat in Parliament. This election, occasioned by Peel's reversal of policy on the Catholic question, not only sharply split the university but also the Oriel fellowship. Hawkins as provost failed to deliver the Oriel votes to Peel and thereafter found himself at odds with many members of his Common Room. To his sister, Newman portrayed Peel's reversal on Catholic Emancipation as part of a larger attack on the church led by "Utilitarians and Schismatics" that required the "Guardians and Guides of Christ's Church" to demonstrate its independence from the state. To his mother, no doubt echoing views derived from conversations with Keble and Froude, he explained that the English Church now confronted the spirit of "latitudinarianism, indifferentism, republicanism, and schism, a spirit which tends to overthrow doctrine, as if the fruit of bigotry, and discipline as if the instrument of priestcraft."[111] Today scholars see this new political alignment of 1829 as marking the beginning of the internal university disruption that would culminate in Tractarianism.

A second event in 1829 soon followed this political disruption, an event about which Newman only hints in the *Apologia*. He, along with Froude, Robert Wilberforce, and Joseph Dornford, the other Oriel tutors, reorganized tutorial instruction in Oriel without consulting Hawkins. During the first half of the next year Hawkins turned back the reform and gradually removed Newman and his fellow tutors from instructional responsibilities by thereafter sending them no new students. This action reduced Newman's income by approximately one-half. After 1832, when his last student took his examinations, Newman provided no other collegiate instruction during his Oxford career. He would later interpret Hawkins's action as having providentially opened the way for him to have time to lead the Tractarian Movement. On other occasions, however, he would complain bitterly about having been deprived of his natural vocation of instructing the young. Hawkins for his part would see the Tractarian Movement and the turbulence it provoked in Oxford

---

111. JHN to Jemima Newman, March 4, 1829, JHN to Mrs. Newman, March 13, 1829, *L&D* 2: 128, 130.

and the English Church as having originated in a college quarrel. As another fallout of the collapsed tutorial reform, Hawkins replaced Newman as tutor with R. D. Hampden, also an Oriel fellow.

During the period of conflict over the Oriel tutorial reform, Newman had also quarreled with local radical Oxford evangelicals and in early 1830 had been ejected from his position as secretary of the Oxford chapter of the Church Missionary Society. By this point he had begun his brilliant criticism of evangelical doctrine, devotional practices, and ecclesiology from the pulpit of St. Mary's.

Just as his career as a college tutor concluded, Newman experienced a second personal professional disappointment. Hugh James Rose and W. R. Lyall, two orthodox, traditional high churchmen, had recruited Newman to write a history of the early church councils. However, when in the autumn of 1832 he submitted the manuscript, which became his volume on *The Arians of the Fourth Century* (1833), Rose and Lyall rejected it as being too sympathetic to Rome and presenting too indeterminate a view of early Christian church doctrine.

Consequently, in December 1832 when Newman set out on a Mediterranean voyage with the Froudes, which plays so important a part in the *Apologia,* he was a deeply disappointed person, having been ousted from the Oriel tutorship by Hawkins and rejected as an author by two traditionally orthodox high churchmen. The Newman who toured the Mediterranean was a man in process of having to establish a new identity and life purpose for himself. He would find that identity, as he had since 1829, by nurturing an increasingly radical high church theology that emphasized sacramental clericalism and that denigrated as ecclesiastically inadequate not only Dissenters but also both evangelicals and traditional high churchmen in the English Church. In April 1833 he wrote from Italy to an Oriel friend: "Why will you not be in the humour to devote yourself to the Apostolical cause? I do not wish you to come back to College, but to join the brotherhood of those who wish a return to the primitive state of the Church, when it was not a mere instrument of civil government, which it approaches to be now." Newman further explained, "I almost think the time has come to form clubs and societies under title of Apostolical — that we may have some approximation towards a system of discipline."[112] Newman thus proposed a high church apostolic brotherhood of radically reforming celibate priests whose activities would go well beyond those of traditional high churchmen. Clerical celibacy and the idea of religious brotherhoods would also become increasingly important in Newman's mind.

---

112. JHN to H. A. Woodgate, April 17, 1833, *L&D* 3: 300.

In Sicily, Newman fell dangerously ill, and he interpreted this near-death experience as his having been providentially spared for a new undertaking. He came to understand what that fresh departure should be upon hearing Keble's Assize Sermon attacking the proposed parliamentary restructuring of the bishoprics of the Church of Ireland as an assault on the apostolic church in the realm. Having been deprived of his instructional identity in Oriel College, Newman generated a new role for himself in the university and the English Church — an identity of his own making. Henceforth, from within the established church he would champion the status of Anglican clergy on the basis of their episcopal ordination, deprecate schismatic Dissent, and denounce virtually all manifestations of evangelical Protestantism within and without the Church of England. He would fashion a new Catholic theology, new avenues of Catholic devotion, and the possible restoration of monastic life in the boundaries of the established church.

A few weeks after hearing Keble's sermon Newman launched the *Tracts for the Times* and pressed steadily for a more radical course of action than more traditional high churchmen such as Rose and William Palmer thought prudent. In terms of the Oriel College fellowship, the *Tracts for the Times* implicitly censured the vocations and ideas of all those fellows feeling comfortable in successful careers within Erastian structures, benefiting from government patronage, embracing moderate reform of the Church of England, and to a greater or lesser degree standing prepared to accommodate the demands of Dissenters. Such prospering, advancing Oriel fellows were the latitudinarian liberals against whom a disappointed, angry Newman now battled as he had for an even longer period denounced evangelicals.

The most outspoken of these Oriel figures was Hampden, an ambitious ecclesiastical liberal and principal of St. Mary Hall, who had replaced Newman as tutor in the college and then in early 1834 defeated him for the appointment as professor of moral philosophy. Later that year in a signed pamphlet designed to gain the attention of the Whigs, whose patronage he sought, Hampden astonished the university by urging the admission of Dissenters without requiring their subscription to the Thirty-Nine Articles, which was already the practice at Cambridge. Hampden would have required Dissenters so admitted to receive instruction in the Anglican articles of faith.

Drawing upon his Bampton Lectures of 1833, Hampden based his broader theological position, which minimized the importance of all creedal statements such as the Thirty-Nine Articles, on his rejection of "the common prejudice, which identifies systems of doctrine — or theological propositions methodically deduced and stated — with Christianity itself — with the simple religion of Jesus Christ, as received into the heart and influencing conduct." Religious dissent, he argued, originated in that "confusion of theological and moral truth with Religion." Distinguishing original Christianity from later theological reasoning that had resulted in creeds, Hampden stated "that no conclusions of human reasoning, however correctly deduced, however logically sound, are properly religious truths — are such as strictly and necessarily belong to human salvation through Christ." He further explained "that *conclusions* from Scripture are not to be placed on a level with truths which Scripture itself simply declares." Thus he concluded that differences among Christian denominations and their varying creeds were not based on matters essential to the Christian faith. Hampden took the even more radical step of refusing to deny the name of *Christian* to Unitarians, no matter how much he disliked their theology, because they professed "to love Christ in sincerity." In evangelical fashion Hampden stated that the true unity of the Church was not one of formal, visible creedal agreement but rather "an invisible one ... the communion of saints; the union of Christians with the Holy Spirit himself."[113]

As already noted, it was this Hampden pamphlet advocating the admission of Dissenters that Newman described in the *Apologia* as "that onset of Liberal principles, of which we were all in immediate anticipation, whether in the Church or in the University" (180) and as "the commencement of the assault of Liberalism upon the old orthodoxy of Oxford" (181). But Newman's ire extended beyond Hampden himself in a fashion not reported in the *Apologia*.

Subsequent to Hampden's pamphlet, Hawkins, whose views differed from those of Hampden, had introduced a proposal before the Oxford Heads of Houses that would have required entering students to make a declaration of willingness to be instructed in the Thirty-Nine Articles in place of subscription to them. He and others of undoubted orthodoxy had long believed that at the time of matriculation Oxford students were too young and inexperienced to understand adequately the Thirty-Nine Articles to which they were required to subscribe.

Soon thereafter Newman elaborately coached his former student and close friend Henry Wilberforce in composing a pamphlet responding to Hawkins's proposal. Newman urged Wilberforce to portray Hampden, Hawkins, Arnold, Whately, and others associated with the Oriel fellowship with whom he differed as supporting a theology that advanced possible Socinianism at Oxford. In his anonymous pamphlet titled *The Foundation of the Faith Assailed at Oxford* Wilberforce named all of those figures and then declared "that in

---

113. Renn Dickson Hampden, *Observations on Religious Dissent: With Particular Reference to the Use of Religious Tests in the University*, 2nd rev. ed. (Oxford: S. Collingwood; London: B. Fellowes and J. G. & F. Rivington, 1834), pp. 3, 7, 8, 11, 20, 28.

the University there exists a party on which I think I should hardly lay an unjust censure were I to apply to them the awful name of SOCINIAN."[114] Wilberforce's pamphlet thus became Newman's vehicle for attacking the orthodoxy and good faith of those Oriel fellows who had frustrated his career while they themselves advanced in the English Church and Oxford.

Two years later in 1836 Newman helped lead the university effort to censure Hampden when Lord Melbourne appointed Hampden regius professor of divinity. On that occasion, the archbishop of Canterbury had submitted to Melbourne the names of Newman, Keble, and Pusey among others (but not Hampden) as acceptable candidates for the professorship. When they were not chosen for the highly lucrative position, they along with many others known as the Corpus Common Room Committee organized a broad effort to challenge the right of a Whig ministry to exercise patronage in the university.[115]

During this university revolt against the Whig ministry Newman composed a notorious, anonymous pamphlet (quoted in the *Apologia*), titled *Elucidations of Dr. Hampden's Theological Statements,* that in ferocity and dubious honesty far outstripped Kingsley's assault of 1864. In a fashion that three decades later Newman would regard as Kingsley poisoning the well, the Corpus Common Room Committee in its public assault on Hampden declared that "no explanation or even recantation of his opinions at this moment can sufficiently restore . . . confidence."[116] The Oxford Convocation duly condemned Hampden on the basis of these trumped-up charges and relieved him of a minor duty associated with the regius professorship, after which he assumed his duties, received his professorial income, and instructed goodly numbers of students. In 1847, after confronting still further high church–instigated controversy, Hampden would become bishop of Hereford. Significantly, Hampden's liberalism had really only extended to criticizing restrictive use of the Thirty-Nine Articles for admission to Oxford. He was later highly critical of the authors of *Essays and Reviews*, an eventuality that might have been pre-

---

114. [Henry Wilberforce], *The Foundation of the Faith Assailed in Oxford: A Letter to His Grace the Archbishop of Canterbury, &c. &c. &c., Visitor of the University; with Particular Reference to the Changes in Its Constitution, Now under Consideration* (London: J. G. & F. Rivington, 1835), pp. 15, 34.

115. See Turner, *John Henry Newman,* pp. 207–254, and Robert Pattison, *The Great Dissent: John Henry Newman and the Liberal Heresy* (New York: Oxford Univ. Press, 1991), pp. 55–96, for differing accounts of the Newman-Hampden relationship and rivalry.

116. Broadsides of March 5, 1836, included in the materials under the Hampden Case, Beinecke Rare Book and Manuscript Library, Yale University [Beinecke Library Mhg 56, Vol. 1].

dicted from his insistence throughout his Oxford career on the primacy of scripture in determining the rule of faith.

As demonstrated most clearly in the Hampden rivalry, what Newman witnessed throughout the 1830s as he led the Tractarian Movement was the rise to positions of prominence in the Church of England and Oxford of other Oriel fellows who achieved the income, influence, and authority that consistently eluded him.

The issue of income forgone was not a minor one for Newman. Until the spring of 1836 when his mother suddenly and unexpectedly died and his two sisters married, Newman had to provide financial support for them as he had for much of the rest of his family during the previous decade. The loss of income from the Oriel tutorship had produced severe financial pressure on him. On July 11, 1836, a few weeks after their mother's death, Newman wrote to his sister Jemima:

> About a year since, when I found myself getting into debt, I began a prayer to this effect, which I continued till May last — "that God would either give me the means of doing what I wished to do towards you all, or remove the necessity —" In the latter clause a number of things suggested themselves to me, and nothing definitely. First I thought it right to say so, not to bind down (as it were) God's providence to one way — again I thought of money being left us, etc etc., I mean, I did not realize (or think to do so) *any* mode, but left it to God. When your engagement was formed, it struck me strangely — and, when we were overtaken with our affliction last May [their mother's death], it seemed just as if I had been praying for the death of her, whom I had always looked forward to as living for many years. You may conceive how I was overcome.

Newman's sense of guilt over this prayer for some kind of relief from his family financial pressures endured for some time. Six years later he wrote to Henry Wilberforce, "I will add that my own Mother's death was a most unintentional and startling, but still a fulfillment of a prayer of mine — which wounded me much at the time, for I seemed, as if, to have been praying that God would take her away."[117]

Throughout the 1836 campaign against Hampden the prospect loomed that if Melbourne retracted the appointment or Hampden resigned, the regius

---

117. JHN to Jemima Mozley, July 11, 1836, *L&D* 5: 322; JHN to Henry Wilberforce, April 25, 1842, *L&D* 8: 511–512. See also JHN to Jemima Mozley, June 26, 1836, and "Memorandum: 'Apology for Myself,'" June 1873, in which Newman discusses his monetary concerns as well as tensions between his mother and himself over his religious views. *L&D* 5: 313–315.

professorship of divinity and its considerable income would then go to someone else in the university, possibly to Newman, who had been on the archbishop of Canterbury's patronage list. At one point during the controversy Newman privately described Hampden, who had his own pressing family obligations, as "worse than a Socinian" and "the most lucre loving, earthly minded, unlovely person one ever set eyes on."[118] Clearly, financial as well as theological concerns informed Newman's furious rivalry with Hampden.

Deep angers rooted in Oriel would continue to stir Newman's mind for many years to come. During the painful spring of 1845, as he pondered moving to Rome, Newman voiced long-standing resentments against Oriel fellows that had accumulated over more than a decade. In April 1845, rehearsing for Henry Wilberforce the injuries he had suffered within Oxford, Newman recounted: "No one has spoken well of me. My friends who have had means of knowing me have spoken against me. Whately and Hawkins have both used opprobrious language about me, till I began to think myself really deceitful and double dealing, as they said.... Others have kept silent in my greatest troubles. The mass of men in Oxford who know me a little have shown a coldness and suspicion which I do not deserve. In the affair of Number 90, few indeed showed me any sympathy, or gave me reason to believe that I was at all in their hearts.... Heads of Houses whom I knew have been unkind to me, and have set the fashion; and now my prime of life is past, and I am nothing." Newman pondered as a personal mystery that while his gifts were that of the "tuition or the oversight of young men," he had "all along been so wonderfully kept out of that occupation." Having recited wrongs he had suffered since being excluded from the Oriel tutorship more than a decade earlier, he concluded, "And now it is all gone and over, and there is no redress, no retrieving." Yet he did not "think any thing of ambition or longing is mixed with these feelings, as far as I can tell."[119] Such was the lingering bitterness and abiding anger that Newman experienced dating from his ouster as Oriel tutor through his reception into the Roman Catholic Church. Without exception, those whom he associated with latitudinarianism and liberalism in the Church of England were those whose career advancement had either blocked or gone beyond his.

Newman and His Family

One of the most remarkable silences in the *Apologia* is that of Newman in regard to his family. To be sure, he did not conceive of the book as a full autobiography, but as the history of his religious opinions. Nonetheless,

---

118. JHN to Simeon Lloyd Pope, March 3, 1836, *L&D* 5: 251.
119. JHN to H. Wilberforce, April 27, 1845, *L&D* 10: 641, 642.

important factors in his family life and his sibling relations touched that more limited history. Indeed, it had been primarily within his family that he first closely encountered both the radical evangelicalism and latitudinarianism he would later denounce under the term liberalism.

Newman was the eldest of six children, three sons and three daughters, in a family that experienced downward social mobility. His father, John Newman, had been a banker whose firm failed in 1816. It was shortly after that event and a serious illness on his own part that John Henry Newman underwent his evangelical conversion at Ealing School under the instruction of Walter Mayers. During those same months Newman came to the decision that he should lead a celibate life. Later that year he was entered at Trinity College, Oxford, taking up residence in 1817. In late 1821 John Newman experienced formal bankruptcy, and all the family goods were sold on the street outside their residence. This family trauma haunted John Henry Newman all his life, and not unnaturally he tried to conceal the experience. From the time of the bankruptcy until 1836 Newman became the major source of financial support for his immediate family and an aunt, initially with income from his Oriel fellowship later supplemented by the Oriel tutorship. By 1826 he was earning the considerable income of 650 pounds a year, later supplemented by a small income from St. Mary's.[120] Nonetheless, he remained deeply concerned about generating enough income to address his responsibilities to his family.

Beginning in 1823, long before significant religious quarrels emerged between himself and other Oriel fellows, Newman encountered theological conflict with his two younger brothers. Charles, who was never stable, had moved into radical political circles and eventually into Owenism. Francis, thanks to having his education financed by John, studied at Worcester College where he attained a double first and a Balliol College fellowship.[121] During this period Francis, who later repaid his brother's expenditures on his behalf, moved toward radical modes of contemporary evangelical religion while John moved in the opposite direction. Some of John's earliest efforts to delineate his

---

120. For Newman's lingering concern over his father's bankruptcy, see JHN to Jemima Mozley, July 2, 1871, *L&D* 25: 351. On the financial background of the Newman family and Newman's subsequent sources of income, see O'Faolain, *Newman's Way*, pp. 1–20, 49–85.

121. See William Robbins, *The Newman Brothers: An Essay in Comparative Intellectual Biography* (Cambridge, Mass.: Harvard Univ. Press, 1966) as well as Francis W. Newman, *Phases of Faith; or, Passages from the History of My Creed* (London: J. Chapman, 1850); *Contributions Chiefly to the Early History of the Late Cardinal Newman* (London: Kegan Paul, Trench, Trübner, 1891); I. Giberne Sievking, *Memoir and Letters of Francis W. Newman* (London: Kegan Paul, Trench, Trübner, 1909).

high churchmanship, particularly in regard to the reading of scripture and the then much contested sacrament of baptism, occurred in correspondence with Charles and Francis. The former eventually went his own way; the latter, however, continued in sharp controversy with John. Both John and Francis attempted to persuade their sisters and mother of the correctness of their views. Indeed, over the years their home became a theological battleground as the two brothers sought to elicit the support and approval of their mother and sisters.

In 1828 in the midst of these conflicts Mary, their youngest sister, died after an illness of less than twenty-four hours. She had feared for her salvation as she lay dying, and it was after her death that John began to embrace in his preaching much more strongly than in the past the doctrine of regeneration through the sacrament of baptism rather than through evangelical conversion. John nursed grief for this young woman his entire life. It was her death as well as an illness of his own about the same time that in the *Apologia* he associated with his own movement away from what he regarded as a personal drift toward liberalism, the details of which he did not significantly delineate.

John and Francis continued to quarrel. Indeed, though not mentioning the subject in the *Apologia,* this fraternal conflict was John's first close, direct encounter with those radical evangelical forces and outlooks that he equated with religious liberalism, and the manner in which he defined liberalism in the *Tracts for the Times* reflected his encounter with Francis. The younger brother had, like John, experienced the long-standing influence of Walter Mayers. When Mayers died in 1828, Francis then became deeply involved with radical Oxford and Irish evangelicals, among whom the most important was John Nelson Darby. Several of these clergy seceded from the English and Irish establishments to found the Plymouth Brethren. As a result of these radical evangelical associations, Francis in 1830 aided the ouster of John as secretary of the Oxford branch of the Church Missionary Society. About the same time, while the conflict over the Oriel tutorial reform also occupied John, Francis resigned his Balliol fellowship because he could no longer subscribe to the Thirty-Nine Articles. During this period John complained to their sister Jemima of Francis's "great dissatisfaction with every thing as it is." Later that summer in his important previously quoted letter to Simeon Lloyd Pope, Newman would describe liberalism as "a thinking established notions worth nothing," the very attitude he had ascribed to and encountered in Francis. Furthermore, John Newman directly criticized Francis for standing among those "in the so-called religious world" who "account themselves Christians because they use Scripture phrases" and consider themselves "to believe in Christ with the heart and to be changed in their moral nature because they assent fully to certain doctrines ... that we can do nothing of ourselves, have no merit, or are saved by faith; — or (again) imagine they have habits or a character when they have only feelings." Francis and others like him applied "high Christian doctrines as medicines," thus too readily offering "truths, which require a faith (to understand and receive them) grounded on deep self-knowledge and a long course of self discipline."[122] These were exactly the same evangelical doctrines that John so brilliantly denounced from the pulpit of St. Mary's and in both his poetry and prose from the late 1820s onward.

The academic achievements that John's work and personal expense had realized in Francis evaporated before his eyes as Francis in 1830 departed Oxford for a Plymouth Brethren missionary journey to Persia to preach the gospel. Francis returned in 1833, thereafter married a woman from the Darbyite sect, and later began to worship with Baptists and occasionally to preach. On November 17, 1835, John reported to Froude that because Francis had undertaken a preaching ministry outside the Church of England, he had broken with him socially. This break included a refusal to meet with Francis in their mother's home. Deploring to Froude his brother's "verging towards liberalism," Newman observed, "That wretched Protestant principle about Scripture, when taken in by an independent and clear mind, is almost certain to lead to errors I do not like to name."[123]

Shortly thereafter John directly told Francis that he now exemplified the popular notion that "latitudinarianism *is* a secret Socinianizing." John explained that he had not realized how deeply Francis had imbibed "that wretched, nay (I may say) cursed Protestant principle, (not a low principle in which our Church has any share, but the low arrogant cruel ultra-Protestant principle)" of private interpretation of scripture. He then demanded of his brother: "On what ground of reason or Scripture do you say that every one may gain the true doctrines of the gospel for himself from the Bible? where is illumination promised an *individual* for this purpose? where is it any where hinted that the aid of teachers is to be superseded? where that the universal testimony of the Church is not a principle of belief as sure and satisfactory as the word of Scripture?" He warned Francis, "You will unravel the web of selfsufficient

---

122. JHN to Jemima Newman, May 27, 1830, *L&D* 2: 226; JHN to Simeon Lloyd Pope, August 15, 1830, *L&D* 2: 264; JHN to F. W. Newman, 1830, *L&D* 2: 183, 184. Regarding John Henry Newman's quarrels with Oxford evangelicals, see Timothy C. F. Stunt, *From Awakening to Secession: Radical Evangelicals in Switzerland and Britain, 1815–1835* (Edinburgh: T&T Clark, 2000), pp. 181–220; T. C. F. Stunt, "John Henry Newman and the Evangelicals," *Journal of Ecclesiastical History* 21 (1970): 65–74; Carter, *Anglican Evangelicals*, pp. 249–311.

123. JHN to Richard Hurrell Froude, November 17, 1835, *L&D* 5: 164.

inquiry." As far as John was concerned, Francis's faith in independent, private interpretation of scripture represented "a snare of the devil."[124] In his self-determined religious journey, his rejection of baptismal regeneration, his voluntaristic preaching, his bibliolatry, and his advocacy of broad religious toleration Francis embodied the antidogmatic principle against which John preached, campaigned, and polemicized.

This extended conflict with Francis occurred in the midst of the struggle that John carried out against Hampden between 1834 and 1836. The latter also had championed the Bible over the Thirty-Nine Articles and had said he would regard as Christians all who loved Christ in sincerity. Francis embodied the very kind of radical Dissenter, including those of Unitarian outlook, whom Hampden would have admitted to Oxford. Much to John Henry Newman's anger and disappointment their mother continued to welcome Francis and his bride to her home until her death in the spring of 1836 just as the Whig government and eventually much of Oxford had embraced Hampden.

By the close of the decade family matters led John and Francis to renew their correspondence. An exchange in 1840 displayed a paradoxical convergence of opinion and remarkable transformation of John's views. Francis wrote to his brother: "*You* call it sectarianism, to promote any church but that of the Establishment: I do not mean to offend, when I say that *I* am conscientiously convinced that every Baptist or Independent meeting in the land is (to speak temperately) *as true* a church as yours, and yours as much a sect as those. . . . It is true that I see much sectarianism in dissenters, but I see a worse sectarianism in the Establishment." Francis stated that his "heart and understanding alike long for something larger far than either."[125] Francis Newman had in this letter very nearly articulated John's own changing view of the English Church and had in the last line directly expressed his brother's deep inner longing in regard to the Church Catholic.

John immediately responded, "I dare say you would be surprised to find how much more I agreed with you in detail than you at present think"; stated that sectarianism could exist without outward separation; and confessed that the establishment "is internally in a sectarian state." In a subsequent letter John indicated that Catholics in the Church of England required the exact comprehensive religious sympathy and latitudinarian charity that Francis believed should be extended to various Christian groups. John further stated, "If

---

124. JHN to Francis William Newman, November 23, 1835, *L&D* 5: 166, 167. For John Henry Newman's scorn for private judgment, see "Submission to Church Authority," preached in November 1829, Newman, *Parochial and Plain Sermons,* 3: 190–205.

125. F. W. Newman to JHN, April 15, 1840, *L&D* 7: 308.

there is at present a party, (if it must be so called) of great *capacity*, of greater *actual* latitude than any other, ours is that one." While still voicing his "great distress and even horror" at the "notion of fraternizing with Unitarians," John nonetheless indicated his willingness "to abide" by Francis's "test of religious truth, the moral peculiarities of a Christian" though he thought that test left similar grounds for disagreement, as did differing estimates of creeds.[126]

Thus by 1840 John, while articulating his views through correspondence with Francis, had placed himself into a mental framework of religious dissent and potential separation. John saw himself ministering in a church where only greater latitude in theology, liturgy, and devotion would permit Catholic truth to assert itself against the smothering excesses of evangelical Protestantism supported by Erastianism. Largely abandoning his earlier ecclesiology and emphasis on dogmatic creeds, John was seeking for himself and his Catholic coterie in the English Church the very kind of latitudinarian liberalism he had decried in the tracts and his campaign against Hampden and would again decry in the *Apologia*. It is worth noting that throughout the late 1850s and 1860s Newman would seek to establish a parallel situation of latitude for liberal English Roman Catholics, oppressed by excesses of the *Dublin Review* ultramontanes, who regarded Newman as seeking to establish his own party or sect within the English Roman Catholic Church.

A final exchange of correspondence occurred between John and Francis in the weeks before John converted to Rome when Francis clearly discerned and brilliantly articulated the schismatic, sectarian drive in his brother's Anglican career.

By the summer of 1845 John Newman was indicating to family and friends that he would soon be leaving the Church of England and resigning his Oriel fellowship. At this time Francis, in a role reversal of two decades earlier, offered to aid his brother financially, an offer his brother did not take up. In August Francis sent John a long letter that sought to help his brother clarify his long-standing confusion and hesitation as to what religious steps to take. Francis wrote, "If you choose the Romish Communion as in *itself good,* you would be in it already, and would long and long since have abandoned your ostensible position." John's delay in choosing, Francis quite correctly perceived, suggested that the Roman Church "must needs have in it points which make you reluctant to enter it." With considerable prescience about the difficulties that for the next two decades John as a convert would encounter, Francis reminded him that upon his conversion he "would at once lose all influence with nine tenths of those who were used to respect" him and that

---

126. JHN to F. W. Newman, April 16, 1840, and May 5, 1840, *L&D* 7: 310, 320.

within the Roman Church he "would be received with condescending pity as a novice who had yet much to learn and to unlearn."[127]

Francis thought John's real challenge was not that of following his conscience but of finding how in a practical fashion to be useful. Given that situation, Francis contended that "it would be better for obtaining what I believe to be your ends, — *not* to join Rome, *but* to stay unconnected with any thing, until you can form and join some independent Episcopal System, similar to that of Scotland or New York." He thought John might well achieve his goal of realizing a fuller Christian unity by taking "even a leading part in organizing the nucleus of an Anglo-Episcopal Free Church with succession of Bishops derived from New York or Scotland." Francis argued that this new religious group need profess "no hostility to Rome," but might rather keep that question "carefully open." This alternative would allow John and like-minded clergy to be linked to an episcopacy with apostolic succession and still provide for a possible eventual union with Rome without John and his followers "*surrendering their own liberties,* which liberties, it strikes me, your friends have never liked to surrender to our English Bishops." Francis urged his brother to "boldly face the charge of 'Schism'" and "not enslave yourself to your past words" by undertaking just such a newly organized church. Francis concluded, "In such a church you would have an immediate sphere of useful actions — and, if you succeeded, you would by it *prepare materials for a future union* [with Rome], such as you desire; and this would be work enough surely for one life."[128]

Francis Newman recognized that for at least the past five years his brother had set a course of establishing a sectarian alternative to the Church of England and the Roman Catholic Church. His perception fits the portrait that Newman at the time and later in the *Apologia* paints of himself during those years — that of Elijah waiting for reform. What Francis could not have known in August 1845 was that the sectarian solution was no longer possible for his brother because John's sectarian followers were fleeing and he could no longer sustain his previous hold over them.

Contingency and Conversion

In Chapter III of the *Apologia Pro Vita Sua* Newman evoked the memory of "three blows which broke me" between July and November 1841 (245), causing him to lose faith in the catholicity of the Church of England and to enter

---

127. Francis Newman to JHN, August 6, 1845, "Copies of Letters Personal and Family, 1817–1845," N. IV, Book 2, Letter 182, Newman Microfilms, Reel 81, Batch 107. Only a partial reprinting of this important letter appears in *L&D* 10: 744–745.

128. Ibid.

upon his "death-bed, as regards my membership with the Anglican Church" (252).[129] These incidents consisted of his perceiving with new intensity the analogy of the English Church, presumably including his own Catholic enclave therein, with the ancient Monophysite communion; the fierce episcopal charges against *Tract 90;* and the launching of the Jerusalem bishopric project. Thereafter, the English Church in his eyes bore all the signs of heresy, heresy that for him would only intensify in coming months.

At another point in Chapter IV of the *Apologia*, commenting on his state of mind three years later, Newman wrote, "I had begun my Essay on the Development of Doctrine in the beginning of 1845 . . . Before I got to the end, I resolved to be received" (317). Here, as in the advertisement to that book and in his first postconversion conversation with Bishop Wiseman, Newman suggested that working through the implications of the concept of development led to his decision to convert.[130] Furthermore, in neither the advertisement nor Wiseman's report of the conversation is anything mentioned about the Monophysite parallel. Yet in the *Apologia* the latter rather than the concept of doctrinal development appears as the chief factor determining Newman's thinking, and he states that he had not even consulted his volume on development for many years.

By 1864 Newman had for fifteen years downplayed the relationship of his conversion to the concept of doctrinal development because upon its publication in 1845 *An Essay on the Development of Christian Doctrine* had encountered a hostile, skeptical reception among both Roman Catholic and Protestant reviewers as well as among Vatican commentators. Hence, begin-

---

129. On the relationship of Newman's image of his deathbed to St. Augustine, see Linda H. Peterson, *Victorian Autobiography: The Tradition of Self-Interpretation* (New Haven, Conn.: Yale Univ. Press, 1986), pp. 111–116.

130. In the *Apologia* Newman places less emphasis on the role of the concept of development as leading to his conversion than he did in the advertisement to *An Essay on the Development of Christian Doctrine* or as he would seem to have stated to Bishop Wiseman during their first interview in late 1845. See John Henry Newman, *An Essay on the Development of Christian Doctrine* (London: James Toovey, 1845), pp. iii–xi, and N. Wiseman to C. Russell, early November 1845, in Wilfrid Ward, *The Life and Times of Cardinal Wiseman,* 2nd ed. (London: Longmans, Green, 1897), 1: 433–436. Once Newman had settled in Rome in 1846, he began to realize the doubts about himself that his book on development had raised in Roman Catholic circles at the Vatican. Consequently, by 1849 he dropped references to development and his conversion and instead noted the effect of Wiseman's 1839 article. He repeated and expanded this statement in 1850 in *Certain Difficulties Felt by Anglicans.* See John Henry Newman, *Discourses Addressed to Mixed Congregations,* 2nd ed. (London: Longman, Brown, Green, and Longmans, 1850), p. vi, and the next footnote.

ning in 1849 Newman had pointed to Bishop Wiseman's article of 1839 as first provoking his doubts about the English Church, and in 1850 he cited the study of the Church Fathers leading to his perception of the Monophysite parallel as "simply and solely the one intellectual cause" accounting for his reception into the Roman Catholic Church.[131] The same retreat from development marked the *Apologia*.

As a matter of the documented record, Newman's account of his decision to convert to Roman Catholicism as related in the *Apologia*, whether based on the Monophysite parallel or the concept of development, is historically inadequate. He does explain the intellectual and theological factors producing "that great revolution of mind" (208) that led him to leave the English Church. He does *not*, however, provide an account of the immediate, concrete factors in 1844 and 1845 that actually drove him to the act itself, an act that he had long postponed. The writings and actions of the Newman of history between 1841 and 1845, as opposed to the voice of the *Apologia*, present a picture not of inevitability or slow development but of unanticipated, contingent events occasioning a sudden decision to be received into the Roman Catholic Church.

In the memorable paragraph of Chapter III, beyond recollecting his deathbed as regarded the English Church, Newman made another significant statement. He noted that he was not allowed to see his Anglican life die in peace, but suffered public intrusions. He then stated, "But in consequence, my narrative must be in great measure documentary, as I cannot rely on my memory, except for definite particulars, positive or negative" (252). He indicated that he would rely on letters he had retained and others recently come into his hands. As a result, the chapter relating the five years leading up to his conversion consists largely of a train of correspondence for which Newman provides a minimum of commentary and far less narrative detail than marks the first three chapters of his book.

The months and years between the publication of *Tract 90* in February 1841 and his reception into the Roman Catholic Church in October 1845 were the most difficult, trying, and confused of Newman's Anglican career. From the close of 1841 forward he conducted himself as a quasi-schismatic priest largely making up his own rules as he went along. He withdrew from his relationship with Pusey and related to Keble almost entirely through correspondence. He founded the Littlemore community, which attracted to him and itself followers profoundly at odds with the Church of England establishment and eagerly desirous of pursuing a highly innovative Catholic religious experiment. Although not always fully agreeing with those followers and criticizing them in

---

131. Newman, *Certain Difficulties*, 1: 367; see also 1: 370–374.

the pages of the *Apologia*, Newman had closely identified with them during the first half of the 1840s. His determined pursuit of a radical Catholic experiment characterized by deep sympathy with Roman Catholicism cost him the support and sympathy of one major high churchman after another. The latter were not about to challenge bishops who had made their criticisms of Newman and his pursuit of the Catholic very clear in their episcopal charges. Newman was also weaving one way and then another during this period, seeking to avoid in action the logical conclusion of his thinking and to retain his followers in a community that he dominated. It was with implicit recognition of all these contradictory words and actions that Newman wrote his sister in February 1845 of his "dread" of "a jealous controversy about my conduct since Number 90" that might arise should any formal examination of his behavior be undertaken. Although he was "really . . . conscious of nothing which I am ashamed of" and trusted that he "should come out of the closest scrutiny undamaged," he still could not "help disliking such inquiries."[132]

In 1864, as in 1845, Newman did not wish to pursue a deep historical examination of his conduct in the years after *Tract 90*. Thus in the *Apologia* he emphasized that a death-bed such as his membership in the Anglican Church had occupied has no history. By reprinting primarily letters from those years, he could emphasize the Monophysite parallel because he mentioned it often to a growing circle of correspondents. The perception of that parallel became his vehicle for an explanation of actions rather than his providing a narration of events and external influences such as he had related in the earlier chapters of the *Apologia*.

Newman's contemporary comments during the months after receiving the three blows of 1841 differed considerably from what he described in the *Apologia*. These differences pertain particularly to the role and function of the Monophysite parallel. Newman dated the first instance of his perceiving the parallel to 1839. As he wrote to Robert Wilberforce in January 1842: "Since then whatever line of early history I look into, I see as in a glass reflected our own Church in the heretical party, and the Roman Church in the Catholic. This is an appalling fact—which, do what I will, I cannot shake off." Between 1839 and 1842 Newman had similarly informed other correspondents, expressing greater and lesser degrees of anxiety. None of these correspondents —including Frederic Rogers, Henry and Robert Wilberforce, William and

---

132. JHN to Jemima Mozley, February 11, 1845, *L&D* 10: 547. Newman feared that some such kind of inquiry might arise if there were an ongoing effort to have *Tract 90* condemned following the assumed proctors' veto of the proposed condemnation in the upcoming meeting of Oxford Convocation.

Catherine Froude, J. B. Mozley, Manning, Gladstone, and Pusey — found the parallel either disturbing or persuasive. More important, it is not altogether certain what significance Newman in the 1840s attached to the parallel since as late as February 1844 he wrote Pusey: "I am too much accustomed to this idea to feel pain at it. I could only feel pain, if I found it led me to action. At present I do not feel any such call."[133]

In early 1842 Newman explained the fearfulness of the Monophysite analogy as arising from contemporary events driven primarily by Anglican evangelicals. He explained to Robert Wilberforce that his thinking had returned to the parallel only when he found that his "fears," which had "slept for very many months," had become "re-animated by our dreadful divisions, the Bishops' charges, and this Prussian affair."[134] Thus in 1842 Newman related the effect of the Monophysite parallel to the episcopal attacks, first initiated by two evangelical bishops, and the establishment of the Jerusalem bishopric, which had been the brainchild of evangelicals led by Lord Shaftsbury and later supported hesitantly by high churchmen. As indicated in various contemporary letters, the heresy about which Newman complained during these and subsequent months was what he regarded as the growing influence of evangelicals on matters large and small within the highest councils of the Church of England.

In the *Apologia* Newman quoted extensively from two letters he wrote in October 1843 to Henry Manning in which, among other things, he appealed to the Monophysite parallel to explain why he no longer believed in the catholicity of the English Church. Newman wrote these letters not only to demonstrate his changing convictions but also to vent his explosive rage at the manner in which high church clerics such as Manning and Palmer and their lay friends, including Gladstone, had dealt with him in recent months. Here and elsewhere in the *Apologia* Newman appealed to his perception of the Monophysite parallel of 1839 long after the fact as a post facto explanation for actions and attitudes that had arisen from his enormous frustration, anger, and isolation after *Tract 90*. As he experienced attacks or abandonment by one group after another in the Church of England, he informed friends of his lack of confidence in the catholicity of that institution based on the Monophysite parallel as well as on perceived parallels with other ancient heresies. Through this device Newman made the church that was disowning him less

---

133. JHN to Robert Wilberforce, January 26, 1842, *L&D* 8: 440; JHN to E. B. Pusey, February 19, 1844, *L&D* 10: 126.

134. JHN to Robert Wilberforce, January 26, 1842, *L&D* 8: 441. See also Robert Wilberforce to JHN, January 21 and 29, 1842, Newman Microfilms, Reel 75, Batch 86.

and less worthy in his eyes not for spurning him but for being in a state of schism with the Roman Catholic Church.

That fury manifested itself in another letter contemporary with those to Manning in which Newman fulsomely denounced the Church of England as a Protestant body, but made no reference to the Monophysite issue. On October 13 Newman wrote H. A. Woodgate that he did "not doubt that the [Thirty-Nine] articles were drawn up by persons either heretics or heretical" and that he did "not believe that the compilers acknowledged *any* Catholic sense," which appeared only with those who received them after their promulgation in 1571 and 1662. Newman further observed, "But leave the Articles in their *intended* meaning and they are Protestant. Well — the Bishops and the body of the Church at this day *have* decided on taking them in their Protestant sense — and the question is whether they have not as much right to do so, as the Convocations of 1571 and 1662 to take them in their Catholic sense." On these grounds Newman had come to regard "our system rotten" because "we have no system over and above the administered one." Since *Tract 90*, those administering the English Church had decided that it "is *not* Catholic, i. e. that it does not hold Catholic doctrine." Two weeks later, writing to J. W. Bowden, Newman deplored the English episcopal bench as "ultra-protestant" and as having "nothing else in them, i. e., speaking of them as Bishops."[135]

By the middle of 1844 Newman undertook a process of self-consciously constructing a narrative of his behavior during the past five years to which he might appeal should he decide to join the Roman Catholic Church. It was a narrative that would avoid all consideration of what had occurred to him personally and to the Tractarian cause in general at the hands of both evangelicals and high churchmen since the publication of *Tract 90*.

In June 1844, Newman wrote to Henry Wilberforce: "I want you, if you do not object, to do this: — to state *historically,* that you know that in 1839 I was very unsettled on the subject of the Catholicity of our Church. You may speak as strongly as your recollection enables you. But I should not like, first, any mention *what my present feelings are* — not, any hint that *I* have put you on doing this." About a month later Newman told Wilberforce, who was uncomfortable with the request, that his friends should know that his present state of mind, which had become increasingly open to the religious truthfulness of Roman Catholicism, was "not an accidental state of mind, but a part of my character or history — that they should not be relying on a person, even if he continued where he is, without knowing what they rely upon. And still more if

---

135. JHN to H. A. Woodgate, October 13, 1843; JHN to J. W. Bowden, October 31, 1843, *L&D* 9: 564–565, 596.

something is to come of it, they ought to be prepared for it."¹³⁶ Thus through the Monophysite parallel Newman provided a calm, rational, theological explanation for his disenchantment with the Church of England predating *Tract 90* and its aftermath when in fact he was deeply angered by his treatment that had resulted from that publication and its aftermath. Furthermore, appealing to the Monophysite parallel allowed him to cast himself as a righteous rebel against an unrighteous church through a privileged interpretation of sacred history.

Various of Newman's friends understood immediate current events to be producing Newman's growing sense of both isolation and alienation. J. B. Mozley warned him of taking too seriously the influence of evangelicals in the English Church. Pusey told Manning that Newman's "mind is so refined, that it may be that if we take its language in an ordinary way, we may be mistranslating it." Pusey, who quite simply painted the situation under which Newman labored and to which he was reacting, explained to Gladstone, "it is not the natural effects of any principles, but the actual state of things, our disorganization, the tolerance of heresy, the conduct of our Bishops" that so disturbed Newman's and others' minds; "Blow comes, after blow."¹³⁷

Some friends attempted to intervene directly with Newman. In June 1844 John Keble dared to ask his friend, whom he served effectively as a confessor: "Do you not think it possible (I dare say I borrow the view from yourself) that the *whole* Church may be so lowered by sin as to hinder one's finding on earth anything which *seems* really to answer to the Church of the Scriptures? and will it not be well to prepare yourself for disappointment, lest you fall into something like scepticism?" For Keble, Newman had become the victim of his own perfectionist ecclesiology. A year later Henry Wilberforce warned Newman against taking action on the basis of being "haunted by feelings of loneliness & desertion as if no one had sympathy or affection for you." Wilberforce

---

136. JHN to Henry Wilberforce, June 8 and July 4, 1844, *L&D* 10: 263, 293. See also JHN to Henry Wilberforce, July 17, 1844, *L&D* 10: 298–299. Consult JHN to Simeon Lloyd Pope, September 18, 1845, *L&D* 10: 762–763, for a succinct version of the personal narrative of his behavior from 1841 onward that Newman had constructed for himself and acquaintances in the days before his reception into the Roman Catholic Church.

137. See J. B. Mozley to JHN, August 31, 1843; September 9, 1843, *L&D* 9: 491–493, 501–502; and August 24, 1844, Newman Microfilms, Reel 67, Batch 56. [In these letters, the first two of which are partially reprinted in *L&D* 9 as cited, Mozley urged Newman to understand that his opponents are evangelicals.] E. B. Pusey to H. Manning, November 17, 1843, Bodleian Library, MS Eng lett c. 654, f. 206; E. B. Pusey to W. E. Gladstone, November 1843, Gladstone Papers, British Library, Add Mss. 44247, f. 192.

gently reminded him: "But is it not true, my dearest Newman, that to a sensitive mind there is nothing so dangerous as the allowing itself to feel unjustly [or] unkindly treated by all around? It is commonly said to be the first sign of mental disorder. I should think it quite as often one of the first causes."[138]

A late twentieth-century scholar pointed to other factors affecting Newman's state of mind during these months. Valerie Pitt observed, "The man had isolated himself at Littlemore, away from his peers and the ordinary activities of his profession, and had given himself up not only to a regimen of study and obsessive self-questioning ... but to ascetic practices, watching or sleeping on the ground, fasting and so on." She went on to note that such a regimen is calculated "to disorient the personality, to shatter and remake a mind-set and induce docility."[139] All of these factors, Pitt contended, led to real physiological and psychological challenges to Newman's mental stability. Furthermore, throughout his last year in the English Church Newman interacted primarily with his most radical followers, who displayed increasing hostility to all manifestations of Protestantism. During this time and under these conditions his position in the Church of England encountered unprecedented challenges.

As Francis Newman understood, in late 1844 and early 1845 John Newman still held adverse views of the Roman Catholic Church. On December 29, 1844, the latter declared to Keble, "No one can have a more unfavorable view than I of the present state of the Roman Catholics — so much so, that any who join them would be like the Cistercians of Fountains, living under trees till their house was built."[140] No evidence exists that he substantially changed his views in the succeeding months. He still hoped that either the English or Roman Church might reform itself to respond to the concerns of his radical Littlemore community. During the next nine months, however, three significant external events transformed his situation in the English Church and precipitated his sudden reception into the Roman Catholic Church. None of these does he mention in the *Apologia*.

By late 1844 Newman's most outspoken radical Catholic follower had generated a new crisis within Oxford. W. G. Ward had published *The Ideal of a Christian Church* in which he claimed that he subscribed to the Thirty-Nine

---

138. John Keble to JHN (II), June 12, 1844, *L&D* 10: 269; Henry Wilberforce to JHN, June 5, 1845, Newman Microfilms, Reel 74, Batch 85.

139. Valerie Pitt, "Demythologising Newman," in *John Henry Newman*, ed. Nicholls and Kerr, p. 24.

140. JHN to JK, December 29, 1844, *L&D* 10: 476. See also JHN to Miss M. R. Giberne, January 8, 1845, *L&D* 10: 484–485.

Articles in a "non-natural" sense and furthermore asserted publicly, as he had for some time privately, that all Roman doctrine could be accepted under the Thirty-Nine Articles by English clergy.[141] Publication of these views led to a successful effort on February 13, 1845, to have Oxford Convocation condemn the book and strip Ward of his degrees. The leaders in this effort had been the Oxford Heads of Houses urged on by Archbishop of Dublin Richard Whately, powerfully disgruntled high churchmen, and perennially hostile evangelicals. Liberals had generally opposed the action.

That same day a second measure appeared before Convocation—a formal condemnation of *Tract 90*. Through a procedural move, however, the proctors vetoed this censure, thus preventing it from coming to a vote. Technically, therefore, *Tract 90* did not receive official condemnation within Oxford and probably, because of the private intervention of the archbishop of Canterbury, would not have again come before Convocation. Newman, however, feared another effort to condemn the tract might well occur.

Rather than arising from within Oxford, the formal condemnation of the principles of *Tract 90* suddenly and unexpectedly originated within the diocese of London, with its powerful bishop, Charles Blomfield. This momentous turn of events arose from a case decided by the Court of Arches in the summer of 1845, only the barest details of which can be related here.

Frederick Oakeley had been one of the chief figures in the radical wing of the second generation of Tractarians. Like Ward, he contended that all Roman doctrine was compatible with the Thirty-Nine Articles. In late December 1845, Oakeley had claimed for himself and other Church of England clergy the right "of holding (as distinct from teaching) all Roman doctrine, and that notwithstanding my subscription to the Thirty-nine Articles." Shortly after Ward's Oxford condemnation, Oakeley reasserted the same position in a public letter to the vice chancellor of Oxford. As a clergyman assigned to the Margaret Chapel in London, Oakeley was accountable to the bishop of London, who immediately challenged him. In a public letter to Blomfield, Oakeley declared his conviction that the articles were "*subscribable* in what may be called an ultra-Catholic sense."[142] After further exchanges, Blomfield took the

---

141. See note 40 above.

142. Frederick Oakeley, *The Subject of Tract XC. Examined, in Connection with the History of the Thirty-Nine Articles, and the Statements of Certain English Divines. To Which Is Added, the Case of Bishop Mountague, in the Reign of King James I*, 2nd rev. ed. (London: James Toovey, 1845), pp. xiii, xiv; Frederick Oakeley, *A Letter to the Lord Bishop of London, on a Subject Connected with the Recent Proceedings at Oxford*

matter to the Court of Arches under the auspices of the Church Discipline Act. No one among the Tractarians doubted the authority of the Court of Arches as a decisive legal authority in ecclesiastical matters.

Sir Herbert Jenner Fust heard the case on June 10 as the prosecution set out to demonstrate "that the Articles of the Church of England have been drawn up in direct opposition to the then recent decrees of the Council of Trent." (Both Newman and Oakeley had asserted that because the Thirty-Nine Articles were adopted before the close of the Council of Trent, they could not condemn official Roman Catholic doctrine as opposed to popular piety.) Handing down his decision on June 30, Fust asserted that Oakeley's "outwardly professing to be a member of one Church, whilst he is inwardly attached to the doctrine of another; and his declaration, that he signs the Thirty-nine Articles in a sense different from their grammatical construction, in which he knows they ought to be signed, can hardly be reconciled with integrity." Fust firmly stated, "No minister of the Church of England has a right to put his own private interpretation upon the Articles, which he has sworn to, and which he has subscribed." Most important, Oakeley possessed no right "to put his own construction upon the Articles of the Church, in order to justify the holding and maintaining of doctrines contrary to the views of that Church."[143] In all these respects, Fust provided the judicial authority of the Court of Arches to the injunctions regarding clerical subscription asserted by several bishops in their charges of 1841 through 1844 castigating *Tract 90.*

Fust finally commented, "where the Articles are plain, distinct, and definite, affording no room for doubt as to their real meaning, no attempt can be sanctioned which goes to distort their language, and so to extort by unfair means, if fair means will not do, a sense consistent with the ultra-Catholic, or Roman Doctrine, which Mr. Oakeley professes." Fust thus repudiated not only Oakeley's advanced position that the articles were compatible with all

---

(London: James Toovey, 1845), pp. 11, 14, 26. The second pamphlet had been preceded by Frederick Oakeley to the Vice Chancellor of Oxford, February 14, 1845, *Times,* February 15, 1845. On the Oakeley case, see Peter Galloway, *A Passionate Humility: Frederick Oakeley and the Oxford Movement* (Leominster: Gracewing, 1999), pp. 147–210, and Turner, *John Henry Newman,* pp. 535–548.

143. A. F. Bayford, ed., *A Full Report of the Proceedings in the Office of the Judge Promoted by Hodgson v. Rev. F. Oakeley, before the Rt. Hon. Sir Herbert Jenner Fust, KT., Dean of the Arches* (London: William Benning & Co., 1845), pp. 11, 134–135, 144, 151. See also Frederick Oakeley, *The Claim to "Hold, as Distinct from Teaching," Explained in a Letter to a Friend,* dated June 25, 1845 (London: James Toovey, 1845).

Roman Catholic doctrine, but also Newman's more moderate position in *Tract 90* of their not being incompatible with certain Roman Catholic doctrines and devotions. As Oakeley would state in 1864, "The judge . . . unwilling to lose so good an opportunity of entering the protest of the highest ecclesiastical court against what were called 'Romanizing opinions,' pronounced a condemnation of Catholic doctrines *seriatim*."[144]

The Oakeley case, despite some Tractarian efforts to contend otherwise, had produced the very kind of official condemnation of the principles of *Tract 90* that Newman for more than four years had strenuously avoided. The Court of Arches decision far more than any article by Bishop Wiseman or perceived parallels between the Tractarian vision and the ancient Monophysites destroyed the via media as Newman had articulated it. Before the Oakeley decision Newman and his followers might have remained a Catholic conventicle gathered unto themselves at Littlemore awaiting the day when their views somehow became officially tolerated within the English Church. After the Oakeley decision the position they hoped to realize over time had become legally, if not necessarily theologically, untenable.

By early September the advanced Catholic party that had once looked to Newman for leadership was rapidly disintegrating around him. Almost immediately after his degradation at Oxford, Ward had flouted the general Tractarian espousal of clerical celibacy by announcing that he would soon marry. Ward also clearly understood the impact of the Oakeley decision on the future of Tractarianism. On August 8, he wrote Newman that whatever Newman's "present feelings" might be "about our position," for his own part he could not "but look on the decisions of the Ecclesiastical Courts as final."[145] He and his wife entered the Roman Catholic Church the first week of September. Others of Newman's Littlemore group followed Ward's example of converting rather than Newman's of waiting. By late September, J. B. Dalgairns, the first person to have joined Newman at Littlemore, and Ambrose St. John — Newman's closest Littlemore friend, with whom almost a half-century later he would be buried — were received into the Roman Church.

On October 7, though still wishing to complete his book on development before his own reception, Newman told Henry Wilberforce that what he termed "this accident" of the approaching visit of the Passionist priest Father Dominic

---

144. Bayford, ed., *A Full Report of the Proceedings*, p. 166; Oakeley, *Historical Notes*, p. 96.

145. W. G. Ward to JHN, August 8, 1845, Newman Microfilms, Reel 74, Batch 80.

Barberi might fulfill his desire for "an external call" indicating he should change religious communions. Newman further confessed, "Also, I suppose the departure of others has had something to do with it, for when they went, it was as if I were losing my own bowels."[146] Newman, who for many weeks had alerted friends and family of his probable conversion, actually joined the Roman Catholic Church only after his quasi-schismatic Littlemore community had already dispersed with no hope of reconstituting itself outside the Roman Catholic communion.

Newman's passage to Rome — like every other of his major actions since early 1841, including the publication of *Tract 90*, the founding of the Littlemore community, the resignation of St. Mary's, the launching of the *Lives of the English Saints* — constituted still another response to a shifting cadre of relentlessly radical young followers with whom Newman desperately wished to preserve friendship, leadership, connection, and community. Although the previous June the *Morning Herald* had claimed, "Tractarianism, in fact, is at an end when Mr. Newman departs," he actually departed the Church of England only after the advanced Tractarian party deserted him as a result of the decision in the Oakeley case.[147] The desire and determination to remain with the followers whose minds and affections he had shaped and cultivated and upon whom his spirit and personal sense of identity had come so much to depend were the key factors leading to Newman's conversion. Whether Newman would have converted, had they not first done so, remains an open historical question. By 1864 Newman's memory of these events and those affections must have been especially painful because with the exception of Ambrose St. John he had broken and fiercely quarreled with almost all those Anglican friends with whom he had converted and who at that time had regarded him as their spiritual mentor. Indeed, within weeks of their joining their new church Newman's one-time followers, much to his anger and chagrin, transformed themselves into not always sympathetic mentors. By 1864 Ward had, of course, become his fiercest English Roman Catholic detractor.

In late September and early October 1845 still another key person was about to leave Newman's life — Richard Bagot, bishop of Oxford. In late September Sir Robert Peel and the archbishop of Canterbury had opened negotiations to transfer Bagot from Oxford to the diocese of Bath and Wells. For many years Newman and other Tractarians had grasped the importance for their cause of the benign and ineffectual bishop of Oxford. Newman voiced

---

146. JHN to H. Wilberforce, October 7, 1845, *L&D* 11: 3.
147. *Morning Herald,* June 20, 1845, p. 10.

his sense of Bagot's personal importance for him and his position in the English Church even after he had resigned St. Mary's.[148]

It is impossible to know with certainty whether Newman knew that Bagot was in the process of changing dioceses. However, it is certainly possible that Newman had heard rumors that a change in the bishopric was in process. He would have understood that Peel would, as he did, appoint a bishop hostile to radical Tractarianism. As late as October 4, 1845, however, Newman had told a correspondent that he might be too busy to be received by Father Dominic, whom he knew would be visiting Littlemore.[149] Over the next two days it may have become public knowledge that Bagot was thinking of leaving because by October 7 the coming visit of Father Dominic appeared providential to Newman, who was received into the Roman Catholic Church on October 9.

The choice of Father Dominic, the priest who had a few days earlier received Dalgairns and had long hoped to receive Newman, guaranteed the fewest possible questions being raised about Newman's motives, his principles, or his personal understanding of Roman Catholic theology, beliefs, and practices. The timing of Newman's conversion avoided any possible conflict with a new, active, inevitably anti-Tractarian bishop of Oxford who could have caused him difficulty and embarrassment, especially if cooperating with Benjamin Symons, the recently elected strongly evangelical vice chancellor of Oxford.

Had Newman entered the Roman communion *after* direct difficulty with his own bishop, he could not have maintained the stance that he acted upon religious conviction rather than in reaction to formal discipline, conflict, or other episcopal unpleasantness. From the standpoint of the Roman Church authorities, it was also well to appear to receive a Newman acting upon principle rather than a Newman seeking a final refuge.

It is admittedly not certain that Bagot's transfer to Bath and Wells served as the immediate catalyst for Newman's conversion. Yet there was, as noted at the time, a precipitous quality about Newman's reception. Newman's conversion took Keble by surprise as a "thunderbolt," and he continued to believe that Newman had acted on impulse rather than long thought. Bishop Wiseman's report of his meeting with Newman on November 1 indicates that he did not wish to examine issues surrounding the "how sudden" conversion,

---

148. JHN to J. R. Hope, October 17, 1841; JHN to R. W. Church, December 24, 1841; JHN to S. Rickards, January 2, 1842; JHN to Charles Crawley, January 2, 1841, *L&D* 8: 300, 384, 408, 404; JHN to Miss Giberne, November 13, 1843, *L&D* 10: 23-24.

149. JHN to Richard Stanton, October 4, 1845, *L&D* 10: 777.

which, he reported, Newman himself had acknowledged to be "accidental" in "mode." Clearly, much was quite consciously left unspoken and unasked during the conversation. As Wiseman told Charles Russell, "I have often said I should be ready to sing my *Nunc dimittis* when Mr. Newman should have joined us; and I must not draw back from my word."[150]

Newman's conversion arose from his failure to establish and hold about himself within the Church of England a stable community of followers. As already seen, in the summer of 1845 Francis Newman could imagine his brother formally establishing a schismatic Catholic group under a Scottish or American bishop. There were numerous examples of seceding clergy in Newman's day who successfully founded congregations that lasted at least one generation. Such was what Newman had in effect been doing at Littlemore, where he had bought land, renovated buildings for worship, and formed a floating cadre of followers whose lives he largely dominated. He had in effect instituted something like an Oxford hall at Littlemore, where he held high table and carried out the instructional role to which he had unsuccessfully aspired in the university. This situation might well have proved tenuously stable had it not been for the Oakeley judgment. With his assurances exploded by the Oakeley decision that Catholic-minded clergy in the Church of England could not subscribe to the Thirty-Nine Articles on the basis of *Tract 90*, Newman lost his personal authority within his own Catholic enclave. Newman's Catholic religious experiment within the English Church had collapsed as its adherents rapidly moved to Rome, leaving him behind.

Biographers and other scholars have badly underestimated the importance that Newman attached to his ongoing life with those followers. After his conversion, he would rejoin some members of that group under Bishop Wiseman's authority at Oscott and attempt (ultimately unsuccessfully) to hold them together. Just a month after entering the Roman Church, he told Dalgairns, "The problem is, how to get education and orders (for those who wish it) yet to keep together." On the same day, he rather more forthrightly told J. W. Bowden's widow that despite the Oscott building that Bishop Wiseman offered him being "dismally ugly," it would nonetheless "bring with it this advantage, which is a great temptation—that my friends could get educated for orders etc. *without separating from each other or from me*" (emphasis added). Newman's determination on this matter caused James Robert Hope,

---

150. N. Wiseman to C. Russell, early November 1845, Ward, *Life and Times of Cardinal Wiseman*, 1: 433, 436. Nor did Wiseman mention Newman's having said anything about the influence of Russell to which Newman attaches so much importance in the *Apologia*.

who throughout the autumn of 1845 advised him on his new position in the Roman Catholic Church, to warn about "the risk of giving a party aspect to your position."[151] It was that same fear twenty years later on the part of English Roman Catholic ultramontanes that led them to oppose Newman's effort to found a Roman Catholic house at Oxford. They could not imagine his undertaking such a project without making himself and his views of the Roman Catholic faith the center of its life and spirit.

Newman's concern with holding his Littlemore party together reflected another significant motivating force in his religious opinions again unmentioned in the *Apologia*. A powerful monastic imperative had long informed much of Newman's own personal devotion, and he attempted to impose that imperative on other men near to him. From the late 1820s to the end of his life Newman sought to live in the company of celibate males. In 1829 he established a dining club among Oxford dons organized around simple meals. Contemporaneously with the launching of *Tracts for the Times,* he published in the *British Magazine* a series of articles that explored and praised ancient monasticism. Later in 1840 he republished those essays as a book titled *Church of the Fathers.* During the years of Newmania at Oxford he drew around himself celibate male followers devoted to Catholicism and explained to friends that these men were dissatisfied with contemporary Anglican devotion and that among other things they wanted monasteries. By the late 1830s he contemplated starting a monastery at Littlemore where he eventually established a monastic retreat house whose celibate male inhabitants pursued a rigorous devotional routine of silence, prayer, and study and an ascetic regimen of eating. This drive toward a monastic experiment in living with other celibate males and away from the company of women may be the single most important of Newman's religious opinions about which he remained silent in the *Apologia*.[152]

That monastic imperative does, however, account for two important passages in the *Apologia*. The first is that containing those previously quoted harsh sentences about the second generation of Tractarians whom he declared had cut across the grain of the original movement (266). It was this group, led by Ward and Oakeley, whose extreme actions regarding Catholic subscription

---

151. JHN to J. D. Dalgairns, November 9, 1845; JHN to Mrs. J. W. Bowden, November 9, 1845, *L&D* 11: 29; J. R. Hope to JHN, November 1, 1845, Newman Microfilms, Reel 42, Batch 35. See also JHN to J. R. Hope, November 28, 1845, in which he desists from the idea of forming his own group. *L&D* 11: 46–48.

152. On the complex issue of the ascetic monastic imperative in Newman's life, see Turner, *John Henry Newman,* pp. 412–436, 623–631, 636–640.

to the Thirty-Nine Articles ultimately led to the collapse of the movement. Furthermore, Ward's marriage in 1845 to a young woman eager to join the Roman Catholic Church and their joint conversion in early September in turn fostered further conversions and the subsequent dispersion of the Littlemore community. The second passage is that standing at the very close of the volume in which Newman pays such a moving tribute of affection to the brothers of the Birmingham Oratory with whom he then was living (352–353). In that sense a neglected narrative of the *Apologia* is that of Newman's journey from two unsuccessful sets of relationships with celibate male communities, that is, the Oriel College fellowship and Littlemore, to the final settled stability of his life in the celibate male community of the Birmingham Oratory.

Victorian Spiritual Crossings

Newman's history of his religious journey profoundly affected contemporary educated Victorian Protestant and secular opinion throughout the transatlantic world. Before the *Apologia* even learned Victorian Protestants described conversion to Roman Catholicism by members of the Church of England in terms of perversion, abandonment of truth, or seduction by diseased imagination. Newman's *Apologia* demonstrated how personal religious development leading to a Roman Catholic conversion could arise from a process of honest, good faith, even if concluded by embracing a religion that English Protestants deplored, and how such a profound transition might grow out of religious sensibilities familiar to a Protestant English audience. He achieved these ends by recounting the history of his religious opinions culminating in his Roman Catholic conversion through the culturally familiar format of a spiritual autobiography. Wanting to be judged as an Englishman, Newman adopted the mode of religious narrative to which English Protestant readers could immediately relate as their own.

Since the seventeenth century English Protestant autobiographies had described transitions of spiritual life and denominational affiliation from spiritual inadequacy to adequacy, from nominal to vital religion, from unbelief to faith, from religious instability to stability, from turmoil to peace. Narrating his own religious journey through these familiar categories, Newman culturally domesticated English conversion to Roman Catholicism.[153] Once so do-

---

153. D. Bruce Hindmarsh, *The Evangelical Conversion Narrative: Spiritual Autobiography in Early Modern England* (New York: Oxford Univ. Press, 2005). Conversions to Roman Catholicism had been portrayed previously in Victorian novels, including his own little-noticed *Loss and Gain* (1848), but the *Apologia* brought the journey of a Protestant to conversion to Roman Catholicism into the tradition of English spiritual

mesticated, his conversion to the Roman Catholic Church fit into other well-known patterns of transition in Victorian religious life and culture. It had been this domestication of Roman Catholic conversion, along with Newman's assertion of a significant sphere of liberty of opinion for Roman Catholics, that the ultramontanes had deplored as softening of commitment to their faith and compromising its distinct place in English culture.

The most prominent of the familiar Victorian cultural patterns into which Newman set his conversion narrative was the search for a new religion to replace an older, inadequate, decayed religion, a process most clearly articulated for his entire generation and that which followed by Thomas Carlyle in *Sartor Resartus* of 1835. Carlyle's account of the spiritual passage of Diogenes Teufelsdrockh from the despair of the Everlasting No through the Centre of Indifference to the triumph of the Everlasting Yea more than any other work of the era had shaped Victorian understanding of contemporary Protestant spiritual angst and religious transformation. Exploring the drive toward personal spiritual regeneration in terms of a demand for new Church-Clothes, Carlyle had explained:

> Church-Clothes, are, in our vocabulary, the Forms, the *Vestures,* under which men have at various periods embodied and represented for themselves the Religious Principle; that is to say, invested the Divine Idea of the World with a sensible and practically active Body, so that it might dwell among them as a living and life-giving Word.... [I]n our era of the World, those same Church-Clothes have gone sorrowfully out-at-elbows: nay, far worse, many of them have become mere hollow Shapes, or Masks, under which no living Figure or Spirit any longer dwells; but only spiders and unclean beetles, in horrid accumulation, drive their trade; and the mask still glares on you with its glass eyes, in ghastly affectation of Life, — some generation-and-half after Religion has quite withdrawn from it, and in unnoticed nooks is weaving for herself new Vestures, wherewith to reappear, and bless us, or our sons or grandsons.

No less than others of his generation Newman saw the English Church establishment into which he had been baptized and which he served first as an evangelical clergyman, then as a radical high churchman, and finally as a quasi-schismatic priest as very much clad in church clothes worn at the elbows. The *Apologia* provided an account of his various attempts to rearrange his ecclesiastical wardrobe, an effort that resonated with the observations and experiences of his readers and reviewers across a wide spectrum of the religious landscape. In his own case, as well as that of other Anglican clergy who

---

autobiography. Joseph Ellis Baker, *The Novel and the Oxford Movement* (Princeton, N.J.: Princeton Univ. Press, 1932).

converted to Rome, Newman did exchange one set of clerical clothing for another as during the years following his resignation from St. Mary's he had worn clothing other than that normally associated with an Anglican priest.[154]

Contemporary journals had long noted the transformative character of Newman's religious opinions. As early as 1862 the *Saturday Review* had characterized Newman as instancing "in his own person his own law of development." Two years later, commenting upon the *Apologia*, the *Spectator* recognized in Newman the culturally familiar figure of the religious enthusiast. The journal observed that over the course of his Anglican years Newman had embodied two different modes of religious enthusiasm: first, "the form in which it appeared in Wesley and other religious reformers, — as a fire of aggressive zeal, carrying him into the thick of the onset against Liberalism and Latitudinarianism," and then later "a thin line of pale ascetic fire just edging the circle of his human sympathies so as to keep them in what he himself has termed a state of 'detachment' from the world, and the life of the world, though without either searing their sensitivities or limiting their range."[155] This judgment very shrewdly characterized Newman's public behavior during the early Tractarian era and his drive toward private asceticism and monasticism in the later years of that era and beyond.

The commentator for the *Saturday Review*, similarly casting Newman in the role of "an enthusiast" and "a visionary of an extremely wild type," portrayed him as the embodiment of the quintessential religious seeker of the day, that is, a person subjectively determining his own course of religious action. On the basis of the *Apologia*, the journal observed that Newman's entire religious career had consisted "in picking up bits of system, and adding to his body of doctrine, in piecing here and patching there" and that from his earliest evangelical activities "to the day when he submitted to the mother and mistress of all Churches, he was in a constant state of transition." The journal

154. Thomas Carlyle, *Sartor Resartus,* Book III, Ch. 2. In July 1846 Newman reported to J. B. Dalgairns his discomfort wearing Roman Catholic clerical garb: "My dislike of marching up the London streets is considerable, not indeed that I have any reluctance to wear a clerical dress, for I need not unless I had wished it, but I am so awkward and gawky that I feel ashamed of myself. The only make-up is that the poor Catholics recognize it as I go along and touch their hats to me; but fancy *me,* who have never been in costume, wearing a straight cut collar to my coat, and having a long skirt to it. I know I look like a fool, from my own great intrinsic absurdity." JHN to J. B. Dalgairns, July 6, 1846, *L&D* 11: 194. Newman had not yet been ordained as a Roman Catholic priest when he reports this incident.

155. "Dr. Newman," *Saturday Review* 14 (1862): 12; "Dr. Newman's Apology [Second Notice]," *Spectator,* 37: 681.

commented, "He was an inquirer all his life; and in one sense he has been the apostle of free thought." The *Saturday Review* concluded: "Books, history, reflection, logic, documents, have brought him to a certain conclusion. . . . This is what is commonly called choosing a religion by the exercise of Private Judgment, however it may be disguised."[156] This and other reviewers clearly recognized that the *Apologia* presented a Protestant mind actively seeking to make its way in the world of the spirit and finally defining a new Roman Catholic religious affiliation via a process thoroughly understandable in Protestant terms.

At least one formidable Victorian freethinker could relate to Newman on those very grounds. On July 13, 1864, the novelist Marianne Evans (George Eliot) wrote a close friend that she had found it impossible to leave the *Apologia* without finishing it. Her interest in the book had arisen initially from a desire to see "Kingsley's mixture of arrogance, coarse impertinence and unscrupulousness with real intellectual *in*competence . . . thoroughly castigated." She then told her correspondent, "But the Apology now mainly affects me as the revelation of a life—how different in form from one's own, yet with how close a fellowship in its needs and burthens—I mean spiritual needs and burthens."[157] Evans herself had passed through family religious turmoil, personal study, and changing friendships, moving from a provincial evangelical youth to Unitarianism to the German higher criticism, translating works of David Friedrich Strauss and Ludwig Feuerbach, and finally to Auguste Comte's religion of humanity. She and other mid-Victorian freethinkers had experienced calumny from the religious press not unlike that which Kingsley had hurled against Newman. Moreover, like Newman, she deeply repudiated the dominance of narrow evangelical theology, bibliolatry, and morality over the wider culture. Her experience, which had also included a period of intense admiration for Francis Newman, resonated with that of both Newman brothers.

At the other end of the Victorian religious spectrum the radical evangelical John Nelson Darby, founder of the Plymouth Brethren and modern fundamentalist dispensationalist theology as well as a one-time mentor to the young Francis Newman, also related personally to John Newman's religious trans-

---

156. *Saturday Review* 17 (1864): 786, 788. The same article compared Newman to Edward Irving, the radical Scottish Protestant, whose charismatic preaching had galvanized London in the early 1830s and whose own religious development had led to the formation of the new Catholic Apostolic Church. Similar comments had been directed toward Newman at the time of his conversion and the publication of *An Essay on the Development of Christian Doctrine*. See Turner, *John Henry Newman*, pp. 577–586.

157. George Eliot to Sara Hennell, July 13, 1864, in *The George Eliot Letters*, ed. Gordon S. Haight (New Haven: Yale Univ. Press, 1955), 4: 158–159.

formations while deploring their outcome. Claiming to have trodden much of Newman's path, Darby recounted his own youthful discontent with the Anglican Church in Ireland and his similar search for a rigorous mode of ascetic, penitential, personal devotion and piety:

> I fasted in Lent so as to be weak in body at the end of it; ate no meat on week days — nothing till evening on Wednesdays, Fridays, and Saturdays, then a little bread or nothing; observed strictly the weekly fasts, too. I went to my clergyman always if I wished to take the sacrament, that he might judge of the matter. I held apostolic succession fully, and the channels of grace to be there only. I held thus Luther and Calvin and their followers to be outside. . . . The union of church and state I held to be Babylonish, that the church ought to govern itself, and that she was in bondage but was the church.[158]

Darby testified that what had saved him from Roman Catholicism was reading the Epistle to the Hebrews with its emphasis on Christ as the great high priest. Thereafter, Darby passed into radical evangelical Protestantism and eventual separation from the Anglican Church of Ireland, in which he was an ordained priest. Both he and Newman had thus become clerical seceders from the Anglican Church. Reading of scripture had clarified the situation for Darby as reading of the history of the ancient Christian heresies had clarified Newman's.

Darby and other contemporary reviewers saw a significant parallel between John Newman's *Apologia* and Francis Newman's *Phases of Faith, or Passages in the History of My Creed* (1850). The latter volume had provided an influential account of Francis's journey from Anglican evangelicalism through radical Protestant evangelicalism to Unitarianism and then to the formulation of his own theistic synthesis. More than a quarter-century after publishing his autobiography, Francis in a private letter succinctly summarized his religious development:

> In my youthful days I grew up an Evangelical of the Church of England. Next I became a Baptist, and a thoroughgoing Biblist. But I never for a moment imagined that I was set free from the duty of searching for and following truth. I thought myself and was in heart, *God's freeman*; though plenty of persons, like our men of material science, had they known me, would have counted my mind *enslaved*, because I looked up to the Bible as a divine

---

158. John Nelson Darby, "Analysis of Dr. Newman's Apologia Pro Vita Sua: With a Glance at the History of Popes, Councils, and the Church," in *The Collected Writings of J. N. Darby*, ed. William Kelley (London: G. Morrish, n.d.), 5: 238. Professor Mark Noll is to be thanked for securing a copy of this remarkable essay for the editor. On Newman's asceticism, see Turner, *John Henry Newman*, pp. 412–425.

authority. But it taught me to enlarge, not contract my heart; and I never learned from it to disuse my faculties, — however timidly I used them, when I perceived incipient difficulties.[159]

How similar for all their differences were the spiritual transformations of the Newman brothers. John Newman during his Anglican years, and for that matter well beyond them, no less than Francis had also powerfully personified "God's freeman," moving from one religious opinion to another, as readers of the *Apologia* had been quick to discern.

The analogous expanding religious mentalities that informed both Newman brothers' narratives particularly impressed Darby. Each brother's account displayed "a mind step by step giving up what they held as true, and finding they were wrong at each step." But this process did not "lead them to distrust themselves." To the contrary, Darby noted, "They would have us embrace the conclusions they have come to . . . and in which they profess to have the greatest confidence, though in every previous step they had found themselves wrong." What this situation demonstrated was "not confidence in the truth . . . but the attaching an immense importance to their own views — I am afraid I must say, to themselves, meaning by that, to the processes of their own mind."[160] Darby had perceived that for each Newman brother his own internal development constituted the subject of highest personal interest.

Darby also explained why the Victorian reading public found the two very different Newman autobiographical narratives so gripping. He asked whether the public would read with the same interest those accounts if "Mr. F. W. Newman or Dr. Newman were to return, the one to Christianity, the other to scriptural truth"? Would "their phases of return, or the history of their religious recovery" evoke the same kind of interest? Darby thought not, asserting that "no bookseller would undertake an edition of the history of their recovery as he would of their fall." He regretted "that it should be so; but the history of their fall away from truth and into evil, this it is that interests" and "this is what their history is a history of."[161]

Darby grasped that much of the fascination provoked by Francis's *Phases of*

---

159. F. W. Newman to W. H. Burrow, October 31, 1877, Francis William Newman Collection, GEN MSS 264, Box 1, Folder 1, Beinecke Rare Book and Manuscript Library, Yale University. For a discussion of the high regard that the London freethinking community of the early 1850s held for Francis Newman and his own religious journey, see Mark Francis, *Herbert Spencer and the Invention of Modern Life* (Ithaca, N.Y.: Cornell University Press, 2007), pp. 115–149.

160. Darby, "Analysis of Dr. Newman's Apologia Pro Vita Sua," 5: 227.

161. Ibid., 5: 229.

Faith and John's *Apologia* originated in their each drawing the reader into a culturally forbidden, liminal arena of contemporary life and thought: the former into radical mid-Victorian free thought and the latter into Roman Catholicism. Both Newman brothers had entered upon intellectual experiments of cultural apostasy as well as of religious apostasy from the dominant evangelical Protestantism of the day. For their readers both brothers had entered and then reported upon a foreign and dangerous spiritual terrain that lay on the borders of contemporary Victorian culture and establishment religion. Those spiritual crossings into forbidden realms provided much of the powerful contemporary attraction of their books. Each had demonstrated that their journeys were compatible with English morality and English truthfulness. Both realms might by the lights of conventional opinion stand condemned, but entering neither required the spiritual explorer to surrender his larger cultural identity as a loyal Englishman. In the 1850s and 1860s Unitarians and Roman Catholics had within living memory been regarded as dangerous to English society, politics, morals, and culture. The religious narratives of the two Newman brothers contributed to the eradication of the broad cultural doubt and hostility extended toward religious freethinkers on one hand and Roman Catholics on the other. Within a few years of the publication of the *Apologia* Victorian religious, scientific, and philosophical writers, including Anglican and Roman Catholic clerics and evolutionary scientists, would gather as members of the Metaphysical Society for evenings of lively, but civil, exchange and debate over sharply differing opinions.[162] Religious and philosophical debate of a determined, but civil character would fill the columns of mainstream journals.

Yet the *Apologia* retains its audience while *Phases of Faith*, for all its interesting virtues, has become a historical curiosity and period piece. At least three factors have accounted for the continuing influence and attraction of John Newman's *Apologia*. First, watching a man defend his own honesty and character in brilliant prose against egregiously nasty accusations continues to draw readers and to elicit their sympathies. Newman's biographers have always emphasized this aspect of his book as much or more than its substantial content. The ongoing immediacy of Kingsley's gratuitous snub and its dramatic repudiation by Newman permanently established the ground for reading all

---

162. On the role of cultural apostasy in Victorian culture, see Turner, *Contesting Cultural Authority*, pp. 38–72. See also Alan Brown, *The Metaphysical Society: Victorian Minds in Crisis, 1869–1880* (New York: Columbia Univ. Press, 1947). John Henry Newman was invited to join this group but declined, not surprisingly, given his age and the necessity of journeying from Birmingham to London for the meetings.

the rest of the volume. The sense of a wrong put right rather than a consideration of the historical accuracy of his account or his important defense of liberal Roman Catholicism continues to achieve the reader's assent to Newman's narrative and polemic. That defense of his personal honesty and that of his fellow Roman Catholic clerics continues to serve as a protective umbrella for his expansive understanding of freedom of opinion for Roman Catholics.

Second, for many Protestant and secular readers Roman Catholicism, even after the Second Vatican Council, still remains something of an arena of mystery asking for explanation (to wit, consider the reaction to Dan Brown's improbable novel *The Da Vinci Code*). Newman's *Apologia* retains its capacity to draw such readers into a religious world and experience that is unfamiliar and challenging of many modern opinions, convictions, and practices yet still deeply beckoning. Newman continues to domesticate Roman Catholicism for those outside that communion and to present it in a manner especially attractive to Protestant readers. In particular, Newman's assertions of Roman Catholic theological latitude have proved attractive and compelling. The power of Newman as a witness for Roman Catholicism in Protestant and secular cultures stands endorsed by the placing of his name on Roman Catholic religious centers on so many North American college and university campuses. Whereas in the Victorian age Charles Kingsley was associated with "Muscular Christianity" and Tractarianism with effeminacy, the Newman of the *Apologia*, by repulsing Kingsley's assault and vigorously defending the Roman Catholic faith against its most prejudiced detractors, has emerged as the champion of a "Muscular Roman Catholicism" that can hold its own in both Protestant and secular cultures as well as challenging and reshaping those cultures.[163]

Finally, spiritual crossings occurred in the twentieth century and continue into the twenty-first, but they much more resemble that of John than Francis Newman. Despite the widespread presence of nondogmatic religions, during the almost century and a half since the *Apologia* appeared, demanding, dogmatic religious and secular faiths more often than not have commanded the day and attracted the true believers. In *Tract 85* while assaulting the Protestant principle of private judgment, Newman declared:

> Religion cannot but be dogmatic, it ever has been. All religions have had doctrines; all have professed to carry with them benefits which could be enjoyed only on condition of believing the word of a supernatural informant, that is, of embracing some doctrines or other. It is a mere idle sophistical

---

163. Donald E. Hall, ed., *Muscular Christianity: Embodying the Victorian Age* (Cambridge: Cambridge Univ. Press, 2006).

theory, to suppose it can be otherwise. *Destroy* religion, make men give it up, if you can; but while it exists, it will profess an insight into the next world, it will profess *important* information about the next world, it will have points of faith, it will have dogmatism, it will have anathemas.[164]

Newman's *Apologia,* for all its defense of theological freedom for Roman Catholics, remains what he intended it to be — a great assertion of the dogmatic principle wherever it may reside, whether or not his own personal religious journey embodied it. It has been dogmatic strains of the Christian, Jewish, and Muslim faiths and dogmatic political ideologies that marked the life of much of the twentieth century and that for the moment flourish around the globe. Newman's was and continues to be the voice championing dogma and authority in a world that he and others have seen rendered senseless by relativism, subjectivity, and usurpations of reason.

In the most powerful prose moment in the *Apologia* Newman wrote that when he looked out of himself "into the world of men" he saw a sight that filled him "with unspeakable distress" (322). He mused that if he looked into a mirror and did not see his face, he should have "the sort of feeling" that actually came upon him when he looked "into this living busy world" and saw "no reflexion of its Creator" (322). While refusing to deny "the real force of the arguments in proof of a God, drawn from the general facts of human society and the course of history," he nonetheless confessed that those arguments "do not warm me or enlighten me; they do not take away the winter of my desolation or make the buds unfold and the leaves grow within me, and my moral being rejoice" (323). For Newman, "the sight of the world" was "nothing else than the prophet's scroll, full of 'lamentations and mourning, and woe'" (323). Such it has been to many in the past century and may well be for much of the present century, and for those who so view or experience the world, the *Apologia Pro Vita Sua* of John Henry Newman and the Newman of the *Apologia* will prove a solace and a source of wisdom.

Yet for others concerned with the history of Victorian religious life, ecclesiastical institutions, theology, and literature, the Newman of history stands apart from that of the *Apologia*. The Newman of history will appear as a brilliant theologian, perhaps the most brilliant of the modern Church of England, and at the same time as a quasi-schismatic priest and typical Victorian

---

164. *Tract 85:* 20. On June 3, 1863, Newman wrote to Edmund S. Foulkes: "Then again, I have personally a great dislike to mixed education in se. I love Oxford too well to wish its dogmatism destroyed, tho' it be a Protestant dogmatism. I had rather it was dogmatic on an error, than not dogmatic at all. At present I had rather it excluded us, from dogmatism, than admitted us, from liberalism." *L&D* 20: 455–456.

religious seeker. He will appear led by personal religious aspirations and by a desire to dwell in and preside over a community of celibate men. He will appear as a person, like so many others of the Victorian age, who could not express his most heartfelt religious convictions with sincere transparency in either communion because they stood in tension with the dominant views of each. The narrative of the Newman of the *Apologia* constitutes a theodicy whereby the Newman of history could make sense of the ever-shifting friendships, opinions, contingencies, happenstances, concealments, and loyalties of the remarkable religious and ecclesiastical journey he had made and about which for so much of his life he had pondered and wondered.[165] The Newman of history stands as the protagonist who for his own deeply personal and public polemical purposes created the powerful, memorable, and to many readers transforming Newman of the *Apologia*.

---

165. Georges Gusdorf, "Conditions and Limits of Autobiography," in *Autobiography: Essays, Theoretical and Critical*, p. 39.

*Apologia Pro Vita Sua:
Being a History of His
Religious Opinions*

"*Commit thy way to the Lord, and trust in Him,
and he will do it. And He will bring forth
thy justice as the light, and thy judgment
as the noonday.*"

Preface

The following History of my Religious Opinions, now that it is detached from the context in which it originally stood, requires some preliminary explanation; and that, not only in order to introduce it generally to the reader, but specially to make him understand, how I came to write a whole book about myself, and about my most private thoughts and feelings.[1] Did I consult indeed my own impulses, I should do my best simply to wipe out of my Volume, and consign to oblivion, every trace of the circumstances to which it is to be ascribed; but its original title of "Apologia" is too exactly borne out by its matter and structure, and these again are too suggestive of correlative circumstances, and those circumstances are of too grave a character, to allow of my indulging so natural a wish. And therefore, though in this new Edition I have

---

1. Authorial prefaces typically preceded nineteenth-century English autobiographies. Their function, originating in the late eighteenth century as autobiography emerged as a genre, as with Newman's, was to provide a justification for the usually deeply personal and self-revelatory autobiographical narrative. Newman's preface thus serves to defend his setting the story of the history of his religious opinions into the world of print culture and the public sphere. In this preface Newman asserts that his autobiography now serves a different function than that of its original 1864 pamphlet edition written in response to Kingsley's accusations. See James Treadwell, *Autobiographical Writing and British Literature, 1783–1834* (New York: Oxford Univ. Press, 2005), pp. 112–121.

managed to omit nearly a hundred pages of my original Volume, which I could safely consider to be of merely ephemeral importance, I am even for that very reason obliged, by way of making up for their absence, to prefix to my Narrative some account of the provocation out of which it arose.

It is now more than twenty years that a vague impression to my disadvantage has rested on the popular mind, as if my conduct towards the Anglican Church, while I was a member of it, was inconsistent with Christian simplicity and uprightness.[2] An impression of this kind was almost unavoidable under the circumstances of the case, when a man, who had written strongly against a cause, and had collected a party round him by virtue of such writings, gradually faltered in his opposition to it, unsaid his words, threw his own friends into perplexity and their proceedings into confusion, and ended by passing over to the side of those whom he had so vigorously denounced.[3] Sensitive then as I have ever been of the imputations which have been so freely cast upon me, I have never felt much impatience under them, as considering them to be a portion of the penalty which I naturally and justly incurred by my change of religion, even though they were to continue as long as I lived. I left their removal to a future day, when personal feelings would have died out, and documents would see the light, which were as yet buried in closets or scattered through the country.

This was my state of mind, as it had been for many years, when, in the beginning of 1864, I unexpectedly found myself publicly put upon my defence, and furnished with an opportunity of pleading my cause before the world, and, as it so happened, with a fair prospect of an impartial hearing. Taken indeed by surprise, as I was, I had much reason to be anxious how I should be able to acquit myself in so serious a matter; however, I had long had a tacit understanding with myself, that, in the improbable event of a challenge being formally made to me, by a person of name, it would be my duty to meet it.[4]

---

2. Newman's emphasis on his refuting long-standing impressions about his behavior as an Anglican serves to downplay his later strong assertions of theological choice and freedom for Roman Catholics in Chapter V. See the introduction to this volume.

3. At least one contemporary reviewer believed Newman had seized the Kingsley controversy to define its issues and to shape his subsequent narrative for his own purpose: "The kind of dishonesty of which he chooses to consider himself accused is nowhere even hinted at by Mr. Kingsley." (Theodore Walrond, "J. H. Newman's *Apologia*," *North British Review* 41 (1864): 86.)

4. For some time Newman had pondered his never having replied to his critics and how a history of the Tractarian Movement and his life might come to be. See JHN to Sister Mary Gabriel Du Boulay, August 18, 1861; JHN to W. J. Copeland, February 23, 1863; JHN to Jemima Mozley, May 18, 1863, *L&D* 20: 29, 413, 442–444. By early March

That opportunity had now occurred; it never might occur again; not to avail myself of it at once would be virtually to give up my cause; accordingly, I took advantage of it, and, as it has turned out, the circumstance that no time was allowed me for any studied statements has compensated, in the equitable judgment of the public, for such imperfections in composition as my want of leisure involved.

It was in the number for January 1864, of a magazine of wide circulation, and in an Article upon Queen Elizabeth, that a popular writer took occasion formally to accuse me by name of thinking so lightly of the virtue of Veracity, as in set terms to have countenanced and defended that neglect of it which he at the same time imputed to the Catholic Priesthood.[5] His words were these:—

"Truth, for its own sake, had never been a virtue with the Roman clergy. Father Newman informs us that it need not, and on the whole ought not to be; that cunning is the weapon which heaven has given to the Saints wherewith to withstand the brute male force of the wicked world which marries and is given in marriage. Whether his notion be doctrinally correct or not, it is at least historically so."

These assertions, going far beyond the popular prejudice entertained against me, had no foundation whatever in fact. I never had said, I never had dreamed of saying, that truth for its own sake, need not, and on the whole ought not to be, a virtue with the Roman Clergy; or that cunning is the weapon which heaven has given to the Saints wherewith to withstand the wicked world. To what work of mine then could the writer be referring? In a correspondence which ensued upon the subject between him and myself, he rested his charge against me on a Sermon of mine, preached, before I was a Catholic, in the pulpit of my Church at Oxford; and he gave me to understand, that, after having done as much as this, he was not bound, over and above such a general reference to my Sermon, to specify the passages of it, in which the doctrine, which he imputed to me, was contained.[6] On my part I considered this not enough; and I demanded of him to bring out his proof of his accusation in form and in detail, or to confess he was unable to do so. But he persevered in his refusal to cite any distinct passages from any writing of mine; and, though he consented to with-

---

1864, Newman had begun to gather materials for an autobiographical response to Kingsley. (JHN to Jemima Mozley, March 4, 1864; JHN to Edward Badeley, March 8, 1864, L&D 21: 70, 73–74.)

5. On this exchange see the introduction to the present volume.

6. The sermon was "Wisdom and Innocence" (1843), reprinted in the editor's appendix to this volume, pp. 478–486.

draw his charge, he would not do so on the issue of its truth or falsehood, but simply on the ground that I assured him that I had had no intention of incurring it. This did not satisfy my sense of justice. Formally to charge me with committing a fault is one thing; to allow that I did not intend to commit it, is another; it is no satisfaction to me, if a man accuses me of *this* offense, for him to profess that he does not accuse me of *that;* but he thought differently. Not being able then to gain redress in the quarter, where I had a right to ask it, I appealed to the public. I published the correspondence in the shape of a Pamphlet, with some remarks of my own at the end, on the course which that correspondence had taken.[7]

This Pamphlet, which appeared in the first weeks of February, received a reply from my accuser towards the end of March, in another Pamphlet of 48 pages, entitled, "What then does Dr. Newman mean?" in which he professed to do that which I had called upon him to do; that is, he brought together a number of extracts from various works of mine, Catholic and Anglican, with the object of showing that, if I was to be acquitted of the crime of teaching and practising deceit and dishonesty, according to his first supposition, it was at the price of my being considered no longer responsible for my actions; for, as he expressed it, "I had a human reason once, no doubt, but I had gambled it away," and I had "worked my mind into that morbid state, in which nonsense was the only food for which it hungered;" and that it could not be called "a hasty or farfetched or unfounded mistake, when he concluded that I did not care for truth for its own sake, or teach my disciples to regard it as a virtue;" and, though "too many prefer the charge of insincerity to that of insipience, Dr. Newman seemed not to be of that number."[8]

He ended his Pamphlet by returning to his original imputation against me, which he had professed to abandon. Alluding by anticipation to my probable answer to what he was then publishing, he professed his heartfelt embarrassment how he was to believe any thing I might say in my exculpation, in the plain and literal sense of the words. "I am henceforth," he said, "in doubt and fear, as much as an honest man can be, concerning every word Dr. Newman may write. How can I tell, that I shall not be the dupe of some cunning equivocation, of one of the three kinds laid down as permissible by the blessed St. Alfonso da Liguori and his pupils, even when confirmed with an oath,

---

7. [John Henry Newman], *Mr. Kingsley and Dr. Newman: A Correspondence on the Question Whether Dr. Newman Teaches That Truth Is No Virtue?* (London: Longman, Green, Longman, Roberts, and Green, 1864).

8. Charles Kingsley, *"What, Then, Does Dr. Newman Mean?" A Reply to a Pamphlet Lately Published by Dr. Newman* (London: Macmillan, 1864).

because 'then we do not deceive our neighbour, but allow him to deceive himself?' . . . How can I tell, that I may not in this Pamphlet have made an accusation, of the truth of which Dr. Newman is perfectly conscious; but that, as I, a heretic Protestant, have no business to make it, he has a full right to deny it?"

Even if I could have found it consistent with my duty to my own reputation to leave such an elaborate impeachment of my moral nature unanswered, my duty to my Brethren in the Catholic Priesthood, would have forbidden such a course. *They* were involved in the charges which this writer, all along, from the original passage in the Magazine, to the very last paragraph of the Pamphlet, had so confidently, so pertinaciously made. In exculpating myself, it was plain I should be pursuing no mere personal quarrel; — I was offering my humble service to a sacred cause. I was making my protest in behalf of a large body of men of high character, of honest and religious minds, and of sensitive honour, — who had their place and their rights in this world, though they were ministers of the world unseen, and who were insulted by my Accuser, as the above extracts from him sufficiently show, not only in my person, but directly and pointedly in their own. Accordingly, I at once set about writing the *Apologia pro vitâ suâ*, of which the present Volume is the Second Edition; and it was a great reward to me to find, as the controversy proceeded, such large numbers of my clerical brethren supporting me by their sympathy in the course which I was pursuing, and, as occasion offered, bestowing on me the formal and public expression of their approbation. These testimonials in my behalf, so important and so grateful to me, are, together with the Letter, sent to me with the same purpose, from my Bishop, contained in the last pages of this Volume.[9]

This Edition differs from the Apologia in the following particulars: — The original work consisted of seven Parts, which were published in series on consecutive Thursdays, between April 21 and June 2. An Appendix, in answer to specific allegations urged against me in the Pamphlet of Accusation, appeared on June 16. Of these Parts 1 and 2, as being for the most part directly controversial, are omitted in this Edition, excepting the latter pages of Part 2, which are subjoined to this Preface, as being necessary for the due explanation of the subsequent five Parts. These, (being 3, 4, 5, 6, 7, of the Apologia,) are here numbered as Chapters 1, 2, 3, 4, 5 respectively. Of the Appendix, about

---

9. See the introduction to this volume and the editor's preface to Newman's Supplemental Matter on the importance of the supporting correspondence that Newman reprints.

half has been omitted, for the same reason as has led to the omission of Parts 1 and 2. The rest of it is thrown into the shape of Notes of a discursive character, with two new ones on Liberalism and the Lives of the English Saints of 1843-4, and another, new in part, on Ecclesiastical Miracles.[10] In the body of the work, the only addition of consequence is the letter which is found at p. 313, a copy of which has recently come into my possession.

I should add that, since writing the Apologia last year, I have seen for the first time Mr. Oakeley's "Notes on the Tractarian Movement."[11] This work remarkably corroborates the substance of my Narrative, while the kind terms in which he speaks of me personally, call for my sincere gratitude.

May 2, 1865.

I make this extract from my Apologia, Part 2, pp. 29–31 and pp. 41–51, in order to set before the reader the drift I had in writing my Volume:[12] —

> What shall be the special imputation, against which I shall throw myself in these pages, out of the thousand and one which my Accuser directs upon me? I mean to confine myself to one, for there is only one about which I much care, — the charge of Untruthfulness. He may cast upon me as many other imputations as he pleases, and they may stick on me, as long as they can, in the course of nature. They will fall to the ground in their season.
>
> And indeed I think the same of the charge of Untruthfulness, and select it from the rest, not because it is more formidable but because it is more serious. Like the rest, it may disfigure me for a time, but it will not stain: Archbishop Whately used to say, "Throw dirt enough, and some will stick;" well, will stick, but not, will stain. I think he used to mean "stain," and I do not agree with him. Some dirt sticks longer than other dirt; but no dirt is immortal. According to the old saying, Prævalebit Veritas. There are virtues indeed, about which the world is not fitted to judge or to uphold, such as faith, hope, and charity: but it can judge about Truthfulness; it can judge about the natural virtues, and Truthfulness is one of them. Natural virtues may also become supernatural; Truthfulness is such; but that does not withdraw it from the jurisdiction of mankind at large. It may be more difficult in this or that particular case for men to take cognizance of it, as it may be difficult for the Court of Queen's Bench at Westminster to try a case fairly which took place in Hindostan: but that is a question of capacity, not of right. Mankind has the

---

10. See the editor's preface to Newman's notes.
11. Frederick Oakeley, *Historical Notes on the Tractarian Movement, A.D. 1833–1845* (London: Longman, Green, Longman, Roberts, and Green, 1865).
12. These passages are taken from the second pamphlet in the original edition of the *Apologia,* which was titled "True Mode of Meeting Mr. Kingsley."

right to judge of Truthfulness in a Catholic, as in the case of a Protestant, of an Italian, or of a Chinese. I have never doubted, that in my hour, in God's hour, my avenger will appear, and the world will acquit me of untruthfulness, even though it be not while I live.

Still more confident am I of such eventual acquittal, seeing that my judges are my own countrymen. I consider, indeed, Englishmen the most suspicious and touchy of mankind; I think them unreasonable, and unjust in their seasons of excitement; but I had rather be an Englishman, (as in fact I am,) than belong to any other race under heaven. They are as generous, as they are hasty and burly; and their repentance for their injustice is greater than their sin.

For twenty years and more I have borne an imputation, of which I am at least as sensitive, who am the object of it, as they can be, who are only the judges. I have not set myself to remove it, first, because I never have had an opening to speak, and, next, because I never saw in them the disposition to hear. I have wished to appeal from Philip drunk to Philip sober. When shall I pronounce him to be himself again? If I may judge from the tone of the public press, which represents the public voice, I have great reason to take heart at this time. I have been treated by contemporary critics in this controversy with great fairness and gentleness, and I am grateful to them for it. However, the decision of the time and mode of my defence has been taken out of my hands; and I am thankful that it has been so. I am bound now as a duty to myself, to the Catholic cause, to the Catholic Priesthood, to give account of myself without any delay, when I am so rudely and circumstantially charged with Untruthfulness. I accept the challenge; I shall do my best to meet it, and I shall be content when I have done so.

It is not my present accuser alone who entertains, and has entertained, so dishonourable an opinion of me and of my writings. It is the impression of large classes of men; the impression twenty years ago and the impression now. There has been a general feeling that I was for years where I had no right to be; that I was a "Romanist" in Protestant livery and service; that I was doing the work of a hostile Church in the bosom of the English Establishment, and knew it, or ought to have known it. There was no need of arguing about particular passages in my writings, when the fact was so patent, as men thought it to be.

First it was certain, and I could not myself deny it, that I scouted the name "Protestant." It was certain again, that many of the doctrines which I professed were popularly and generally known as badges of the Roman Church, as distinguished from the faith of the Reformation. Next, how could I have come by them? Evidently, I had certain friends and advisers who did not appear; there was some underground communication between Stonyhurst or Oscott and my rooms at Oriel. Beyond a doubt, I was advocating certain doctrines, not by accident, but on an understanding with ecclesiastics of the old religion. Then men went further, and said that I had actually been received into that religion, and withal had leave given me to profess myself a Protestant still. Others went even further, and gave it out to the world, as a matter of fact, of which they themselves had the proof in their hands, that I was actually a Jesuit. And when the opinions which I advocated spread, and younger men went further than I, the feeling against me waxed stronger and took a wider range.

And now indignation arose at the knavery of a conspiracy such as this:— and it became of course all the greater in consequence of its being the received belief of the public at large, that craft and intrigue, such as they fancied they beheld with their eyes, were the very instruments to which the Catholic Church has in these last centuries been indebted for her maintenance and extension.

There was another circumstance still, which increased the irritation and aversion felt by the large classes, of whom I have been speaking, against the preachers of doctrines, so new to them and so unpalatable; and that was, that they developed them in so measured a way. If they were inspired by Roman theologians, (and this was taken for granted,) why did they not speak out at once? Why did they keep the world in such suspense and anxiety as to what was coming next, and what was to be the upshot of the whole? Why this reticence, and half-speaking, and apparent indecision? It was plain that the plan of operations had been carefully mapped out from the first, and that these men were cautiously advancing towards its accomplishment, as far as was safe at the moment; that their aim and their hope was to carry off a large body with them of the young and the ignorant; that they meant gradually to leaven the minds of the rising generation, and to open the gates of that city, of which they were the sworn defenders, to the enemy who lay in ambush outside of it. And when in spite of the many protestations of the party to the contrary, there was at length an actual movement among their disciples, and one went over to Rome, and then another, the worst anticipations and the worst judgments which had been formed of them received their justification. And, lastly, when men first had said of me, "You will see, *he* will go, he is only biding his time, he is waiting the word of command from Rome," and, when after all, after my arguments and denunciations of former years, at length I did leave the Anglican Church for the Roman, then they said to each other, "It is just as we said: we knew it would be so."

This was the state of mind of masses of men twenty years ago, who took no more than an external and common sense view of what was going on. And partly the tradition, partly the effect of that feeling, remains to the present time. Certainly I consider that, in my own case, it is the great obstacle in the way of my being favourably heard, as at present, when I have to make my defence. Not only am I now a member of a most un-English communion, whose great aim is considered to be the extinction of Protestantism and the

Protestant Church, and whose means of attack are popularly supposed to be unscrupulous cunning and deceit, but how came I originally to have any relations with the Church of Rome at all? did I, or my opinions, drop from the sky? how came I, in Oxford, *in gremio Universitatis,* to present myself to the eyes of men in that full blown investiture of Popery? How could I dare, how could I have the conscience, with warnings, with prophecies, with accusations against me, to persevere in a path which steadily advanced towards, which ended in, the religion of Rome? And how am I now to be trusted, when long ago I was trusted, and was found wanting?

It is this which is the strength of the case of my Accuser against me; — not the articles of impeachment which he has framed from my writings, and which I shall easily crumble into dust, but the bias of the court. It is the state of the atmosphere; it is the vibration all around, which will echo his bold assertion of my dishonesty; it is that prepossession against me, which takes it for granted that, when my reasoning is convincing it is only ingenious, and that when my statements are unanswerable, there is always something put out of sight or hidden in my sleeve; it is that plausible, but cruel conclusion to which men are apt to jump, that when much is imputed, much must be true, and that it is more likely that one should be to blame, than that many should be mistaken in blaming him; — these are the real foes which I have to fight, and the auxiliaries to whom my Accuser makes his advances.[13]

Well, I must break through this barrier of prejudice against me if I can; and I think I shall be able to do so. When first I read the Pamphlet of Accusation, I almost despaired of meeting effectively such a heap of misrepresentations and such a vehemence of animosity. What was the good of answering first one point, and then another, and going through the whole circle of its abuse; when my answer to the first point would be forgotten, as soon as I got to the second? What was the use of bringing out half a hundred separate principles or views for the refutation of the separate counts in the Indictment, when rejoinders of this sort would but confuse and torment the reader by their number and their diversity? What hope was there of condensing into a pamphlet of a readable length, matter which ought freely to expand itself into half a dozen volumes? What means was there, except the expenditure of interminable pages, to set right even one of that series of "single passing hints," to use my Assailant's own language, which, "as with his finger tip he had delivered" against me?

---

13. On the manner in which the issue of truthfulness resonated with Newman's audience, see the introduction to this volume, pp. 38–54. See also Frank M. Turner, *Contesting Cultural Authority: Essays in Victorian Intellectual Life* (Cambridge: Cambridge Univ. Press, 1993), pp. 38–72, for the manner in which Newman was defending himself as much against cultural apostasy as a change in religious communion as he set out to prove that a religion his contemporaries regarded as un-English did not fundamentally challenge everyday English values.

All those separate charges had their force in being illustrations of one and the same great imputation. He had already a positive idea to illuminate his whole matter, and to stamp it with a force, and to quicken it with an interpretation. He called me a *liar* — a simple, a broad, an intelligible, to the English public a plausible arraignment; but for me, to answer in detail charge one by reason one, and charge two by reason two, and charge three by reason three, and so on through the whole string both of accusations and replies, each of which was to be independent of the rest, this would be certainly labour lost as regards any effective result. What I needed was a corresponding antagonist unity in my defence, and where was that to be found? We see, in the case of commentators on the prophecies of Scripture, an exemplification of the principle on which I am insisting; viz. how much more powerful even a false interpretation of the sacred text is than none at all; — how a certain key to the visions of the Apocalypse, for instance, may cling to the mind (I have found it so in the case of my own), because the view, which it opens on us, is positive and objective, in spite of the fullest demonstration that it really has no claim upon our reception. The reader says, "What else can the prophecy mean?" just as my Accuser asks, "What, then, does Dr. Newman mean?" . . . . . I reflected, and I saw a way out of my perplexity.

Yes, I said to myself, his very question is about my *meaning;* "What does Dr. Newman mean?" It points in the very same direction as that into which my musings had turned me already. He asks what I *mean;* not about my words, not about my arguments, not about my actions, as his ultimate point, but about that living intelligence, by which I write, and argue, and act. He asks about my Mind and its Beliefs and its sentiments; and he shall be answered; — not for his own sake, but for mine, for the sake of the Religion which I profess, and of the Priesthood in which I am unworthily included, and of my friends and of my foes, and of that general public which consists of neither one nor the other, but of well-wishers, lovers of fair play, sceptical cross-questioners, interested inquirers, curious lookers-on, and simple strangers, unconcerned yet not careless about the issue, — for the sake of all these he shall be answered.

My perplexity had not lasted half an hour. I recognized what I had to do, though I shrank from both the task and the exposure which it would entail. I must, I said, give the true key to my whole life; I must show what I am, that it may be seen what I am not, and that the phantom may be extinguished which gibbers instead of me. I wish to be known as a living man, and not as a scarecrow which is dressed up in my clothes. False ideas may be refuted indeed by argument, but by true ideas alone are they expelled. I will vanquish, not my Accuser, but my judges. I will indeed answer his charges and criticisms on me one by one,* lest any one should say that they are unanswerable, but

---

*[Newman's Note] This was done in the Appendix, of which the more important parts are preserved in the Notes.

such a work shall not be the scope nor the substance of my reply. I will draw out, as far as may be, the history of my mind; I will state the point at which I began, in what external suggestion or accident each opinion had its rise, how far and how they developed from within, how they grew, were modified, were combined, were in collision with each other, and were changed; again how I conducted myself towards them, and how, and how far, and for how long a time, I thought I could hold them consistently with the ecclesiastical engagements which I had made and with the position which I held. I must show, — what is the very truth, — that the doctrines which I held, and have held for so many years, have been taught me (speaking humanly) partly by the suggestions of Protestant friends, partly by the teaching of books, and partly by the action of my own mind: and thus I shall account for that phenomenon which to so many seems so wonderful, that I should have left "my kindred and my father's house" for a Church from which once I turned away with dread; — so wonderful to them! as if forsooth a Religion which has flourished through so many ages, among so many nations, amid such varieties of social life, in such contrary classes and conditions of men, and after so many revolutions, political and civil, could not subdue the reason and overcome the heart, without the aid of fraud in the process and the sophistries of the schools.

What I had proposed to myself in the course of half-an-hour, I determined on at the end of ten days. However, I have many difficulties in fulfilling my design. How am I to say all that has to be said in a reasonable compass? And then as to the materials of my narrative; I have no autobiographical notes to consult, no written explanations of particular treatises or of tracts which at the time gave offence, hardly any minutes of definite transactions or conversations, and few contemporary memoranda, I fear, of the feelings or motives under which from time to time I acted. I have an abundance of letters from friends with some copies or drafts of my answers to them, but they are for the most part unsorted; and, till this process has taken place, they are even too numerous and various to be available at a moment for my purpose. Then, as to the volumes which I have published, they would in many ways serve me, were I well up in them: but though I took great pains in their composition, I have thought little about them, when they were once out of my hands, and for the most part the last time I read them has been when I revised their last proof sheets.

Under these circumstances my sketch will of course be incomplete. I now for the first time contemplate my course as a whole; it is a first essay, but it will contain, I trust, no serious or substantial mistake, and so far will answer the purpose for which I write it. I purpose to set nothing down in it as certain, for which I have not a clear memory, or some written memorial, or the corroboration of some friend. There are witnesses enough up and down the country to verify, or correct, or complete it; and letters moreover of my own in abundance, unless they have been destroyed.

Moreover, I mean to be simply personal and historical: I am not expounding Catholic doctrine, I am doing no more than explaining myself, and my opinions and actions. I wish, as far as I am able, simply to state facts, whether they are ultimately determined to be for me or against me. Of course there will be room enough for contrariety of judgment among my readers, as to the necessity, or appositeness, or value, or good taste, or religious prudence, of the details which I shall introduce. I may be accused of laying stress on little things, of being beside the mark, of going into impertinent or ridiculous details, of sounding my own praise, of giving scandal; but this is a case above all others, in which I am bound to follow my own lights and to speak out my own heart. It is not at all pleasant for me to be egotistical; nor to be criticized for being so. It is not pleasant to reveal to high and low, young and old, what has gone on within me from my early years. It is not pleasant to be giving to every shallow or flippant disputant the advantage over me of knowing my most private thoughts, I might even say the intercourse between myself and my Maker. But I do not like to be called to my face a liar and a knave; nor should I be doing my duty to my faith or to my name, if I were to suffer it. I know I have done nothing to deserve such an insult, and if I prove this, as I hope to do, I must not care for such incidental annoyances as are involved in the process.

Chapter I.

History of My Religious Opinions to the Year 1833

It may easily be conceived how great a trial it is to me to write the following history of myself; but I must not shrink from the task. The words, "Secretum meum mihi," keep ringing in my ears;[1] but as men draw towards their end, they care less for disclosures. Nor is it the least part of my trial, to anticipate that, upon first reading what I have written, my friends may consider much in it irrelevant to my purpose; yet I cannot help thinking that, viewed as a whole, it will effect what I propose to myself in giving it to the public.

I was brought up from a child to take great delight in reading the Bible; but I had no formed religious convictions till I was fifteen. Of course I had a perfect knowledge of my Catechism.

After I was grown up, I put on paper my recollections of the thoughts and feelings on religious subjects, which I had at the time that I was a child and a boy, — such as had remained on my mind with sufficient prominence to make me then consider them worth recording. Out of these, written in the Long Vacation of 1820, and transcribed with additions in 1823, I select two, which

1. "My secret is my own," Isaiah 24:16.

are at once the most definite among them, and also have a bearing on my later convictions.

1. "I used to wish the Arabian Tales were true: my imagination ran on unknown influences, on magical powers, and talismans. . . . . I thought life might be a dream, or I an Angel, and all this world a deception, my fellow-angels by a playful device concealing themselves from me, and deceiving me with the semblance of a material world."

Again: "Reading in the Spring of 1816 a sentence from [Dr. Watts's] 'Remnants of Time,' entitled 'the Saints unknown to the world,' to the effect, that 'there is nothing in their figure or countenance to distinguish them,' &c., &c., I supposed he spoke of Angels who lived in the world, as it were disguised."[2]

2. The other remark is this: "I was very superstitious, and for some time previous to my conversion" [when I was fifteen] "used constantly to cross myself on going into the dark."

Of course I must have got this practice from some external source or other; but I can make no sort of conjecture whence; and certainly no one had ever spoken to me on the subject of the Catholic religion, which I only knew by name. The French master was an *émigré* Priest, but he was simply made a butt, as French masters too commonly were in that day, and spoke English very imperfectly. There was a Catholic family in the village, old maiden ladies we used to think; but I knew nothing about them. I have of late years heard that there were one or two Catholic boys in the school; but either we were carefully kept from knowing this, or the knowledge of it made simply no impression on our minds. My brother will bear witness how free the school was from Catholic ideas.[3]

I had once been into Warwick Street Chapel, with my father, who, I believe, wanted to hear some piece of music; all that I bore away from it was the recollection of a pulpit and a preacher, and a boy swinging a censer.

When I was at Littlemore,[4] I was looking over old copybooks of my school

---

2. Isaac Watts (1674–1748) was an English Dissenting minister famous for his hymns and as the author of *Remnants of Time Employed in Prose and Verse* (1753).

3. John Henry Newman and his brother Francis William Newman attended Ealing School located outside London. There, both came under the influence of the evangelical classics master and clergyman Walter Mayers (1790–1828).

4. Littlemore is a village outside Oxford. Its parish was technically part of Newman's parish of St. Mary the Virgin in the city of Oxford. He oversaw the construction of a new church in the village in 1836. From 1842 to 1845 Newman spent increasing amounts of time there and established a monastic retreat house. He was received into the Roman Catholic Church at Littlemore in October 1845.

days, and I found among them my first Latin verse-book; and in the first page of it there was a device which almost took my breath away with surprise. I have the book before me now, and have just been showing it to others. I have written in the first page, in my school-boy hand, "John H. Newman, February 11th, 1811, Verse Book;" then follow my first Verses. Between "Verse" and "Book" I have drawn the figure of a solid cross upright, and next to it is, what may indeed be meant for a necklace, but what I cannot make out to be any thing else than a set of beads suspended, with a little cross attached. At this time I was not quite ten years old. I suppose I got these ideas from some romance, Mrs. Radcliffe's or Miss Porter's;[5] or from some religious picture; but the strange thing is, how, among the thousand objects which meet a boy's eyes, these in particular should so have fixed themselves in my mind, that I made them thus practically my own. I am certain there was nothing in the churches I attended, or the prayer books I read, to suggest them. It must be recollected that Anglican churches and prayer books were not decorated in those days as I believe they are now.

When I was fourteen, I read Paine's Tracts against the Old Testament, and found pleasure in thinking of the objections which were contained in them.[6] Also, I read some of Hume's Essays; and perhaps that on Miracles.[7] So at least I gave my Father to understand; but perhaps it was a brag. Also, I recollect copying out some French verses, perhaps Voltaire's, in denial of the immortality of the soul, and saying to myself something like "How dreadful, but how plausible!"[8]

When I was fifteen, (in the autumn of 1816,) a great change of thought took place in me. I fell under the influences of a definite Creed, and received into my intellect impressions of dogma, which, through God's mercy, have never been effaced or obscured. Above and beyond the conversations and sermons of the excellent man, long dead, the Rev. Walter Mayers, of Pembroke College, Oxford, who was the human means of this beginning of divine faith in me, was

---

5. Mrs. Ann Radcliffe (1764–1823) was an early nineteenth-century English novelist, as were the sisters Jane (1776–1850) and Anna Maria (1778–1832) Porter.

6. Thomas Paine (1737–1809) was a deist, a transatlantic political radical, and author of revolutionary writings related to both the American and French revolutions. Here, Newman refers to Paine's *Age of Reason* (1794–1795).

7. David Hume (1711–1776) was a major Scottish philosopher and historian whose famous skeptical chapter on miracles appeared in his *An Enquiry Concerning Human Understanding* (1748).

8. Voltaire (1694–1778), the foremost author associated with the French Enlightenment, wrote verse, plays, history, social commentary, and philosophy. He was a deist and a major eighteenth-century critic of Christianity.

the effect of the books which he put into my hands, all of the school of Calvin.[9] One of the first books I read was a work of Romaine's;[10] I neither recollect the title nor the contents, except one doctrine, which of course I do not include among those which I believe to have come from a divine source, viz. the doctrine of final perseverance. I received it at once, and believed that the inward conversion of which I was conscious, (and of which I still am more certain than that I have hands and feet,) would last into the next life, and that I was elected to eternal glory. I have no consciousness that this belief had any tendency whatever to lead me to be careless about pleasing God. I retained it till the age of twenty-one, when it gradually faded away; but I believe that it had some influence on my opinions, in the direction of those childish imaginations which I have already mentioned, viz. in isolating me from the objects which surrounded me, in confirming me in my mistrust of the reality of material phenomena, and making me rest in the thought of two and two only absolute and luminously self-evident beings, myself and my Creator; — for while I considered myself predestined to salvation, my mind did not dwell upon others, as fancying them simply passed over, not predestined to eternal death. I only thought of the mercy to myself.

The detestable doctrine last mentioned is simply denied and abjured, unless my memory strangely deceives me, by the writer who made a deeper impression on my mind than any other, and to whom (humanly speaking) I almost owe my soul, — Thomas Scott of Aston Sandford.[11] I so admired and delighted in his writings, that, when I was an under-graduate, I thought of making a visit to his Parsonage, in order to see a man whom I so deeply revered. I hardly think I could have given up the idea of this expedition, even after I had taken my degree; for the news of his death in 1821 came upon me as a disappointment as well as a sorrow. I hung upon the lips of Daniel Wilson, afterwards Bishop of Calcutta, as in two sermons at St. John's Chapel he gave the history

---

9. The French theologian John Calvin (1509–1564) was the primary founder of the reformed tradition of Protestant theology. He is particularly associated with the doctrines of original sin and predestination. In the early nineteenth-century English Calvinists often regarded a personal conversion experience as a sign of election to eternal salvation.

10. William Romaine (1714–1795) was a major English evangelical Calvinist clergyman and author. He was a firm member of the Church of England who argued for the essentially Calvinist character of the Thirty-Nine Articles.

11. Thomas Scott (1747–1821) was an influential evangelical minister and biblical commentator. His autobiographical *The Force of Truth* (1779) traced his religious journey from Socinianism to Calvinism. Newman patterned the structure of the early parts of his *Apologia* after Scott's personal narrative.

of Scott's life and death.[12] I had been possessed of his "Force of Truth" and Essays from a boy; his Commentary I bought when I was an under-graduate.

What, I suppose, will strike any reader of Scott's history and writings, is his bold unworldliness and vigorous independence of mind. He followed truth wherever it led him, beginning with Unitarianism, and ending in a zealous faith in the Holy Trinity. It was he who first planted deep in my mind that fundamental truth of religion. With the assistance of Scott's Essays, and the admirable work of Jones of Nayland,[13] I made a collection of Scripture texts in proof of the doctrine, with remarks (I think) of my own upon them, before I was sixteen; and a few months later I drew up a series of texts in support of each verse of the Athanasian Creed.[14] These papers I have still.

Besides his unworldliness, what I also admired in Scott was his resolute opposition to Antinomianism, and the minutely practical character of his writings.[15] They show him to be a true Englishman, and I deeply felt his influence; and for years I used almost as proverbs what I considered to be the scope and issue of his doctrine, "Holiness rather than peace," and "Growth the only evidence of life."

Calvinists make a sharp separation between the elect and the world; there is much in this that is cognate or parallel to the Catholic doctrine; but they go on

---

12. Daniel Wilson (1778–1858) was a major English evangelical who, after ministering for many years in London, became bishop of Calcutta in 1832.

13. William Jones (1726–1800) was the author of *The Catholic Doctrine of the Trinity* (1756), a major eighteenth-century apology for the doctrine. Jones also defended the traditional authority of the Church of England, championed the seventeenth-century Anglican Caroline divines, and firmly defended the concept of apostolic succession within the English Church. He and others like him emphasized the need in the Christian life for personal devotion and piety instead of conversion experience. In these respects his thought prefigured that of the later Tractarians.

14. The Athanasian Creed was drawn up by the Western Christian Church and associated with St. Athanasius (d. 373) though it would appear to have originated several centuries after him. The creed was used in the Church of England during the early nineteenth century but gradually became less used because of its strong language regarding damnation. It remains in the Book of Common Prayer.

15. Antinomianism is a view that Christians need only have faith in Christ for salvation without obeying moral law. It emerged from the idea that Christians lived under the dispensation of grace rather than of the law. Throughout both his Anglican and Roman Catholic careers Newman emphasized the necessity of personal holiness in the Christian life. Newman emphasized the need of preaching Christian obedience in contrast to preaching a subjective experience of faith in Christ, declaring, "In truth men *do* think that a saving state is one, where the mind merely looks to Christ—a virtual antinomianism." (JHN to Samuel Wilberforce, February 4, 1835, *L&D* 5: 22.)

to say, as I understand them, very differently from Catholicism, — that the converted and the unconverted can be discriminated by man, that the justified are conscious of their state of justification, and that the regenerate cannot fall away. Catholics on the other hand shade and soften the awful antagonism between good and evil, which is one of their dogmas, by holding that there are different degrees of justification, that there is a great difference in point of gravity between sin and sin, that there is the possibility and the danger of falling away, and that there is no certain knowledge given to any one that he is simply in a state of grace, and much less that he is to persevere to the end: — of the Calvinistic tenets the only one which took root in my mind was the fact of heaven and hell, divine favour and divine wrath, of the justified and the unjustified. The notion that the regenerate and the justified were one and the same, and that the regenerate, as such, had the gift of perseverance, remained with me not many years, as I have said already.

This main Catholic doctrine of the warfare between the city of God and the powers of darkness was also deeply impressed upon my mind by a work of a character very opposite to Calvinism, Law's "Serious Call."[16]

From this time I have held with a full inward assent and belief the doctrine of eternal punishment, as delivered by our Lord Himself, in as true a sense as I hold that of eternal happiness; though I have tried in various ways to make that truth less terrible to the intellect.

Now I come to two other works, which produced a deep impression on me in the same Autumn of 1816, when I was fifteen years old, each contrary to each, and planting in me the seeds of an intellectual inconsistency which disabled me for a long course of years. I read Joseph Milner's Church History, and was nothing short of enamoured of the long extracts from St. Augustine, St. Ambrose, and the other Fathers which I found there.[17] I read them as being the religion of the primitive Christians: but simultaneously with Milner I read Newton on the Prophecies, and in consequence became most firmly convinced that the Pope was the Antichrist predicted by Daniel, St. Paul, and St. John.[18]

---

16. William Law (1686–1761) composed *A Serious Call to a Devout and Holy Life* (1729) as a guide to the practical living of a devout Christian life. Newman contrasts it to Calvinism because Law emphasized the necessity of holy living for Christians rather than predestined election. Law was deeply influenced by the Christian mystical tradition.

17. Joseph Milner (1745–1797), working with his brother Isaac (1750–1820), was the evangelical author of the immensely influential five-volume *History of the Church of Christ* (1794–1809). While reading this work, Newman first encountered the history of the early Church Fathers.

18. Thomas Newton (1704–1782) was bishop of Bristol in the Church of England whose most important work was *Dissertations on the Prophecies, Which have remark-*

My imagination was stained by the effects of this doctrine up to the year 1843; it had been obliterated from my reason and judgment at an earlier date; but the thought remained upon me as a sort of false conscience. Hence came that conflict of mind, which so many have felt besides myself; — leading some men to make a compromise between two ideas, so inconsistent with each other, — driving others to beat out the one idea or the other from their minds, — and ending in my own case, after many years of intellectual unrest, in the gradual decay and extinction of one of them, — I do not say in its violent death, for why should I not have murdered it sooner, if I murdered it at all?

I am obliged to mention, though I do it with great reluctance, another deep imagination, which at this time, the autumn of 1816, took possession of me, — there can be no mistake about the fact; viz. that it would be the will of God that I should lead a single life. This anticipation, which has held its ground almost continuously ever since, — with the break of a month now and a month then, up to 1829, and, after that date, without any break at all, — was more or less connected in my mind with the notion, that my calling in life would require such a sacrifice as celibacy involved; as, for instance, missionary work among the heathen, to which I had a great drawing for some years. It also strengthened my feeling of separation from the visible world, of which I have spoken above.

In 1822 I came under very different influences from those to which I had hitherto been subjected.[19] At that time, Mr. Whately, as he was then, afterwards Archbishop of Dublin, for the few months he remained in Oxford, which he was leaving for good, showed great kindness to me.[20] He renewed it in 1825, when he became Principal of Alban Hall, making me his Vice-

---

ably been fulfilled, and at this time are fulfilling in the world (1754). Both in his adolescence and early adulthood Newman was deeply interested in biblical prophecy. Newton's work included a strong strain of antipapal bias, which is one of the sources of Newman's own long-standing association during his Anglican years of the papacy with the Antichrist.

19. In 1822 Newman was elected to the Oriel College fellowship, a group known for the sprightliness and sharp wittedness of its conversation. These conversations in the Oriel Common Room introduced Newman to ideas very different from those of his evangelical years. However, the Oriel Fellowship was known to be friendly to evangelicals and also was regarded as one of the more religiously serious fellowships within Oxford. See H. C. G. Matthew, "Noetics, Tractarians, and the Reform of the University of Oxford in the Nineteenth Century," *History of Universities* 9 (1990): 195–225.

20. Richard Whately (1787–1863), a fellow of Oriel College and later archbishop of Dublin, wrote in numerous fields of theology, philosophy, and religious controversy. He befriended Newman as a young man, but they later parted ways, and Whately became an implacable enemy of the Tractarian Movement.

Principal and Tutor. Of Dr. Whately I will speak presently: for from 1822 to 1825 I saw most of the present Provost of Oriel, Dr. Hawkins, at that time Vicar of St. Mary's; and, when I took orders in 1824 and had a curacy in Oxford, then, during the Long Vacations, I was especially thrown into his company.[21] I can say with a full heart that I love him, and have never ceased to love him; and I thus preface what otherwise might sound rude, that in the course of the many years in which we were together afterwards, he provoked me very much from time to time, though I am perfectly certain that I have provoked him a great deal more. Moreover, in me such provocation was unbecoming, both because he was the Head of my College, and because, in the first years that I knew him, he had been in many ways of great service to my mind.

He was the first who taught me to weigh my words, and to be cautious in my statements. He led me to that mode of limiting and clearing my sense in discussion and in controversy, and of distinguishing between cognate ideas, and of obviating mistakes by anticipation, which to my surprise has been since considered, even in quarters friendly to me, to savour of the polemics of Rome. He is a man of most exact mind himself, and he used to snub me severely, on reading, as he was kind enough to do, the first Sermons that I wrote, and other compositions which I was engaged upon.

Then as to doctrine, he was the means of great additions to my belief. As I have noticed elsewhere, he gave me the "Treatise on Apostolical Preaching," by Sumner, afterwards Archbishop of Canterbury, from which I was led to give up my remaining Calvinism, and to receive the doctrine of Baptismal Regeneration.[22] In many other ways too he was of use to me, on subjects semi-religious and semi-scholastic.

---

21. Edward Hawkins (1789–1882), a fellow of Oriel College, preceded Newman as vicar of St. Mary the Virgin Church in Oxford. In 1828 Hawkins was elected provost of Oriel. Although Hawkins and Newman were friends in the mid-twenties, Hawkins as provost deprived Newman of his tutorship in Oriel and later became one of the staunchest Oxford opponents of the Tractarians.

22. John Bird Sumner (1780–1862) assumed the bishopric of Chester in 1828 and became archbishop of Canterbury in 1848. He was a moderate evangelical who, along with his brother Charles Sumner (1790–1874), bishop of Winchester, was highly critical of the Tractarians and of Newman's *Tract 90*. Sumner's *Apostolic Preaching Considered in an Examination of St. Paul's Epistles* (1815) deeply influenced Newman in the mid-1820s. During the nineteenth century there were various understandings of the doctrine of baptismal regeneration, but all of them upheld in some fashion the view that the sacrament of baptism marks the initiation of spiritual renewal. Baptismal regeneration thus stood in opposition to the Calvinist doctrine of predestined election. Those clergy who upheld baptismal regeneration also generally saw themselves as opposing evangelicals,

It was Dr. Hawkins too who taught me to anticipate that, before many years were over, there would be an attack made upon the books and the canon of Scripture. I was brought to the same belief by the conversation of Mr. Blanco White, who also led me to have freer views on the subject of inspiration than were usual in the Church of England at the time.[23]

There is one other principle, which I gained from Dr. Hawkins, more directly bearing upon Catholicism, than any that I have mentioned; and that is the doctrine of Tradition. When I was an Under-graduate, I heard him preach in the University Pulpit his celebrated sermon on the subject, and recollect how long it appeared to me, though he was at that time a very striking preacher; but, when I read it and studied it as his gift, it made a most serious impression upon me.[24] He does not go one step, I think, beyond the high Anglican doctrine, nay he does not reach it; but he does his work thoroughly, and his view was in him original, and his subject was a novel one at the time. He lays down a proposition, self-evident as soon as stated, to those who have at all examined the structure of Scripture, viz. that the sacred text was never intended to teach doctrine, but only to prove it, and that, if we would learn doctrine, we must have recourse to the formularies of the Church; for instance to the Catechism,

---

who normally emphasized a personal conversion experience as marking the moment of spiritual renewal. Sumner himself argued that baptism planted the seeds that came to later fruition through a conversion experience. He was an enormously effective bishop in Chester and served as archbishop of Canterbury during a very trying time for the English Church. See Nigel Scotland, *John Bird Sumner: Evangelical Archbishop* (Leominster: Gracewing, 1995).

23. Joseph Blanco White (1775–1841) was a Spanish Roman Catholic priest who moved first toward an appreciation of the Church of England and then eventually into Unitarianism. He was associated with Oriel College for many years and was a friend of Newman. He left Oxford in 1832 before the beginning of the Tractarian Movement, which he deeply deplored. Newman, as he moved closer to converting to Roman Catholicism, found himself haunted by the example of White's various religious transitions. See Martin Murphy, *Blanco White: Self-Banished Spaniard* (New Haven, Conn.: Yale Univ. Press, 1989).

24. Edward Hawkins's sermon titled *A Dissertation upon the Use and Importance of Unauthoritative Tradition as an Introduction to the Christian Doctrines* (preached 1818; published 1819) argued that the informed reading of the Bible must always occur within a context of Christian teachers and mentors. Newman would take this view much further as he upheld the authority of church tradition in one area of theological and ecclesiastical life after another. Hawkins's moderate view of tradition deeply impressed Newman because the evangelical writers whom he had studied taught that individuals could and should read and interpret the Bible on their own.

and to the Creeds. He considers, that, after learning from them the doctrines of Christianity, the inquirer must verify them by Scripture. This view, most true in its outline, most fruitful in its consequences, opened upon me a large field of thought. Dr. Whately held it too. One of its effects was to strike at the root of the principle on which the Bible Society was set up.[25] I belonged to its Oxford Association; it became a matter of time when I should withdraw my name from its subscription-list, though I did not do so at once.

It is with pleasure that I pay here a tribute to the memory of the Rev. William James, then Fellow of Oriel; who, about the year 1823, taught me the doctrine of Apostolical Succession, in the course of a walk, I think, round Christ Church meadow; I recollect being somewhat impatient of the subject at the time.[26]

It was at about this date, I suppose, that I read Bishop Butler's Analogy; the study of which has been to so many, as it was to me, an era in their religious opinions.[27] Its inculcation of a visible Church, the oracle of truth and a pattern of sanctity, of the duties of external religion, and of the historical character of Revelation, are characteristics of this great work which strike the reader at once; for myself, if I may attempt to determine what I most gained from it, it lay in two points, which I shall have an opportunity of dwelling on in the sequel; they are the underlying principles of a great portion of my teaching. First, the very idea of an analogy between the separate works of God leads to the conclusion that the system which is of less importance is economically or sacramentally connected with the more momentous system,* and of this conclusion the

---

*[Newman's Note] It is significant that Butler begins his work with a quotation from Origen.

---

25. The British and Foreign Bible Society was a major evangelical society founded in 1804 to encourage the dispersion of Bibles throughout Britain and abroad. It was an ecumenical group, with both clerical and lay leadership. It emphasized the importance of individuals reading and interpreting the Bible on their own. Newman became a member in 1824 and resigned from it in 1830. On the phenomenon of the Victorian Bible societies, see Leslie Howsam, *Cheap Bibles: Nineteenth-Century Publishing and the British and Foreign Bible Society* (Cambridge: Cambridge Univ. Press, 1991).

26. William James was an Oriel fellow. The doctrine of apostolic succession holds that the government of the church and the right to ordain clergy pertain to bishops who have themselves been ordained by bishops in a line of succession going back to the age of the apostles. This doctrine became one of the chief cornerstones of Tractarian theology and ecclesiology.

27. Joseph Butler (1692–1752) was bishop of Bristol and then of Durham. His *Analogy of Religion, Natural and Revealed, to the Constitution and Course of Nature* (1736) constitutes one of the most influential works of English theology. He emphasized the role of conscience and saw probability as providing a fundamental ground for religious belief.

theory, to which I was inclined as a boy, viz. the unreality of material phenomena, is an ultimate resolution. At this time I did not make the distinction between matter itself and its phenomena, which is so necessary and so obvious in discussing the subject. Secondly, Butler's doctrine that Probability is the guide of life, led me, at least under the teaching to which a few years later I was introduced, to the question of the logical cogency of Faith, on which I have written so much. Thus to Butler I trace those two principles of my teaching, which have led to a charge against me both of fancifulness and of scepticism.

And now as to Dr. Whately. I owe him a great deal. He was a man of generous and warm heart. He was particularly loyal to his friends, and to use the common phrase, "all his geese were swans." While I was still awkward and timid in 1822, he took me by the hand, and acted towards me the part of a gentle and encouraging instructor. He, emphatically, opened my mind, and taught me to think and to use my reason. After being first noticed by him in 1822, I became very intimate with him in 1825, when I was his Vice-Principal at Alban Hall. I gave up that office in 1826, when I became Tutor of my College, and his hold upon me gradually relaxed.[28] He had done his work towards me or nearly so, when he had taught me to see with my own eyes and to walk with my own feet. Not that I had not a good deal to learn from others still, but I influenced them as well as they me, and co-operated rather than merely concurred with them. As to Dr. Whately, his mind was too different from mine for us to remain long on one line. I recollect how dissatisfied he was with an Article of mine in the London Review, which Blanco White, good-humouredly, only called Platonic. When I was diverging from him in opinion (which he did not like), I thought of dedicating my first book to him, in words to the effect that he had not only taught me to think, but to think for myself. He left Oxford in 1831; after that, as far as I can recollect, I never saw him but twice, — when he visited the University; once in the street in 1834, once in a room in 1838. From

---

28. In 1829 Newman, Richard Hurrell Froude, Robert I. Wilberforce, and Joseph Dornford reorganized the tutorial instruction in Oriel without consulting Hawkins. Their intention was to provide stronger students with more personal instruction and pastoral care. Early in 1830 Hawkins ended the experiment and thereafter sent no more students to any of these tutors, who ceased to offer instruction after completing the tuition of those students then under their care. This event, which removed Newman from the instructional life of Oriel, was one of the most momentous in his life and one of the most important that he does not extensively discuss in the *Apologia*. See John Henry Newman, "Autobiographical Memoir," in John Henry Newman, *Autobiographical Writings,* ed. Henry Tristram (New York: Sheed and Ward, 1957), pp. 86–107; *L&D* 2: 202–250; A. Dwight Culler, *The Imperial Intellect: A Study of Newman's Educational Ideal* (New Haven, Conn.: Yale Univ. Press, 1955), pp. 96–122.

the time that he left, I have always felt a real affection for what I must call his memory; for, at least from the year 1834, he made himself dead to me. He had practically indeed given me up from the time that he became Archbishop in 1831; but in 1834 a correspondence took place between us, which, though conducted in the most friendly language on both sides, was the expression of differences of opinion which acted as a final close to our intercourse. My reason told me that it was impossible we could have got on together longer, had he stayed in Oxford; yet I loved him too much to bid him farewell without pain. After a few years had passed, I began to believe that his influence on me in a higher respect than intellectual advance, (I will not say through his fault,) had not been satisfactory. I believe that he has inserted sharp things in his later works about me. They have never come in my way, and I have not thought it necessary to seek out what would pain me so much in the reading.

What he did for me in point of religious opinion, was, first, to teach me the existence of the Church, as a substantive body or corporation; next to fix in me those anti-Erastian views of Church polity, which were one of the most prominent features of the Tractarian movement. On this point, and, as far as I know, on this point alone, he and Hurrell Froude intimately sympathized, though Froude's development of opinion here was of a later date.[29] In the year 1826, in the course of a walk, he said much to me about a work then just published, called "Letters on the Church by an Episcopalian."[30] He said that it would make my blood boil. It was certainly a most powerful composition. One of our common friends told me, that, after reading it, he could not keep still, but went on walking up and down his room. It was ascribed at once to Whately; I gave eager expression to the contrary opinion; but I found the belief of Oxford in the affirmative to be too strong for me; rightly or wrongly I yielded to the

---

29. Richard Hurrell Froude (1803–1836), an Oriel fellow, became a close friend of and collaborator with Newman after about 1828. He came from a high church family and was known for his extreme views and quick style of conversation. His thought and personality pushed Newman toward the more extreme positions associated with Tractarianism. Froude was a champion of clerical celibacy and a strong opponent of Erastianism. Very few other contemporaries admired Froude as much as Newman did. See Piers Brenden, *Hurrell Froude and the Oxford Movement* (London: Paul Elek, 1974).

30. Richard Whately was the anonymous author of *Letters on the Church by an Episcopalian* (1826), which made a strong case for the independence of the Church of England from the state. This view would grow steadily in Newman's mind. He and other Tractarians urged that the standing of the Church of England should be based not on its relationship to the state but on its being the branch of the Holy Catholic Apostolic Church in England. See Donald Harman Akenson, *Protestant in Purgatory: Richard Whately, Archbishop of Dublin* (Hamden: Archon Books, 1981).

general voice; and I have never heard, then or since, of any disclaimer of authorship on the part of Dr. Whately.

The main positions of this able essay are these; first that Church and State should be independent of each other: — he speaks of the duty of protesting "against the profanation of Christ's kingdom, by that *double usurpation*, the interference of the Church in temporals, of the State in spirituals," p. 191; and, secondly, that the Church may justly and by right retain its property, though separated from the State. "The clergy," he says p. 133, "though they ought not to be the hired servants of the Civil Magistrate, may justly retain their revenues; and the State, though it has no right of interference in spiritual concerns, not only is justly entitled to support from the ministers of religion, and from all other Christians, but would, under the system I am recommending, obtain it much more effectually." The author of this work, whoever he may be, argues out both these points with great force and ingenuity, and with a thoroughgoing vehemence, which perhaps we may refer to the circumstance, that he wrote, not in *propriâ personâ*, and as thereby answerable for every sentiment that he advanced, but in the professed character of a Scotch Episcopalian. His work had a gradual, but a deep effect on my mind.

I am not aware of any other religious opinion which I owe to Dr. Whately. For his special theological tenets I had no sympathy. In the next year, 1827, he told me he considered that I was Arianizing.[31] The case was this: though at that time I had not read Bishop Bull's *Defensio* nor the Fathers, I was just then very strong for that ante-Nicene view of the Trinitarian doctrine, which some writers, both Catholic and non-Catholic, have accused of wearing a sort of Arian exterior.[32] This is the meaning of a passage in Froude's Remains, in which he seems to accuse me of speaking against the Athanasian Creed.[33] I had

---

31. The charge of Arianizing was lodged against people who believed that Jesus was not of the same substance with God the Father. It refers to the ancient Arian heresy, about which Newman would write his first book, *The Arians of the Fourth Century* (1833). The ideas of Arius (AD 280–336) were repudiated at the Council of Nicea (AD 325), where St. Athanasius led the opposition. Newman would develop a close sense of personal spiritual and theological identity with St. Athanasius. It was also a commonplace of eighteenth- and early nineteenth-century English religious polemics for high churchmen to charge their opponents with an ill-defined Arianism or Socinianism or some other form of lack of Trinitarian orthodoxy.

32. George Bull (1634–1710) was bishop of St. David's, the author of *Defensio Fidei Nicaenae* (1685), and the foremost Caroline Anglican defender of the doctrine of the Trinity.

33. Newman and John Keble published the four-volume *Remains of the Late Reverend Richard Hurrell Froude, M.A.* in 1838 and 1839.

contrasted the two aspects of the Trinitarian doctrine, which are respectively presented by the Athanasian Creed and the Nicene.[34] My criticisms were to the effect that some of the verses of the former Creed were unnecessarily scientific. This is a specimen of a certain disdain for Antiquity which had been growing on me now for several years. It showed itself in some flippant language against the Fathers in the Encyclopædia Metropolitana, about whom I knew little at the time, except what I had learnt as a boy from Joseph Milner. In writing on the Scripture Miracles in 1825–6, I had read Middleton on the Miracles of the early Church, and had imbibed a portion of his spirit.[35]

The truth is, I was beginning to prefer intellectual excellence to moral; I was drifting in the direction of the liberalism of the day.* I was rudely awakened from my dream at the end of 1827 by two great blows—illness and bereavement.[36]

In the beginning of 1829, came the formal break between Dr. Whately and me; the affair of Mr. Peel's re-election was the occasion of it. I think in 1828 or 1827 I had voted in the minority, when the Petition to Parliament against the Catholic Claims was brought into Convocation. I did so mainly on the views suggested to me by the theory of the Letters of an Episcopalian. Also I disliked the bigoted "two-bottle-orthodox," as they were invidiously called. Accordingly I took part against Mr. Peel, on a simple academical, not at all an ecclesiastical or a political ground; and this I professed at the time.[37] I considered

---

*[Newman's Note] Vide Note A, *Liberalism,* at the end of the volume.

---

34. The Nicene Creed, promulgated by the Council of Nicea (AD 325), devotes special attention to the relationship of the Son to the Father in the doctrine of the Trinity and was designed to repudiate Arianism.

35. Conyers Middleton (1683–1750) was a Church of England clergyman and the author of *A Free Inquiry into the Miraculous Powers, Which are Supposed to have Subsisted in the Christian Church, from the Earliest Ages through Several Successive Centuries* (1749), a work skeptical of the veracity of miracles alleged to have occurred after the age of the apostles.

36. Newman suffered three major illnesses from late adolescence through 1833. One of these occurred in 1821 when he performed poorly on his undergraduate examinations; the second happened in 1827; the last and by far the most serious struck him when he visited Sicily in 1833 and produced a powerful impression on him. He interpreted each illness in providential terms. He does not explain what he meant by the liberalism from which the relatively mild illness of 1827 deflected him. The bereavement noted here is the death of his youngest and most deeply loved sister, Mary, which occurred very suddenly on January 5, 1828.

37. Many scholars regard the Peel election of 1829 as the origin of the Tractarian Movement. After resisting Catholic Emancipation for all his career, Peel as leader of the

that Mr. Peel had taken the University by surprise; that his friends had no right to call upon us to turn round on a sudden, and to expose ourselves to the imputation of time-serving; and that a great University ought not to be bullied even by a great Duke of Wellington. Also by this time I was under the influence of Keble and Froude; who, in addition to the reasons I have given, disliked the Duke's change of policy as dictated by liberalism.[38]

Whately was considerably annoyed at me, and he took a humourous revenge, of which he had given me due notice beforehand. As head of a house he had duties of hospitality to men of all parties; he asked a set of the least intellectual men in Oxford to dinner, and men most fond of port; he made me one of this party; placed me between Provost This and Principal That, and then asked me if I was proud of my friends. However, he had a serious meaning in his act; he saw, more clearly than I could do, that I was separating from his own friends for good and all.

Dr. Whately attributed my leaving his *clientela* to a wish on my part to be the head of a party myself. I do not think that this charge was deserved. My habitual feeling then and since has been, that it was not I who sought friends, but friends who sought me. Never man had kinder or more indulgent friends than I have had; but I expressed my own feeling as to the mode in which I gained them, in this very year 1829, in the course of a copy of verses. Speaking of my blessings, I said, "Blessings of friends, which to my door *unasked, unhoped,* have come." They have come, they have gone; they came to my great

---

House of Commons in the duke of Wellington's ministry prepared to guide the measure through the House. Having reversed policy, Peel, who had represented Oxford since 1817, returned to stand for reelection. In this election he was defeated through the efforts of younger dons, including Newman, who believed that Peel had taken the university for granted. Moreover, this election marked a long-lasting division between those younger dons and the older Heads of Oxford Houses who had attempted to turn out the votes for Peel. From 1829 onward there existed a deep animosity between Peel and those who had voted against him, a group that included many of the future Tractarians. Peel was re-elected from another borough and carried Catholic Emancipation through the Commons. The election and the passage of Catholic Emancipation sharply divided the Tory party, with Newman and his friends emerging on the more conservative side. See Peter Nockles, "'Lost Causes and . . . impossible loyalties': The Oxford Movement and the University," in *The History of the University of Oxford,* ed. M. B. Brocke and M. C. Curthoys (Oxford: Clarendon Press, 1997), pp. 195–267.

38. John Keble (1792–1866) was an Oriel fellow and the author of *The Christian Year* (1827), a popular and influential volume of devotional poetry. He would become one of the major leaders of the Tractarian Movement. Throughout the Tractarian years Newman confided in Keble and sought spiritual direction from him. See Georgina Battiscombe, *John Keble: A Study in Limitations* (New York: Alfred A. Knopf, 1963).

joy, they went to my great grief. He who gave took away. Dr. Whately's impression about me, however, admits of this explanation: —

During the first years of my residence at Oriel, though proud of my College, I was not quite at home there. I was very much alone, and I used often to take my daily walk by myself. I recollect once meeting Dr. Copleston, then Provost, with one of the Fellows.[39] He turned round, and with the kind courteousness which sat so well on him, made me a bow and said, "Nunquam minus solus, quàm cùm solus."[40] At that time indeed (from 1823) I had the intimacy of my dear and true friend Dr. Pusey, and could not fail to admire and revere a soul so devoted to the cause of religion, so full of good works, so faithful in his affections; but he left residence when I was getting to know him well.[41] As to Dr. Whately himself, he was too much my superior to allow of my being at my ease with him; and to no one in Oxford at this time did I open my heart fully and familiarly. But things changed in 1826. At that time I became one of the Tutors of my College, and this gave me position; besides, I had written one or two Essays which had been well received. I began to be known. I preached my first University Sermon. Next year I was one of the Public Examiners for the B.A. degree. In 1828 I became Vicar of St. Mary's. It was to me like the feeling of spring weather after winter; and, if I may so speak, I came out of my shell; I remained out of it till 1841.

The two persons who knew me best at that time are still alive, beneficed clergymen, no longer my friends. They could tell better than any one else what I was in those years. From this time my tongue was, as it were, loosened, and I spoke spontaneously and without effort. One of the two, a shrewd man, said

---

39. Edward Copleston (1776–1849) served as provost of Oriel from 1814 to 1827. He then became bishop of Llandaff and later was a moderate critic of the Tractarians.

40. "Never less alone than when alone." Cicero, *De Officiis* 3:1.

41. Edward Bouverie Pusey (1800–1882) was a fellow of Oriel who became regius professor of Hebrew in 1828 and thereafter moved to Christchurch. He was a major leader of the Tractarian Movement, whose followers were often called "Puseyites" in the popular press. Pusey's thought represented a strongly ascetic side of Tractarianism. His rigorous views on baptismal regeneration separated him and the Tractarians from most other parties in the English Church. Over the years of the movement he and Newman drifted apart, especially as Newman became more critical of the English Church and friendly to the Roman Catholic Church. See Frank M. Turner, *John Henry Newman: The Challenge to Evangelical Religion* (New Haven, Conn.: Yale Univ. Press, 2002), pp. 187–193; David Forrester, *Young Doctor Pusey: A Study in Development* (London: Mowbray, 1989); Perry Butler, *Pusey Rediscovered* (London: SPCK, 1983); H. C. G. Matthew, "Edward Bouverie Pusey: From Scholar to Tractarian," *Journal of Theological Studies* NS 32 (1981): 101–124.

of me, I have been told, "Here is a fellow who, when he is silent, will never begin to speak; and when he once begins to speak, will never stop." It was at this time that I began to have influence, which steadily increased for a course of years. I gained upon my pupils, and was in particular intimate and affectionate with two of our probationer Fellows, Robert Isaac Wilberforce (afterwards Archdeacon) and Richard Hurrell Froude.[42] Whately then, an acute man, perhaps saw around me the signs of an incipient party, of which I was not conscious myself. And thus we discern the first elements of that movement afterwards called Tractarian.

The true and primary author of it, however, as is usual with great motive-powers, was out of sight. Having carried off as a mere boy the highest honours of the University, he had turned from the admiration which haunted his steps, and sought for a better and holier satisfaction in pastoral work in the country. Need I say that I am speaking of John Keble? The first time that I was in a room with him was on occasion of my election to a fellowship at Oriel, when I was sent for into the Tower, to shake hands with the Provost and Fellows. How is that hour fixed in my memory after the changes of forty-two years, forty-two this very day on which I write! I have lately had a letter in my hands, which I sent at the time to my great friend, John William Bowden, with whom I passed almost exclusively my Under-graduate years.[43] "I had to hasten to the Tower," I say to him, "to receive the congratulations of all the Fellows. I bore it till Keble took my hand, and then felt so abashed and unworthy of the honour done me, that I seemed desirous of quite sinking into the ground." His had been the first name which I had heard spoken of, with reverence rather than admiration, when I came up to Oxford. When one day I was walking in High Street with my dear earliest friend just mentioned, with what eagerness did he cry out, "There's Keble!" and with what awe did I look at him! Then at another time I heard a Master of Arts of my College give an account how he had just then had occasion to introduce himself on some business to Keble, and how gentle, courteous, and unaffected Keble had been, so as almost to put him out of countenance. Then too it was reported, truly or falsely, how a rising man of brilliant reputation, the present Dean of St. Paul's, Dr. Milman, admired and loved him, adding, that somehow he was strangely unlike any one

---

42. Robert Isaac Wilberforce (1802–1857) was a fellow of Oriel and one of the four tutors associated with the abortive Oriel tutorial experiment. A distinguished theologian of the Incarnation, he would convert to the Roman Catholic Church in 1851 as a result of the Gorham Judgment.

43. John William Bowden (1798–1844) was Newman's closest Oxford friend from his undergraduate days.

else.⁴⁴ However, at the time when I was elected Fellow of Oriel he was not in residence, and he was shy of me for years in consequence of the marks which I bore upon me of the evangelical and liberal schools. At least so I have ever thought. Hurrell Froude brought us together about 1828: it is one of the sayings preserved in his "Remains," — "Do you know the story of the murderer who had done one good thing in his life? Well; if I was ever asked what good deed I had ever done, I should say that I had brought Keble and Newman to understand each other."

The Christian Year made its appearance in 1827.⁴⁵ It is not necessary, and scarcely becoming, to praise a book which has already become one of the classics of the language. When the general tone of religious literature was so nerveless and impotent, as it was at that time, Keble struck an original note and woke up in the hearts of thousands a new music, the music of a school, long unknown in England. Nor can I pretend to analyze, in my own instance, the effect of religious teaching so deep, so pure, so beautiful. I have never till now tried to do so; yet I think I am not wrong in saying, that the two main intellectual truths which it brought home to me, were the same two, which I had learned from Butler, though recast in the creative mind of my new master. The first of these was what may be called, in a large sense of the word, the Sacramental system; that is, the doctrine that material phenomena are both the types and the instruments of real things unseen, — a doctrine, which embraces in its fulness, not only what Anglicans, as well as Catholics, believe about Sacraments properly so called; but also the article of "the Communion of Saints;" and likewise the Mysteries of the faith. The connexion of this philosophy of religion with what is sometimes called "Berkeleyism" has been mentioned above; I knew little of Berkeley at this time except by name; nor have I ever studied him.⁴⁶

---

44. Henry Hart Milman (1791–1868) was a major early Victorian historian of biblical and early church history, poet, writer of hymns, and after 1849 to his death dean of St. Paul's Cathedral. Newman was highly critical of his scholarship and saw it as representative of liberalism.

45. On Keble's *Christian Year*, see G. B. Tennyson, *Victorian Devotional Poetry: The Tractarian Mode* (Cambridge, Mass.: Harvard Univ. Press, 1981).

46. Berkeleyism refers to the philosophy of George Berkeley (1685–1753), bishop of Cloyne, who contended that the human mind cannot extend its knowledge beyond its perceptions. Thus the external world has existence only in terms of the perceptions of the human mind. Newman admits little direct knowledge of this philosophy, but his view of the external world and most particularly of the Christian sacraments was that their existence represented manifestations of an unseen spiritual power.

On the second intellectual principle which I gained from Mr. Keble, I could say a great deal; if this were the place for it. It runs through very much that I have written, and has gained for me many hard names. Butler teaches us that probability is the guide of life. The danger of this doctrine, in the case of many minds, is, its tendency to destroy in them absolute certainty, leading them to consider every conclusion as doubtful, and resolving truth into an opinion, which it is safe indeed to obey or to profess, but not possible to embrace with full internal assent. If this were to be allowed, then the celebrated saying, "O God, if there be a God, save my soul, if I have a soul!" would be the highest measure of devotion: — but who can really pray to a Being, about whose existence he is seriously in doubt?

I considered that Mr. Keble met this difficulty by ascribing the firmness of assent which we give to religious doctrine, not to the probabilities which introduced it, but to the living power of faith and love which accepted it. In matters of religion, he seemed to say, it is not merely probability which makes us intellectually certain, but probability as it is put to account by faith and love. It is faith and love which give to probability a force which it has not in itself. Faith and love are directed towards an Object; in the vision of that Object they live; it is that Object, received in faith and love, which renders it reasonable to take probability as sufficient for internal conviction. Thus the argument from Probability, in the matter of religion, became an argument from Personality, which in fact is one form of the argument from Authority.

In illustration, Mr. Keble used to quote the words of the Psalm: "I will guide thee with mine *eye*. Be ye not like to horse and mule, which have no understanding; whose mouths must be held with bit and bridle, lest they fall upon thee." This is the very difference, he used to say, between slaves, and friends or children. Friends do not ask for literal commands; but, from their knowledge of the speaker, they understand his half-words, and from love of him they anticipate his wishes. Hence it is, that in his Poem for St. Bartholomew's Day, he speaks of the "Eye of God's word;" and in the note quotes Mr. Miller, of Worcester College, who remarks in his Bampton Lectures, on the special power of Scripture, as having "this Eye, like that of a portrait, uniformly fixed upon us, turn where we will."[47] The view thus suggested by Mr. Keble, is brought forward in one of the earliest of the "Tracts for the Times." In No. 8 I

---

47. The Bampton Lectures were an endowed lectureship at Oxford dating from 1780. The lectures here referenced are those of John Miller (1787–1858) delivered in 1817 and then published as *The Divine Authority of Holy Scripture Asserted, from its Adaptation to the Real State of Human Nature*.

say, "The Gospel is a Law of Liberty. We are treated as sons, not as servants; not subjected to a code of formal commandments, but addressed as those who love God, and wish to please Him."

I did not at all dispute this view of the matter, for I made use of it myself; but I was dissatisfied, because it did not go to the root of the difficulty. It was beautiful and religious, but it did not even profess to be logical; and accordingly I tried to complete it by considerations of my own, which are to be found in my University Sermons, Essay on Ecclesiastical Miracles, and Essay on Development of Doctrine.[48] My argument is in outline as follows: that that absolute certitude which we were able to possess, whether as to the truths of natural theology, or as to the fact of a revelation, was the result of an *assemblage* of concurring and converging probabilities, and that, both according to the constitution of the human mind and the will of its Maker; that certitude was a habit of mind, that certainty was a quality of propositions; that probabilities which did not reach to logical certainty, might suffice for a mental certitude; that the certitude thus brought about might equal in measure and strength the certitude which was created by the strictest scientific demonstration; and that to possess such certitude might in given cases and to given individuals be a plain duty, though not to others in other circumstances: —

Moreover, that as there were probabilities which sufficed for certitude, so there were other probabilities which were legitimately adapted to create opinion; that it might be quite as much a matter of duty in given cases and to given persons to have about a fact an opinion of a definite strength and consistency, as in the case of greater or of more numerous probabilities it was a duty to have a certitude; that accordingly we were bound to be more or less sure, on a sort of (as it were) graduated scale of assent, viz. according as the probabilities attaching to a professed fact were brought home to us, and as the case might be, to entertain about it a pious belief, or a pious opinion, or a religious conjecture, or at least, a tolerance of such belief, or opinion or conjecture in others; that on the other hand, as it was a duty to have a belief, of more or less strong texture, in given cases, so in other cases it was a duty not to believe, not to opine, not to conjecture, not even to tolerate the notion that a professed fact was true, inasmuch as it would be credulity or superstition, or some other

---

48. Newman's *Essay on Ecclesiastical Miracles* of 1842 was among the most controversial of his Anglican writings. In it he contended that miracles presumed to have occurred after the age of the apostles could not be denied without also denying the miracles of the age of the apostles and of scripture on the same grounds. Traditionally, Protestants had seen the age of miracles as ending with the apostles. See Robert Bruce Mullin, *Miracles and the Modern Religious Imagination* (New Haven, Conn.: Yale Univ. Press, 1996).

moral fault, to do so. This was the region of Private Judgment in religion; that is, of a Private Judgment, not formed arbitrarily and according to one's fancy or liking, but conscientiously, and under a sense of duty.

Considerations such as these throw a new light on the subject of Miracles, and they seem to have led me to re-consider the view which I had taken of them in my Essay in 1825–6. I do not know what was the date of this change in me, nor of the train of ideas on which it was founded. That there had been already great miracles, as those of Scripture, as the Resurrection, was a fact establishing the principle that the laws of nature had sometimes been suspended by their Divine Author, and since what had happened once might happen again, a certain probability, at least no kind of improbability, was attached to the idea taken in itself, of miraculous intervention in later times, and miraculous accounts were to be regarded in connexion with the verisimilitude, scope, instrument, character, testimony, and circumstances, with which they presented themselves to us; and, according to the final result of those various considerations, it was our duty to be sure, or to believe, or to opine, or to surmise, or to tolerate, or to reject, or to denounce. The main difference between my Essay on Miracles in 1826 and my Essay in 1842 is this: that in 1826 I considered that miracles were sharply divided into two classes, those which were to be received, and those which were to be rejected; whereas in 1842 I saw that they were to be regarded according to their greater or less probability, which was in some cases sufficient to create certitude about them, in other cases only belief or opinion.

Moreover, the argument from Analogy, on which this view of the question was founded, suggested to me something besides, in recommendation of the Ecclesiastical Miracles. It fastened itself upon the theory of Church History which I had learned as a boy from Joseph Milner. It is Milner's doctrine, that upon the visible Church come down from above, at certain intervals, large and temporary *Effusions* of divine grace. This is the leading idea of his work. He begins by speaking of the Day of Pentecost, as marking "the first of those *Effusions* of the Spirit of God, which from age to age have visited the earth since the coming of Christ." Vol. i. p. 3. In a note he adds that "in the term 'Effusion' there is *not* here included the idea of the miraculous or extraordinary operations of the Spirit of God;" but still it was natural for me, admitting Milner's general theory, and applying to it the principle of analogy, not to stop short at his abrupt *ipse dixit*, but boldly to pass forward to the conclusion, on other grounds plausible, that as miracles accompanied the first effusion of grace, so they might accompany the later. It is surely a natural and on the whole, a true anticipation (though of course there are exceptions in particular cases), that gifts and graces go together; now, according to the ancient Catholic doctrine, the gift of miracles was viewed as the attendant and shadow of transcendent sanctity: and moreover, since such sanctity was not of every day's occurrence, nay further, since one period of Church history differed widely from another, and, as Joseph Milner would say, there have been generations or centuries of degeneracy or disorder, and times of revival, and since one region might be in the mid-day of religious fervour, and another in twilight or gloom, there was no force in the popular argument, that, because we did not see miracles with our own eyes, miracles had not happened in former times, or were not now at this very time taking place in distant places:—but I must not dwell longer on a subject, to which in a few words it is impossible to do justice.*

Hurrell Froude was a pupil of Keble's, formed by him, and in turn reacting upon him. I knew him first in 1826, and was in the closest and most affectionate friendship with him from about 1829 till his death in 1836. He was a man of the highest gifts,—so truly many-sided, that it would be presumptuous in me to attempt to describe him, except under those aspects in which he came before me. Nor have I here to speak of the gentleness and tenderness of nature, the playfulness, the free elastic force and graceful versatility of mind, and the patient winning considerateness in discussion, which endeared him to those to whom he opened his heart; for I am all along engaged upon matters of belief and opinion, and am introducing others into my narrative, not for their own sake, or because I love and have loved them, so much as because, and so far as, they have influenced my theological views. In this respect then, I speak of Hurrell Froude,—in his intellectual aspect,—as a man of high genius, brimful and overflowing with ideas and views, in him original, which were too many and strong even for his bodily strength, and which crowded and jostled against each other in their effort after distinct shape and expression. And he had an intellect as critical and logical as it was speculative and bold. Dying prematurely, as he did, and in the conflict and transition-state of opinion, his religious views never reached their ultimate conclusion, by the very reason of their multitude and their depth. His opinions arrested and influenced me, even when they did not gain my assent. He professed openly his admiration of the Church of Rome, and his hatred of the Reformers. He delighted in the notion of an hierarchical system, of sacerdotal power, and of full ecclesiastical liberty. He felt scorn of the maxim, "The Bible and the Bible only is the religion of Protestants;" and he gloried in accepting Tradition as a main instrument of religious teaching. He had a high severe idea of the intrinsic excellence of Virginity; and he considered the Blessed Virgin its great Pattern. He delighted in

---

*[Newman's Note] Vide Note B, *Ecclesiastical Miracles,* at the end of the volume.

thinking of the Saints; he had a vivid appreciation of the idea of sanctity, its possibility and its heights; and he was more than inclined to believe a large amount of miraculous interference as occurring in the early and middle ages. He embraced the principle of penance and mortification. He had a deep devotion to the Real Presence, in which he had a firm faith. He was powerfully drawn to the Medieval Church, but not to the Primitive.

He had a keen insight into abstract truth; but he was an Englishman to the backbone in his severe adherence to the real and the concrete. He had a most classical taste, and a genius for philosophy and art; and he was fond of historical inquiry, and the politics of religion. He had no turn for theology as such. He set no sufficient value on the writings of the Fathers, on the detail or development of doctrine, on the definite traditions of the Church viewed in their matter, on the teaching of the Ecumenical Councils, or on the controversies out of which they arose. He took an eager courageous view of things on the whole. I should say that his power of entering into the minds of others did not equal his other gifts; he could not believe, for instance, that I really held the Roman Church to be Antichristian. On many points he would not believe but that I agreed with him, when I did not. He seemed not to understand my difficulties. His were of a different kind, the contrariety between theory and fact. He was a high Tory of the Cavalier stamp, and was disgusted with the Toryism of the opponents of the Reform Bill. He was smitten with the love of the Theocratic Church; he went abroad and was shocked by the degeneracy which he thought he saw in the Catholics of Italy.

It is difficult to enumerate the precise additions to my theological creed which I derived from a friend to whom I owe so much. He taught me to look with admiration towards the Church of Rome, and in the same degree to dislike the Reformation. He fixed deep in me the idea of devotion to the Blessed Virgin, and he led me gradually to believe in the Real Presence.

There is one remaining source of my opinions to be mentioned, and that far from the least important. In proportion as I moved out of the shadow of that liberalism which had hung over my course, my early devotion towards the Fathers returned; and in the Long Vacation of 1828 I set about to read them chronologically, beginning with St. Ignatius and St. Justin. About 1830 a proposal was made to me by Mr. Hugh Rose, who with Mr. Lyall (afterwards Dean of Canterbury) was providing writers for a Theological Library, to furnish them with a History of the Principal Councils.[49] I accepted it, and at once

---

49. Hugh James Rose (1795–1838) was a high church clergyman educated at Cambridge. In the 1820s he had warned of the rising danger of German thought for tradi-

set to work on the Council of Nicæa. It was to launch myself on an ocean with currents innumerable; and I was drifted back first to the ante-Nicene history, and then to the Church of Alexandria. The work at last appeared under the title of "The Arians of the Fourth Century;" and of its 422 pages, the first 117 consisted of introductory matter, and the Council of Nicæa did not appear till the 254th, and then occupied at most twenty pages.

    I do not know when I first learnt to consider that Antiquity was the true exponent of the doctrines of Christianity and the basis of the Church of England; but I take it for granted that the works of Bishop Bull, which at this time I read, were my chief introduction to this principle. The course of reading, which I pursued in the composition of my volume, was directly adapted to develope it in my mind. What principally attracted me in the ante-Nicene period was the great Church of Alexandria, the historical centre of teaching in those times. Of Rome for some centuries comparatively little is known. The battle of Arianism was first fought in Alexandria; Athanasius, the champion of the truth, was Bishop of Alexandria; and in his writings he refers to the great religious names of an earlier date, to Origen, Dionysius, and others, who were the glory of its see, or of its school.[50] The broad philosophy of Clement and Origen carried me away; the philosophy, not the theological doctrine; and I have drawn out some features of it in my volume, with the zeal and freshness, but with the partiality, of a neophyte. Some portions of their teaching, magnificent in themselves, came like music to my inward ear, as if the response to ideas, which, with little external to encourage them, I had cherished so long. These were based on the mystical or sacramental principle, and spoke of the various Economies or Dispensations of the Eternal. I understood these pas-

---

tional theology. He and William Rowe Lyall (1788–1857) had recruited Newman to write a history of the early church councils. Instead, Newman produced *The Arians of the Fourth Century,* which these two high churchmen rejected for their series as too friendly to Roman Catholicism. Newman then found another publisher, and the book appeared in 1833. Rose and Lyall represented the older kind of high churchmen whom Newman and Froude found too timid in their response to the dangers of Dissent and the reform of the English Church. See Richard Sharp, "New Perspectives on the High Church Tradition: Historical Background 1730–1780," and Peter Nockles, "The Oxford Movement: Historical Background 1780–1833," in *Tradition Renewed: The Oxford Movement Conference Papers,* ed. Geoffrey Rowell (London: Darton, Longman, and Todd, 1986), pp. 4–50.

    50. On the importance of thinking about ancient heresy for Newman, see Stephen Thomas, *Newman and Heresy: The Anglican Years* (Cambridge: Cambridge Univ. Press, 1991). For a recent treatment of Arianism, see Rowan Williams, *Arius: Heresy and Tradition,* rev. ed. (Grand Rapids, Mich.: Wm. B. Eerdmans, 2002).

sages to mean that the exterior world, physical and historical, was but the manifestation to our senses of realities greater than itself. Nature was a parable: Scripture was an allegory: pagan literature, philosophy, and mythology, properly understood, were but a preparation for the Gospel. The Greek poets and sages were in a certain sense prophets; for "thoughts beyond their thought to those high bards were given." There had been a directly divine dispensation granted to the Jews; but there had been in some sense a dispensation carried on in favour of the Gentiles. He who had taken the seed of Jacob for His elect people had not therefore cast the rest of mankind out of His sight. In the fulness of time both Judaism and Paganism had come to nought; the outward framework, which concealed yet suggested the Living Truth, had never been intended to last, and it was dissolving under the beams of the Sun of Justice which shone behind it and through it. The process of change had been slow; it had been done not rashly, but by rule and measure, "at sundry times and in divers manners," first one disclosure and then another, till the whole evangelical doctrine was brought into full manifestation. And thus room was made for the anticipation of further and deeper disclosures, of truths still under the veil of the letter, and in their season to be revealed. The visible world still remains without its divine interpretation; Holy Church in her sacraments and her hierarchical appointments, will remain, even to the end of the world, after all but a symbol of those heavenly facts which fill eternity. Her mysteries are but the expressions in human language of truths to which the human mind is unequal. It is evident how much there was in all this in correspondence with the thoughts which had attracted me when I was young, and with the doctrine which I have already associated with the Analogy and the Christian Year.

It was, I suppose, to the Alexandrian school and to the early Church, that I owe in particular what I definitely held about the Angels. I viewed them, not only as the ministers employed by the Creator in the Jewish and Christian dispensations, as we find on the face of Scripture, but as carrying on, as Scripture also implies, the Economy of the Visible World. I considered them as the real causes of motion, light, and life, and of those elementary principles of the physical universe, which, when offered in their developments to our senses, suggest to us the notion of cause and effect, and of what are called the laws of nature. This doctrine I have drawn out in my Sermon for Michaelmas day, written in 1831. I say of the Angels, "Every breath of air and ray of light and heat, every beautiful prospect, is, as it were, the skirts of their garments, the waving of the robes of those whose faces see God." Again, I ask what would be the thoughts of a man who, "when examining a flower, or a herb, or a pebble, or a ray of light, which he treats as something so beneath him in the scale of existence, suddenly discovered that he was in the presence of some powerful being who was hidden behind the visible things he was inspecting, — who, though concealing his wise hand, was giving them their beauty, grace, and perfection, as being God's instrument for the purpose, — nay, whose robe and ornaments those objects were, which he was so eager to analyze?" and I therefore remark that "we may say with grateful and simple hearts with the Three Holy Children, 'O all ye works of the Lord, &c., &c., bless ye the Lord, praise Him, and magnify Him for ever.'"

Also, besides the hosts of evil spirits, I considered there was a middle race, δαιμόνια, neither in heaven, nor in hell; partially fallen, capricious, wayward; noble or crafty, benevolent or malicious, as the case might be. These beings gave a sort of inspiration or intelligence to races, nations, and classes of men. Hence the action of bodies politic and associations, which is often so different from that of the individuals who compose them. Hence the character and the instinct of states and governments, of religious communities and communions. I thought these assemblages had their life in certain unseen Powers. My preference of the Personal to the Abstract would naturally lead me to this view. I thought it countenanced by the mention of "the Prince of Persia" in the Prophet Daniel; and I think I considered that it was of such intermediate beings that the Apocalypse spoke, in its notice of "the Angels of the Seven Churches."

In 1837 I made a further development of this doctrine. I said to an intimate and dear friend, Samuel Francis Wood,[51] in a letter which came into my hands on his death, "I have an idea. The mass of the Fathers (Justin, Athenagoras, Irenæus, Clement, Tertullian, Origen, Lactantius, Sulpicius, Ambrose, Nazianzen,) hold that, though Satan fell from the beginning, the Angels fell before the deluge, falling in love with the daughters of men. This has lately come across me as a remarkable solution of a notion which I cannot help holding. Daniel speaks as if each nation had its guardian Angel. I cannot but think that there are beings with a great deal of good in them, yet with great defects, who are the animating principles of certain institutions, &c., &c. . . . . Take England with many high virtues, and yet a low Catholicism. It seems to me that John Bull is a spirit neither of heaven nor hell. . . . Has not the Christian Church, in its parts, surrendered itself to one or other of these simulations of the truth? . . . . How are we to avoid Scylla and Charybdis and go straight on to the very image of Christ?" &c., &c.

I am aware that what I have been saying will, with many men, be doing credit to my imagination at the expense of my judgment—"Hippoclides doesn't care;" I am not setting myself up as a pattern of good sense or of any thing else: I

---

51. Samuel Francis Wood (1810–1843) studied with Newman and became a strong supporter of the Tractarians.

am but giving a history of my opinions, and that, with the view of showing that I have come by them through intelligible processes of thought and honest external means. The doctrine indeed of the Economy has in some quarters been itself condemned as intrinsically pernicious, — as if leading to lying and equivocation, when applied, as I have applied it in my remarks upon it in my History of the Arians, to matters of conduct. My answer to this imputation I postpone to the concluding pages of my Volume.

While I was engaged in writing my work upon the Arians, great events were happening at home and abroad, which brought out into form and passionate expression the various beliefs which had so gradually been winning their way into my mind. Shortly before, there had been a Revolution in France; the Bourbons had been dismissed: and I held that it was unchristian for nations to cast off their governors, and, much more, sovereigns who had the divine right of inheritance. Again, the great Reform Agitation was going on around me as I wrote. The Whigs had come into power; Lord Grey had told the Bishops to set their house in order, and some of the Prelates had been insulted and threatened in the streets of London. The vital question was, how were we to keep the Church from being liberalized? there was such apathy on the subject in some quarters, such imbecile alarm in others; the true principles of Churchmanship seemed so radically decayed, and there was such distraction in the councils of the Clergy. Blomfield, the Bishop of London of the day, an active and openhearted man, had been for years engaged in diluting the high orthodoxy of the Church by the introduction of members of the Evangelical body into places of influence and trust.[52] He had deeply offended men who agreed in opinion with myself, by an off-hand saying (as it was reported) to the effect that belief in the Apostolical succession had gone out with the Non-jurors.[53] "We can count you," he said to some of the gravest and most venerated persons of the old school. And the Evangelical party itself, with their late successes, seemed to have lost that simplicity and unworldliness which I admired so much in Milner

---

52. Charles James Blomfield (1786–1857) served as bishop of London from 1828 to 1856. He was arguably the most powerful bishop of his day and worked with both Whig and Conservative governments to carry out the reform of the Church of England during the 1830s. He was a strong opponent of Tractarianism.

53. The Nonjurors were a group of bishops and clergy who in 1689 refused to swear an oath of allegiance to William III, believing themselves still bound by their previous oath to James II, who had been deposed by the Revolution of 1688. They left the state church and ordained their own successors. The line of nonjuring clergy had died out by the middle of the eighteenth century. See Robert D. Cornwall, *Visible and Apostolic: The Constitution of the Church in High Church Anglican and Non-Juror Thought* (Newark: Univ. of Delaware Press, 1993).

and Scott. It was not that I did not venerate such men as Ryder,[54] the then Bishop of Lichfield, and others of similar sentiments, who were not yet promoted out of the ranks of the Clergy, but I thought little of the Evangelicals as a class.[55] I thought they played into the hands of the Liberals. With the Establishment thus divided and threatened, thus ignorant of its true strength, I compared that fresh vigorous Power of which I was reading in the first centuries. In her triumphant zeal on behalf of that Primeval Mystery, to which I had had so great a devotion from my youth, I recognized the movement of my Spiritual Mother. "Incessu patuit Dea."[56] The self-conquest of her Ascetics, the patience of her Martyrs, the irresistible determination of her Bishops, the joyous swing of her advance, both exalted and abashed me. I said to myself, "Look on this picture and on that;"[57] I felt affection for my own Church, but not tenderness; I felt dismay at her prospects, anger and scorn at her do-nothing perplexity. I thought that if Liberalism once got a footing within her, it was sure of the victory in the event. I saw that Reformation principles were powerless to rescue her. As to leaving her, the thought never crossed my imagination; still I ever kept before me that there was something greater than the Established Church, and that that was the Church Catholic and Apostolic, set up from the beginning, of which she was but the local presence and the organ. She was nothing, unless she was this. She must be dealt with strongly, or she would be lost. There was need of a second reformation.[58]

At this time I was disengaged from College duties, and my health had suffered from the labour involved in the composition of my Volume. It was ready

---

54. Henry Ryder (1777–1836) became bishop of Gloucester in 1815 and of Lichfield and Coventry from 1824 to 1836, the first strong evangelical appointed as bishop in the Church of England.

55. Newman here is referring to important changes that had occurred among British evangelicals during the 1820s as a new generation of evangelical leaders began to take a more radical path of biblical literalism and explication of prophecies concerning the last days. These were the type of evangelicals to whom his brother Francis was attracted. On these developments see Turner, *John Henry Newman*, pp. 39–41, 46–52, and W. H. Oliver, *Prophets and Millennialists: The Uses of Biblical Prophecy in England from the 1790s to the 1840s* (Oxford: Oxford Univ. Press, 1978). For Newman's own extensive critique of contemporary evangelicalism as embodying a declension from its eighteenth-century roots, consult JHN to Lord Lifford, September 12, 1837, *L&D* 6: 128–133.

56. "By her step she revealed herself as a goddess," Aeneid 1:404.

57. Shakespeare, *Hamlet*, III, iv. 53.

58. *Tract* 41 had called for "a SECOND REFORMATION" (p. 12), by which was meant a purification of the English Church from what the Tractarians believed to be the novel Protestant practices arising in the past century as a result of the evangelical revival.

for the Press in July, 1832, though not published till the end of 1833. I was easily persuaded to join Hurrell Froude and his Father, who were going to the south of Europe for the health of the former.

We set out in December, 1832. It was during this expedition that my Verses which are in the Lyra Apostolica were written; — a few indeed before it, but not more than one or two of them after it.[59] Exchanging, as I was, definite Tutorial work, and the literary quiet and pleasant friendships of the last six years, for foreign countries and an unknown future, I naturally was led to think that some inward changes, as well as some larger course of action, were coming upon me. At Whitchurch, while waiting for the down mail to Falmouth, I wrote the verses about my Guardian Angel, which begin with these words: "Are these the tracks of some unearthly Friend?" and which go on to speak of "the vision" which haunted me: — that vision is more or less brought out in the whole series of these compositions.

I went to various coasts of the Mediterranean; parted with my friends at Rome; went down for the second time to Sicily without companion, at the end of April; and got back to England by Palermo in the early part of July. The strangeness of foreign life threw me back into myself; I found pleasure in historical sites and beautiful scenes, not in men and manners. We kept clear of Catholics throughout our tour. I had a conversation with the Dean of Malta, a most pleasant man, lately dead; but it was about the Fathers, and the Library of the great church. I knew the Abbate Santini, at Rome, who did no more than copy for me the Gregorian tones. Froude and I made two calls upon Monsignore (now Cardinal) Wiseman at the Collegio Inglese, shortly before we left Rome.[60] Once we heard him preach at a church in the Corso. I do not recollect being in a room with any other ecclesiastics, except a Priest at Castro-Giovanni

---

59. *Lyra Apostolica* (Derby: Henry Mozley and Sons; London: J. G. & F. Rivington, 1836) was a volume of relatively short poems infused with Tractarian principles published by Newman and other Tractarians in 1836 and reprinted for many years thereafter. Many of these relatively brief poems had been previously published in the *British Magazine*.

60. Nicholas Wiseman (1802–1865) was the formidable Roman Catholic churchman who first presided over the English College in Rome, where Newman and Froude met him in 1833; later directed the Roman Catholic Oscott College located near Birmingham; and then in 1850 as cardinal-archbishop of Westminster oversaw the reestablishment of the Roman Catholic hierarchy in England. After Newman converted to the Roman Catholic Church, he and Wiseman had an often tense and not mutually trusting relationship. See E. R. Norman, *The English Catholic Church in the Nineteenth Century* (Oxford: Clarendon Press, 1984); R. J. Schiefen, *Nicholas Wiseman and the Transformation of English Catholicism* (Shepherdstown, W.Va.: Patmos Press, 1984); B. Fothergill, *Nicholas Wiseman* (London: Faber and Faber, 1963).

in Sicily, who called on me when I was ill, and with whom I wished to hold a controversy. As to Church Services, we attended the Tenebræ, at the Sestine, for the sake of the Miserere; and that was all. My general feeling was, "All, save the spirit of man, is divine." I saw nothing but what was external; of the hidden life of Catholics I knew nothing. I was still more driven back into myself, and felt my isolation. England was in my thoughts solely, and the news from England came rarely and imperfectly. The Bill for the Suppression of the Irish Sees was in progress, and filled my mind.[61] I had fierce thoughts against the Liberals.

It was the success of the Liberal cause which fretted me inwardly. I became fierce against its instruments and its manifestations. A French vessel was at Algiers; I would not even look at the tricolour. On my return, though forced to stop twenty-four hours at Paris, I kept indoors the whole time, and all that I saw of that beautiful city was what I saw from the Diligence. The Bishop of London had already sounded me as to my filling one of the Whitehall preacherships, which he had just then put on a new footing; but I was indignant at the line which he was taking, and from my Steamer I had sent home a letter declining the appointment by anticipation, should it be offered to me. At this time I was specially annoyed with Dr. Arnold, though it did not last into later years.[62] Some one, I think, asked, in conversation at Rome, whether a certain

---

61. In 1833 Parliament passed a major reform of the Church of Ireland, the Anglican Church in Ireland, which was till then supported by various taxes on the overwhelmingly Roman Catholic population. Through a process of gradual elimination (not suppression, as Newman states) the bill reduced the number of Irish archbishoprics from four to two and the number of bishoprics from eighteen to ten. In 1833 Newman and other high churchmen saw the measure, particularly before certain clauses were removed, as an assault on the ecclesiastical establishment by a reformed Parliament whose members legislating over the established church included Roman Catholics and Protestant Dissenters as well as people of no formal religious affiliation. Once a Roman Catholic, Newman had a lower opinion of the Church of Ireland. See Stewart J. Brown, *The National Churches of England, Ireland, and Scotland 1801–1846* (Oxford: Oxford Univ. Press, 2002).

62. Thomas Arnold (1795–1842) had been an Oriel fellow and was then appointed headmaster of Rugby in 1827 where he gained great fame for reforming the school. He was also a distinguished historian of the ancient world. In 1833 he published a highly controversial pamphlet titled *Principles of Church Reform* in which he proposed significant accommodation with Dissenters as a vehicle for protecting the established church. That pamphlet made any advancement in the Church of England impossible for Arnold and was the chief basis for his reputation for liberalism. He became one of the most vigorous and outspoken critics of the Tractarians though he would oppose efforts to condemn Newman and *Tract 90*. Newman thought his views on the Bible liberal although in some respects Newman held similar views regarding the composition of the Old Testament. See Eugene L. Williamson, *The Liberalism of Thomas Arnold: A Study of*

interpretation of Scripture was Christian? it was answered that Dr. Arnold took it; I interposed, "But is *he* a Christian?" The subject went out of my head at once; when afterwards I was taxed with it, I could say no more in explanation, than (what I believe was the fact) that I must have had in mind some free views of Dr. Arnold about the Old Testament:—I thought I must have meant, "Arnold answers for the interpretation, but who is to answer for Arnold?" It was at Rome, too, that we began the Lyra Apostolica which appeared monthly in the British Magazine. The motto shows the feeling of both Froude and myself at the time: we borrowed from M. Bunsen a Homer,[63] and Froude chose the words in which Achilles, on returning to the battle, says, "You shall know the difference, now that I am back again."

Especially when I was left by myself, the thought came upon me that deliverance is wrought, not by the many but by the few, not by bodies but by persons. Now it was, I think, that I repeated to myself the words, which had ever been dear to me from my school days, "Exoriare aliquis!"[64]—now too, that Southey's beautiful poem of Thalaba, for which I had an immense liking, came forcibly to my mind.[65] I began to think that I had a mission. There are sentences of my letters to my friends to this effect, if they are not destroyed. When we took leave of Monsignore Wiseman, he had courteously expressed a wish that we might make a second visit to Rome; I said with great gravity, "We have a work to do in England." I went down at once to Sicily, and the presentiment grew stronger. I struck into the middle of the island, and fell ill of a fever at Leonforte. My servant thought that I was dying, and begged for my last directions. I gave them, as he wished; but I said, "I shall not die." I repeated, "I shall not die, for I have not sinned against light, I have not sinned against light." I never have been able to make out at all what I meant.[66]

His Religious and Political Writings (Tuscaloosa: Univ. of Alabama Press, 1964), and Tod E. Jones, *The Broad Church: A Biography of a Movement* (New York: Lexington Books, 2003), pp. 51–128.

63. C. J. K. Bunsen (1791–1860) served as a Prussian diplomat in Rome and later in Britain. He was a scholar and a person quite active in Prussian ecclesiastical matters. He was sympathetic to evangelical causes and was one of the prime movers behind the establishment of the Jerusalem bishopric, which caused Newman such anger and pain in 1841.

64. *Exoriare aliquis!* (Aeneid 4:625) is the beginning of a speech by Dido that demands some avenger for Aeneas's abandonment of her.

65. *Thalaba the Destroyer* (1801) was a poem by Robert Southey about the revenge a young Arab carries out over the death of his father. In it, Allah protects the boy through the completion of his mission.

66. Newman's fever in Sicily was one of the key moments in his life and an event to

I got to Castro-Giovanni, and was laid up there for nearly three weeks. Towards the end of May I left for Palermo, taking three days for the journey. Before starting from my inn in the morning of May 26th or 27th, I sat down on my bed, and began to sob bitterly. My servant, who had acted as my nurse, asked what ailed me. I could only answer him, "I have a work to do in England."

I was aching to get home; yet for want of a vessel I was kept at Palermo for three weeks. I began to visit the Churches, and they calmed my impatience, though I did not attend any services. I knew nothing of the Presence of the Blessed Sacrament there. At last I got off in an orange-boat, bound for Marseilles. We were becalmed a whole week in the Straits of Bonifacio. Then it was that I wrote the lines, "Lead, kindly light," which have since become well known. I was writing verses the whole time of my passage. At length I got to Marseilles, and set off for England. The fatigue of travelling was too much for me, and I was laid up for several days at Lyons. At last I got off again, and did not stop night or day, (excepting the compulsory delay at Paris,) till I reached England, and my mother's house. My brother had arrived from Persia only a few hours before.[67] This was on the Tuesday. The following Sunday, July 14th, Mr. Keble preached the Assize Sermon in the University Pulpit. It was published under the title of "National Apostasy." I have ever considered and kept the day, as the start of the religious movement of 1833.[68]

---

which he referred over the course of his life. He deeply believed his life had been spared so that he might carry out a providential mission. It was in this state of mind that he heard and interpreted John Keble's Assize Sermon on July 14, 1833.

67. Francis Newman (1805–1897) had resigned his Balliol College fellowship in 1830, joined the Plymouth Brethren, and undertaken an unsuccessful missionary journey to Baghdad. He returned to England in June 1833. See William Robbins, *The Newman Brothers: An Essay in Comparative Intellectual Biography* (Cambridge, Mass.: Harvard Univ. Press, 1966).

68. The assizes were the courts held in particular towns by judges who traveled that judicial circuit. Keble's sermon attacked the Irish Church legislation and presented the Church of England as the only true church in the nation. Except for Newman's reaction the sermon seems to have roused little contemporary interest. See John Keble, "National Apostasy," in *The Oxford Movement,* ed. Eugene R. Fairweather (New York: Oxford Univ. Press, 1964), pp. 17–50, and F. L. Cross, *John Henry Newman* (London: Philip Allan, 1933), pp. 162–163.

Chapter II.

History of My Religious Opinions from 1833 to 1839

In spite of the foregoing pages, I have no romantic story to tell; but I have written them, because it is my duty to tell things as they took place. I have not exaggerated the feelings with which I returned to England, and I have no desire to dress up the events which followed, so as to make them in keeping with the narrative which has gone before. I soon relapsed into the every-day life which I had hitherto led; in all things the same, except that a new object was given me. I had employed myself in my own rooms in reading and writing, and in the care of a Church, before I left England, and I returned to the same occupations when I was back again. And yet perhaps those first vehement feelings which carried me on, were necessary for the beginning of the Movement; and afterwards, when it was once begun, the special need of me was over.

When I got home from abroad, I found that already a movement had commenced, in opposition to the specific danger which at that time was threatening the religion of the nation and its Church.[1] Several zealous and able men had united their counsels, and were in correspondence with each other. The principal of these were Mr. Keble, Hurrell Froude, who had reached home long before me, Mr. William Palmer of Dublin and Worcester College (not Mr.

---

1. Newman is referring to the parliamentary measure to reform the Church of Ireland.

William Palmer of Magdalen, who is now a Catholic), Mr. Arthur Perceval, and Mr. Hugh Rose.[2]

To mention Mr. Hugh Rose's name is to kindle in the minds of those who knew him a host of pleasant and affectionate remembrances. He was the man above all others fitted by his cast of mind and literary powers to make a stand, if a stand could be made, against the calamity of the times. He was gifted with a high and large mind, and a true sensibility of what was great and beautiful; he wrote with warmth and energy; and he had a cool head and cautious judgment. He spent his strength and shortened his life, Pro Ecclesia Dei, as he understood that sovereign idea. Some years earlier he had been the first to give warning, I think from the University Pulpit at Cambridge, of the perils to England which lay in the biblical and theological speculations of Germany. The Reform agitation followed, and the Whig Government came into power; and he anticipated in their distribution of Church patronage the authoritative introduction of liberal opinions into the country. He feared that by the Whig party a door would be opened in England to the most grievous of heresies, which never could be closed again. In order under such grave circumstances to unite Churchmen together, and to make a front against the coming danger, he had in 1832 commenced the British Magazine, and in the same year he came to Oxford in the summer term, in order to beat up for writers for his publication; on that occasion I became known to him through Mr. Palmer. His reputation and position came in aid of his obvious fitness, in point of character and intellect, to become the centre of an ecclesiastical movement, if such a movement were to depend on the action of a party. His delicate health, his prema-

---

2. The three figures mentioned here in addition to Keble and Froude were traditional high churchmen. Hugh James Rose (see Chapter I, note 49) of Cambridge had long been concerned with the changing position of the Church of England but would later become doubtful of the direction of the Tractarians. William Palmer (1803–1885) of Worcester College was a scholar of ancient Christian liturgy who was doubtful from the beginning of the radical rhetoric of the tracts. He formally broke with the movement in 1843, publishing a highly critical pamphlet titled *A Narrative of Events Connected with the Publication of the Tracts for the Times*. (Palmer of Worcester is not to be confused with William Palmer of Magdalen [1811–1879], who was interested in the Russian Orthodox Church and sought to promote relations between it and the Church of England, but played no significant part in the Tractarian Movement.) Arthur Perceval (1799–1853) was a royal chaplain to George IV, William IV, and Queen Victoria and a strong supporter of the early Tractarian Movement. He contributed to the tracts and initially defended Newman regarding *Tract 90* but later distanced himself from the Tractarians. For the background of such traditional high churchmen, see Peter B. Nockles, *The Oxford Movement in Context: Anglican High Churchmanship, 1760–1857* (Cambridge: Cambridge Univ. Press, 1994).

ture death, would have frustrated the expectation, even though the new school of opinion had been more exactly thrown into the shape of a party, than in fact was the case. But he zealously backed up the first efforts of those who were principals in it; and, when he went abroad to die, in 1838, he allowed me the solace of expressing my feelings of attachment and gratitude to him by addressing him, in the dedication of a volume of my Sermons, as the man "who, when hearts were failing, bade us stir up the gift that was in us, and betake ourselves to our true Mother."

But there were other reasons, besides Mr. Rose's state of health, which hindered those who so much admired him from availing themselves of his close co-operation in the coming fight. United as both he and they were in the general scope of the Movement, they were in discordance with each other from the first in their estimate of the means to be adopted for attaining it.[3] Mr. Rose had a position in the Church, a name, and serious responsibilities; he had direct ecclesiastical superiors; he had intimate relations with his own University, and a large clerical connexion through the country. Froude and I were nobodies; with no characters to lose, and no antecedents to fetter us. Rose could not go a-head across country, as Froude had no scruples in doing. Froude was a bold rider, as on horseback, so also in his speculations. After a long conversation with him on the logical bearing of his principles, Mr. Rose said of him with quiet humour, that "he did not seem to be afraid of inferences." It was simply the truth; Froude had that strong hold of first principles, and that keen perception of their value, that he was comparatively indifferent to the revolutionary action which would attend on their application to a given state of things; whereas in the thoughts of Rose, as a practical man, existing facts had the precedence of every other idea, and the chief test of the soundness of a line of policy lay in the consideration whether it would work. This was one of the first questions, which, as it seemed to me, on every occasion occurred to his mind. With Froude, Erastianism, — that is, the union (so he viewed it) of Church and State, — was the parent, or if not the parent, the serviceable and sufficient tool, of liberalism.[4] Till that union was snapped, Christian doctrine never could be safe; and, while he well knew how high and

---

3. Rose, Palmer, Perceval, and Froude had met at Rose's rectory in Hadleigh, Suffolk, in July 1833. This meeting, which included neither Newman nor Keble, became legendary within Tractarian hagiography as one of the key events leading to the launching of the movement. In fact, the gathering persuaded Froude and then Newman that traditional high churchmen were much too timid in their response to the perceived threats against the English Church.

4. Erastianism is a term describing a relationship of church and state in which the church stands in subordination to state institutions.

unselfish was the temper of Mr. Rose, yet he used to apply to him an epithet, reproachful in his own mouth; — Rose was a "conservative." By bad luck, I brought out this word to Mr. Rose in a letter of my own, which I wrote to him in criticism of something he had inserted in his Magazine: I got a vehement rebuke for my pains, for though Rose pursued a conservative line, he had as high a disdain, as Froude could have, of a worldly ambition, and an extreme sensitiveness of such an imputation.

But there was another reason still, and a more elementary one, which severed Mr. Rose from the Oxford Movement. Living movements do not come of committees, nor are great ideas worked out through the post, even though it had been the penny post. This principle deeply penetrated both Froude and myself from the first, and recommended to us the course which things soon took spontaneously, and without set purpose of our own. Universities are the natural centres of intellectual movements. How could men act together, whatever was their zeal, unless they were united in a sort of individuality? Now, first, we had no unity of place. Mr. Rose was in Suffolk, Mr. Perceval in Surrey, Mr. Keble in Gloucestershire; Hurrell Froude had to go for his health to Barbadoes. Mr. Palmer was indeed in Oxford; this was an important advantage, and told well in the first months of the Movement; — but another condition, besides that of place, was required.

A far more essential unity was that of antecedents, — a common history, common memories, an intercourse of mind with mind in the past, and a progress and increase in that intercourse in the present. Mr. Perceval, to be sure, was a pupil of Mr. Keble's; but Keble, Rose, and Palmer, represented distinct parties, or at least tempers, in the Establishment. Mr. Palmer had many conditions of authority and influence. He was the only really learned man among us. He understood theology as a science; he was practised in the scholastic mode of controversial writing; and, I believe, was as well acquainted, as he was dissatisfied, with the Catholic schools. He was as decided in his religious views, as he was cautious and even subtle in their expression, and gentle in their enforcement. But he was deficient in depth; and besides, coming from a distance, he never had really grown into an Oxford man, nor was he generally received as such; nor had he any insight into the force of personal influence and congeniality of thought in carrying out a religious theory, — a condition which Froude and I considered essential to any true success in the stand which had to be made against Liberalism. Mr. Palmer had a certain connexion, as it may be called, in the Establishment, consisting of high Church dignitaries, Archdeacons, London Rectors, and the like, who belonged to what was commonly called the high-and-dry school. They were far more opposed than even he was to the irresponsible action of individuals. Of course their *beau idéal* in ecclesiastical action was a board of safe, sound, sensible men. Mr. Palmer was their organ and representative; and he wished for a Committee, an Association, with rules and meetings, to protect the interests of the Church in its existing peril. He was in some measure supported by Mr. Perceval.

I, on the other hand, had out of my own head begun the Tracts; and these, as representing the antagonist principle of personality, were looked upon by Mr. Palmer's friends with considerable alarm. The great point at the time with these good men in London, — some of them men of the highest principle, and far from influenced by what we used to call Erastianism, — was to put down the Tracts. I, as their editor, and mainly their author, was of course willing to give way. Keble and Froude advocated their continuance strongly, and were angry with me for consenting to stop them. Mr. Palmer shared the anxiety of his own friends; and, kind as were his thoughts of us, he still not unnaturally felt, for reasons of his own, some fidget and nervousness at the course which his Oriel friends were taking. Froude, for whom he had a real liking, took a high tone in his project of measures for dealing with bishops and clergy, which must have shocked and scandalized him considerably. As for me, there was matter enough in the early Tracts to give him equal disgust; and doubtless I much tasked his generosity, when he had to defend me, whether against the London dignitaries or the country clergy. Oriel, from the time of Dr. Copleston to Dr. Hampden, had had a name far and wide for liberality of thought;[5] it had received a formal recognition from the Edinburgh Review, if my memory serves me truly, as the school of speculative philosophy in England; and on one occasion, in 1833, when I presented myself, with some of the first papers of the Movement, to a country clergyman in Northamptonshire, he paused awhile, and then, eyeing me with significance, asked, "Whether Whately was at the bottom of them?"

Mr. Perceval wrote to me in support of the judgment of Mr. Palmer and the dignitaries. I replied in a letter, which he afterwards published. "As to the Tracts," I said to him (I quote my own words from his Pamphlet), "every one has his own taste. You object to some things, another to others. If we altered to please every one, the effect would be spoiled. They were not intended as symbols è cathedrâ, but as the expression of individual minds; and individuals,

---

5. Renn Dickson Hampden (1793–1868) was a fellow of Oriel College and associated with the Noetics. Provost Edward Hawkins recruited him to replace Newman at the time of the end of the Oriel tutorial reform project. Hampden became the object of Tractarian persecution in 1834 when he advocated admission of Dissenters to Oxford and of a formal condemnation by the Oxford Convocation in 1836 upon his appointment as regius professor of divinity. He was a Whig supporter and appointee. In 1847 Hampden again with much controversy was appointed bishop of Hereford.

feeling strongly, while on the one hand, they are incidentally faulty in mode or language, are still peculiarly effective. No great work was done by a system; whereas systems rise out of individual exertions. Luther was an individual. The very faults of an individual excite attention; he loses, but his cause (if good and he powerful-minded) gains. This is the way of things; we promote truth by a self-sacrifice."

The visit which I made to the Northamptonshire Rector was only one of a series of similar expedients, which I adopted during the year 1833. I called upon clergy in various parts of the country, whether I was acquainted with them or not, and I attended at the houses of friends where several of them were from time to time assembled. I do not think that much came of such attempts, nor were they quite in my way. Also I wrote various letters to clergymen, which fared not much better, except that they advertised the fact, that a rally in favour of the Church was commencing. I did not care whether my visits were made to high Church or low Church; I wished to make a strong pull in union with all who were opposed to the principles of liberalism, whoever they might be. Giving my name to the Editor, I commenced a series of letters in the Record Newspaper:[6] they ran to a considerable length; and were borne by him with great courtesy and patience. The heading given to them was, "Church Reform." The first was on the revival of Church Discipline; the second, on its Scripture proof; the third, on the application of the doctrine; the fourth was an answer to objections; the fifth was on the benefits of discipline. And then the series was abruptly brought to a termination. I had said what I really felt, and what was also in keeping with the strong teaching of the Tracts, but I suppose the Editor discovered in me some divergence from his own line of thought; for at length he sent a very civil letter, apologizing for the non-appearance of my sixth communication, on the ground that it contained an attack upon "Temperance Societies," about which he did not wish a controversy in his columns. He added, however, his serious regret at the character of the Tracts. I had subscribed a small sum in 1828 towards the first start of the Record.

Acts of the officious character, which I have been describing, were uncongenial to my natural temper, to the genius of the Movement, and to the historical mode of its success: — they were the fruit of that exuberant and joyous

6. The *Record*, founded in 1828, was the major evangelical publication of the day and generally reflected the more recent radical direction in evangelical thought. It appeared weekly and because of the absence of alternative publications also served as a general newspaper for Church of England concerns. Although Newman sent the letters he mentions to the *Record*, by the close of 1833 the newspaper had already voiced criticism of the early *Tracts for the Times*. Newman's letters had outlined typical Tractarian positions, which directly opposed evangelical theology and ecclesiology.

energy with which I had returned from abroad, and which I never had before or since. I had the exultation of health restored, and home regained. While I was at Palermo and thought of the breadth of the Mediterranean, and the wearisome journey across France, I could not imagine how I was ever to get to England; but now I was amid familiar scenes and faces once more. And my health and strength came back to me with such a rebound, that some friends at Oxford, on seeing me, did not well know that it was I, and hesitated before they spoke to me.[7] And I had the consciousness that I was employed in that work which I had been dreaming about, and which I felt to be so momentous and inspiring. I had a supreme confidence in our cause; we were upholding that primitive Christianity which was delivered for all time by the early teachers of the Church, and which was registered and attested in the Anglican formularies and by the Anglican divines. That ancient religion had well nigh faded away out of the land, through the political changes of the last 150 years, and it must be restored. It would be in fact a second Reformation: — a better reformation, for it would be a return not to the sixteenth century, but to the seventeenth.[8] No time was to be lost, for the Whigs had come to do their worst, and the rescue might come too late.[9] Bishopricks were already in course of suppression; Church property was in course of confiscation; Sees would soon be receiving unsuitable occupants. We knew enough to begin preaching upon, and there was no one else to preach. I felt as on board a vessel, which first gets under weigh, and then the deck is cleared out, and luggage and live stock stowed away into their proper receptacles.

Nor was it only that I had confidence in our cause, both in itself, and in its

---

7. One reason that during the summer and fall of 1833 friends may not have recognized Newman was that as a result of his illness in Sicily he had temporarily lost all of his hair.

8. Newman traced the political changes in the life of the Church of England to the Revolution of 1688. In contemporary correspondence he also complained of the changes wrought in the life and worship of the English Church as a result of the evangelical revival dating from the late 1730s. The Tractarians used the term *Second Reformation* in two ways: resistance to the Erastian relationship of church and state, and removal of what they regarded as ultra-Protestant or evangelical innovations in worship and devotion since the 1730s.

9. For considerations of the religious policies of the Whigs taking a less hostile view than Newman voices, see Stewart J. Brown, *The National Churches of England, Ireland, and Scotland 1801–1846* (Oxford: Oxford Univ. Press, 2002); Richard Brent, *Liberal Anglican Politics: Whiggery, Religion, and Reform, 1830–1841* (Oxford: Clarendon Press, 1987); G. I. T. Machin, *Politics and the Churches in Great Britain, 1832 to 1868* (Oxford: Clarendon Press, 1977); and Geoffrey Best, *Temporal Pillars: Queen Anne's Bounty, the Ecclesiastical Commissioners, and the Church of England* (Cambridge: Cambridge Univ. Press, 1964).

polemical force, but also, on the other hand, I despised every rival system of doctrine and its arguments too. As to the high Church and the low Church, I thought that the one had not much more of a logical basis than the other;[10] while I had a thorough contempt for the controversial position of the latter. I had a real respect for the character of many of the advocates of each party, but that did not give cogency to their arguments; and I thought, on the contrary, that the Apostolical form of doctrine was essential and imperative, and its grounds of evidence impregnable. Owing to this supreme confidence, it came to pass at that time, that there was a double aspect in my bearing towards others, which it is necessary for me to enlarge upon. My behaviour had a mixture in it both of fierceness and of sport; and on this account, I dare say, it gave offence to many; nor am I here defending it.

I wished men to agree with me, and I walked with them step by step, as far as they would go; this I did sincerely; but if they would stop, I did not much care about it, but walked on, with some satisfaction that I had brought them so far. I liked to make them preach the truth without knowing it, and encouraged them to do so. It was a satisfaction to me that the Record had allowed me to say so much in its columns, without remonstrance. I was amused to hear of one of the Bishops, who, on reading an early Tract on the Apostolical Succession, could not make up his mind whether he held the doctrine or not. I was not distressed at the wonder or anger of dull and self-conceited men, at propositions which they did not understand. When a correspondent, in good faith, wrote to a newspaper, to say that the "Sacrifice of the Holy Eucharist," spoken of in the Tract, was a false print for "Sacrament," I thought the mistake too pleasant to be corrected before I was asked about it.[11] I was not unwilling to

---

10. The meaning of the terms *high church* and *low church* did and continue to change over time. During the 1830s high church referred to clergy who held strong views on the authority of bishops, saw the sacraments as channels of grace, looked to both the Bible and the practices of Christian antiquity through about the fifth century for the rule of faith, and firmly supported the Church of England as an establishment. Low church tended to refer to evangelicals who saw the church as a voluntary association of believers, emphasized the necessity of a conversion experience, and looked to the Bible for the rule of faith. Many Church of England evangelicals were no less strong supporters of establishment than were their high church counterparts. The Tractarians originated among high churchmen but created their own radical alternative in their frequent criticism of the connection between the English Church and the English state. See Nockles, *Oxford Movement in Context*, pp. 25–43.

11. The use of the term *sacrifice* was in violation of Article 31, which rejects the presence of a sacrifice in the celebration of the Eucharist. In *Tract 4* Keble had written of the power of apostolically ordained clergy to make their congregations "Partakers of the

draw an opponent on step by step, by virtue of his own opinions, to the brink of some intellectual absurdity, and to leave him to get back as he could. I was not unwilling to play with a man, who asked me impertinent questions. I think I had in my mouth the words of the Wise man, "Answer a fool according to his folly," especially if he was prying or spiteful. I was reckless of the gossip which was circulated about me; and, when I might easily have set it right, did not deign to do so. Also I used irony in conversation, when matter-of-fact-men would not see what I meant.

This kind of behaviour was a sort of habit with me. If I have ever trifled with my subject, it was a more serious fault. I never used arguments which I saw clearly to be unsound. The nearest approach which I remember to such conduct, but which I consider was clear of it nevertheless, was in the case of Tract 15. The matter of this Tract was furnished to me by a friend, to whom I had applied for assistance, but who did not wish to be mixed up with the publication. He gave it me, that I might throw it into shape, and I took his arguments as they stood. In the chief portion of the Tract I fully agreed; for instance, as to what it says about the Council of Trent;[12] but there were arguments, or some argument, in it which I did not follow; I do not recollect what it was. Froude, I think, was disgusted with the whole Tract, and accused me of *economy* in publishing it. It is principally through Mr. Froude's Remains that this word has got into our language. I think, I defended myself with arguments such as these: — that, as every one knew, the Tracts were written by various persons who agreed together in their doctrine, but not always in the arguments by which it was to be proved; that we must be tolerant of difference of opinion among ourselves; that the author of the Tract had a right to his own opinion,

---

Body and Blood of Christ" (*Tract 4*: 2). In the first edition of *Tract 10* Newman had written of such clergy as being "intrusted with the awful and mysterious gift of making the bread and wine CHRIST's body and blood" (*Tract 10*: 4). These statements received sharp criticism from otherwise strong Tractarian supporters. See A. Hardelin, *The Tractarian Understanding of the Eucharist* (Uppsala and Stockholm: Almqvist and Wiksell, 1965). For a discussion of the ongoing revisions introduced into the tracts in their varying editions, consult Rune Imberg, *Tracts for the Times: A Complete Survey of All the Editions* (Lund: Lund Univ. Press, 1987), pp. 143–164. The different editions of the tracts did not give notice of these changes.

12. The Council of Trent met between 1548 and 1563 and reasserted numerous Roman Catholic doctrines in the face of the challenges of the Protestant Reformation. The first edition of *Tract 15* had stated: "True, Rome may be so considered [heretical] now; but she was not heretical in the primitive ages. If she has apostatized, it was at the time of the Council of Trent. Then, if at any time, surely not before, did the Roman Communion bind itself in covenant to the cause of Antichrist."

and that the argument in question was ordinarily received; that I did not give my own name or authority, nor was asked for my personal belief, but only acted instrumentally, as one might translate a friend's book into a foreign language. I account these to be good arguments; nevertheless I feel also that such practices admit of easy abuse and are consequently dangerous; but then, again, I feel also this, — that if all such mistakes were to be severely visited, not many men in public life would be left with a character for honour and honesty.[13]

This absolute confidence in my cause, which led me to the negligence or wantonness which I have been instancing, also laid me open, not unfairly, to the opposite charge of fierceness in certain steps which I took, or words which I published. In the Lyra Apostolica, I have said that before learning to love, we must "learn to hate;" though I had explained my words by adding "hatred of sin." In one of my first Sermons I said, "I do not shrink from uttering my firm conviction that it would be a gain to the country were it vastly more superstitious, more bigoted, more gloomy, more fierce in its religion than at present it shows itself to be." I added, of course, that it would be an absurdity to suppose such tempers of mind desirable in themselves. The corrector of the press bore these strong epithets till he got to "more fierce," and then he put in the margin a *query*. In the very first page of the first Tract, I said of the Bishops, that, "black event though it would be for the country, yet we could not wish them a more blessed termination of their course, than the spoiling of their goods and martyrdom." In consequence of a passage in my work upon the Arian History, a Northern dignitary wrote to accuse me of wishing to re-establish the blood and torture of the Inquisition. Contrasting heretics and heresiarchs, I had said, "The latter should meet with no mercy: he assumes the office of the Tempter; and, so far forth as his error goes, must be dealt with by the competent authority, as if he were embodied evil. To spare him is a false and dangerous pity. It is to endanger the souls of thousands, and it is uncharitable towards himself." I cannot deny that this is a very fierce passage; but Arius was banished, not burned; and it is only fair to myself to say that neither at this, nor any other time of my life, not even when I was fiercest, could I have even cut off a Puritan's ears, and I think the sight of a Spanish *auto-da-fè* would have been the death of me. Again, when one of my friends, of liberal and evangelical opinions, wrote to expostulate with me on the course I was taking, I said that we would ride over him and his, as Othniel prevailed over Chushan-rishathaim, king of Mesopotamia. Again, I would have no dealings

---

13. See the introduction to this volume on the issue of economy and truthfulness as well as Newman's Notes F and G.

with my brother, and I put my conduct upon a syllogism. I said, "St. Paul bids us avoid those who cause divisions; you cause divisions: therefore I must avoid you." I dissuaded a lady from attending the marriage of a sister who had seceded from the Anglican Church. No wonder that Blanco White, who had known me under such different circumstances, now hearing the general course that I was taking, was amazed at the change which he recognized in me. He speaks bitterly and unfairly of me in his letters contemporaneously with the first years of the Movement; but in 1839, on looking back, he uses terms of me, which it would be hardly modest in me to quote, were it not that what he says of me in praise occurs in the midst of blame. He says: "In this party [the anti-Peel, in 1829] I found, to my great surprise, my dear friend, Mr. Newman of Oriel. As he had been one of the annual Petitioners to Parliament for Catholic Emancipation, his sudden union with the most violent bigots was inexplicable to me. That change was the first manifestation of the mental revolution, which has suddenly made him one of the leading persecutors of Dr. Hampden, and the most active and influential member of that association called the Puseyite party, from which we have those very strange productions, entitled, Tracts for the Times. While stating these public facts, my heart feels a pang at the recollection of the affectionate and mutual friendship between that excellent man and myself; a friendship, which his principles of orthodoxy could not allow him to continue in regard to one, whom he now regards as inevitably doomed to eternal perdition. Such is the venomous character of orthodoxy. What mischief must it create in a bad heart and narrow mind, when it can work so effectually for evil, in one of the most benevolent of bosoms, and one of the ablest of minds, in the amiable, the intellectual, the refined John Henry Newman!" (Vol. iii. p. 131.) He adds that I would have nothing to do with him, a circumstance which I do not recollect, and very much doubt.

I have spoken of my firm confidence in my position; and now let me state more definitely what the position was which I took up, and the propositions about which I was so confident. These were three: —

1. First was the principle of dogma: my battle was with liberalism; by liberalism I mean the anti-dogmatic principle and its developments. This was the first point on which I was certain. Here I make a remark: persistence in a given belief is no sufficient test of its truth: but departure from it is at least a slur upon the man who has felt so certain about it. In proportion, then, as I had in 1832 a strong persuasion of the truth of opinions which I have since given up, so far a sort of guilt attaches to me, not only for that vain confidence, but for all the various proceedings which were the consequence of it. But under this first head I have the satisfaction of feeling that I have nothing to retract, and

nothing to repent of. The main principle of the movement is as dear to me now, as it ever was. I have changed in many things: in this I have not. From the age of fifteen, dogma has been the fundamental principle of my religion: I know no other religion; I cannot enter into the idea of any other sort of religion; religion, as a mere sentiment, is to me a dream and a mockery. As well can there be filial love without the fact of a father, as devotion without the fact of a Supreme Being. What I held in 1816, I held in 1833, and I hold in 1864. Please God, I shall hold it to the end. Even when I was under Dr. Whately's influence, I had no temptation to be less zealous for the great dogmas of the faith, and at various times I used to resist such trains of thought on his part as seemed to me (rightly or wrongly) to obscure them. Such was the fundamental principle of the Movement of 1833.

2. Secondly, I was confident in the truth of a certain definite religious teaching, based upon this foundation of dogma; viz. that there was a visible Church, with sacraments and rites which are the channels of invisible grace. I thought that this was the doctrine of Scripture, of the early Church, and of the Anglican Church.[14] Here again, I have not changed in opinion; I am as certain now on this point as I was in 1833, and have never ceased to be certain. In 1834 and the following years I put this ecclesiastical doctrine on a broader basis, after reading Laud, Bramhall, and Stillingfleet and other Anglican divines on the one hand, and after prosecuting the study of the Fathers on the other;[15] but the doctrine of 1833 was strengthened in me, not changed. When I began the Tracts for the Times I rested the main doctrine, of which I am speaking, upon Scripture, on the Anglican Prayer Book, and on St. Ignatius's Epistles. (1) As to the existence of a visible Church, I especially argued out the point from Scripture, in Tract 11, viz. from the Acts of the Apostles and the Epistles. (2) As to the Sacraments and Sacramental rites, I stood on the Prayer Book. I appealed to the Ordination Service, in which the Bishop says, "Receive the Holy Ghost;" to the Visitation Service, which teaches confession and absolution; to the Baptismal Service, in which the Priest speaks of the child after baptism as regenerate; to the Catechism, in which Sacramental Communion is receiving "verily and indeed the Body and Blood of Christ;" to the Commina-

---

14. Newman's emphasis on the visible church directly contrasted with the evangelical emphasis on an invisible church of the saved in Christ through the ages. This distinction was a major feature of Tractarian thought and theology.

15. William Laud (1573–1645) was the archbishop of Canterbury under Charles I. A vigorous opponent of Puritanism, he was executed during the rule of the Long Parliament. John Bramhall (1594–1663) was bishop of Derry, a strong royalist during the English Civil War, and an opponent of both the Roman Catholic Church and Puritanism; in 1661 he was appointed archbishop of Armagh. Edward Stillingfleet (1635–1699), bishop of Worcester, was regarded as a religious moderate in his day.

tion Service, in which we are told to do "works of penance;" to the Collects, Epistles, and Gospels, to the calendar and rubrics, portions of the Prayer Book, wherein we find the festivals of the Apostles, notice of certain other Saints, and days of fasting and abstinence.

(3.) And further, as to the Episcopal system, I founded it upon the Epistles of St. Ignatius, which inculcated it in various ways. One passage especially impressed itself upon me: speaking of cases of disobedience to ecclesiastical authority, he says, "A man does not deceive that Bishop whom he sees, but he practises rather with the Bishop Invisible, and so the question is not with flesh, but with God, who knows the secret heart." I wished to act on this principle to the letter, and I may say with confidence that I never consciously transgressed it. I loved to act as feeling myself in my Bishop's sight, as if it were the sight of God. It was one of my special supports and safeguards against myself; I could not go very wrong while I had reason to believe that I was in no respect displeasing him. It was not a mere formal obedience to rule that I put before me, but I desired to please him personally, as I considered him set over me by the Divine Hand. I was strict in observing my clerical engagements, not only because they *were* engagements, but because I considered myself simply as the servant and instrument of my Bishop. I did not care much for the Bench of Bishops, except as they might be the voice of my Church: nor should I have cared much for a Provincial Council; nor for a Diocesan Synod presided over by my Bishop; all these matters seemed to me to be *jure ecclesiastico,* but what to me was *jure divino* was the voice of my Bishop in his own person. My own Bishop was my Pope; I knew no other; the successor of the Apostles, the Vicar of Christ. This was but a practical exhibition of the Anglican theory of Church Government, as I had already drawn it out myself, after various Anglican Divines. This continued all through my course; when at length, in 1845, I wrote to Bishop Wiseman, in whose Vicariate I found myself, to announce my conversion, I could find nothing better to say to him than that I would obey the Pope as I had obeyed my own Bishop in the Anglican Church. My duty to him was my point of honour; his disapprobation was the one thing which I could not bear. I believe it to have been a generous and honest feeling; and in consequence I was rewarded by having all my time for ecclesiastical superior a man, whom, had I had a choice, I should have preferred, out and out, to any other Bishop on the Bench, and for whose memory I have a special affection, Dr. Bagot—a man of noble mind, and as kind-hearted and as considerate as he was noble.[16] He ever sympathized with me in my trials which followed; it was

---

16. Richard Bagot (1782–1854) served as bishop of Oxford throughout the entire history of the Tractarian Movement. He was generally sympathetic to the Tractarians though he voiced occasional modest criticism. Newman valued him as a bishop more

my own fault, that I was not brought into more familiar personal relations with him, than it was my happiness to be. May his name be ever blessed!

And now in concluding my remarks on the second point on which my confidence rested, I repeat that here again I have no retraction to announce as to its main outline. While I am now as clear in my acceptance of the principle of dogma, as I was in 1833 and 1816, so again I am now as firm in my belief of a visible Church, of the authority of Bishops, of the grace of the sacraments, of the religious worth of works of penance, as I was in 1833. I have added Articles to my Creed; but the old ones, which I then held with a divine faith, remain.

3. But now, as to the third point on which I stood in 1833, and which I have utterly renounced and trampled upon since, — my then view of the Church of Rome; — I will speak about it as exactly as I can. When I was young, as I have said already, and after I was grown up, I thought the Pope to be Antichrist. At Christmas 1824–5 I preached a sermon to that effect. But in 1827 I accepted eagerly the stanza in the Christian Year, which many people thought too charitable, "Speak *gently* of thy sister's fall." From the time that I knew Froude I got less and less bitter on the subject. I spoke (successively, but I cannot tell in what order or at what dates) of the Roman Church as being bound up with "the *cause* of Antichrist," as being *one* of the "*many* antichrists" foretold by St. John, as being influenced by "the *spirit* of Antichrist," and as having something "very Antichristian" or "unchristian" about her.[17] From my boyhood and in 1824 I considered, after Protestant authorities, that St. Gregory I. about A.D. 600 was the first Pope that was Antichrist, though, in spite of this, he was also a great and holy man; but in 1832–3 I thought the Church of Rome was

---

highly than did any of his contemporaries. Newman's conversion to the Roman Catholic Church in October 1845 and Bagot's decision to accept appointment as bishop of Bath and Wells occurred within days of each other.

17. During his Anglican years Newman was deeply interested in biblical prophecy. *Tract 83* was titled *Advent Sermons on Antichrist*. Other Tractarians also speculated on the person of the Antichrist. Most believed like other English Protestants that the Antichrist was embodied in the Roman Catholic Church or the papacy. By the early 1840s some Tractarians, including Pusey, had come to see the Antichrist as arising from evangelical Protestantism. Newman's views on the subject changed over the years of the Tractarian Movement. When he visited Rome in 1833, he came to believe that the spirit of the Antichrist lay over the city rather than being embodied in the Roman Catholic Church itself. See Sheridan Gilley, "Newman and Prophecy, Evangelical and Catholic," *Journal of the United Reformed Church History Society* 3 (1985): 160–188, and Paul Misner, "Newman and the Tradition Concerning the Papal Antichrist," *Church History* 42 (1973): 377–395. On Victorian anti-Catholicism, consult John Wolffe, *The Protestant Crusade in Britain* (Oxford: Clarendon Press, 1990).

bound up with the cause of Antichrist by the Council of Trent. When it was that in my deliberate judgment I gave up the notion altogether in any shape, that some special reproach was attached to her name, I cannot tell; but I had a shrinking from renouncing it, even when my reason so ordered me, from a sort of conscience or prejudice, I think up to 1843. Moreover, at least during the Tract Movement, I thought the essence of her offence to consist in the honours which she paid to the Blessed Virgin and the Saints; and the more I grew in devotion, both to the Saints and to our Lady, the more impatient was I at the Roman practices, as if those glorified creations of God must be gravely shocked, if pain could be theirs, at the undue veneration of which they were the objects.

On the other hand, Hurrell Froude in his familiar conversations was always tending to rub the idea out of my mind. In a passage of one of his letters from abroad, alluding, I suppose, to what I used to say in opposition to him, he observes: "I think people are injudicious who talk against the Roman Catholics for worshipping Saints, and honouring the Virgin and images, &c. These things may perhaps be idolatrous; I cannot make up my mind about it; but to my mind it is the Carnival that is real practical idolatry, as it is written, 'the people sat down to eat and drink, and rose up to play.' "[18] The Carnival, I observe in passing, is, in fact, one of those very excesses, to which, for at least three centuries, religious Catholics have ever opposed themselves, as we see in the life of St. Philip, to say nothing of the present day; but this we did not then know.[19] Moreover, from Froude I learned to admire the great medieval Pontiffs; and, of course, when I had come to consider the Council of Trent to be the turning-point of the history of Christian Rome, I found myself as free, as I was rejoiced, to speak in their praise. Then, when I was abroad, the sight of so many great places, venerable shrines, and noble churches, much impressed my imagination. And my heart was touched also. Making an expedition on foot across some wild country in Sicily, at six in the morning, I came upon a small church; I heard voices, and I looked in. It was crowded, and the congregation was singing. Of course it was the mass, though I did not know it at the time. And, in my weary days at Palermo, I was not ungrateful for the comfort which I had received in frequenting the churches; nor did I ever forget it. Then, again, her zealous maintenance of the doctrine and the rule of celibacy, which I recognized as Apostolic, and her faithful agreement with Antiquity in so many other points which were dear to me, was an argument as well as a plea in

---

18. Exodus 32:6.
19. St. Philip Neri (1515–1595) founded the Congregation of the Oratory, an order of secular priests that Newman brought to England upon his return from Rome in 1848.

favour of the great Church of Rome. Thus I learned to have tender feelings towards her; but still my reason was not affected at all. My judgment was against her, when viewed as an institution, as truly as it ever had been.

This conflict between reason and affection I expressed in one of the early Tracts, published July, 1834. "Considering the high gifts and the strong claims of the Church of Rome and its dependencies on our admiration, reverence, love, and gratitude; how could we withstand it, as we do, how could we refrain from being melted into tenderness, and rushing into communion with it, but for the words of Truth itself, which bid us prefer It to the whole world? 'He that loveth father or mother more than Me, is not worthy of me.' How could 'we learn to be severe, and execute judgment,' but for the warning of Moses against even a divinely-gifted teacher, who should preach new gods; and the anathema of St. Paul even against Angels and Apostles, who should bring in a new doctrine?" — *Records*, No. 24. My feeling was something like that of a man, who is obliged in a court of justice to bear witness against a friend; or like my own now, when I have said, and shall say, so many things on which I had rather be silent.

As a matter, then, of simple conscience, though it went against my feelings, I felt it to be a duty to protest against the Church of Rome. But besides this, it was a duty, because the prescription of such a protest was a living principle of my own Church, as expressed not simply in a *catena*, but by a *consensus* of her divines, and by the voice of her people. Moreover, such a protest was necessary as an integral portion of her controversial basis; for I adopted the argument of Bernard Gilpin, that Protestants "were *not able* to give any *firm and solid* reason of the separation besides this, to wit, that the Pope is Antichrist."[20] But while I thus thought such a protest to be based upon truth, and to be a religious duty, and a rule of Anglicanism, and a necessity of the case, I did not at all like the work. Hurrell Froude attacked me for doing it; and, besides, I felt that my language had a vulgar and rhetorical look about it. I believed, and really measured, my words, when I used them; but I knew that I had a temptation, on the other hand, to say against Rome as much as ever I could, in order to protect myself against the charge of Popery.[21]

---

20. Bernard Gilpin (1516–1584), a clergyman of the Church of England during the English Reformation, had reluctantly broken with Rome and did not fully accept the Reformation until the Council of Trent when he came to the conclusion that the pope was the Antichrist.

21. In the *Apologia* Newman stresses his negative criticism of the Roman Catholic Church during his Anglican career. He did so because he needed to explain how he had moved from such criticism to entering the Roman communion. However, during

And now I come to the very point, for which I have introduced the subject of my feelings about Rome. I felt such confidence in the substantial justice of the charges which I advanced against her, that I considered them to be a safeguard and an assurance that no harm could ever arise from the freest exposition of what I used to call Anglican principles. All the world was astounded at what Froude and I were saying: men said that it was sheer Popery. I answered, "True, we seem to be making straight for it; but go on awhile, and you will come to a deep chasm across the path, which makes real approximation impossible." And I urged in addition, that many Anglican divines had been accused of Popery, yet had died in their Anglicanism; — now, the ecclesiastical principles which I professed, they had professed also; and the judgment against Rome which they had formed, I had formed also. Whatever deficiencies then had to be supplied in the existing Anglican system, and however boldly I might point them out, any how that system would not in the process be brought nearer to the special creed of Rome, and might be mended in spite of her. In that very agreement of the two forms of faith, close as it might seem, would really be found, on examination, the elements and principles of an essential discordance.

It was with this absolute persuasion on my mind that I fancied that there could be no rashness in giving to the world in fullest measure the teaching and the writings of the Fathers. I thought that the Church of England was substantially founded upon them. I did not know all that the Fathers had said, but I felt that, even when their tenets happened to differ from the Anglican, no harm could come of reporting them. I said out what I was clear they had said; I spoke vaguely and imperfectly, of what I thought they said, or what some of them had said. Any how, no harm could come of bending the crooked stick the other way, in the process of straightening it; it was impossible to break it.[22] If there was any thing in the Fathers of a startling character, this would be only for a time; it would admit of explanation, or it might suggest something profitable to Anglicans; it could not lead to Rome. I express this view of the matter in a passage of the Preface to the first volume, which I edited, of the

---

those Anglican years his criticism of evangelical Protestantism and then later of mainstream historical Protestantism had been far more extensive and vitriolic than his critique of the Roman Catholic Church. See Frank M. Turner, *John Henry Newman: The Challenge to Evangelical Religion* (New Haven, Conn.: Yale Univ. Press, 2002), pp. 110–207, 255–292.

22. The metaphor of bending the stick meant that Newman believed the Church of England had been directed for a century far too much toward evangelical Protestantism and that to introduce the early Church Fathers was to bend it in the opposite direction.

Library of the Fathers.[23] Speaking of the strangeness at first sight, in the judgment of the present day, of some of their principles and opinions, I bid the reader go forward hopefully, and not indulge his criticism till he knows more about them, than he will learn at the outset. "Since the evil," I say, "is in the nature of the case itself, we can do no more than have patience, and recommend patience to others, and with the racer in the Tragedy, look forward steadily and hopefully to the *event,* τῷ τέλει πίστιν φέρων,[24] when, as we trust, all that is inharmonious and anomalous in the details, will at length be practically smoothed."

Such was the position, such the defences, such the tactics, by which I thought that it was both incumbent on us, and possible for us, to meet that onset of Liberal principles, of which we were all in immediate anticipation, whether in the Church or in the University. And during the first year of the Tracts, the attack upon the University began. In November, 1834, was sent to me by the author the second edition of a Pamphlet, entitled, "Observations on Religious Dissent, with particular reference to the use of religious tests in the University."[25] In this Pamphlet it was maintained, that "Religion is distinct from Theological Opinion," pp. 1. 28. 30, &c.; that it is but a common prejudice to identify theological propositions methodically deduced and stated, with the simple religion of Christ, p. 1; that under Theological Opinion were to be placed the Trinitarian doctrine, p. 27, and the Unitarian, p. 19; that a dogma was a theological opinion formally insisted on, pp. 20, 21; that speculation always left an opening for improvement, p. 22; that the Church of England was not dogmatic in its spirit, though the wording of its formularies might often carry the sound of dogmatism, p. 23.

---

23. The *Library of the Fathers of the Holy Catholic Church, Anterior to the Division of the East and the West* was a fifty-volume series of writings of the early Church Fathers instigated by E. B. Pusey in the mid-1830s. Its volumes were published from 1838 to 1885. Pusey initiated the series with the publication of St. Augustine's *Confessions,* thus bringing that classic back into circulation in England.

24. From Sophocles, *Electra,* line 735. Newman has translated the line in the clause before the quote.

25. In 1834 R. D. Hampden published *Observations on Religious Dissent* in which he advocated the admission of Dissenters, including Unitarians, into Oxford with the provision that they receive instruction in the faith and practice of the Church of England. Hampden wrote the pamphlet to gain favor with the Whig Party, which had introduced a bill in Parliament for the removal of religious tests in the universities. The bill failed. A long, deeply acrimonious conflict erupted in the university over Hampden, continuing into 1836 when at the time of his appointment as regius professor of divinity, Hampden was condemned by Oxford Convocation. See Turner, *John Henry Newman,* pp. 207–254.

I acknowledged the receipt of this work in the following letter:—

"The kindness which has led to your presenting me with your late Pamphlet, encourages me to hope that you will forgive me, if I take the opportunity it affords of expressing to you my very sincere and deep regret that it has been published. Such an opportunity I could not let slip without being unfaithful to my own serious thoughts on the subject.

"While I respect the tone of piety which the Pamphlet displays, I dare not trust myself to put on paper my feelings about the principles contained in it; tending as they do, in my opinion, altogether to make shipwreck of Christian faith.[26] I also lament, that, by its appearance, the first step has been taken towards interrupting that peace and mutual good understanding which has prevailed so long in this place, and which, if once seriously disturbed, will be succeeded by dissensions the more intractable, because justified in the minds of those who resist innovation by a feeling of imperative duty."

Since that time Phaeton has got into the chariot of the sun; we, alas! can only look on, and watch him down the steep of heaven. Meanwhile, the lands, which he is passing over, suffer from his driving.

Such was the commencement of the assault of Liberalism upon the old orthodoxy of Oxford and England; and it could not have been broken, as it was, for so long a time, had not a great change taken place in the circumstances of that counter-movement which had already started with the view of resisting it. For myself, I was not the person to take the lead of a party; I never was, from first to last, more than a leading author of a school; nor did I ever wish to be anything else.[27] This is my own account of the matter; and I say it, neither as

---

26. The phrase "a shipwreck of Christian faith" appeared in a letter of 1834 that Newman sent to Hampden. In a draft of that letter Newman had originally charged that Hampden's principles legitimately led to "formal Socinianism," but in the sent version he replaced that accusation with the vague phrase about making "a shipwreck of Christian faith." [Newman Microfilms, Yale University Library, Reel 95, Batch 140.] It is clear from Hampden's response that the word *Socinian* had not appeared in the letter he received. When Newman authorized the reprinting of this letter in 1871, *Socinian* did not appear in that reprinting. [Henry Wilberforce, "Dr. Hampden and Anglicanism," *Dublin Review* 69 (1871): 79.] In later reprintings of this letter, however, the word *Socinian* did appear, apparently as editors used the original manuscript of the unsent letter rather than looking to what Newman printed in the *Apologia*. See Anne Mozley, ed., *Letters and Correspondence of John Henry Newman during His Life in the English Church* (London: Longmans, Green, 1890), 2: 69, and Henry Parry Liddon, *Life of Edward Bouverie Pusey* (London: Longmans, Green, 1893), 1: 302. See also *L&D* 4:371, n4.

27. In this account Newman gives too modest a portrait of his role. He was the driving

intending to disown the responsibility of what was done, or as if ungrateful to those who at that time made more of me than I deserved, and did more for my sake and at my bidding than I realized myself. I am giving my history from my own point of sight, and it is as follows: — I had lived for ten years among my personal friends; the greater part of the time, I had been influenced, not influencing; and at no time have I acted on others, without their acting upon me. As is the custom of a University, I had lived with my private, nay, with some of my public, pupils, and with the junior fellows of my College, without form or distance, on a footing of equality. Thus it was through friends, younger, for the most part, than myself, that my principles were spreading. They heard what I said in conversation, and told it to others. Under-graduates in due time took their degree, and became private tutors themselves. In their new *status,* they in turn preached the opinions, with which they had already become acquainted. Others went down to the country, and became curates of parishes. Then they had down from London parcels of the Tracts, and other publications. They placed them in the shops of local booksellers, got them into newspapers, introduced them to clerical meetings, and converted more or less their Rectors and their brother curates. Thus the Movement, viewed with relation to myself, was but a floating opinion; it was not a power. It never would have been a power, if it had remained in my hands. Years after, a friend, writing to me in remonstrance at the excesses, as he thought them, of my disciples, applied to me my own verse about St. Gregory Nazianzen, "Thou couldst a people raise, but couldst not rule."[28] At the time that he wrote to me, I had special impediments in the way of such an exercise of power; but at no time could I exercise over others that authority, which under the circumstances was imperatively required. My great principle ever was, Live and let live. I never had the staidness or dignity necessary for a leader. To the last I never recognized the hold I had over young men. Of late years I have read and heard that they even imitated me in various ways. I was quite unconscious of it, and I think my immediate friends knew too well how disgusted I should be at such proceedings, to have the heart to tell me. I felt great impatience at our being called a

---

force of the movement against Hampden and wrote the most influential pamphlet attacking him, the anonymous *Elucidations of Dr. Hampden's Theological Statements* (Oxford: J. H. Parker, 1836). This pamphlet provided most members of Oxford Convocation and the press with the information upon which they based their criticism of Hampden. Upon actually reading Hamden's works after his condemnation, various of the people who had voted against him, including William Gladstone, Samuel Wilberforce, W. F. Hook, and Roundell Palmer, changed their minds and felt that they had been misled. See Turner, *John Henry Newman,* pp. 245–246.

28. St. Gregory Nazianzen (ca. 330–390) was bishop of Constantinople.

party, and would not allow that we were such. I had a lounging, free-and-easy way of carrying things on. I exercised no sufficient censorship upon the Tracts. I did not confine them to the writings of such persons as agreed in all things with myself; and, as to my own Tracts, I printed on them a notice to the effect, that any one who pleased, might make what use he would of them, and reprint them with alterations if he chose, under the conviction that their main scope could not be damaged by such a process. It was the same with me afterwards, as regards other publications. For two years I furnished a certain number of sheets for the British Critic from myself and my friends, while a gentleman was editor, a man of splendid talent, who, however, was scarcely an acquaintance of mine, and had no sympathy with the Tracts. When I was Editor myself, from 1838 to 1841, in my very first number I suffered to appear a critique unfavorable to my work on Justification, which had been published a few months before, from a feeling of propriety, because I had put the book into the hands of the writer who so handled it.[29] Afterwards I suffered an article against the Jesuits to appear in it, of which I did not like the tone. When I had to provide a curate for my new church at Littlemore, I engaged a friend, by no fault of his, who, before he had entered into his charge, preached a sermon, either in depreciation of baptismal regeneration, or of Dr. Pusey's view of it. I showed a similar easiness as to the Editors who helped me in the separate volumes of Fleury's Church History;[30] they were able, learned, and excellent men, but their after-history has shown, how little my choice of them was influenced by any notion I could have had of any intimate agreement of opinion between them and myself. I shall have to make the same remark in its place concerning the Lives of the English Saints, which subsequently appeared. All this may seem inconsistent with what I have said of my fierceness. I am not bound to account for it; but there have been men before me, fierce in act, yet tolerant and moderate in their reasonings; at least, so I read history. However, such was the case, and such its effect upon the Tracts. These at first starting were short, hasty, and some of them ineffective; and at the end of the year, when collected into a volume, they had a slovenly appearance.

It was under these circumstances, that Dr. Pusey joined us. I had known him well since 1827–8, and had felt for him an enthusiastic admiration. I used to

---

29. The *British Critic* from 1838 to 1843 became the chief journalistic organ for Tractarian opinion, first under Newman's editorship and from 1841 under that of his brother-in-law Thomas Mozley. See S. A. Skinner, "Newman, the Tractarians and the British Critic," *Journal of Ecclesiastical History* 50 (1999): 716–759.

30. "Fleury's Church History" refers to *Histoire Ecclésiastique* composed by Claude Fleury (1640–1723) between 1691 and 1720.

call him ὁ μέγας.³¹ His great learning, his immense diligence, his scholarlike mind, his simple devotion to the cause of religion, overcame me; and great of course was my joy, when in the last days of 1833 he showed a disposition to make common cause with us. His Tract on Fasting appeared as one of the series with the date of December 21. He was not, however, I think, fully associated in the Movement till 1835 and 1836, when he published his Tract on Baptism, and started the Library of the Fathers.³² He at once gave to us a position and a name. Without him we should have had little chance, especially at the early date of 1834, of making any serious resistance to the Liberal aggression. But Dr. Pusey was a Professor and Canon of Christ Church; he had a vast influence in consequence of his deep religious seriousness, the munificence of his charities, his Professorship, his family connexions, and his easy relations with University authorities. He was to the Movement all that Mr. Rose might have been, with that indispensable addition, which was wanting to Mr. Rose, the intimate friendship and the familiar daily society of the persons who had commenced it. And he had that special claim on their attachment, which lies in the living presence of a faithful and loyal affectionateness. There was henceforth a man who could be the head and centre of the zealous people in every part of the country, who were adopting the new opinions; and not only so, but there was one who furnished the Movement with a front to the world, and gained for it a recognition from other parties in the University. In 1829, Mr. Froude, or Mr. Robert Wilberforce, or Mr. Newman were but individuals; and, when they ranged themselves in the contest of that year on the side of Sir Robert Inglis,³³ men on either side only asked with surprise how they got there, and attached no significancy to the fact; but Dr. Pusey was, to use the common expression, a host in himself; he was able to give a name, a form, and a personality, to what was without him a sort of mob; and when various parties had to meet together in order to resist the liberal acts of the Government, we of the Movement took our place by right among them.

Such was the benefit which he conferred on the Movement externally; nor were the internal advantages at all inferior to it. He was a man of large designs; he had a hopeful, sanguine mind; he had no fear of others; he was haunted by no intellectual perplexities. People are apt to say that he was once nearer to the Catholic Church than he is now; I pray God that he may be one day far nearer to the Catholic Church than he was then; for I believe that, in his reason and

---

31. "the great one."
32. Pusey, unlike other authors of *Tracts for the Times,* signed his tracts.
33. Sir Robert Inglis (1786–1855) had defeated Sir Robert Peel in the 1829 Oxford election.

judgment, all the time that I knew him, he never was near to it at all. When I became a Catholic, I was often asked, "What of Dr. Pusey?" when I said that I did not see symptoms of his doing as I had done, I was sometimes thought uncharitable. If confidence in his position is, (as it is,) a first essential in the leader of a party, this Dr. Pusey possessed pre-eminently. The most remarkable instance of this, was his statement, in one of his subsequent defences of the Movement, when moreover it had advanced a considerable way in the direction of Rome, that among its more hopeful peculiarities was its "stationariness." He made it in good faith; it was his subjective view of it.

Dr. Pusey's influence was felt at once. He saw that there ought to be more sobriety, more gravity, more careful pains, more sense of responsibility in the Tracts and in the whole Movement. It was through him that the character of the Tracts was changed. When he gave to us his Tract on Fasting, he put his initials to it. In 1835 he published his elaborate Treatise on Baptism, which was followed by other Tracts from different authors, if not of equal learning, yet of equal power and appositeness. The Catenas of Anglican divines, projected by me, which occur in the Series, were executed with a like aim at greater accuracy and method.[34] In 1836 he advertised his great project for a Translation of the Fathers: — but I must return to myself. I am not writing the history either of Dr. Pusey or of the Movement; but it is a pleasure to me to have been able to introduce here reminiscences of the place which he held in it, which have so direct a bearing on myself, that they are no digression from my narrative.

I suspect it was Dr. Pusey's influence and example which set me, and made me set others, on the larger and more careful works in defence of the principles of the Movement which followed in a course of years, — some of them demanding and receiving from their authors, such elaborate treatment that they did not make their appearance till both its temper and its fortunes had changed. I set about a work at once; one in which was brought out with precision the relation in which we stood to the Church of Rome. We could not move a step in comfort, till this was done. It was of absolute necessity and a plain duty from the first, to provide as soon as possible a large statement, which would encourage and reassure our friends, and repel the attacks of our opponents. A cry was heard on all sides of us, that the Tracts and the writings of the Fathers would lead us to become Catholics, before we were aware of it.

34. The Catenas of Anglican divines were collections of writings from earlier Anglican clergy with whom the Tractarians agreed. They appeared as *Tracts 74* and *76*. The contents of both tracts was edited in a highly selective manner.

This was loudly expressed by members of the Evangelical party, who in 1836 had joined us in making a protest in Convocation against a memorable appointment of the Prime Minister.[35] These clergymen even then avowed their desire, that the next time they were brought up to Oxford to give a vote, it might be in order to put down the Popery of the Movement. There was another reason still, and quite as important. Monsignore Wiseman, with the acuteness and zeal which might be expected from that great Prelate, had anticipated what was coming, had returned to England by 1836, had delivered Lectures in London on the doctrines of Catholicism, and created an impression through the country, shared in by ourselves, that we had for our opponents in controversy, not only our brethren, but our hereditary foes.[36] These were the circumstances, which led to my publication of "The Prophetical office of the Church viewed relatively to Romanism and Popular Protestantism."[37]

This work employed me for three years, from the beginning of 1834 to the end of 1836, and was published in 1837. It was composed, after a careful consideration and comparison of the principal Anglican divines of the 17th century. It was first written in the shape of controversial correspondence with a learned French Priest; then it was re-cast, and delivered in Lectures at St. Mary's; lastly, with considerable retrenchments and additions, it was re-written for publication.

It attempts to trace out the rudimental lines on which Christian faith and teaching proceed, and to use them as means of determining the relation of the Roman and Anglican systems to each other. In this way it shows that to confuse the two together is impossible, and that the Anglican can be as little said to tend to the Roman, as the Roman to the Anglican. The spirit of the Volume is not so gentle to the Church of Rome, as Tract 71 published the year before; on the contrary, it is very fierce; and this I attribute to the circumstance that the Volume is theological and didactic, whereas the Tract, being contro-

---

35. In 1836 evangelicals had joined the Tractarians to condemn the appointment of R. D. Hampden as regius professor. They very soon thereafter distanced themselves from this action.

36. Nicholas Wiseman's lectures of 1835 and 1836 appeared as *Lectures on the Principal Doctrines and Practices of the Catholic Church* (1836). Before these lectures the Tractarians appeared to have believed that they did not need to confront Roman Catholicism. Once Wiseman had made his views known to an English audience, the Tractarians had to distinguish between their Catholicism and Roman Catholicism.

37. Newman's *Prophetical Office of the Church: Viewed Relatively to Romanism and Popular Protestantism* (1837) is regarded as his most important statement of the position he termed the via media. See the discussion of Newman's use of this concept in the introduction to this volume.

versial, assumes as little and grants as much as possible on the points in dispute, and insists on points of agreement as well as of difference. A further and more direct reason is, that in my Volume I deal with "Romanism" (as I call it), not so much in its formal decrees and in the substance of its creed, as in its traditional action and its authorized teaching as represented by its prominent writers; — whereas the Tract is written as if discussing the differences of the Churches with a view to a reconciliation between them. There is a further reason too, which I will state presently.

But this Volume had a larger scope than that of opposing the Roman system. It was an attempt at commencing a system of theology on the Anglican idea, and based upon Anglican authorities.[38] Mr. Palmer, about the same time, was projecting a work of a similar nature in his own way. It was published, I think, under the title, "A Treatise on the Christian Church."[39] As was to be expected from the author, it was a most learned, most careful composition; and in its form, I should say, polemical. So happily at least did he follow the logical method of the Roman Schools, that Father Perrone in his Treatise on dogmatic theology, recognized in him a combatant of the true cast, and saluted him as a foe worthy of being vanquished.[40] Other soldiers in that field he seems to have thought little better than the *Lanzknechts* of the middle ages, and, I dare say, with very good reason. When I knew that excellent and kind-hearted man at Rome at a later time, he allowed me to put him to ample penance for those light thoughts of me, which he had once had, by encroaching on his valuable time with my theological questions. As to Mr. Palmer's book, it was one which no Anglican could write but himself, — in no sense, if I recollect aright, a tentative work. The ground of controversy was cut into squares, and then every objection had its answer. This is the proper method to adopt in teaching authoritatively young men; and the work in fact was intended for students in theology. My own book, on the other hand, was of a directly tentative and empirical character. I wished to build up an Anglican theology out of the

---

38. Although here Newman emphasizes the anti-Roman aspects of his *Prophetical Office of the Church,* far more of the volume attacks evangelical Protestantism. At the time of the publication of the book he wrote to his sister Jemima that his forthcoming remarks about evangelicals were "so strong that everything I have as yet said is milk and water to it," resembling the "difference between drifting snow and a hard snow ball," and, he thought, would have an effect "like hitting the Peculiars, etc. a most uncommon blow in the face." JHN to Jemima Mozley, January 5, 1837, *L&D* 6: 6. See also JHN to F. Rogers, January 7, 1837, *L&D* 6: 8.

39. William Palmer's volume was *A Treatise on the Church of Christ* (London, 1838).

40. Giovanni Perrone (1794–1876) was a Jesuit who taught Roman Catholic theology in Rome.

stores which already lay cut and hewn upon the ground, the past toil of great divines. To do this could not be the work of one man; much less, could it be at once received into Anglican theology, however well it was done. This I fully recognized; and, while I trusted that my statements of doctrine would turn out to be true and important, still I wrote, to use the common phrase, "under correction."

There was another motive for my publishing, of a personal nature, which I think I should mention. I felt then, and all along felt, that there was an intellectual cowardice in not finding a basis in reason for my belief, and a moral cowardice in not avowing that basis. I should have felt myself less than a man, if I did not bring it out, whatever it was. This is one principal reason why I wrote and published the "Prophetical Office." It was from the same feeling, that in the spring of 1836, at a meeting of residents on the subject of the struggle then proceeding against a Whig appointment,[41] when some one wanted us all merely to act on college and conservative grounds (as I understood him), with as few published statements as possible, I answered, that the person whom we were resisting had committed himself in writing, and that we ought to commit ourselves too. This again was a main reason for the publication of Tract 90. Alas! it was my portion for whole years to remain without any satisfactory basis for my religious profession, in a state of moral sickness, neither able to acquiesce in Anglicanism, nor able to go to Rome. But I bore it, till in course of time my way was made clear to me. If here it be objected to me, that as time went on, I often in my writings hinted at things which I did not fully bring out, I submit for consideration whether this occurred except when I was in great difficulties, how to speak, or how to be silent, with due regard for the position of mind or the feelings of others. However, I may have an opportunity to say more on this subject. But to return to the "Prophetical Office."

I thus speak in the Introduction to my Volume: —

"It is proposed," I say, "to offer helps towards the formation of a recognized Anglican theology in one of its departments. The present state of our divinity is as follows: the most vigorous, the clearest, the most fertile minds, have through God's mercy been employed in the service of our Church: minds too as reverential and holy, and as fully imbued with Ancient Truth, and as well versed in the writings of the Fathers, as they were intellectually gifted. This is God's great mercy indeed, for which we must ever be thankful. Primitive doctrine has been explored for us in every direction, and the original principles of the Gospel and the Church patiently brought to light. But one thing is still wanting: our champions and teachers have lived in stormy times: political and

---

41. The Whig appointment refers to R. D. Hampden.

other influences have acted upon them variously in their day, and have since obstructed a careful consolidation of their judgments. We have a vast inheritance, but no inventory of our treasures. All is given us in profusion; it remains for us to catalogue, sort, distribute, select, harmonize, and complete. We have more than we know how to use; stores of learning, but little that is precise and serviceable; Catholic truth and individual opinion, first principles and the guesses of genius, all mingled in the same works, and requiring to be discriminated. We meet with truths overstated or misdirected, matters of detail variously taken, facts incompletely proved or applied, and rules inconsistently urged or discordantly interpreted. Such indeed is the state of every deep philosophy in its first stages, and therefore of theological knowledge. What we need at present for our Church's well-being, is not invention, nor originality, nor sagacity, nor even learning in our divines, at least in the first place, though all gifts of God are in a measure needed, and never can be unseasonable when used religiously, but we need peculiarly a sound judgment, patient thought, discrimination, a comprehensive mind, an abstinence from all private fancies and caprices and personal tastes, — in a word, Divine Wisdom."

The subject of the Volume is the doctrine of the *Via Media*, a name which had already been applied to the Anglican system by writers of name. It is an expressive title, but not altogether satisfactory, because it is at first sight negative. This had been the reason of my dislike to the word "Protestant;" viz. it did not denote the profession of any particular religion at all, and was compatible with infidelity. A *Via Media* was but a receding from extremes, — therefore it needed to be drawn out into a definite shape and character: before it could have claims on our respect, it must first be shown to be one, intelligible, and consistent. This was the first condition of any reasonable treatise on the *Via Media*. The second condition, and necessary too, was not in my power. I could only hope that it would one day be fulfilled. Even if the *Via Media* were ever so positive a religious system, it was not as yet objective and real; it had no original any where of which it was the representative. It was at present a paper religion. This I confess in my Introduction; I say, "Protestantism and Popery are real religions . . . but the *Via Media*, viewed as an integral system, has scarcely had existence except on paper." I grant the objection, though I endeavour to lessen it: — "It still remains to be tried, whether what is called Anglo-Catholicism, the religion of Andrewes, Laud, Hammond, Butler, and Wilson,[42] is capable of being professed, acted on, and maintained on a large

---

42. Lancelot Andrewes (1555–1626), Henry Hammond (1605–1660), and Thomas Wilson (1663–1755), along with William Laud and Joseph Butler, stood among those earlier Anglican divines whom Newman and other Tractarians saw as their predecessors.

sphere of action, or whether it be a mere modification or transition-state of either Romanism or popular Protestantism." I trusted that some day it would prove to be a substantive religion.

Lest I should be misunderstood, let me observe that this hesitation about the validity of the theory of the *Via Media* implied no doubt of the three fundamental points on which it was based, as I have described them above, dogma, the sacramental system, and anti-Romanism.

Other investigations which had to be followed up were of a still more tentative character. The basis of the *Via Media*, consisting of the three elementary points, which I have just mentioned, was clear enough; but, not only had the house itself to be built upon them, but it had also to be furnished, and it is not wonderful if, after building it, both I and others erred in detail in determining what its furniture should be, what was consistent with the style of building, and what was in itself desirable. I will explain what I mean.

I had brought out in the "Prophetical Office" in what the Roman and the Anglican systems differed from each other, but less distinctly in what they agreed. I had indeed enumerated the Fundamentals, common to both, in the following passage:—"In both systems the same Creeds are acknowledged. Besides other points in common, we both hold, that certain doctrines are necessary to be believed for salvation; we both believe in the doctrines of the Trinity, Incarnation, and Atonement; in original sin; in the necessity of regeneration; in the supernatural grace of the Sacraments; in the Apostolical succession; in the obligation of faith and obedience, and in the eternity of future punishment,"—pp. 55, 56. So much I had said, but I had not said enough. This enumeration implied a great many more points of agreement than were found in those very Articles which were fundamental. If the two Churches were thus the same in fundamentals, they were also one and the same in such plain consequences as were contained in those fundamentals and in such natural observances as outwardly represented them. It was an Anglican principle that "the abuse of a thing doth not take away the lawful use of it;" and an Anglican Canon in 1603 had declared that the English Church had no purpose to forsake all that was held in the Churches of Italy, France, and Spain, and reverenced those ceremonies and particular points which were Apostolic. Excepting then such exceptional matters, as are implied in this avowal, whether they were many or few, all these Churches were evidently to be considered as one with the Anglican. The Catholic Church in all lands had been one from the first for many centuries; then, various portions had followed their own way to the injury, but not to the destruction, whether of truth or of charity. These portions or branches were mainly three:—the Greek,

Latin, and Anglican.[43] Each of these inherited the early undivided Church *in solido* as its own possession. Each branch was identical with that early undivided Church, and in the unity of that Church it had unity with the other branches. The three branches agreed together in *all but* their later accidental errors. Some branches had retained in detail portions of Apostolical truth and usage, which the others had not; and these portions might be and should be appropriated again by the others which had let them slip. Thus, the middle age belonged to the Anglican Church, and much more did the middle age of England. The Church of the 12th century was the Church of the 19th. Dr. Howley sat in the seat of St. Thomas the Martyr;[44] Oxford was a medieval University. Saving our engagements to Prayer Book and Articles, we might breathe and live and act and speak, as in the atmosphere and climate of Henry III.'s day, or the Confessor's, or of Alfred's. And we ought to be indulgent to all that Rome taught now, as to what Rome taught then, saving our protest. We might boldly welcome, even what we did not ourselves think right to adopt. And, when we were obliged on the contrary boldly to denounce, we should do so with pain, not with exultation. By very reason of our protest, which we had made, and made *ex animo,* we could agree to differ. What the members of the Bible Society did on the basis of Scripture, we could do on the basis of the Church; Trinitarian and Unitarian were further apart than Roman and Anglican. Thus we had a real wish to co-operate with Rome in all lawful things, if she would let us, and if the rules of our own Church let us; and we thought there was no better way towards the restoration of doctrinal purity and unity. And we thought that Rome was not committed by her formal decrees to all that she actually taught: and again, if her disputants had been unfair to us, or her rulers tyrannical, we bore in mind that on our side too there had been rancour and slander in our controversial attacks upon her, and violence in our political measures. As to ourselves being direct instruments in

---

43. Within high church theology there existed what was known as the *branch theory* of the church. This theory held that because of its possession of apostolic succession, the Church of England, like the Roman Catholic Church and the Orthodox Church, was a branch of the Holy Catholic and Apostolic Church.

44. William Howley (1766–1848) was archbishop of Canterbury from 1828 to 1848. Although he had resisted the Reform Act and the Irish Temporalities Act, Howley nonetheless extended little sympathy to the Tractarian cause and demanded that the tracts cease being published after the appearance of *Tract 90*. See James Garrard, "Archbishop Howley and the Oxford Movement," in *From Oxford to the People: Reconsidering Newman & the Oxford Movement,* ed. Paul Vaiss (Leominster: Gracewing, 1996), pp. 255–268.

improving her belief or practice, I used to say, "Look at home; let us first, (or at least let us the while,) supply our own shortcomings, before we attempt to be physicians to any one else." This is very much the spirit of Tract 71, to which I referred just now. I am well aware that there is a paragraph inconsistent with it in the Prospectus to the Library of the Fathers; but I do not consider myself responsible for it. Indeed, I have no intention whatever of implying that Dr. Pusey concurred in the ecclesiastical theory, which I have been now drawing out; nor that I took it up myself except by degrees in the course of ten years. It was necessarily the growth of time. In fact, hardly any two persons, who took part in the Movement, agreed in their view of the limit to which our general principles might religiously be carried.

And now I have said enough on what I consider to have been the general objects of the various works, which I wrote, edited, or prompted in the years which I am reviewing. I wanted to bring out in a substantive form a living Church of England, in a position proper to herself, and founded on distinct principles; as far as paper could do it, as far as earnestly preaching it and influencing others towards it, could tend to make it a fact; — a living Church, made of flesh and blood, with voice, complexion, and motion and action, and a will of its own. I believe I had no private motive, and no personal aim. Nor did I ask for more than "a fair stage and no favour," nor expect the work would be accomplished in my days; but I thought that enough would be secured to continue it in the future, under, perhaps, more hopeful circumstances and prospects than the present.

I will mention in illustration some of the principal works, doctrinal and historical, which originated in the object which I have stated.[45]

I wrote my Essay on Justification in 1837; it was aimed at the Lutheran dictum that justification by faith only was the cardinal doctrine of Christianity. I considered that this doctrine was either a paradox or a truism, — a paradox in Luther's mouth, a truism in Melanchthon's. I thought that the Anglican Church followed Melanchthon, and that in consequence between Rome and Anglicanism, between high Church and low Church, there was no real intellectual difference on the point. I wished to fill up a ditch, the work of man. In this Volume again, I express my desire to build up a system of theology out of the Anglican divines, and imply that my dissertation was a tentative

---

45. In this passage Newman casually lists some of his most remarkable and substantial works of theology and polemic, which constitute a major portion of his statement of his religious and theological opinion while in the Church of England. It is remarkable that in a work on the history of his religious opinions he writes so little about this body of his thought.

Inquiry. I speak in the Preface of "offering suggestions towards a work, which must be uppermost in the mind of every true son of the English Church at this day, — the consolidation of a theological system, which, built upon those formularies, to which all clergymen are bound, may tend to inform, persuade, and absorb into itself religious minds, which hitherto have fancied, that, on the peculiar Protestant questions, they were seriously opposed to each other." — P. vii.

In my University Sermons there is a series of discussions upon the subject of Faith and Reason; these again were the tentative commencement of a grave and necessary work, viz. an inquiry into the ultimate basis of religious faith, prior to the distinction into Creeds.

In like manner in a Pamphlet, which I published in the summer of 1838, is an attempt at placing the doctrine of the Real Presence on an intellectual basis. The fundamental idea is consonant to that to which I had been so long attached: it is the denial of the existence of space except as a subjective idea of our minds.

The Church of the Fathers is one of the earliest productions of the Movement, and appeared in numbers in the British Magazine, being written with the aim of introducing the religious sentiments, views, and customs of the first ages into the modern Church of England.

The Translation of Fleury's Church History was commenced under these circumstances: — I was fond of Fleury for a reason which I express in the Advertisement; because it presented a sort of photograph of ecclesiastical history without any comment upon it. In the event, that simple representation of the early centuries had a good deal to do with unsettling me in my Anglicanism; but how little I could anticipate this, will be seen in the fact that the publication of Fleury was a favourite scheme with Mr. Rose. He proposed it to me twice, between the years 1834 and 1837; and I mention it as one out of many particulars curiously illustrating how truly my change of opinion arose, not from foreign influences, but from the working of my own mind, and the accidents around me. The date, from which the portion actually translated began, was determined by the Publisher on reasons with which we were not concerned.

Another historical work, but drawn from original sources, was given to the world by my old friend Mr. Bowden, being a Life of Pope Gregory VII. I need scarcely recall to those who have read it, the power and the liveliness of the narrative. This composition was the author's relaxation, on evenings and in his summer vacations, from his ordinary engagements in London. It had been suggested to him originally by me, at the instance of Hurrell Froude.

The Series of the Lives of the English Saints was projected at a later period, under circumstances which I shall have in the sequel to describe.[46] Those beautiful compositions have nothing in them, as far as I recollect, simply inconsistent with the general objects which I have been assigning to my labours in these years, though the immediate occasion which led to them, and the tone in which they were written, had little that was congenial with Anglicanism.

At a comparatively early date I drew up the Tract on the Roman Breviary.[47] It frightened my own friends on its first appearance; and several years afterwards, when younger men began to translate for publication the four volumes *in extenso,* they were dissuaded from doing so by advice to which from a sense of duty they listened. It was an apparent accident, which introduced me to the knowledge of that most wonderful and most attractive monument of the devotion of saints. On Hurrell Froude's death, in 1836, I was asked to select one of his books as a keepsake. I selected Butler's Analogy; finding that it had been already chosen, I looked with some perplexity along the shelves as they stood before me, when an intimate friend at my elbow said, "Take that." It was the Breviary which Hurrell had had with him at Barbadoes. Accordingly I took it, studied it, wrote my Tract from it, and have it on my table in constant use till this day.

That dear and familiar companion, who thus put the Breviary into my hands, is still in the Anglican Church. So, too, is that early venerated long-loved friend, together with whom I edited a work which, more perhaps than any other, caused disturbance and annoyance in the Anglican world,—Froude's Remains;[48] yet, however judgments might run as to the prudence of publishing it, I never heard any one impute to Mr. Keble the very shadow of dishonesty or treachery towards his Church in so acting.

The annotated Translation of the Treatises of St. Athanasius was of course in no sense of a tentative character; it belongs to another order of thought. This historico-dogmatic work employed me for years. I had made preparations for following it up with a doctrinal history of the heresies which succeeded to the Arian.

I should make mention also of the British Critic. I was Editor of it for three

---

46. On *Lives of the English Saints,* see pp. 27 and 356–357 of this volume.

47. See Donald A. Withey, *John Henry Newman: The Liturgy and the Breviary, Their Influence on His Life as an Anglican* (London: Sheed and Ward, 1992) for an excellent discussion of the breviary in Newman's Tractarian thought and devotional life.

48. *The Remains of the Late Reverend Richard Hurrell Froude* (4 vols., 1838–1839), with diaries of Froude's ascetic spiritual observances and with writings critical of the English Reformation and sympathetic toward Roman Catholicism, proved to be one of the chief turning points in the Tractarian Movement and cost the Tractarians the support of many Anglican high churchmen.

years, from July 1838 to July 1841. My writers belonged to various schools, some to none at all. The subjects are various, — classical, academical, political, critical, and artistic, as well as theological, and upon the Movement none are to be found which do not keep quite clear of advocating the cause of Rome.

So I went on for years up to 1841. It was, in a human point of view, the happiest time of my life. I was truly at home. I had in one of my volumes appropriated to myself the words of Bramhall, "Bees, by the instinct of nature, do love their hives, and birds their nests." I did not suppose that such sunshine would last, though I knew not what would be its termination. It was the time of plenty, and, during its seven years, I tried to lay up as much as I could for the dearth which was to follow it. We prospered and spread. I have spoken of the doings of these years, since I was a Catholic, in a passage, part of which I will here quote:

"From beginnings so small," I said, "from elements of thought so fortuitous, with prospects so unpromising, the Anglo-Catholic party suddenly became a power in the National Church, and an object of alarm to her rulers and friends. Its originators would have found it difficult to say what they aimed at of a practical kind: rather, they put forth views and principles for their own sake, because they were true, as if they were obliged to say them; and, as they might be themselves surprised at their earnestness in uttering them, they had as great cause to be surprised at the success which attended their propagation. And, in fact, they could only say that those doctrines were in the air; that to assert was to prove, and that to explain was to persuade; and that the Movement in which they were taking part was the birth of a crisis rather than of a place. In a very few years a school of opinion was formed, fixed in its principles, indefinite and progressive in their range; and it extended itself into every part of the country. If we inquire what the world thought of it, we have still more to raise our wonder; for, not to mention the excitement it caused in England, the Movement and its party-names were known to the police of Italy and to the back-woodmen of America. And so it proceeded, getting stronger and stronger every year, till it came into collision with the Nation, and that Church of the Nation, which it began by professing especially to serve."

The greater its success, the nearer was that collision at hand. The first threatenings of what was coming were heard in 1838. At that time, my Bishop in a Charge made some light animadversions, but they *were* animadversions, on the Tracts for the Times.[49] At once I offered to stop them. What took place

---

49. In his Triennial Charge of August 14, 1838, Bishop Richard Bagot had commented in regard to the Tractarian Movement then beginning to move in a more radical direction:

on the occasion I prefer to state in the words, in which I related it in a Pamphlet addressed to him in a later year, when the blow actually came down upon me.

"In your Lordship's Charge for 1838," I said, "an allusion was made to the Tracts for the Times. Some opponents of the Tracts said that you treated them with undue indulgence.... I wrote to the Archdeacon on the subject, submitting the Tracts entirely to your Lordship's disposal. What I thought about your Charge will appear from the words I then used to him. I said, 'A Bishop's lightest word *ex cathedrâ* is heavy. His judgment on a book cannot be light. It is a rare occurrence.' And I offered to withdraw any of the Tracts over which I had control, if I were informed which were those to which your Lordship had objections. I afterwards wrote to your Lordship to this effect, that 'I trusted I might say sincerely, that I should feel a more lively pleasure in knowing that I was submitting myself to your Lordship's expressed judgment in a matter of that kind, than I could have even in the widest circulation of the volumes in question.' Your Lordship did not think it necessary to proceed to such a measure, but I felt, and always have felt, that, if ever you determined on it, I was bound to obey."

That day at length came, and I conclude this portion of my narrative, with relating the circumstances of it.

From the time that I had entered upon the duties of Public Tutor at my College, when my doctrinal views were very different from what they were in 1841, I had meditated a comment upon the Articles. Then, when the Movement was in its swing, friends had said to me, "What will you make of the Articles?" but I did not share the apprehension which their question implied.[50]

"I have more fear of the Disciples than of the Teachers. In speaking therefore of the Authors of the Tracts in question, I would say, that I think their desire to restore the ancient discipline of the Church most praiseworthy; I rejoice in their attempts to secure a stricter attention to the Rubrical directions in the Book of Common Prayer; and I heartily approve the spirit which would restore a due observance of the Fasts and Festivals of the Church; *but* I would implore them, by the purity of their intentions, to be cautious, both in their writings and actions, to take heed lest their good be evil spoken of; lest in their exertions to re-establish unity, they unhappily create fresh schism; lest in their admiration of antiquity, they revert to practices which heretofore have ended in superstition." (Bagot quoted in *L&D* 6: 285–286.)

50. The "Articles" refer to the Thirty-Nine Articles of the Church of England. There had been several statements of such articles in the course of the English Reformation. The articles were finalized at the number of thirty-nine in 1562. The content of those articles has generally been considered more distinctly Protestant and reflective of the continental Reformation than the contents of the Church of England Book of Common Prayer.

Whether, as time went on, I should have been forced, by the necessities of the original theory of the Movement, to put on paper the speculations which I had about them, I am not able to conjecture. The actual cause of my doing so, in the beginning of 1841, was the restlessness, actual and prospective, of those who neither liked the *Via Media*, nor my strong judgment against Rome. I had been enjoined, I think by my Bishop, to keep these men straight, and I wished so to do: but their tangible difficulty was subscription to the Articles; and thus the question of the Articles came before me. It was thrown in our teeth; "How can you manage to sign the Articles? they are directly against Rome." "Against Rome?" I made answer, "What do you mean by 'Rome?'" and then I proceeded to make distinctions, of which I shall now give an account.

By "Roman doctrine" might be meant one of three things: 1, the *Catholic teaching* of the early centuries; or 2, the *formal dogmas of Rome* as contained in the later Councils, especially the Council of Trent, and as condensed in the Creed of Pope Pius IV.;[51] 3, the *actual popular beliefs and usages* sanctioned by Rome in the countries in communion with it, over and above the dogmas; and these I called "dominant errors." Now Protestants commonly thought that in all three senses, "Roman doctrine" was condemned in the Articles: I thought that the *Catholic teaching* was not condemned; that the *dominant errors* were; and as to the *formal dogmas*, that some were, some were not, and that the line had to be drawn between them. Thus, 1. The use of Prayers for the dead was a Catholic doctrine, — not condemned in the Articles; 2. The prison of Purgatory was a Roman dogma, — which was condemned in them; but the infallibility of Ecumenical Councils was a Roman dogma, — not condemned; and 3. The fire of Purgatory was an authorized and popular error, not a dogma, — which was condemned.

Further, I considered that the difficulties, felt by the persons whom I have mentioned, mainly lay in their mistaking, 1, Catholic teaching, which was not condemned in the Articles, for Roman dogma which was condemned; and 2, Roman dogma, which was not condemned in the Articles, for dominant

---

Before 1865 Church of England clergy at the time of ordination were required to subscribe to the articles; thereafter, they have been required to affirm that the articles conform to the Word of God. Students matriculating at Oxford during the Tractarian era and after were required to subscribe to the Thirty-Nine Articles. During the 1830s and 1840s enormous conflict occurred within Oxford University over the propriety of continuing the requirement of subscription at the time of matriculation, over the historically situated character of the articles, and after Newman's *Tract 90* over the meaning of the articles.

51. The Creed of Pope Pius IV, consisting of twelve articles, was the creed drawn up to convey the decisions and doctrines set forth by the Council of Trent. Roman Catholic priests and converts were expected to accept this creed.

error which was. If they went further than this, I had nothing more to say to them.

A further motive which I had for my attempt, was the desire to ascertain the ultimate points of contrariety between the Roman and Anglican creeds, and to make them as few as possible. I thought that each creed was obscured and misrepresented by a dominant circumambient "Popery" and "Protestantism."

The main thesis then of my Essay was this: — the Articles do not oppose Catholic teaching; they but partially oppose Roman dogma; they for the most part oppose the dominant errors of Rome. And the problem was, as I have said, to draw the line as to what they allowed and what they condemned.[52]

Such being the object which I had in view, what were my prospects of widening and of defining their meaning? The prospect was encouraging; there was no doubt at all of the elasticity of the Articles; to take a palmary instance, the seventeenth was assumed by one party to be Lutheran, by another Calvinistic, though the two interpretations were contradictory of each other; why then should not other Articles be drawn up with a vagueness of an equally intense character? I wanted to ascertain what was the limit of that elasticity in the direction of Roman dogma. But next, I had a way of inquiry of my own, which I state without defending. I instanced it afterwards in my Essay on Doctrinal Development.[53] That work, I believe, I have not read since I published it, and I do not doubt at all I have made many mistakes in it; — partly, from my ignorance of the details of doctrine, as the Church of Rome holds them, but partly from my impatience to clear as large a range for the *principle* of doctrinal Development (waiving the question of historical *fact*) as was consistent with the strict Apostolicity and identity of the Catholic Creed. In like manner, as regards the 39 Articles, my method of inquiry was to leap *in medias res*. I wished to institute an inquiry how far, in critical fairness, the text *could* be opened; I was aiming far more at ascertaining what a man who subscribed it might hold than what he must, so that my conclusions were

---

52. In this passage Newman provides a summary of his general argument in *Tract 90*. Even some non-Tractarians who might have agreed with his argument broadly construed completely rejected the specific arguments he made in support of that broader argument. In particular, he said the articles were not to be interpreted according to the intention of their composers. The Tractarians themselves very quickly became sharply divided over the meaning and advisability of the tract. See Peter Nockles, "Oxford, Tract 90 and the Bishops," in *John Henry Newman: Reason, Rhetoric and Romanticism*, ed. David Nicholls and Fergus Kerr (Carbondale and Edwardsville: Southern Illinois Univ. Press, 1991), pp. 28–87; Turner, *John Henry Newman*, pp. 358–382.

53. Newman published *An Essay on the Development of Christian Doctrine* (London: J. Toovey, 1845) in late 1845 after entering the Roman Catholic Church.

Chapter II 199

negative rather than positive. It was but a first essay. And I made it with the full recognition and consciousness, which I had already expressed in my Prophetical Office, as regards the *Via Media*, that I was making only "a first approximation to the required solution;" — "a series of illustrations supplying hints for the removal" of a difficulty, and with full acknowledgment "that in minor points, whether in question of fact or of judgment, there was room for difference or error of opinion," and that I "should not be ashamed to own a mistake, if it were proved against me, nor reluctant to bear the just blame of it." — Proph. Off. p. 31.

I will add, I was embarrassed in consequence of my wish to go as far as was possible in interpreting the Articles in the direction of Roman dogma, without disclosing what I was doing to the parties whose doubts I was meeting; who, if they understood at once the full extent of the licence which the Articles admitted, might be thereby encouraged to proceed still further than at present they found in themselves any call to go.

1. But in the way of such an attempt comes the prompt objection that the Articles were actually drawn up against "Popery," and therefore it was transcendently absurd and dishonest to suppose that Popery, in any shape, — patristic belief, Tridentine dogma, or popular corruption authoritatively sanctioned, — would be able to take refuge under their text. This premiss I denied. Not any religious doctrine at all, but a political principle, was the primary English idea of "Popery" at the date of the Reformation. And what was that political principle, and how could it best be suppressed in England? What was the great question in the days of Henry and Elizabeth? The *Supremacy;* — now, was I saying one single word in favour of the Supremacy of the Holy See, in favour of the foreign jurisdiction? No; I did not believe in it myself. Did Henry VIII. religiously hold Justification by faith only? did he disbelieve Purgatory? Was Elizabeth zealous for the marriage of the Clergy? or had she a conscience against the Mass? The Supremacy of the Pope was the essence of the "Popery" to which, at the time of the composition of the Articles, the Supreme Head or Governor of the English Church was so violently hostile.

2. But again I said this: — let "Popery" mean what it would in the mouths of the compilers of the Articles, let it even, for argument's sake, include the doctrines of that Tridentine Council, which was not yet over when the Articles were drawn up, and against which they could not be simply directed, yet, consider, what was the object of the Government in their imposition? merely to get rid of "Popery?" No; it had the further object of gaining the "Papists." What then was the best way to induce reluctant or wavering minds, and these, I supposed, were the majority, to give in their adhesion to the new symbol? how had the Arians drawn up their Creeds? was it not on the principle of using

vague ambiguous language, which to the subscribers would seem to bear a Catholic sense, but which, when worked out on the long run, would prove to be heterodox? Accordingly, there was great antecedent probability, that, fierce as the Articles might look at first sight, their bark would prove worse than their bite. I say antecedent probability, for to what extent that surmise might be true, could only be ascertained by investigation.

3. But a consideration came up at once, which threw light on this surmise: — what if it should turn out that the very men who drew up the Articles, in the very act of doing so, had avowed, or rather in one of those very Articles themselves had imposed on subscribers, a number of those very "Papistical" doctrines, which they were now thought to deny, as part and parcel of that very Protestantism, which they were now thought to consider divine? and this was the fact, and I showed it in my Essay.

Let the reader observe: — the 35th Article says: "The second Book of Homilies doth contain *a godly and wholesome doctrine, and necessary for* these times, as doth the former Book of Homilies."[54] Here the *doctrine* of the Homilies is recognized as godly and wholesome, and concurrence in that recognition is imposed on all subscribers of the Articles. Let us then turn to the Homilies, and see what this godly doctrine is; I quoted from them to the following effect:

1. They declare that the so-called "apocryphal" book of Tobit is the teaching of the Holy Ghost, and is Scripture.

2. That the so-called "apocryphal" book of Wisdom is Scripture, and the infallible and undeceivable word of God.

3. That the Primitive Church, next to the Apostles' time, and, as they imply, for almost 700 years, is no doubt most pure.

4. That the Primitive Church is specially to be followed.

5. That the Four first General Councils belong to the Primitive Church.

6. That there are Six Councils which are allowed and received by all men.

7. Again, they speak of a certain truth which they are enforcing, as declared by God's word, the sentences of the ancient doctors, and judgment of the Primitive Church.

---

54. The Books of Homilies were sets of sixteenth-century sermons intended for the use of clergy who had difficulty in composing their own sermons. They are commended in the Thirty-Nine Articles. In the *Apologia* Newman indicates the religious views and doctrines that he deduced from quotations from the homilies. In *Tract 90,* however, the supporting quotations were extremely brief and widely considered to be often taken out of context. His use of those quotations was the subject of much of the criticism of his rhetorical tactics in *Tract 90.* Within the *Apologia* Newman does not cite any of his far more tendentious claims in the tract regarding various of the other articles.

8. Of the learned and holy Bishops and doctors of the Church of the first eight centuries being of great authority and credit with the people.

9. Of the declaration of Christ and His Apostles and all the rest of the Holy Fathers.

10. Of the authority both of Scripture and also of Augustine.

11. Of Augustine, Chrysostom, Ambrose, Jerome, and about thirty other Fathers, to some of whom they give the title of "Saint," to others of "ancient Catholic Fathers and doctors, &c."

12. They declare that, not only the holy Apostles and disciples of Christ, but the godly Fathers also, before and since Christ, were endued without doubt with the Holy Ghost.

13. That the ancient Catholic Fathers say that the "Lord's Supper" is the salve of immortality, the sovereign preservative against death, the food of immortality, the healthful grace.

14. That the Lord's Blessed Body and Blood are received under the form of bread and wine.

15. That the meat in the Sacrament is an invisible meat and a ghostly substance.

16. That the holy Body and Blood of thy God ought to be touched with the mind.

17. That Ordination is a Sacrament.

18. That Matrimony is a Sacrament.

19. That there are other Sacraments besides "Baptism and the Lord's Supper," though not "such as" they.

20. That the souls of the Saints are reigning in joy and in heaven with God.

21. That alms-deeds purge the soul from the infection and filthy spots of sin, and are a precious medicine, an inestimable jewel.

22. That mercifulness wipes out and washes away sins, as salves and remedies to heal sores and grievous diseases.

23. That the duty of fasting is a truth more manifest than it should need to be proved.

24. That fasting, used with prayer, is of great efficacy and weigheth much with God; so the Angel Raphael told Tobias.

25. That the puissant and mighty Emperor Theodosius was, in the Primitive Church which was most holy and godly, excommunicated by St. Ambrose.

26. That Constantine, Bishop of Rome, did condemn Philippicus, then Emperor, not without a cause indeed, but very justly.

Putting altogether aside the question how far these separate theses came under the matter to which subscription was to be made, it was quite plain, that in the minds of the men who wrote the Homilies, and who thus incorporated them into the Anglican system of doctrine, there was no such nice discrimination between the Catholic and the Protestant faith, no such clear recognition of formal Protestant principles and tenets, no such accurate definition of "Roman doctrine," as is received at the present day: — hence great probability accrued to my presentiment, that the Articles were tolerant, not only of what I called "Catholic teaching," but of much that was "Roman."

4. And here was another reason against the notion that the Articles directly attacked the Roman dogmas as declared at Trent and as promulgated by Pius the Fourth: — the Council of Trent was not over, nor its Canons promulgated at the date when the Articles were drawn up,* so that those Articles must be aiming at something else? What was that something else? The Homilies tell us: the Homilies are the best comment upon the Articles. Let us turn to the Homilies, and we shall find from first to last that, not only is not the Catholic teaching of the first centuries, but neither again are the dogmas of Rome, the objects of the protest of the compilers of the Articles, but the dominant errors, the popular corruptions, authorized or suffered by the high name of Rome. The eloquent declamation of the Homilies finds its matter almost exclusively in the dominant errors. As to Catholic teaching, nay as to Roman dogma, of such theology those Homilies, as I have shown, contained no small portion themselves.

5. So much for the writers of the Articles and Homilies; — they were witnesses, not authorities, and I used them as such; but in the next place, who were the actual authorities imposing them? I reasonably considered the authority *imponens* to be the Convocation of 1571; but here again, it would be found that the very Convocation, which received and confirmed the 39 Articles, also enjoined by Canon that "preachers should be *careful,* that they should *never* teach aught in a sermon, to be religiously held and believed by the people, except that which is agreeable to the doctrine of the Old and New Testament, and *which the Catholic Fathers and ancient Bishops have collected* from that very doctrine." Here, let it be observed, an appeal is made by the Convocation *imponens* to the very same ancient authorities, as had been mentioned with such profound veneration by the writers of the Homilies and the Articles, and thus, if the Homilies contained views of doctrine which now would be called Roman, there seemed to me to be an extreme probability that the Convocation of 1571 also countenanced and received, or at least did not reject, those doctrines.

---

*[Newman's Note] The Pope's Confirmation of the Council, by which its Canons became *de fide,* and his Bull *super confirmatione* by which they were promulgated to the world, are dated January 26, 1564. The Articles are dated 1562.

6. And further, when at length I came actually to look into the text of the Articles, I saw in many cases a patent justification of all that I had surmised as to their vagueness and indecisiveness, and that, not only on questions which lay between Lutherans, Calvinists, and Zuinglians, but on Catholic questions also; and I have noticed them in my Tract. In the conclusion of my Tract I observe: The Articles are "evidently framed on the principle of leaving open large questions on which the controversy hinges. They state broadly extreme truths, and are silent about their adjustment. For instance, they say that all necessary faith must be proved from Scripture; but do not say *who* is to prove it. They say, that the Church has authority in controversies; they do not say *what* authority. They say that it may enforce nothing beyond Scripture, but do not say *where* the remedy lies when it does. They say that works *before* grace *and* justification are worthless and worse, and that works *after* grace *and* justification are acceptable, but they do not speak at all of works *with* God's aid *before* justification. They say that men are lawfully called and sent to minister and preach, who are chosen and called by men who have public authority *given* them in the Congregation; but they do not add *by whom* the authority is to be given. They say that Councils called by *princes* may err; they do not determine whether Councils called in the name of Christ may err."

Such were the considerations which weighed with me in my inquiry how far the Articles were tolerant of a Catholic, or even a Roman interpretation; and such was the defence which I made in my Tract for having attempted it. From what I have already said, it will appear that I have no need or intention at this day to maintain every particular interpretation which I suggested in the course of my Tract, nor indeed had I then. Whether it was prudent or not, whether it was sensible or not, any how I attempted only a first essay of a necessary work, an essay which, as I was quite prepared to find, would require revision and modification by means of the lights which I should gain from the criticism of others. I should have gladly withdrawn any statement, which could be proved to me to be erroneous; I considered my work to be faulty and open to objection in the same sense in which I now consider my Anglican interpretations of Scripture to be erroneous; but in no other sense. I am surprised that men do not apply to the interpreters of Scripture generally the hard names which they apply to the author of Tract 90. He held a large system of theology, and applied it to the Articles: Episcopalians, or Lutherans, or Presbyterians, or Unitarians, hold a large system of theology and apply it to Scripture. Every theology has its difficulties; Protestants hold justification by faith only, though there is no text in St. Paul which enunciates it, and though St. James expressly denies it; do we therefore call Protestants dishonest? they deny that the Church has a divine mission, though St. Paul says that it is "the Pillar and ground of

Truth;" they keep the Sabbath, though St. Paul says, "Let no man judge you in meat or drink or in respect of . . . the sabbath days." Every creed has texts in its favour, and again texts which run counter to it: and this is generally confessed. And this is what I felt keenly: — how had I done worse in Tract 90 than Anglicans, Wesleyans, and Calvinists did daily in their Sermons and their publications? how had I done worse, than the Evangelical party in their *ex animo* reception of the Services for Baptism and Visitation of the Sick?* Why was I to be dishonest and they immaculate? There was an occasion on which our Lord gave an answer, which seemed to be appropriate to my own case, when the tumult broke out against my Tract: — "He that is without sin among you, let him first cast a stone at him." I could have fancied that a sense of their own difficulties of interpretation would have persuaded the great party I have mentioned to some prudence, or at least moderation, in opposing a teacher of an opposite school. But I suppose their alarm and their anger overcame their sense of justice.

In the sudden storm of indignation with which the Tract was received throughout the country on its appearance, I recognize much of real religious feeling, much of honest and true principle, much of straightforward ignorant common sense. In Oxford there was genuine feeling too; but there had been a smouldering, stern, energetic animosity, not at all unnatural, partly rational, against its author. A false step had been made; now was the time for action. I am told that, even before the publication of the Tract, rumours of its contents had got into the hostile camp in an exaggerated form; and not a moment was lost in proceeding to action, when I was actually fallen into the hands of the

---

*[Newman's Note] For instance, let candid men consider the form of Absolution contained in that Prayer Book, of which all clergymen, Evangelical and Liberal as well as high Church, and (I think) all persons in University office declare that "it containeth *nothing contrary to the Word of God.*"

I challenge, in the sight of all England, Evangelical clergymen generally, to put on paper an interpretation of this form of words, consistent with their sentiments, which shall be less forced than the most objectionable of the interpretations which Tract 90 puts upon any passage in the Articles.

"Our Lord Jesus Christ, who hath left *power* to His Church to absolve all sinners who truly repent and believe in Him, of His great mercy forgive thee thine offences; and by *His authority committed to me, I absolve thee from all thy sins,* in the Name of the Father, and of the Son, and of the Holy Ghost. Amen."

I subjoin the Roman form, as used in England and elsewhere: "Dominus noster Jesus Christus te absolvat; et ego auctoritate ipsius te absolvo, ab omni vinculo excommunicationis et interdicti, in quantum possum et tu indiges. Deinde ego te absolvo à peccatis tuis, in nomine Patris et Filii et Spiritûs Sancti. Amen."

Philistines. I was quite unprepared for the outbreak, and was startled at its violence. I do not think I had any fear. Nay, I will add, I am not sure that it was not in one point of view a relief to me.

I saw indeed clearly that my place in the Movement was lost; public confidence was at an end; my occupation was gone. It was simply an impossibility that I could say any thing henceforth to good effect, when I had been posted up by the marshal on the buttery-hatch of every College of my University, after the manner of discommoned pastry-cooks, and when in every part of the country and every class of society, through every organ and opportunity of opinion, in newspapers, in periodicals, at meetings, in pulpits, at dinner-tables, in coffee-rooms, in railway carriages, I was denounced as a traitor who had laid his train and was detected in the very act of firing it against the time-honoured Establishment. There were indeed men, besides my own immediate friends, men of name and position, who gallantly took my part, as Dr. Hook,[55] Mr. Palmer, and Mr. Perceval; it must have been a grievous trial for themselves; yet what after all could they do for me? Confidence in me was lost;—but I had already lost full confidence in myself. Thoughts had passed over me a year and a half before in respect to the Anglican claims, which for the time had profoundly troubled me. They had gone: I had not less confidence in the power and the prospects of the Apostolical movement than before; not less confidence than before in the grievousness of what I called the "dominant errors" of Rome: but how was I any more to have absolute confidence in myself? how was I to have confidence in my present confidence? how was I to be sure that I should always think as I thought now? I felt that by this event a kind Providence had saved me from an impossible position in the future.

First, if I remember right, they wished me to withdraw the Tract. This I refused to do: I would not do so for the sake of those who were unsettled or in danger of unsettlement. I would not do so for my own sake; for how could I acquiesce in a mere Protestant interpretation of the Articles? how could I range myself among the professors of a theology, of which it put my teeth on edge even to hear the sound?

Next they said, "Keep silence; do not defend the Tract;" I answered, "Yes, if you will not condemn it,—if you will allow it to continue on sale." They

---

55. Dr. Walter Farquhar Hook (1798–1875) was the longtime Anglican vicar of Leeds and after 1859 the dean of Chicester. He was sympathetic to the Tractarians and even defended *Tract 90* until the radical ideas of W. G. Ward came to the fore. Later in life he hostilely criticized Newman and the tactics of the Tractarians toward their enemies. In particular, he regretted his own acquiescence in the 1836 Oxford Convocation that condemned R. D. Hampden.

pressed on me whenever I gave way; they fell back when they saw me obstinate. Their line of action was to get out of me as much as they could; but upon the point of their tolerating the Tract I *was* obstinate. So they let me continue it on sale; and they said they would not condemn it. But they said that this was on condition that I did not defend it, that I stopped the series, and that I myself published my own condemnation in a letter to the Bishop of Oxford. I impute nothing whatever to him, he was ever most kind to me. Also, they said they could not answer for what some individual Bishops might perhaps say about the Tract in their own charges. I agreed to their conditions. My one point was to save the Tract.[56]

Not a line in writing was given me, as a pledge of the observance of the main article on their side of the engagement. Parts of letters from them were read to me, without being put into my hands. It was an "understanding." A clever man had warned me against "understandings" some six years before: I have hated them ever since.[57]

56. Throughout his negotiation with Bishop Bagot in March 1841, Newman's goal was to avoid having *Tract 90* formally condemned as opposed to its being harshly criticized. Moreover, in all of his writings at the time, including pamphlets written to Dr. Richard Jelf and to Bishop Bagot, Newman sought to include elements of what he regarded as Catholic doctrine so he might say that the contents of these pamphlets, having been published and received without specific criticism, was therefore approved. Regarding his *Letter Addressed to the Right Reverend Father in God, Richard, Lord Bishop of Oxford*, written as part of his negotiation with Bagot, Newman told Keble that he was "sanguine" about his letter to the bishop, into which he had "managed to wedge in a good many bits of Catholicism, which *now* come out with the Bishop's sanction." In another letter written the same day he told Keble, "We have got the *principle* of our interpretation admitted in that it has not been condemned." JHN to J. Keble, April 1, 1841 (I) and (II), *L&D* 8: 148–149.

57. Newman sincerely believed that he had been given an "understanding" that if he brought the tracts to a conclusion, *Tract 90* would not receive wide criticism. The reverse, of course, happened. Newman consequently thought that he had been betrayed by Church of England authorities. Pusey claimed to have received Bagot's assurance on this point not only on the basis of Bagot's word but also of other authority. See *L&D* 8: 106n, 119n, and 123n for extensive references on the question. Furthermore, on March 22, 1841, Bishop Blomfield wrote R. W. Jelf: "With regard to the Bishops, it is most probable that some of them will notice the Tract [No. 90] in their charges, as they have already noticed others of the series: but I have no reason to apprehend that there will be any formal censure of it by the Bishops collectively. Indeed neither the Archbishop, nor myself, would consent to such a measure in the present posture of the question." [C. Blomfield to Dr. Jelf, March 22, 1841, Letterbook No. 28, f. 33, Blomfield Papers, Lambeth Palace Library, London.] Blomfield then advised the discontinuation of the tracts. If Jelf either showed Pusey, Bagot, or much less likely Newman, this letter or

In the last words of my letter to the Bishop of Oxford I thus resigned my place in the Movement: —

"I have nothing to be sorry for," I say to him, "except having made your Lordship anxious, and others whom I am bound to revere. I have nothing to be sorry for, but everything to rejoice in and be thankful for. I have never taken pleasure in seeming to be able to move a party, and whatever influence I have had, has been found, not sought after. I have acted because others did not act, and have sacrificed a quiet which I prized. May God be with me in time to come, as He has been hitherto! and He will be, if I can but keep my hand clean and my heart pure. I think I can bear, or at least will try to bear, any personal humiliation, so that I am preserved from betraying sacred interests, which the Lord of grace and power has given into my charge."

---

simply conveyed by paraphrase this passage, Newman might well have concluded that a firm assurance on the basis of authority had been given that he would not be censured by the bishops. See also Thomas Gornall, "Newman's Lapses into Subjectivity," *Heythrop Journal* 23 (1982): 46–50.

Chapter III.

History of My Religious Opinions from 1839 to 1841

And now that I am about to trace, as far as I can, the course of that great revolution of mind, which led me to leave my own home, to which I was bound by so many strong and tender ties, I feel overcome with the difficulty of satisfying myself in my account of it, and have recoiled from the attempt, till the near approach of the day, on which these lines must be given to the world, forces me to set about the task.[1] For who can know himself, and the multitude of subtle influences which act upon him? And who can recollect, at the distance of twenty-five years, all that he once knew about his thoughts and his deeds, and that, during a portion of his life, when, even at the time, his observation, whether of himself or of the external world, was less than before or after, by very reason of the perplexity and dismay which weighed upon him, — when, in spite of the light given to him according to his need amid his darkness, yet a darkness it emphatically was? And who can suddenly gird himself

---

1. Here and elsewhere in the *Apologia* Newman emphasizes "that great revolution of mind" that occurred in his thinking about the Church of England and the Roman Catholic Church. He says conspicuously little about *what factors led him to act* upon changes in his thinking. In his correspondence from 1839 through 1845 on more than one occasion he indicates that his thinking did not compel action but had led him instead into a state of near paralysis.

to a new and anxious undertaking, which he might be able indeed to perform well, were full and calm leisure allowed him to look through every thing that he had written, whether in published works or private letters? but, on the other hand, as to that calm contemplation of the past, in itself so desirable, who can afford to be leisurely and deliberate, while he practises on himself a cruel operation, the ripping up of old griefs, and the venturing again upon the "infandum dolorem" of years, in which the stars of this lower heaven were one by one going out?[2] I could not in cool blood, nor except upon the imperious call of duty, attempt what I have set myself to do. It is both to head and heart an extreme trial, thus to analyze what has so long gone by, and to bring out the results of that examination. I have done various bold things in my life: this is the boldest: and, were I not sure I should after all succeed in my object, it would be madness to set about it.

In the spring of 1839 my position in the Anglican Church was at its height. I had supreme confidence in my controversial *status,* and I had a great and still growing success, in recommending it to others. I had in the foregoing autumn been somewhat sore at the Bishop's Charge, but I have a letter which shows that all annoyance had passed from my mind. In January, if I recollect aright, in order to meet the popular clamour against myself and others, and to satisfy the Bishop, I had collected into one all the strong things which they, and especially I, had said against the Church of Rome, in order to their insertion among the advertisements appended to our publications. Conscious as I was that my opinions in religion were not gained, as the world said, from Roman sources, but were, on the contrary, the birth of my own mind and of the circumstances in which I had been placed, I had a scorn of the imputations which were heaped upon me. It was true that I held a large bold system of religion, very unlike the Protestantism of the day, but it was the concentration and adjustment of the statements of great Anglican authorities, and I had as much right to hold it, as the Evangelical, and more right than the Liberal party could show, for asserting their own respective doctrines.[3] As I declared on

2. *infandum dolorem,* "unutterable woe," Aeneid 2:3.
3. This passage is one of Newman's most straightforward statements of the manner in which his religious and theological development had arisen through the exercise of his private judgment. He also makes clear that he was attempting to establish a safe space in the Church of England for what he termed Catholic opinion. He saw this Catholic frame of mind as pushing the devotional boundaries of the English Church in a new direction, just as the evangelical revival of the past century had pushed it in a more radically Protestant direction than originally embodied in its formularies. On March 14, 1843, in discussing the prospect of resigning St. Mary's, Newman wrote to John Keble: "What

occasion of Tract 90, I claimed, in behalf of who would in the Anglican Church, the right of holding with Bramhall a comprecation with the Saints, and the Mass all but Transubstantiation with Andrewes, or with Hooker that Transubstantiation itself is not a point for Churches to part communion upon, or with Hammond that a General Council, truly such, never did, never shall err in a matter of faith, or with Bull that man had in paradise and lost on the fall, a supernatural habit of grace, or with Thorndike that penance is a propitiation for post-baptismal sin, or with Pearson that the all-powerful name of Jesus is no otherwise given than in the Catholic Church.[4] "Two can play at that," was often in my mouth, when men of Protestant sentiments appealed to the Articles, Homilies, or Reformers; in the sense that, if they had a right to speak loud, I had the liberty to speak out as well as they, and had the means, by the same or parallel appeals, of giving them tit for tat. I thought that the Anglican Church was tyrannized over by a mere party,[5] and I aimed at bringing into effect the promise contained in the motto to the Lyra, "They shall know the difference now." I only asked to be allowed to show them the difference.

What will best describe my state of mind at the early part of 1839, is an Article in the British Critic for that April. I have looked over it now, for the first time since it was published; and have been struck by it for this reason: — it contains the last words which I ever spoke as an Anglican to Anglicans. It may now be read as my parting address and valediction, made to my friends. I little knew it at the time. It reviews the actual state of things, and it ends by looking towards the future. It is not altogether mine; for my memory goes to this, — that I had asked a friend to do the work; that then, the thought came on me, that I would do it myself: and that he was good enough to put into my hands what he had with great appositeness written, and that I embodied it in my

---

men learn from me, who learn any thing, is to lean towards doctrines and practices which our Church does not sanction. . . . I cannot deny, first, that my interpretation [of the Thirty-Nine Articles in *Tract 90*] has never been drawn out, to say the least, before — and I suspect our Catholic-minded Divines have rather had recourse to the expedient of looking on the Articles as Articles of Peace — and next I am conscious too, as I have said above, that I am not advocating, that I am not promoting, the Anglican system of doctrine, but one very much more resembling in matter of fact, the doctrine of the Roman Church." (JHN to John Keble, March 14, 1843, *L&D* 9: 279–280.)

4. Richard Hooker (1554–1600), Herbert Thorndike (1597?–1672), and John Pearson (1613–1686) were major Anglican writers of their day; all were highly regarded by the Tractarians.

5. Newman believed the evangelical party had tyrannized the Church of England since the late 1730s.

Article. Every one, I think, will recognize the greater part of it as mine. It was published two years before the affair of Tract 90, and was entitled "The State of Religious Parties."[6]

In this Article, I begin by bringing together testimonies from our enemies to the remarkable success of our exertions. One writer said: "Opinions and views of a theology of a very marked and peculiar kind have been extensively adopted and strenuously upheld, and are daily gaining ground among a considerable and influential portion of the members, as well as ministers of the Established Church." Another: The Movement has manifested itself "with the most rapid growth of the hot-bed of these evil days." Another: "The *Via Media* is crowded with young enthusiasts, who never presume to argue, except against the propriety of arguing at all." Another: "Were I to give you a full list of the works, which they have produced within the short space of five years, I should surprise you. You would see what a task it would be to make yourself complete master of their system, even in its present probably immature state. The writers have adopted the motto, 'In quietness and confidence shall be your strength.' With regard to confidence, they have justified their adopting it; but as to quietness, it is not very quiet to pour forth such a succession of controversial publications." Another: "The spread of these doctrines is in fact now having the effect of rendering all other distinctions obsolete, and of severing the religious community into two portions, fundamentally and vehemently opposed one to the other. Soon there will be no middle ground left; and every man, and especially every clergyman, will be compelled to make his choice between the two." Another: "The time has gone by, when those unfortunate and deeply regretted publications can be passed over without notice, and the hope that their influence would fail is now dead." Another: "These doctrines had already made fearful progress. One of the largest churches in Brighton is crowded to hear them; so is the church at Leeds. There are few towns of note, to which they have not extended. They are preached in small towns in Scotland. They obtain in Elginshire, 600 miles north of London. I found them myself in the heart of the highlands of Scotland. They are advocated in the newspaper and periodical press. They have even insinuated themselves into the House of Commons." And, lastly, a bishop in a charge:—It "is daily assuming a more serious and alarming aspect. Under the specious pretence of deference to Antiquity and respect for primitive models, the foundations of the Protestant Church are undermined by men, who dwell within her walls, and those who sit in the Reformers' seat are traducing the Reformation."

After thus stating the phenomenon of the time, as it presented itself to those

---

6. "State of Religious Parties," *British Critic* 25 (1839): 395–426.

who did not sympathize in it, the Article proceeds to account for it; and this it does by considering it as a re-action from the dry and superficial character of the religious teaching and the literature of the last generation, or century, and as a result of the need which was felt both by the hearts and the intellects of the nation for a deeper philosophy, and as the evidence and as the partial fulfilment of that need, to which even the chief authors of the then generation had borne witness.[7] First, I mentioned the literary influence of Walter Scott, who turned men's minds in the direction of the middle ages. "The general need," I said, "of something deeper and more attractive, than what had offered itself elsewhere, may be considered to have led to his popularity; and by means of his popularity he re-acted on his readers, stimulating their mental thirst, feeding their hopes, setting before them visions, which, when once seen, are not easily forgotten, and silently indoctrinating them with nobler ideas, which might afterwards be appealed to as first principles."

Then I spoke of Coleridge, thus: "While history in prose and verse was thus made the instrument of Church feelings and opinions, a philosophical basis for the same was laid in England by a very original thinker, who, while he indulged a liberty of speculation, which no Christian can tolerate, and advocated conclusions which were often heathen rather than Christian, yet after all installed a higher philosophy into inquiring minds, than they had hitherto been accustomed to accept. In this way he made trial of his age, and succeeded in interesting its genius in the cause of Catholic truth."

Then come Southey and Wordsworth, "two living poets, one of whom in the department of fantastic fiction, the other in that of philosophical meditation, have addressed themselves to the same high principles and feelings, and carried forward their readers in the same direction."

Then comes the prediction of this re-action hazarded by "a sagacious observer withdrawn from the world, and surveying its movements from a distance," Mr. Alexander Knox.[8] He had said twenty years before the date of my Article: "No Church on earth has more intrinsic excellence than the English Church, yet no Church probably has less practical influence. . . . The rich provision, made by the grace and providence of God, for habits of a noble

---

7. Newman here associates the Tractarian Party and its views with the ideas and sentiments of major British Romantic writers: Walter Scott, Samuel Taylor Coleridge, Robert Southey, and William Wordsworth. See David Goslee, *Romanticism and the Anglican Newman* (Athens: Ohio Univ. Press, 1996).

8. Alexander Knox (1757–1831) was an Irish layman who produced important theological writings that appealed to many Tractarians. Although a close friend to Methodists and evangelicals, his theology of baptism, justification, and ecclesiology was deeply high church. He was also sympathetic to Roman Catholicism.

kind, is evidence that men shall arise, fitted both by nature and ability, to discover for themselves, and to display to others, whatever yet remains undiscovered, whether in the words or works of God." Also I referred to "a much venerated clergyman of the last generation," who said shortly before his death, "Depend on it, the day will come, when those great doctrines, now buried, will be brought out to the light of day, and then the effect will be fearful." I remarked upon this, that they who "now blame the impetuosity of the current, should rather turn their animadversions upon those who have dammed up a majestic river, till it has become a flood."

These being the circumstances under which the Movement began and progressed, it was absurd to refer it to the act of two or three individuals. It was not so much a movement as a "spirit afloat;" it was within us, "rising up in hearts where it was least suspected, and working itself, though not in secret, yet so subtly and impalpably, as hardly to admit of precaution or encounter on any ordinary human rules of opposition. It is," I continued, "an adversary in the air, a something one and entire, a whole wherever it is, unapproachable and incapable of being grasped, as being the result of causes far deeper than political or other visible agencies, the spiritual awakening of spiritual wants."

To make this clear, I proceed to refer to the chief preachers of the revived doctrines at that moment, and to draw attention to the variety of their respective antecedents. Dr. Hook and Mr. Churton represented the high Church dignitaries of the last century;[9] Mr. Perceval, the Tory aristocracy; Mr. Keble came from a country parsonage; Mr. Palmer from Ireland; Dr. Pusey from the Universities of Germany, and the study of Arabic MSS.; Mr. Dodsworth from the study of Prophecy;[10] Mr. Oakeley had gained his views, as he himself expressed it, "partly by study, partly by reflection, partly by conversation with one or two friends, inquirers like himself:"[11] while I speak of myself as being

---

9. Edward Churton (1800–1874) was a conservative high churchman initially sympathetic to the Tractarian Movement but quickly and lastingly dissuaded by its extreme positions.

10. William Dodsworth (1798–1861) was an Anglican clergyman sympathetic to Tractarianism and after the Gorham Judgment a convert to Roman Catholicism. In the mid-1830s he published articles on the second coming of Christ and the vanquishing of the Antichrist.

11. Frederick Oakeley (1802–1880) was a student at Christ Church, Oxford, with strong evangelical training and ties until the late 1830s when he was drawn to the later Tractarian Movement under the influence of Froude's *Remains* and his friendship with W. G. Ward. In the wake of *Tract 90* Oakeley, by then minister of Margaret Chapel in London, advanced increasingly radical anti-Protestant ideas and argued that a clergyman of the Church of England could hold but not teach all Roman Catholic doctrine. See the

"much indebted to the friendship of Archbishop Whately." And thus I am led on to ask, "What head of a sect is there? What march of opinions can be traced from mind to mind among preachers such as these? They are one and all in their degree the organs of one Sentiment, which has risen up simultaneously in many places very mysteriously."

My train of thought next led me to speak of the disciples of the Movement, and I freely acknowledged and lamented that they needed to be kept in order. It is very much to the purpose to draw attention to this point now, when such extravagances as then occurred, whatever they were, are simply laid to my door, or to the charge of the doctrines which I advocated. A man cannot do more than freely confess what is wrong, say that it need not be, that it ought not to be, and that he is very sorry that it should be. Now I said in the Article, which I am reviewing, that the great truths themselves, which we were preaching, must not be condemned on account of such abuse of them. "Aberrations there must ever be, whatever the doctrine is, while the human heart is sensitive, capricious, and wayward. A mixed multitude went out of Egypt with the Israelites." "There will ever be a number of persons," I continued, "professing the opinions of a movement party, who talk loudly and strangely, do odd or fierce things, display themselves unnecessarily, and disgust other people; persons, too young to be wise, too generous to be cautious, too warm to be sober, or too intellectual to be humble. Such persons will be very apt to attach themselves to particular persons, to use particular names, to say things merely because others do, and to act in a party-spirited way."

While I thus republish what I then said about such extravagances as occurred in these years, at the same time I have a very strong conviction that those extravagances furnished quite as much the welcome excuse for those who were jealous or shy of us, as the stumbling-blocks of those who were well inclined to our doctrines. This too we felt at the time; but it was our duty to see that our good should not be evil-spoken of; and accordingly, two or three of the writers of the Tracts for the Times had commenced a Series of what they called "Plain Sermons" with the avowed purpose of discouraging and correct-

---

introduction to this volume for the circumstances surrounding Oakeley's condemnation by the Court of Arches in the summer of 1845, a decision that precipitated several Tractarian conversions to Roman Catholicism. These provided the occasion for Newman's own conversion. Oakeley himself converted to the Roman Catholic Church on October 29, 1845. See also Peter Galloway, *A Passionate Humility: Frederick Oakeley and the Oxford Movement* (Leominster: Gracewing, 1999), pp. 147–210, and Frank M. Turner, *John Henry Newman: The Challenge to Evangelical Religion* (New Haven, Conn.: Yale Univ. Press, 2002), pp. 535–548.

ing whatever was uppish or extreme in our followers: to this Series I contributed a volume myself.

Its conductors say in their Preface: "If therefore as time goes on, there shall be found persons, who admiring the innate beauty and majesty of the fuller system of Primitive Christianity, and seeing the transcendent strength of its principles, *shall become loud and voluble advocates* in their behalf, speaking the more freely, *because they do not feel them deeply as founded* in divine and eternal truth, of such persons *it is our duty to declare plainly,* that, as we should contemplate their condition with serious misgiving, *so would they be the last persons from whom we should* seek support.

"But if, on the other hand, there shall be any, who, in the silent humility of their lives, and in their unaffected reverence for holy things, show that they in truth accept these principles as real and substantial, and by habitual purity of heart and serenity of temper, give proof of their deep veneration for sacraments and sacramental ordinances, those persons, *whether our professed adherents or not,* best exemplify the kind of character which the writers of the Tracts for the Times have wished to form."

These clergymen had the best of claims to use these beautiful words, for they were themselves, all of them, important writers in the Tracts, the two Mr. Kebles, and Mr. Isaac Williams.[12] And this passage, with which they ushered their Series into the world, I quoted in the Article, of which I am giving an account, and I added, "What more can be required of the preachers of neglected truth, than that they should admit that some, who do not assent to their preaching, are holier and better men than some who do?" They were not answerable for the intemperance of those who dishonoured a true doctrine, provided they protested, as they did, against such intemperance. "They were not answerable for the dust and din which attends any great moral movement. The truer doctrines are, the more liable they are to be perverted."

---

12. The "two Mr. Kebles" refer to John Keble and his brother Thomas Keble (1793–1875). The latter contributed to collections of Tractarian sermons and also to *Tracts for the Times.* Isaac Williams (1802–1865) was a Tractarian and early Victorian poet. He wrote *Tract 80* and *Tract 87,* titled *On Reserve in Communicating Religious Knowledge* (1837; 1840), which except for *Tract 90* were the most controversial of all Tractarian publications. Williams, as he explained in his autobiography, directed the two tracts against the evangelical practice of preaching forgiveness through the atonement of Christ to the virtual exclusion of other Christian truths and doctrines. Williams urged that the preaching of such forgiveness should follow, not proceed, a life of good works and virtuous behavior. See Isaac Williams, *The Autobiography of Isaac Williams,* ed. George Prevost (London: Longmans, Green, 1892), pp. 91, 92, and O. W. Jones, *Isaac Williams and His Circle* (London, SPCK, 1971).

The notice of these incidental faults of opinion or temper in adherents of the Movement, led on to a discussion of the secondary causes, by means of which a system of doctrine may be embraced, modified, or developed, of the variety of schools which may all be in the One Church, and of the succession of one phase of doctrine to another, while that doctrine is ever one and the same. Thus I was brought on to the subject of Antiquity, which was the basis of the doctrine of the *Via Media,* and by which was not to be understood a servile imitation of the past, but such a reproduction of it as is really new, while it is old. "We have good hope," I say, "that a system will be rising up, superior to the age, yet harmonizing with, and carrying out its higher points, which will attract to itself those who are willing to make a venture and to face difficulties, for the sake of something higher in prospect. On this, as on other subjects, the proverb will apply, 'Fortes fortuna adjuvat.' "[13]

Lastly, I proceeded to the question of that future of the Anglican Church, which was to be a new birth of the Ancient Religion.[14] And I did not venture to pronounce upon it. "About the future, we have no prospect before our minds whatever, good or bad. Ever since that great luminary, Augustine, proved to be the last bishop of Hippo, Christians have had a lesson against attempting to foretell, *how* Providence will prosper and" [or?] "bring to an end, what it begins." Perhaps the lately-revived principles would prevail in the Anglican Church; perhaps they would be lost in "some miserable schism, or some more miserable compromise; but there was nothing rash in venturing to predict that "neither Puritanism nor Liberalism had any permanent inheritance within her."

Then I went on: "As to Liberalism, we think the formularies of the Church will ever, with the aid of a good Providence, keep it from making any serious inroads upon the clergy. Besides, it is too cold a principle to prevail with the multitude." But as regarded what was called Evangelical Religion or Puritanism, there was more to cause alarm.[15] I observed upon its organization; but on the other hand it had no intellectual basis; no internal idea, no principle of unity, no theology. "Its adherents," I said, "are already separating from each

---

13. "Fortune favors the strong."

14. In discussing his views of the future of the Anglican Church as "a new birth of the Ancient Religion," Newman indicates his determination to redirect the English Church through an articulation of what he believed to be the religion of the ancient Catholic Church. He envisioned radical change through the device of restoring an ancient pristine past.

15. As Newman here indirectly indicates, his remarks on liberalism in this article were minimal while his criticisms of evangelical and mainstream Protestantism were quite extensive.

other; they will melt away like a snow-drift. It has no straightforward view on any one point, on which it professes to teach, and to hide its poverty, it has dressed itself out in a maze of words. We have no dread of it at all; we only fear what it may lead to. It does not stand on intrenched ground, or make any pretence to a position; it does but occupy the space between contending powers, Catholic Truth and Rationalism. Then indeed will be the stern encounter, when two real and living principles, simple, entire, and consistent, one in the Church, the other out of it, at length rush upon each other, contending not for names and words, or half-views, but for elementary notions and distinctive moral characters."

Whether the ideas of the coming age upon religion were true or false, at least they would be real. "In the present day," I said, "mistiness is the mother of wisdom. A man who can set down a half-a-dozen general propositions, which escape from destroying one another only by being diluted into truisms, who can hold the balance between opposites so skilfully as to do without fulcrum or beam, who never enunciates a truth without guarding himself against being supposed to exclude the contradictory, — who holds that Scripture is the only authority, yet that the Church is to be deferred to, that faith only justifies, yet that it does not justify without works, that grace does not depend on the sacraments, yet is not given without them, that bishops are a divine ordinance, yet those who have them not are in the same religious condition as those who have, — this is your safe man and the hope of the Church; this is what the Church is said to want, not party men, but sensible, temperate, sober, well-judging persons, to guide it through the channel of no-meaning, between the Scylla and Charybdis of Aye and No."

This state of things, however, I said, could not last, if men were to read and think. They "will not keep in that very attitude which you call sound Church-of-Englandism or orthodox Protestantism. They cannot go on for ever standing on one leg, or sitting without a chair, or walking with their feet tied, or like Tityrus's stags grazing in the air.[16] They will take one view or another, but it will be a consistent view. It may be Liberalism, or Erastianism, or Popery, or Catholicity; but it will be real."

I concluded the Article by saying, that all who did not wish to be "democratic, or pantheistic, or popish," must "look out for *some* Via Media which will preserve us from what threatens, though it cannot restore the dead. The spirit of Luther is dead; but Hildebrand and Loyola are alive.[17] Is it sensible,

---

16. "Tityrus's stags" refers to a shepherd in Virgil's Ecologue I.
17. Hildebrand refers to Pope Gregory VII (1021?–1085); St. Ignatius Loyola (1491–1556) founded the Jesuit order.

sober, judicious, to be so very angry with those writers of the day, who point to the fact, that our divines of the seventeenth century have occupied a ground which is the true and intelligible mean between extremes? Is it wise to quarrel with this ground, because it is not exactly what we should choose, had we the power of choice? Is it true moderation, instead of trying to fortify a middle doctrine, to fling stones at those who do? ... Would you rather have your sons and daughters members of the Church of England or of the Church of Rome?"

And thus I left the matter. But, while I was thus speaking of the future of the Movement, I was in truth winding up my accounts with it, little dreaming that it was so to be; — while I was still, in some way or other, feeling about for an available *Via Media*, I was soon to receive a shock which was to cast out of my imagination all middle courses and compromises for ever. As I have said, this Article appeared in the April number of the British Critic; in the July number, I cannot tell why, there is no Article of mine; before the number for October, the event had happened to which I have alluded.

But before I proceed to describe what happened to me in the summer of 1839, I must detain the reader for a while, in order to describe the *issue* of the controversy between Rome and the Anglican Church, as I viewed it. This will involve some dry discussion; but it is as necessary for my narrative, as plans of buildings and homesteads are often found to be in the proceedings of our law courts.

I have said already that, though the object of the Movement was to withstand the Liberalism of the day, I found and felt this could not be done by mere negatives.[18] It was necessary for us to have a positive Church theory erected on a definite basis. This took me to the great Anglican divines; and then of course I found at once that it was impossible to form any such theory, without cutting across the teaching of the Church of Rome. Thus came in the Roman controversy.

When I first turned myself to it, I had neither doubt on the subject, nor suspicion that doubt would ever come upon me. It was in this state of mind that I began to read up Bellarmine on the one hand, and numberless Anglican writers on the other.[19] But I soon found, as others had found before me, that it was a tangled and manifold controversy, difficult to master, more difficult to put out of hand with neatness and precision. It was easy to make points, not

18. For a discussion of Newman's pursuit of the Catholic during the 1830s, see Turner, *John Henry Newman*, pp. 293–403.

19. Robert Bellarmine (1542–1621) was a Roman Catholic cardinal and a major voice of the Catholic Reformation criticism of Protestantism.

easy to sum up and settle. It was not easy to find a clear issue for the dispute, and still less by a logical process to decide it in favour of Anglicanism. This difficulty, however, had no tendency whatever to harass or perplex me: it was a matter which bore not on convictions, but on proofs.

First I saw, as all see who study the subject, that a broad distinction had to be drawn between the actual state of belief and of usage in the countries which were in communion with the Roman Church, and her formal dogmas; the latter did not cover the former. Sensible pain, for instance, is not implied in the Tridentine decree upon Purgatory; but it was the tradition of the Latin Church, and I had seen the pictures of souls in flames in the streets of Naples. Bishop Lloyd had brought this distinction out strongly in an Article in the British Critic in 1825;[20] indeed, it was one of the most common objections made to the Church of Rome, that she dared not commit herself by formal decree, to what nevertheless she sanctioned and allowed. Accordingly, in my Prophetical Office, I view as simply separate ideas, Rome quiescent, and Rome in action. I contrasted her creed on the one hand, with her ordinary teaching, her controversial tone, her political and social bearing, and her popular beliefs and practices, on the other.

While I made this distinction between the decrees and the traditions of Rome, I drew a parallel distinction between Anglicanism quiescent, and Anglicanism in action. In its formal creed Anglicanism was not at a great distance from Rome: far otherwise, when viewed in its insular spirit, the traditions of its establishment, its historical characteristics, its controversial rancour, and its private judgment. I disavowed and condemned those excesses, and called them "Protestantism" or "Ultra-Protestantism:"[21] I wished to find a parallel disclaimer, on the part of Roman controversialists, of that popular system of beliefs and usages in their own Church, which I called "Popery." When that hope was a dream, I saw that the controversy lay between the book-theology of Anglicanism on the one side, and the living system of what I called Roman

---

20. Charles Lloyd (1784–1829) became regius professor of divinity at Oxford in 1822 and continued to hold the position during his brief time as bishop of Oxford. Newman had attended his lectures in the 1820s in which Lloyd related the liturgy and prayer book of the Church of England to ancient and medieval sources. In 1829 he supported Peel and Wellington's policy of enacting Catholic Emancipation. See William J. Baker, *Beyond Port and Prejudice: Charles Lloyd of Oxford, 1784–1829* (Orono: Univ. of Maine at Orono Press, 1981).

21. In Tractarian writings the terms *Ultra-Protestantism* and *popular Protestantism* denoted evangelical religion, whether found in the Church of England or among Protestant Dissenters. *Protestantism* generally meant historical Protestantism deriving from either the Lutheran or continental reformed traditions.

corruption on the other. I could not get further than this; with this result I was forced to content myself.

These then were the *parties* in the controversy: — the Anglican *Via Media* and the popular religion of Rome. And next, as to the *issue,* to which the controversy between them was to be brought, it was this: — the Anglican disputant took his stand upon Antiquity or Apostolicity, the Roman upon Catholicity.[22] The Anglican said to the Roman: "There is but One Faith, the Ancient, and you have not kept to it;" the Roman retorted: "There is but One Church, the Catholic, and you are out of it." The Anglican urged "Your special beliefs, practices, modes of action, are nowhere in Antiquity;" the Roman objected: "You do not communicate with any one Church besides your own and its offshoots, and you have discarded principles, doctrines, sacraments, and usages, which are and ever have been received in the East and the West." The true Church, as defined in the Creeds, was both Catholic and Apostolic; now, as I viewed the controversy in which I was engaged, England and Rome had divided these notes or prerogatives between them: the cause lay thus, Apostolicity *versus* Catholicity.

However, in thus stating the matter, of course I do not wish it supposed that I allowed the note of Catholicity really to belong to Rome, to the disparagement of the Anglican Church; but I considered that the special point or plea of Rome in the controversy was Catholicity, as the Anglican plea was Antiquity. Of course I contended that the Roman idea of Catholicity was not ancient and aspostolic. It was in my judgment at the utmost only natural, becoming, expedient, that the whole of Christendom should be united in one visible body; while such a unity might, on the other hand, be nothing more than a mere heartless and political combination. For myself, I held with the Anglican divines, that, in the Primitive Church, there was a very real mutual independence between its separate parts, though, from a dictate of charity, there was in fact a close union between them. I considered that each See and Diocese might be compared to a crystal, and that each was similar to the rest, and that the sum total of them all was only a collection of crystals. The unity of the Church lay, not in its being a polity, but in its being a family, a race, coming down by apostolical descent from its first founders and bishops. And I considered this

---

22. *Apostolicity* referred to the claim of the Church of England to link its bishops to the long line of episcopal successors to the apostles. *Catholicity* referred to the ability of the Church of England to understand itself as part of the Holy Catholic and Apostolic Church. It was over the latter issue that Newman would ultimately come to rethink the basis of his religious affiliation as he came to believe that a church could not be part of the universal Christian Church if it stood apart from the see of Rome.

truth brought out, beyond the possibility of dispute, in the Epistles of St. Ignatius, in which the Bishop is represented as the one supreme authority in the Church, that is, in his own place, with no one above him, except as, for the sake of ecclesiastical order and expedience, arrangements had been made by which one was put over or under another. So much for our own claim to Catholicity, which was so perversely appropriated by our opponents to themselves: — on the other hand, as to our special strong point, Antiquity, while, of course, by means of it, we were able to condemn most emphatically the novel claim of Rome to domineer over other Churches, which were in truth her equals, further than that, we thereby especially convicted her of the intolerable offence of having added to the Faith. This was the critical head of accusation urged against her by the Anglican disputant; and as he referred to St. Ignatius in proof that he himself was a true Catholic, in spite of being separated from Rome, so he triumphantly referred to the Treatise of Vincentius of Lerins upon the "Quod semper, quod ubique, quod ab omnibus," in proof that the controversialists of Rome, in spite of their possession of the Catholic name, were separated in their creed from the Apostolical and primitive faith.[23]

Of course those controversialists had their own mode of answering him, with which I am not concerned in this place; here I am only concerned with the issue itself, between the one party and the other — Antiquity *versus* Catholicity.

Now I will proceed to illustrate what I have been saying of the *status* of the controversy, as it presented itself to my mind, by extracts from my writings of the dates of 1836, 1840, and 1841. And I introduce them with a remark, which especially applies to the paper, from which I shall quote first, of the date of 1836. That paper appeared in the March and April numbers of the British Magazine of that year, and was entitled "Home Thoughts Abroad."[24] Now it will be found, that, in the discussion which it contains, as in various other writings of mine, when I was in the Anglican Church, the argument in behalf of Rome is stated with considerable perspicuity and force. And at the time my friends and supporters cried out, "How imprudent!" and, both at the time, and especially at a later date, my enemies have cried out, "How insidious!" Friends and foes virtually agreed in their criticism; I had set out the cause which I was combating to the best advantage: this was an offence; it might be from imprudence, it might be with a traitorous design. It was from neither the

---

23. Vincentius of Lerins (d. ca. 434) defined true doctrine as distinguished from heresy as those doctrines that had been taught and believed "everywhere, in all times, by all people."

24. "Home Thoughts Abroad," *British Magazine* 5 (1834): 1–11, 121–131; 9 (1836): 237–248, 357–369.

one nor the other; but for the following reasons. First, I had a great impatience, whatever was the subject, of not bringing out the whole of it, as clearly as I could; next I wished to be as fair to my adversaries as possible; and thirdly I thought that there was a great deal of shallowness among our own friends, and that they undervalued the strength of the argument in behalf of Rome, and that they ought to be roused to a more exact apprehension of the position of the controversy. At a later date, (1841,) when I really felt the force of the Roman side of the question myself, as a difficulty which had to be met, I had a fourth reason for such frankness in argument, and that was, because a number of persons were unsettled far more than I was, as to the Catholicity of the Anglican Church. It was quite plain that, unless I was perfectly candid in stating what could be said against it, there was no chance that any representations, which I felt to be in its favour, or at least to be adverse to Rome, would have had any success with the persons in question. At all times I had a deep conviction, to put the matter on the lowest ground, that "honesty was the best policy." Accordingly, in July 1841, I expressed myself thus on the Anglican difficulty: "This is an objection which we must honestly say is deeply felt by many people, and not inconsiderable ones; and the more it is openly avowed to be a difficulty, the better; for there is then the chance of its being acknowledged, and in the course of time obviated, as far as may be, by those who have the power. Flagrant evils cure themselves by being flagrant; and we are sanguine that the time is come when so great an evil as this is, cannot stand its ground against the good feeling and common sense of religious persons. It is the very strength of Romanism against us; and, unless the proper persons take it into their serious consideration, they may look for certain to undergo the loss, as time goes on, of some whom they would least like to be lost to our Church." The measure which I had especially in view in this passage, was the project of a Jerusalem Bishopric, which the then Archbishop of Canterbury was at that time concocting with M. Bunsen, and of which I shall speak more in the sequel. And now to return to the Home Thoughts Abroad of the spring of 1836:—

The discussion contained in this composition runs in the form of a dialogue. One of the disputants says: "You say to me that the Church of Rome is corrupt. What then? to cut off a limb is a strange way of saving it from the influence of some constitutional ailment. Indigestion may cause cramp in the extremities; yet we spare our poor feet notwithstanding. Surely there is such a religious *fact* as the existence of a great Catholic body, union with which is a Christian privilege and duty. Now, we English are separate from it."

The other answers: "The present is an unsatisfactory, miserable state of things, yet I can grant no more. The Church is founded on a doctrine, — on the gospel of Truth; it is a means to an end. Perish the Church, (though, blessed be the promise! this cannot be,) yet let it perish *rather* than the Truth should fail. Purity of faith is more precious to the Christian than unity itself. If Rome has erred grievously in doctrine, then it is a duty to separate even from Rome."

His friend, who takes the Roman side of the argument, refers to the image of the Vine and its branches, which is found, I think, in St. Cyprian, as if a branch cut from the Catholic Vine must necessarily die. Also he quotes a passage from St. Augustine in controversy with the Donatists to the same effect;[25] viz. that, as being separated from the body of the Church, they were *ipso facto* cut off from the heritage of Christ. And he quotes St. Cyril's argument drawn from the very title Catholic, which no body or communion of men has ever dared or been able to appropriate, besides one. He adds, "Now I am only contending for the fact, that the communion of Rome constitutes the main body of the Church Catholic, and that we are split off from it, and in the condition of the Donatists."

The other replies by denying the fact that the present Roman communion is like St. Augustine's Catholic Church, inasmuch as there must be taken into account the large Anglican and Greek communions. Presently he takes the offensive, naming distinctly the points, in which Rome has departed from Primitive Christianity, viz. "the practical idolatry, the virtual worship of the Virgin and Saints, which are the offence of the Latin Church, and the degradation of moral truth and duty, which follows from these." And again: "We cannot join a Church, did we wish it ever so much, which does not acknowledge our orders, refuses us the Cup, demands our acquiescence in image-worship, and excommunicates us, if we do not receive it and all other decisions of the Tridentine Council."

His opponent answers these objections by referring to the doctrine of "developments of gospel truth." Besides, "The Anglican system itself is not found complete in those early centuries; so that the [Anglican] principle [of Antiquity] is self-destructive." "When a man takes up this *Via Media*, he is a mere *doctrinaire;*" he is like those, "who, in some matter of business, start up to suggest their own little crotchet, and are ever measuring mountains with a pocket ruler, or improving the planetary courses." "The *Via Media* has slept in libraries; it is a substitute of infancy for manhood."

It is plain, then, that at the end of 1835 or beginning of 1836, I had the whole state of the question before me, on which, to my mind, the decision between the Churches depended. It is observable that the question of the position of the Pope, whether as the centre of unity, or as the source of jurisdic-

---

25. The Donatists were a fourth-century schism that flourished in North Africa.

tion, did not come into my thoughts at all; nor did it, I think I may say, to the end. I doubt whether I ever distinctly held any of his powers to be *de jure divino,* while I was in the Anglican Church; — not that I saw any difficulty in the doctrine; not that in connexion with the history of St. Leo, of which I shall speak by and by, the idea of his infallibility did not cross my mind, for it did, — but after all, in my view the controversy did not turn upon it; it turned upon the Faith and the Church. This was my issue of the controversy from the beginning to the end. There was a contrariety of claims between the Roman and Anglican religions, and the history of my conversion is simply the process of working it out to a solution. In 1838 I illustrated it by the contrast presented to us between the Madonna and Child, and a Calvary. The peculiarity of the Anglican theology was this, — that it "supposed the Truth to be entirely objective and detached, not" (as in the theology of Rome) "lying hid in the bosom of the Church as if one with her, clinging to and (as it were) lost in her embrace, but as being sole and unapproachable, as on the Cross or at the Resurrection, with the Church close by, but in the back-ground."

As I viewed the controversy in 1836 and 1838, so I viewed it in 1840 and 1841.[26] In the British Critic of January 1840, after gradually investigating how the matter lies between the Churches by means of a dialogue, I end thus: "It would seem, that, in the above discussion, each disputant has a strong point: our strong point is the argument from Primitiveness, that of Romanists from Universality. It is a fact, however it is to be accounted for, that Rome has added to the Creed; and it is a fact, however we justify ourselves, that we are estranged from the great body of Christians over the world. And each of these two facts is at first sight a grave difficulty in the respective systems to which they belong." Again, "While Rome, though not deferring to the Fathers, recognizes them, and England, not deferring to the large body of the Church, recognizes it, both Rome and England have a point to clear up."

And still more strongly, in July, 1841:

"If the Note of schism, on the one hand, lies against England, an antagonist disgrace lies upon Rome, the Note of idolatry. Let us not be mistaken here; we are neither accusing Rome of idolatry nor ourselves of schism; we think neither charge tenable; but still the Roman Church practises what is so like idolatry, and the English Church makes much of what is so very like schism, that without deciding what is the duty of a Roman Catholic towards the Church of England in her present state, we do seriously think that members of the English Church have a providential direction given them, how to comport themselves towards the Church of Rome, while she is what she is."

26. John Henry Newman, "The Catholicity of the English Church," and "Private Judgment," *British Critic* 27 (1840): 40–88; 30 (1841): 280–331.

Chapter III   225

One remark more about Antiquity and the *Via Media*. As time went on, without doubting the strength of the Anglican argument from Antiquity, I felt also that it was not merely our special plea, but our only one. Also I felt that the *Via Media*, which was to represent it, was to be a sort of remodelled and adapted Antiquity. This I advanced both in Home Thoughts Abroad and in the Article of the British Critic which I have analyzed above. But this circumstance, that after all we must use private judgment upon Antiquity, created a sort of distrust of my theory altogether, which in the conclusion of my Volume on the Prophetical Office (1836–7) I express thus: "Now that our discussions draw to a close, the thought, with which we entered on the subject, is apt to recur, when the excitement of the inquiry has subsided, and weariness has succeeded, that what has been said is but a dream, the wanton exercise, rather than the practical conclusions of the intellect." And I conclude the paragraph by anticipating a line of thought into which I was, in the event, almost obliged to take refuge: "After all," I say, "the Church is ever invisible in its day, and faith only apprehends it." What was this, but to give up the Notes of a visible Church altogether, whether the Catholic Note or the Apostolic?

The Long Vacation of 1839 began early. There had been a great many visitors to Oxford from Easter to Commemoration; and Dr. Pusey's party had attracted attention, more, I think, than in any former year. I had put away from me the controversy with Rome for more than two years. In my Parochial Sermons the subject had at no time been introduced: there had been nothing for two years, either in my Tracts or in the British Critic, of a polemical character. I was returning, for the Vacation, to the course of reading which I had many years before chosen as especially my own. I have no reason to suppose that the thoughts of Rome came across my mind at all. About the middle of June I began to study and master the history of the Monophysites.[27]

---

27. The Monophysites were a variety of heretical groups in the fifth and sixth centuries, all holding to versions of the teaching that Christ had a single "physis," or nature. They arose in opposition to the Nestorians, who contended that the human and the divine in Christ remained distinct and that only the human nature of Christ suffered during the crucifixion. The Monophysites argued that the human and the divine constituted a single entity in Christ, with the divine subsuming the human. On one hand, this theology presented a very high view of Christ; on the other, it was understood as actually denying that Christ had been human. In 448 a church council had condemned Eutyches, who lived near Constantinople as abbot of a monastery, for holding Monophysite views though he appealed to ancient authorities and scripture. After attempts to reverse the condemnation of Eutyches, the Council of Chalcedon in 451 continued the condemnation and championed the authority of the Church of Rome. Thereafter, the Monophysite churches of Egypt refused to acknowledge the authority of Rome. Newman appears to

I was absorbed in the doctrinal question. This was from about June 13th to August 30th. It was during this course of reading that for the first time a doubt came upon me of the tenableness of Anglicanism. I recollect on the 30th of July mentioning to a friend, whom I had accidentally met, how remarkable the history was; but by the end of August I was seriously alarmed.

I have described in a former work, how the history affected me. My stronghold was Antiquity; now here, in the middle of the fifth century, I found, as it seemed to me, Christendom of the sixteenth and the nineteenth centuries reflected. I saw my face in that mirror, and I was a Monophysite. The Church of the *Via Media* was in the position of the Oriental communion, Rome was, where she now is; and the Protestants were the Eutychians. Of all passages of history, since history has been, who would have thought of going to the sayings and doings of old Eutyches, that *delirus senex*, as (I think) Petavius calls him, and to the enormities of the unprincipled Dioscorus, in order to be converted to Rome!28

Now let it be simply understood that I am not writing controversially, but with the one object of relating things as they happened to me in the course of my conversion. With this view I will quote a passage from the account, which I gave in 1850, of my reasonings and feelings in 1839:

"It was difficult to make out how the Eutychians or Monophysites were heretics, unless Protestants and Anglicans were heretics also; difficult to find arguments against the Tridentine Fathers, which did not tell against the Fathers of Chalcedon; difficult to condemn the Popes of the sixteenth century,

---

have believed that he and his Anglican followers, as well as the entire Church of England, stood to modern Rome as had the ancient Monophysites. In other words, he and the Church of England appeared as schismatics from the authority of the Roman Catholic Church. Newman had originally explained his sense of the parallel between his position in the Church of England and the Monophysites in *An Essay on the Development of Christian Doctrine* (London: J. Toovey, 1845), pp. 297ff, and John Henry Newman, *Certain Difficulties Felt by Anglicans in Catholic Teaching Considered: In Twelve Lectures Addressed in 1850 to the Party of the Religious Movement of 1833* (London: Longmans, Green, 1918), 1: 1, 363–400. See Stephen Thomas, *Newman and Heresy: The Anglican Years* (Cambridge: Cambridge Univ. Press, 1991), pp. 203–227. Thomas makes a very strong case that Newman's understanding of the Monophysites and his own position was a retrospective construct. Moreover, on November 17, 1839, Newman wrote his sister: "Our Church is not at one with itself—there is no denying it. We have an heretical spirit in us." Here he was directly referring to the evangelicals, not to his perception of either his group or the English Church as a whole resembling the Monophysites. (JHN to Jemima Mozley, November 17, 1839, *L&D* 7: 183).

28. Dionysius Petavius (1583–1652) was a seventeenth-century French Jesuit theologian who wrote on ancient Christian doctrine.

without condemning the Popes of the fifth. The drama of religion, and the combat of truth and error, were ever one and the same. The principles and proceedings of the Church now, were those of the Church then; the principles and proceedings of heretics then, were those of Protestants now. I found it so, — almost fearfully; there was an awful similitude, more awful, because so silent and unimpassioned, between the dead records of the past and the feverish chronicle of the present. The shadow of the fifth century was on the sixteenth. It was like a spirit rising from the troubled waters of the old world, with the shape and lineaments of the new. The Church then, as now, might be called peremptory and stern, resolute, overbearing, and relentless; and heretics were shifting, changeable, reserved, and deceitful, ever courting civil power, and never agreeing together, except by its aid; and the civil power was ever aiming at comprehensions, trying to put the invisible out of view, and substituting expediency for faith. What was the use of continuing the controversy, or defending my position, if, after all, I was forging arguments for Arius or Eutyches, and turning devil's advocate against the much-enduring Athanasius and the majestic Leo? Be my soul with the Saints! and shall I lift up my hand against them? Sooner may my right hand forget her cunning, and wither outright, as his who once stretched it out against a prophet of God! anathema to a whole tribe of Cranmers, Ridleys, Latimers, and Jewels![29] perish the names of Bramhall, Ussher, Taylor, Stillingfleet, and Barrow from the face of the earth, ere I should do ought but fall at their feet in love and in worship, whose image was continually before my eyes, and whose musical words were ever in my ears and on my tongue!"[30]

Hardly had I brought my course of reading to a close, when the Dublin Review of that same August was put into my hands, by friends who were more favourable to the cause of Rome than I was myself. There was an article in it on the "Anglican Claim" by Dr. Wiseman.[31] This was about the middle of September. It was on the Donatists, with an application to Anglicanism. I read it, and did not see much in it. The Donatist controversy was known to me for some years, as has appeared already. The case was not parallel to that of the

---

29. Thomas Cranmer (1489–1556), Nicholas Ridley (1502–1555), Hugh Latimer (ca. 1485–1555), and John Jewel (1522–1571) were the bishops of the English Reformation; the first three were martyrs executed during the reign of Mary I.

30. James Ussher (1581–1656), Jeremy Taylor (1613–1667), and Isaac Barrow (1630–1677), along with Bramhall, were seventeenth-century Church of England theologians whom Newman and other Tractarians believed to have set forth Catholic rather than Protestant teaching.

31. The article that Newman read in the summer of 1839 was Nicholas Wiseman, "The Anglican Claim of Apostolic Succession," *Dublin Review* 7 (1839): 138–180.

Anglican Church. St. Augustine in Africa wrote against the Donatists in Africa. They were a furious party who made a schism within the African Church, and not beyond its limits. It was a case of Altar against Altar, of two occupants of the same See, as that between the Non-jurors in England and the Established Church; not the case of one Church against another, as Rome against the Oriental Monophysites. But my friend, an anxiously religious man, now, as then, very dear to me, a Protestant still, pointed out the palmary words of St. Augustine, which were contained in one of the extracts made in the Review, and which had escaped my observation. "Securus judicat orbis terrarum."[32] He repeated these words again and again, and, when he was gone, they kept ringing in my ears. "Securus judicat orbis terrarum;" they were words which went beyond the occasion of the Donatists: they applied to that of the Monophysites. They gave a cogency to the Article, which had escaped me at first. They decided ecclesiastical questions on a simpler rule than that of Antiquity; nay, St. Augustine was one of the prime oracles of Antiquity; here then Antiquity was deciding against itself. What a light was hereby thrown upon every controversy in the Church! not that, for the moment, the multitude may not falter in their judgment, — not that, in the Arian hurricane, Sees more than can be numbered did not bend before its fury, and fall off from St. Athanasius, — not that the crowd of Oriental Bishops did not need to be sustained during the contest by the voice and the eye of St. Leo; but that the deliberate judgment, in which the whole Church at length rests and acquiesces, is an infallible prescription and a final sentence against such portions of it as protest and secede. Who can account for the impressions which are made on him? For a mere sentence, the words of St. Augustine, struck me with a power which I never had felt from any words before. To take a familiar instance, they were like the "Turn again Whittington" of the chime; or, to take a more serious one, they were like the "Tolle, lege,—Tolle, lege," of the child, which converted St. Augustine himself. "Securus judicat orbis terrarum!"[33] By those

---

32. A quotation from St. Augustine, *Contra epistolam Parmeniani* iii. 24: *Securus judicat orbis terrarum, bonos non esse qui se dividunt ab orbe terrarum in quacumque parte terrarum* ("Wherefore, the entire world judges *with security*, that they are not good, who separate themselves from the entire world, in whatever part of the entire world"). Wiseman's translation, as cited in N. Wiseman, "The Anglican Claim of Apostolical Succession," *Dublin Review* 7 (1839): 153–154.

33. "Turn again Whittington" refers to a tale of a runaway apprentice who heard the bells of London toll out sounds that he interpreted as "Turn again, Whittington, Lord Mayor of London." He returned and in time became Lord Mayor. "Tolle, lege—Tolle, lege"—Take up and Read—from St. Augustine's *Confessions*, Book VIII, ch. 12, marking

great words of the ancient Father, interpreting and summing up the long and varied course of ecclesiastical history, the theory of the *Via Media* was absolutely pulverized.

I became excited at the view thus opened upon me. I was just starting on a round of visits; and I mentioned my state of mind to two most intimate friends: I think to no others.[34] After a while, I got calm, and at length the vivid impression upon my imagination faded away. What I thought about it on reflection, I will attempt to describe presently. I had to determine its logical value, and its bearing upon my duty. Meanwhile, so far as this was certain, — I had seen the shadow of a hand upon the wall. It was clear that I had a good deal to learn on the question of the Churches, and that perhaps some new light was coming upon me. He who has seen a ghost, cannot be as if he had never seen it. The heavens had opened and closed again. The thought for the moment had been, "The Church of Rome will be found right after all;" and then it had vanished. My old convictions remained as before.

At this time, I wrote my Sermon on Divine Calls, which I published in my volume of Plain Sermons. It ends thus: —

"O that we could take that simple view of things, as to feel that the one thing which lies before us is to please God! What gain is it to please the world, to please the great, nay even to please those whom we love, compared with this? What gain is it to be applauded, admired, courted, followed, — compared with this one aim, of not being disobedient to a heavenly vision? What can this world offer comparable with that insight into spiritual things, that keen faith, that heavenly peace, that high sanctity, that everlasting righteousness, that hope of glory, which they have, who in sincerity love and follow our Lord Jesus Christ? Let us beg and pray Him day by day to reveal Himself to our souls more fully, to quicken our senses, to give us sight and hearing, taste and touch of the world to come; so to work within us, that we may sincerely say, 'Thou shalt guide me with Thy counsel, and after that receive me with glory. Whom have I in heaven but Thee? and there is none upon earth that I desire in

---

the moment when he began to read St. Paul's Epistle to the Romans, which persuaded him to become a Christian.

34. Over the years Newman spoke or wrote privately of his perception of the Monophysite parallel to a number of people. He did so usually when he had become angry about his treatment in the university or the Church of England. He also made clear to some of those people that he did not see the perceived parallel as a reason to change his church. It should be added that his sense of the parallel which he communicated to his friends neither moved nor convinced any of them as it did him. See Turner, *John Henry Newman*, pp. 603–613.

comparison of Thee. My flesh and my heart faileth, but God is the strength of my heart, and my portion for ever.'"

Now to trace the succession of thoughts, and the conclusions, and the consequent innovations on my previous belief, and the general conduct, to which I was led, upon this sudden visitation. And first, I will say, whatever comes of saying it, for I leave inferences to others, that for years I must have had something of an habitual notion, though it was latent, and had never led me to distrust my own convictions, that my mind had not found its ultimate rest, and that in some sense or other I was on journey. During the same passage across the Mediterranean in which I wrote "Lead kindly light," I also wrote the verses, which are found in the Lyra under the head of "Providences," beginning, "When I look back." This was in 1833; and, since I have begun this narrative, I have found a memorandum under the date of September 7, 1829, in which I speak of myself, as "now in my rooms in Oriel College, slowly advancing &c. and led on by God's hand blindly, not knowing whither He is taking me." But, whatever this presentiment be worth, it was no protection against the dismay and disgust, which I felt, in consequence of the dreadful misgiving, of which I have been relating the history. The one question was, what was I to do? I had to make up my mind for myself, and others could not help me. I determined to be guided, not by my imagination, but by my reason. And this I said over and over again in the years which followed, both in conversation and in private letters. Had it not been for this severe resolve, I should have been a Catholic sooner than I was. Moreover, I felt on consideration a positive doubt, on the other hand, whether the suggestion did not come from below. Then I said to myself, Time alone can solve that question. It was my business to go on as usual, to obey those convictions to which I had so long surrendered myself, which still had possession of me, and on which my new thoughts had no direct bearing. That new conception of things should only so far influence me, as it had a logical claim to do so. If it came from above, it would come again; — so I trusted, — and with more definite outlines and greater cogency and consistency of proof. I thought of Samuel, before "he knew the word of the Lord;" and therefore I went, and lay down to sleep again. This was my broad view of the matter, and my *primâ facie* conclusion.

However, my new historical fact had already to a certain point a logical force. Down had come the *Via Media* as a definite theory or scheme, under the blows of St. Leo. My "Prophetical Office" had come to pieces; not indeed as an argument against "Roman errors," nor as against Protestantism, but as in behalf of England. I had no longer a distinctive plea for Anglicanism, unless I would be a Monophysite. I had, most painfully, to fall back upon my three original points of belief, which I have spoken so much of in a former passage, — the principle of dogma, the sacramental system, and anti-Romanism. Of these three, the first two were better secured in Rome than in the Anglican Church. The Apostolical Succession, the two prominent sacraments, and the primitive Creeds, belonged, indeed, to the latter; but there had been and was far less strictness on matters of dogma and ritual in the Anglican system than in the Roman: in consequence, my main argument for the Anglican claims lay in the positive and special charges, which I could bring against Rome. I had no positive Anglican theory. I was very nearly a pure Protestant. Lutherans had a sort of theology, so had Calvinists; I had none.

However, this pure Protestantism, to which I was gradually left, was really a practical principle. It was a strong, though it was only a negative ground, and it still had great hold on me. As a boy of fifteen, I had so fully imbibed it, that I had actually erased in my *Gradus ad Parnassum,* such titles, under the word "Papa," as "Christi Vicarius," "sacer interpres," and "sceptra gerens," and substituted epithets so vile that I cannot bring myself to write them down here.[35] The effect of this early persuasion remained as, what I have already called it, a "stain upon my imagination." As regards my reason, I began in 1833 to form theories on the subject, which tended to obliterate it; yet by 1838 I had got no further than to consider Antichrist, as not the Church of Rome, but the spirit of the old pagan city, the fourth monster of Daniel, which was still alive, and which had corrupted the Church which was planted there. Soon after this indeed, and before my attention was directed to the Monophysite controversy, I underwent a great change of opinion. I saw that, from the nature of the case, the true Vicar of Christ must ever to the world seem like Antichrist, and be stigmatized as such, because a resemblance must ever exist between an original and a forgery; and thus the fact of such a calumny was almost one of the notes of the Church. But we cannot unmake ourselves or change our habits in a moment. Though my reason was convinced, I did not throw off, for some time after, — I could not have thrown off, — the unreasoning prejudice and suspicion, which I cherished about her at least by fits and starts, in spite of this conviction of my reason. I cannot prove this, but I believe it to have been the case from what I recollect of myself. Nor was there any thing in the history of St. Leo and the Monophysites to undo the

---

35. *Gradus ad Parnassum* was a Latin thesaurus for schoolboys. The Latin words Newman had erased under the Latin entry for *pope* ("Papa") meant in English Vicar of Christ, sacred mediator, and scepter-bearing.

firm belief I had in the existence of what I called the practical abuses and excesses of Rome.[36]

To her inconsistencies then, to her ambition and intrigue, to her sophistries (as I considered them to be) I now had recourse in my opposition to her, both public and personal. I did so by way of a relief. I had a great and growing dislike, after the summer of 1839, to speak against the Roman Church herself or her formal doctrines. I was very averse to speaking against doctrines, which might possibly turn out to be true, though at the time I had no reason for thinking they were; or against the Church, which had preserved them. I began to have misgivings, that, strong as my own feelings had been against her, yet in some things which I had said, I had taken the statements of Anglican divines for granted without weighing them for myself. I said to a friend in 1840, in a letter, which I shall use presently, "I am troubled by doubts whether as it is, I have not, in what I have published, spoken too strongly against Rome, though I think I did it in a kind of faith, being determined to put myself into the English system, and say all that our divines said, whether I had fully weighed it or not." I was sore about the great Anglican divines, as if they had taken me in, and made me say strong things, which facts did not justify. Yet I *did* still hold in substance all that I had said against the Church of Rome in my Prophetical Office. I felt the force of the usual Protestant objections against her; I believed that we had the Apostolical succession in the Anglican Church, and the grace of the sacraments; I was not sure that the difficulty of its isolation might not be overcome, though I was far from sure that it could. I did not see any clear proof that it had committed itself to any heresy, or had taken part against the truth; and I was not sure that it would not revive into full Apostolic purity and strength, and grow into union with Rome herself (Rome explaining her doctrines and guarding against their abuse), that is, if we were but patient and hopeful. I began to wish for union between the Anglican Church and Rome, if, and when, it was possible; and I did what I could to gain weekly prayers for that object. The ground which I felt to be good against her was the moral ground: I felt I could not be wrong in striking at her political and social line of action. The alliance of a dogmatic religion with liberals, high or low, seemed to me a providential direction against moving towards Rome, and a better "Preservative against Popery," than the three volumes in folio, in which, I think,

---

36. As late as December 29, 1844, Newman declared to Keble, "No one can have a more unfavorable view than I of the present state of the Roman Catholics — so much so, that any who join them would be like the Cistercians of Fountains, living under trees till their house was built. If I must account for it, I should say that the want of unity has injured both them and us." (JHN to John Keble, December 29, 1844, *L&D* 10: 476.)

that prophylactic is to be found. However, on occasions which demanded it, I felt it a duty to give out plainly all that I thought, though I did not like to do so. One such instance occurred, when I had to publish a Letter about Tract 90.[37] In that Letter, I said, "Instead of setting before the soul the Holy Trinity, and heaven and hell, the Church of Rome does seem to me, as a popular system, to preach the Blessed Virgin and the Saints, and purgatory." On this occasion I recollect expressing to a friend the distress it gave me thus to speak; but, I said, "How can I help saying it, if I think it? and I *do* think it; my Bishop calls on me to say out what I think; and that is the long and the short of it." But I recollected Hurrell Froude's words to me, almost his dying words, "I must enter another protest against your cursing and swearing. What good can it do? and I call it uncharitable to an excess. How mistaken we may ourselves be, on many points that are only gradually opening on us!"

Instead then of speaking of errors in doctrine, I was driven, by my state of mind, to insist upon the political conduct, the controversial bearing, and the social methods and manifestations of Rome. And here I found a matter ready to my hand, which affected me the more sensibly for the reason that it lay at our very doors. I can hardly describe too strongly my feeling upon it. I had an unspeakable aversion to the policy and acts of Mr. O'Connell, because, as I thought, he associated himself with men of all religions and no religion against the Anglican Church, and advanced Catholicism by violence and intrigue.[38] When then I found him taken up by the English Catholics, and, as I supposed, at Rome, I considered I had a fulfilment before my eyes how the Court of Rome played fast and loose, and justified the serious charges which I had seen put down in books against it. Here we saw what Rome was in action, whatever she might be when quiescent. Her conduct was simply secular and political.

This feeling led me into the excess of being very rude to that zealous and most charitable man, Mr. Spencer, when he came to Oxford in January, 1840,

---

37. John Henry Newman, *Letter to the Right Reverend Father in God, Richard, Lord Bishop of Oxford* (Oxford: J. H. Parker, 1841). This pamphlet was reprinted in John Henry Newman, *The Via Media of the Anglican Church. Illustrated in Lectures, Letters, and Tracts Written between 1830 and 1841* (London: Longmans, Green, 1899) 2: 395–424.

38. Daniel O'Connell (1775–1847) was the foremost leader of Irish nationalism during Newman's Anglican years. He was a Roman Catholic whose political tactics had forced the hand of the British government regarding Catholic Emancipation. During the 1830s and 1840s Newman disliked his tactic of appealing to and mobilizing popular opinion in Ireland and the support O'Connell received from the Irish Roman Catholic Church.

to get Anglicans to set about praying for Unity.[39] I myself, at that time, or soon after, drew up such prayers; their desirableness was one of the first thoughts which came upon me after my shock; but I was too much annoyed with the political action of the Catholic body in these islands to wish to have any thing to do with them personally. So glad in my heart was I to see him, when he came to my rooms with Mr. Palmer of Magdalen, that I could have laughed for joy; I think I did laugh; but I was very rude to him, I would not meet him at dinner, and that, (though I did not say so,) because I considered him "in loco apostatæ" from the Anglican Church, and I hereby beg his pardon for it.[40] I wrote afterwards with a view to apologize, but I dare say he must have thought that I made the matter worse, for these were my words to him: —

"The news that you are praying for us is most touching, and raises a variety of indescribable emotions. . . . May their prayers return abundantly into their own bosoms. . . . Why then do I not meet you in a manner conformable with these first feelings? For this single reason, if I may say it, that your acts are contrary to your words. You invite us to a union of hearts, at the same time that you are doing all you can, not to restore, not to reform, not to re-unite, but to destroy our Church. You go further than your principles require. You are leagued with our enemies. 'The voice is Jacob's voice, but the hands are the hands of Esau.' This is what especially distresses us; this is what we cannot understand; how Christians, like yourselves, with the clear view you have that a warfare is ever waging in the world between good and evil, should, in the present state of England, ally yourselves with the side of evil against the side of good. . . . Of parties now in the country, you cannot but allow, that next to yourselves we are nearest to revealed truth. We maintain great and holy principles; we profess Catholic doctrines. . . . So near are we as a body to yourselves in modes of thinking, as even to have been taunted with the nicknames which belong to you; and, on the other hand, if there are professed infidels, scoffers, sceptics, unprincipled men, rebels, they are found among our opponents. And yet you take part with them against us. . . . You consent to act hand in hand [with these and others] for our overthrow. Alas! all this it is that impresses us irresistibly with the notion that you are a political, not a religious party; that in order to gain an end on which you set your hearts, — an open stage for yourselves in England, — you ally yourselves with those who hold nothing against those who hold something. This is what distresses my own mind so greatly, to speak of myself, that, with limitations which need not now be mentioned, I

---

39. George Spencer (1799–1864) was a convert to Roman Catholicism who worked for the union of the Church of England and the Roman Catholic Church.

40. *in loco apostatæ,* "in effect an apostate."

cannot meet familiarly any leading persons of the Roman Communion, and least of all when they come on a religious errand. Break off, I would say, with Mr. O'Connell in Ireland and the liberal party in England, or come not to us with overtures for mutual prayer and religious sympathy."

And here came in another feeling, of a personal nature, which had little to do with the argument against Rome, except that, in my prejudice, I viewed what happened to myself in the light of my own ideas of the traditionary conduct of her advocates and instruments. I was very stern in the case of any interference in our Oxford matters on the part of charitable Catholics, and of any attempt to do me good personally. There was nothing, indeed, at the time more likely to throw me back. "Why do you meddle? why cannot you let me alone? You can do me no good; you know nothing on earth about me; you may actually do me harm; I am in better hands than yours. I know my own sincerity of purpose; and I am determined upon taking my time." Since I have been a Catholic, people have sometimes accused me of backwardness in making converts; and Protestants have argued from it that I have no great eagerness to do so. It would be against my nature to act otherwise than I do; but besides, it would be to forget the lessons which I gained in the experience of my own history in the past.

This is the account which I have to give of some savage and ungrateful words in the British Critic of 1840 against the controversialists of Rome: "By their fruits ye shall know them. . . . We see it attempting to gain converts among us by unreal representations of its doctrines, plausible statements, bold assertions, appeals to the weaknesses of human nature, to our fancies, our eccentricities, our fears, our frivolities, our false philosophies. We see its agents, smiling and nodding and ducking to attract attention, as gipsies make up to truant boys, holding out tales for the nursery, and pretty pictures, and gilt gingerbread, and physic concealed in jam, and sugar-plums for good children. Who can but feel shame when the religion of Ximenes, Borromeo, and Pascal, is so overlaid?[41] Who can but feel sorrow, when its devout and earnest defenders so mistake its genius and its capabilities? We Englishmen like manliness, openness, consistency, truth. Rome will never gain on us, till she learns these virtues, and uses them; and then she *may* gain us, but it will be by ceasing to be what we now mean by Rome, by having a right, not to 'have dominion over our faith,' but to gain and possess our affections in the bonds of the

---

41. Francisco Ximenes de Cisneros (1436–1517), a Spanish prelate; St. Carlo Borromeo (1538–1584), an Italian prelate; and Blaise Pascal (1623–1662), a French mathematician and religious writer, were exemplars to Newman of Roman Catholics of great accomplishment and personal piety.

gospel. Till she ceases to be what she practically is, a union is impossible between her and England; but, if she does reform, (and who can presume to say that so large a part of Christendom never can?) then it will be our Church's duty at once to join in communion with the continental Churches, whatever politicians at home may say to it, and whatever steps the civil power may take in consequence. And though we may not live to see that day, at least we are bound to pray for it; we are bound to pray for our brethren that they and we may be led together into the pure light of the gospel, and be one as we once were one. It was most touching news to be told, as we were lately, that Christians on the Continent were praying together for the spiritual well-being of England. May they gain light, while they aim at unity, and grow in faith while they manifest their love! We too have our duties to them; not of reviling, not of slandering, not of hating, though political interests require it; but the duty of loving brethren still more abundantly in spirit, whose faces, for our sins and their sins, we are not allowed to see in the flesh."

No one ought to indulge in insinuations; it certainly diminishes my right to complain of slanders uttered against myself, when, as in this passage, I had already spoken in disparagement of the controversialists of that religious body, to which I myself now belong.

I have thus put together, as well as I can, what has to be said about my general state of mind from the autumn of 1839 to the summer of 1841; and, having done so, I go on to narrate how my new misgivings affected my conduct, and my relations towards the Anglican Church.

When I got back to Oxford in October, 1839, after the visits which I had been paying, it so happened, there had been, in my absence, occurrences of an awkward character, compromising me both with my Bishop and also with the authorities of the University; and this drew my attention at once to the state of the Movement party there, and made me very anxious for the future.[42] In the spring of the year, as has been seen in the Article analyzed above, I had spoken of the excesses which were to be found among persons commonly included in it: — at that time I thought little of such an evil, but the new views, which had

---

42. By 1839 Newman's younger followers were acting quite independently of him, causing embarrassment and risking discipline from university and church authorities. John B. Morris (1812–1880) had preached a sermon from the pulpit of St. Mary's that the vice chancellor of the university thought Romanish and for which he formally criticized him. J. R. Bloxam (1807–1891) was reported to have assisted in the celebration of a Roman Catholic mass, a false report that nonetheless disturbed Bishop Bagot. From this date until the time of his reception into the Roman Catholic Church, Newman found himself driven to increasingly radical positions by such advanced, restless followers.

come on me during the Long Vacation, on the one hand made me comprehend it, and on the other took away my power of effectually meeting it. A firm and powerful control was necessary to keep men straight; I never had a strong wrist, but at the very time, when it was most needed, the reins had broken in my hands. With an anxious presentiment on my mind of the upshot of the whole inquiry, which it was almost impossible for me to conceal from men who saw me day by day, who heard my familiar conversation, who came perhaps for the express purpose of pumping me, and having a categorical *yes* or *no* to their questions, — how could I expect to say any thing about my actual, positive, present belief, which would be sustaining or consoling to such persons as were haunted already by doubts of their own? Nay, how could I, with satisfaction to myself, analyze my own mind, and say what I held and what I did not hold? or how could I say with what limitations, shades of difference, or degrees of belief, I still held that body of Anglican opinions which I had openly professed and taught? how could I deny or assert this point or that, without injustice to the new light, in which the whole evidence for those old opinions presented itself to my mind?

However, I had to do what I could, and what was best, under the circumstances; I found a general talk on the subject of the Article in the Dublin Review; and, if it had affected me, it was not wonderful, that it affected others also. As to myself, I felt no kind of certainty that the argument in it was conclusive. Taking it at the worst, granting that the Anglican Church had not the Note of Catholicity; yet there were many Notes of the Church. Some belonged to one age or place, some to another. Bellarmine had reckoned Temporal Prosperity among the Notes of the Church; but the Roman Church had not any great popularity, wealth, glory, power, or prospects, in the nineteenth century. It was not at all certain as yet, even that we had not the Note of Catholicity; but, if not this, we had others. My first business then, was to examine this question carefully, and see, whether a great deal could not be said after all for the Anglican Church, in spite of its acknowledged short-comings. This I did in an Article "on the Catholicity of the English Church," which appeared in the British Critic of January, 1840. As to my personal distress on the point, I think it had gone by February 21st in that year, for I wrote then to Mr. Bowden about the important Article in the Dublin, thus: "It made a great impression here [Oxford]; and, I say what of course I would only say to such as yourself, it made me for a while very uncomfortable in my own mind. The great speciousness of his argument is one of the things which have made me despond so much," that is, as anticipating its effect upon others.

But, secondly, the great stumbling-block lay in the 39 Articles. It was urged that here was a positive Note *against* Anglicanism: — Anglicanism claimed to hold, that the Church of England was nothing else than a continuation in this country, (as the Church of Rome might be in France or Spain,) of that one Church of which in old times Athanasius and Augustine were members. But, if so, the doctrine must be the same; the doctrine of the Old Church must live and speak in Anglican formularies, in the 39 Articles. Did it? Yes, it did; that is what I maintained; it did in substance, in a true sense. Man had done his worst to disfigure, to mutilate, the old Catholic Truth; but there it was, in spite of them, in the Articles still. It was there, — but this must be shown. It was a matter of life and death to us to show it. And I believed that it could be shown; I considered that those grounds of justification, which I gave above, when I was speaking of Tract 90, were sufficient for the purpose; and therefore I set about showing it at once. This was in March, 1840, when I went up to Littlemore. And, as it was a matter of life and death with us, all risks must be run to show it. When the attempt was actually made, I had got reconciled to the prospect of it, and had no apprehensions as to the experiment; but in 1840, while my purpose was honest, and my grounds of reason satisfactory, I did nevertheless recognize that I was engaged in an *experimentum crusis*.[43] I have no doubt that then I acknowledged to myself that it would be a trial of the Anglican Church, which it had never undergone before, — not that the Catholic sense of the Articles had not been held or at least suffered by their framers and promulgators, not that it was not implied in the teaching of Andrewes or Beveridge,[44] but that it had never been publicly recognized, while the interpretation of the day was Protestant and exclusive. I observe also, that, though my Tract was an experiment, it was, as I said at the time, "no *feeler*"; the event showed this; for, when my principle was not granted, I did not draw back, but gave up. I would not hold office in a Church which would not allow my sense of the Articles.[45] My tone was, "This is necessary for us, and have it we must and will, and, if it tends to bring men to look less bitterly on the Church of Rome, so much the better."

This then was the second work to which I set myself; though when I got to

43. "crucial experiment"; in late 1840 Newman told Keble that the Tractarians had not "yet made fair trial how much the English Church will bear" and that this trial was "a hazardous experiment, like proving Cannon," but they must not "take it for granted the metal will burst in the operation." (JHN to J. Keble, November 6, 1840, *L&D* 7: 433).

44. William Beveridge (1637–1708) was bishop of St. Asaph and one of the seventeenth-century Anglican divines whom Newman admired.

45. Hostile contemporaries publicly disparaged the Tractarians for their idiosyncratic interpretation of the Thirty-Nine Articles. The *Christian Observer,* a major evangelical journal, in 1842 described the Tractarians as "the sect of the Ninety Articles." (*Christian Observer* 42 (1842): 35.)

Littlemore, other things interfered to prevent my accomplishing it at the moment. I had in mind to remove all such obstacles as lay in the way of holding the Apostolic and Catholic character of the Anglican teaching; to assert the right of all who chose, to say in the face of day, "Our Church teaches the Primitive Ancient faith." I did not coneal this: in Tract 90, it is put forward as the first principle of all, "It is a duty which we owe both to the Catholic Church, and to our own, to take our reformed confessions in the most Catholic sense they will admit: we have no duties towards their framers." And still more pointedly in my Letter, explanatory of the Tract, addressed to Dr. Jelf, I say: "The only peculiarity of the view I advocate, if I must so call it, is this — that whereas it is usual at this day to make the *particular belief of their writers* their true interpretation, I would make the *belief of the Catholic Church such*. That is, as it is often said that infants are regenerated in Baptism, not on the faith of their parents, but of the Church, so in like manner I would say that the Articles are received, not in the sense of their framers, but (as far as the wording will admit or any ambiguity requires it) in the one Catholic sense."[46]

A third measure which I distinctly contemplated, was the resignation of St. Mary's, whatever became of the question of the 39 Articles; and as a first step I meditated a retirement to Littlemore. Littlemore was an integral part of St. Mary's Parish, and between two and three miles distant from Oxford. I had built a Church there several years before; and I went there to pass the Lent of 1840, and gave myself up to teaching in the Parish School, and practising the choir. At the same time, I had in view a monastic house there. I bought ten acres of ground and began planting; but this great design was never carried out. I mention it, because it shows how little I had really the idea at that time of ever leaving the Anglican Church. That I contemplated even the further step of giving up St. Mary's itself as early as 1839, appears from a letter which I wrote in October, 1840, to the friend whom it was most natural for me to consult on such a point. It ran as follows: —

"For a year past a feeling has been growing on me that I ought to give up St. Mary's, but I am no fit judge in the matter. I cannot ascertain accurately my own impressions and convictions, which are the basis of the difficulty, and

---

46. John Henry Newman, *Letter Addressed to the Rev. R. W. Jelf* (reprinted in Newman, *The Via Media of the Anglican Church*, 2: 365–394). Newman claimed that he was interpreting the Thirty-Nine Articles not in the sense of their framers but in the sense of what he regarded as Catholic tradition, of which he presented himself as the sure interpreter. If the articles were compatible with Catholic tradition, as Newman argued, then in subscribing to them at the time of ordination, his followers were not rejecting Catholic tradition. It was the reading of this pamphlet that caused the archbishop of Canterbury to decide that the *Tracts for the Times* must be discontinued.

though you cannot of course do this for me, yet you may help me generally, and perhaps supersede the necessity of my going by them at all.

"First, it is certain that I do not know my Oxford parishioners; I am not conscious of influencing them, and certainly I have no insight into their spiritual state. I have no personal, no pastoral acquaintance with them. To very few have I any opportunity of saying a religious word. Whatever influence I exert on them is precisely that which I may be exerting on persons out of my parish. In my excuse I am accustomed to say to myself that I am not adapted to get on with them, while others are. On the other hand, I am conscious that by means of my position at St. Mary's, I do exert a considerable influence on the University, whether on Undergraduates or Graduates. It seems, then, on the whole that I am using St. Mary's, to the neglect of its direct duties, for objects not belonging to it; I am converting a parochial charge into a sort of University office.

"I think I may say truly that I have begun scarcely any plan but for the sake of my parish, but every one has turned, independently of me, into the direction of the University. I began Saints'-days Services, daily Services, and Lectures in Adam de Brome's Chapel,[47] for my parishioners; but they have not come to them. In consequence I dropped the last mentioned, having, while it lasted, been naturally led to direct it to the instruction of those who did come, instead of those who did not. The Weekly Communion, I believe, I did begin for the sake of the University.

"Added to this the authorities of the University, the appointed guardians of those who form great part of the attendants on my Sermons, have shown a dislike of my preaching. One dissuades men from coming; — the late Vice-Chancellor threatens to take his own children away from the Church; and the present, having an opportunity last spring of preaching in my parish pulpit, gets up and preaches against doctrine with which I am in good measure identified. No plainer proof can be given of the feeling in these quarters, than the absurd myth, now a second time put forward, 'that Vice-Chancellors cannot be got to take the office on account of Puseyism.'

"But further than this, I cannot disguise from myself that my preaching is not calculated to defend that system of religion which has been received for 300 years, and of which the Heads of Houses are the legitimate maintainers in this place. They exclude me, as far as may be, from the University Pulpit; and, though I never have preached strong doctrine in it, they do so rightly, so far as

---

47. Adam de Brome's Chapel was a small side chapel in the Church of St. Mary the Virgin. Newman reported that few people attended those lectures.

this, that they understand that my sermons are calculated to undermine things established. I cannot disguise from myself that they are. No one will deny that most of my sermons are on moral subjects, not doctrinal; still I am leading my hearers to the Primitive Church, if you will, but not to the Church of England. Now, ought one to be disgusting the minds of young men with the received religion, in the exercise of a sacred office, yet without a commission, and against the wish of their guides and governors?

"But this is not all. I fear I must allow that, whether I will or no, I am disposing them towards Rome. First, because Rome is the only representative of the Primitive Church besides ourselves; in proportion then as they are loosened from the one, they will go to the other. Next, because many doctrines which I have held have far greater, or their only scope, in the Roman system. And, moreover, if, as is not unlikely, we have in process of time heretical Bishops or teachers among us, an evil which *ipso facto* infects the whole community to which they belong, and if, again (what there are at this moment symptoms of), there be a movement in the English Roman Catholics to break the alliance of O'Connell and of Exeter Hall, strong temptations will be placed in the way of individuals, already imbued with a tone of thought congenial to Rome, to join her Communion."[48]

"People tell me, on the other hand, that I am, whether by sermons or otherwise, exerting at St. Mary's a beneficial influence on our prospective clergy; but what if I take to myself the credit of seeing further than they, and of having in the course of the last year discovered that what they approve so much is very likely to end in Romanism?

"The *arguments* which I have published against Romanism seem to myself as cogent as ever, but men go by their sympathies, not by argument; and if I feel the force of this influence myself, who bow to the arguments, why may not others still more, who never have in the same degree admitted the arguments?

"Nor can I counteract the danger by preaching or writing against Rome. I seem to myself almost to have shot my last arrow in the Article on English Catholicity. It must be added, that the very circumstance that I have committed myself against Rome has the effect of setting to sleep people suspicious about me, which is painful now that I begin to have suspicions about myself. I mentioned my general difficulty to Rogers a year since, than whom I know no

---

48. Exeter Hall was a large auditorium in London that was the center for London and national evangelical gatherings. Newman had written a devastating satire of these meetings in the *British Critic* 24 (1838): 190–210.

one of a more fine and accurate conscience, and it was his spontaneous idea that I should give up St. Mary's, if my feelings continued.[49] I mentioned it again to him lately, and he did not reverse his opinion, only expressed great reluctance to believe it must be so."

My friend's judgment was in favour of my retaining my living; at least for the present; what weighed with me most was his saying, "You must consider, whether your retiring either from the Pastoral Care only, or from writing and printing and editing in the cause, would not be a sort of scandalous thing, unless it were done very warily. It would be said, 'You see he can go on no longer with the Church of England, except in mere Lay Communion;' or people might say you repented of the cause altogether. Till you see [your way to mitigate, if not remove this evil] I certainly should advise you to stay." I answered as follows: —

"Since you think I *may* go on, it seems to follow that, under the circumstances, I *ought* to do so. There are plenty of reasons for it, directly it is allowed to be lawful. The following considerations have much reconciled my feelings to your conclusion.

"1. I do not think that we have yet made fair trial how much the English Church will bear. I know it is a hazardous experiment, — like proving cannon. Yet we must not take it for granted that the metal will burst in the operation. It has borne at various times, not to say at this time, a great infusion of Catholic truth without damage. As to the result, viz. whether this process will not approximate the whole English Church, as a body, to Rome, that is nothing to us. For what we know, it may be the providential means of uniting the whole Church in one, without fresh schismatizing or use of private judgment."

Here I observe, that, what was contemplated was the bursting of the *Catholicity* of the Anglican Church, that is, my *subjective idea* of that Church. Its bursting would not hurt her with the world, but would be a discovery that she was purely and essentially Protestant, and would be really the "hoisting of the engineer with his own petard." And this was the result. I continue: —

"2. Say, that I move sympathies for Rome: in the same sense does Hooker, Taylor, Bull, &c. Their *arguments* may be against Rome, but the sympathies they raise must be towards Rome, *so far* as Rome maintains truths which our Church does not teach or enforce. Thus it is a question of *degree* between our divines and me. I may, if so be, go further; I may raise sympathies *more;* but

---

49. Frederic Rogers, later Baron Blachford (1811–1889), had been one of Newman's successful students who continued as a friend until he broke with Newman, thinking him having moved too close to Roman Catholicism. Rogers and Newman reestablished their relationship at the time of the Kingsley controversy.

I am but urging minds in the same direction as they do. I am doing just the very thing which all our doctors have ever been doing. In short, would not Hooker, if Vicar of St. Mary's, be in my difficulty?" — Here it may be objected, that Hooker could preach against Rome and I could not; but I doubt whether he could have preached effectively against Transubstantiation better than I, though neither he nor I held that doctrine.

"3. Rationalism is the great evil of the day.[50] May not I consider my post at St. Mary's as a place of protest against it? I am more certain that the Protestant [spirit], which I oppose, leads to infidelity, than that which I recommend, leads to Rome. Who knows what the state of the University may be, as regards Divinity Professors in a few years hence? Any how, a great battle may be coming on, of which Milman's book is a sort of earnest.[51] The whole of *our* day may be a battle with this spirit. May we not leave to another age *its own* evil, — to settle the question of Romanism?"

I may add that from this time I had a curate at St. Mary's, who gradually took more and more of my work.

Also, this same year, 1840, I made arrangements for giving up the British Critic, in the following July, which were carried into effect at that date.

Such was about my state of mind, on the publication of Tract 90 in February 1841. I was indeed in prudence taking steps towards eventually withdrawing from St. Mary's, and I was not confident about my permanent adhesion to the Anglican creed; but I was in no actual perplexity or trouble of mind. Nor did the immense commotion consequent upon the publication of the Tract unsettle me again; for I fancied I had weathered the storm, as far as the Bishops were concerned: the Tract had not been condemned: that was the great point, and I made much of it.[52]

To illustrate my feelings during this trial, I will make extracts from my letters addressed severally to Mr. Bowden and another friend, which have come into my possession.

---

50. Tractarian writers used the term *rationalism* in a variety of ways. Sometimes they applied it to evangelicals who looked for precise meanings in scripture. Other times they applied it to writers influenced by German historical criticism. The full context of this letter to Keble suggests both. See JHN to John Keble, November 6, 1840, *L&D* 7: 433–434, and Turner, *John Henry Newman*, pp. 234–244.

51. Milman is Henry Hart Milman (1791–1868), whose *History of Christianity to the Abolition of Paganism in the Roman Empire* (1840) Newman critically reviewed in the *British Critic* early in 1841. In that same history, however, Milman himself had sharply criticized some of the more advanced German theological writing of the day.

52. See footnote 57, p. 206.

1. March 15. — "The Heads, I believe, have just done a violent act: they have said that my interpretation of the Articles is an *evasion*.[53] Do not think that this will pain me. You see, no *doctrine* is censured, and my shoulders shall manage to bear the charge. If you knew all, or were here, you would see that I have asserted a great principle, and I *ought* to suffer for it: — that the Articles are to be interpreted, not according to the meaning of the writers, but (as far as the wording will admit) according to the sense of the Catholic Church."

2. March 25. — "I do trust I shall make no false step, and hope my friends will pray for me to this effect. If, as you say, a destiny hangs over us, a single false step may ruin all. I am very well and comfortable; but we are not yet out of the wood."

3. April 1. — "The Bishop sent me word on Sunday to write a Letter to him '*instanter*.' So I wrote it on Monday: on Tuesday it passed through the press: on Wednesday it was out: and to-day [Thursday] it is in London.

"I trust that things are smoothing now; and that we have made a *great step* is certain. It is not right to boast, till I am clear out of the wood, i. e. till I know how the Letter is received in London. You know, I suppose, that I am to stop the Tracts; but you will see in the Letter, though I speak *quite* what I feel, yet I have managed to take out on *my* side my snubbing's worth. And this makes me anxious how it will be received in London.

"I have not had a misgiving for five minutes from the first: but I do not like to boast, lest some harm come."

4. April 4. — "Your letter of this morning was an exceedingly great gratification to me; and it is confirmed, I am thankful to say, by the opinion of others. The Bishop sent me a message that my Letter had his unqualified approbation; and since that, he has sent me a note to the same effect, only going more into detail. It is most pleasant too to my feelings, to have such a testimony to the substantial truth and importance of No. 90, as I have had from so many of my friends, from those who, from their cautious turn of mind, I was least sanguine about. I have not had one misgiving myself about it throughout; and I do trust that what has happened will be overruled to subserve the great cause we all have at heart."

5. May 9. — "The Bishops are very desirous of hushing the matter up: and I certainly have done my utmost to co-operate with them, on the understanding that the Tract is not to be withdrawn or condemned."

---

53. "The Heads" refers to the Oxford Heads of Houses (colleges and residential halls), who were the chief authoritative body in the university at this time. They were also known as the Hebdomadal Board because they met weekly.

Upon this occasion several Catholics wrote to me; I answered one of my correspondents in the same tone: —

"April 8. — You have no cause to be surprised at the discontinuance of the Tracts. We feel no misgivings about it whatever, as if the cause of what we hold to be Catholic truth would suffer thereby. My letter to my Bishop has, I trust, had the effect of bringing the preponderating *authority* of the Church on our side. No stopping of the Tracts can, humanly speaking, stop the spread of the opinions which they have inculcated.

"The Tracts are not *suppressed*. No doctrine or principle has been conceded by us, or condemned by authority. The Bishop has but said that a certain Tract is 'objectionable,' no reason being stated. I have no intention whatever of yielding any one point which I hold on conviction; and that the authorities of the Church know full well."

In the summer of 1841, I found myself at Littlemore without any harass or anxiety on my mind. I had determined to put aside all controversy, and I set myself down to my translation of St. Athanasius; but, between July and November, I received three blows which broke me.

1. I had got but a little way in my work, when my trouble returned on me. The ghost had come a second time. In the Arian History I found the very same phenomenon, in a far bolder shape, which I had found in the Monophysite. I had not observed it in 1832. Wonderful that this should come upon me! I had not sought it out; I was reading and writing in my own line of study, far from the controversies of the day, on what is called a "metaphysical" subject; but I saw clearly, that in the history of Arianism, the pure Arians were the Protestants, the semi-Arians were the Anglicans, and that Rome now was what it was then. The truth lay, not with the *Via Media*, but with what was called "the extreme party." As I am not writing a work of controversy, I need not enlarge upon the argument; I have said something on the subject in a Volume, from which I have already quoted.

2. I was in the misery of this new unsettlement, when a second blow came upon me.[54] The Bishops one after another began to charge against me. It was a

---

54. During the summer of 1841 several of the bishops issued charges to the clergy of their respective dioceses in which they sharply criticized Newman and *Tract 90* as well as Isaac Williams's tracts *On Reserve*. Evangelical bishops initially took the lead, including John Bird Sumner, who would become the archbishop of Canterbury. Similarly critical charges from high church bishops soon followed those of evangelical bishops. No bishop in any manner suggested approval of *Tract 90* though some indicated sympathy for its

formal, determinate movement. This was the real "understanding;" that, on which I had acted on the first appearance of Tract 90, had come to nought. I think the words, which had then been used to me, were, that "perhaps two or three of them might think it necessary to say something in their charges;" but by this time they had tided over the difficulty of the Tract, and there was no one to enforce the "understanding." They went on in this way, directing charges at me, for three whole years. I recognized it as a condemnation; it was the only one that was in their power. At first I intended to protest; but I gave up the thought in despair.

On October 17th, I wrote thus to a friend: "I suppose it will be necessary in some shape or other to re-assert Tract 90; else, it will seem, after these Bishops' Charges, as if it were silenced, which it has not been, nor do I intend it should be. I wish to keep quiet; but if Bishops speak, I will speak too. If the view were silenced, I could not remain in the Church, nor could many others; and therefore, since it is *not* silenced, I shall take care to show that it isn't."

A day or two after, Oct. 22, a stranger wrote to me to say, that the Tracts for the Times had made a young friend of his a Catholic, and to ask, "would I be so good as to convert him back;" I made answer:

"If conversions to Rome take place in consequence of the Tracts for the Times, I do not impute blame to them, but to those who, instead of acknowledging such Anglican principles of theology and ecclesiastical polity as they contain, set themselves to oppose them. Whatever be the influence of the Tracts, great or small, they may become just as powerful for Rome, if our Church refuses them, as they would be for our Church if she accepted them. If our rulers speak either against the Tracts, or not at all, if any number of them, not only do not favour, but even do not suffer the principles contained in them, it is plain that our members may easily be persuaded either to give up those principles, or to give up the Church. If this state of things goes on, I mournfully prophesy, not one or two, but many secessions to the Church of Rome."

Two years afterwards, looking back on what had passed, I said, "There were no converts to Rome, till after the condemnation of No. 90."

3. As if all this were not enough, there came the affair of the Jerusalem Bishopric; and, with a brief mention of it, I shall conclude.[55]

---

broad argument, but not for its specific contentions. See Peter Nockles, "Oxford, Tract 90 and the Bishops," in *John Henry Newman: Reason, Rhetoric and Romanticism*, ed. David Nicholls and Fergus Kerr (Carbondale and Edwardsville: Southern Illinois Univ. Press, 1991), pp. 28–87, and Turner, *John Henry Newman*, pp. 389–395, 436–446. A selection from the charges appears as appendix 5 in *L&D* 8: 569–592.

55. The establishment of the Jerusalem bishopric is one of the obscure events of

I think I am right in saying that it had been long a desire with the Prussian Court to introduce Episcopacy into the new Evangelical Religion, which was intended in that country to embrace both the Lutheran and Calvinistic bodies. I almost think I heard of the project, when I was at Rome in 1833, at the Hotel of the Prussian Minister, M. Bunsen, who was most hospitable and kind, as to other English visitors, so also to my friends and myself. The idea of Episcopacy, as the Prussian king understood it, was, I suppose, very different from that taught in the Tractarian School: but still, I suppose also, that the chief authors of that school would have gladly seen such a measure carried out in Prussia, had it been done without compromising those principles which were necessary to the being of a Church. About the time of the publication of Tract 90, M. Bunsen and the then Archbishop of Canterbury were taking steps for its execution, by appointing and consecreting a Bishop for Jerusalem. Jerusalem, it would seem, was considered a safe place for the experiment; it was too far from Prussia to awaken the susceptibilities of any party at home; if the project failed, it failed without harm to any one; and, if it succeeded, it gave Protestantism a *status* in the East, which, in association with the Monophysite or Jacobite and the Nestorian bodies, formed a political instrument for England, parallel to that which Russia had in the Greek Church, and France in the Latin.[56]

Accordingly, in July 1841, full of the Anglican difficulty on the question of

---

nineteenth-century ecclesiastical history that would long ago have been forgotten except for its effect on Newman. In 1841 the Church of England and the established church of Prussia, recently reorganized to include both Lutherans and Calvinists, decided to send a bishop to Jerusalem to minister to Protestants, with each church nominating a cleric in turn. The proposal had the strong support of evangelicals in England and was seen as an evangelical project. Newman objected to it because he by then regarded both Lutheranism and Calvinism as heresies. From his standpoint the cooperation of the Church of England represented cooperation with heresy and still one more indication of what he perceived to be growing evangelical influence on the highest echelons of the English Church. He was further disappointed when many high churchmen in the English Church supported the project. As with other of his comments regarding contemporary events, several of Newman's friends thought he was overreacting. The Jerusalem bishopric proved unsuccessful and was dissolved in 1886. See Robert Ornsby, *Memoirs of James Robert Hope-Scott of Abbotsford* (London: John Murray, 1884), 1: 283–331; David E. Barclay, *Frederick William IV and the Prussian Monarchy, 1840–1861* (Oxford: Oxford Univ. Press, 1995), pp. 33–34, 74–84; R. W. Greaves, "The Jerusalem Bishopric, 1841," *English Historical Review* 64 (1949): 328–352.

56. The term *Jacobite* here refers not to the eighteenth-century followers of the Stuart dynasty, but to a Monophysite church founded in Syria in the sixth century by Jacob Baradaeus.

Catholicity, I thus spoke of the Jerusalem scheme in an Article in the British Critic: "When our thoughts turn to the East, instead of recollecting that there are Christian Churches there, we leave it to the Russians to take care of the Greeks, and the French to take care of the Romans, and we content ourselves with erecting a Protestant Church at Jerusalem, or with helping the Jews to rebuild their Temple there, or with becoming the august protectors of Nestorians, Monophysites, and all the heretics we can hear of, or with forming a league with the Mussulman against Greeks and Romans together."

I do not pretend, so long after the time, to give a full or exact account of this measure in detail. I will but say that in the Act of Parliament, under date of October 5, 1841, (if the copy, from which I quote, contains the measure as it passed the Houses,) provision is made for the consecration of "British subjects, or the subjects or citizens of any foreign state, to be Bishops in any foreign country, whether such foreign subjects or citizens be or be not subjects or citizens of the country in which they are to act, and. . . . without requiring such of them as may be subjects or citizens of any foreign kingdom or state to take the oaths of allegiance and supremacy, and the oath of due obedience to the Archbishop for the time being" . . . also "that such Bishop or Bishops, so consecrated, may exercise, within such limits, as may from time to time be assigned for that purpose in such foreign countries by her Majesty, spiritual jurisdiction over the ministers of British congregations of the United Church of England and Ireland, and over *such other Protestant* Congregations, as may be desirous of placing themselves under his or their authority."

Now here, at the very time that the Anglican Bishops were directing their censure upon me for avowing an approach to the Catholic Church not closer than I believed the Anglican formularies would allow, they were on the other hand, fraternizing, by their act or by their sufferance, with Protestant bodies, and allowing them to put themselves under an Anglican Bishop, without any renunciation of their errors or regard to their due reception of baptism and confirmation; while there was great reason to suppose that the said Bishop was intended to make converts from the orthodox Greeks, and the schismatical Oriental bodies, by means of the influence of England. This was the third blow, which finally shattered my faith in the Anglican Church. That Church was not only forbidding any sympathy or concurrence with the Church of Rome, but it actually was courting an intercommunion with Protestant Prussia and the heresy of the Orientals. The Anglican Church might have the Apostolical succession, as had the Monophysites; but such acts as were in progress led me to the gravest suspicion, not that it would soon cease to be a Church, but that, since the 16th century, it had never been a Church all along.

On October 12th, I thus wrote to Mr. Bowden:—"We have not a single

Anglican in Jerusalem; so we are sending a Bishop to *make* a communion, not to govern our own people. Next, the excuse is, that there are converted Anglican Jews there who require a Bishop; I am told there are not half-a-dozen. But for *them* the Bishop is sent out, and for them he is a Bishop of the *circumcision*" (I think he was a converted Jew, who boasted of his Jewish descent), "against the Epistle to the Galatians pretty nearly. Thirdly, for the sake of Prussia, he is to take under him all the foreign Protestants who will come; and the political advantages will be so great, from the influence of England, that there is no doubt they *will* come. They are to sign the Confession of Augsburg, and there is nothing to show that they hold the doctrine of Baptismal Regeneration.

"As to myself, I shall do nothing whatever publicly, unless indeed it were to give my signature to a Protest; but I think it would be out of place in *me* to agitate, having been in a way silenced; but the Archbishop is really doing most grave work, of which we cannot see the end."

I did make a solemn Protest, and sent it to the Archbishop of Canterbury, and also sent it to my own Bishop, with the following letter:[57] —

"It seems as if I were never to write to your Lordship, without giving you pain, and I know that my present subject does not specially concern your Lordship; yet, after a great deal of anxious thought, I lay before you the enclosed Protest.

"Your Lordship will observe that I am not asking for any notice of it, unless you think that I ought to receive one. I do this very serious act in obedience to my sense of duty.

"If the English Church is to enter on a new course, and assume a new aspect, it will be more pleasant to me hereafter to think, that I did not suffer so grievous an event to happen, without bearing witness against it.

"May I be allowed to say, that I augur nothing but evil, if we in any respect prejudice our title to be a branch of the Apostolic Church? That Article of the Creed, I need hardly observe to your Lordship, is of such constraining power, that, if *we* will not claim it, and use it for ourselves, *others* will use it in their own behalf against us. Men who learn whether by means of documents or measures, whether from the statements or the acts of persons in authority, that

---

57. Newman's protest over the Jerusalem bishopric is dated November 11, 1843, and the letter sending it to Bishop Bagot is dated November 13, 1843. See *L&D* 8: 327–328. In addition to Bagot, Newman sent the letter to Benjamin Harrison, a chaplain to the archbishop of Canterbury. The document equating both Lutheranism and Calvinism to heresy is one of the most extreme anti-Protestant statements Newman composed while in the Church of England. Keble dissuaded him from making it public.

our communion is not a branch of the One Church, I foresee with much grief, will be tempted to look out for that Church elsewhere.

"It is to me a subject of great dismay, that, as far as the Church has lately spoken out, on the subject of the opinions which I and others hold, those opinions are, not merely not *sanctioned* (for that I do not ask), but not even *suffered*.

"I earnestly hope that your Lordship will excuse my freedom in thus speaking to you of some members of your Most Rev. and Right Rev. Body. With every feeling of reverent attachment to your Lordship,

"I am, &c."

PROTEST.

"Whereas the Church of England has a claim on the allegiance of Catholic believers only on the ground of her own claim to be considered a branch of the Catholic Church:

"And whereas the recognition of heresy, indirect as well as direct, goes far to destroy such claim in the case of any religious body:

"And whereas to admit maintainers of heresy to communion, without formal renunciation of their errors, goes far towards recognizing the same:

"And whereas Lutheranism and Calvinism are heresies, repugnant to Scripture, springing up three centuries since, and anathematized by East as well as West:

"And whereas it is reported that the Most Reverend Primate and other Right Reverend of our Church have consecrated a Bishop with a view to exercising spiritual jurisdiction over Protestant, that is, Lutheran and Calvinist congregations in the East (under the provisions of an Act made in the last session of Parliament to amend an Act made in the 26th year of the reign of his Majesty King George the Third, intituled, 'An Act to empower the Archbishop of Canterbury, or the Archbishop of York for the time being, to consecrate to the office of Bishop persons being subjects or citizens of countries out of his Majesty's dominions'), dispensing at the same time, not in particular cases and accidentally, but as if on principle and universally, with any abjuration of error on the part of such congregations, and with any reconciliation to the Church on the part of the presiding Bishop; thereby giving some sort of formal recognition to the doctrines which such congregations maintain:

"And whereas the dioceses in England are connected together by so close an intercommunion, that what is done by authority in one, immediately affects the rest:

"On these grounds, I in my place, being a priest of the English Church and Vicar of St. Mary the Virgin's, Oxford, by way of relieving my conscience, do hereby solemnly protest against the measure aforesaid, and disown it, as removing our Church from her present ground and tending to her disorganization.

"John Henry Newman.
"November 11, 1841."

Looking back two years afterwards on the above-mentioned and other acts, on the part of Anglican Ecclesiastical authorities, I observed: "Many a man might have held an abstract theory about the Catholic Church, to which it was difficult to adjust the Anglican, — might have admitted a suspicion, or even painful doubts about the latter, — yet never have been impelled onwards, had our Rulers preserved the quiescence of former years; but it is the corroboration of a present, living, and energetic heterodoxy, which realizes and makes them practical; it has been the recent speeches and acts of authorities, who had so long been tolerant of Protestant error, which have given to inquiry and to theory its force and its edge."

As to the project of a Jerusalem Bishopric, I never heard of any good or harm it has ever done, except what it has done for me; which many think a great misfortune, and I one of the greatest of mercies. It brought me on to the beginning of the end.

Chapter IV.

History of My Religious Opinions from 1841 to 1845

§ 1.

From the end of 1841, I was on my death-bed, as regards my membership with the Anglican Church, though at the time I became aware of it only by degrees. I introduce what I have to say with this remark, by way of accounting for the character of this remaining portion of my narrative. A death-bed has scarcely a history; it is a tedious decline, with seasons of rallying and seasons of falling back; and since the end is foreseen, or what is called a matter of time, it has little interest for the reader, especially if he has a kind heart. Moreover, it is a season when doors are closed and curtains drawn, and when the sick man neither cares nor is able to record the stages of his malady. I was in these circumstances, except so far as I was not allowed to die in peace, — except so far as friends, who had still a full right to come in upon me, and the public world which had not, have given a sort of history to those last four years. But in consequence, my narrative must be in great measure documentary, as I cannot rely on my memory, except for definite particulars, positive or negative.[1] Letters of mine to friends since dead have come into my hands; others

---

1. It is not surprising that Newman here notes the difficulty he encountered in remembering the details of his last four years in the Church of England. These were years during which he continued to feel betrayed in his negotiations over *Tract 90*, when he encoun-

have been kindly lent me for the occasion; and I have some drafts of others, and some notes which I made, though I have no strictly personal or continuous memoranda to consult, and have unluckily mislaid some valuable papers.

And first as to my position in the view of duty; it was this: — 1. I had given up my place in the Movement in my letter to the Bishop of Oxford in the spring of 1841; but 2. I could not give up my duties towards the many and various minds who had more or less been brought into it by me; 3. I expected or intended gradually to fall back into Lay Communion; 4. I never contemplated leaving the Church of England; 5. I could not hold office in its service, if I were not allowed to hold the Catholic sense of the Articles; 6. I could not go to Rome, while she suffered honours to be paid to the Blessed Virgin and the Saints which I thought in my conscience to be incompatible with the Supreme, Incommunicable Glory of the One Infinite and Eternal; 7. I desired a union with Rome under conditions, Church with Church; 8. I called Littlemore my Torres Vedras,[2] and thought that some day we might advance again within the Anglican Church, as we had been forced to retire; 9. I kept back all persons who were disposed to go to Rome with all my might.

And I kept them back for three or four reasons; 1. because what I could not in conscience do myself, I could not suffer them to do; 2. because I thought that in various cases they were acting under excitement; 3. because I had duties to my Bishop and to the Anglican Church; and 4. in some cases, because I had received from their Anglican parents or superiors direct charge of them.

This was my view of my duty from the end of 1841, to my resignation of

---

tered a first slow then precipitous evaporation of support from former high church allies and sympathizers, when certain of his followers pursued a line of radical Catholicism with which he did not fully sympathize but from which he did not publicly disassociate himself, and when his tactic of holding his coterie within the English Church on the basis of *Tract 90* collapsed. Throughout this period he was increasingly isolated in the Littlemore community, pursuing a rigorously ascetic devotional and personal life, relentlessly attacked, and largely paralyzed in terms of taking action. Had he recounted the events of these years along with the history of his religious opinions, it would have become clear that his conversion to Roman Catholicism was a contingent event and one of several different paths he might have taken. In the *Apologia* he cites certain letters from this period of his life, but in the now completed *Letters and Diaries of John Henry Newman* the correspondence of those years constitutes approximately two and a half printed volumes.

2. Torres Vedras was the site in Spain where in 1810 during the Peninsular War the Duke of Wellington established a powerful defensive base from which he would later move his forces for engagement with the enemy. During late 1841 and early 1842 when Newman first withdrew to Littlemore, he did not use this military metaphor in his sermons, but rather portrayed himself as the prophet Elijah.

St. Mary's in the autumn of 1843. And now I shall relate my view, during that time, of the state of the controversy between the Churches.

As soon as I saw the hitch in the Anglican argument, during my course of reading in the summer of 1839, I began to look about, as I have said, for some ground which might supply a controversial basis for my need. The difficulty in question had affected my view both of Antiquity and Catholicity; for, while the history of St. Leo showed me that the deliberate and eventual consent of the great body of the Church ratified a doctrinal decision as a part of revealed truth, it also showed that the rule of Antiquity was not infringed, though a doctrine had not been publicly recognized as so revealed, till centuries after the time of the Apostles. Thus, whereas the Creeds tell us that the Church is One, Holy, Catholic, and Apostolic, I could not prove that the Anglican communion was an integral part of the One Church, on the ground of its teaching being Apostolic or Catholic, without reasoning in favour of what are commonly called the Roman corruptions; and I could not defend our separation from Rome and her faith without using arguments prejudicial to those great doctrines concerning our Lord, which are the very foundation of the Christian religion. The *Via Media* was an impossible idea; it was what I had called "standing on one leg;" and it was necessary, if my old issue of the controversy was to be retained, to go further either one way or the other.

Accordingly, I abandoned that old ground and took another. I deliberately quitted the old Anglican ground as untenable; though I did not do so all at once, but as I became more and more convinced of the state of the case. The Jerusalem Bishopric was the ultimate condemnation of the old theory of the *Via Media*: — if its establishment did nothing else, at least it demolished the sacredness of diocesan rights.[3] If England could be in Palestine, Rome might be in England. But its bearing upon the controversy, as I have shown in the foregoing chapter, was much more serious than this technical ground. From that time the Anglican Church was, in my mind, either not a normal portion of

---

3. By "diocesan rights" Newman means that he believed that only one branch of the Holy Catholic Church could appoint a bishop to a particular geographical area. He thought the Jerusalem bishopric, establishing a jointly administered diocese in Jerusalem, had confused that situation with the Church of England and the Prussian state church intruding into an area where another Orthodox bishop already presided. If that were to be the case, Newman believed there was no longer any reason that the Roman Catholic Church could not establish its own set of dioceses in England alongside those of the Church of England. What Newman is here expressing is the collapse of his previously held ecclesiology into what he regarded as a state of confusion. Few of his contemporaries, including those personally sympathetic to him, shared these views. This passage illustrates the kind of isolation into which he had set himself.

that One Church to which the promises were made, or at least in an abnormal state; and from that time I said boldly (as I did in my Protest, and as indeed I had even intimated in my Letter to the Bishop of Oxford), that the Church in which I found myself had no claim on me, except on condition of its being a portion of the One Catholic Communion, and that that condition must ever be borne in mind as a practical matter, and had to be distinctly proved. All this is not inconsistent with my saying above that, at this time, I had no thought of leaving the Church of England; because I felt some of my old objections against Rome as strongly as ever. I had no right, I had no leave, to act against my conscience. That was a higher rule than any argument about the Notes of the Church.

Under these circumstances I turned for protection to the Note of Sanctity, with a view of showing that we had at least one of the necessary Notes, as fully as the Church of Rome; or, at least, without entering into comparisons, that we had it in such a sufficient sense as to reconcile us to our position, and to supply full evidence, and a clear direction, on the point of practical duty. We had the Note of Life,—not any sort of life, not such only as can come of nature, but a supernatural Christian life, which could only come directly from above. Thus, in my Article in the British Critic, to which I have so often referred, in January, 1840 (before the time of Tract 90), I said of the Anglican Church that "she has the note of possession, the note of freedom from party titles, the note of life,—a tough life and a vigorous; she has ancient descent, unbroken continuance, agreement in doctrine with the Ancient Church."[4] Presently I go on to speak of sanctity: "Much as Roman Catholics may denounce us at present as schismatical, they could not resist us if the Anglican communion had but that one note of the Church upon it,—sanctity. The Church of the day [4th century] could not resist Meletius; his enemies were fairly overcome by him, by his meekness and holiness, which melted the most jealous of them."[5] And I continue, "We are almost content to say to Romanists, account us not yet as a branch of the Catholic Church, though we be a branch, till we are like a branch, provided that when we do become like a branch, then you consent to acknowledge us," &c. And so I was led on in the Article to that sharp attack on English Catholics, for their shortcomings as regards this Note, a good portion of which I have already quoted in another

---

4. John Henry Newman, "The Catholicity of the English Church," *British Critic* 27 (1840): 40–88. This article was Newman's most extensive discussion of this subject immediately before the publication of *Tract 90* in early 1841.

5. St. Meletius (d. 381) was bishop of Antioch who, during the Arian controversy, endured a period of exile from his diocese for standing up against the heresy. Meletius was one of a number of ancient Christians whom Newman admired for having dwelled outside traditional ecclesiastical boundaries and institutions.

place. It is there that I speak of the great scandal which I took at their political, social, and controversial bearing; and this was a second reason why I fell back upon the Note of Sanctity, because it took me away from the necessity of making any attack upon the doctrines of the Roman Church, nay, from the consideration of her popular beliefs, and brought me upon a ground on which I felt I could not make a mistake; for what is a higher guide for us in speculation and in practice, than that conscience of right and wrong, of truth and falsehood, those sentiments of what is decorous, consistent, and noble, which our Creator has made a part of our original nature? Therefore I felt I could not be wrong in attacking what I fancied was a fact, — the unscrupulousness, the deceit, and the intriguing spirit of the agents and representatives of Rome.

This reference to Holiness as the true test of a Church was steadily kept in view in what I wrote in connexion with Tract 90. I say in its Introduction, "The writer can never be party to forcing the opinions or projects of one school upon another; religious changes should be the act of the whole body. No good can come of a change which is not a development of feelings springing up freely and calmly within the bosom of the whole body itself; every change in religion" must be "attended by deep repentance; changes" must be "nurtured in mutual love; we cannot agree without a supernatural influence;" we must come "together to God to do for us what we cannot do for ourselves." In my Letter to the Bishop I said, "I have set myself against suggestions for considering the differences between ourselves and the foreign Churches with a view to their adjustment." (I meant in the way of negotiation, conference, agitation, or the like.) "Our business is with ourselves, — to make ourselves more holy, more self-denying, more primitive, more worthy of our high calling. To be anxious for a composition of differences is to begin at the end. Political reconciliations are but outward and hollow, and fallacious. And till Roman Catholics renounce political efforts, and manifest in their public measures the light of holiness and truth, perpetual war is our only prospect."

According to this theory, a religious body is part of the One Catholic and Apostolic Church, if it has the succession and the creed of the Apostles, with the note of holiness of life; and there is much in such a view to approve itself to the direct common sense and practical habits of an Englishman. However, with the events consequent upon Tract 90, I sunk my theory to a lower level. For what could be said in apology, when the Bishops and the people of my Church, not only did not suffer, but actually rejected primitive Catholic doctrine, and tried to eject from their communion all who held it? after the Bishops' charges? after the Jerusalem "abomination?"* Well, this could be said; still we were not nothing: we could not be as if we never had been a

---

*[Newman's Note] Matt. xxiv. 15.

Church; we were "Samaria."⁶ This then was that lower level on which I placed myself, and all who felt with me, at the end of 1841.

To bring out this view was the purpose of Four Sermons preached at St. Mary's in December of that year.⁷ Hitherto I had not introduced the exciting topics of the day into the Pulpit;* on this occasion I did. I did so, for the moment was urgent; there was great unsettlement of mind among us, in consequence of those same events which had unsettled me. One special anxiety, very obvious, which was coming on me now, was, that what was "one man's meat was another man's poison." I had said even of Tract 90, "It was addressed to one set of persons, and has been used and commented on by another;"⁸ still more was it true now, that whatever I wrote for the service of those whom I knew to be in trouble of mind, would become on the one hand matter of suspicion and slander in the mouths of my opponents, and of distress and surprise to those on the other hand, who had no difficulties of faith at all. Accordingly, when I published these Four Sermons at the end of 1843, I introduced them with a recommendation that none should read them who did not need them. But in truth the virtual condemnation of Tract 90, after that the whole difficulty seemed to have been weathered, was an enormous disappointment and trial. My Protest also against the Jerusalem Bishopric was an

---

*[Newman's Note] Vide Note C, *Sermon on Wisdom and Innocence.*

---

6. By "Samaria" Newman intended to indicate that his group within the Church of England had become like those tribes of ancient Israel that established their capital in Samaria apart from Jerusalem, the site of the temple. By this point in his life Newman had come to see himself and those around him as a saving remnant of the true Catholic Church dwelling outside both the Church of England and the Roman Catholic Church.

7. These four sermons, preached between November 28 and December 19, 1841, were later republished in a revised form in *Sermons, Bearing on Subjects of the Day* (1843). They were titled "Invisible Presence of Christ," "Outward and Inward Notes of the Church," "Grounds for Steadfastness in our Religious Profession," and "Elijah the Prophet of the Latter Days." In these sermons Newman urged his followers to remain in the Church of England despite the trials of the past year, including the condemnations of *Tract 90* and the establishment of the Jerusalem bishopric. He emphasized that Catholics in the Church of England must look to their own inner sense of spiritual and religious certitude because, as he wrote, "The Church of God is under eclipse among us." (John Henry Newman, *Sermons, Bearing on Subjects of the Day* (Oxford: J. G. F. & J. Rivington, 1843), p. 379.) In the last of these sermons he compared his own position to that of Elijah, who did not worship in the temple at Jerusalem and who had broken idols, but who did not seek to accomplish more than that finite task.

8. This statement, written to explain the explosion of controversy around *Tract 90*, had persuaded many readers in 1841 and after that Newman was providing a kind of esoteric advice to his own coterie and could not be fully honest.

unavoidable cause of excitement in the case of many; but it calmed them too, for the very fact of a Protest was a relief to their impatience. And so, in like manner, as regards the Four Sermons, of which I speak, though they acknowledged freely the great scandal which was involved in the recent episcopal doings, yet at the same time they might be said to bestow upon the multiplied disorders and shortcomings of the Anglican Church a sort of place in the Revealed Dispensation, and an intellectual position in the controversy, and the dignity of a great principle, for unsettled minds to take and use, — a principle which might teach them to recognize their own consistency, and to be reconciled to themselves, and which might absorb and dry up a multitude of their grudgings, discontents, misgivings, and questionings, and lead the way to humble, thankful, and tranquil thoughts; — and this was the effect which certainly it produced on myself.

The point of these Sermons is, that, in spite of the rigid character of the Jewish law, the formal and literal force of its precepts, and the manifest schism, and worse than schism, of the Ten Tribes, yet in fact they were still recognized as a people by the Divine Mercy; that the great prophets Elias and Eliseus were sent to them; and not only so, but were sent to preach to them and reclaim them, without any intimation that they must be reconciled to the line of David and the Aaronic priesthood, or go up to Jerusalem to worship. They were not in the Church, yet they had the means of grace and the hope of acceptance with their Maker. The application of all this to the Anglican Church was immediate; — whether, under the circumstances, a man could assume or exercise ministerial functions, or not, might not clearly appear (though it must be remembered that England had the Apostolic Priesthood, whereas Israel had no priesthood at all), but so far was clear, that there was no call at all for an Anglican to leave his Church for Rome, though he did not believe his own to be part of the One Church: — and for this reason, because it was a fact that the kingdom of Israel was cut off from the Temple; and yet its subjects, neither in a mass, nor as individuals, neither the multitudes on Mount Carmel, nor the Shunammite and her household, had any command given them, though miracles were displayed before them, to break off from their own people, and to submit themselves to Judah.*

It is plain, that a theory such as this, — whether the marks of a divine presence and life in the Anglican Church were sufficient to prove that she was actually within the covenant, or only sufficient to prove that she was at least

---

*[Newman's Note] As I am not writing controversially, I will only here remark upon this argument, that there is a great difference between a command, which presupposes physical, material, and political conditions, and one which is moral. To go to Jerusalem was a matter of the body, not of the soul.

enjoying extraordinary and uncovenanted mercies, — not only lowered her level in a religious point of view, but weakened her controversial basis. Its very novelty made it suspicious; and there was no guarantee that the process of subsidence might not continue, and that it might not end in a submersion. Indeed, to many minds, to say that England was wrong was even to say that Rome was right; and no ethical or casuistic reasoning whatever could overcome in their case the argument from prescription and authority. To this objection, as made to my new teaching, I could only answer that I did not make my circumstances. I fully acknowledged the force and effectiveness of the genuine Anglican theory, and that it was all but proof against the disputants of Rome; but still like Achilles, it had a vulnerable point, and that St. Leo had found it out for me, and that I could not help it; — that, were it not for matter of fact, the theory would be great indeed; it would be irresistible, if it were only true. When I became a Catholic, the Editor of the Christian Observer,[9] Mr. Wilkes, who had in former days accused me, to my indignation, of tending towards Rome, wrote to me to ask, which of the two was now right, he or I? I answered him in a letter, part of which I here insert, as it will serve as a sort of leave-taking of the great theory, which is so specious to look upon, so difficult to prove, and so hopeless to work.

"Nov. 8, 1845. I do not think, at all more than I did, that the Anglican principles which I advocated at the date you mention, lead men to the Church of Rome. If I must specify what I mean by 'Anglican principles,' I should say, e. g. taking *Antiquity*, not the *existing Church*, as the oracle of truth; and holding that the *Apostolical Succession* is a sufficient guarantee of Sacramental Grace, *without union with the Christian Church throughout the world*. I think these still the firmest, strongest ground against Rome — that is, *if they can be held*" [as truths or facts]. "They *have* been held by many, and are far more difficult to refute in the Roman controversy, than those of any other religious body.

"For myself, I found *I could not* hold them. I left them. From the time I began to suspect their unsoundness, I ceased to put them forward. When I was fairly sure of their unsoundness, I gave up my Living. When I was fully confident that the Church of Rome was the only true Church, I joined her.

"I have felt all along that Bp. Bull's theology was the only theology on which the English Church could stand. I have felt, that opposition to the Church of Rome was *part* of that theology; and that he who could not protest against the Church of Rome was no true divine in the English Church. I have never said, nor attempted to say, that any one in office in the En-

---

9. The *Christian Observer* was the major publication of moderate Church of England evangelicals.

glish Church, whether Bishop or incumbent, could be otherwise than in hostility to the Church of Rome."

The *Via Media* then disappeared for ever, and a Theory, made expressly for the occasion, took its place. I was pleased with my new view. I wrote to an intimate friend, Samuel F. Wood, Dec. 13, 1841: "I think you will give me the credit, Carissime,[10] of not undervaluing the strength of the feelings which draw one [to Rome], and yet I am (I trust) quite clear about my duty to remain where I am; indeed, much clearer than I was some time since. If it is not presumptuous to say, I have ... a much more definite view of the promised inward Presence of Christ with us in the Sacraments now that the outward notes of it are being removed. And I am content to be with Moses in the desert, or with Elijah excommunicated from the Temple. I say this, putting things at the strongest."

However, my friends of the moderate Apostolical party, who were my friends for the very reason of my having been so moderate and Anglican myself in general tone in times past, who had stood up for Tract 90 partly from faith in me, and certainly from generous and kind feeling, and had thereby shared an obloquy which was none of theirs, were naturally surprised and offended at a line of argument, novel, and, as it appeared to them, wanton, which threw the whole controversy into confusion, stultified my former principles, and substituted, as they would consider, a sort of methodistic self-contemplation,[11] especially abhorrent both to my nature and to my past professions, for the plain and honest tokens, as they were commonly received, of a divine mission in the Anglican Church. They could not tell whither I was going; and were still further annoyed when I persisted in viewing the reception of Tract 90 by the public and the Bishops as so grave a matter, and when I threw about what they considered mysterious hints of "eventualities," and would not simply say, "An Anglican I was born, and an Anglican I will die." One of my familiar friends, Mr. Church, who was in the country at Christmas, 1841-2, reported to me the feeling that prevailed about me,[12] and how I felt towards it will appear in the following letter of mine, written in answer: —

10. "Carissime," or "dearest friend," was a term that Newman sometimes introduced into letters written to his closest friends.

11. Newman associated Methodism and evangelical religion in general with modes of extreme religious subjectivity.

12. Richard W. Church (1815-1890) had been an Oriel fellow and close friend of Newman during the 1840s and had contributed one of the *Lives of the English Saints*. In 1845 while serving as university proctor, Church vetoed the measure coming before Oxford Convocation to condemn *Tract 90*. He became reacquainted with Newman at the time of the Kingsley controversy and would write one of the early histories of the Tractarian Movement, *The Oxford Movement: Twelve Years 1833-1845* (1891).

"Oriel, Dec. 24, 1841. Carissime, you cannot tell how sad your account of Moberly has made me.[13] His view of the sinfulness of the decrees of Trent is as much against union of Churches as against individual conversions. To tell the truth, I never have examined those decrees with this object, and have no view; but that is very different from having a deliberate view against them. Could not he say *which* they are? I suppose Transubstantiation is one. Charles Marriott,[14] though of course he would not like to have it repeated,* does not scruple at that. I have not my mind clear. Moberly must recollect that Palmer [of Worcester] thinks they all bear a Catholic interpretation. For myself, this only I see, that there is indefinitely more in the Fathers against our own state of alienation from Christendom than against the Tridentine Decrees.

"The only thing I can think of," [that I can have said of a startling character,] "is this, that there were persons who, if our Church committed herself to heresy,[15] *sooner* than think that there was no Church any where, would believe the Roman to be the Church; and therefore would on faith accept what they could not otherwise acquiesce in. I suppose, it would be no relief to him to insist upon the circumstance that there is no immediate danger. Individuals can never be answered for of course; but I should think lightly of that man, who, for some act of the Bishops, should all at once leave the Church. Now, considering how the Clergy really are improving, considering that this row is even making them read the Tracts, is it not possible we may all be in a better state of mind seven years hence to consider these matters? and may we not leave them meanwhile to the will of Providence? I *cannot* believe this work has been of man; God has a right to His own work, to do what He will with it. May we not try to leave it in His hands, and be content?

---

*[Newman's Note] As things stand now, I do not think he would have objected to his opinion being generally known.

---

13. George Moberly (1803–1885) served as a tutor in Balliol College, then as headmaster of Winchester School, and finally as bishop of Salisbury. He was regarded as a high churchman.

14. Charles Marriott (1811–1858) was a fellow and tutor of Oriel and a strong Tractarian supporter. He furnished part of the money with which Newman bought land at Littlemore. He continued the Tractarian cause at Oxford after Newman's conversion. In 1850 he became vicar of St. Mary the Virgin Church in Oxford, carried out a very active ministry, and died of cholera, which he contracted helping others struck with the disease.

15. In this context by "heresy" Newman meant specifically evangelical doctrine, most particularly in regard to baptism. Throughout the early 1840s Newman was deeply sensitive to any act, however minor, of friendliness toward evangelicals on the part of the bishops and the archbishop of Canterbury. The use of the term *heresy* in regard to evangelicals in the English Church had begun with high churchmen before the Tractarian Movement and was then adopted into Tractarian polemical rhetoric.

"If you learn any thing about Barter,[16] which leads you to think that I can relieve him by a letter, let me know. The truth is this, — our good friends do not read the Fathers; they assent to us from the common sense of the case: then, when the Fathers, and we, say *more* than their common sense, they are dreadfully shocked.

"The Bishop of London has rejected a man, 1. For holding *any* Sacrifice in the Eucharist. 2. The Real Presence. 3. That there is a grace in Ordination.*

"Are we quite sure that the Bishops will not be drawing up some stringent declarations of faith? Is this what Moberly fears? Would the Bishop of Oxford accept them? If so, I should be driven into the Refuge for the Destitute [Littlemore]. But I promise Moberly, I would do my utmost to catch all dangerous persons and clap them into confinement there."

Christmas Day, 1841. "I have been dreaming of Moberly all night. Should not he and the like see, that it is unwise, unfair, and impatient to ask others, What will you do under circumstances, which have not, which may never come? Why bring fear, suspicion, and disunion into the camp about things which are merely *in posse?*[17] Natural, and exceedingly kind as Barter's and another friend's letters were, I think they have done great harm. I speak most sincerely when I say, that there are things which I neither contemplate, nor wish to contemplate; but, when I am asked about them ten times, at length I begin to contemplate them.

"He surely does not mean to say, that *nothing* could separate a man from the English Church, e. g. its avowing Socinianism;[18] its holding the Holy

---

*[Newman's Note] I cannot prove this at this distance of time, but I do not think it wrong to introduce here the passage containing it, as I am imputing to the Bishop nothing which the world would think disgraceful, but, on the contrary, what a large religious body would approve.

---

16. William Brudenell Barter (1811–1858) was an Oriel fellow who broke with Newman at the time of his conversion.

17. "as possible."

18. Socinianism, a form of Unitarianism named for Lelio Sozzini (1525–1562) and Fausto Sozzini (1539–1604), originated in sixteenth- and seventeenth-century Poland. Its proponents argued that Jesus Christ was a man and not by nature divine. They regarded the Bible as properly understood through reason. The Socinian view of the Eucharist differed from that of other groups in seeing its celebration as a thanksgiving for the high moral example of Christ without imputing divinity to him. In nineteenth-century Britain the term *Socinian* was often used as a negative epithet hurled by religious combatants without particularly substantive meaning being attached to it. W. F. Hook once wrote: "When I speak of that class of persons [i.e., evangelicals] represented by the 'Patriot,' the 'Record," &c., as Socinianizing Christians, I deal with them as they deal with [high]

Eucharist in a Socinian sense. Yet, he would say, it was not *right* to contemplate such things.

"Again, our case is [diverging] from that of Ken's.[19] To say nothing of the last miserable century, which has given us to *start* from a much lower level and with much less to *spare* than a Churchman in the 17th century, questions of *doctrine* are now coming in; with him, it was a question of discipline.

"If such dreadful events were realized, I cannot help thinking we should all be vastly more agreed than we think now. Indeed, is it possible (humanly speaking) that those, who have so much the same heart, should widely differ? But let this be considered, as to alternatives. *What* communion could we join? Could the Scotch or American sanction the presence of its Bishops and congregations in England, without incurring the imputation of schism, unless indeed (and is that likely?) they denounced the English as heretical?[20]

"Is not this a time of strange providences? is it not our safest course, without looking to consequences, to do simply *what we think right* day by day? shall we not be sure to go wrong, if we attempt to trace by anticipation the course of divine Providence?

"Has not all our misery, as a Church, arisen from people being afraid to look difficulties in the face? They have palliated acts, when they should have denounced them. There is that good fellow, Worcester Palmer, can whitewash the Ecclesiastical Commission and the Jerusalem Bishopric.[21] And what is the consequence? that our Church has, through centuries, ever been sinking lower and lower, till good part of its pretensions and professions is a mere sham,

---

churchmen. They contend that [high] church principles lead to popery, and therefore, trusting on the infallibility of their logic, they call us papists. Now we think that it is only their ignorance of logic which prevents their perceiving how *their* principles, if properly carried out, lead on to Socinianism. It is therefore on the same principle that we call them Socinians, as they call us papists." (*British Magazine* 14 (1838): 26.)

19. Thomas Ken (1637–1711) was a bishop of Bath and Wells who after the Revolution of 1688 became a Nonjuror.

20. Here Newman is speculating on what would be the position and possible function of either American or Scottish Episcopal Church bishops in England if they believed the Church of England itself had become heretical. At various points in the 1840s people around Newman, including his brother Francis in 1845, suggested that he and his group put themselves under the authority of a Scottish or American bishop whom they might regard as orthodox in contrast to their growing suspicion of and hostility toward Church of England bishops.

21. The Ecclesiastical Commission was the vehicle Parliament established in 1835 with the support of both Conservatives and Whigs as well as reforming bishops, such as Charles Blomfield of London, to reform the finances and administration of the Church of England. Newman saw its activity as an example of the danger of Erastianism.

though it be a duty to make the best of what we have received. Yet, though bound to make the best of other men's shams, let us not incur any of our own. The truest friends of our Church are they, who say boldly when her rulers are going wrong, and the consequences; and (to speak catachrestically) *they* are most likely to die in the Church, who are, under these black circumstances, most prepared to leave it.

"And I will add, that, considering the traces of God's grace which surround us, I am very sanguine, or rather confident, (if it is right so to speak,) that our prayers and our alms will come up as a memorial before God, and that all this miserable confusion tends to good.

"Let us not then be anxious, and anticipate differences in prospect, when we agree in the present.

"P. S. I think when friends" [i. e. the extreme party] "get over their first unsettlement of mind and consequent vague apprehensions, which the new attitude of the Bishops, and our feelings upon it, have brought about, they will get contented and satisfied. They will see that they exaggerated things. . . . Of course it would have been wrong to anticipate what one's feelings would be under such a painful contingency as the Bishops' charging as they have done, — so it seems to me nobody's fault. Nor is it wonderful that others" [moderate men] "are startled" [i. e. at my Protest, &c. &c.]; "yet they should recollect that the more implicit the reverence one pays to a Bishop, the more keen will be one's perception of heresy in him. The cord is binding and compelling, till it snaps.

"Men of reflection would have seen this, if they had looked that way. Last spring, a very high churchman talked to me of resisting my Bishop, of asking him for the Canons under which he acted, and so forth; but those, who have cultivated a loyal feeling towards their superiors, are the most loving servants, or the most zealous protestors. If others became so too, if the clergy of Chester denounced the heresy of their diocesan, they would be doing their duty, and relieving themselves of the share which they otherwise have in any possible defection of their brethren.[22]

"St. Stephen's [Day, December 26]. How I fidget! I now fear that the note I

---

22. In 1841 Bishop John Bird Sumner, the evangelical bishop of Chester and later archbishop of Canterbury, denounced *Tract 90* in his episcopal charge. Thereafter, Newman wrote in private letters that the diocese of Chester lay under the authority of a person guilty of heresy. During the early 1840s when Newman used the term *heresy* or its cognates in reference to current events, he was denoting evangelical religion. See JHN to J. Keble, October 5 and 24, 1841, *L&D* 8: 286, 305–306.

wrote yesterday only makes matters worse by *disclosing* too much. This is always my great difficulty.

"In the present state of excitement on both sides, I think of leaving out altogether my reassertion of No. 90 in my Preface to Volume 6 [of Parochial Sermons], and merely saying, 'As many false reports are at this time in circulation about him, he hopes his well-wishers will take this Volume as an indication of his real thoughts and feelings: those who are not, he leaves in God's hand to bring them to a better mind in His own time.' What do you say to the logic, sentiment, and propriety of this?"

An old friend, at a distance from Oxford, Archdeacon Robert I. Wilberforce, must have said something to me at this time, I do not know what, which challenged a frank reply; for I disclosed to him, I do not know in what words, my frightful suspicion, hitherto only known to two persons, viz. his brother Henry,[23] and Mr. (now Sir Frederic) Rogers, that, as regards my Anglicanism, perhaps I might break down in the event, — that perhaps we were both out of the Church. I think I recollect expressing my difficulty, as derived from the Arian and Monophysite history, in a form in which it would be most intelligible to him, as being in fact an admission of Bishop Bull's; viz. that in the controversies of the early centuries the Roman Church was ever on the right side, which was of course a *primâ facie* argument in favour of Rome and against Anglicanism now. He answered me thus, under date of Jan. 29, 1842: "I don't think that I ever was so shocked by any communication, which was ever made to me, as by your letter of this morning. It has quite unnerved me. . . . I cannot but write to you, though I am at a loss where to begin. . . . I know of no act by which we have dissevered ourselves from the communion of the Church Universal. . . . The more I study Scripture, the more am I impressed with the resemblance between the Romish principle in the Church and the Babylon of St. John. . . . I am ready to grieve that I ever directed my thoughts to theology, if it is indeed so uncertain, as your doubts seem to indicate."

While my old and true friends were thus in trouble about me, I suppose they felt not only anxiety but pain, to see that I was gradually surrendering myself to the influence of others, who had not their own claims upon me, younger

---

23. Henry William Wilberforce (1807–1873) had studied with Newman at Oriel and became a close friend for all of his life. He converted to Roman Catholicism in 1850 in the wake of the Gorham Judgment. For the classic account of the relationship of the Wilberforce family to the Tractarian Movement, see David Newsome, *The Wilberforces and Henry Manning: The Parting of Friends* (Cambridge, Mass.: Harvard Univ. Press, 1966).

men, and of a cast of mind in no small degree uncongenial to my own. A new school of thought was rising, as is usual in doctrinal inquiries, and was sweeping the original party of the Movement aside, and was taking its place.[24] The most prominent person in it, was a man of elegant genius, of classical mind, of rare talent in literary composition:—Mr. Oakeley. He was not far from my own age; I had long known him, though of late years he had not been in residence at Oxford; and quite lately, he has been taking several signal occasions of renewing that kindness, which he ever showed towards me when we were both in the Anglican Church. His tone of mind was not unlike that which gave a character to the early Movement; he was almost a typical Oxford man, and, as far as I recollect, both in political and ecclesiastical views, would have been of one spirit with the Oriel party of 1826–1833. But he had entered late into the Movement; he did not know its first years; and, beginning with a new start, he was naturally thrown together with that body of eager, acute, resolute minds who had begun their Catholic life about the same time as he, who knew nothing about the *Via Media*, but had heard much about Rome. This new party rapidly formed and increased, in and out of Oxford, and, as it so happened, contemporaneously with that very summer, when I received so serious a blow to my ecclesiastical views from the study of the Monophysite controversy. These men cut into the original Movement at an angle, fell across its line of thought, and then set about turning that line in its own direction. They were most of them keenly religious men, with a true concern for their souls as the first matter of all, with a great zeal for me, but giving little certainty at the time as to which way they would ultimately turn. Some in the event have remained firm to Anglicanism, some have become Catholics, and some have found a

---

24. This passage refers to the emergence of a more radical group of generally younger Tractarians who had not been part of the original movement. The two most important figures in this group were William George Ward (1812–1882) and Frederick Oakeley, both of whom published radical articles in the *British Critic*. Ward was quite close to Newman in the early 1840s. The hostility in this passage arises from the manner in which Ward and Oakeley took increasingly extreme positions in regard to interpreting the Thirty-Nine Articles in conformity with Roman Catholic doctrine, precipitating events that led to the judicial condemnation of *Tract 90* and Newman's eventual conversion, as discussed in the introduction to this volume. Ward preceded Newman into the Roman Catholic Church; Oakeley converted after him. By the 1860s Newman and Ward were at loggerheads in the English Roman Catholic Church, with the former being regarded as a liberal and the latter as an ultramontane. See Wilfrid Philip Ward, *William George Ward and the Oxford Movement* (New York: Macmillan, 1890), and Peter Galloway, *A Passionate Humility: Frederick Oakeley and the Oxford Movement* (Leominster: Gracewing, 1999).

refuge in Liberalism. Nothing was clearer concerning them, than that they needed to be kept in order; and on me who had had so much to do with the making of them, that duty was as clearly incumbent; and it is equally clear, from what I have already said, that I was just the person, above all others, who could not undertake it. There are no friends like old friends; but of those old friends, few could help me, few could understand me, many were annoyed with me, some were angry, because I was breaking up a compact party, and some, as a matter of conscience, could not listen to me. When I looked round for those whom I might consult in my difficulties, I found the very hypothesis of those difficulties acting as a bar to their giving me their advice. Then I said, bitterly, "You are throwing me on others, whether I will or no." Yet still I had good and true friends around me of the old sort, in and out of Oxford too, who were a great help to me. But on the other hand, though I neither was so fond (with a few exceptions) of the persons, nor of the methods of thought, which belonged to this new school, as of the old set, though I could not trust in their firmness of purpose, for, like a swarm of flies, they might come and go, and at length be divided and dissipated, yet I had an intense sympathy in their object and in the direction in which their path lay, in spite of my old friends, in spite of my old life-long prejudices. In spite of my ingrained fears of Rome, and the decision of my reason and conscience against her usages, in spite of my affection for Oxford and Oriel, yet I had a secret longing love of Rome the Mother of English Christianity, and I had a true devotion to the Blessed Virgin, in whose College I lived, whose Altar I served, and whose Immaculate Purity I had in one of my earliest printed Sermons made much of. And it was the consciousness of this bias in myself, if it is so to be called, which made me preach so earnestly against the danger of being swayed in religious inquiry by our sympathy rather than by our reason. And moreover, the members of this new school looked up to me, as I have said, and did me true kindnesses, and really loved me, and stood by me in trouble, when others went away, and for all this I was grateful; nay, many of them were in trouble themselves, and in the same boat with me, and that was a further cause of sympathy between us; and hence it was, when the new school came on in force, and into collision with the old, I had not the heart, any more than the power, to repel them; I was in great perplexity, and hardly knew where I stood; I took their part; and, when I wanted to be in peace and silence, I had to speak out, and I incurred the charge of weakness from some men, and of mysteriousness, shuffling, and underhand dealing from the majority.

Now I will say here frankly, that this sort of charge is a matter which I cannot properly meet, because I cannot duly realize it. I have never had any suspicion of my own honesty; and, when men say that I was dishonest, I cannot grasp the accusation as a distinct conception, such as it is possible to encounter. If a man said to me, "On such a day and before such persons you said a thing was white, when it was black," I understand what is meant well enough, and I can set myself to prove an *alibi* or to explain the mistake; or if a man said to me, "You tried to gain me over to your party, intending to take me with you to Rome, but you did not succeed," I can give him the lie, and lay down an assertion of my own as firm and as exact as his, that not from the time that I was first unsettled, did I ever attempt to gain any one over to myself or to my Romanizing opinions, and that it is only his own coxcombical fancy which has bred such a thought in him: but my imagination is at a loss in presence of those vague charges, which have commonly been brought against me, charges, which are made up of impressions, and understandings, and inferences, and hearsay, and surmises. Accordingly, I shall not make the attempt, for, in doing so, I should be dealing blows in the air; what I shall attempt is to state what I know of myself and what I recollect, and leave to others its application.

While I had confidence in the *Via Media*, and thought that nothing could overset it, I did not mind laying down large principles, which I saw would go further than was commonly perceived. I considered that to make the *Via Media* concrete and substantive, it must be much more than it was in outline; that the Anglican Church must have a ceremonial, a ritual, and a fulness of doctrine and devotion, which it had not at present, if it were to compete with the Roman Church with any prospect of success. Such additions would not remove it from its proper basis, but would merely strengthen and beautify it: such, for instance, would be confraternities, particular devotions, reverence for the Blessed Virgin, prayers for the dead, beautiful churches, munificent offerings to them and in them, monastic houses, and many other observances and institutions, which I used to say belonged to us as much as to Rome, though Rome had appropriated them and boasted of them, by reason of our having let them slip from us. The principle, on which all this turned, is brought out in one of the Letters I published on occasion of Tract 90. "The age is moving," I said, "towards something; and most unhappily the one religious communion among us, which has of late years been practically in possession of this something, is the Church of Rome. She alone, amid all the errors and evils of her practical system, has given free scope to the feelings of awe, mystery, tenderness, reverence, devotedness, and other feelings which may be especially called Catholic. The question then is, whether we shall give them up to the Roman Church or claim them for ourselves. . . . But if we do give them up, we must give up the men who cherish them. We must consent either to give up the men, or to admit their principles." With these feelings I frankly admit, that, while I was working simply for the sake of the Anglican Church, I did not at all mind, though I found myself laying down principles in its defence, which went beyond that particular kind of defence which high-and-dry men thought perfection, and even though I ended in framing a kind of defence, which they might call a revolution, while I thought it a restoration. Thus, for illustration, I might discourse upon the "Communion of Saints" in such a manner, (though I do not recollect doing so,) as might lead the way towards devotion to the Blessed Virgin and the Saints on the one hand, and towards prayers for the dead on the other. In a memorandum of the year 1844 or 1845, I thus speak on this subject: "If the Church be not defended on establishment grounds, it must be upon principles, which go far beyond their immediate object. Sometimes I saw these further results, sometimes not. Though I saw them, I sometimes did not say that I saw them:—so long as I thought they were inconsistent, *not* with our Church, but only with the existing opinions, I was not unwilling to insinuate truths into our Church, which I thought had a right to be there."

To so much I confess; but I do not confess, I simply deny that I ever said any thing which secretly bore against the Church of England, knowing it myself, in order that others might unwarily accept it. It was indeed one of my great difficulties and causes of reserve, as time went on, that I at length recognized in principles which I had honestly preached as if Anglican, conclusions favourable to the cause of Rome. Of course I did not like to confess this; and, when interrogated, was in consequence in perplexity. The prime instance of this was the appeal to Antiquity; St. Leo had overset, in my own judgment, its force as the special argument for Anglicanism; yet I was committed to Antiquity, together with the whole Anglican school; what then was I to say, when acute minds urged this or that application of it against the *Via Media?* it was impossible that, in such circumstances, any answer could be given which was not unsatisfactory, or any behaviour adopted which was not mysterious. Again, sometimes in what I wrote I went just as far as I saw, and could as little say more, as I could see what is below the horizon; and therefore, when asked as to the consequences of what I had said, I had no answer to give. Again, sometimes when I was asked, whether certain conclusions did not follow from a certain principle, I might not be able to tell at the moment, especially if the matter were complicated; and for this reason, if for no other, because there is great difference between a conclusion in the abstract and a conclusion in the concrete, and because a conclusion may be modified in fact by a conclusion from some opposite principle. Or it might so happen that my head got simply confused, by the very strength of the logic which was administered to me, and thus I gave my sanction to conclusions which really were not mine; and when the report of those conclusions came round to me through others, I had to unsay them. And then again, perhaps I did not like to see men scared or scandalized by unfeeling logical inferences, which would not have troubled them to the day of their death, had they not been forced to recognize them. And then I felt altogether the force of the maxim of St. Ambrose, "Non in dialecticâ complacuit Deo salvum facere populum suum;"[25] — I had a great dislike of paper logic. For myself, it was not logic that carried me on; as well might one say that the quicksilver in the barometer changes the weather. It is the concrete being that reasons; pass a number of years, and I find my mind in a new place; how? the whole man moves; paper logic is but the record of it. All the logic in the world would not have made me move faster towards Rome than I did; as well might you say that I have arrived at the end of my journey, because I see the village church before me, as venture to assert that the miles, over which my soul had to pass before it got to Rome, could be annihilated, even though I had been in possession of some far clearer view than I then had, that Rome was my ultimate destination. Great acts take time. At least this is what I felt in my own case; and therefore to come to me with methods of logic had in it the nature of a provocation, and, though I do not think I ever showed it, made me somewhat indifferent how I met them, and perhaps led me, as a means of relieving my impatience, to be mysterious or irrelevant, or to give in because I could not meet them to my satisfaction. And a greater trouble still than these logical mazes, was the introduction of logic into every subject whatever, so far, that is, as it was done. Before I was at Oriel, I recollect an acquaintance saying to me that "the Oriel Common Room stank of Logic." One is not at all pleased when poetry, or eloquence, or devotion, is considered as if chiefly intended to feed syllogisms. Now, in saying all this, I am saying nothing against the deep piety and earnestness which were characteristics of this second phase of the Movement, in which I had taken so prominent a part. What I have been observing is, that this phase had a tendency to bewilder and to upset me; and, that, instead of saying so, as I ought to have done, perhaps from a sort of laziness I gave answers at random, which have led to my appearing close or inconsistent.

I have turned up two letters of this period, which in a measure illustrate what I have been saying. The first was written to the Bishop of Oxford on occasion of Tract 90:

"March 20, 1841. No one can enter into my situation but myself. I see a great many minds working in various directions and a variety of principles with multiplied bearings; I act for the best. I sincerely think that matters would not have gone better for the Church, had I never written. And if I write I have a

---

25. "It did not please God to save his people by logic." St. Ambrose, *De Fide* 1. 42.

choice of difficulties. It is easy for those who do not enter into those difficulties to say, 'He ought to say this and not say that,' but things are wonderfully linked together, and I cannot, or rather I would not be dishonest. When persons too interrogate me, I am obliged in many cases to give an opinion, or I seem to be underhand. Keeping silence looks like artifice. And I do not like people to consult or respect me, from thinking differently of my opinions from what I know them to be. And (again to use the proverb) what is one man's food is another man's poison. All these things make my situation very difficult. But that collision must at some time ensue between members of the Church of opposite sentiments, I have long been aware. The time and mode has been in the hand of Providence; I do not mean to exclude my own great imperfections in bringing it about; yet I still feel obliged to think the Tract necessary."

The second is taken from the notes of a letter which I sent to Dr. Pusey in the next year:[26]

"October 16, 1842. As to my being entirely with A., I do not know the limits of my own opinions, If A. says that this or that is a development from what I have said, I cannot say Yes or No. It is plausible, it *may* be true. Of course the fact that the Roman Church *has* so developed and maintained, adds great weight to the antecedent plausibility. I cannot assert that it is not true; but I cannot, with that keen perception which some people have, appropriate it. It is a nuisance to me to be *forced* beyond what I can fairly accept."

There was another source of the perplexity with which at this time I was encompassed, and of the reserve and mysteriousness, of which that perplexity gained for me the credit. After Tract 90 the Protestant world would not let me alone; they pursued me in the public journals to Littlemore. Reports of all kinds were circulated about me. "Imprimis, why did I go up to Littlemore at all? For no good purpose certainly; I dared not tell why." Why, to be sure, it was hard that I should be obliged to say to the Editors of newspapers that I went up there to say my prayers; it was hard to have to tell the world in confidence, that I had a certain doubt about the Anglican system, and could not at that moment resolve it, or say what would come of it; it was hard to have to confess that I had thought of giving up my Living a year or two before,

---

26. This letter to Pusey followed approximately a year after a triangulated exchange of the autumn of 1841 among Ward, Pusey, and Newman in which Ward had made clear to Pusey, and Newman confirmed, that the latter was much more sympathetic to Roman Catholicism than Pusey had allowed himself to believe. The full correspondence also reveals that Newman and Ward in 1841 were far closer than Newman admits in the *Apologia*. See Frank M. Turner, *John Henry Newman: The Challenge to Evangelical Religion* (New Haven, Conn.: Yale Univ. Press, 2002), pp. 382–389.

and that this was a first step to it. It was hard to have to plead, that, for what I knew, my doubts would vanish, if the newspapers would be so good as to give me time and let me alone. Who would ever dream of making the world his confidant? yet I was considered insidious, sly, dishonest, if I would not open my heart to the tender mercies of the world. But they persisted: "What was I doing at Littlemore?" Doing there! have I not retreated from you? have I not given up my position and my place? am I alone, of Englishmen, not to have the privilege to go where I will, no questions asked? am I alone to be followed about by jealous prying eyes, who note down whether I go in at a back door or at the front, and who the men are who happen to call on me in the afternoon? Cowards! if I advanced one step, you would run away; it is not you that I fear: "Di me terrent, et Jupiter hostis."[27] It is because the Bishops still go on charging against me, though I have quite given up: it is that secret misgiving of heart which tells me that they do well, for I have neither lot nor part with them: this it is which weighs me down. I cannot walk into or out of my house, but curious eyes are upon me. Why will you not let me die in peace? Wounded brutes creep into some hole to die in, and no one grudges it them. Let me alone, I shall not trouble you long. This was the keen feeling which pierced me, and, I think, these are the very words in which I expressed it to myself. I asked, in the words of a great motto, "Ubi lapsus? quid feci?"[28] One day when I entered my house, I found a flight of Under-graduates inside. Heads of Houses, as mounted patrols, walked their horses round those poor cottages. Doctors of Divinity dived into the hidden recesses of that private tenement uninvited, and drew domestic conclusions from what they saw there. I had thought that an Englishman's house was his castle; but the newspapers thought otherwise, and at last the matter came before my good Bishop. I insert his letter, and a portion of my reply to him:—

"April 12, 1842. So many of the charges against yourself and your friends which I have seen in the public journals have been, within my own knowledge, false and calumnious, that I am not apt to pay much attention to what is asserted with respect to you in the newspapers.

"In" [a newspaper] "however, of April 9, there appears a paragraph in which it is asserted, as a matter of notoriety, that a 'so-called Anglo-Catholic Monastery is in a process of erection at Littlemore, and that the cells of dormitories, the chapel, the refectory, the cloisters all may be seen advancing to perfection, under the eye of a Parish Priest of the Diocese of Oxford.'

"Now, as I have understood that you really are possessed of some tenements

---

27. "I fear the gods and the enmity of Jove," Aeneid 7:895.
28. "Where is my fault? What have I done?"

at Littlemore, — as it is generally believed that they are destined for the purposes of study and devotion, — and as much suspicion and jealousy are felt about the matter, I am anxious to afford you an opportunity of making me an explanation on the subject.

"I know you too well not to be aware that you are the last man living to attempt in my Diocese a revival of the Monastic orders (in any thing approaching to the Romanist sense of the term) without previous communication with me, — or indeed that you should take upon yourself to originate any measure of importance without authority from the heads of the Church, — and therefore I at once exonerate you from the accusation brought against you by the newspaper I have quoted, but I feel it nevertheless a duty to my Diocese and myself, as well as to you, to ask you to put it in my power to contradict what, if uncontradicted, would appear to imply a glaring invasion of all ecclesiastical discipline on *your* part, or of inexcusable neglect and indifference to my duties on *mine*."

I wrote in answer as follows: —

"April 14, 1842. I am very much obliged by your Lordship's kindness in allowing me to write to you on the subject of my house at Littlemore; at the same time I feel it hard both on your Lordship and myself that the restlessness of the public mind should oblige you to require an explanation of me.

"It is now a whole year that I have been the subject of incessant misrepresentation. A year since I submitted entirely to your Lordship's authority; and, with the intention of following out the particular act enjoined upon me, I not only stopped the series of Tracts, on which I was engaged, but withdrew from all public discussion of Church matters of the day, or what may be called ecclesiastical politics. I turned myself at once to the preparation for the Press of the translations of St. Athanasius to which I had long wished to devote myself, and I intended and intend to employ myself in the like theological studies, and in the concerns of my own parish and in practical works.

"With the same view of personal improvement I was led more seriously to a design which had been long on my mind.[29] For many years, at least thirteen, I

---

29. Beginning in the late 1830s Newman had envisioned the refounding of monastic life in the Church of England and more particularly at Littlemore. This ascetic, monastic imperative was one of the key elements in late Tractarianism and was recognized as such by both supporters and detractors of the movement in the early 1840s. See A. M. Allchin, *Silent Rebellion: Anglican Religious Communities, 1845–1900* (London: SCM Press, 1958); Michael Hill, *Religious Order: A Study of Virtuoso Religion and Its Legitimation in the Nineteenth-Century Church of England* (London: Heinemann Educational, 1973); R. D. Cox, "Newman, Littlemore, and a Tractarian Attempt at Community," *Anglican and Episcopal History* 62/3 (1993): 343–376.

have wished to give myself to a life of greater religious regularity than I have hitherto led; but it is very unpleasant to confess such a wish even to my Bishop, because it seems arrogant, and because it is committing me to a profession which may come to nothing. For what have I done that I am to be called to account by the world for my private actions, in a way in which no one else is called? Why may I not have that liberty which all others are allowed? I am often accused of being underhand and uncandid in respect to the intentions to which I have been alluding: but no one likes his own good resolutions noised about, both from mere common delicacy and from fear lest he should not be able to fulfil them. I feel it very cruel, though the parties in fault do not know what they are doing, that very sacred matters between me and my conscience are made a matter of public talk. May I take a case parallel though different? suppose a person in prospect of marriage; would he like the subject discussed in newspapers, and parties, circumstances, &c., &c., publicly demanded of him, at the penalty of being accused of craft and duplicity?

"The resolution I speak of has been taken with reference to myself alone, and has been contemplated quite independent of the co-operation of any other human being, and without reference to success or failure other than personal, and without regard to the blame or approbation of man. And being a resolution of years, and one to which I feel God has called me, and in which I am violating no rule of the Church any more than if I married, I should have to answer for it, if I did not pursue it, as a good Providence made openings for it. In pursuing it then I am thinking of myself alone, not aiming at any ecclesiastical or external effects. At the same time of course it would be a great comfort to me to know that God had put it into the hearts of others to pursue their personal edification in the same way, and unnatural not to wish to have the benefit of their presence and encouragement, or not to think it a great infringement on the rights of conscience if such personal and private resolutions were interfered with. Your Lordship will allow me to add my firm conviction that such religious resolutions are most necessary for keeping a certain class of minds firm in their allegiance to our Church; but still I can as truly say that my own reason for any thing I have done has been a personal one, without which I should not have entered upon it, and which I hope to pursue whether with or without the sympathies of others pursuing a similar course. . . . .

"As to my intentions, I purpose to live there myself a good deal, as I have a resident curate in Oxford. In doing this, I believe I am consulting for the good of my parish, as my population at Littlemore is at least equal to that of St. Mary's in Oxford, and the *whole* of Littlemore is double of it. It has been very much neglected; and in providing a parsonage-house at Littlemore, as this will be, and will be called, I conceive I am doing a very great benefit to my people.

At the same time it has appeared to me that a partial or temporary retirement from St. Mary's Church might be expedient under the prevailing excitement.

"As to the quotation from the [newspaper], which I have not seen, your Lordship will perceive from what I have said, that no 'monastery is in process of erection;' there is no 'chapel;' no 'refectory,' hardly a dining-room or parlour. The 'cloisters' are my shed connecting the cottages. I do not understand what 'cells of dormitories' means. Of course I can repeat your Lordship's words that 'I am not attempting a revival of the Monastic Orders, in any thing approaching to the Romanist sense of the term,' or 'taking on myself to originate any measure of importance without authority from the Heads of the Church.' I am attempting nothing ecclesiastical, but something personal and private, and which can only be made public, not private, by newspapers and letter-writers, in which sense the most sacred and conscientious resolves and acts may certainly be made the objects of an unmannerly and unfeeling curiosity."[30]

One calumny there was which the Bishop did not believe, and of which of course he had no idea of speaking. It was that I was actually in the service of the enemy. I had forsooth been already received into the Catholic Church, and was rearing at Littlemore a nest of Papists, who, like me, were to take the Anglican oaths which they disbelieved, by virtue of a dispensation from Rome, and thus in due time were to bring over to that unprincipled Church great numbers of the Anglican Clergy and Laity. Bishops gave their countenance to this imputation against me. The case was simply this: — as I made Littlemore a place of retirement for myself, so did I offer it to others. There were young men in Oxford, whose testimonials for Orders had been refused by their Colleges; there were young clergymen, who had found themselves unable from conscience to go on with their duties, and had thrown up their parochial engagements. Such men were already going straight to Rome, and I interposed; I interposed for the reasons I have given in the beginning of this portion of my

---

30. Newman was less than candid with Bishop Bagot in this letter. Technically, Littlemore was not a monastery, but Newman had on more than one occasion written privately of hoping to establish a monastery there. Various contemporaries, including Dr. Richard Jelf and Frederick Oakeley, wrote of Littlemore as a monastery. (R. W. Jelf to E. B. Pusey, December 10 and 12, 1841, Jelf-Pusey Correspondence [transcripts], Pusey House; F. Oakeley to F. Kilvert, January 19, 1843, Bodleian Library, Ms. Don. d. 120, f. 132.) On April 25, 1842, thirteen days after the letter to Bishop Bagot, Newman confided in Henry Wilberforce: "we are a small household here, small indeed — but we have begun the Breviary Service here this morning, . . . Do not tell, please, *any* one, what we are doing; it would be sure to be misinterpreted" (JHN to Henry Wilberforce, April 25, 1842, *L&D* 8: 512). See also Turner, *John Henry Newman*, pp. 412–436.

narrative. I interposed from fidelity to my clerical engagements, and from duty to my Bishop; and from the interest which I was bound to take in them, and from belief that they were premature or excited. Their friends besought me to quiet them, if I could. Some of them came to live with me at Littlemore. They were laymen, or in the place of laymen. I kept some of them back for several years from being received into the Catholic Church. Even when I had given up my living, I was still bound by my duty to their parents or friends, and I did not forget still to do what I could for them. The immediate occasion of my resigning St. Mary's, was the unexpected conversion of one of them. After that, I felt it was impossible to keep my post there, for I had been unable to keep my word with my Bishop.[31]

The following letters refer, more or less, to these men, whether they were actually with me at Littlemore or not:—

1. "March 6, 1842. Church doctrines are a powerful weapon; they were not sent into the world for nothing. God's word does not return unto Him void: If I have said, as I have, that the doctrines of the Tracts for the Times would build up our Church and destroy parties, I meant, if they were used, not if they were denounced. Else, they will be as powerful against us, as they might be powerful for us.

"If people who have a liking for another, hear him called a Roman Catholic, they will say, 'Then after all Romanism is no such bad thing.' All these persons, who are making the cry, are fulfilling their own prophecy. If all the world agree in telling a man, he has no business in our Church, he will at length begin to think he has none. How easy is it to persuade a man of any thing, when numbers affirm it! so great is the force of imagination. Did every one who met you in the streets look hard at you, you would think you were somehow in fault. I do not know any thing so irritating, so unsettling, especially in the case of young persons, as, when they are going on calmly and unconsciously, obeying their Church and following its divines, (I am speaking from facts,) as suddenly to their surprise to be conjured not to make a leap, of which they have not a dream and from which they are far removed."

2. 1843 or 1844. "I did not explain to you sufficiently the state of mind of

---

31. William Lockhardt (1820–1892) was the follower who converted to Roman Catholicism in what Newman regarded as a precipitous manner. He had lived at Littlemore for some time, having promised Newman he would not enter the Roman Catholic Church without the latter's permission. High churchman Edward Churton described the conversion as "the defection of that rogue, Lockhardt; who has played the *Monastery* a thorough Jesuitical trick, and left N. to bear the obloquy" (Edward Churton to Joshua Watson, September 18, 1843, Churton Papers, CHUR 2/3/8, Pusey House).

those who were in danger. I only spoke of those who were convinced that our Church was external to the Church Catholic, though they felt it unsafe to trust their own private convictions; but there are two other states of mind; 1. that of those who are unconsciously near Rome, and whose *despair* about our Church would at once develop into a state of conscious approximation, or a *quasi*-resolution to go over; 2. those who feel they can with a safe conscience remain with us *while* they are allowed to *testify* in behalf of Catholicism, i. e. as if by such acts they were putting our Church, or at least that portion of it in which they were included, in the position of catechumens."

3. "June 20, 1843. I return the very pleasing letter you have permitted me to read. What a sad thing it is, that it should be a plain duty to restrain one's sympathies, and to keep them from boiling over; but I suppose it is a matter of common prudence.

"Things are very serious here; but I should not like you to say so, as it might do no good. The Authorities find, that, by the Statutes, they have more than military power; and the general impression seems to be, that they intend to exert it, and put down Catholicism at any risk. I believe that by the Statutes, they can pretty nearly suspend a Preacher, as *seditiosus* or causing dissension, without assigning their grounds in the particular case, nay, banish him, or imprison him. If so, all holders of preferment in the University should make as quiet an *exit* as they can. There is more exasperation on both sides at this moment, as I am told, than ever there was."

4. "July 16, 1843. I assure you that I feel, with only too much sympathy, what you say. You need not be told that the whole subject of our position is a subject of anxiety to others beside yourself. It is no good attempting to offer advice, when perhaps I might raise difficulties instead of removing them. It seems to me quite a case, in which you should, as far as may be, make up your mind for yourself. Come to Littlemore by all means. We shall all rejoice in your company; and, if quiet and retirement are able, as they very likely will be, to reconcile you to things as they are, you shall have your fill of them. How distressed poor Henry Wilberforce must be! Knowing how he values you, I feel for him; but, alas! he has his own position, and every one else has his own, and the misery is that no two of us have exactly the same.

"It is very kind of you to be so frank and open with me, as you are; but this is a time which throws together persons who feel alike. May I without taking a liberty sign myself, yours affectionately, &c."

5. "August 30, 1843. A. B. has suddenly conformed to the Church of Rome.[32]

---

32. "A. B." is William Lockhardt.

He was away for three weeks. I suppose I must say in my defence, that he promised me distinctly to remain in our Church three years, before I received him here."

6. "June 17, 1845. I am concerned to find you speak of me in a tone of distrust. If you knew me ever so little, instead of hearing of me from persons who do not know me at all, you would think differently of me, whatever you thought of my opinions. Two years since, I got your son to tell you my intention of resigning St. Mary's, before I made it public, thinking you ought to know it. When you expressed some painful feeling upon it, I told him I could not consent to his remaining here, painful as it would be to me to part with him, without your written sanction. And this you did me the favour to give.

"I believe you will find that it has been merely a delicacy on your son's part, which has delayed his speaking to you about me for two months past; a delicacy, lest he should say either too much or too little about me. I have urged him several times to speak to you.

"Nothing can be done after your letter, but to recommend him to go to A. B. (his home) at once. I am very sorry to part with him."

7. The following letter is addressed to Cardinal Wiseman, then Vicar Apostolic, who accused me of coldness in my conduct towards him: —

"April 16, 1845. I was at that time in charge of a ministerial office in the English Church, with persons entrusted to me, and a Bishop to obey; how could I possibly write otherwise than I did without violating sacred obligations and betraying momentous interests which were upon me? I felt that my immediate, undeniable duty, clear if any thing was clear, was to fulfil that trust. It might be right indeed to give it up, that was another thing; but it never could be right to hold it, and to act as if I did not hold it. . . . . . If you knew me, you would acquit me, I think, of having ever felt towards your Lordship in an unfriendly spirit, or ever having had a shadow on my mind (as far as I dare witness about myself) of what might be called controversial rivalry or desire of getting the better, or fear lest the world should think I had got the worse, or irritation of any kind. You are too kind indeed to imply this, and yet your words lead me to say it. And how in like manner, pray believe, though I cannot explain it to you, that I am encompassed with responsibilities, so great and so various, as utterly to overcome me, unless I have mercy from Him, who all through my life has sustained and guided me, and to whom I can now submit myself, though men of all parties are thinking evil of me."

Such fidelity, however, was taken *in malam partem* by the high Anglican authorities; they thought it insidious. I happen still to have a correspondence which took place in 1843, in which the chief place is filled by one of the most eminent Bishops of the day, a theologian and reader of the Fathers, a moderate man, who at one time was talked of as likely on a vacancy to succeed to the Primacy.[33] A young clergyman in his diocese became a Catholic; the papers at once reported on authority from "a very high quarter," that, after his reception, "the Oxford men had been recommending him to retain his living." I had reasons for thinking that the allusion was made to me, and I authorized the Editor of a Paper, who had inquired of me on the point, to "give it, as far as I was concerned, an unqualified contradiction;" — when from a motive of delicacy he hesitated, I added "my direct and indignant contradiction." "Whoever is the author of it," I continued to the Editor, "no correspondence or intercourse of any kind, direct or indirect, has passed between Mr. S. and myself, since his conforming to the Church of Rome, except my formally and merely acknowledging the receipt of his letter, in which he informed me of the fact, without, as far as I recollect, my expressing any opinion upon it. You may state this as broadly as I have set it down." My denial was told to the Bishop; what took place upon it is given in a letter from which I copy. "My father showed the letter to the Bishop, who, as he laid it down, said, 'Ah, those Oxford men are not ingenuous.' 'How do you mean?' asked my father. 'Why,' said the Bishop, 'they advised Mr. B. S. to retain his living after he turned Catholic. I know that to be a fact, because A. B. told me so.'" "The Bishop," continues the letter, "who is perhaps the most influential man in reality on the bench, evidently believes it to be the truth." Upon this Dr. Pusey wrote in my behalf to the Bishop; and the Bishop instantly beat a retreat. "I have the honour," he says in the autograph which I transcribe, "to acknowledge the receipt of your note, and to say in reply that it has not been stated by me, (though such a statement has, I believe, appeared in some of the Public Prints,) that Mr. Newman had advised Mr. B. S. to retain his living, after he had forsaken our Church. But it has been stated to me, that Mr. Newman was in close correspondence with Mr. B. S., and, being fully aware of his state of opinions and feelings, yet advised him to continue in our communion. Allow me to add," he says to Dr. Pusey, "that neither your name, nor that of Mr. Keble, was mentioned to me in connexion with that of Mr. B. S."

I was not going to let the Bishop off on this evasion, so I wrote to him myself. After quoting his Letter to Dr. Pusey, I continued, "I beg to trouble your Lordship with my own account of the two allegations" [*close correspondence* and *fully aware*, &c.] "which are contained in your statement, and which have led to your speaking of me in terms which I hope never to deserve. 1. Since Mr. B. S. has been in your Lordship's diocese, I have seen him in Common rooms

---

33. The bishop to whom Newman refers is Bishop John Kaye of Lincoln (1783–1853).

or private parties in Oxford two or three times, when I never (as far as I can recollect) had any conversation with him. During the same time I have, to the best of my memory, written to him three letters. One was lately, in acknowledgment of his informing me of his change of religion. Another was last summer, when I asked him (to no purpose) to come and stay with me in this place. The earliest of the three letters was written just a year since, as far as I recollect, and it certainly was on the subject of his joining the Church of Rome. I wrote this letter at the earnest wish of a friend of his. I cannot be sure that, on his replying, I did not send him a brief note in explanation of points in my letter which he had misapprehended. I cannot recollect any other correspondence between us.

"2. As to my knowledge of his opinions and feelings, as far as I remember, the only point of perplexity which I knew, the only point which to this hour I know, as pressing upon him, was that of the Pope's supremacy. He professed to be searching Antiquity whether the see of Rome had formerly that relation to the whole Church which Roman Catholics now assign to it. My letter was directed to the point, that it was his duty not to perplex himself with arguments on [such] a question, . . . and to put it altogether aside. . . . It is hard that I am put upon my memory, without knowing the details of the statement made against me, considering the various correspondence in which I am from time to time unavoidably engaged . . . Be assured, my Lord, that there are very definite limits, beyond which persons like me would never urge another to retain preferment in the English Church, nor would retain it themselves; and that the censure which has been directed against them by so many of its Rulers has a very grave bearing upon those limits." The Bishop replied in a civil letter, and sent my own letter to his original informant, who wrote to me the letter of a gentleman. It seems that an anxious lady had said something or other which had been misinterpreted, against her real meaning, into the calumny which was circulated, and so the report vanished into thin air. I closed the correspondence with the following Letter to the Bishop: —

"I hope your Lordship will believe me when I say, that statements about me, equally incorrect with that which has come to your Lordship's ears, are from time to time reported to me as credited and repeated by the highest authorities in our Church, though it is very seldom that I have the opportunity of denying them. I am obliged by your Lordship's letter to Dr. Pusey as giving me such an opportunity." Then I added, with a purpose, "Your Lordship will observe that in my Letter I had no occasion to proceed to the question, whether a person holding Roman Catholic opinions can in honesty remain in our Church. Lest then any misconception should arise from my silence, I here take the liberty of adding, that I see nothing wrong in such a person's continuing in communion with us, provided he holds no preferment or office, abstains from the management of ecclesiastical matters, and is bound by no subscription or oath to our doctrines."

This was written on March 8, 1843, and was in anticipation of my own retirement into lay communion. This again leads me to a remark: — for two years I was in lay communion, not indeed being a Catholic in my convictions, but in a state of serious doubt, and with the probable prospect of becoming some day, what as yet I was not. Under these circumstances I thought the best thing I could do was to give up duty and to throw myself into lay communion, remaining an Anglican. I could not go to Rome, while I thought what I did of the devotions she sanctioned to the Blessed Virgin and the Saints. I did not give up my fellowship, for I could not be sure that my doubts would not be reduced or overcome, however unlikely I might consider such an event. But I gave up my living; and, for two years before my conversion, I took no clerical duty. My last Sermon was in September, 1843; then I remained at Littlemore in quiet for two years.[34] But it was made a subject of reproach to me at the time, and is at this day, that I did not leave the Anglican Church sooner. To me this seems a wonderful charge; why, even had I been quite sure that Rome was the true Church, the Anglican Bishops would have had no just subject of complaint against me, provided I took no Anglican oath, no clerical duty, no ecclesiastical administration. Do they force all men who go to their Churches to believe in the 39 Articles, or to join in the Athanasian Creed? However, I was to have other measure dealt to me; great authorities ruled it so; and a learned controversialist in the North thought it a shame that I did not leave the Church of England as much as ten years sooner than I did. He said this in print between the years 1847 and 1849. His nephew, an Anglican clergyman, kindly wished to undeceive him on this point. So, in the latter year, after some correspondence, I wrote the following letter, which will be of service to this narrative, from its chronological notes: —

"Dec. 6, 1849. Your uncle says, 'If he (Mr. N.) will declare, *sans phrase*, as the French say, that I have laboured under an entire mistake, and that he was not a concealed Romanist during the ten years in question,' (I suppose, the last ten years of my membership with the Anglican Church,) 'or during any part of the time, my controversial antipathy will be at an end, and I will readily express to him that I am truly sorry that I have made such a mistake.'

---

34. During this period Newman remained an Oriel fellow and received the income derived from that fellowship through the payment of October 1845.

"So candid an avowal is what I should have expected from a mind like your uncle's. I am extremely glad he has brought it to this issue.

"By a 'concealed Romanist' I understand him to mean one, who, professing to belong to the Church of England, in his heart and will intends to benefit the Church of Rome, at the expense of the Church of England. He cannot mean by the expression merely a person who in fact is benefiting the Church of Rome, while he is intending to benefit the Church of England, for that is no discredit to him morally, and he (your uncle) evidently means to impute blame.

"In the sense in which I have explained the words, I can simply and honestly say that I was not a concealed Romanist during the whole, or any part of, the years in question.

"For the first four years of the ten, (up to Michaelmas, 1839,) I honestly wished to benefit the Church of England, at the expense of the Church of Rome:

"For the second four years I wished to benefit the Church of England without prejudice to the Church of Rome:

"At the beginning of the ninth year (Michaelmas, 1843) I began to despair of the Church of England, and gave up all clerical duty; and then, what I wrote and did was influenced by a mere wish not to injure it, and not by the wish to benefit it:

"At the beginning of the tenth year I distinctly contemplated leaving it, but I also distinctly told my friends that it was in my contemplation.

"Lastly, during the last half of that tenth year I was engaged in writing a book (Essay on Development) in favour of the Roman Church, and indirectly against the English; but even then, till it was finished, I had not absolutely intended to publish it, wishing to reserve to myself the chance of changing my mind when the argumentative views which were actuating me had been distinctly brought out before me in writing.[35]

"I wish this statement, which I make from memory, and without consulting any document, severely tested by my writings and doings, as I am confident it

---

35. Newman's *Essay on the Development of Christian Doctrine* (1845) was less clearly against the English Church and for the Roman Church than he suggests in this passage. In the book Newman defended various modes of devotion and the monastic life that he wished to pursue in the Church of England. He sought to demonstrate that these devotional practices had developed in the course of Christian history and were legitimate even though they had emerged after the fifth century when high church Anglicans believed corruption had set into the Christian Church. Reviewers at the time noted that Newman's specific case for the modern Roman Catholic Church appeared to have been introduced late into the book.

will, on the whole, be borne out, whatever real or apparent exceptions (I suspect none) have to be allowed by me in detail.

"Your uncle is at liberty to make what use he pleases of this explanation."

I have now reached an important date in my narrative, the year 1843; but before proceeding to the matters which it contains, I will insert portions of my letters from 1841 to 1843, addressed to Catholic acquaintances.[36]

1. "April 8, 1841. . . . The unity of the Church Catholic is very near my heart, only I do not see any prospect of it in our time; and I despair of its being effected without great sacrifices on all hands. As to resisting the Bishop's will, I observe that no point of doctrine or principle was in dispute, but a course of action, the publication of certain works. I do not think you sufficiently understood our position. I suppose you would obey the Holy See in such a case; now, when we were separated from the Pope, his authority reverted to our Diocesans. Our Bishop is our Pope. It is our theory, that each diocese is an integral Church, intercommunion being a duty, (and the breach of it a sin,) but not essential to Catholicity. To have resisted my Bishop, would have been to place myself in an utterly false position, which I never could have recovered. Depend upon it, the strength of any party lies in its being *true to its theory.* Consistency is the life of a movement.

"I have no misgivings whatever that the line I have taken can be other than a prosperous one: that is, in itself, for of course Providence may refuse to us its legitimate issues for our sins.

"I am afraid, that in one respect you may be disappointed. It is my trust, though I must not be too sanguine, that we shall not have individual members of our communion going over to yours. What one's duty would be under other circumstances, what our duty ten or twenty years ago, I cannot say; but I do think that there is less of private judgment in going with one's Church, than in leaving it. I can earnestly desire a union between my Church and yours. I cannot listen to the thought of your being joined by individuals among us."

2. "April 26, 1841. My only anxiety is lest your branch of the Church should not meet us by those reforms which surely are *necessary.* It never could

---

36. The remarkable letters that follow here indicate a vast leap of the religious imagination on Newman's part and an openness to a kind of ecumenical dialogue that only small groups in either the Church of England or Roman Catholic Church could share. Newman speaks for himself and his surrounding Catholic group, not for the Church of England in general. He assumes, along with his then followers such as Ward, that what is required for ecumenical cooperation would be a series of internal reforms on the part of both communions, which he does not see occurring in his own lifetime.

be, that so large a portion of Christendom should have split off from the communion of Rome, and kept up a protest for 300 years for nothing. I think I never shall believe that so much piety and earnestness would be found among Protestants, if there were not some very grave errors on the side of Rome. To suppose the contrary is most unreal, and violates all one's notions or moral probabilities. All aberrations are founded on, and have their life in, some truth or other—and Protestantism, so widely spread and so long enduring, must have in it, and must be witness for, a great truth or much truth. That I am an advocate for Protestantism, you cannot suppose;—but I am forced into a *Via Media*, short of Rome, as it is at present."

3. "May 5, 1841. While I most sincerely hold that there is in the Roman Church a traditionary system which is not necessarily connected with her essential formularies, yet, were I ever so much to change my mind on this point, this would not tend to bring me from my present position, providentially appointed in the English Church. That your communion was unassailable, would not prove that mine was indefensible. Nor would it at all affect the sense in which I receive our Articles; they would still speak against certain definite errors, though you had reformed them.

"I say this lest any lurking suspicion should be left in the mind of your friends that persons who think with me are likely, by the growth of their present views, to find it imperative on them to pass over to your communion. Allow me to state strongly, that if you have any such thoughts, and proceed to act upon them, your friends will be committing a fatal mistake. We have (I trust) the principle and temper of obedience too intimately wrought into us to allow of our separating ourselves form our ecclesiastical superiors because in many points we may sympathize with others. We have too great a horror of the principle of private judgment to trust it in so immense a matter as that of changing from one communion to another. We may be cast out of our communion, or it may decree heresy to be truth,—you shall say whether such contingencies are likely; but I do not see other conceivable causes of our leaving the Church in which we were baptized.

"For myself, persons must be well acquainted with what I have written before they venture to say whether I have much changed my main opinions and cardinal views in the course of the last eight years. That my *sympathies* have grown towards the religion of Rome I do not deny; that my *reasons* for *shunning* her communion have lessened or altered it would be difficult perhaps to prove. And I wish to go by reason, not by feeling."

4. "June 18, 1841. You urge persons whose views agree with mine to commence a movement in behalf of a union between the Churches. Now in the letters I have written, I have uniformly said that I did not expect that union in

our time, and have discouraged the notion of all sudden proceedings with a view to it. I must ask your leave to repeat on this occasion most distinctly, that I cannot be party to any agitation, but mean to remain quiet in my own place, and to do all I can to make others take the same course. This I conceive to be my simple duty; but, over and above this, I will not set my teeth on edge with sour grapes.[37] I know it is quite within the range of possibilities that one or another of our people should go over to your communion; however, it would be a greater misfortune to you than grief to us. If your friends wish to put a gulf between themselves and us, let them make converts, but not else. Some months ago, I ventured to say that I felt it a painful duty to keep aloof from all Roman Catholics who came with the intention of opening negotiations for the union of the Churches: when you now urge us to petition our Bishops for a union, this, I conceive, is very like an act of negotiation."

5. I have the first sketch or draft of a letter, which I wrote to a zealous Catholic layman: it runs as follows, as far as I have preserved it, but I think there were various changes and additions:—"September 12, 1841. It would rejoice all Catholic minds among us, more than words can say, if you could persuade members of the Church of Rome to take the line in politics which you so earnestly advocate. Suspicion and distrust are the main causes at present of the separation between us, and the nearest approaches in doctrine will but increase the hostility, which, alas, our people feel towards yours, while these causes continue. Depend upon it, you must not rely upon our Catholic tendencies till they are removed. I am not speaking of myself, or of any friends of mine; but of our Church generally. Whatever *our* personal feelings may be, we shall but tend to raise and spread a *rival* Church to yours in the four quarters of the world, unless *you* do what none but you *can* do. Sympathies, which would flow over to the Church of Rome, as a matter of course, did she admit them, will but be developed in the consolidation of our own system, if she continues to be the object of our suspicions and fears. I wish, of course I do, that our own Church may be built up and extended, but still, not at the cost of the Church of Rome, not in opposition to it. I am sure, that, while you suffer, we suffer too from the separation; *but we cannot remove the obstacles;* it is with you to do so. You do not fear us; we fear you. Till we cease to fear you, we cannot love you.

"While you are in your present position, the friends of Catholic unity in our Church are but fulfilling the prediction of those of your body who are averse to them, viz. that they will be merely strengthening a rival communion to yours. Many of you say that *we* are your greatest enemies; we have said so ourselves:

---

37. Ezekiel 18:2.

so we are, so we shall be, as things stand at present. We are keeping people from you, by supplying their wants in our own Church. We *are* keeping persons from you: do you wish us to keep them from you for a time or for ever? It rests with you to determine. I do not fear that you will succeed among us; you will not supplant our Church in the affections of the English nation; only through the English Church can you act upon the English nation. I wish of course our Church should be consolidated, with and through and in your communion, for its sake, and your sake, and for the sake of unity.

"Are you aware that the more serious thinkers among us are used, as far as they dare form an opinion, to regard the spirit of Liberalism as the characteristic of the destined Antichrist? In vain does any one clear the Church of Rome from the badges of Antichrist, in which Protestants would invest her, if she deliberately takes up her position in the very quarter, whither we have cast them, when we took them off from her. Antichrist is described as the ἄνομος,[38] as exalting himself above the yoke of religion and law. The spirit of lawlessness came in with the Reformation, and Liberalism is its offspring.

"And now I fear I am going to pain you by telling you, that you consider the approaches in doctrine on our part towards you, closer than they really are. I cannot help repeating what I have many times said in print, that your services and devotions to St. Mary in matter of fact do most deeply pain me. I am only stating it as a fact.

"Again, I have nowhere said that I can accept the decrees of Trent throughout, nor implied it. The doctrine of Transubstantiation is a great difficulty with me, as being, as I think, not primitive. Nor have I said that our Articles in all respects admit of a Roman interpretation; the very word 'Transubstantiation' is disowned in them.

"Thus, you see, it is not merely on grounds of expedience that we do not join you. There are positive difficulties in the way of it. And, even if there were not, we shall have no divine warrant for doing so, while we think that the Church of England is a branch of the true Church, and that intercommunion with the rest of Christendom is necessary, not for the life of a particular Church, but for its health only. I have never disguised that there are actual circumstances in the Church of Rome, which pain me much; of the removal of these I see no chance, while we join you one by one; but if our Church were prepared for a union, she might make her terms; she might gain the cup; she might protest against the extreme honours paid to St. Mary; she might make some explanation of the doctrine of Transubstantiation. I am not prepared to say that a reform in other branches of the Roman Church would be necessary for our uniting with them, however desirable in itself, so that we were allowed to make a reform in our

---

38. "lawless one."

own country. We do not look towards Rome as believing that its communion is infallible, but that union is a duty."

6. The following letter was occasioned by the present made to me of a book by the friend to whom it is written; more will be said on the subject of it presently:—

"Nov. 22, 1842. I only wish that your Church were more known among us by such writings. You will not interest us in her, till we see her, not in politics, but in her true functions of exhorting, teaching, and guiding. I wish there were a chance of making the leading men among you understand, what I believe is no novel thought to yourself. It is not by learned discussions, or acute arguments, or reports of miracles, that the heart of England can be gained. It is by men 'approving themselves,' like the Apostle, 'ministers of Christ.'

"As to your question, whether the Volume you have sent is not calculated to remove my apprehensions that another gospel is substituted for the true one in your practical instructions, before I can answer it in any way, I ought to know how far the Sermons which it comprises are *selected* from a number, or whether they are the whole, or such as the whole, which have been published of the author's. I assure you, or at least I trust, that, if it is ever clearly brought home to me that I have been wrong in what I have said on this subject, my public avowal of that conviction will only be a question of time with me.

"If, however, you saw our Church as we see it, you would easily understand that such a change of feeling, did it take place, would have no necessary tendency, which you seem to expect, to draw a person from the Church of England to that of Rome. There is a divine life among us, clearly manifested, in spite of all our disorders, which is as great a note of the Church, as any can be. Why should we seek our Lord's presence elsewhere, when He vouchsafes it to us where we are? What *call* have we to change our communion?

"Roman Catholics will find this to be the state of things in time to come, whatever promise they may fancy there is of a large secession to their Church. This man or that may leave us, but there will be no general movement. There is, indeed, an incipient movement of our *Church* towards yours, and this your leading men are doing all they can to frustrate by their unwearied efforts at all risks to carry off individuals. When will they know their position, and embrace a larger and wiser policy?"

§ 2.

The letter which I have last inserted, is addressed to my dear friend, Dr. Russell, the present President of Maynooth.[39] He had, perhaps, more to do

---

39. Dr. Charles Russell (1812–1880) was professor of humanity at the Roman Catholic Maynooth College in Ireland. He would later become president of that institution.

with my conversion than any one else. He called upon me, in passing through Oxford in the summer of 1841, and I think I took him over some of the buildings of the University. He called again another summer, on his way from Dublin to London. I do not recollect that he said a word on the subject of religion on either occasion. He sent me at different times several letters; he was always gentle, mild, unobtrusive, uncontroversial. He let me alone. He also gave me one or two books. Veron's Rule of Faith and some Treatises of the Wallenburghs was one; a volume of St. Alfonso Liguori's Sermons was another; and it is to those Sermons that my letter to Dr. Russell relates.[40]

Now it must be observed that the writings of St. Alfonso, as I knew them by the extracts commonly made from them, prejudiced me as much against the Roman Church as any thing else, on account of what was called their "Mariolatry;" but there was nothing of the kind in this book. I wrote to ask Dr. Russell whether any thing had been left out in the translation; he answered that there certainly were omissions in one Sermon about the Blessed Virgin. This omission, in the case of a book intended for Catholics, at least showed that such passages as are found in the works of Italian Authors were not acceptable to every part of the Catholic world. Such devotional manifestations in honour of our Lady had been my great *crux* as regards Catholicism; I say frankly, I do not fully enter into them now; I trust I do not love her the less, because I cannot enter into them.[41] They may be fully explained and defended; but sentiment and taste do not run with logic: they are suitable for Italy, but they are not suitable for England. But, over and above England, my own case was special; from a boy I had been led to consider that my Maker and I, His creature, were the two beings, luminously such, *in rerum naturâ*. I will not here speculate, however, about my own feelings. Only this I know full well now, and did not know then, that the Catholic Church allows no image of any sort, material or immaterial, no dogmatic symbol, no rite, no sacrament, no Saint, not even the Blessed Virgin herself, to come between the soul and its Creator. It is face to face, "solus cum solo," in all matters between man and his God. He alone creates; He alone has redeemed; before His awful eyes we go in death; in the vision of Him is our eternal beatitude.

    40. François Véron (1575–1625) was a writer of the Catholic Reformation who criticized Protestantism. Adrian (d. 1669) and Peter (d. 1675) von Wallenburgh were seventeenth-century Roman Catholic controversialists. Both served as auxiliary bishops in Cologne, Germany. On St. Alfonso Liguori, see the introduction to this volume.

    41. Newman was quite open about his difficulty with Italianate Marian devotion, about which ultramontanes faulted him. However, Bishop Ullathorne wrote a letter defending him on this matter. See W. B. Ullathorne to the Editor of the *Tablet,* April 4, 1866, *L&D* 24: 341–344.

1. Solus cum solo:[42]—I recollect but indistinctly what I gained from the Volume of which I have been speaking; but it must have been something considerable. At least I had got a key to a difficulty; in these Sermons, (or rather heads of sermons, as they seem to be, taken down by a hearer,) there is much of what would be called legendary illustration; but the substance of them is plain, practical, awful preaching upon the great truths of salvation. What I can speak of with greater confidence is the effect produced on me a little later by studying the Exercises of St. Ignatius.[43] For here again, in a matter consisting in the purest and most direct acts of religion, — in the intercourse between God and the soul, during a season of recollection, of repentance, of good resolution, of inquiry into vocation, — the soul was "sola cum solo;" there was no cloud interposed between the creature and the Object of his faith and love. The command practically enforced was, "My son, give Me thy heart." The devotions then to Angels and Saints as little interfered with the incommunicable glory of the Eternal, as the love which we bear our friends and relations, our tender human sympathies, are inconsistent with that supreme homage of the heart to the Unseen, which really does but sanctify and exalt, not jealously destroy, what is of earth. At a later date Dr. Russell sent me a large bundle of penny or half-penny books of devotion, of all sorts, as they are found in the booksellers' shops at Rome; and, on looking them over, I was quite astonished to find how different they were from what I had fancied, how little there was in them to which I could really object. I have given an account of them in my Essay on the Development of Doctrine. Dr. Russell sent me St. Alfonso's book at the end of 1842; however, it was still a long time before I got over my difficulty, on the score of the devotions paid to the Saints; perhaps, as I judge from a letter I have turned up, it was some way into 1844 before I could be said fully to have got over it.

2. I am not sure that I did not also at this time feel the force of another consideration. The idea of the Blessed Virgin was as it were *magnified* in the Church of Rome, as time went on, — but so were all the Christian ideas; as that of the Blessed Eucharist. The whole scene of pale, faint, distant Apostolic Christianity is seen in Rome, as through a telescope or magnifier. The harmony of the whole, however, is of course what it was. It is unfair then to take one Roman idea, that of the Blessed Virgin, out of what may be called its context.

3. Thus I am brought to the principle of development of doctrine in the

---

42. "I am alone with myself."

43. St. Ignatius Loyola was the author of the *Spiritual Exercises*, the chief document of Jesuit devotional literature.

Christian Church, to which I gave my mind at the end of 1842.[44] I had made mention of it in the passage, which I quoted many pages back (vide p. 223), in "Home Thoughts Abroad," published in 1836; and even at an earlier date I had introduced it into my History of the Arians in 1832; nor had I ever lost sight of it in my speculations. And it is certainly recognized in the Treatise of Vincent of Lerins, which has so often been taken as the basis of Anglicanism. In 1843 I began to consider it attentively; I made it the subject of my last University Sermon on February 2; and the general view to which I came is stated thus in a letter to a friend of the date of July 14, 1844; — it will be observed that, now as before, my *issue* is still Creed *versus* Church: —

"The kind of considerations which weighs with me are such as the following: — 1. I am far more certain (according to the Fathers) that we *are* in a state of culpable separation, *than* that developments do *not* exist under the Gospel, and that the Roman developments are not the true ones. 2. I am far more certain, that *our* (modern) doctrines are wrong, *than* that the *Roman* (modern) doctrines are wrong. 3. Granting that the Roman (special) doctrines are not found drawn out in the early Church, yet I think there is sufficient trace of them in it, to recommend and prove them, *on the hypothesis* of the Church having a divine guidance, though not sufficient to prove them by itself. So that the question simply turns on the nature of the promise of the Spirit, made to the Church. 4. The proof of the Roman (modern) doctrine is as strong (or stronger) in Antiquity, as that of certain doctrines which both we and Romans hold: e. g. there is more of evidence in Antiquity for the necessity of Unity, than for the Apostolical Succession; for the Supremacy of the See of Rome, than for the Presence in the Eucharist; for the practice of Invocation, than for certain books in the present Canon of Scripture, &c. &c. 5. The analogy of the Old Testament, and also of the New, leads to the acknowledgment of doctrinal developments."

4. And thus I was led on to a further consideration. I saw that the principle of development not only accounted for certain facts, but was in itself a remarkable philosophical phenomenon, giving a character to the whole course

---

44. During the early 1840s Newman began to articulate a concept of the development of Christian doctrine that culminated in his *Essay on the Development of Christian Doctrine,* published in 1845. Newman contended that Christian doctrine and practice had developed across the centuries and was not limited by the Bible or by the writings of Christian antiquity. Contemporaries in both the Church of England and the Roman Catholic Church saw Newman as having set forth a highly indeterminate understanding of the form and contents of Christian truth and doctrine. See Owen Chadwick, *From Bossuet to Newman: The Idea of Doctrinal Development,* 2nd ed. (Cambridge: Cambridge Univ. Press, 1987), and Turner, *John Henry Newman,* pp. 557–586.

of Christian thought. It was discernible from the first years of the Catholic teaching up to the present day, and gave to that teaching a unity and individuality. It served as a sort of test, which the Anglican could not exhibit, that modern Rome was in truth ancient Antioch, Alexandria, and Constantinople, just as a mathematical curve has its own law and expression.

5. And thus again I was led on to examine more attentively what I doubt not was in my thoughts long before, viz. the concatenation of argument by which the mind ascends from its first to its final religious idea; and I came to the conclusion that there was no medium, in true philosophy, between Atheism and Catholicity, and that a perfectly consistent mind, under those circumstances in which it finds itself here below, must embrace either the one or the other.[45] And I hold this still: I am a Catholic by virtue of my believing in a God; and if I am asked why I believe in a God, I answer that it is because I believe in myself, for I feel it impossible to believe in my own existence (and of that fact I am quite sure) without believing also in the existence of Him, who lives as a Personal, All-seeing, All-judging Being in my conscience. Now, I dare say, I have not expressed myself with philosophical correctness, because I have not given myself to the study of what metaphysicians have said on the subject; but I think I have a strong true meaning in what I say which will stand examination.

6. Moreover, I found a corroboration of the fact of the logical connexion of Theism with Catholicism in a consideration parallel to that which I had adopted on the subject of development of doctrine. The fact of the operation from first to last of that principle of development in the truths of Revelation, is an argument in favour of the identity of Roman and Primitive Christianity; but as there is a law which acts upon the subject-matter of dogmatic theology, so is there a law in the matter of religious faith. In the first chapter of this Narrative I spoke of certitude as the consequence, divinely intended and enjoined upon us, of the accumulative force of certain given reasons which, taken one by one, were only probabilities.[46] Let it be recollected that I am historically relating my state of mind, at the period of my life which I am surveying. I am not speaking theologically, nor have I any intention of going into controversy, or of defending myself; but speaking historically of what I held in 1843-4, I say, that I believed in a God on a ground of probability, that I believed in Christianity on

---

45. Contemporary reviewers noted that whatever the merit of Newman's logical claim here, it was empirically falsified by millions of people who were professing Christians while rejecting both Roman Catholicism and atheism.

46. Much of Newman's personal religious belief and theology was based on approaching those issues on the basis of probability rather than through conviction based on natural religion or biblical revelation.

a probability, and that I believed in Catholicism on a probability, and that these three grounds of probability, distinct from each other of course in subject matter, were still all of them one and the same in nature of proof, as being probabilities—probabilities of a special kind, a cumulative, a transcendent probability but still probability; inasmuch as He who made us has so willed, that in mathematics indeed we should arrive at certitude by rigid demonstration, but in religious inquiry we should arrive at certitude by accumulated probabilities;—He has willed, I say, that we should so act, and, as willing it, He co-operates with us in our acting, and thereby enables us to do that which He wills us to do, and carries us on, if our will does but co-operate with His, to a certitude which rises higher than the logical force of our conclusions. And thus I came to see clearly, and to have a satisfaction in seeing, that, in being led on into the Church of Rome, I was not proceeding on any secondary or isolated grounds of reason, or by controversial points in detail, but was protected and justified, even in the use of those secondary or particular arguments, by a great and broad principle. But, let it be observed, that I am stating a matter of fact, not defending it; and if any Catholic says in consequence that I have been converted in a wrong way, I cannot help that now.

I have nothing more to say on the subject of the change in my religious opinions. On the one hand I came gradually to see that the Anglican Church was formally in the wrong, on the other that the Church of Rome was formally in the right; then, that no valid reasons could be assigned for continuing in the Anglican, and again that no valid objections could be taken to joining the Roman. Then, I had nothing more to learn; what still remained for my conversion, was, not further change of opinion, but to change opinion itself into the clearness and firmness of intellectual conviction.

Now I proceed to detail the acts, to which I committed myself during this last stage of my inquiry.

In 1843, I took two very significant steps:—1. In February, I made a formal Retractation of all the hard things which I had said against the Church of Rome.[47] 2. In September, I resigned the Living of St. Mary's, Littlemore included:—I will speak of these two acts separately.

 1. The words, in which I made my Retractation, have given rise to much criticism. After quoting a number of passages from my writings against the Church of Rome, which I withdrew, I ended thus:—"If you ask me how an

---

47. Newman published these retractions anonymously in the *Oxford Conservative Journal* (December 12, 1842) and the *Oxford University Herald* (February 1843). They are reprinted in *L&D* 9: 167–172.

individual could venture, not simply to hold, but to publish such views of a communion so ancient, so wide-spreading, so fruitful in Saints, I answer that I said to myself, 'I am not speaking my own words, I am but following almost a *consensus* of the divines of my own Church. They have ever used the strongest language against Rome, even the most able and learned of them. I wish to throw myself into their system. While I say what they say, I am safe. Such views, too, are necessary for our position.' Yet I have reason to fear still, that such language is to be ascribed, in no small measure, to an impetuous temper, a hope of approving myself to persons I respect, and a wish to repel the charge of Romanism."

These words have been, and are, again and again cited against me, as if a confession that, when in the Anglican Church, I said things against Rome which I did not really believe.

For myself, I cannot understand how any impartial man can so take them; and I have explained them in print several times. I trust that by this time their plain meaning has been satisfactorily brought out by what I have said in former portions of this Narrative; still I have a word or two to say in addition to my former remarks upon them.

In the passage in question I apologize for *saying out* in controversy charges against the Church of Rome, which withal I affirm that I fully *believed* at the time when I made them. What is wonderful in such an apology? There are surely many things a man may hold, which at the same time he may feel that he has no right to say publicly, and which it may annoy him that he has said publicly. The law recognizes this principle. In our own time, men have been imprisoned and fined for saying true things of a bad king. The maxim has been held, that, "The greater the truth, the greater is the libel." And so as to the judgment of society, a just indignation would be felt against a writer who brought forward wantonly the weaknesses of a great man, though the whole world knew that they existed. No one is at liberty so speak ill of another without a justifiable reason, even though he knows he is speaking truth, and the public knows it too. Therefore, though I believed what I said against the Roman Church, nevertheless I could not religiously speak it out, unless I was really justified, not only in believing ill, but in speaking ill. I did believe what I said on what I thought to be good reasons; but had I also a just cause for saying out what I believed? I thought I had, and it was this, viz. that to say out what I believed was simply necessary in the controversy for self-defence. It was impossible to let it alone: the Anglican position could not be satisfactorily maintained, without assailing the Roman. In this, as in most cases of conflict, one was right or the other, not both; and the best defence was to attack. Is not this almost a truism in the Roman controversy? Is it not what every one says, who speaks on the subject at all? does any serious man abuse the Church of Rome, for the sake of abusing her, or because that abuse justifies his own religious position? What is the meaning of the very word "Protestantism," but that there is a call to speak out? This then is what I said; "I know I spoke strongly against the Church of Rome; but it was no mere abuse, for I had a serious reason for doing so."

But, not only did I think such language necessary for my Church's religious position, but I recollected that all the great Anglican divines had thought so before me. They had thought so, and they had acted accordingly. And therefore I observe in the passage in question, with much propriety, that I had not used strong language simply out of my own head, but that in doing so I was following the track, or rather reproducing the teaching, of those who had preceded me.

I was pleading guilty to using violent language, but I was pleading also that there were extenuating circumstances in the case. We all know the story of the convict, who on the scaffold bit off his mother's ear. By doing so he did not deny the fact of his own crime, for which he was to hang; but he said that his mother's indulgence when he was a boy, had a good deal to do with it. In like manner I had made a charge, and I had made it *ex animo;* but I accused others of having, by their own example, led me into believing it and publishing it.

I was in a humour, certainly, to bite off their ears. I will freely confess, indeed I said it some pages back, that I was angry with the Anglican divines. I thought they had taken me in; I had read the Fathers with their eyes; I had sometimes trusted their quotations or their reasonings; and from reliance on them, I had used words or made statements, which by right I ought rigidly to have examined myself. I had thought myself safe, while I had their warrant for what I said. I had exercised more faith than criticism in the matter. This did not imply any broad misstatements on my part, arising from reliance on their authority, but it implied carelessness in matters of detail. And this of course was a fault.

But there was a far deeper reason for my saying what I said in this matter, on which I have not hitherto touched; and it was this: — The most oppressive thought, in the whole process of my change of opinion, was the clear anticipation, verified by the event, that it would issue in the triumph of Liberalism. Against the Anti-dogmatic principle I had thrown my whole mind; yet now I was doing more than any one else could do, to promote it. I was one of those who had kept it at bay in Oxford for so many years; and thus my very retirement was its triumph. The men who had driven me from Oxford were distinctly the Liberals; it was they who had opened the attack upon Tract 90, and it was they who would gain a second benefit, if I went on to abandon the

Anglican Church. But this was not all.⁴⁸ As I have already said, there are but two alternatives, the way to Rome, and the way to Atheism: Anglicanism is the halfway house on the one side, and Liberalism is the halfway house on the other. How many men were there, as I knew full well, who would not follow me now in my advance from Anglicanism to Rome, but would at once leave Anglicanism and me for the Liberal camp. It is not at all easy (humanly speaking) to wind up an Englishman to a dogmatic level. I had done so in good measure, in the case both of young men and of laymen, the Anglican *Via Media* being the representative of dogma. The dogmatic and the Anglican principle were one, as I had taught them; but I was breaking the *Via Media* to pieces, and would not dogmatic faith altogether be broken up, in the minds of a great number, by the demolition of the *Via Media?* Oh! how unhappy this made me! I heard once from an eye-witness the account of a poor sailor whose legs were shattered by a ball, in the action off Algiers in 1816, and who was taken below for an operation. The surgeon and the chaplain persuaded him to have a leg off; it was done and the tourniquet applied to the wound. Then, they broke it to him that he must have the other off too. The poor fellow said, "You should have told me that, gentlemen," and deliberately unscrewed the instrument and bled to death. Would not that be the case with many friends of my own? How could I ever hope to make them believe in a second theology, when I had cheated them in the first? with what face could I publish a new edition of a dogmatic creed, and ask them to receive it as gospel? Would it not be plain to them that no certainty was to be found any where? Well, in my defence I could but make a lame apology; however, it was the true one, viz. that I had not read the Fathers cautiously enough; that in such nice points, as those which determine the angle of divergence between the two Churches, I had made considerable miscalculations. But how came this about? why, the fact was, unpleasant as it was to avow, that I had leaned too much upon the assertions of Ussher, Jeremy Taylor, or Barrow, and had been deceived by them. Valeat quantum,⁴⁹ — it was all that *could* be said. This then was a chief reason of that wording of the Retractation, which has given so much offence, because the bitterness, with which it was written, was not understood; — and the following letter will illustrate it: —

---

48. On this claim by Newman, consult Peter Nockles, "Oxford, Tract 90 and the Bishops," in *John Henry Newman: Reason, Rhetoric and Romanticism,* ed. David Nicholls and Fergus Kerr (Carbondale and Edwardsville: Southern Illinois Univ. Press, 1991), pp. 28–87.

49. "For whatever it may be worth."

"April 3, 1844. I wish to remark on William's chief distress,[50] that my changing my opinion seemed to unsettle one's confidence in truth and falsehood as external things, and led one to be suspicious of the new opinion as one became distrustful of the old. Now in what I shall say, I am not going to speak in favour of my second thoughts in comparison of my first, but against such scepticism and unsettlement about truth and falsehood generally, the idea of which is very painful.

"The case with me, then, was this, and not surely an unnatural one: — as a matter of feeling and of duty I threw myself into the system which I found myself in. I saw that the English Church had a theological idea or theory as such, and I took it up. I read Laud on Tradition, and thought it (as I still think it) very masterly. The Anglican Theory was very distinctive. I admired it and took it on faith. It did not (I think) occur to me to doubt it; I saw that it was able, and supported by learning, and I felt it was a duty to maintain it. Further, on looking into Antiquity and reading the Fathers, I saw such portions of it as I examined, fully confirmed (e. g. the supremacy of Scripture). There was only one question about which I had a doubt, viz. whether it would *work,* for it has never been more than a paper system. . . .

"So far from my change of opinion having any fair tendency to unsettle persons as to truth and falsehood viewed as objective realities, it should be considered whether such change is not *necessary,* if truth be a real objective thing, and be made to confront a person who has been brought up in a system *short of* truth. Surely the *continuance* of a person, who wishes to go right, in a wrong system, and not his *giving it up,* would be that which militated against the objectiveness of Truth, leading, as it would, to the suspicion, that one thing and another were equally pleasing to our Maker, where men were sincere.

"Nor surely is it a thing I need be sorry for, that I defended the system in which I found myself, and thus have had to unsay my words. For is it not one's duty, instead of beginning with criticism, to throw oneself generously into that form of religion which is providentially put before one? Is it right, or is it wrong, to begin with private judgment? May we not, on the other hand, look for a blessing *through* obedience even to an erroneous system, and a guidance even by means of it out of it? Were those who were strict and conscientious in their Judaism, or those who were lukewarm and sceptical, more likely to be led into Christianity, when Christ came? Yet in proportion to their previous

---

50. William Froude (1810–1879) was the brother of Richard Hurrell Froude and an engineer with whom Newman carried on a wide-ranging correspondence, as he did with Froude's wife, Catherine, to whom this particular letter is addressed.

zeal, would be their appearance of inconsistency. Certainly, I have always contended that obedience even to an erring conscience was the way to gain light, and that it mattered not where a man began, so that he began on what came to hand, and in faith; and that any thing might become a divine method of Truth; that to the pure all things are pure, and have a self-correcting virtue and a power of germinating. And though I have no right at all to assume that this mercy is granted to me, yet the fact, that a person in my situation *may* have it granted to him, seems to me to remove the perplexity which my change of opinion may occasion.

"It may be said,—I have said it to myself,—'Why, however, did you *publish?* had you waited quietly, you would have changed your opinion without any of the misery, which now is involved in the change, of disappointing and distressing people.' I answer, that things are so bound up together, as to form a whole, and one cannot tell what is or is not a condition of what. I do not see how possibly I could have published the Tracts, or other works professing to defend our Church, without accompanying them with a strong protest or argument against Rome. The one obvious objection against the whole Anglican line is, that it is Roman; so that I really think there was no alternative between silence altogether, and forming a theory and attacking the Roman system."[51]

2. And now, in the next place, as to my Resignation of St. Mary's, which was the second of the steps which I took in 1843. The ostensible, direct, and sufficient reason for my doing so was the persevering attack of the Bishops on Tract 90. I alluded to it in the letter which I have inserted above, addressed to one of the most influential among them. A series of their *ex cathedrâ* judgments, lasting through three years, and including a notice of no little severity in a Charge of my own Bishop, came as near to a condemnation of my Tract, and, so far, to a repudiation of the ancient Catholic doctrine, which was the scope of the Tract, as was possible in the Church of England. It was in order to shield the Tract from such a condemnation, that I had at the time of its publication in 1841 so simply put myself at the disposal of the higher powers in London. At that time, all that was distinctly contemplated in the way of censure, was contained in the message which my Bishop sent me, that it was "objectionable." That I thought was the end of the matter. I had refused to suppress it, and they had yielded that point. Since I published the former portions of this

---

51. By "Anglican line" Newman means the more general Tractarian frame of theology, which from its earliest publications had encountered accusations of being Romanish. Hence to counter those polemics, he had undertaken criticism of Roman Catholicism.

Narrative, I have found what I wrote to Dr. Pusey on March 24, while the matter was in progress. "The more I think of it," I said, "the more reluctant I am to suppress Tract 90, though *of course* I will do it if the Bishop wishes it; I cannot, however, deny that I shall feel it a severe act." According to the notes which I took of the letters or messages which I sent to him in the course of that day, I presently wrote to him, "My first feeling was to obey without a word; I will obey still; but my judgment has steadily risen against it ever since." Then in the Postscript, "If I have done any good to the Church, I do ask the Bishop this favour, as my reward for it, that he would not insist on a measure, from which I think good will not come. However, I will submit to him." Afterwards, I got stronger still and wrote: "I have almost come to the resolution, if the Bishop publicly intimates that I must suppress the Tract, or speaks strongly in his charge against it, to suppress it indeed, but to resign my living also. I could not in conscience act otherwise. You may show this in any quarter you please."

All my then hopes, all my satisfaction at the apparent fulfilment of those hopes was at an end in 1843. It is not wonderful then, that in May of that year, when two out of the three years were gone, I wrote on the subject of my retiring from St. Mary's to the same friend, whom I had consulted upon it in 1840. But I did more now; I told him my great unsettlement of mind on the question of the Churches. I will insert portions of two of my letters: —

"May 4, 1843. . . . . At present I fear, as far as I can analyze my own convictions, I consider the Roman Catholic Communion to be the Church of the Apostles, and that what grace is among us (which, through God's mercy, is not little) is extraordinary, and from the over-flowings of His dispensation. I am very far more sure that England is in schism, than that the Roman additions to the Primitive Creed may not be developments, arising out of a keen and vivid realizing of the Divine Depositum of Faith.

"You will now understand what gives edge to the Bishops' Charges, without any undue sensitiveness on my part. They distress me in two ways: — first, as being in some sense protests and witnesses to my conscience against my own unfaithfulness to the English Church, and next, as being samples of her teaching, and tokens how very far she is from even aspiring to Catholicity.

"Of course my being unfaithful to a trust is my great subject of dread, — as it has long been, as you know."

When he wrote to make natural objections to my purpose, such as the apprehension that the removal of clerical obligations might have the indirect effect of propelling me towards Rome, I answered: —

"May 18, 1843. . . . My office or charge at St. Mary's is not a mere *state*, but a continual *energy*. People assume and assert certain things of me in consequence. With what sort of sincerity can I obey the Bishop? how am I to act in the frequent cases, in which one way or another the Church of Rome comes into consideration? I have to the utmost of my power tried to keep persons from Rome, and with some success; but even a year and a half since, my arguments, though more efficacious with the persons I aimed at than any others could be, were of a nature to infuse great suspicion of me into the minds of lookers-on.

"By retaining St. Mary's, I am an offence and a stumbling-block. Persons are keen-sighted enough to make out what I think on certain points, and then they infer that such opinions are compatible with holding situations of trust in our Church. A number of younger men take the validity of their interpretation of the Articles, &c. from me on *faith*. Is not my present position a cruelty, as well as a treachery towards the Church?

"I do not see how I can either preach or publish again, while I hold St. Mary's;—but consider again the following difficulty in such a resolution, which I must state at some length.

"Last Long Vacation the idea suggested itself to me of publishing the Lives of the English Saints; and I had a conversation with [a publisher] upon it. I thought it would be useful, as employing the minds of men who were in danger of running wild, bringing them from doctrine to history, and from speculation to fact;—again, as giving them an interest in the English soil, and the English Church, and keeping them from seeking sympathy in Rome, as she is; and further, as tending to promote the spread of right views.

"But, within the last month, it has come upon me, that, if the scheme goes on, it will be a practical carrying out of No. 90, from the character of the usages and opinions of ante-reformation times.

"It is easy to say, 'Why *will* you do *any* thing? why won't you keep quiet? what business had you to think of any such plan at all?' But I cannot leave a number of poor fellows in the lurch. I am bound to do my best for a great number of people both in Oxford and elsewhere. If *I* did not act, others would find means to do so.

"Well, the plan has been taken up with great eagerness and interest. Many men are setting to work. I set down the names of men, most of them engaged, the rest half engaged and probable, some actually writing." About thirty names follow, some of them at that time of the school of Dr. Arnold, others of Dr. Pusey's, some my personal friends and of my own standing, others whom I hardly knew, while of course the majority were of the party of the new Movement. I continue:—

"The plan has gone so far, that it would create surprise and talk, were it now suddenly given over. Yet how is it compatible with my holding St. Mary's, being what I am?"

Such was the object and the origin of the projected Series of the English Saints;[52] and, since the publication was connected, as has been seen, with my resignation of St. Mary's, I may be allowed to conclude what I have to say on the subject here, though it may read like a digression. As soon then as the first of the Series got into print, the whole project broke down. I had already anticipated that some portions of the Series would be written in a style inconsistent with the professions of a beneficed clergyman, and therefore I had given up my Living; but men of great weight went further in their misgivings than I, when they saw the Life of St. Stephen Harding, and decided that it was of a character inconsistent even with its proceeding from an Anglican publisher: and so the scheme was given up at once.[53] After the two first numbers, I retired from the Editorship, and those Lives only were published in addition, which were then already finished, or in advanced preparation. The following passages from what I or others wrote at the time will illustrate what I have been saying: —

In November, 1844, I wrote thus to the author of one of them: "I am not Editor, I have no direct control over the Series. It is T.'s work;[54] he may admit what he pleases; and exclude what he pleases. I was to have been Editor. I did edit the two first numbers. I was responsible for them, in the way in which an Editor is responsible. Had I continued Editor, I should have exercised a control over all. I laid down in the Preface that doctrinal subjects were, if possible, to

52. The brief lives published in the five-volume *Lives of the English Saints* (1844–1845) were written by Newman's friends. They generally supported the historical validity of medieval miracles, championed medieval monasticism, and included numerous comments on issues of monastic celibacy, chastity, and virginity that many contemporary readers regarded as immodest. Those same readers saw the lives as both Roman Catholic in sympathy and dangerous to family life. Their publication was another of the reasons high churchmen deserted the Tractarian cause. See Turner, *John Henry Newman*, pp. 479–496.

53. John Dobrée Dalgairns (1818–1876) was the author of *Life of St. Stephen Harding* and had been one of Newman's earliest recruits to the Littlemore community. After the two men quarreled in the mid-1850s, Dalgairns left Birmingham for the London Oratory.

54. James Toovey was the publisher who assumed editorial responsibility when Newman withdrew as editor. Newman continued to be interested in the project; however, he was deeply angered at the hostile response of high churchmen to the initial lives, telling one correspondent, "I assure you, to find that the English Church cannot bear the lives of her Saints . . . does not tend to increase my faith and confidence in her." (JHN to J. R. Hope, December 11, 1843, *L&D* 10: 55.)

be excluded. But, even then, I also set down that no writer was to be held answerable for any of the Lives but his own. When I gave up the Editorship, I had various engagements with friends for separate Lives remaining on my hands. I should have liked to have broken from them all, but there were some from which I could not break, and I let them take their course. Some have come to nothing; others like yours have gone on. I have seen such, either in MS. or Proof. As time goes on, I shall have less and less to do with the Series. I think the engagement between you and me should come to an end. I have any how abundant responsibility on me, and too much. I shall write to T. that if he wants the advantage of your assistance, he must write to you direct."

In accordance with this letter, I had already advertised in January 1844, ten months before it, that "other Lives," after St. Stephen Harding, would "be published by their respective authors on their own responsibility." This notice was repeated in February, in the advertisement to the second number entitled "The Family of St. Richard," though to this number, for some reason which I cannot now recollect, I also put my initials. In the Life of St. Augustine, the author, a man of nearly my own age, says in like manner, "No one but himself is responsible for the way in which these materials have been used." I have in MS. another advertisement to the same effect, but I cannot tell whether it ever appeared in print.

I will add, since the authors have been considered "hot-headed fanatic young men," whom I was in charge of, and whom I suffered to do intemperate things, that, while the writer of St. Augustine was in 1844 past forty, the author of the proposed Life of St. Boniface, Mr. Bowden, was forty-six; Mr. Johnson, who was to write St. Aldhelm, forty-three;[55] and most of the others were on one side or other of thirty. Three, I think, were under twenty-five. Moreover, of these writers some became Catholics, some remained Anglicans, and others have professed what are called free or liberal opinions.*

The immediate cause of the resignation of my Living is stated in the following letter, which I wrote to my Bishop: —

"August 29, 1843. It is with much concern that I inform your Lordship, that Mr. A. B., who has been for the last year an inmate of my house here, has just conformed to the Church of Rome.[56] As I have ever been desirous, not only of faithfully discharging the trust, which is involved in holding a living in your

---

*[Newman's Note] Vide Note D, *Series of Saints' Lives of 1843–4.*

---

55. Manuel Johnson (1805–1859) was an astronomer in charge of the Radcliffe observatory. A strong Tractarian supporter, he actually did not publish his proposed saint's life.
56. "A. B." is William Lockhardt.

Lordship's diocese, but of approving myself to your Lordship, I will for your information state one or two circumstances connected with this unfortunate event..... I received him on condition of his promising me, which he distinctly did, that he would remain quietly in our Church for three years. A year has passed since that time, and, though I saw nothing in him which promised that he would eventually be contented with his present position, yet for the time his mind became as settled as one could wish, and he frequently expressed his satisfaction at being under the promise which I had exacted of him."

I felt it impossible to remain any longer in the service of the Anglican Church, when such a breach of trust, however little I had to do with it, would be laid at my door. I wrote in a few days to a friend:

"September 7, 1843. I this day ask the Bishop leave to resign St. Mary's. Men whom you little think, or at least whom I little thought, are in almost a hopeless way. Really we may expect any thing. I am going to publish a Volume of Sermons, including those Four against moving."

I resigned my living on September the 18th. I had not the means of doing it legally at Oxford. The late Mr. Goldsmid was kind enough to aid me in resigning it in London.[57] I found no fault with the Liberals; they had beaten me in a fair field. As to the act of the Bishops, I thought, to borrow a Scriptural image from Walter Scott, that they had "seethed the kid in his mother's milk."[58]

I said to a friend: —

"Victrix causa diis placuit, sed victa Catoni."[59]

And now I may be almost said to have brought to an end, as far as is necessary for a sketch such as this is, the history both of my changes of religious opinion and of the public acts which they involved.

I had one final advance of mind to accomplish, and one final step to take. That further advance of mind was to be able honestly to say that I was *certain* of the conclusions at which I had already arrived. That further step, imperative when such certitude was attained, was my *submission* to the Catholic Church.

This submission did not take place till two full years after the resignation of my living in September 1843; nor could I have made it at an earlier day, without doubt and apprehension, that is, with any true conviction of mind or certitude.

In the interval, of which it remains to speak, viz. between the autumns of

---

57. Nathaniel Goldsmid (1807–1860) was a London lawyer sympathetic to the Tractarians.

58. Exodus 23:19.

59. "The victorious cause pleased the gods, but the vanquished one pleased Cato." Lucan, Pharsalia, I. 128.

1843 and 1845, I was in lay communion with the Church of England, attending its services as usual, and abstaining altogether from intercourse with Catholics, from their places of worship, and from those religious rites and usages, such as the Invocation of Saints, which are characteristics of their creed. I did all this on principle; for I never could understand how a man could be of two religions at once.

What I have to say about myself between these two autumns I shall almost confine to this one point,—the difficulty I was in, as to the best mode of revealing the state of my mind to my friends and others, and how I managed to reveal it.

Up to January, 1842, I had not disclosed my state of unsettlement to more than three persons, as has been mentioned above, and as is repeated in the course of the letters which I am now about to give to the reader. To two of them, intimate and familiar companions, in the Autumn of 1839: to the third, an old friend too, whom I have named above, when, I suppose, I was in great distress of mind upon the affair of the Jerusalem Bishopric. In May, 1843, I made it known, as has been seen, to the friend, by whose advice I wished, as far as possible, to be guided. To mention it on set purpose to any one, unless indeed I was asking advice, I should have felt to be a crime. If there is any thing that was abhorrent to me, it was the scattering doubts, and unsettling consciences without necessity. A strong presentiment that my existing opinions would ultimately give way, and that the grounds of them were unsound, was not a sufficient warrant for disclosing the state of my mind. I had no guarantee yet, that that presentiment would be realized. Supposing I were crossing ice, which came right in my way, which I had good reasons for considering sound, and which I saw numbers before me crossing in safety, and supposing a stranger from the bank, in a voice of authority, and in an earnest tone, warned me that it was dangerous, and then was silent, I think I should be startled, and should look about me anxiously, but I think too that I should go on, till I had better grounds for doubt; and such was my state, I believe, till the end of 1842. Then again, when my dissatisfaction became greater, it was hard at first to determine the point of time, when it was too strong to suppress with propriety. Certitude of course is a point, but doubt is a progress; I was not near certitude yet. Certitude is a reflex action; it is to know that one knows. Of that I believe I was not possessed, till close upon my reception into the Catholic Church. Again, a practical, effective doubt is a point too, but who can easily ascertain it for himself? Who can determine when it is, that the scales in the balance of opinion begin to turn, and what was a greater probability in behalf of a belief becomes a positive doubt against it?

In considering this question in its bearing upon my conduct in 1843, my own simple answer to my great difficulty had been, *Do what your present state of opinion requires in the light of duty, and let that doing tell: speak by acts*. This I had done; my first *act* of the year had been in February. After three months' deliberation I had published my retractation of the violent charges which I had made against Rome: I could not be wrong in doing so much as this; but I did no more at the time: I did not retract my Anglican teaching. My second *act* had been in September in the same year; after much sorrowful lingering and hesitation, I had resigned my Living. I tried indeed, before I did so, to keep Littlemore for myself, even though it was still to remain an integral part of St. Mary's. I had given to it a Church and a sort of Parsonage; I had made it a Parish, and I loved it; I thought in 1843 that perhaps I need not forfeit my existing relations towards it. I could indeed submit to become the curate at will of another, but I hoped an arrangement was possible, by which, while I had the curacy, I might have been my own master in serving it. I had hoped an exception might have been made in my favour, under the circumstances; but I did not gain my request. Perhaps I was asking what was impracticable, and it is well for me that it was so.

These had been my two acts of the year, and I said, "I cannot be wrong in making them; let that follow which must follow in the thoughts of the world about me, when they see what I do." And, as time went on, they fully answered my purpose. What I felt it a simple duty to do, did create a general suspicion about me, without such responsibility as would be involved in my initiating any direct act for the sake of creating it. Then, when friends wrote me on the subject, I either did not deny or I confessed my state of mind, according to the character and need of their letters. Sometimes in the case of intimate friends, whom I should otherwise have been leaving in ignorance of what others knew on every side of them, I invited the question.

And here comes in another point for explanation. While I was fighting in Oxford for the Anglican Church, then indeed I was very glad to make converts, and, though I never broke away from that rule of my mind, (as I may call it,) of which I have already spoken, of finding disciples rather than seeking them, yet, that I made advances to others in a special way, I have no doubt; this came to an end, however, as soon as I fell into misgivings as to the true ground to be taken in the controversy. For then, when I gave up my place in the Movement, I ceased from any such proceedings: and my utmost endeavour was to tranquilize such persons, especially those who belonged to the new school, as were unsettled in their religious views, and, as I judged, hasty in their conclusions. This went on till 1843; but, at that date, as soon as I turned my face Romeward, I gave up, as far as ever was possible, the thought of in any respect and in any shape acting upon others. Then I myself was simply my own concern. How could I in any sense direct others, who had to be guided in so momentous a matter myself? How could I be considered in a position, even to say a word to them one way or the other? How could I presume to unsettle them, as I was unsettled, when I had no means of bringing them out of such unsettlement? And, if they were unsettled already, how could I point to them a place of refuge, when I was not sure that I should choose it for myself? My only line, my only duty, was to keep simply to my own case. I recollected Pascal's words, "Je mourrai seul."[60] I deliberately put out of my thoughts all other works and claims, and said nothing to any one, unless I was obliged.

But this brought upon me a great trouble. In the newspapers there were continual reports about my intentions; I did not answer them; presently strangers or friends wrote, begging to be allowed to answer them; and, if I still kept to my resolution and said nothing, then I was thought to be mysterious, and a prejudice was excited against me. But, what was far worse, there were a number of tender, eager hearts, of whom I knew nothing at all, who were watching me, wishing to think as I thought, and to do as I did, if they could but find it out; who in consequence were distressed, that, in so solemn a matter, they could not see what was coming, and who heard reports about me this way or that, on a first day and on a second; and felt the weariness of waiting, and the sickness of delayed hope, and did not understand that I was as perplexed as they were, and, being of more sensitive complexion of mind than myself, were made ill by the suspense. And they too of course for the time thought me mysterious and inexplicable. I ask their pardon as far as I was really unkind to them. There was a gifted and deeply earnest lady, who in a parabolical account of that time, has described both my conduct as she felt it, and that of such as herself. In a singularly graphic, amusing vision of pilgrims, who were making their way across a bleak common in great discomfort, and who were ever warned against, yet continually nearing, "the king's highway" on the right, she says, "All my fears and disquiets were speedily renewed by seeing the most daring of our leaders, (the same who had first forced his way through the palisade, and in whose courage and sagacity we all put implicit trust,) suddenly stop short, and declare that he would go on no further. He did not, however, take the leap at once, but quietly sat down on the top of the fence with his feet hanging towards the road, as if he meant to take his time about it, and let himself down easily." I do not wonder at all that I thus seemed so unkind to a lady, who at that time had never seen me. We were both in trial in our different ways. I am far from denying that I was acting selfishly both in her

60. "I shall die alone."

case and in that of others; but it was a religious selfishness. Certainly to myself my own duty seemed clear. They that are whole can heal others; but in my case it was, "Physician, heal thyself." My own soul was my first concern, and it seemed an absurdity to my reason to be converted in partnership. I wished to go to my Lord by myself, and in my own way, or rather His way. I had neither wish, nor, I may say, thought of taking a number with me. Moreover, it is but the truth to say, that it had ever been an annoyance to me to seem to be the head of a party; and that even from fastidiousness of mind, I could not bear to find a thing done elsewhere, simply or mainly because I did it myself, and that, from distrust of myself, I shrank from the thought, whenever it was brought home to me, that I was influencing others. But nothing of this could be known to the world.

The following three letters are written to a friend, who had every claim upon me to be frank with him: — it will be seen that I disclose the real state of my mind in proportion as he presses me.[61]

1. "October 14, 1843. I would tell you in a few words why I have resigned St. Mary's, as you seem to wish, were it possible to do so. But it is most difficult to bring out in brief, or even *in extenso,* any just view of my feelings and reasons.

"The nearest approach I can give to a general account of them is to say, that it has been caused by the general repudiation of the view, contained in No. 90, on the part of the Church. I could not stand against such an unanimous expression of opinion from the Bishops, supported, as it has been, by the concurrence, or at least silence, of all classes in the Church, lay and clerical. If there ever was a case, in which an individual teacher has been put aside and virtually put away by a community, mine is one. No decency has been observed in the attacks upon me from authority; no protests have been offered

---

61. These three letters were written to Henry Edward Manning, who shared them with William Gladstone. Both men, who had deeply believed Newman's previous anti-Roman statements, were appalled by the content of the letters. With enormous insight into the indeterminacy of Newman's mind, Gladstone observed, "The Newman of 1843 is not the Newman of 1842, nor is he of 1842 the same with him of 1841: and how different, how far drifted down, are any of these from the Newman of the 'Romanism and Popular Protestantism.'" Gladstone further found Newman's remarks about his *Letter to the Right Reverend Father in God, Richard, Lord Bishop of Oxford,* written in early 1841 as part of the negotiation over *Tract 90,* "frightful" and "more like the expressions of some Faust gambling for his soul, than the records of the inner life of a great Christian teacher." (Gladstone to Manning, October 24 and 28, 1843, *Correspondence on Church and Religion of William Ewart Gladstone,* ed. D. C. Lathbury (New York: Macmillan, 1910), 1: 281, 284.)

against them. It is felt, — I am far from denying, justly felt, — that I am a foreign material, and cannot assimilate with the Church of England.

"Even my own Bishop has said that my mode of interpreting the Articles makes them mean *any thing* or *nothing*. When I heard this delivered, I did not believe my ears. I denied to others that it was said. . . . Out came the charge, and the words could not be mistaken. This astonished me the more, because I published that Letter to him, (how unwillingly you know,) on the understanding that *I* was to deliver his judgment on No. 90 *instead* of him. A year elapses, and a second and heavier judgment came forth. I did not bargain for this, — nor did he, but the tide was too strong for him.

"I fear that I must confess, that, in proportion as I think the English Church is showing herself intrinsically and radically alien from Catholic principles, so do I feel the difficulties of defending her claims to be a branch of the Catholic Church. It seems a dream to call a communion Catholic, when one can neither appeal to any clear statement of Catholic doctrine in its formularies, nor interpret ambiguous formularies by the received and living Catholic sense, whether past or present. Men of Catholic views are too truly but a party in our Church. I cannot deny that many other independent circumstances, which it is not worth while entering into, have led me to the same conclusion.

"I do not say all this to every body, as you may suppose; but I do not like to make a secret of it to you."

2. "Oct. 25, 1843. You have engaged in a dangerous correspondence; I am deeply sorry for the pain I shall give you.

"I must tell you then frankly, (but I combat arguments which to me, alas, are shadows,) that it is not from disappointment, irritation, or impatience, that I have, whether rightly or wrongly, resigned St. Mary's; but because I think the Church of Rome the Catholic Church, and ours not part of the Catholic Church, because not in communion with Rome; and because I feel that I could not honestly be a teacher in it any longer."

"This thought came to me last summer four years . . . I mentioned it to two friends in the autumn . . . It arose in the first instance from the Monophysite and Donatist controversies, the former of which I was engaged with in the course of theological study to which I had given myself. This was at a time when no Bishop, I believe, had declared against us,* and when all was progress and hope. I do not think I have ever felt disappointment or impatience, certainly not then; for I never looked forward to the future, nor do I realize it now.

"My first effort was to write that article on the Catholicity of the English Church; for two years it quieted me. Since the summer of 1839 I have written

---

*[Newman's Note] I think Sumner, Bishop of Chester, must have done so already.

little or nothing on modern controversy ... You know how unwillingly I wrote my letter to the Bishop in which I committed myself again, as the safest course under circumstances. The article I speak of quieted me till the end of 1841, over the affair of No. 90, when that wretched Jerusalem Bishopric (no personal matter) revived all my alarms. They have increased up to this moment. At that time I told my secret to another person in addition.

"You see then that the various ecclesiastical and quasi-ecclesiastical acts, which have taken place in the course of the last two years and a half, are not the *cause* of my state of opinion, but are keen stimulants and weighty confirmations of a conviction forced upon me, while engaged in the *course of duty,* viz. that theological reading to which I had given myself. And this last-mentioned circumstance is a fact, which has never, I think, come before me till now that I write to you.

"It is three years since, on account of my state of opinion, I urged the Provost in vain to let St. Mary's be separated from Littlemore; thinking I might with a safe conscience serve the latter, though I could not comfortably continue in so public a place as a University. This was before No. 90.

"Finally, I have acted under advice, and that, not of my own choosing, but what came to me in the way of duty, nor the advice of those only who agree with me, but of near friends who differ from me.

"I have nothing to reproach myself with, as far as I see, in the matter of impatience; i. e. practically or in conduct. And I trust that He, who has kept me in the slow course of change hitherto, will keep me still from hasty acts, or resolves with a doubtful conscience.

"This I am sure of, that such interposition as yours, kind as it is, only does what *you* would consider harm. It makes me realize my own views to myself; it makes me see their consistency; it assures me of my own deliberateness; it suggests to me the traces of a Providential Hand; it takes away the pain of disclosures; it relieves me of a heavy secret.

"You may make what use of my letters you think right."

3. My correspondent wrote to me once more, and I replied thus: "October 31, 1843. Your letter has made my heart ache more, and caused me more and deeper sighs than any I have had a long while, though I assure you there is much on all sides of me to cause sighing and heartache. On all sides: — I am quite haunted by the one dreadful whisper repeated from so many quarters, and causing the keenest distress to friends. You know but a part of my present trial, in knowing that I am unsettled myself.

"Since the beginning of this year I have been obliged to tell the state of my mind to some others; but never, I think, without being in a way obliged, as from friends writing to me as you did, or guessing how matters stood. No one in Oxford knows it or here" [Littlemore], "but one near friend whom I felt I could not help telling the other day. But, I suppose, many more suspect it."

On receiving these letters, my correspondent, if I recollect rightly, at once communicated the matter of them to Dr. Pusey, and this will enable me to describe, as nearly as I can, the way in which he first became aware of my changed state of opinion.[62]

I had from the first a great difficulty in making Dr. Pusey understand such differences of opinion as existed between himself and me. When there was a proposal about the end of 1838 for a subscription for a Cranmer Memorial, he wished us both to subscribe together to it. I could not, of course, and wished him to subscribe by himself.[63] That he would not do; he could not bear the thought of our appearing to the world in separate positions, in a matter of importance. And, as time went on, he would not take any hints, which I gave him, on the subject of my growing inclination to Rome. When I found him so determined, I often had not the heart to go on. And then I knew, that, from affection to me, he so often took up and threw himself into what I said, that I felt the great responsibility I should incur, if I put things before him just as I might view them myself. And, not knowing him so well as I did afterwards, I feared lest I should unsettle him. And moreover, I recollected well, how prostrated he had been with illness in 1832, and I used always to think that the start of the Movement had given him a fresh life. I fancied that his physical energies even depended on the presence of a vigorous hope and bright prospects for his imagination to feed upon; so much so, that when he was so unworthily treated by the authorities of the place in 1843, I recollect writing to

62. E. B. Pusey told Manning in regard to Newman's letters: "I have been gradually recovering since the very painful letters wh. you showed me, & I cannot but strongly hope that in all practical bearings they seemed to us to say more than they do. I have not said any thing of them to the writer; I shd expect only harm wd come of it; it is so sensitive a mind & so shrinks from speaking of itself, that for years I have found that I would be violating a sanctuary by wishing it to do so. Thus in a quick sharp way, as if it was almost avenging itself on itself for doing so. Then also that mind is so refined, that it may be that if we take its language in an ordinary way, we may be mistranslating it." (E. B. Pusey to H. Manning, November 17, 1843, Bodleian Library, MS Eng lett c. 654, f. 206.)

63. The "Cranmer Memorial" refers to a monument, the Martyrs' Memorial, honoring Thomas Cranmer, Hugh Latimer, and Nicholas Ridley, Protestant martyrs in the English Reformation. It was completed in 1843 but had been proposed some years earlier. The subscription fund to finance the monument was a vehicle devised in the aftermath of the publication of Froude's *Remains* to divide the Oxford and larger Anglican Church community into those who would associate themselves with the English Reformation and those who would not. The monument stands in Oxford at the intersection of St. Giles, Magdalen Street, and Beaumont Street.

the late Mr. Dodsworth to state my anxiety, lest, if his mind became dejected in consequence, his health should suffer seriously also.[64] These were difficulties in my way; and then again, another difficulty was, that, as we were not together under the same roof, we only saw each other at set times; others indeed, who were coming in or out of my rooms freely, and according to the need of the moment, knew all my thoughts easily; but for him to know them well, formal efforts were necessary. A common friend of ours broke it all to him in 1841, as far as matters had gone at that time, and showed him clearly the logical conclusions which must lie in propositions to which I had committed myself; but somehow or other in a little while, his mind fell back into its former happy state, and he could not bring himself to believe that he and I should not go on pleasantly together to the end.[65] But that affectionate dream needs must have been broken at last; and two years afterwards, that friend to whom I wrote the letters which I have just now inserted, set himself, as I have said, to break it. Upon that, I too begged Dr. Pusey to tell in private to any one he would, that I thought in the event I should leave the Church of England. However, he would not do so; and at the end of 1844 had almost relapsed into his former thoughts about me, if I may judge from a letter of his which I have found. Nay, at the Commemoration of 1845, a few months before I left the Anglican Church, I think he said about me to a friend, "I trust after all we shall keep him."

In that autumn of 1843, at the time I spoke to Dr. Pusey, I asked another friend also to communicate in confidence, to whom he would, the prospect which lay before me.[66]

---

64. In July 1843 Pusey was suspended from preaching in the university for two years by a body of six doctors who were Heads of Houses. The incident grew from a complaint lodged against Pusey for a sermon he had preached on the Eucharist that was regarded as Romanish. Newman saw the event as another university attack on Catholic truth. See Turner, *John Henry Newman*, pp. 455–459. William Dodsworth (1798–1861) was a London Anglican cleric who in 1851 converted to Roman Catholicism.

65. Although from the publication of *Tract 90* onward Pusey had gradually separated himself from Newman, he refused to concede that Newman's views might actually be very close to those of the radical men who now composed his coterie. It had been W. G. Ward who explained to Pusey how sympathetic Newman had become to Roman Catholicism. See note 26, p. 271.

66. In June 1844, Newman wrote Henry Wilberforce: "I want you, if you do not object, to do this: — to state *historically*, that you know that in 1839 I was very unsettled on the subject of the Catholicity of our Church. You may speak as strongly as your recollection enables you. But I should not like, first, any mention what my *present feelings are* — not, any hint that *I* have put you on doing this. . . . I don't care who knows it. The

To another friend, Mr. James Hope, now Mr. Hope Scott, I gave the opportunity of knowing it, if he would, in the following Postscript to a letter:[67] —

"While I write, I will add a word about myself. You may come near a person or two who, owing to circumstances, know more exactly my state of feeling than you do, though they would not tell you. Now I do not like that you should not be aware of this, though I see no *reason* why you should know what they happen to know. Your wishing it would *be* a reason."

I had a dear and old friend, near his death; I never told him my state of mind. Why should I unsettle that sweet calm tranquillity, when I had nothing to offer him instead? I could not say, 'Go to Rome;" else I should have shown him the way. Yet I offered myself for his examination. One day he led the way to my speaking out; but, rightly or wrongly, I could not respond. My reason was, "I have no certainty on the matter myself. To say 'I think' is to tease and to distress, not to persuade."

I wrote to him on Michaelmas Day, 1843: "As you may suppose, I have nothing to write to you about, pleasant. I *could* tell you some very painful things; but it is best not to anticipate trouble, which after all can but happen, and, for what one knows, may be averted. You are always so kind, that sometimes, when I part with you, I am nearly moved to tears, and it would be a relief to be so, at your kindness and at my hardness. I think no one ever had such kind friends as I have."

The next year, January 22, I wrote to him: "Pusey has quite enough on him, and generously takes on himself more than enough, for me to add burdens when I am not obliged; particularly too, when I am very conscious, that there *are* burdens, which I am or shall be obliged to lay upon him some time or other, whether I will or no."

And on February 21: "Half-past ten. I am just up, having a bad cold; the like has not happened to me (except twice in January) in my memory. You may think you have been in my thoughts, long before my rising. Of course you are so continually, as you well know. I could not come to see you; I am not worthy of friends. With my opinions, to the full of which I dare not confess, I feel like a guilty person with others, though I trust I am not so. People kindly think that I have much to bear externally, disappointment, slander, &c. No, I have nothing to bear, but the anxiety which I feel for my friends' anxiety for me, and their perplexity. This is a better Ash-Wednesday than birthday present;" [his

---

only fear is, that, being so long ago, people may think I have got over it." (JHN to Henry Wilberforce, June 8, 1844, *L&D* 10: 263.)

67. James R. Hope-Scott (1812–1873) was a London lawyer and friend of Newman from whom the latter often took advice. He converted to Roman Catholicism in 1851.

birthday was the same day as mine; it was Ash-Wednesday that year;] "but I cannot help writing about what is uppermost. And now, my dear A., all kindest and best wishes to you, my oldest friend, whom I must not speak more about, and with reference to myself, lest you should be angry." It was not in his nature to have doubts: he used to look at me with anxiety, and wonder what had come over me.

On Easter Monday: "All that is good and gracious descend upon you and yours from the influences of this Blessed Season; and it will be so, (so be it!) for what is the life of you all, as day passes after day, but a simple endeavour to serve Him, from whom all blessing comes? Though we are separated in place, yet this we have in common, that you are living a calm and cheerful time, and I am enjoying the thought of you. It is your blessing to have a clear heaven, and peace around, according to the blessing pronounced on Benjamin.* So it is, my dear A., and so may it ever be."

He was in simple good faith. He died in September of the same year. I had expected that his last illness would have brought light to my mind, as to what I ought to do. It brought none. I made a note, which runs thus: "I sobbed bitterly over his coffin, to think that he left me still dark as to what the way of truth was, and what I ought to do in order to please God and fulfil His will." I think I wrote to Charles Marriott to say, that at that moment, with the thought of my friend before me, my strong view in favour of Rome remained just what it was. On the other hand, my firm belief that grace was to be found within the Anglican Church remained too.** I wrote to another friend thus:—

"Sept. 16, 1844. I am full of wrong and miserable feelings, which it is useless to detail, so grudging and sullen, when I should be thankful. Of course, when one sees so blessed an end, and that, the termination of so blameless a life, of one who really fed on our ordinances and got strength from them, and see the same continued in a whole family, the little children finding quite a solace of their pain in the Daily Prayer, it is impossible not to feel more at ease in our Church, as at least a sort of Zoar, a place of refuge and temporary rest, because of the steepness of the way. Only, may we be kept from unlawful security, lest we have Moab and Ammon for our progeny, the enemies of Israel."

I could not continue in this state, either in the light of duty or of reason. My difficulty was this: I had been deceived greatly once; how could I be sure that I was not deceived a second time? I thought myself right then; how was I to be certain that I was right now? How many years had I thought myself sure of

---

*[Newman's Note] Deut. xxxiii. 12.

**[Newman's Note] On this subject, vide my Third Lecture on "Anglican Difficulties," also Note E, *The Anglican Church*.

what I now rejected? how could I ever again have confidence in myself? As in 1840 I listened to the rising doubt in favour of Rome, now I listened to the waning doubt in favour of the Anglican Church. To be certain is to know that one knows; what inward test had I, that I should not change again, after that I had become a Catholic? I had still apprehension of this, though I thought a time would come, when it would depart. However, some limit ought to be put to these vague misgivings; I must do my best and then leave it to a higher Power to prosper it. So, at the end of 1844, I came to the resolution of writing an Essay on Doctrinal Development; and then, if, at the end of it, my convictions in favour of the Roman Church were not weaker, of taking the necessary steps for admission into her fold.

By this time the state of my mind was generally known, and I made no great secret of it. I will illustrate it by letters of mine which have been put into my hands.

"November 16, 1844. I am going through what must be gone through; and my trust only is that every day of pain is so much taken from the necessary draught which must be exhausted. There is no fear (humanly speaking) of my moving for a long time yet. This has got out without my intending it; but it is all well. As far as I know myself, my one great distress is the perplexity, unsettlement, alarm, scepticism, which I am causing to so many; and the loss of kind feeling and good opinion on the part of so many, known and unknown, who have wished well to me. And of these two sources of pain it is the former that is the constant, urgent, unmitigated one. I had for days a literal ache all about my heart; and from time to time all the complaints of the Psalmist seemed to belong to me.

"And as far as I know myself, my one paramount reason for contemplating a change is my deep, unvarying conviction that our Church is in schism, and that my salvation depends on my joining the Church of Rome. I may use *argumenta ad hominem* to this person or that;* but I am not conscious of resentment, or disgust, at any thing that has happened to me. I have no visions whatever of hope, no schemes of action, in any other sphere more suited to me. I have no existing sympathies with Roman Catholics; I hardly ever, even abroad, was at one of their services; I know none of them, I do not like what I hear of them.

"And then, how much I am giving up in so many ways! and to me sacrifices irreparable, not only from my age, when people hate changing, but from my especial love of old associations and the pleasures of memory. Nor am I con-

---

*[Newman's Note] Vide supr. p. 306, &c. Letter of Oct. 14, 1843, compared with that of Oct. 25.

scious of any feeling, enthusiastic or heroic, of pleasure in the sacrifice; I have nothing to support me here.

"What keeps me yet is what has kept me long; a fear that I am under a delusion; but the conviction remains firm under all circumstances, in all frames of mind. And this most serious feeling is growing on me; viz. that the reasons for which I believe as much as our system teaches, *must* lead me to believe more, and that not to believe more is to fall back into scepticism.

"A thousand thanks for your most kind and consoling letter; though I have not yet spoken of it, it was a great gift."

Shortly after I wrote to the same friend thus: "My intention is, if nothing comes upon me, which I cannot foresee, to remain quietly *in statu quo* for a considerable time, trusting that my friends will kindly remember me and my trial in their prayers. And I should give up my fellowship some time before any thing further took place."

There was a lady, who was very anxious on the subject, and I wrote to her the following letters: —

1. "November 7, 1844. I am still where I was; I am not moving. Two things, however, seem plain, that every one is prepared for such an event, next, that every one expects it of me. Few, indeed, who do not think it suitable, fewer still, who do not think it likely. However, I do not think it either suitable or likely. I have very little reason to doubt about the issue of things, but the when and the how are known to Him, from whom, I trust, both the course of things and the issue come. The expression of opinion, and the latent and habitual feeling about me, which is on every side and among all parties, has great force. I insist upon it, because I have a great dread of going by my own feelings, lest they should mislead me. By one's sense of duty one must go; but external facts support one in doing so."

2. "January 8, 1845. What am I to say in answer to your letter? I know perfectly well, I ought to let you know more of my feelings and state of mind than you do know. But how is that possible in a few words? Any thing I say must be abrupt; nothing can I say which will not leave a bewildering feeling, as needing so much to explain it, and being isolated, and (as it were) unlocated, and not having any thing with it to show its bearings upon other parts of the subject.

"At present, my full belief is, in accordance with your letter, that, if there is a move in our Church, very few persons indeed will be partners to it. I doubt whether one or two at the most among residents at Oxford. And I don't know whether I can wish it. The state of the Roman Catholics is at present so unsatisfactory. This I am sure of, that nothing but a simple, direct call of duty is a warrant for any one leaving our Church; no preference of another Church, no delight in its services, no hope of greater religious advancement in it, no indignation, no disgust, at the persons and things, among which we may find ourselves in the Church of England. The simple question is, Can *I* (it is personal, not whether another, but can *I*) be saved in the English Church? am *I* in safety, were I to die to-night? Is it a mortal sin in *me*, not joining another communion?

"P.S. I hardly see my way to concur in attendance, though occasional, in the Roman Catholic chapel, unless a man has made up his mind pretty well to join it eventually. Invocations are not *required* in the Church of Rome; somehow, I do not like using them except under the sanction of the Church, and this makes me unwilling to admit them in members of our Church."

3. "March 30. Now I will tell you more than any one knows except two friends. My own convictions are as strong as I suppose they can become: only it is so difficult to know whether it is a call of *reason* or of conscience. I cannot make out, if I am impelled by what seems *clear*, or by a sense of *duty*. You can understand how painful this doubt is; so I have waited, hoping for light, and using the words of the Psalmist, 'Show some token upon me.' But I suppose I have no right to wait for ever for this. Then I am waiting, because friends are most considerately bearing me in mind, and asking guidance for me; and, I trust, I should attend to any new feelings which came upon me, should that be the effect of their kindness. And then this waiting subserves the purpose of preparing men's minds. I dread shocking, unsettling people. Any how, I can't avoid giving incalculable pain. So, if I had my will, I should like to wait till the summer of 1846, which would be a full seven years from the time that my convictions first began to fall on me. But I don't think I shall last so long.

"My present intention is to give up my Fellowship in October, and to publish some work or treatise between that and Christmas. I wish people to know *why* I am acting, as well as *what* I am doing; it takes off that vague and distressing surprise, 'What *can* have made him?'"

4. "June 1. What you tell me of yourself makes it plain that it is your duty to remain quietly and patiently, till you see more clearly where you are; else you are leaping in the dark."

In the early part of this year, if not before, there was an idea afloat that my retirement from the Anglican Church was owing to the feeling that I had so been thrust aside, without any one's taking my part. Various measures were, I believe, talked of in consequence of this surmise. Coincidently with it appeared an exceedingly kind article about me in a Quarterly, in its April number. The writer praised me in feeling and beautiful language far above my deserts. In the course of his remarks, he said, speaking of me as Vicar of St. Mary's: "He had the future race of clergy hearing him. Did he value and feel tender about, and cling to his position?.... Not at all.... No sacrifice to him perhaps, he did not care about such things."

There was a censure implied, however covertly, in these words; and it is alluded to in the following letter, addressed to a very intimate friend:—

"April 3, 1845.... Accept this apology, my dear Church, and forgive me. As I say so, tears come into my eyes;—that arises from the accident of this time, when I am giving up so much I love. Just now I have been overset by A.'s article in the Christian Remembrancer; yet really, my dear Church, I have never for an instant had even the temptation of repenting my leaving Oxford. The feeling of repentance has not even come into my mind. How could it? How could I remain at St. Mary's a hypocrite? how could I be answerable for souls, (and life so uncertain,) with the convictions, or at least persuasions, which I had upon me? It is indeed a responsibility to act as I am doing; and I feel His hand heavy on me without intermission, who is all Wisdom and Love, so that my heart and mind are tired out, just as the limbs might be from a load on one's back. That sort of dull aching pain is mine; but my responsibility really is nothing to what it would be, to be answerable for souls, for confiding loving souls, in the English Church, with my convictions. My love to Marriott, and save me the pain of sending him a line."

In July a Bishop thought it worth while to give out to the world that "the adherents of Mr. Newman are few in number. A short time will now probably suffice to prove this fact. It is well known that he is preparing for secession; and, when that event takes place, it will be seen how few will go with him."

I am now close upon the date of my reception into the Catholic Church; and have reserved for this place some sentences from a letter addressed to me at the beginning of the year by a very dear friend, now no more, Charles Marriott. I quote them for the love which I bear him, and the value that I set on his good word.

"January 15, 1845. You know me well enough to be aware, that I never see through any thing at first. Your letter to Badeley casts a gloom over the future, which you can understand, if you have understood me, as I believe you have. But I may speak out at once, of what I see and feel at once, and doubt not that I shall ever feel: that your whole conduct towards the Church of England and towards us, who have striven and are still striving to seek after God for ourselves, and to revive true religion among others, under her authority and guidance, has been generous and considerate, and, were that word appropriate, dutiful, to a degree that I could scarcely have conceived possible, more unsparing of self than I should have thought nature could sustain. I have felt with pain every link that you have severed, and I have asked no questions, because I felt that you ought to measure the disclosure of your thoughts according to the occasion, and the capacity of those to whom you spoke. I write in haste, in the midst of engagements engrossing in themselves, but partly made tasteless, partly embittered by what I have heard; but I am willing to trust even you, whom I love best on earth, in God's Hand, in the earnest prayer that you may be so employed as is best for the Holy Catholic Church."

I had begun my Essay on the Development of Doctrine in the first months of 1845, and I was hard at it all through the year till October. As I advanced, my view so cleared that instead of speaking any more of "the Roman Catholics," I boldly called them Catholics. Before I got to the end, I resolved to be received, and the book remains in the state in which it was then, unfinished.[68]

One of my friends at Littlemore had been received into the Church on Michaelmas Day, at the Passionist House at Aston, near Stone, by Father Dominic, the Superior.[69] At the beginning of October the latter was passing through London to Belgium; and, as I was in some perplexity what steps to take for being received myself, I assented to the proposition made to me that the good priest should take Littlemore in his way, with a view to his doing for me the same charitable service as he had done to my friend.

On October the 8th I wrote to a number of friends the following letter: —

"Littlemore, October 8th, 1845. I am this night expecting Father Dominic, the Passionist, who, from his youth, has been led to have distinct and direct thoughts, first of the countries of the North, then of England. After thirty years' (almost) waiting, he was without his own act sent here. But he has had little to do with conversions. I saw him here for a few minutes on St. John Baptist's day last year.

"He is a simple, holy man; and withal gifted with remarkable powers. He does not know of my intention; but I mean to ask of him admission into the One Fold of Christ...

"I have so many letters to write, that this must do for all who choose to ask about me. With my best love to dear Charles Marriott, who is over your head, &c., &c.

"P.S. This will not go till all is over. Of course it requires no answer."

For a while after my reception, I proposed to betake myself to some secular calling. I wrote thus in answer to a very gracious letter of congratulation sent me by Cardinal Acton: —

"Nov. 25, 1845. I hope you will have anticipated, before I express it, the

---

68. See the introduction to this volume on the immediate circumstances — about which Newman remains silent in the *Apologia* — surrounding Newman's reception into the Roman Catholic Church.

69. Father Domenic Barberi (1792–1849) was an Italian Passionist priest who had long hoped to be the person to receive Newman. He had received some of Newman's circle in the weeks earlier.

great gratification which I received from your Eminence's letter. That gratification, however, was tempered by the apprehension, that kind and anxious well-wishers at a distance attach more importance to my step than really belongs to it. To me indeed personally it is of course an inestimable gain; but persons and things look great at a distance, which are not so when seen close; and, did your Eminence know me, you would see that I was one, about whom there has been far more talk for good and bad than he deserves, and about whose movements far more expectation has been raised than the event will justify.

"As I never, I do trust, aimed at any thing else than obedience to my own sense of right, and have been magnified into the leader of a party without my wishing it or acting as such, so now, much as I may wish to the contrary, and earnestly as I may labour (as is my duty) to minister in a humble way to the Catholic Church, yet my powers will, I fear, disappoint the expectations of both my own friends, and of those who pray for the peace of Jerusalem.

"If I might ask of your Eminence a favour, it is that you would kindly moderate those anticipations. Would it were in my power to do, what I do not aspire to do! At present certainly I cannot look forward to the future, and, though it would be a good work if I could persuade others to do as I have done, yet it seems as if I had quite enough to do in thinking of myself."

Soon, Dr. Wiseman, in whose Vicariate Oxford lay, called me to Oscott; and I went there with others; afterwards he sent me to Rome, and finally placed me in Birmingham.

I wrote to a friend: —

"January 20, 1846. You may think how lonely I am. 'Obliviscere populum tuum et domum patris tui,'[70] has been in my ears for the last twelve hours. I realize more that we are leaving Littlemore, and it is like going on the open sea."

I left Oxford for good on Monday, February 23, 1846. On the Saturday and Sunday before, I was in my house at Littlemore simply by myself, as I had been for the first day or two when I had originally taken possession of it. I slept on Sunday night at my dear friend's, Mr. Johnson's, at the Observatory. Various friends came to see the last of me; Mr. Copeland, Mr. Church, Mr. Buckle, Mr. Pattison, and Mr. Lewis. Dr. Pusey too came up to take leave of me; and I called on Dr. Ogle, one of my very oldest friends, for he was my private Tutor, when I was an Undergraduate.[71] In him I took leave of my first College,

---

70. "Forget . . . thine own people and thy father's house," Psalms 44:11 (Vulg.), 45:10 (AV).

71. These friends were Manuel Johnson, the Oxford astronomer; W. J. Copeland (1804–1885), who served as Newman's curate at Littlemore and who many years later

Trinity, which was so dear to me, and which held on its foundation so many who had been kind to me both when I was a boy, and all through my Oxford life. Trinity had never been unkind to me. There used to be much snap-dragon growing on the walls opposite my freshman's rooms there, and I had for years taken it as the emblem of my own perpetual residence even unto death in my University.

On the morning of the 23rd I left the Observatory. I have never seen Oxford since, excepting its spires, as they are seen from the railway.[72]

---

would oversee the publication of Newman's sermons; Richard Church, Oriel fellow; George Buckle (1820–1900), a young acquaintance and later an Oriel fellow; Mark Pattison (1813–1884), who, like Church, had written one of the *Lives of the English Saints* and who would in 1860 become one of the contributors to *Essays and Reviews*; and David Lewis (1814–1895) of Jesus College, who would also become a Roman Catholic convert. Dr. James Adey Ogle (1792–1857) had served as Newman's undergraduate tutor at Trinity College.

72. Newman would return to Oxford on February 26, 1878, to be made an honorary fellow of Trinity College.

Chapter V.

Position of My Mind since 1845

From the time that I became a Catholic, of course I have no further history of my religious opinions to narrate.[1] In saying this, I do not mean to say that my mind has been idle, or that I have given up thinking on theological subjects; but that I have had no variations to record, and have had no anxiety of heart whatever. I have been in perfect peace and contentment; I never have had one doubt. I was not conscious to myself, on my conversion, of any change, intellectual or moral, wrought in my mind. I was not conscious of firmer faith in the fundamental truths of Revelation, or of more self-command; I had not more fervour; but it was like coming into port after a rough sea; and my happiness on that score remains to this day without interruption.

Nor had I any trouble about receiving those additional articles, which are not found in the Anglican Creed. Some of them I believed already, but not any one of them was a trial to me. I made a profession of them upon my reception

---

1. By saying he had no further history of his religious opinion to narrate since he had become a Roman Catholic, Newman sought to obviate the ultramontane suspicions of shifting and ever-developing theological opinions on his part arising from his *Rambler* article "On Consulting the Faithful," *Rambler* ns 1 (1859): 198–230. See the introduction to John Henry Newman, *On Consulting the Faithful in Matters of Doctrine*, ed. John Coulson (New York: Sheed and Ward, 1961).

with the greatest ease, and I have the same ease in believing them now. I am far of course from denying that every article of the Christian Creed, whether as held by Catholics or by Protestants, is beset with intellectual difficulties; and it is simple fact, that, for myself, I cannot answer those difficulties. Many persons are very sensitive of the difficulties of Religion; I am as sensitive of them as any one; but I have never been able to see a connexion between apprehending those difficulties, however keenly, and multiplying them to any extent, and on the other hand doubting the doctrines to which they are attached. Ten thousand difficulties do not make one doubt, as I understand the subject; difficulty and doubt are incommensurate. There of course may be difficulties in the evidence; but I am speaking of difficulties intrinsic to the doctrines themselves, or to their relations with each other. A man may be annoyed that he cannot work out a mathematical problem, of which the answer is or is not given to him, without doubting that it admits of an answer, or that a certain particular answer is the true one. Of all points of faith, the being of a God is, to my own apprehension, encompassed with most difficulty, and yet borne in upon our minds with most power.

People say that the doctrine of Transubstantiation is difficult to believe; I did not believe the doctrine till I was a Catholic. I had no difficulty in believing it, as soon as I believed that the Catholic Roman Church was the oracle of God, and that she had declared this doctrine to be part of the original revelation. It is difficult, impossible, to imagine, I grant; — but how is it difficult to believe? Yet Macaulay thought it so difficult to believe, that he had need of a believer in it of talents as eminent as Sir Thomas More, before he could bring himself to conceive that the Catholics of an enlightened age could resist "the overwhelming force of the argument against it."[2] "Sir Thomas More," he says, "is one of the choice specimens of wisdom and virtue; and the doctrine of transubstantiation is a kind of proof charge. A faith which stands that test, will stand any test." But for myself, I cannot indeed prove it, I cannot tell *how* it is; but I say, "Why should it not be? What's to hinder it? What do I know of substance or matter? just as much as the greatest philosophers, and that is nothing at all;" — so much is this the case, that there is a rising school of philosophy now, which considers phenomena to constitute the whole of our knowledge in physics. The Catholic doctrine leaves phenomena alone. It does not say that the phenomena go; on the contrary, it says that they remain; nor does it say that the

---

2. Thomas Babington Macaulay (1800–1859), the most famous Whig historian of the nineteenth century, had commented on Sir Thomas More in his essay on Leopold Von Ranke's *History of the Popes* published in the *Edinburgh Review* in 1840 and then reprinted in the many editions of Macaulay's essays.

same phenomena are in several places at once. It deals with what no one on earth knows any thing about, the material substances themselves. And, in like manner, of that majestic Article of the Anglican as well as of the Catholic Creed, — the doctrine of the Trinity in Unity. What do I know of the Essence of the Divine Being? I know that my abstract idea of three is simply incompatible with my idea of one; but when I come to the question of concrete fact, I have no means of proving that there is not a sense in which one and three can equally be predicated of the Incommunicable God.

But I am going to take upon myself the responsibility of more than the mere Creed of the Church; as the parties accusing me are determined I shall do. They say, that now, in that I am a Catholic, though I may not have offences of my own against honesty to answer for, yet, at least, I am answerable for the offences of others, of my co-religionists, of my brother priests, of the Church herself. I am quite willing to accept the responsibility; and, as I have been able, as I trust, by means of a few words, to dissipate, in the minds of all those who do not begin with disbelieving me, the suspicion with which so many Protestants start, in forming their judgment of Catholics, viz. that our Creed is actually set up in inevitable superstition and hypocrisy, as the original sin of Catholicism; so now I will proceed, as before, identifying myself with the Church and vindicating it, — not of course denying the enormous mass of sin and error which exists of necessity in that world-wide multiform Communion, — but going to the proof of this one point, that its system is in no sense dishonest, and that therefore the upholders and teachers of that system, as such, have a claim to be acquitted in their own persons of that odious imputation.

Starting then with the being of a God, (which, as I have said, is as certain to me as the certainty of my own existence, though when I try to put the grounds of that certainty into logical shape I find a difficulty in doing so in mood and figure to my satisfaction,) I look out of myself into the world of men, and there I see a sight which fills me with unspeakable distress. The world seems simply to give the lie to that great truth, of which my whole being is so full; and the effect upon me is, in consequence, as a matter of necessity, as confusing as if it denied that I am in existence myself. If I looked into a mirror, and did not see my face, I should have the sort of feeling which actually comes upon me, when I look into this living busy world, and see no reflexion of its Creator. This is, to me, one of those great difficulties of this absolute primary truth, to which I referred just now. Were it not for this voice, speaking so clearly in my conscience and my heart, I should be an atheist, or a pantheist, or a polytheist when I looked into the world. I am speaking for myself only; and I am far from denying the real force of the arguments in proof of a God, drawn from the general facts of human society and the course of history, but these do not warm me or enlighten me; they do not take away the winter of my desolation, or make the buds unfold and the leaves grow within me, and my moral being rejoice. The sight of the world is nothing else than the prophet's scroll, full of "lamentations, and mourning, and woe."[3]

To consider the world in its length and breadth, its various history, the many races of man, their starts, their fortunes, their mutual alienation, their conflicts; and then their ways, habits, governments, forms of worship; their enterprises, their aimless courses, their random achievements and acquirements, the impotent conclusion of long-standing facts, the tokens so faint and broken of a superintending design, the blind evolution of what turn out to be great powers or truths, the progress of things, as if from unreasoning elements, not towards final causes, the greatness and littleness of man, his far-reaching aims, his short duration, the curtain hung over his futurity, the disappointments of life, the defeat of good, the success of evil, physical pain, mental anguish, the prevalence and intensity of sin, the pervading idolatries, the corruptions, the dreary hopeless irreligion, that condition of the whole race, so fearfully yet exactly described in the Apostle's words, "having no hope and without God in the world,"[4] — all this is a vision to dizzy and appal; and inflicts upon the mind the sense of a profound mystery, which is absolutely beyond human solution.[5]

What shall be said to this heart-piercing, reason-bewildering fact? I can only answer, that either there is no Creator, or this living society of men is in a true sense discarded from His presence. Did I see a boy of good make and mind, with the tokens on him of a refined nature, cast upon the world without provision, unable to say whence he came, his birth-place or his family connexions, I should conclude that there was some mystery connected with his history, and that he was one, of whom, from one cause or other, his parents were ashamed. Thus only should I be able to account for the contrast between the promise and the condition of his being. And so I argue about the world; — *if* there be a God, *since* there is a God, the human race is implicated in some terrible aboriginal calamity. It is out of joint with the purposes of its Creator.

3. Ezekiel 2:9–10.
4. Ephesians 2:12.
5. In pointing to the futility of human solutions furnishing an explanation of the condition of the human race and the world in this and the immediately subsequent paragraphs, Newman directly distanced himself from the various nineteenth-century philosophies of history that sought to provide secular theodicies. In other publications he similarly rejected various versions of nineteenth-century natural theology that presented similar optimistic visions of nature.

This is a fact, a fact as true as the fact of its existence; and thus the doctrine of what is theologically called original sin becomes to me almost as certain as that the world exists, and as the existence of God.

And now, supposing it were the blessed and loving will of the Creator to interfere in this anarchical condition of things, what are we to suppose would be the methods which might be necessarily or naturally involved in His purpose of mercy? Since the world is in so abnormal a state, surely it would be no surprise to me, if the interposition were of necessity equally extraordinary — or what is called miraculous. But that subject does not directly come into the scope of my present remarks. Miracles as evidence, involve a process of reason, or an argument; and of course I am thinking of some mode of interference which does not immediately run into argument. I am rather asking what must be the face-to-face antagonist, by which to withstand and baffle the fierce energy of passion and the all-corroding, all-dissolving scepticism of the intellect in religious inquiries? I have no intention at all of denying, that truth is the real object of our reason, and that, if it does not attain to truth, either the premise or the process is in fault; but I am not speaking here of right reason, but of reason as it acts in fact and concretely in fallen man. I know that even the unaided reason, when correctly exercised, leads to a belief in God, in the immortality of the soul, and in a future retribution; but I am considering the faculty of reason actually and historically; and in this point of view, I do not think I am wrong in saying that its tendency is towards a simple unbelief in matters of religion. No truth, however sacred, can stand against it, in the long run; and hence it is that in the pagan world, when our Lord came, the last traces of the religious knowledge of former times were all but disappearing from those portions of the world in which the intellect had been active and had had a career.

And in these latter days, in like manner, outside the Catholic Church things are tending, — with far greater rapidity than in that old time from the circumstance of the age, — to atheism in one shape or other. What a scene, what a prospect, does the whole of Europe present at this day! and not only Europe, but every government and every civilization through the world, which is under the influence of the European mind! Especially, for it most concerns us, how sorrowful, in the view of religion, even taken in its most elementary, most attenuated form, is the spectacle presented to us by the educated intellect of England, France, and Germany! Lovers of their country and of their race, religious men, external to the Catholic Church, have attempted various expedients to arrest fierce wilful human nature in its onward course, and to bring it into subjection. The necessity of some form of religion for the interests of humanity, has been generally acknowledged: but where was the concrete representative of things invisible, which would have the force and the toughness necessary to be a breakwater against the deluge? Three centuries ago the establishment of religion, material, legal, and social, was generally adopted as the best expedient for the purpose, in those countries which separated from the Catholic Church; and for a long time it was successful; but now the crevices of those establishments are admitting the enemy. Thirty years ago, education was relied upon: ten years ago there was a hope that wars would cease for ever, under the influence of commercial enterprise and the reign of the useful and fine arts; but will any one venture to say that there is any thing any where on this earth, which will afford a fulcrum for us, whereby to keep the earth from moving onwards?

The judgment, which experience passes whether on establishments or on education, as a means of maintaining religious truth in this anarchical world, must be extended even to Scripture, though Scripture be divine. Experience proves surely that the Bible does not answer a purpose for which it was never intended. It may be accidentally the means of the conversion of individuals; but a book, after all, cannot make a stand against the wild living intellect of man, and in this day it begins to testify, as regards its own structure and contents, to the power of that universal solvent, which is so successfully acting upon religious establishments.[6]

Supposing then it to be the Will of the Creator to interfere in human affairs, and to make provisions for retaining in the world a knowledge of Himself, so definite and distinct as to be proof against the energy of human scepticism, in such a case, — I am far from saying that there was no other way, — but there is nothing to surprise the mind, if He should think fit to introduce a power into the world, invested with the prerogative of infallibility in religious matters.

---

6. Throughout his Anglican years as part of his challenge to evangelical religion, Newman had questioned the Bible as a source of doctrinal teaching. His two most important statements on the subject occurred in *Tract 85* (1838), titled "Lectures on the Scripture Proof of the Doctrines of the Church," and in *An Essay on the Development of Christian Doctrine* (London: J. Toovey, 1845). Newman believed that the Bible required a dogmatic authority to provide its interpretation. He also thought that placing the entire burden of Christian teaching upon the Bible alone opened the way for a shattering of the faith of individuals when advanced critical scholarship became applied to the text of scripture. See Jaak Seynaeve, *Cardinal Newman's Doctrine on Holy Scripture* (Louvain: Publications Universitaires de Louvain, 1953), for a discussion of the difficult subject of Newman and scripture as well as John Henry Newman, *On the Inspiration of Scripture*, ed. J. Derek Holmes and Robert Murray (London: G. Chapman, 1967), and Rowan A. Greer, *Anglican Approaches to Scripture: From the Reformation to the Present* (London: Herder and Herder, 2006).

Such a provision would be a direct, immediate, active, and prompt means of withstanding the difficulty; it would be an instrument suited to the need; and, when I find that this is the very claim of the Catholic Church, not only do I feel no difficulty in admitting the idea, but there is a fitness in it, which recommends it to my mind. And thus I am brought to speak of the Church's infallibility, as a provision, adapted by the mercy of the Creator, to preserve religion in the world, and to restrain that freedom of thought, which of course in itself is one of the greatest of our natural gifts, and to rescue it from its own suicidal excesses. And let it be observed that, neither here nor in what follows, shall I have occasion to speak directly of Revelation in its subject-matter, but in reference to the sanction which it gives to truths which may be known independently of it, — as it bears upon the defence of natural religion. I say, that a power, possessed of infallibility in religious teaching, is happily adapted to be a working instrument, in the course of human affairs, for smiting hard and throwing back the immense energy of the aggressive, capricious, untrustworthy intellect: — and in saying this, as in the other things that I have to say, it must still be recollected that I am all along bearing in mind my main purpose, which is a defence of myself.

I am defending myself here from a plausible charge brought against Catholics, as will be seen better as I proceed. The charge is this: — that I, as a Catholic, not only make profession to hold doctrines which I cannot possibly believe in my heart, but that I also believe in the existence of a power on earth, which at its own will imposes upon men any new set of *credenda*, when it pleases, by a claim to infallibility; in consequence, that my own thoughts are not my own property; that I cannot tell that to-morrow I may not have to give up what I hold to-day, and that the necessary effect of such a condition of mind must be a degrading bondage, or a bitter inward rebellion relieving itself in secret infidelity, or the necessity of ignoring the whole subject of religion in a sort of disgust, and of mechanically saying every thing that the Church says, and leaving to others the defence of it. As then I have above spoken of the relation of my mind towards the Catholic Creed, so now I shall speak of the attitude which it takes up in the view of the Church's infallibility.

And first, the initial doctrine of the infallible teacher must be an emphatic protest against the existing state of mankind. Man had rebelled against his Maker. It was this that caused the divine interposition: and to proclaim it must be the first act of the divinely-accredited messenger. The Church must denounce rebellion as of all possible evils the greatest. She must have no terms with it; if she would be true to her Master, she must ban and anathematize it. This is the meaning of a statement of mine, which has furnished matter for one of those special accusations to which I am at present replying: I have, however, no fault at all to confess in regard to it; I have nothing to withdraw, and in consequence I here deliberately repeat it. I said, "The Catholic Church holds it better for the sun and moon to drop from heaven, for the earth to fail, and for all the many millions on it to die of starvation in extremest agony, as far as temporal affliction goes, than that one soul, I will not say, should be lost, but should commit one single venial sin, should tell one wilful untruth, or should steal one poor farthing without excuse."[7] I think the principle here enunciated to be the mere preamble in the formal credentials of the Catholic Church, as an Act of Parliament might begin with a *"Whereas."* It is because of the intensity of the evil which has possession of mankind, that a suitable antagonist has been provided against it; and the initial act of that divinely-commissioned power is of course to deliver her challenge and to defy the enemy. Such a preamble then gives a meaning to her position in the world, and an interpretation to her whole course of teaching and action.

In like manner she has ever put forth, with most energetic distinctness, those other great elementary truths, which either are an explanation of her mission or give a character to her work. She does not teach that human nature is irreclaimable, else wherefore should she be sent? not, that it is to be shattered and reversed, but to be extricated, purified, and restored; not, that it is a mere mass of hopeless evil, but that it has the promise upon it of great things, and even now, in its present state of disorder and excess, has a virtue and a praise proper to itself. But in the next place she knows and she preaches that such a restoration, as she aims at effecting in it, must be brought about, not simply through certain outward provisions of preaching and teaching, even though they be her own, but from an inward spiritual power or grace imparted directly from above, and of which she is the channel. She has it in charge to rescue human nature from its misery, but not simply by restoring it on its own level, but by lifting it up to a higher level than its own. She recognizes in it real moral excellence though degraded, but she cannot set it free from earth except by exalting it towards heaven. It was for this end that a renovating grace was put into her hands; and therefore from the nature of the gift, as well as from the reasonableness of the case, she goes on, as a further point, to insist, that all true conversion must begin with the first springs of thought, and to teach that each individual man must be in his own person one whole and perfect temple of God, while he is also one of the living stones which build up a visible religious community. And thus the distinctions between nature and grace, and

---

7. Newman had made this argument in *Certain Difficulties Felt by Anglicans in Catholic Teaching Considered: In Twelve Lectures Addressed in 1850 to the Party of the Religious Movement of 1833* (London: Longmans, Green, 1918), 1: 240.

between outward and inward religion, become two further articles in what I have called the preamble of her divine commission.

Such truths as these she vigorously reiterates, and pertinaciously inflicts upon mankind; as to such she observes no half-measures, no economical reserve, no delicacy or prudence. "Ye must be born again," is the simple, direct form of words which she uses after her Divine Master:[8] "your whole nature must be re-born; your passions, and your affections, and your aims, and your conscience, and your will, must all be bathed in a new element, and reconsecrated to your Maker,—and, the last not the least, your intellect." It was for repeating these points of her teaching in my own way, that certain passages of one of my Volumes have been brought into the general accusation which has been made against my religious opinions. The writer has said that I was demented if I believed, and unprincipled if I did not believe, in my own statement, that a lazy, ragged, filthy, story-telling beggar-woman, if chaste, sober, cheerful, and religious, had a prospect of heaven, such as was absolutely closed to an accomplished statesman, or lawyer, or noble, be he ever so just, upright, generous, honourable, and conscientious, unless he had also some portion of the divine Christian graces;[9]—yet I should have thought myself defended from criticism by the words which our Lord used to the chief priests, "The publicans and harlots go into the kingdom of God before you."[10] And I was subjected again to the same alternative of imputations, for having ventured to say that consent to an unchaste wish was indefinitely more heinous than any lie viewed apart from its causes, its motives, and its consequences: though a lie, viewed under the limitation of these conditions, is a random utterance, an almost outward act, not directly from the heart, however disgraceful and despicable it may be, however prejudicial to the social contract, however deserving of public reprobation; whereas we have the express words of our Lord to the doctrine that "whoso looketh on a woman to lust after her, hath committed adultery with her already in his heart."[11] On the strength of these texts, I have surely as much right to believe in these doctrines which have caused so much surprise, as to believe in original sin, or that there is a supernatural revelation, or that a Divine Person suffered, or that punishment is eternal.

Passing now from what I have called the preamble of that grant of power,

8. John 3:7.

9. Newman had made this statement in *Certain Difficulties Felt by Anglicans*, 1: 249–250, and Kingsley had used it against him in *"What, Then, Does Dr. Newman Mean?"*

10. Matthew 21:31.

11. Matthew 5:2.

which is made to the Church, to that power itself, Infallibility, I premise two brief remarks: — 1. on the one hand, I am not here determining any thing about the essential seat of that power, because that is a question doctrinal, not historical and practical;[12] 2. nor, on the other hand, am I extending the direct subject-matter, over which that power of Infallibility has jurisdiction, beyond religious opinion: — and now as to the power itself.

This power, viewed in its fulness, is as tremendous as the giant evil which has called for it. It claims, when brought into exercise but in the legitimate manner, for otherwise of course it is but quiescent, to know for certain the very meaning of every portion of that Divine Message in detail, which was committed by our Lord to His Apostles. It claims to know its own limits, and to decide what it can determine absolutely and what it cannot. It claims, moreover, to have a hold upon statements not directly religious, so far as this, — to determine whether they indirectly relate to religion, and, according to its own definitive judgment, to pronounce whether or not, in a particular case, they are simply consistent with revealed truth. It claims to decide magisterially, whether as within its own province or not, that such and such statements are or are not prejudicial to the *Depositum* of faith, in their spirit or in their consequences, and to allow them, or condemn and forbid them, accordingly. It claims to impose silence at will on any matters, or controversies, of doctrine, which on its own *ipse dixit,* it pronounces to be dangerous, or inexpedient, or inopportune. It claims that, whatever may be the judgment of Catholics upon such acts, these acts should be received by them with those outward marks of reverence, submission, and loyalty, which Englishmen, for instance, pay to the presence of their sovereign, without expressing any criticism on them on the ground that in their matter they are inexpedient, or in their manner violent or harsh. And lastly, it claims to have the right of inflicting spiritual punishment, of cutting off from the ordinary channels of the divine life, and of simply excommunicating, those who refuse to submit themselves to its formal declarations. Such is the infallibility lodged in the Catholic Church, viewed in the concrete, as clothed and surrounded by the appendages of its high sovereignty: it is, to repeat what I said above, a supereminent prodigious power sent upon earth to encounter and master a giant evil.

12. The *Apologia* appeared six years before the First Vatican Council ruled on papal infallibility. In a letter to William Monsell, January 12, 1865, Newman stated that the infallibility of the pope was not an article of faith. (*L&D* 21: 386.) On Newman's complicated views of the papacy, see Paul Misner, *Papacy and Development: Newman and the Primacy of the Pope* (Leiden: Brill, 1976), and John R. Page, *What Will Dr. Newman Do?: John Henry Newman and Papal Infallibility, 1865–1875* (Collegeville, Minn.: Liturgical Press, 1994).

And now, having thus described it, I profess my own absolute submission to its claim. I believe the whole revealed dogma as taught by the Apostles, as committed by the Apostles to the Church, and as declared by the Church to me. I receive it, as it is infallibly interpreted by the authority to whom it is thus committed, and (implicitly) as it shall be, in like manner, further interpreted by that same authority till the end of time. I submit, moreover, to the universally received traditions of the Church, in which lies the matter of those new dogmatic definitions which are from time to time made, and which in all times are the clothing and the illustration of the Catholic dogma as already defined. And I submit myself to those other decisions of the Holy See, theological or not, through the organs which it has itself appointed, which, waiving the question of their infallibility, on the lowest ground come to me with a claim to be accepted and obeyed. Also, I consider that, gradually and in the course of ages, Catholic inquiry has taken certain definite shapes, and has thrown itself into the form of a science, with a method and a phraseology of its own, under the intellectual handling of great minds, such as St. Athanasius, St. Augustine, and St. Thomas; and I feel no temptation at all to break in pieces the great legacy of thought thus committed to us for these latter days.

All this being considered as the profession which I make *ex animo,* as for myself, so also on the part of the Catholic body, as far as I know it, it will at first sight be said that the restless intellect of our common humanity is utterly weighed down, to the repression of all independent effort and action whatever, so that, if this is to be the mode of bringing it into order, it is brought into order only to be destroyed. But this is far from the result, far from what I conceive to be the intention of that high Providence who has provided a great remedy for a great evil, — far from borne out by the history of the conflict between Infallibility and Reason in the past, and the prospect of it in the future. The energy of the human intellect "does from opposition grow;" it thrives and is joyous, with a tough elastic strength, under the terrible blows of the divinely-fashioned weapon, and is never so much itself as when it has lately been overthrown. It is the custom with Protestant writers to consider that, whereas there are two great principles in action in the history of religion, Authority and Private Judgment, they have all the Private Judgment to themselves, and we have the full inheritance and the superincumbent oppression of Authority. But this is not so; it is the vast Catholic body itself, and it only, which affords an arena for both combatants in that awful, never-dying duel. It is necessary for the very life of religion, viewed in its large operations and its history, that the warfare should be incessantly carried on. Every exercise of Infallibility is brought out into act by an intense and varied operation of the Reason, both as its ally and as its opponent, and provokes again, when it has done its work, a re-action of Reason against it; and, as in a civil polity the State exists and endures by means of the rivalry and collision, the encroachments and defeats of its constituent parts, so in like manner Catholic Christendom is no simple exhibition of religious absolutism, but presents a continuous picture of Authority and Private Judgment alternately advancing and retreating as the ebb and flow of the tide; — it is a vast assemblage of human beings with wilful intellects and wild passions, brought together into one by the beauty and the Majesty of a Superhuman Power, — into what may be called a large reformatory or training-school, not as if into a hospital or into a prison, not in order to be sent to bed, not to be buried alive, but (if I may change my metaphor) brought together as if into some moral factory, for the melting, refining, and moulding, by an incessant, noisy process, of the raw material of human nature, so excellent, so dangerous, so capable of divine purposes.

St. Paul says in one place that his Apostolical power is given him to edification, and not to destruction. There can be no better account of the Infallibility of the Church. It is a supply for a need, and it does not go beyond that need. Its object is, and its effect also, not to enfeeble the freedom or vigour of human thought in religious speculation, but to resist and control its extravagance. What have been its great works? All of them in the distinct province of theology: — to put down Arianism, Eutychianism, Pelagianism, Manichæism, Lutheranism, Jansenism.[13] Such is the broad result of its action in the past; — and now as to the securities which are given us that so it ever will act in time to come.

First, Infallibility cannot act outside of a definite circle of thought, and it must in all its decisions, or *definitions,* as they are called, profess to be keeping within it. The great truths of the moral law, of natural religion, and of Apostolical faith, are both its boundary and its foundation. It must not go beyond them, and it must ever appeal to them. Both its subject-matter, and its articles in that subject-matter, are fixed. And it must ever profess to be guided by Scripture and by tradition. It must refer to the particular Apostolic truth which it is enforcing, or (what is called) *defining.* Nothing, then, can be presented to me, in time to come, as part of the faith, but what I ought already to have received, and hitherto have been kept from receiving, (if so,) merely because it has not been brought home to me. Nothing can be imposed upon me different in kind from what I hold already, — much less contrary to it. The new truth

---

13. The first four of these were heresies in the ancient church. Lutheranism arose with the Protestant Reformation in Germany. Jansenism was a heresy arising in the seventeenth century from the Dutch Roman Catholic theologian Cornelius Jansen but became most prominent in France.

which is promulgated, if it is to be called new, must be at least homogeneous, cognate, implicit, viewed relatively to the old truth. It must be what I may even have guessed, or wished, to be included in the Apostolic revelation; and at least it will be of such a character, that my thoughts readily concur in it or coalesce with it, as soon as I hear it. Perhaps I and others actually have always believed it, and the only question which is now decided in my behalf, is, that I have henceforth the satisfaction of having to believe, that I have only been holding all along what the Apostles held before me.

Let me take the doctrine which Protestants consider our greatest difficulty, that of the Immaculate Conception.[14] Here I entreat the reader to recollect my main drift, which is this. I have no difficulty in receiving the doctrine; and that, because it so intimately harmonizes with that circle of recognized dogmatic truths, into which it has been recently received; — but if *I* have no difficulty, why may not another have no difficulty also? why may not a hundred? a thousand? Now I am sure that Catholics in general have not any intellectual difficulty at all on the subject of the Immaculate Conception; and that there is no reason why they should. Priests have no difficulty. You tell me that they *ought* to have a difficulty; — but they have not. Be large-minded enough to believe, that men may reason and feel very differently from yourselves; how is it that men, when left to themselves, fall into such various forms of religion, except that there are various types of mind among them, very distinct from each other? From my testimony then about myself, if you believe it, judge of others also who are Catholics: we do not find the difficulties which you do in the doctrines which we hold; we have no intellectual difficulty in that doctrine in particular, which you call a novelty of this day. We priests need not be hypocrites, though we be called upon to believe in the Immaculate Conception. To that large class of minds, who believe in Christianity after our manner, — in the particular temper, spirit, and light, (whatever word is used,) in which Catholics believe it, — there is no burden at all in holding that the Blessed Virgin was conceived without original sin; indeed, it is a simple fact to say, that Catholics have not come to believe it because it is defined, but that it was defined because they believed it.

So far from the definition in 1854 being a tyrannical infliction on the Catholic world, it was received every where on its promulgation with the greatest enthusiasm. It was in consequence of the unanimous petition, presented from all parts of the Church to the Holy See, in behalf of an *ex cathedrâ* declaration

---

14. The doctrine of the immaculate conception, enunciated as official doctrine in 1854 by Pope Pius IX, holds that the Virgin Mary was conceived without the contamination of original sin.

that the doctrine was Apostolic, that it was declared so to be. I never heard of one Catholic having difficulties in receiving the doctrine, whose faith on other grounds was not already suspicious. Of course there were grave and good men, who were made anxious by the doubt whether it could be formally proved to be Apostolical either by Scripture or tradition, and who accordingly, though believing it themselves, did not see how it could be defined by authority and imposed upon all Catholics as a matter of faith; but this is another matter. The point in question is, whether the doctrine is a burden. I believe it to be none. So far from it being so, I sincerely think that St. Bernard and St. Thomas, who scrupled at it in their day, had they lived into this, would have rejoiced to accept it for its own sake.[15] Their difficulty, as I view it, consisted in matters of words, ideas, and arguments. They thought the doctrine inconsistent with other doctrines; and those who defended it in that age had not that precision in their view of it, which has been attained by means of the long disputes of the centuries which followed. And in this want of precision lay the difference of opinion, and the controversy.

Now the instance which I have been taking suggests another remark; the number of those (so called) new doctrines will not oppress us, if it takes eight centuries to promulgate even one of them. Such is about the length of time through which the preparation has been carried on for the definition of the Immaculate Conception. This of course is an extraordinary case; but it is difficult to say what is ordinary, considering how few are the formal occasions on which the voice of Infallibility has been solemnly lifted up. It is to the Pope in Ecumenical Council that we look, as to the normal seat of Infallibility: now there have been only eighteen such Councils since Christianity was, — an average of one to a century, — and of these Councils some passed no doctrinal decree at all, others were employed on only one, and many of them were concerned with only elementary points of the Creed. The Council of Trent embraced a large field of doctrine certainly; but I should apply to its Canons a remark contained in that University Sermon of mine, which has been so ignorantly criticized in the Pamphlet which has been the occasion of this Volume; — I there have said that the various verses of the Athanasian Creed are only repetitions in various shapes of one and the same idea; and in like manner, the Tridentine Decrees are not isolated from each other, but are occupied in bringing out in detail, by a number of separate declarations, as if into bodily form, a few necessary truths. I should make the same remark on the various theological censures, promulgated by Popes, which the Church has received,

---

15. Neither St. Bernard of Clairvaux (1090–1153) nor St. Thomas Aquinas had taught that the Virgin Mary was immaculately conceived.

and on their dogmatic decisions generally. I own that at first sight those decisions seem from their number to be a greater burden on the faith of individuals than are the Canons of Councils; still I do not believe that in matter of fact they are so at all, and I give this reason for it: — it is not that a Catholic, layman or priest, is indifferent to the subject, or, from a sort of recklessness, will accept any thing that is placed before him, or is willing, like a lawyer, to speak according to his brief, but that in such condemnations the Holy See is engaged, for the most part, in repudiating one or two great lines of error, such as Lutheranism or Jansenism, principally ethical not doctrinal, which are divergent from the Catholic mind, and that it is but expressing what any good Catholic, of fair abilities, though unlearned, would say himself, from common and sound sense, if the matter could be put before him.

Now I will go on in fairness to say what I think *is* the great trial to the Reason, when confronted with that august prerogative of the Catholic Church, of which I have been speaking. I enlarged just now upon the concrete shape and circumstances, under which pure infallible authority presents itself to the Catholic. That authority has the prerogative of an indirect jurisdiction on subject-matters which lie beyond its own proper limits, and it most reasonably has such a jurisdiction. It could not act in its own province, unless it had a right to act out of it. It could not properly defend religious truth, without claiming for that truth what may be called its *pomœria*;[16] or, to take another illustration, without acting as we act, as a nation, in claiming as our own, not only the land on which we live, but what are called British waters. The Catholic Church claims, not only to judge infallibly on religious questions, but to animadvert on opinions in secular matters which bear upon religion, on matters of philosophy, of science, of literature, of history, and it demands our submission to her claim. It claims to censure books, to silence authors, and to forbid discussions. In this province, taken as a whole, it does not so much speak doctrinally, as enforce measures of discipline. It must of course be obeyed without a word, and perhaps in process of time it will tacitly recede from its own injunctions. In such cases the question of faith does not come in at all; for what is matter of faith is true for all times, and never can be unsaid. Nor does it at all follow, because there is a gift of infallibility in the Catholic Church, that therefore the parties who are in possession of it are in all their proceedings infallible. "O, it is excellent," says the poet, "to have a giant's strength, but tyrannous, to use it like a giant."[17] I think history supplies us with instances in the Church, where legitimate power has been harshly used.

---

16. *Pomœria*, a limit or boundary.
17. Shakespeare, *Measure for Measure*, II, ii. 107–109.

To make such admission is no more than saying that the divine treasure, in the words of the Apostle, is "in earthen vessels;"[18] nor does it follow that the substance of the acts of the ruling power is not right and expedient, because its manner may have been faulty. Such high authorities act by means of instruments; we know how such instruments claim for themselves the name of their principals, who thus get the credit of faults which really are not theirs. But granting all this to an extent greater than can with any show of reason be imputed to the ruling power in the Church, what difficulty is there in the fact of this want of prudence or moderation more than can be urged, with far greater justice, against Protestant communities and institutions? What is there in it to make us hypocrites, if it has not that effect upon Protestants? We are called upon, not to profess any thing, but to submit and be silent, as Protestant Churchmen have before now obeyed the royal command to abstain from certain theological questions. Such injunctions as I have been contemplating are laid merely upon our actions, not upon our thoughts. How, for instance, does it tend to make a man a hypocrite, to be forbidden to publish a libel? his thoughts are as free as before: authoritative prohibitions may tease and irritate, but they have no bearing whatever upon the exercise of reason.

So much at first sight; but I will go on to say further, that, in spite of all that the most hostile critic may urge about the encroachments or severities of high ecclesiastics, in times past, in the use of their power, I think that the event has shown after all, that they were mainly in the right, and that those whom they were hard upon were mainly in the wrong. I love, for instance, the name of Origen: I will not listen to the notion that so great a soul was lost; but I am quite sure that, in the contest between his doctrine and followers and the ecclesiastical power, his opponents were right, and he was wrong. Yet who can speak with patience of his enemy and the enemy of St. John Chrysostom, that Theophilus, bishop of Alexandria?[19] who can admire or revere Pope Virgilius?[20] And here another consideration presents itself to my thoughts. In reading ecclesiastical history, when I was an Anglican, it used to be forcibly brought home to me, how the initial error of what afterwards became heresy was the urging forward some truth against the prohibition of authority at an

18. II Corinthians 4:7.
19. Theophilus (d. 412) was a late fourth- and early fifth-century patriarch of Alexandria known for his cruelty against his enemies, who included St. John Chrysostom (ca. 347–407), one of the greatest of the ancient doctors of the church as well as bishop of Constantinople.
20. Virgilius was pope from 537 to 555. He came to office through politically opportunistic leniency toward heretics and bribery and then turned on those whose support he had sought.

unseasonable time. There is a time for every thing, and many a man desires a reformation of an abuse, or the fuller development of a doctrine, or the adoption of a particular policy, but forgets to ask himself whether the right time for it is come; and, knowing that there is no one who will be doing any thing towards its accomplishment in his own lifetime unless he does it himself, he will not listen to the voice of authority, and he spoils a good work in his own century, in order that another man, as yet unborn, may not have the opportunity of bringing it happily to perfection in the next. He may seem to the world to be nothing else than a bold champion for the truth and a martyr to free opinion, when he is just one of those persons whom the competent authority ought to silence; and, though the case may not fall within that subject-matter in which that authority is infallible, or the formal conditions of the exercise of that gift may be wanting, it is clearly the duty of authority to act vigorously in the case. Yet its act will go down to posterity as an instance of a tyrannical interference with private judgment, and of the silencing of a reformer, and of a base love of corruption or error; and it will show still less to advantage, if the ruling power happens in its proceedings to evince any defect of prudence or consideration. And all those who take the part of that ruling authority will be considered as time-servers, or indifferent to the cause of uprightness and truth; while, on the other hand, the said authority may be accidentally supported by a violent ultra party, which exalts opinions into dogmas, and has it principally at heart to destroy every school of thought but its own.

Such a state of things may be provoking and discouraging at the time, in the case of two classes of persons; of moderate men who wish to make differences in religious opinion as little as they fairly can be made; and of such as keenly perceive, and are honestly eager to remedy, existing evils, — evils, of which doctrines in this or that foreign country know nothing at all, and which even at home, where they exist, it is not every one who has the means of estimating. This is a state of things both of past time and of the present. We live in a wonderful age; the enlargement of the circle of secular knowledge just now is simply a bewilderment, and the more so, because it has the promise of continuing, and that with greater rapidity, and more signal results. Now these discoveries, certain or probable, have in matter of fact an indirect bearing upon religious opinions, and the question arises how are the respective claims of revelation and of natural science to be adjusted. Few minds in earnest can remain at ease without some sort of rational grounds for their religious belief; to reconcile theory and fact is almost an instinct of the mind. When then a flood of facts, ascertained or suspected, comes pouring in upon us, with a multitude of others in prospect, all believers in Revelation, be they Catholic or not, are roused to consider their bearing upon themselves, both for the honour of God, and from tenderness for those many souls who, in consequence of the confident tone of the schools of secular knowledge, are in danger of being led away into a bottomless liberalism of thought.

I am not going to criticize here that vast body of men, in the mass, who at this time would profess to be liberals in religion; and who look towards the discoveries of the age, certain or in progress, as their informants, direct or indirect, as to what they shall think about the unseen and the future. The Liberalism which gives a colour to society now, is very different from that character of thought which bore the name thirty or forty years ago. Now it is scarcely a party; it is the educated lay world. When I was young, I knew the word first as giving name to a periodical, set up by Lord Byron and others.[21] Now, as then, I have no sympathy with the philosophy of Byron. Afterwards, Liberalism was the badge of a theological school, of a dry and repulsive character, not very dangerous in itself, though dangerous as opening the door to evils which it did not itself either anticipate or comprehend. At present it is nothing else than that deep, plausible scepticism, of which I spoke above, as being the development of human reason, as practically exercised by the natural man.

The Liberal religionists of this day are a very mixed body, and therefore I am not intending to speak against them. There may be, and doubtless is, in the hearts of some or many of them a real antipathy or anger against revealed truth, which it is distressing to think of. Again; in many men of science or literature there may be an animosity arising from almost a personal feeling; it being a matter of party, a point of honour, the excitement of a game, or a satisfaction to the soreness or annoyance occasioned by the acrimony or narrowness of apologists for religion, to prove that Christianity or that Scripture is untrustworthy. Many scientific and literary men, on the other hand, go on, I am confident, in a straightforward impartial way, in their own province and on their own line of thought, without any disturbance from religious difficulties in themselves, or any wish at all to give pain to others by the result of their investigations. It would ill become me, as if I were afraid of truth of any kind, to blame those who pursue secular facts, by means of the reason which God has given them, to their logical conclusions: or to be angry with science, because religion is bound in duty to take cognizance of its teaching. But putting these particular classes of men aside, as having no special call on the

---

21. Newman here refers to a short-lived journal called the *Liberal,* which appeared in 1822 and then ceased publication. It was associated with radical romantic writers such as Byron, Shelley, and Leigh Hunt.

sympathy of the Catholic, of course he does most deeply enter into the feelings of a fourth and large class of men, in the educated portions of society, of religious and sincere minds, who are simply perplexed,—frightened or rendered desperate, as the case may be,—by the utter confusion into which late discoveries or speculations have thrown their most elementary ideas of religion. Who does not feel for such men? who can have one unkind thought of them? I take up in their behalf St. Augustine's beautiful words, "Illi in vos sæviant," &c.[22] Let them be fierce with you who have no experience of the difficulty with which error is discriminated from truth, and the way of life is found amid the illusions of the world. How many a Catholic has in his thoughts followed such men, many of them so good, so true, so noble! how often has the wish risen in his heart that some one from among his own people should come forward as the champion of revealed truth against its opponents! Various persons, Catholic and Protestant, have asked me to do so myself; but I had several strong difficulties in the way. One of the greatest is this, that at the moment it is so difficult to say precisely what it is that is to be encountered and overthrown. I am far from denying that scientific knowledge is really growing, but it is by fits and starts; hypotheses rise and fall; it is difficult to anticipate which of them will keep their ground, and what the state of knowledge in relation to them will be from year to year. In this condition of things, it has seemed to me to be very undignified for a Catholic to commit himself to the work of chasing what might turn out to be phantoms, and, in behalf of some special objections, to be ingenious in devising a theory, which, before it was completed, might have to give place to some theory newer still, from the fact that those former objections had already come to nought under the uprising of others. It seemed to be specially a time, in which Christians had a call to be patient, in which they had no other way of helping those who were alarmed, than that of exhorting them to have a little faith and fortitude, and to "beware," as the poet says, "of dangerous steps."[23] This seemed so clear to me, the more I thought of the matter, as to make me surmise, that, if I attempted what had so little promise in it, I should find that the highest Catholic Authority was against the attempt, and that I should have spent my time and my thought, in doing what either it would be imprudent to bring before the public at all, or what, did I do so, would only complicate matters further which were already complicated, without my interference, more than enough. And I interpret recent acts of that authority as fulfilling my expectation; I interpret them as

22. "They rage against you."
23. From William Cowper (1731–1800), "The needless Alarm."

tying the hands of a controversialist, such as I should be, and teaching us that true wisdom, which Moses inculcated on his people, when the Egyptians were pursuing them, "Fear ye not, stand still; the Lord shall fight for you, and ye shall hold your peace."[24] And so far from finding a difficulty in obeying in this case, I have cause to be thankful and to rejoice to have so clear a direction in a matter of difficulty.

But if we would ascertain with correctness the real course of a principle, we must look at it at a certain distance, and as history represents it to us. Nothing carried on by human instruments, but has its irregularities, and affords ground for criticism, when minutely scrutinized in matters of detail. I have been speaking of that aspect of the action of an infallible authority, which is most open to invidious criticism from those who view it from without; I have tried to be fair, in estimating what can be said to its disadvantage, as witnessed at a particular time in the Catholic Church, and now I wish its adversaries to be equally fair in their judgment upon its historical character. Can, then, the infallible authority, with any show of reason, be said in fact to have destroyed the energy of the Catholic intellect? Let it be observed, I have not here to speak of any conflict which ecclesiastical authority has had with science, for this simple reason, that conflict there has been none; and that, because the secular sciences, as they now exist, are a novelty in the world, and there has been no time yet for a history of relations between theology and these new methods of knowledge, and indeed the Church may be said to have kept clear of them, as is proved by the constantly cited case of Galileo.[25] Here "exceptio probat regulam:"[26] for it is the one stock argument. Again, I have not to speak of any relations of the Church to the new sciences, because my simple question all along has been whether the assumption of infallibility by the proper authority is adapted to make me a hypocrite, and till that authority passes decrees on pure physical subjects and calls on me to subscribe them, (which it never will do, because it has not the power,) it has no tendency to interfere by any of its acts with my private judgment on those points. The simple question is, whether authority has so acted upon the reason of individuals, that they can have no opinion of

---

24. Exodus 14:13–14.

25. In 1632 the church condemned Galileo Galilei (1564–1642) for his Copernican writings. This became the single most famous case of the clash of the Roman Catholic Church with science and was inevitably cited by anti-Catholic writers. Recent scholarship has emphasized the complexity of the case. See David C. Lindberg, "Galileo, the Church, and the Cosmos," in *When Science and Christianity Meet,* ed. Ronald L. Numbers and David C. Lindberg (Chicago: Univ. of Chicago Press, 2003), pp. 33–60.

26. "The exception proves the rule."

their own, and have but an alternative of slavish superstition or secret rebellion of heart; and I think the whole history of theology puts an absolute negative upon such a supposition.

It is hardly necessary to argue out so plain a point. It is individuals, and not the Holy See, that have taken the initiative, and given the lead to the Catholic mind, in theological inquiry. Indeed, it is one of the reproaches urged against the Roman Church, that it has originated nothing, and has only served as a sort of *remora* or break in the development of doctrine. And it is an objection which I really embrace as a truth; for such I conceive to be the main purpose of its extraordinary gift. It is said, and truly, that the Church of Rome possessed no great mind in the whole period of persecution. Afterwards for a long while, it has not a single doctor to show; St. Leo, its first, is the teacher of one point of doctrine; St. Gregory, who stands at the very extremity of the first age of the Church, has no place in dogma or philosophy. The great luminary of the western world is, as we know, St. Augustine; he, no infallible teacher, has formed the intellect of Christian Europe; indeed to the African Church generally we must look for the best early exposition of Latin ideas. Moreover, of the African divines, the first in order of time, and not the least influential, is the strong-minded and heterodox Tertullian. Nor is the Eastern intellect, as such, without its share in the formation of the Latin teaching. The free thought of Origen is visible in the writings of the Western Doctors, Hilary and Ambrose; and the independent mind of Jerome has enriched his own vigorous commentaries on Scripture, from the stores of the scarcely orthodox Eusebius.[27] Heretical questionings have been transmuted by the living power of the Church into salutary truths. The case is the same as regards the Ecumenical Councils. Authority in its most imposing exhibition, grave bishops, laden with the traditions and rivalries of particular nations or places, have been guided in their decisions by the commanding genius of individuals, sometimes young and of inferior rank. Not that uninspired intellect overruled the super-human gift which was committed to the Council, which would be a self-contradictory assertion, but that in that process of inquiry and deliberation, which ended in an infallible enunciation, individual reason was paramount. Thus Malchion, a mere presbyter, was the instrument of the great Council of Antioch in the third century in meeting and refuting, for the assembled Fathers, the heretical Patriarch of that see. Parallel to this instance is the influence, so well known, of a young deacon, St. Athanasius, with the 318 Fathers at Nicæa. In mediæval times we read of St. Anselm at Bari, as the champion of the Council there held,

---

27. Tertullian, Hilary, Ambrose, Jerome, and Eusebius were major Christian writers of the fourth century.

against the Greeks. At Trent, the writings of St. Bonaventure, and, what is more to the point, the address of a Priest and theologian, Salmeron, had a critical effect on some of the definitions of dogma.[28] In some of these cases the influence might be partly moral, but in others it was that of a discursive knowledge of ecclesiastical writers, a scientific acquaintance with theology, and a force of thought in the treatment of doctrine.

There are of course intellectual habits which theology does not tend to form, as for instance the experimental, and again the philosophical; but that is because it *is* theology, not because of the gift of infallibility. But, as far as this goes, I think it could be shown that physical science on the other hand, or again mathematical, affords but an imperfect training for the intellect. I do not see then how any objection about the narrowness of theology comes into our question, which simply is, whether the belief in an infallible authority destroys the independence of the mind; and I consider that the whole history of the Church, and especially the history of the theological schools, gives a negative to the accusation. There never was a time when the intellect of the educated class was more active, or rather more restless, than in the middle ages. And then again all through Church history from the first, how slow is authority in interfering! Perhaps a local teacher, or a doctor in some local school, hazards a proposition, and a controversy ensues. It smoulders or burns in one place, no one interposing; Rome simply lets it alone. Then it comes before a Bishop; or some priest, or some professor in some other seat of learning takes it up; and then there is a second stage of it. Then it comes before a University, and it may be condemned by the theological faculty. So the controversy proceeds year after year, and Rome is still silent. An appeal perhaps is next made to a seat of authority inferior to Rome; and then at last after a long while it comes before the supreme power. Meanwhile, the question has been ventilated and turned over and over again, and viewed on every side of it, and authority is called upon to pronounce a decision, which has already been arrived at by reason. But even then, perhaps the supreme authority hesitates to do so, and nothing is determined on the point for years: or so generally and vaguely, that the whole controversy has to be gone through again, before it is ultimately determined. It is manifest how a mode of proceeding, such as this, tends not only to the

---

28. Malchion was a Christian priest in Antioch who during the third century opposed the authority of his local bishop. St. Anselm (1033–1109) was a major medieval Christian philosopher and theologian as well as archbishop of Canterbury. St. Bonaventure (1221–1274) was a medieval Franciscan philosopher and theologian. Alphonsus Salmeron (1515–1585) was a sixteenth-century Jesuit who advised the popes during the Council of Trent.

liberty, but to the courage, of the individual theologian or controversialist. Many a man has ideas, which he hopes are true, and useful for his day, but he is not confident about them, and wishes to have them discussed. He is willing, or rather would be thankful, to give them up, if they can be proved to be erroneous or dangerous, and by means of controversy he obtains his end. He is answered, and he yields; or on the contrary he finds that he is considered safe. He would not dare to do this, if he knew an authority, which was supreme and final, was watching every word he said, and made signs of assent or dissent to each sentence, as he uttered it. Then indeed he would be fighting, as the Persian soldiers, under the lash, and the freedom of his intellect might truly be said to be beaten out of him. But this has not been so: — I do not mean to say that, when controversies run high, in schools or even in small portions of the Church, an interposition may not advisably take place; and again, questions may be of that urgent nature, that an appeal must, as a matter of duty, be made at once to the highest authority in the Church; but if we look into the history of controversy, we shall find, I think, the general run of things to be such as I have represented it. Zosimus treated Pelagius and Cœlestius with extreme forbearance; St. Gregory VII. was equally indulgent with Berengarius: — by reason of the very power of the Popes they have commonly been slow and moderate in their use of it.[29]

And here again is a further shelter for the legitimate exercise of the reason: — the multitude of nations which are within the fold of the Church will be found to have acted for its protection, against any narrowness, on the supposition of narrowness, in the various authorities at Rome, with whom lies the practical decision of controverted questions. How have the Greek traditions been respected and provided for in the later Ecumenical Councils, in spite of the countries that held them being in a state of schism! There are important points of doctrine which have been (humanly speaking) exempted from the infallible sentence, by the tenderness with which its instruments, in framing it, have treated the opinions of particular places. Then, again, such national influences have a providential effect in moderating the bias which the local influences of Italy may exert upon the See of St. Peter. It stands to reason that,

29. Zosimus was pope from 417 to 418 and had to deal with Coelestius, a disciple of the heretic Pelagius. St. Gregory VII, who was pope from 1073 to 1085, had had to confront Berengarius (999–1088), the eleventh-century bishop of Tours, whose views on the Eucharist were adjudged heretical. In this passage Newman is attempting to persuade readers that popes used their very considerable power with restraint. In this respect he was trying to refute the views of the mid-Victorian English ultramontanes, who argued for a vast spectrum to papal authority. See Newman's letter to William Lockhardt, October 26, 1865, *L&D* 22: 84–85.

as the Gallican Church has in it a French element, so Rome must have in it an element of Italy; and it is no prejudice to the zeal and devotion with which we submit ourselves to the Holy See to admit this plainly. It seems to me, as I have been saying, that Catholicity is not only one of the notes of the Church, but, according to the divine purposes, one of its securities. I think it would be a very serious evil, which Divine Mercy avert! that the Church should be contracted in Europe within the range of particular nationalities. It is a great idea to introduce Latin civilization into America, and to improve the Catholics there by the energy of French devotedness; but I trust that all European races will ever have a place in the Church, and assuredly I think that the loss of the English, not to say the German element, in its composition has been a most serious misfortune. And certainly, if there is one consideration more than another which should make us English grateful to Pius the Ninth, it is that, by giving us a Church of our own, he has prepared the way for our own habits of mind, our own manner of reasoning, our own tastes, and our own virtues, finding a place and thereby a sanctification, in the Catholic Church.[30]

There is only one other subject, which I think it necessary to introduce here, as bearing upon the vague suspicions which are attached in this country to the Catholic Priesthood. It is one of which my accusers have before now said much,—the charge of reserve and economy. They found it in no slight degree on what I have said on the subject in my History of the Arians, and in a note upon one of my Sermons in which I refer to it. The principle of Reserve is also advocated by an admirable writer in two numbers of the Tracts for the Times, and of these I was the Editor.[31]

Now, as to the Economy itself,* it is founded upon the words of our Lord, "Cast not your pearls before swine;"[32] and it was observed by the early Christians more or less, in their intercourse with the heathen populations among whom they lived. In the midst of the abominable idolatries and impurities of that fearful time, the Rule of the Economy was an imperative duty. But that rule, at least as I have explained and recommended it, in anything that I have

---

*[Newman's Note] Vide Note F, *The Economy*.

30. Here Newman refers to the restoration of the Roman Catholic hierarchy in England by Cardinal Nicholas Wiseman acting under the authority of Pope Pius IX in 1850, an event that had stirred enormous religious and political controversy at the time.

31. The principle of reserve had been advocated by Isaac Williams in *Tracts 80 and 87*, titled *On Reserve in Communicating Religious Knowledge*. In these tracts Williams sharply criticized the open preaching of forgiveness through the atonement.

32. Matthew 7:6.

written, did not go beyond (1) the concealing the truth when we could do so without deceit, (2) stating it only partially, and (3) representing it under the nearest form possible to a learner or inquirer, when he could not possibly understand it exactly. I conceive that to draw Angels with wings is an instance of the third of these economical modes; and to avoid the question, "Do Christians believe in a Trinity?" by answering, "They believe in only one God," would be an instance of the second. As to the first, it is hardly an Economy, but comes under what is called the "Disciplina Arcani."[33] The second and third economical modes Clement calls *lying;* meaning that a partial truth is in some sense a lie, as is also a representative truth. And this, I think, is about the long and the short of the ground of the accusation which has been so violently urged against me, as being a patron of the Economy.[34]

Of late years I have come to think, as I believe most writers do, that Clement meant more than I have said. I used to think he used the word "lie" as an hyperbole, but I now believe that he, as other early Fathers, thought that, under certain circumstances, it was lawful to tell a lie. This doctrine I never maintained, though I used to think, as I do now, that the theory of the subject is surrounded with considerable difficulty; and it is not strange that I should say so, considering that great English writers declare without hesitation that in certain extreme cases, as to save life, honour, or even property, a lie is allowable. And thus I am brought to the direct question of truth, and of the truthfulness of Catholic priests generally in their dealings with the world, as bearing on the general question of their honesty, and of their internal belief in their religious professions.

It would answer no purpose, and it would be departing from the line of writing which I have been observing all along, if I entered into any formal discussion on this question; what I shall do here, as I have done in the foregoing pages, is to give my own testimony on the matter in question, and there to leave it. Now first I will say, that, when I became a Catholic, nothing struck me more at once than the English out-spoken manner of the Priests. It was the same at Oscott, at Old Hall Green, at Ushaw;[35] there was nothing of that smoothness, or mannerism, which is commonly imputed to them, and they

---

33. *Disciplina Arcani* refers to the practice among some sections of the early church of reserving the teaching of certain Christian doctrines to Christians alone rather than preaching them openly to the heathen world. Newman had been interested in this practice from the time of the publication of *The Arians of the Fourth Century* (1833). The term itself was not ancient but dated from the seventeenth century.

34. On the issue of truthfulness and lying, see the introduction to this volume.

35. Oscott, Old Green Hall, and Ushaw were Roman Catholic seminaries in England.

were more natural and unaffected than many an Anglican clergyman. The many years, which have passed since, have only confirmed my first impression. I have ever found it in the priests of this Diocese; did I wish to point out a straightforward Englishman, I should instance the Bishop, who has, to our great benefit, for so many years presided over it.[36]

And next, I was struck, when I had more opportunity of judging of the Priests, by the simple faith in the Catholic Creed and system, of which they always gave evidence, and which they never seemed to feel, in any sense at all, to be a burden. And now that I have been in the Church nineteen years, I cannot recollect hearing of a single instance in England of an infidel priest. Of course there are men from time to time, who leave the Catholic Church for another religion, but I am speaking of cases, when a man keeps a fair outside to the world and is a hollow hypocrite in his heart.

I wonder that the self-devotion of our priests does not strike a Protestant in this point of view. What do they gain by professing a Creed, in which, if their enemies are to be credited, they really do not believe? What is their reward for committing themselves to a life of self-restraint and toil, and perhaps to a premature and miserable death? The Irish fever cut off between Liverpool and Leeds thirty priests and more, young men in the flower of their days, old men who seemed entitled to some quiet time after their long toil. There was a bishop cut off in the North; but what had a man of his ecclesiastical rank to do with the drudgery and danger of sick calls, except that Christian faith and charity constrained him? Priests volunteered for the dangerous service. It was the same with them on the first coming of the cholera, that mysterious awe-inspiring infliction. If they did not heartily believe in the Creed of the Church, then I will say that the remark of the Apostle had its fullest illustration: — "If in this life only we have hope in Christ, we are of all men most miserable."[37] What could support a set of hypocrites in the presence of a deadly disorder, one of them following another in long order up the forlorn hope, and one after another perishing? And such, I may say, in its substance, is every Mission-Priest's life. He is ever ready to sacrifice himself for his people. Night and day, sick or well himself, in all weathers, off he is, on the news of a sick call. The fact of a parishioner dying without the Sacraments through his fault is terrible to him; why terrible, if he has not a deep absolute faith, which he acts upon with a free service? Protestants admire this, when they see it; but they do not seem to see as clearly, that it excludes the very notion of hypocrisy.

---

36. This bishop was William Bernard Ullathorne (1806–1889), who as the Roman Catholic bishop of Birmingham provided much support to Newman.
37. I Corinthians 15:19.

Sometimes, when they reflect upon it, it leads them to remark on the wonderful discipline of the Catholic priesthood; they say that no Church has so well ordered a clergy, and that in that respect it surpasses their own; they wish they could have such exact discipline among themselves. But is it an excellence which can be purchased? is it a phenomenon which depends on nothing else than itself, or is it an effect which has a cause? You cannot buy devotion at a price. "It hath never been heard of in the land of Chanaan, neither hath it been seen in Theman. The children of Agar, the merchants of Meran, none of these have known its way."[38] What then is that wonderful charm, which makes a thousand men act all in one way, and infuses a prompt obedience to rule, as if they were under some stern military compulsion? How difficult to find an answer, unless you will allow the obvious one, that they believe intensely what they profess!

I cannot think what it can be, in a day like this, which keeps up the prejudice of this Protestant country against us, unless it be the vague charges which are drawn from our books of Moral Theology; and with a short notice of the work in particular which by our accusers is especially thrown into our teeth, I shall bring these observations to a close.

St. Alfonso Liguori, then, it cannot be denied, lays down that an equivocation, (that is, a play upon words, in which one sense is taken by the speaker, and another sense intended by him for the hearer,) is allowable, if there is a just cause, that is, in an extraordinary case, and may even be confirmed by an oath. I shall give my opinion on this point as plainly as any Protestant can wish; and therefore I avow at once that in this department of morality, much as I admire the high points of the Italian character, I like the English rule of conduct better; but, in saying so, I am not, as will shortly be seen, saying any thing disrespectful to St. Alfonso, who was a lover of truth, and whose intercession I trust I shall not lose, though, on the matter under consideration, I follow other guidance in preference to his.

Now I make this remark first: — great English authors, Jeremy Taylor, Milton, Paley, Johnson, men of very different schools of thought, distinctly say, that under certain extraordinary circumstances it is allowable to tell a lie. Taylor says: "To tell a lie for charity, to save a man's life, the life of a friend, of a husband, of a prince, of a useful and a public person, hath not only been done at all times, but commended by great and wise and good men. Who would not save his father's life, at the charge of a harmless lie, from persecutors or tyrants?" Again, Milton says: "What man in his senses would deny, that there

---

38. Baruch 3:22–23 (Apocrypha).

are those whom we have the best grounds for considering that we ought to deceive, — as boys, madmen, the sick, the intoxicated, enemies, men in error, thieves? I would ask, by which of the commandments is a lie forbidden? You will say, by the ninth. If then my lie does not injure my neighbour, certainly it is not forbidden by this commandment." Paley says: "There are falsehoods, which are not lies, that is, which are not criminal." Johnson: "The general rule is, that truth should never be violated; there must, however, be some exceptions. If, for instance, a murderer should ask you which way a man is gone."[39]

Now, I am not using these instances as an *argumentum ad hominem;* but the purpose to which I put them is this: —

1. First, I have set down the distinct statements of Taylor, Milton, Paley, and Johnson: — now, would any one give ever so little weight to these statements, in forming a real estimate of the veracity of the writers, if they now were alive? Were a man, who is so fierce with St. Alfonso, to meet Paley or Johnson, tomorrow in society, would he look upon him as a liar, a knave, as dishonest and untrustworthy? I am sure he would not. Why then does he not deal out the same measure to Catholic priests? If a copy of Scavini, which speaks of equivocation as being in a just cause allowable, be found in a student's room at Oscott, not Scavini himself, but even the unhappy student, who has what a Protestant calls a bad book in his possession, is judged to be for life unworthy of credit.[40] Are all Protestant text-books, which are used at the University, immaculate? Is it necessary to take for gospel every word of Aristotle's Ethics, or every assertion of Hey or Burnet on the Articles?[41] Are text-books the ultimate authority, or rather are they not manuals in the hands of a lecturer, and the groundwork of his remarks? But, again, let us suppose, not the case of a student, or of a professor, but of Scavini himself, or of St. Alfono; now here again I ask, since you would not scruple in holding Paley for an honest man, in spite of his defence of lying, why do you scruple at holding St. Alfono honest? I

---

39. The quotations are taken from Jeremy Taylor, *The Rule of Conscience;* John Milton, *De Doctrina Christiana;* William Paley, *Moral and Political Philosophy;* and James Boswell, *Life of Johnson.* In choosing to quote these authors Newman was giving examples from writers of the strongest possible Protestant credentials. It is significant, however, that Newman does not quote from late eighteenth- and early nineteenth-century evangelical moralists, whose views on truth were much less compromising than that of these authors. On the subject of Victorian views of truthfulness and truth-telling, see the introduction to this volume.

40. Petro Scavini was a nineteenth-century Italian Roman Catholic interpreter of Liguori.

41. John Hey (1734–1815) and Gilbert Burnet (1643–1715) had written widely influential books interpreting the Thirty-Nine Articles.

am perfectly sure that you would not scruple at Paley personally; you might not agree with him, but you would not go further than to call him a bold thinker: then why should St. Alfonso's person be odious to you, as well as his doctrine?

Now I wish to tell you why you are not afraid of Paley; because, you would say, when he advocated lying, he was taking *extreme* or *special cases*. You would have no fear of a man who you knew had shot a burglar dead in his own house, because you know you are *not* a burglar: so you would not think that Paley had a habit of telling lies in society, because in the case of a cruel alternative he thought it the lesser evil to tell a lie. Then why do you show such suspicion of a Catholic theologian, who speaks of certain extraordinary cases in which an equivocation in a penitent cannot be visited by his confessor as if it were a sin? for this is the exact point of the question.

But again, why does Paley, why does Jeremy Taylor, when no practical matter is actually before him, lay down a maxim about the lawfulness of lying, which will startle most readers? The reason is plain. He is forming a theory of morals, and he must treat every question in turn as it comes. And this is just what St. Alfonso or Scavini is doing. You only try your hand yourself at a treatise on the rules of morality, and you will see how difficult the work is. What is the *definition* of a lie? Can you give a better than that it is a sin against justice, as Taylor and Paley consider it? but, if so, how can it be a sin at all, if your neighbour is not injured? If you do not like this definition, take another; and then, by means of that, perhaps you will be defending St. Alfonso's equivocation. However, this is what I insist upon; that St. Alfonso, as Paley, is considering the different portions of a large subject, and he must, on the subject of lying, give his judgment, though on that subject it is difficult to form any judgment which is satisfactory.

But further still: you must not suppose that a philosopher or moralist uses in his own case the licence which his theory itself would allow him. A man in his own person is guided by his own conscience; but in drawing out a system of rules he is obliged to go by logic, and follow the exact deduction of conclusion from conclusion, and must be sure that the whole system is coherent and one. You hear of even immoral or irreligious books being written by men of decent character; there is a late writer who says that David Hume's sceptical works are not at all the picture of the man. A priest might write a treatise which was really lax on the subject of lying, which might come under the condemnation of the Holy See, as some treatises on that score have already been condemned, and yet in his own person be a rigorist. And, in fact, it is notorious from St. Alfonso's Life, that he, who has the repute of being so lax a moralist, had one of the most scrupulous and anxious of consciences himself. Nay, further than this, he was originally in the Law, and on one occasion he was betrayed into the commission of what seemed like a deceit, though it was an accident; and that was the very occasion of his leaving the profession and embracing the religious life.

The account of this remarkable occurrence is told us in his Life: —

"Notwithstanding he had carefully examined over and over the details of the process, he was completely mistaken regarding the sense of one document, which constituted the right of the adverse party. The advocate of the Grand Duke perceived the mistake, but he allowed Alfonso to continue his eloquent address to the end without interruption; as soon, however, as he had finished, he rose, and said with cutting coolness, 'Sir, the case is not exactly what you suppose it to be; if you will review the process, and examine this paper attentively, you will find there precisely the contrary of all you have advanced.' 'Willingly,' replied Alfonso, without hesitating; 'the decision depends on this question — whether the fief were granted under the law of Lombardy, or under the French Law.' The paper being examined, it was found that the Grand Duke's advocate was in the right. 'Yes,' said Alfonso, holding the paper in his hand, 'I am wrong, I have been mistaken.' A discovery so unexpected, and the fear of being accused of unfair dealing filled him with consternation, and covered him with confusion, so much so, that every one saw his emotion. It was in vain that the President Caravita, who loved him, and knew his integrity, tried to console him, by telling him that such mistakes were not uncommon, even among the first men at the bar. Alfonso would listen to nothing, but, overwhelmed with confusion, his head sunk on his breast, he said to himself, 'World, I know you now; courts of law, never shall you see me again!' And turning his back on the assembly, he withdrew to his own house, incessantly repeating to himself, 'World, I know you now.' What annoyed him most was, that having studied and re-studied the process during a whole month, without having discovered this important flaw, he could not understand how it had escaped his observation."

And this is the man, so easily scared at the very shadow of trickery, who is so flippantly pronounced to be a patron of lying.

But, in truth, a Catholic theologian has objects in view which men in general little compass; he is not thinking of himself, but of a multitude of souls, sick souls, sinful souls, carried away by sin, full of evil, and he is trying with all his might to rescue them from their miserable state; and, in order to save them from more heinous sins, he tries, to the full extent that his conscience will allow him to go, to shut his eyes to such sins, as are, though sins, yet lighter in character or degree. He knows perfectly well that, if he is as strict as he would wish to be, he shall be able to do nothing at all with the run of men; so he is as indulgent with them as ever he can be. Let it not be for an instant supposed, that I allow of the maxim of doing evil that good may come; but, keeping clear of this, there is a way of winning men from greater sins by winking for the time at the less, or at mere improprieties or faults; and this is the key to the difficulty which Catholic books of moral theology so often cause to the Protestant. They are intended for the Confessor, and Protestants view them as intended for the Preacher.

2. And I observe upon Taylor, Milton, and Paley thus: What would a Protestant clergyman say to me, if I accused him of teaching that a lie was allowable; and if, when he asked for my proof, I said in reply that such was the doctrine of Taylor and Milton? Why, he would sharply retort, "*I am not bound by Taylor or Milton;*" and if I went on urging that "Taylor was one of his authorities," he would answer that Taylor was a great writer, but great writers were not therefore infallible. This is pretty much the answer which I make, when I am considered in this matter a disciple of St. Alfonso.

I plainly and positively state, and without any reserve, that I do not at all follow this holy and charitable man in this portion of his teaching. There are various schools of opinion allowed in the Church: and on this point I follow others. I follow Cardinal Gerdil, and Natalis Alexander, nay, St. Augustine.[42] I will quote one passage from Natalis Alexander: — "They certainly lie, who utter the words of an oath, without the will to swear or bind themselves: or who make use of mental reservations and *equivocations* in swearing, since they signify by words what they have not in mind, contrary to the end for which language was instituted, viz. as signs of ideas. Or they mean something else than the words signify in themselves and the common custom of speech." And, to take an instance: I do not believe any priest in England would dream of saying, "My friend is not here;" meaning, "He is not in my pocket or under my shoe." Nor should any consideration make me say so myself. I do not think St. Alfonso would in his own case have said so; and he would have been as much shocked at Taylor and Paley, as Protestants are at him.*

And now, if Protestants wish to know what our real teaching is, as on other subjects, so on that of lying, let them look, not at our books of casuistry, but at our catechisms. Works on pathology do not give the best insight into the form and the harmony of the human frame; and, as it is with the body, so is it with the mind. The Catechism of the Council of Trent was drawn up for the express

---

*[Newman's Note] Vide Note G, *Lying and Equivocation.*

42. Hyacinthe Gerdil (1718–1802) and Natalis Alexander (1639–1724) were important Roman Catholic apologists of their day.

purpose of providing preachers with subjects for their Sermons; and, as my whole work has been a defence of myself, I may here say that I rarely preach a Sermon, but I go to this beautiful and complete Catechism to get both my matter and my doctrine. There we find the following notices about the duty of Veracity: —

" 'Thou shalt not bear false witness,' &c.: let attention be drawn to two laws contained in this commandment: — the one, forbidding false witness; the other bidding, that removing all pretence and deceits, we should measure our words and deeds by simple truth, as the Apostle admonished the Ephesians of that duty in these words: 'Doing truth in charity, let us grow in Him through all things.'

"To deceive by a lie in joke or for the sake of compliment, though to no one there accrues loss or gain in consequence, nevertheless is altogether unworthy: for thus the Apostle admonishes, 'Putting aside lying, speak ye truth.' For therein is great danger of lapsing into frequent and more serious lying, and from lies in joke men gain the habit of lying, whence they gain the character of not being truthful. And thence again, in order to gain credence to their words, they find it necessary to make a practice of swearing.

"Nothing is more necessary [for us] than truth of testimony, in those things, which we neither know ourselves, nor can allowably be ignorant of, on which point there is extant that maxim of St. Augustine's; Whoso conceals the truth, and whoso puts forth a lie, each is guilty; the one because he is not willing to do a service, the other because he has a wish to do a mischief.

"It is lawful at times to be silent about the truth, but out of a court of law; for in court, when a witness is interrogated by the judge according to law, the truth is wholly to be brought out.

"Witnesses, however, must beware, lest, from over-confidence in their memory, they affirm for certain, what they have not verified.

"In order that the faithful may with more good will avoid the sin of lying, the Parish Priest shall set before them the extreme misery and turpitude of this wickedness. For, in holy writ, the devil is called the father of a lie; for, in that he did not remain in Truth, he is a liar, and the father of a lie. He will add, with the view of ridding men of so great a crime, the evils which follow upon lying; and, whereas they are innumerable, he will point out [at least] the sources and the general heads of these mischiefs and calamities, viz. 1. How great is God's displeasure and how great His hatred of a man who is insincere and a liar. 2. What little security there is that a man who is specially hated by God may not be visited by the heaviest punishments. 3. What more unclean and foul, as St. James says, than . . . . that a fountain by the same jet should send out sweet water and bitter? 4. For that tongue, which just now praised God, next, as far as in it lies, dishonours Him by lying. 5. In consequence, liars are shut out from the possession of heavenly beatitude. 6. That too is the worst evil of lying, that that disease of the mind is generally incurable.

"Moreover, there is this harm too, and one of vast extent, and touching men generally, that by insincerity and lying faith and truth are lost, which are the firmest bonds of human society, and, when they are lost, supreme confusion follows in life, so that men seem in nothing to differ from devils.

"Lastly, the Parish Priest will set those right who excuse their insincerity and allege the example of wise men, who, they say, are used to lie for an occasion. He will tell them, what is most true, that the wisdom of the flesh is death. He will exhort his hearers to trust in God, when they are in difficulties and straits, nor to have recourse to the expedient of a lie.

"They who throw the blame of their own lie on those who have already by a lie deceived them, are to be taught that men must not revenge themselves, nor make up for one evil by another.". . . .

There is much more in the Catechism to the same effect, and it is of universal obligation; whereas the decision of a particular author in morals need not be accepted by any one.

To one other authority I appeal on this subject, which commands from me attention of a special kind, for it is the teaching of a Father. It will serve to bring my work to a conclusion.

"St. Philip," says the Roman Oratorian who wrote his Life, "had a particular dislike of affectation both in himself and others, in speaking, in dressing, or in any thing else.

"He avoided all ceremony which savoured of worldly compliment, and always showed himself a great stickler for Christian simplicity in every thing; so that, when he had to deal with men of worldly prudence, he did not very readily accommodate himself to them.

"And he avoided, as much as possible, having any thing to do with *two-faced persons,* who did not go simply and straightforwardly to work in their transactions.

"*As for liars, he could not endure them,* and he was *continually reminding* his spiritual children, *to avoid them as they would a pestilence.*"

These are the principles on which I have acted before I was a Catholic; these are the principles which, I trust, will be my stay and guidance to the end.

I have closed this history of myself with St. Philip's name upon St. Philip's feast-day; and, having done so, to whom can I more suitably offer it, as a memorial of affection and gratitude, than to St. Philip's sons, my dearest brothers of this House, the Priests of the Birmingham Oratory, AMBROSE ST. JOHN, HENRY AUSTIN MILLS, HENRY BITTLESTON, EDWARD CASWALL, WILLIAM PAINE NEVILLE, and HENRY IGNATIUS DUDLEY RYDER?[43] who have been so faithful to me; who have been so sensitive of my needs; who have been so indulgent to my failings; who have carried me through so many trials; who have grudged no sacrifice, if I asked for it; who have been so cheerful under discouragements of my causing; who have done so many good works, and let me have the credit of them; — with whom I have lived so long, with whom I hope to die.

And to you especially, dear AMBROSE ST. JOHN;[44] whom God gave me, when He took every one else away; who are the link between my old life and my new; who have now for twenty-one years been so devoted to me, so patient, so zealous, so tender; who have let me lean so hard upon you; who have watched me so narrowly; who have never thought of yourself, if I was in question.

And in you I gather up and bear in memory those familiar affectionate companions and counsellors, who in Oxford were given to me, one after another, to be my daily solace and relief; and all those others, of great name and high example, who were my thorough friends, and showed me true attachment in times long past; and also those many younger men, whether I knew them or not, who have never been disloyal to me by word or deed; and of all these, thus various in their relations to me, those more especially who have since joined the Catholic Church.

And I earnestly pray for this whole company, with a hope against hope, that all of us, who once were so united, and so happy in our union, may even now be brought at length, by the Power of the Divine Will, into One Fold and under One Shepherd.

May 26, 1864.
In Festo Corp. Christ.

---

43. These are the Oratorians with whom Newman was then living at the Oratory of St. Philip Neri in Birmingham.

44. Newman is buried in a common grave with Ambrose St. John.

Editor's Preface to Newman's Notes

In the spring of 1865, when Newman republished *Apologia Pro Vita Sua* in its revised edition under the title *History of My Religious Opinions*, he added seven notes after the main text. These notes have received at best modest attention from Newman scholars, but they are of considerable importance in understanding Newman's immediate goals in the climate of the mid-1860s.

The first of these notes "Note A, Liberalism" was new to the revised edition, as was "Note D, Series of Saints' Lives" and a portion of "Note B, Ecclesiastical Miracles." The other notes and part of Note B derived from materials that had appeared in Newman's "Appendix: Answers in Detail to Mr. Kingsley's Accusations" in the 1864 pamphlet edition of the *Apologia* and related directly to accusations Kingsley had launched against Newman in "*What, Then, Does Dr. Newman Mean?*" *A Reply to a Pamphlet Lately Published by Dr. Newman.*

"Note A, Liberalism" has received extensive consideration in the introduction to this volume.

In "Note B, Ecclesiastical Miracles" Newman addressed an issue long debated between Roman Catholics and Protestants. Both believed that the miracles recorded in the Bible had occurred. Protestants, however, generally believed that the age of miracles had ended with the death of the last of Jesus' disciples. Roman Catholics believed that the age of miracles extended into the early centuries of the Christian Church and beyond. Protestants, such as Kingsley, regarded the latter outlook as evidence of Roman Catholic superstition. Kingsley had attempted to equate such belief in ecclesiastical miracles with personal and intellectual dishonesty, an accusation that persuaded few contemporary reviewers.

In 1842 Newman had published *An Essay on the Miracles Recorded in the Ecclesiastical History of the Early Ages* in which he defended the historical validity of miracles alleged to have occurred in Christian communities after the age of the apostles. In this essay he argued among other things that the same philosophical or historical criticism that denied postapostolic miracles could be turned against the miracles recorded in the Bible. He contended that postapostolic miracles served to demonstrate the divine mission of the Church Catholic, which in 1842 Newman did not yet identify solely with the Roman Catholic Church. Yet in this essay Newman also admitted that the postapostolic miracles were not of the same power as those of the apostolic age. He knew that Protestant authors regarded belief in ecclesiastical miracles as evidence of superstition, but he had declared, "Superstition is a corruption of Christianity, not merely of the Church; and if it discredits the Divine origin of the Church, it discredits the Divine origin of Christianity also."[1] Contemporaries in the 1840s, including other Tractarians and their supporters, had been less than receptive to both the substance and skeptical argumentative strategies of Newman's essay. Kingsley had attacked Newman for this discussion of miracles and for his subsequent presentation of miracles in the *Lives of the English Saints*, of which more shortly.

In Note B of the *Apologia* Newman returned to this issue, but now defending belief in ecclesiastical miracles as part of the Roman Catholic faith. In this note he presented miracles as associated with "holy men" (371) and also as answers to faithful prayer. He then explored the logic involved in belief in miracles and referenced his earlier 1826 essay on miracles. But Newman quickly moved forward to his Roman Catholic years to present his faith in particular miraculous occurrences, most important the medicinal oil associated with the corpse of Saint Walburga. Newman further defended the arguments in his 1842 discussion of miracles and the specific postapostolic miracles he had discussed there. He also pointed to a miracle that he thought Roman

---

1. John Henry Newman, *An Essay on the Miracles Recorded in the Ecclesiastical History of the Early Ages* (London: J. G. & F. Rivington, 1843), p. cxiii. The essay first appeared in 1842 as a supplement to *The Ecclesiastical History of M. L'Abbé Fleury, from the Second Ecumenical Council to the End of the Fourth Century* and was then separately reprinted in 1843.

Catholics should refrain from believing until properly proved. Beyond seeking to defend faith in postapostolic and contemporary miraculous events, Newman intended his note to defend the personal truthfulness of Roman Catholic priests who believed in and taught the validity of such miracles. Some contemporary secular reviewers saw no difference between faith in biblical and postapostolic miracles; others saw no tension between faith in miracles past and present and the practice of everyday personal honesty.

In "Note C, Sermon on Wisdom and Innocence" Newman revisited the document that Kingsley had seen as the key to his charge that Newman did not believe in truth for its own sake. Kingsley had also contended that the sermon was Roman Catholic in character. In the note Newman discussed the sermon, but did not reprint it, having been advised against that step by a lawyer friend. (The sermon appears in the editor's appendix of the present volume.) Newman argued that the sermon as printed in *Sermons on Subjects of the Day* (1843) was an essay rather than a sermon. He also explored what he understood as the meaning and context of his Tractarian-era sermons. This discussion makes reasonably clear how the Tractarian view of theology, ecclesiology, and Christian history differed from that of other groups in the Church of England.

In this note Newman also related with considerable openness the pressures and criticisms that swirled around him after the publication of *Tract 90* and made further interesting comments on the character of his preaching during those months. Newman's final sermon in the Church of England, "The Parting of Friends," preached in October 1843 and included in the editor's appendix to this volume, also demonstrates the anger and disappointment Newman felt by then toward disillusioned high churchmen such as William Gladstone and William Palmer who in the autumn of 1843 had publicly attacked the Tractarians as overly sympathetic to Roman Catholicism.

That anger had only been confirmed and energized by the subject of the next note. Newman's "Note D, Series of Saints' Lives of 1843–4" addressed what, except for Froude's *Remains*, *Tract 90* and Isaac Williams's tracts on *Reserve in Communicating Religious Knowledge*, had proved to be the most controversial of all publications associated with the Tractarians. When Newman resigned his pulpit at St. Mary's in September 1843, he was deeply worried that his followers might convert to Roman Catholicism and hence bring to an end his Anglo-Catholic experiment in the Church of England. He believed that he must find some kind of project to engage their time and energies. To achieve that goal, in cooperation with the publishing house of Rivington and then after their abandonment of the project with James Toovey, Newman proposed a series of lives of English saints. The purpose of the project was to create a body of historical literature exploring certain holy men and women of the pre-Reformation English Church.

When the manuscript of the first life, that of St. Stephen Harding by J. B. Dalgairns, was circulated among high churchmen in late 1843, the project provoked an immediate hostile response. The critical charges against the series involved first, the reading of the historical sources whereby miraculous medieval occurrences were reported with little critical commentary by the authors; second, the praise of monastic and conventual life on the part of both men and women that was regarded as being hostile to Victorian family conventions; and, third, the outright love of Rome as the center of Christianity that permeated many of the lives. Kingsley had pointed to the series in his charges against Newman as still another example of superstition and lack of critical attention to historical truth. Newman's note presents the scope of the entire proposed project.

In "Note E, The Anglican Church" Newman modified his earlier public statements regarding the Church of England and set distance between himself and Henry Edward Manning, his English Catholic ultramontane opponent. As discussed more fully in the introduction to the present volume, Newman between his conversion in 1845 and the early 1860s had made numerous statements critical of and hostile to the Church of England. In the wake of Kingsley's attack, however, numerous friends from his years in the English Church came to his aid and several old friendships blossomed again. Moreover, at this time Newman was hoping to establish a Roman Catholic college or house in Oxford. Consequently, in the appendix to the 1864 pamphlet edition of the *Apologia* and in Note E he made friendly statements about the English Church and its historic role in English Christianity.

In Note E Newman repeated much of his original commentary of 1864 on the English Church and more fully established his own position toward that institution, which differed substantially from that of Manning and other ultramontane Roman Catholics. Newman specifically restated, "Doubtless the National Church has hitherto been a serviceable breakwater against doctrinal errors, more fundamental than its own" (410). He also specified what he believed were benefits religious and other that he had received from the Church of England. Newman further directly stated that he entertained no intention of seeking to undermine the Church of England. Newman in this note hoped to lay the groundwork for at least a friendly relationship of respect, if also of profound difference, between the two communions. Throughout the note he clarified his differences from the English Church and the manner in which his onetime faith in it had dissolved after his conversion. But the rhetoric of this note, like that throughout much of the *Apologia* toward the Church of England as an institution, might have allowed for a cooperative atmosphere between himself and some Anglicans had he returned to Oxford, and in the course of events it very much did pave the way for friendlier relations between Roman Catholics and Anglicans by allowing the latter to see the former as less than diehard hostile foes to their church.

Newman was less successful in leading Roman Catholics to a friendlier outlook toward Anglicans. Both the tenor of Newman's remarks of 1864 and 1865 regarding the Church of England and his willingness to see the English Roman Catholic Church present in Oxford and at peace with the wider English culture offended his now long-standing ultramontane critics. In September 1864, about three months after the remarks in Newman's appendix had appeared, Manning delivered a sermon on *The Workings of the Holy Spirit in the Church of England* in which he declared, "If the Church of England be a barrier to infidelity by the truths which yet remain in it, I must submit that it is a source of unbelief by all the denials of other truths which it has rejected."[2] These comments, directed against Newman personally and against the *Apologia*, were intended to influence the thinking of the English bishops in regard to the proposed Roman Catholic establishment at Oxford and Newman's possible role therein. Newman's reassertion in the spring of 1865 of his view of the summer of 1864 regarding the English Church replied directly to Manning and the policies that the latter successfully imposed on English Roman Catholic bishops about their relationship to the Church of England and their refusal to permit English Roman Catholics to attend Oxford and Cambridge.

The issues of "Note F, The Economy" and "Note G, Lying and Equivocation" have been discussed in the introduction to this volume. It should be observed that Newman sought to demonstrate that both Protestant and secular English people in effect commonly practiced economy and equivocation in personal and public life and also believed that lying was justified under certain narrow circumstances without at the same time disparaging truth telling.

---

2. Henry Edward Manning, *The Workings of the Holy Spirit in the Church of England: A Letter to the Rev. E. B. Pusey, D.D.,* 2nd ed. (London: Longman, Green, Longman, Roberts, and Green, 1865), p. 31.

Note A. On Page 144.

Liberalism

I have been asked to explain more fully what it is I mean by "Liberalism," because merely to call it the Anti-dogmatic Principle is to tell very little about it.[1] An explanation is the more necessary, because such good Catholics and distinguished writers as Count Montalembert and Father Lacordaire use the word in a favorable sense, and claim to be Liberals themselves.[2] "The only singularity," says the former of the two in describing his friend, "was his

---

1. For a full exploration of this note and other of Newman's comments on liberalism, see the introduction to this volume.
2. Charles Forbes René, Comte de Montalembert (1810–1870) was a French Roman Catholic layman. Jean-Baptiste Lacordaire (1802–1861) was a French Dominican priest. Both urged that the Roman Catholic Church in France function independent of state or government support. This was regarded as a liberal stance in the French political and ecclesiastical context. In this paragraph Newman is seeking to distinguish this French Roman Catholic liberalism from the Protestant liberalism he perceives functioning over the years in English culture and through its influence on the state affecting the character and doctrine of the Church of England. In the weeks before composing the *Apologia* Newman had expressed private concern and sympathy for Montalembert as well as the German liberal Catholic J. J. I. von Döllinger. See JHN to William Monsell, January 20, 1864; JHN to T. W. Allies, February 12, 1864, *L&D* 21: 40–41, 47–49. The latter letter was marked *"Most Private."*

Liberalism. By a phenomenon, at that time unheard of, this convert, this seminarist, this confessor of nuns, was just as stubborn a liberal, as in the days when he was a student and a barrister." — Life (transl.), p. 19.

I do not believe that it is possible for me to differ in any important matter from two men whom I so highly admire. In their general line of thought and conduct I enthusiastically concur, and consider them to be before their age. And it would be strange indeed if I did not read with a special interest, in M. de Montalembert's beautiful volume, of the unselfish aims, the thwarted projects, the unrequited toils, the grand and tender resignation of Lacordaire. If I hesitate to adopt their language about Liberalism, I impute the necessity of such hesitation to some differences between us in the use of words or in the circumstances of country; and thus I reconcile myself to remaining faithful to my own conception of it, though I cannot have their voices to give force to mine. Speaking then in my own way, I proceed to explain what I meant as a Protestant by Liberalism, and to do so in connexion with the circumstances under which that system of opinion came before me at Oxford.

If I might presume to contrast Lacordaire and myself, I should say, that we had been both of us inconsistent; — he, a Catholic, in calling himself a Liberal; I, a Protestant, in being an Anti-liberal; and moreover, that the cause of this inconsistency had been in both cases one and the same. That is, we were both of us such good conservatives, as to take up with what we happened to find established in our respective countries, at the time when we came into active life. Toryism was the creed of Oxford; he inherited, and made the best of, the French Revolution.

When, in the beginning of the present century, not very long before my own time, after many years of moral and intellectual declension, the University of Oxford woke up to a sense of its duties, and began to reform itself, the first instruments of this change, to whose zeal and courage we all owe so much, were naturally thrown together for mutual support, against the numerous obstacles which lay in their path, and soon stood out in relief from the body of residents, who, though many of them men of talent themselves, cared little for the object which the others had at heart.[3] These Reformers, as they may be called, were for some years members of scarcely more than three or four Colleges; and their own Colleges, as being under their direct influence, of

---

3. On the reform of Oxford University in the early and mid-nineteenth century see W. R. Ward, *Victorian Oxford* (London: Cass, 1965), and Peter Nockles, "'Lost Causes and... impossible loyalties': The Oxford Movement and the University," in *The History of the University of Oxford,* ed. M. B. Brocke and M. C. Curthoys (Oxford: Clarendon Press, 1997), pp. 195–267.

course had the benefit of those stricter views of discipline and teaching, which they themselves were urging on the University. They had, in no long time, enough of real progress in their several spheres of exertion, and enough of reputation out of doors, to warrant them in considering themselves the *élite* of the place; and it is not wonderful if they were in consequence led to look down upon the majority of Colleges, which had not kept pace with the reform, or which had been hostile to it. And, when those rivalries of one man with another arose, whether personal or collegiate, which befall literary and scientific societies, such disturbances did but tend to raise in their eyes the value which they had already set upon academical distinction, and increase their zeal in pursuing it. Thus was formed an intellectual circle or class in the University, — men, who felt they had a career before them, as soon as the pupils, whom they were forming, came into public life; men, whom non-residents, whether country parsons or preachers of the Low Church, on coming up from time to time to the old place, would look at, partly with admiration, partly with suspicion, as being an honour indeed to Oxford, but withal exposed to the temptation of ambitious views, and to the spiritual evils signified in what is called the "pride of reason."

Nor was this imputation altogether unjust; for, as they were following out the proper idea of a University, of course they suffered more or less from the moral malady incident to such a pursuit. The very object of such great institutions lies in the cultivation of the mind and the spread of knowledge: if this object, as all human objects, has its dangers at all times, much more would these exist in the case of men, who were engaged in a work of reformation, and had the opportunity of measuring themselves, not only with those who were their equals in intellect, but with the many, who were below them. In this select circle or class of men, in various Colleges, the direct instruments and the choice fruit of real University Reform, we see the rudiments of the Liberal party.

Whenever men are able to act at all, there is the chance of extreme and intemperate action; and therefore, when there is exercise of mind, there is the chance of wayward or mistaken exercise. Liberty of thought is in itself a good; but it gives an opening to false liberty. Now by Liberalism I mean false liberty of thought, or the exercise of thought upon matters, in which, from the constitution of the human mind, thought cannot be brought to any successful issue, and therefore is out of place. Among such matters are first principles of whatever kind; and of these the most sacred and momentous are especially to be reckoned the truths of Revelation. Liberalism then is the mistake of subjecting to human judgment those revealed doctrines which are in their nature beyond and independent of it, and of claiming to determine on intrinsic grounds the truth and value of propositions which rest for their reception simply on the external authority of the Divine Word.

Now certainly the party of whom I have been speaking, taken as a whole, were of a character of mind out of which Liberalism might easily grow up, as in fact it did; certainly they breathed around an influence which made men of religious seriousness shrink into themselves. But, while I say as much as this, I have no intention whatever of implying that the talent of the University, in the years before and after 1820, was liberal in its theology, in the sense in which the bulk of the educated classes through the country are liberal now. I would not for the world be supposed to detract from the Christian earnestness, and the activity in religious works, above the average of men, of many of the persons in question. They would have protested against their being supposed to place reason before faith, or knowledge before devotion; yet I do consider that they unconsciously encouraged and successfully introduced into Oxford a licence of opinion which went far beyond them. In their day they did little more than take credit to themselves for enlightened views, largeness of mind, liberality of sentiment, without drawing the line between what was just and what was inadmissible in speculation, and without seeing the tendency of their own principles; and engrossing, as they did, the mental energy of the University, they met for a time with no effectual hindrance to the spread of their influence, except (what indeed at the moment was most effectual, but not of an intellectual character) the thorough-going Toryism and traditionary Church-of-England-ism of the great body of the Colleges and Convocation.[4]

Now and then a man of note appeared in the Pulpit or Lecture Rooms of the University, who was a worthy representative of the more religious and devout Anglicans. These belonged chiefly to the High-Church party; for the party called Evangelical never has been able to breathe freely in the atmosphere of Oxford, and at no time has been conspicuous, as a party, for talent or learning. But of the old High Churchmen several exerted some sort of Anti-liberal influence in the place, at least from time to time, and that influence of an intellectual nature. Among these especially may be mentioned Mr. John Miller, of Worcester College, who preached the Bampton Lecture in the year 1817. But, as far as I know, he who turned the tide, and brought the talent of the University round to the side of the old theology, and against what was familiarly called "march-of-mind," was Mr. Keble. In and from Keble the mental activity of Oxford took that contrary direction which issued in what was called Tractarianism.

4. On the role of Convocation in Tractarian-era controversies, see note 40 of the editor's introduction.

Keble was young in years, when he became a University celebrity, and younger in mind. He had the purity and simplicity of a child. He had few sympathies with the intellectual party, who sincerely welcomed him as a brilliant specimen of young Oxford. He instinctively shut up before literary display, and pomp and donnishness of manner, faults which always will beset academical notabilities. He did not respond to their advances. His collision with them (if it may be so called) was thus described by Hurrell Froude in his own way. "Poor Keble!" he used gravely to say, "he was asked to join the aristocracy of talent, but he soon found his level." He went into the country, but his instance serves to prove that men need not, in the event, lose that influence which is rightly theirs, because they happen to be thwarted in the use of the channels natural and proper to its exercise. He did not lose his place in the minds of men because he was out of their sight.

Keble was a man who guided himself and formed his judgments, not by processes of reason, by inquiry or by argument, but, to use the word in a broad sense, by authority. Conscience is an authority; the Bible is an authority; such is the Church; such is Antiquity; such are the words of the wise; such are hereditary lessons; such are ethical truths; such are historical memories, such are legal saws and state maxims; such are proverbs; such are sentiments, presages, and prepossessions. It seemed to me as if he ever felt happier, when he could speak or act under some such primary or external sanction; and could use argument mainly as a means of recommending or explaining what had claims on his reception prior to proof. He even felt a tenderness, I think, in spite of Bacon, for the Idols of the Tribe and the Den, of the Market and the Theatre. What he hated instinctively was heresy, insubordination, resistance to things established, claims of independence, disloyalty, innovation, a critical, censorious spirit. And such was the main principle of the school which in the course of years was formed around him; nor is it easy to set limits to its influence in its day; for multitudes of men, who did not profess its teaching, or accept its peculiar doctrines, were willing nevertheless, or found it to their purpose, to act in company with it.

Indeed for a time it was practically the champion and advocate of the political doctrines of the great clerical interest through the country, who found in Mr. Keble and his friends an intellectual, as well as moral support to their cause, which they looked for in vain elsewhere. His weak point, in their eyes, was his consistency; for he carried his love of authority and old times so far, as to be more than gentle towards the Catholic Religion, with which the Toryism of Oxford and of the Church of England had no sympathy. Accordingly, if my memory be correct, he never could get himself to throw his heart into the opposition made to Catholic Emancipation, strongly as he revolted from the politics and the instruments by means of which that Emancipation was won. I fancy he would have had no difficulty in accepting Dr. Johnson's saying about "the first Whig;" and it grieved and offended him that the "Via prima salutis" should be opened to the Catholic body from the Whig quarter. In spite of his reverence for the Old Religion, I conceive that on the whole he would rather have kept its professors beyond the pale of the Constitution with the Tories, than admit them on the principles of the Whigs. Moreover, if the Revolution of 1688 was too lax in principle for him and his friends, much less, as is very plain, could they endure to subscribe to the revolutionary doctrines of 1776 and 1789, which they felt to be absolutely and entirely out of keeping with theological truth.

The Old Tory or Conservative party in Oxford had in it no principle or power of development, and that from its very nature and constitution: it was otherwise with the Liberals. They represented a new idea, which was but gradually learning to recognize itself, to ascertain its characteristics and external relations, and to exert an influence upon the University. The party grew, all the time that I was in Oxford, even in numbers, certainly in breadth and definiteness of doctrine, and in power. And, what was a far higher consideration, by the accession of Dr. Arnold's pupils, it was invested with an elevation of character which claimed the respect even of its opponents.[5] On the other hand, in proportion as it became more earnest and less self-applauding, it became more free-spoken; and members of it might be found who, from the mere circumstance of remaining firm to their original professions, would in the judgment of the world, as to their public acts, seem to have left it for the Conservative camp. Thus, neither in its component parts nor in its policy, was it the same in 1832, 1836, and 1841, as it was in 1845.

These last remarks will serve to throw light upon a matter personal to myself, which I have introduced into my Narrative, and to which my attention has been pointedly called, now that my Volume is coming to a second edition.

It has been strongly urged upon me to re-consider the following passages which occur in it: "The men who had driven me from Oxford were distinctly the Liberals, it was they who had opened the attack upon Tract 90," p. 294, and "I found no fault with the Liberals; they had beaten me in a fair field," p. 302.[6]

---

5. In fact Thomas Arnold's students from Rugby held no influential positions in Oxford during the era about which Newman comments here.

6. For a sharp contestation of this assertion, see Peter Nockles, "Oxford, Tract 90 and the Bishops," in *John Henry Newman: Reason, Rhetoric and Romanticism,* ed. David Nicholls and Fergus Kerr (Carbondale and Edwardsville: Southern Illinois Univ. Press, 1991), p. 66.

I am very unwilling to seem ungracious, or to cause pain in any quarter; still I am sorry to say I cannot modify these statements. It is surely a matter of historical fact that I left Oxford upon the University proceedings of 1841; and in those proceedings, whether we look to the Heads of Houses or the resident Masters, the leaders, if intellect and influence make men such, were members of the Liberal party. Those who did not lead, concurred or acquiesced in them, — I may say, felt a satisfaction. I do not recollect any Liberal who was on my side on that occasion. Excepting the Liberal, no other party, as a party, acted against me. I am not complaining of them; I deserved nothing else at their hands. They could not undo in 1845, even had they wished it, (and there is no proof they did,) what they had done in 1841. In 1845, when I had already given up the contest for four years, and my part in it had passed into the hands of others, then some of those who were prominent against me in 1841, feeling (what they had not felt in 1841) the danger of driving a number of my followers to Rome, and joined by younger friends who had come into University importance since 1841 and felt kindly towards me, adopted a course more consistent with their principles, and proceeded to shield from the zeal of the Hebdomadal Board, not me, but, professedly, all parties through the country, — Tractarians, Evangelicals, Liberals in general, — who had to subscribe to the Anglican formularies, on the ground that those formularies, rigidly taken, were, on some point or other, a difficulty to all parties alike.

However, besides the historical fact, I can bear witness to my own feeling at the time, and my feeling was this: — that those who in 1841 had considered it to be a duty to act against me, had then done their worst. What was it to me what they were doing in the matter of the New Test proposed by the Hebdomadal Board?[7] I owed them no thanks for their trouble. I took no interest at all, in February, 1843, in the proceedings of the Heads of Houses and of the Convocation. I felt myself *dead* as regarded my relations to the Anglican Church. My leaving it was all but a matter of time. I believe I did not even thank my real friends, the two Proctors, who in Convocation stopped by their Veto the condemnation of Tract 90; nor did I make any acknowledgment to Mr. Rogers, nor to Mr. James Mozley, nor, as I think, to Mr. Hussey,[8] for their pamphlets in my behalf. My frame of mind is best described by the sentiment

---

7. The New Test was a proposal arising in late 1844 that would have permitted the vice chancellor of Oxford to require any member of the university to make a new subscription to the Thirty-Nine Articles. The idea was to use the test to root out people who would subscribe only within the arguments of *Tract 90*. The proposal was withdrawn before coming to a vote before Convocation because many parties in the university realized that such a test could be used against themselves as well as the Tractarians.

8. Robert Hussey (1801–1856), regius professor of ecclesiastical history at Oxford, like other non-Tractarians, wrote against the proposal for a New Test.

of the passage in Horace, which at the time I was fond of quoting, as expressing my view of the relation that existed between the Vice-Chancellor and myself.⁹

> "Pentheu,
> Rector Thebarum, quid me perferre patique
> Indignum cogas?" "Adimam bona." "Nempe pecus, rem,
> Lectos, argentum; tollas licet." "In manicis et
> Compedibus, sævo te sub custode tenebo." (*viz. the* 39 *Articles.*)
> "*Ipse Deus, simul atque volam, me solvet.*" Opinor,
> Hoc sentit: *Moriar. Mors ultima linea rerum est.*¹⁰

I conclude this notice of Liberalism in Oxford, and the party which was antagonistic to it, with some propositions in detail, which, as a member of the latter, and together with the High Church, I earnestly denounced and abjured.¹¹

1. No religious tenet is important, unless reason shows it to be so.

> Therefore, e. g. the doctrine of the Athanasian Creed is not to be insisted on, unless it tends to convert the soul; and the doctrine of the Atonement is to be insisted on, if it does convert the soul.

2. No one can believe what he does not understand.

> Therefore, e. g. there are no mysteries in true religion.

3. No theological doctrine is any thing more than an opinion which happens to be held by bodies of men.

> Therefore, e. g. no creed, as such, is necessary for salvation.

9. The vice chancellor at the time was Benjamin P. Symons (1785–1878), warden of Wadham College, a strong evangelical, and longtime opponent of the Tractarians.
10. Horace, Epistles I, no. xvi, 71–79; tr. John Conington:

> The wise and good, like Bacchus in the play,
> When Fortune threats, will have the nerve to say:
> "Great king of Thebes, what pains can you devise
> The man who will not serve you to chastise?"
> "I'll take your goods." "My flocks, my land, to wit,
> My plate, my couches: do, if you think fit."
> "I'll keep you chained and guarded in close thrall."
> "A god will come to free me when I call."
> Yes, he will die; 'tis that the bard intends;
> For when Death comes, the power of Fortune ends.

11. See the introduction to this volume for a consideration of the relationship of Newman's propositions and papal pronouncements of late 1865.

4. It is dishonest in a man to make an act of faith in what he has not had brought home to him by actual proof.

> Therefore, e. g. the mass of men ought not absolutely to believe in the divine authority of the Bible.

5. It is immoral in a man to believe more than he can spontaneously receive as being congenial to his moral and mental nature.

> Therefore, e. g. a given individual is not bound to believe in eternal punishment.

6. No revealed doctrines or precepts may reasonably stand in the way of scientific conclusions.

> Therefore, e. g. Political Economy may reverse our Lord's declarations about poverty and riches, or a system of Ethics may teach that the highest condition of body is ordinarily essential to the highest state of mind.

7. Christianity is necessarily modified by the growth of civilization, and the exigencies of times.

> Therefore, e. g. the Catholic priesthood, though necessary in the Middle Ages, may be superseded now.

8. There is a system of religion more simply true than Christianity as it has ever been received.

> Therefore, e. g. we may advance that Christianity is the "corn of wheat" which has been dead for 1800 years, but at length will bear fruit; and that Mahometanism is the manly religion, and existing Christianity the womanish.

9. There is a right of Private Judgment: that is, there is no existing authority on earth competent to interfere with the liberty of individuals in reasoning and judging for themselves about the Bible and its contents, as they severally please.

> Therefore, e. g. religious establishments requiring subscription are Antichristian.

10. There are rights of conscience such, that every one may lawfully advance a claim to profess and teach what is false and wrong in matters, religious, social, and moral, provided that to his private conscience it seems absolutely true and right.

> Therefore, e. g. individuals have a right to preach and practise fornication and polygamy.

11. There is no such thing as a national or state conscience.

> Therefore, e. g. no judgments can fall upon a sinful or infidel nation.

12. The civil power has no positive duty, in a normal state of things, to maintain religious truth.

> Therefore, e. g. blasphemy and sabbath-breaking are not rightly punishable by law.

13. Utility and expedience are the measure of political duty.

> Therefore, e. g. no punishment may be enacted, on the ground that God commands it: e. g. on the text, "Whoso sheddeth man's blood, by man shall his blood be shed."

14. The Civil Power may dispose of Church property without sacrilege.

> Therefore, e. g. Henry VIII. committed no sin in his spoliations.

15. The Civil Power has the right of ecclesiastical jurisdiction and administration.

> Therefore, e. g. Parliament may impose articles of faith on the Church or suppress Dioceses.

16. It is lawful to rise in arms against legitimate princes.

> Therefore, e. g. the Puritans in the 17th century, and the French in the 18th, were justifiable in their Rebellion and Revolution respectively.

17. The people are the legitimate source of power.

> Therefore, e. g. Universal Suffrage is among the natural rights of man.

18. Virtue is the child of knowledge, and vice of ignorance.

> Therefore, e. g. education, periodical literature, railroad travelling, ventilation, drainage, and the arts of life, when fully carried out, serve to make a population moral and happy.

All of these propositions, and many others too, were familiar to me thirty years ago, as in the number of the tenets of Liberalism, and, while I gave into none of them except No. 12, and perhaps No. 11, and partly No. 1, before I began to publish, so afterwards I wrote against most of them in some part or other of my Anglican works.

If it is necessary to refer to a work, not simply my own, but of the Tractarian school, which contains a similar protest, I should name the *Lyra Apostolica*. This volume, which by accident has been left unnoticed, except incidentally, in my Narrative, was collected together from the pages of the "British Magazine," in which its contents originally appeared, and published in a separate form, immediately after Hurrell Froude's death in 1836. Its signatures, α, β, γ, δ, ε, ζ, denote respectively the authorship of Mr. Bowden, Mr. Hurrell Froude, Mr. Keble, myself, Mr. Robert Wilberforce, and Mr. Isaac Williams.

There is one poem on "Liberalism," beginning "Ye cannot halve the Gospel of God's grace;" which bears out the account of Liberalism as above given.[12] Another upon "the Age to come," defining from its own point of view the position and prospects of Liberalism, shall be quoted *in extenso*.

> When I would search the truths that in me burn,
> And mould them into rule and argument,
> A hundred reasoners cried, — "Hast thou to learn
> Those dreams are scattered now, those fires are spent?"
> And, did I mount to simpler thoughts, and try
> Some theme of peace, 'twas still the same reply.
>
> Perplexed, I hoped my heart was pure of guile,
> But judged me weak in wit, to disagree;
> But now I see, that men are mad awhile,
> And joy the Age to come will think of me;
> 'Tis the old history: — Truth without a home,
> Despised and slain; then, rising from the tomb.

---

12. See the introduction (p. 60) to this volume for a full citation of Newman's poem "Liberalism."

Note B. On Page 152.

Ecclesiastical Miracles[1]

The writer, who gave occasion for the foregoing Narrative, was very severe with me for what I had said about Miracles in the Preface to the Life of St. Walburga. I observe therefore as follows:[2] —

Catholics believe that miracles happen in any age of the Church, though not for the same purposes, in the same number, or with the same evidence, as in Apostolic times. The Apostles wrought them in evidence of their divine mission; and with this object they have been sometimes wrought by Evangelists of countries since, as even Protestants allow. Hence we hear of them in the history of St. Gregory in Pontus, and St. Martin in Gaul; and in their case, as in

---

1. The charges to which Newman replies in this note arose from his 1842 *Essay on Ecclesiastical Miracles* and the *Lives of the English Saints*, which he launched in 1843 and for a time edited. On the issue of Newman and miracles, see the editor's preface to these notes as well as Frank M. Turner, *John Henry Newman: The Challenge to Evangelical Religion* (New Haven, Conn.: Yale Univ. Press, 2000), 475–479, and Robert Bruce Mullin, *Miracles and the Modern Religious Imagination* (New Haven, Conn.: Yale Univ. Press, 1996).

2. It is important to note that Newman says nothing of his other comments on the veracity of historical accounts of medieval miracles, which in various comments in *Lives of the English Saints* he had embraced without significant criticism. See Turner, *John Henry Newman*, pp. 484–485.

that of the Apostles, they were both numerous and clear.³ As they are granted to Evangelists, so are they granted, though in less measure and evidence, to other holy men; and as holy men are not found equally at all times and in all places, therefore miracles are in some places and times more than in others. And since, generally, they are granted to faith and prayer, therefore in a country in which faith and prayer abound, they will be more likely to occur, than where and when faith and prayer are not; so that their occurrence is irregular. And further, as faith and prayer obtain miracles, so still more commonly do they gain from above the ordinary interventions of Providence; and, as it is often very difficult to distinguish between a providence and a miracle, and there will be more providences than miracles, hence it will happen that many occurrences will be called miraculous, which, strictly speaking, are not such, that is, not more than providential mercies, or what are sometimes called "*grazie*" or "favours."

Persons, who believe all this, in accordance with Catholic teaching, as I did and do, they, on the report of a miracle, will of necessity, the necessity of good logic, be led to say, first, "It *may* be," and secondly, "But I must have *good evidence* in order to believe it."

1. It *may* be, because miracles take place in all ages; it must be clearly *proved*, because perhaps after all it may be only a providential mercy, or an exaggeration, or a mistake, or an imposture. Well, this is precisely what I had said, which the writer, who has given occasion to this Volume, considered so irrational. I had said, as he quotes me, "In this day, and under our present circumstances, we can only reply, that there is no reason why they should not be." Surely this is good logic, *provided* that miracles *do* occur in all ages; and so again I am logical in saying, "There is nothing, *primâ facie*, in the miraculous accounts in question, to repel a *properly taught* or religiously disposed mind." What is the matter with this statement? My assailant does not pretend to say *what* the matter is, and he cannot; but he expresses a rude, unmeaning astonishment. Accordingly, in the passage which he quotes, I observe, "Miracles are the kind of facts proper to ecclesiastical history, just as instances of sagacity or daring, personal prowess, or crime, are the facts proper to secular history." What is the harm of this?

2. But, though a miracle be conceivable, it has to be *proved*. *What* has to be proved? (1.) That the event occurred as stated, and is not a false report or an exaggeration. (2.) That it is clearly miraculous, and not a mere providence or answer to prayer within the order of nature. What is the fault of saying this?

---

3. St. Gregory in Pontus (ca. 213–ca. 270) was a saint in Asia Minor, and St. Martin (d. 397), a saint in Gaul. Both were credited with numerous miracles.

The inquiry is parallel to that which is made about some extraordinary fact in secular history. Supposing I hear that King Charles II. died a Catholic, I am led to say: It *may* be, but what is your *proof?*

In my Essay on Miracles of the year 1826, I proposed three questions about a professed miraculous occurrence:[4] 1. is it antecedently *probable?* 2. is it in its *nature* certainly miraculous? 3. has it sufficient *evidence?* To these three heads I had regard in my Essay of 1842; and under them I still wish to conduct the inquiry into the miracles of Ecclesiastical History.

So much for general principles; as to St. Walburga,[5] though I have no intention at all of denying that numerous miracles have been wrought by her intercession, still, neither the Author of her Life, nor I, the Editor, felt that we had grounds for binding ourselves to the belief of certain alleged miracles in particular. I made, however, one exception; it was the medicinal oil which flows from her relics. Now as to the *verisimilitude,* the *miraculousness,* and the *fact,* of this medicinal oil.

1. The *verisimilitude*. It is plain there is nothing extravagant in this report of her relics having a supernatural virtue; and for this reason, because there are such instances in Scripture, and Scripture cannot be extravagant. For instance, a man was restored to life by touching the relics of the Prophet Eliseus. The sacred text runs thus: — "And Elisha died, and they buried him. And the bands of the Moabites invaded the land at the coming in of the year. And it came to pass, as they were burying a man, that, behold, they spied a band of men; and they cast the man into the sepulchre of Elisha. And, when the man was let down, *and touched the bones of Elisha, he revived,* and stood upon his feet." Again, in the case of an inanimate substance, which had touched a living Saint: "And God wrought *special miracles* by the hands of Paul; so that *from his body* were brought unto the sick *handkerchiefs or aprons,* and *the diseases departed from them.*" And again in the case of a pool: "An *Angel went down* at a certain season into the pool, and troubled the water; whosoever then first, after the troubling of the water, stepped in, *was made whole of whatsoever*

---

4. For a modern reprint of the 1826 essay as well as the subsequent essay see John Henry Newman, *Two Essays on Miracles* (Eugene, Ore.: Wipf and Stock, 1998).

5. St. Walburga (ca. 710–777), born in England, became a missionary to Germany. Credited with many miracles and other wondrous occurrences in her life, she later became an abbess. Years after her death, her body was exhumed and found to be surrounded by oil. The story and reality of the oil became long debated. The incident was recounted in the life of St. Walburga written by Thomas Meyrick (1817–1903) for the *Lives of the English Saints* series.

disease he had." 2 Kings [4 Kings] xiii. 20, 21. Acts xix. 11, 12. John v. 4. Therefore there is nothing *extravagant* in the *character* of the miracle.

2. Next, the *matter of fact:*— is there an oil flowing from St. Walburga's tomb, which is medicinal? To this question I confined myself in my Preface. Of the accounts of medieval miracles, I said that there was no *extravagance* in their *general character,* but I could not affirm that there was always *evidence* for them. I could not simply accept them as *facts,* but I could not reject them in their *nature;*— they *might* be true, for they were not impossible; but they were *not proved* to be true, because there was not trustworthy testimony. However, as to St. Walburga, I repeat, I made *one* exception, the fact of the medicinal oil, since for that miracle there was distinct and successive testimony. And then I went on to give a chain of witnesses. It was my duty to state what those witnessees said in their very words; so I gave the testimonies in full, tracing them from the Saint's death. I said, "She is one of the principal Saints of her age and country." Then I quoted Basnage, a Protestant, who says, "Six writers are extant, who have employed themselves in relating the deeds or miracles of Walburga."[6] Then I said that her "renown was not the mere natural *growth* of ages, but begins with the very century of the Saint's death." Then I observed that only two miracles seem to have been "distinctly reported of her as occurring in her lifetime; and they were handed down apparently by tradition." Also, that such miracles are said to have commenced about A.D. 777. Then I spoke of the medicinal oil as having testimony to it in 893, in 1306, after 1450, in 1615, and in 1620. Also, I said that Mabillon seems not to have believed some of her miracles; and that the earliest witness had got into trouble with his Bishop.[7] And so I left the matter, as a question to be decided by evidence, not deciding any thing myself.

What was the harm of all this? but my Critic muddled it together in a most extraordinary manner, and I am far from sure that he knew himself the definite categorical charge which he intended it to convey against me. One of his remarks is, "What has become of the holy oil for the last 240 years, Dr. Newman does not say," p. 25. Of course I did not, because I did not know; I gave the evidence as I found it; he assumes that I had a point to prove, and then asks why I did not make the evidence larger than it was.

I can tell him more about it now: the oil still flows; I have had some of it in my possession; it is medicinal still. This leads to the third head.

3. Its *miraculousness.* On this point, since I have been in the Catholic

---

6. Jacques Basnage (1653–1723) was a French Protestant clerical author.
7. Jean Mabillon (1632–1707) was a French Roman Catholic clerical historian.

Church, I have found there is a difference of opinion. Some persons consider that the oil is the natural produce of the rock, and has ever flowed from it; others, that by a divine gift it flows from the relics; and others, allowing that it now comes naturally from the rock, are disposed to hold that it was in its origin miraculous, as was the virtue of the pool of Bethsaida.

This point must be settled of course before the virtue of the oil can be ascribed to the sanctity of St. Walburga; for myself, I neither have, nor ever have had, the means of going into the question; but I will take the opportunity of its having come before me, to make one or two remarks, supplemental of what I have said on other occasions.

1. I frankly confess that the present advance of science tends to make it probable that various facts take place, and have taken place, in the order of nature, which hitherto have been considered by Catholics as simply supernatural.[8]

2. Though I readily make this admission, it must not be supposed in consequence that I am disposed to grant at once, that every event was natural in point of fact, which *might* have taken place by the laws of nature; for it is obvious, no Catholic can bind the Almighty to act only in one and the same way, or to the observance always of His own laws. An event which is possible in the way of nature, is certainly possible too to Divine Power without the sequence of natural cause and effect at all. A conflagration, to take a parallel, may be the work of an incendiary, or the result of a flash of lightning; nor would a jury think it safe to find a man guilty of arson, if a dangerous thunderstorm was raging at the very time when the fire broke out. In like manner, upon the hypothesis that a miraculous dispensation is in operation, a recovery from diseases to which medical science is equal, may nevertheless in matter of fact have taken place, not by natural means, but by a supernatural interposition. That the Lawgiver always acts through His own laws, is an assumption, of which I never saw proof. In a given case, then, the possibility of assigning a human cause for an event does not *ipso facto* prove that it is not miraculous.

3. So far, however, is plain, that, till some *experimentum crucis* can be found, such as to be decisive against the natural cause or the supernatural, an occurrence of this kind will as little convince an unbeliever that there has been a divine interference in the case, as it will drive the Catholic to admit that there has been no interference at all.

4. Still there is this gain accruing to the Catholic cause from the larger views we now possess of the operation of natural causes, viz. that our opponents will

---

8. Throughout his Roman Catholic career Newman was very sympathetic to the discoveries of contemporary science.

not in future be so ready as hitherto, to impute fraud and falsehood to our priests and their witnesses, on the ground of their pretending or reporting things that are incredible. Our opponents have again and again accused us of false witness, on account of statements which they now allow are either true, or may have been true. They account indeed for the strange facts very differently from us; but still they allow that facts they were. It is a great thing to have our characters cleared; and we may reasonably hope that, the next time our word is vouched for occurrences which appear to be miraculous, our facts will be investigated, not our testimony impugned.

5. Even granting that certain occurrences, which we have hitherto accounted miraculous, have not absolutely a claim to be so considered, nevertheless they constitute an argument still in behalf of Revelation and the Church. Providences, or what are called *grazie*, though they do not rise to the order of miracles, yet, if they occur again and again in connexion with the same persons, institutions, or doctrines, may supply a cumulative evidence of the fact of a supernatural presence in the quarter in which they are found. I have already alluded to this point in my Essay on Ecclesiastical Miracles, and I have a particular reason, as will presently be seen, for referring here to what I said in the course of it.

In that Essay, after bringing its main argument to an end, I append to it a review of "the evidence for particular alleged miracles." "It does not strictly fall within the scope of the Essay," I observe, "to pronounce upon the truth or falsehood of this or that miraculous narrative, as it occurs in ecclesiastical history; but only to furnish such general considerations, as may be useful in forming a decision in particular cases," p. cv. However, I thought it right to go farther and "to set down the evidence for and against certain miracles as we meet with them," ibid. In discussing these miracles separately, I make the following remarks, to which I have just been referring.

After discussing the alleged miracle of the Thundering Legion,[9] I observe:— "Nor does it concern us much to answer the objection, that there is nothing strictly miraculous in such an occurrence, because sudden thunderclouds after drought are not unfrequent; for, I would answer, Grant me such miracles ordinarily in the early Church, and I will ask no other; grant that, upon prayer,

---

9. The Thundering Legion had been one of the ecclesiastical miracles Newman had defended in his 1842 essay. It refers to an incident during Marcus Aurelius's war against the Germans. A group of Christian soldiers were reportedly surrounded by the enemy and dying from lack of water. After they prayed, a thunderstorm occurred, frightening off the enemy and providing them with much needed water.

benefits are vouchsafed, deliverances are effected, unhoped-for results obtained, sicknesses cured, tempests laid, pestilences put to flight, famines remedied, judgments inflicted, and there will be no need of analyzing the causes, whether supernatural or natural, to which they are to be referred. They may, or they may not, in this or that case, follow or surpass the laws of nature, and they may do so plainly or doubtfully, but the common sense of mankind will call them miraculous; for by a miracle is popularly meant, whatever be its formal definition, an event which impresses upon the mind the immediate presence of the Moral Governor of the world. He may sometimes act through nature, sometimes beyond or against it; but those who admit the fact of such interferences, will have little difficulty in admitting also their strictly miraculous character, if the circumstances of the case require it, and those who deny miracles to the early Church will be equally strenuous against allowing her the grace of such intimate influence (if we may so speak) upon the course of divine Providence, as is here in question, even though it be not miraculous." — p. cxxi.

And again, speaking of the death of Arius:[10] "But after all, was it a miracle? for, if not, we are labouring at a proof of which nothing comes. The more immediate answer to this question has already been suggested several times. When a Bishop with his flock prays night and day against a heretic, and at length begs of God to take him away, and when he *is* suddenly taken away, almost at the moment of his triumph, and that by a death awfully significant, from its likeness to one recorded in Scripture, is it not trifling to ask whether such an occurrence comes up to the definition of a miracle? The question is not whether it is formally a miracle, but whether it is an event, the like of which persons, who deny that miracles continue, will consent that the Church should be considered still able to perform. If they are willing to allow to the Church such extraordinary protection, it is for them to draw the line to the satisfaction of people in general, between these and strictly miraculous events; if, on the other hand, they deny their occurrence in the times of the Church, then there is sufficient reason for our appealing here to the history of Arius in proof of the affirmative." — p. clxxii.

These remarks, thus made upon the Thundering Legion and the death of Arius, must be applied, in consequence of investigations made since the date of my Essay, to the apparent miracle wrought in favour of the African confessors

---

10. Arius, whose thought had been the origin of the most important ancient heresy, died unexpectedly the night before he was to be readmitted to the church on order of the Emperor Constantine. Bishop Alexander had prayed that Arius might die rather than be so readmitted to church fellowship.

in the Vandal persecution. Their tongues were cut out by the Arian tyrant, and yet they spoke as before. In my Essay I insisted on this fact as being strictly miraculous.[11] Among other remarks (referring to the instances adduced by Middleton and others in disparagement of the miracle, viz. of a "a girl born without a tongue, who yet talked as distinctly and easily, as if she had enjoyed the full benefit of that organ," and of a boy who lost his tongue at the age of eight or nine, yet retained his speech, whether perfectly or not,) I said, "Does Middleton mean to say, that, if certain of men lost their tongues *at the command of a tyrant* for the *sake of their religion,* and then spoke *as plainly* as before, nay *if only one person was so mutilated* and so gifted, it would not be a miracle?"—p. ccx. And I enlarged upon the minute details of the fact as reported to us by eye-witnesses and contemporaries. "Out of the seven writers adduced, six are contemporaries; three, if not four, are eye-witnesses of the miracle. One reports from an eye-witness, and one testifies to a fervent record at the burial-place of the subjects of it. All seven were living, or had been staying, at one or other of the two places which are mentioned as their abode. One is a Pope, a second a Catholic Bishop, a third a Bishop of a schismatical party, a fourth an emperor, a fifth a soldier, a politician, and a suspected infidel, a sixth a statesman and courtier, a seventh a rhetorician and philosopher. 'He cut out the tongues by the roots,' says Victor, Bishop of Vito; 'I perceived the tongues entirely gone by the roots,' Æneas; 'as low down as the throat,' says Procopius; 'at the roots,' says Justinian and St. Gregory; 'he spoke like an educated man, without impediment,' says Victor of Vito; 'with articulateness,' says Æneas; 'better than before;' 'they talked without any impediment,' says Procopius; 'speaking with perfect voice,' says Marcellinus; 'they spoke perfectly, even to the end,' says the second Victor; 'the words were formed, full, and perfect,' says St. Gregory."—p. ccviii.

However, a few years ago an Article appeared in "Notes and Queries" (No. for May 22, 1858), in which various evidence was adduced to show that the tongue is not necessary for articulate speech.

1. Col. Churchill, in his "Lebanon," speaking of the cruelties of Djezzar Pacha, in extracting to the root the tongues of some Emirs, adds, "It is a curious fact, however, that the tongues grow again sufficiently for the purposes of speech."

2. Sir John Malcom, in his "Sketches of Persia," speaks of Zâb, Khan of Khisht, who was condemned to lose his tongue. "This mandate," he says, "was

---

11. In this remarkable passage Newman cites several ancient and modern writers to suggest that even if a tongue has been cut from a person's mouth, the person may in some manner retain the capacity for speech.

imperfectly executed, and the loss of half this member deprived him of speech. Being afterwards persuaded that its being cut close to the root would enable him to speak so as to be understood, he submitted to the operation; and the effect has been, that his voice, though indistinct and thick, is yet intelligible to persons accustomed to converse with him. . . . I am not an anatomist, and I cannot therefore give a reason, why a man, who could not articulate with half a tongue, should speak when he had none at all; but the facts are as stated."

3. And Sir John McNeill says, "In answer to your inquiries about the powers of speech retained by persons who have had their tongues cut out, I can state from personal observation, that several persons whom I knew in Persia, who had been subjected to that punishment, spoke so intelligibly as to be able to transact important business. . . . The conviction in Persia is universal, that the power of speech is destroyed by merely cutting off the tip of the tongue; and is to a useful extent restored by cutting off another portion as far back as a perpendicular section can be made of the portion that is free from attachment at the lower surface. . . . I never had to meet with a person who had suffered this punishment, who could not speak so as to be quite intelligible to his familiar associates."

I should not be honest, if I professed to be simply converted, by these testimonies, to the belief that there was nothing miraculous in the case of the African confessors. It is quite as fair to be sceptical on one side of the question as on the other; and if Gibbon is considered worthy of praise for his stubborn incredulity in receiving the evidence for this miracle, I do not see why I am to be blamed, if I wish to be quite sure of the full appositeness of the recent evidence which is brought to its disadvantage. Questions of fact cannot be disproved by analogies or presumptions; the inquiry must be made into the particular case in all its parts, as it comes before us. Meanwhile, I fully allow that the points of evidence brought in disparagement of the miracle are *primâ facie* of such cogency, that, till they are proved to be irrelevant, Catholics are prevented from appealing to it for controversial purposes.

Note C. On Page 257.

Sermon on Wisdom and Innocence[1]

The professed basis of the charge of lying and equivocation made against me, and, in my person, against the Catholic clergy, was, as I have already noticed in the Preface, a certain Sermon of mine on "Wisdom and Innocence," being the 20th in a series of "Sermons on Subjects of the Day," written, preached, and published while I was an Anglican. Of this Sermon my accuser spoke thus in his Pamphlet: —

> "It is occupied entirely with the attitude of 'the world' to 'Christians' and 'the Church.' By the world appears to be signified, especially, the Protestant public of these realms; what Dr. Newman means by Christians, and the Church, he has not left in doubt; for in the preceding Sermon he says: 'But if the truth must be spoken, what are the humble monk and the holy nun, and other regulars, as they are called, but Christians after the very pattern given us in Scripture, &c.'. . . . This is his definition of Christians. And in the Sermon itself, he sufficiently defines what he means by 'the Church,' in two notes of her character, which he shall give in his own words: 'What, for instance, though we grant that sacramental confession and the celibacy of the clergy do tend to consolidate the body politic in the relation of rulers and subjects, or, in other words, to aggrandize the priesthood? for how can the Church be one body without such relation?' " — Pp. 8, 9.

---

1. See the introduction to this volume and the preface to Newman's notes for a discussion of Newman's sermon "Wisdom and Innocence."

He then proceeded to analyze and comment on it at great length, and to criticize severely the method and tone of my Sermons generally. Among other things, he said: —

"What, then, did the Sermon *mean?* Why was it preached? To insinuate that a Church which had sacramental confession and a celibate clergy was the only true Church? Or to insinuate that the admiring young gentlemen who listened to him stood to their fellow-countrymen in the relation of the early Christians to the heathen Romans? Or that Queen Victoria's Government was to the Church of England what Nero's or Dioclesian's was to the Church of Rome? It may have been so. I know that men used to suspect Dr. Newman, — I have been inclined to do so myself, — of writing a whole Sermon, not for the sake of the text or of the matter, but for the sake of one single passing hint — one phrase, one epithet, one little barbed arrow, which, as he swept magnificently past on the stream of his calm eloquence, seemingly unconscious of all presences, save those unseen, he delivered unheeded, as with his finger-tip, to the very heart of an initiated hearer, never to be withdrawn again. I do not blame him for that. It is one of the highest triumphs of oratoric power, and may be employed honestly and fairly by any person who has the skill to do it honestly and fairly; but then, Why did he entitle his Sermon 'Wisdom and Innocence?'

"What, then, could I think that Dr. Newman *meant?* I found a preacher bidding Christians imitate, to some undefined point, the 'arts' of the basest of animals, and of men, and of the devil himself. I found him, by a strange perversion of Scripture, insinuating that St Paul's conduct and manner were such as naturally to bring down on him the reputation of being a crafty deceiver. I found him — horrible to say it — even hinting the same of one greater than St. Paul. I found him denying or explaining away the existence of that Priestcraft, which is a notorious fact to every honest student of history, and justifying (as far as I can understand him) that double-dealing by which prelates, in the middle age, too often played off alternately the sovereign against the people, and the people against the sovereign, careless which was in the right, so long as their own power gained by the move. I found him actually using of such (and, as I thought, of himself and his party likewise) the words 'They yield outwardly; to assent inwardly were to betray the faith. Yet they are called deceitful and double-dealing, because they do as much as they can, and not more than they may.' I found him telling Christians that they will always seem 'artificial,' and 'wanting in openness and manliness;' that they will always be 'a mystery' to the world, and that the world will always think them rogues; and bidding them glory in what the world (i. e. the rest of their countrymen), disown, and say with Mawworm, 'I like to be despised.'

"Now, how was I to know that the preacher, who had the reputation of being the most acute man of his generation, and of having a specially intimate acquaintance with the weaknesses of the human heart, was utterly blind to the broad meaning and the plain practical result of a Sermon like this, delivered before fanatic and hot-headed young men, who hung upon his every word? that he did not foresee that they would think that they obeyed him by becoming affected, artificial, sly, shifty, ready for concealments and equivocations?" &c. &c. — Pp. 14-16.

My accuser asked in this passage what did the Sermon *mean,* and why was it preached. I will here answer this question; and with this view will speak, first of the *matter* of the Sermon, then of its *subject,* then of its *circumstances.*

1. It was one of the last six Sermons which I wrote when I was an Anglican. It was one of the five Sermons I preached in St. Mary's between Christmas and Easter, 1843, the year when I gave up my Living. The MS. of the Sermon is destroyed; but I believe, and my memory too bears me out, as far as it goes, that the sentence in question about Celibacy and Confession, of which this writer would make so much, *was not preached at all.* The Volume, in which this Sermon is found, was published *after* that I had given up St. Mary's, when I had no call on me to restrain the expression of any thing which I might hold: and I stated an important fact about it in the Advertisement, in these words: —

> "In preparing [these Sermons] for publication, *a few words and sentences* have in several places been *added,* which will be found to express more *of private or personal opinion,* than it was expedient to introduce into the *instruction* delivered in Church to a parochial Congregation. Such introduction, however, seems unobjectionable in the case of compositions, which are *detached* from the sacred place and service to which they once belonged, and *submitted to the reason* and judgment of the general reader."

This Volume of Sermons then cannot be criticized at all as *preachments;* they are *essays;* essays of a man who, at the time of publishing them, was *not* a preacher. Such passages, as that in question, are just the very ones which I added *upon* my publishing them; and, as I always was on my guard in the pulpit against saying any thing which looked towards Rome, I shall believe that I did not preach the obnoxious sentence till some one is found to testify that he heard it.

At the same time I cannot conceive why the mention of Sacramental Confession, or of Clerical Celibacy, had I made it, was inconsistent with the position of an Anglican Clergyman. For Sacramental Confession and Absolution actually form a portion of the Anglican Visitation of the Sick; and though the 32nd Article says that "Bishops, priests, and deacons, are not *commanded* by God's law either to vow the state of single life or to abstain from marriage," and "therefore it is *lawful* for them to marry," this proposition I did not dream of denying, nor is it inconsistent with St. Paul's doctrine, which I held, that it is "*good* to abide even as he," i. e. in celibacy.

But I have more to say on this point. This writer says, "I know that men used to suspect Dr. Newman, —I have been inclined to do so myself, — of *writing a whole Sermon, not for the sake of the text or of the matter,* but for the sake of one simple passing hint, — one phrase, one epithet." Now observe; can there be a plainer testimony borne to the practical character of my Sermons at St. Mary's than this gratuitous insinuation? Many a preacher of Tractarian doctrine has been accused of not letting his parishioners alone, and of teasing them with his private theological notions. The same report was spread about me twenty years ago as this writer spreads now, and the world believed that my Sermons at St. Mary's were full of red-hot Tractarianism. Then strangers came to hear me preach, and were astonished at their own disappointment. I recollect the wife of a great prelate from a distance coming to hear me, and then expressing her surprise to find that I preached nothing but a plain humdrum Sermon. I recollect how, when on the Sunday before Commemoration one year, a number of strangers came to hear me, and I preached in my usual way, residents in Oxford, of high position, were loud in their satisfaction that on a great occasion, I had made a simple failure, for after all there was nothing in the Sermon to hear. Well, but they were not going to let me off, for all my common-sense view of duty. Accordingly they got up the charitable theory which this Writer revives. They said that there was a double purpose in those plain addresses of mine, and that my Sermons were never so artful as when they seemed common-place; that there were sentences which redeemed their apparent simplicity and quietness. So they watched during the delivery of a Sermon, which to them was too practical to be useful, for the concealed point of it, which they could at least imagine, if they could not discover. "Men used to suspect Dr. Newman," he says, "of writing a *whole* Sermon, *not* for the sake of *the text or of the matter,* but for the sake of one single passing hint, . . . *one* phrase, *one* epithet, *one* little barbed arrow, which, as he *swept magnificently* past on the stream of his calm eloquence, *seemingly* unconscious of all presences, save those unseen, he delivered unheeded," &c. To all appearance, he says, I was "unconscious of all presences." He is not able to deny that the "*whole* Sermon" had the *appearance* of being "*for the sake* of the text and matter;" therefore he suggests that perhaps it wasn't.

2. And now as to the subject of the Sermon. The Sermons of which the Volume consists are such as are, more or less, exceptions to the rule which I ordinarily observed, as to the subjects which I introduced into the pulpit of St. Mary's. They are not purely ethical or doctrinal. They were for the most part caused by circumstances of the day or of the moment, and they belong to

various years. One was written in 1832, two in 1836, two in 1838, five in 1840, five in 1841, four in 1842, seven in 1843. Many of them are engaged on one subject, viz. in viewing the Church in its relation to the world. By the world was meant, not simply those multitudes which were not in the Church, but the existing body of human society, whether in the Church or not, whether Catholics, Protestants, Greeks, or Mahometans, theists or idolaters, as being ruled by principles, maxims, and instincts of their own, that is, of an unregenerate nature, whatever their supernatural privileges might be, greater or less, according to their form of religion. This view of the relation of the Church to the world as taken apart from questions of ecclesiastical politics, as they may be called, is often brought out in my Sermons. Two occur to me at once; No. 3 of my Plain Sermons, which was written in 1829, and No. 15 of my Third Volume of Parochial, written in 1835. On the other hand, by Church I meant, — in common with all writers connected with the Tract Movement, whatever their shades of opinion, and with the whole body of English divines, except those of the Puritan or Evangelical School, — the whole of Christendom, from the Apostles' time till now, whatever their later divisions into Latin, Greek, and Anglican. I have explained this view of the subject above at pp. 190-192 of this Volume. When then I speak, in the particular Sermon before us, of the members, or the rulers, or the action of "the Church," I mean neither the Latin, nor the Greek, nor the English, taken by itself, but of the whole Church as one body: of Italy as one with England, of the Saxon or Norman as one with the Caroline Church. *This* was specially the one Church, and the points in which one branch or one period differed from another were not and could not be Notes of the Church, because Notes necessarily belong to the whole of the Church every where and always.

This being my doctrine as to the relation of the Church to the world, I laid down in the Sermon three principles concerning it, and there left the matter. The first is, that Divine Wisdom had framed for its action laws, which man, if left to himself, would have antecedently pronounced to be the worst possible for its success, and which in all ages have been called by the world, as they were in the Apostles' days, "foolishness;" that man ever relies on physical and material force, and on carnal inducements, — as Mahomet with his sword and his houris, or indeed almost as that theory of religion, called, since the Sermon was written, "muscular Christianity;" but that our Lord, on the contrary, has substituted meekness for haughtiness, passiveness for violence, and innocence for craft: and that the event has shown the high wisdom of such an economy, for it has brought to light a set of natural laws, unknown before, by which the seeming paradox that weakness should be stronger than might, and simplicity than wordly policy, is readily explained.

Secondly, I said that men of the world, judging by the event, and not recognizing the secret causes of the success, viz. a higher order of natural laws, — natural, though their source and action were supernatural, (for "the meek inherit the earth," by means of a meekness which comes from above,) — these men, I say, concluded, that the success which they witnessed must arise from some evil secret which the world had not mastered, — by means of magic, as they said in the first ages, by cunning as they say now. And accordingly they thought that the humility and inoffensiveness of Christians, or of Churchmen, was a mere pretence and blind to cover the real causes of that success, which Christians could explain and would not; and that they were simply hypocrites.

Thirdly, I suggested that shrewd ecclesiastics, who knew very well that there was neither magic nor craft in the matter, and, from their intimate acquaintance with what actually went on within the Church, discerned what were the real causes of its success, were of course under the temptation of substituting reason for conscience, and, instead of simply obeying the command, were led to do good that good might come, that is, to act *in order* to secure success, and not from a motive of faith. Some, I said, did yield to the temptation more or less, and their motives became mixed; and in this way the world in a more subtle shape had got into the Church; and hence it had come to pass, that, looking at its history from first to last, we could not possibly draw the line between good and evil there, and say either that every thing was to be defended, or certain things to be condemned. I expressed the difficulty, which I supposed to be inherent in the Church, in the following words. I said, "*Priestcraft has ever been considered the badge,* and its imputation is a kind of Note of the Church: and *in part indeed truly,* because the presence of powerful enemies, and the sense of their own weakness, *has sometimes tempted Christians to the abuse, instead of the use of Christian wisdom, to be wise without being harmless;* but partly, nay, for the most part, not truly, but slanderously, and merely because the world called their wisdom craft, when it was found to be a match for its own numbers and power."

Such is the substance of the Sermon: and as to the main drift of it, it was this; that I was, there and elsewhere, scrutinizing the course of the Church as a whole, as if philosophically, as an historical phenomenon, and observing the laws on which it was conducted. Hence the Sermon, or Essay as it more truly is, is written in a dry and unimpassioned way: it shows as little of human warmth of feeling as a Sermon of Bishop Butler's. Yet, under that calm exterior there was a deep and keen sensitiveness, as I shall now proceed to show.

3. If I mistake not, it was written with a secret thought about myself. Every one preaches according to his frame of mind, at the time of preaching. One heaviness especially oppressed me at that season, which this Writer, twenty

years afterwards, has set himself with a good will to renew: it arose from the sense of the base calumnies which were heaped upon me on all sides. It is worth observing that this Sermon is exactly contemporaneous with the report spread by a Bishop (*vid. supr.* p. 278–279), that I had advised a clergyman converted to Catholicism to retain his Living. This report was in circulation in February 1843, and my Sermon was preached on the 19th. In the trouble of mind into which I was thrown by such calumnies as this, I gained, while I reviewed the history of the Church, at once an argument and a consolation. My argument was this: if I, who knew my own innocence, was so blackened by party prejudice, perhaps those high rulers and those servants of the Church, in the many ages which intervened between the early Nicene times and the present, who were laden with such grievous accusations, were innocent also; and this reflection served to make me tender towards those great names of the past, to whom weaknesses or crimes were imputed, and reconciled me to difficulties in ecclesiastical proceedings, which there were no means now of properly explaining. And the sympathy thus excited for them, re-acted on myself, and I found comfort in being able to put myself under the shadow of those who had suffered as I was suffering, and who seemed to promise me their recompense, since I had a fellowship in their trial. In a letter to my Bishop at the time of Tract 90, part of which I have quoted, I said that I had ever tried to "keep innocency;" and now two years had passed since then, and men were louder and louder in heaping on me the very charges, which this Writer repeats out of my Sermon, of "fraud and cunning," "craftiness and deceitfulness," "double-dealing," "priestcraft," of being "mysterious, dark, subtle, designing," when I was all the time conscious to myself, in my degree, and after my measure, of "sobriety, self-restraint, and control of word and feeling." I had had experience how my past success had been imputed to "secret management;" and how, when I had shown surprise at that success, that surprise again was imputed to "deceit;" and how my honest heartfelt submission to authority had been called, as it was called in a foreign Bishop's charge, "mystic humility;" and how my silence was called an "hypocrisy;" and my faithfulness to my clerical engagements a secret correspondence with the enemy. And I found a way of destroying my sensitiveness about these things which jarred upon my sense of justice, and otherwise would have been too much for me, by the contemplation of a large law of the Divine Dispensation, and felt myself more and more able to bear in my own person a present trial, of which in my past writings I had expressed an anticipation.

For thus feeling and thus speaking this Writer compares me to "Mawworm." "I found him telling Christians," he says, "that they will always seem 'artificial,' and 'wanting in openness and manliness;' that they will always be 'a mystery' to the world; and that the world will always think them rogues; and bidding them glory in what the world (that is, the rest of their fellow-countrymen) disown, and say with Mawworm,[2] 'I like to be despised.' Now how was I to know that the preacher . . . was utterly blind to the broad meaning and the plain practical result of a Sermon like this delivered before fanatic and hot-headed young men, who hung upon his every word?" — Fanatic and hot-headed young men, who hung on my every word! If he had undertaken to write a history, and not a romance, he would have easily found out, as I have said above, that from 1841 I had severed myself from the younger generation of Oxford, that Dr. Pusey and I had then closed our theological meetings at his house, that I had brought my own weekly evening parties to an end, that I preached only by fits and starts at St. Mary's, so that the attendance of young men was broken up, that in those very weeks from Christmas till over Easter, during which this Sermon was preached, I was but five times in the pulpit there. He would have found, that it was written at a time when I was shunned rather than sought, when I had great sacrifices in anticipation, when I was thinking much of myself; that I was ruthlessly tearing myself away from my own followers, and that, in the musings of that Sermon, I was at the very utmost only delivering a testimony in my behalf for time to come, not sowing my rhetoric broadcast for the chance of present sympathy.[3]

Again, he says: "I found him actually using of such [prelates], (and, as I thought, of himself and his party likewise,) the words 'They yield outwardly; to assent inwardly were to betray the faith. Yet they are called deceitful and double-dealing, because they do as much as they can, not more than they may.'" This too is a proof of my duplicity! Let this writer, in his dealings with some one else, go just a little further than he has gone with me; and let him get into a court of law for libel; and let him be convicted; and let him still fancy that his libel, though a libel, was true, and let us then see whether he will not in such a case "yield outwardly," without assenting internally; and then again whether we should please him, if we called him "deceitful and double-dealing," because "he did as much as he could, not more than he ought to do." But Tract 90 will supply a real illustration of what I meant. I yielded to the Bishops in outward act, viz. in not defending the Tract, and in closing the Series; but, not only did I not assent inwardly to any condemnation of it, but I opposed myself to the proposition of a condemnation on the part of authority.

2. Mawworm was a character in a play of Isaac Bickerstaffe (1735–1812) titled *The Hypocrite* (1769).

3. Newman actually preached more frequently than he acknowledges in this passage. This error may well have been a lapse of memory on his part.

Yet I was then by the public called "deceitful and double-dealing," as this Writer calls me now, "because I did as much as I felt I could do, and not more than I felt I could honestly do." Many were the publications of the day and the private letters, which accused me of shuffling, because I closed the Series of Tracts, yet kept the Tracts on sale, as if I ought to comply not only with what my Bishop asked, but with what he did not ask, and perhaps did not wish. However, such teaching, according to this Writer, was likely to make young men "suspect, that truth was not a virtue for its own sake, but only for the sake of the spread of 'Catholic opinions,' and the 'salvation of their own souls;' and that cunning was the weapon which heaven had allowed to them to defend themselves against the persecuting Protestant public." — p. 16.

And now I draw attention to a further point. He says, "How was I to know that the preacher . . did not foresee, that [fanatic and hot-headed young men] would think that they obeyed him, by becoming affected, artificial, sly, shifty, ready for concealments and *equivocations?*" "How should he know!" What! I suppose that we are to think every man a knave till he is proved not to be such. Know! had he no friend to tell him whether I was "affected" or "artificial" myself? Could he not have done better than impute *equivocations* to me, at a time when I was in no sense answerable for the *amphibologia* of the Roman casuists? Had he a single fact which belongs to me personally or by profession to couple my name with equivocation in 1843? "How should he know" that I was not sly, smooth, artificial, non-natural! he should know by that common manly frankness, by which we put confidence in others, till they are proved to have forfeited it; he should know it by my own words in that very Sermon, in which I say it is best to be natural, and that reserve is at best but an unpleasant necessity. For I say there expressly:—

> "I do not deny that there is something very engaging in a frank and unpretending manner; some persons have it more than others; in *some persons it is a great grace.* But it must be recollected that I am speaking of *times of persecution and oppression* to Christians, such as the text foretells; and then surely frankness will become nothing else than indignation at the oppressor, and vehement speech, if it is permitted. Accordingly, as persons have deep feelings, so they will find the necessity of self-control, lest they should say what they ought not."

He sums up thus:

> "If [Dr. Newman] would ... persist (as in this Sermon) in dealing with matters dark, offensive, doubtful, sometimes actually forbidden, at least according to the notions of the great majority of English Churchmen; if he would always do so in a tentative, paltering way, seldom or never letting the world know

how much he believed, how far he intended to go; if, in a word, his method of teaching was a suspicious one, what wonder if the minds of men were filled with suspicions of him?" — p. 17.

Now, in the course of my Narrative, I have frankly admitted that I was tentative in such of my works as fairly allowed of the introduction into them of religious inquiry; but he is speaking of my Sermons; where, then, is his proof that in my Sermons I dealt in matters dark, offensive, doubtful, actually forbidden? He must show that I was tentative in my Sermons; and he has the range of eight volumes to gather evidence in. As to the ninth, my University Sermons, of course I was tentative in them; but not because "I would seldom or never let the world know how much I believed, or how far I intended to go;" but because University Sermons are commonly, and allowably, of the nature of disquisitions, as preached before a learned body; and because in deep subjects, which had not been fully investigated, I said as much as I believed, and about as far as I saw I could go; and a man cannot do more; and I account no man to be a philosopher who attempts to do more.

Note D. On Page 301.

Series of Saints' Lives of 1843–4

I have here an opportunity of preserving, what otherwise would be lost, the Catalogue of English Saints which I formed, as preparatory to the Series of their Lives which was begun in the above years. It is but a first Essay, and has many obvious imperfections; but it may be useful to others as a step towards a complete hagiography for England. For instance St. Osberga is omitted; I suppose because it was not easy to learn any thing about her. Boniface of Canterbury is inserted, though passed over by the Bollandists on the ground of the absence of proof of a *cultus* having been paid to him.[1] The Saints of Cornwall were too numerous to be attempted. Among the men of note, not Saints, King Edward II. is included from piety towards the founder of Oriel College. With these admissions I present my Paper to the reader.[2]

---

1. The Bollandists are a group of Belgian Jesuits who, beginning in the seventeenth century, published the *Acta Sanctorum,* a broad collection of lives and legends of Christian saints.

2. Newman's statement of the goals and purpose of the proposed series on *Lives of the English Saints* is an important document in setting forth his religious sensibilities and ecclesiastical goals during the period immediately before his resignation from St. Mary's. At this point in his life and in that of his followers, he understood himself to be a priest of the English branch of the Holy Catholic Church, which he believed to retain faithfulness to primitive Christian tradition not present in either the Church of England or the Roman Catholic Church.

Preparing for Publication, in Periodical Numbers, in small 8vo, The Lives of the English Saints, Edited by the Rev. John Henry Newman, B.D., Fellow of Oriel College.

It is the compensation of the disorders and perplexities of these latter times of the Church that we have the history of the foregoing. We indeed of this day have been reserved to witness a disorganization of the City of God, which it never entered into the minds of the early believers to imagine: but we are witnesses also of its triumphs and of its luminaries through those many ages which have brought about the misfortunes which at present overshadow it. If they were blessed who lived in primitive times, and saw the fresh traces of their Lord, and heard the echoes of Apostolic voices, blessed too are we whose special portion it is to see that same Lord revealed in His Saints. The wonders of His grace in the soul of man, its creative power, its inexhaustible resources, its manifold operation, all this we know, as they knew it not. They never heard the names of St. Gregory, St. Bernard, St. Francis, and St. Louis. In fixing our thoughts then, as in an undertaking like the present, on the History of the Saints, we are but availing ourselves of that solace and recompense of our peculiar trials whcih has been provided for our need by our Gracious Master.

And there are special reasons at this time for recurring to the Saints of our own dear and glorious, most favoured, yet most erring and most unfortunate England. Such a recurrence may serve to make us love our country better, and on truer grounds, than heretofore; to teach us to invest her territory, her cities and villages, her hills and springs, with sacred associations; to give us an insight into her present historical position in the course of the Divine Dispensation; to instruct us in the capabilities of the English character; and to open upon us the duties and the hopes to which that Church is heir, which was in former times the Mother of St. Boniface and St. Ethelreds.

Even a selection or specimens of the Hagiology of our country may suffice for some of these high purposes; and in so wide and rich a field of research it is almost presumptuous in one undertaking to aim at more than such a partial exhibition. The list that follows, though by no means so large as might have been drawn up, exceeds the limits which the Editor proposes to his hopes, if not to his wishes; but, whether it is allowed him to accomplish a larger or smaller portion of it, it will be his aim to complete such subjects or periods as he begins before bringing it to a close. It is hardly necessary to observe that any list that is producible in this stage of the undertaking can but approximate to correctness and completeness in matters of detail, and even in the names which are selected to compose it.

He has considered himself at liberty to include in the Series such saints as have been born in England, though they have lived and laboured out of it; and such, again, as have been in any sufficient way connected with our country, though born out of it; for instance, Missionaries or Preachers in it, or spiritual or temporal rulers, or founders of religious institutions or houses.

He has also included in the Series a few eminent or holy persons, who, though not in the Sacred Catalogue, are recommended to our religious memory by their fame, learning, or the benefits they have conferred on posterity. These have been distinguished from the Saints by printing their names in italics.

It is proposed to page all the longer Lives separately; the shorter will be thrown together in one. They will be published in monthly issues of not more than 128 pages each; and no regularity, whether of date or of subject, will be observed in the order of publication. But they will be so numbered as to admit ultimately of a general chronological arrangement.

The separate writers are distinguished by letters subjoined to each Life: and it should be added, to prevent misapprehension, that, since under the present circumstances of our Church, they are necessarily of various, though not divergent, doctrinal opinions, no one is answerable for any composition but his own. At the same time, the work professing an historical and ethical character, questions of theology will be, as far as possible, thrown into the back ground.

J. H. N.

Littlemore, Sept. 9, 1843.

Calendar of English Saints

JANUARY

1 Elvan, B. and Medwyne, C.
2 Martyrs of Lichfield.
3 Melorus, M.
4
5 Edward, K.C.
6 Peter, A.
7 Cedd, B.
8 Pega, V. Wulsin, B.
9 Adrian, A. Bertwald, Archb.
10 Sethrida, V.
11 Egwin, B.
12 Benedict Biscop, A. Aelred, A.
13 Kentigern, B.
14 Beuno, A.
15 Ceolulph, K. Mo.
16 Henry, Hermit. Fursey, A.
17 Mildwida, V.
18 Ulfrid or Wolfrid, M.
19 Wulstan, B. Henry, B.
20
21
22 Brithwold, B.
23 Boisil, A.
24 Cadoc, A.
25
26 Theoritgida, V.
27 Bathildis, Queen.
28
29 Gildas, A.
30
31 Adamnan, Mo. Serapion, M.

FEBRUARY

1
2 Laurence, Archb.

3 Wereburga, V.
4 Gilbert, A. Liephard, B.M.
5
6 Ina, K. Mo.
7 Augulus, B.M. Richard, K.
8 Elfleda, A. Cuthman, C.
9 Theliau, B.
10 Trumwin, B.
11
12 Ethelwold, B. of Lindisfarne.
    Cedmon, Mo.
13 Ermenilda, Q.A.
14
15 Sigefride, B.
16 Finan, B.
17
18
19
20 Ulric, H.
21
22
23 Milburga, V.
24 Luidhard, B. Ethelbert of Kent, K.
25 Walburga, V.A.
26
27 Alnoth, H.M.
28 Oswald, B.
29

MARCH

1 David, Archb. Swibert, B.
2 Chad, B. Willeik, C. Joavan, B.
3 Winwaloe, A.
4 Owin, Mo.
5
6 Kineburga, &c., and Tibba, VV.
    Balther, C. and Bilfrid, H.
7 Easterwin, A. William, Friar.
8 Felix, B.
9 Bosa, B.
10
11
12 Elphege, B. Paul de Leon, B.C.

13
14 Robert, H.
15 Eadgith, A.
16
17 Withburga, V.
18 Edward, K.M.
19 Alemund, M.
20 Cuthbert, B. Herbert, B.
21
22
23 Ædelwald, H.
24 Hildelitha, A.
25 Alfwold of Sherborne, B. and
    William, M.
26
27
28
29 Gundleus, H.
30 Merwenna, A.
31

APRIL

1
2
3 Richard, B.
4
5
6
7
8
9 Frithstan, B.
10
11 Guthlake, H.
12
13 Caradoc, H.
14 *Richard of Bury, B.*
15 Paternus, B.
16
17 Stephen, A.
18
19 Elphege, Archb.
20 Adelhare, M. Cedwalla, K.
21 Anselm, Archb. Doctor.

22
23 George, M.
24 Mellitus, Archb. Wilfrid, Archb. Egbert, C.
25
26
27
28
29 Wilfrid II. Archb.
30 Erconwald, B. Suibert, B. *Maud, Q.*

MAY

1 Asaph, B. Ultan, A. Brioc, B.C.
2 Germanus, M.
3
4
5 Ethelred, K. Mo.
6 Eadbert, A.
7 John, Archb. of Beverley.
8
9
10
11 Fremund, M.
12
13
14
15
16 Simon Stock, H.
17
18 Elgiva, Q.
19 Dunstan, Archb. *B. Alcuin, A.*
20 Ethelbert, K.M.
21 Godric, H.
22 Winewald, A. Berethun, A. Henry, K.
23
24 Ethelburga, Q.
25 Aldhelm, B.
26 Augustine, Archb.
27 Bede, D. Mo.

28 *Lanfranc, Archb.*
29
30 Walston, C.
31 Jurmin, C.

JUNE

1 Wistan, K.M.
2
3
4 Petroc, A.
5 Boniface, Archb. M.
6 Gudwall, B.
7 Robert, A.
8 William, Archb.
9
10 Ivo, B. and Ithamar, B.
11
12 Eskill, B.M.
13
14 Elerius, A.
15 Edburga, V.
16
17 Botulph, A. John, Fr.
18
19
20 Idaberga, V.
21 Egelmund, A.
22 Alban, and Amphibolus, MM.
23 Ethelreda, V.A.
24 Bartholomew, H.
25 Adelbert, C.
26
27 John, C. of Moutier.
28
29 *Margaret, Countess of Richmond.*
30

JULY

1 Julius, Aaron, MM. Rumold, B. Leonorus, B.
2 Oudoceus, B. Swithun, B.
3 Gunthiern, A.
4 Odo, Archb.

5 Modwenna, V.A.
6 Sexburga, A.
7 Edelburga; V.A. Hedda, B.
   Willibald, B. Ercongota, V.
8 Grimbald, and Edgar, K.
9 *Stephen Langton, Archb.*
10
11
12
13 Mildreda, V.A.
14 Marchelm, C. Boniface, Archb.
15 Deusdedit, Archb. Plechelm,
   B. David, A. and Editha of
   Tamworth, Q.V.
16 Helier, H.M.
17 Kenelm, K.M.
18 Edburga and Edgitha of
   Aylesbury, V.V. Frederic, B.M.
19
20
21
22
23
24 Wulfud and Ruffin, MM.
   Lewinna, V.M.
25
26
27 Hugh, M.
28 Sampson, B.
29 Lupus, B.
30 Tatwin, Archb. and
   Ermenigitha, V.
31 Germanus, B. and Neot, H.

AUGUST

1 Ethelwold, B. of Winton.
2 Etheldritha, V.
3 Walthen, A.
4
5 Oswald, K.M. Thomas, Mo. M.
   of Dover.
6
7
8 Colman, B.
9
10
11 *William of Waynfleet, B.*
12
13 Wigbert, A. Walter, A.
14 Werenfrid, C.
15
16
17
18 Helen, Empress.
19
20 Oswin, K.M.
21 Richard, B. of Andria.
22 Sigfrid, A.
23 Ebba, V.A.
24
25 Ebba, V.A.M.
26 Bregwin, Archb. *Bradwardine,
   Archb.*
27 Sturmius, A.
28
29 Sebbus, K.
30
31 Eanswida, V.A. Aidan, A.B.
   Cuthburga, Q.V.

SEPTEMBER

1
2 William, B. of Roschid. William, Fr.
3
4
5
6 Bega, A.
7 Alcmund, A. Tilhbert, A.
8
9 Bertelin, H. Wulfhilda or Vulfridis,
   A.
10 Otger, C.
11 *Robert Kilwardby, Archb.*
12
13
14 *Richard Fox, B.*

15
16 Ninian, B. Edith, daughter of Edgar, V.
17 Socrates and Stephen, MM.
18
19 Theodore, Archb.
20
21 Hereswide, Q. *Edward II. K.*
22
23
24
25 Ceolfrid, A.
26
27 *William of Wykeham, B.*
28 Lioba, V.A.
29 *B. Richard of Hampole, H.*
30 Honorius, Archb.

OCTOBER

1 Roger, B.
2 Thomas of Hereford, B.
3 Ewalds (two) MM.
4
5 *Walter Stapleton, B.*
6 Ywy, C.
7 Ositha, Q.V.M.
8 Ceneu, V.
9 Lina, V. and *Robert Grostete, B.*
10 Paulinus, Archb. John, C. of Bridlington.
11 Edilburga, V.A.
12 Edwin, K.
13
14 Burchard, B.
15 Tecla, V.A.
16 Lullus, Archb.
17 Ethelred, Ethelbright, MM.
18 *Walter de Merton, B.*
19 Frideswide, V. and Ethbin, A.
20
21 Ursula, V.M.
22 Mello, B.C.
23

24 Magloire, B.
25 *John of Salisbury, B.*
26 Eata, B.
27 Witta, B.
28 *B. Alfred.*
29 Sigebert, K. Elfreda, A.
30
31 Foillan, B.M.

NOVEMBER

1
2
3 Wenefred, V.M. Rumwald, C.
4 Brinstan, B. Clarus, M.
5 Cungar, H.
6 Iltut, A. and Winoc, A.
7 Willebrord, B.
8 Willehad, B. Tyssilio, B.
9
10 Justus, Archb.
11
12 Lebwin, C.
13 Eadburga of Menstrey, A.
14 Dubricius, B.C.
15 Malo, B.
16 Edmund, B.
17 Hilda, A. Hugh, B.
18
19 Ermenburga, Q.
20 Edmund, K.M. Humbert, B.M. Acca, B.
21
22 Paulinus, A.
23 Daniel, B.C.
24
25
26
27
28 Edwold, M.
29
30

DECEMBER

1
2 Weede, V.
3 Birinus, B. Lucius, K. and Sola, H.
4 Osmund, B.
5 Christina, V.
6
7
8 *John Peckham, Archb.*
9
10
11 Elfleda, A.
12 Corentin, B.C.
13 Ethelburga, Q. wife of Edwin.
14
15
16
17
18 Winebald, A.
19
20
21 Eadburga, V.A.
22
23
24
25
26 Tathai, C.
27 Gerald, A.B.
28
29 Thomas, Archb. M.
30
31

N.B. *St. William, Austin-Friar, Ingulphus,* and *Peter of Blois* have not been introduced into the above Calendar, their days of death or festival not being as yet ascertained.

Chronological Arrangement

SECOND CENTURY

182 Dec. 3.	Lucius, K. of the British.
Jan. 1.	Elvan, B. and Medwyne, C. envoys from St. Lucius to Rome.

FOURTH CENTURY

300 Oct. 22.	Mello, B. C. of Ronen.
303 Ap. 23.	George, M. under Dioclesian. Patron of England.
June 22.	Alban and Amphibalus, MM.
July 1.	Julius and Aaron, MM. of Caerleon.
304 Jan. 2.	Martyrs of Lichfield.
Feb. 7.	Augulus, B.M. of London.
328 Aug. 18.	Helen, Empress, mother of Constantine.
388 Sept. 17.	Socrates and Stephen, M.M. perhaps in Wales.
411 Jan. 3.	Melorus, M. in Cornwall.

FIFTH CENTURY

432 Sept. 16.	Ninian, B. Apostle of the Southern Picts.
429 July 31.	Germanus, B. C. of Auxerre.

Note D. Series of Saints' Lives of 1843-4   397

July 29.	Lupus, B. C. of Troyes.
502 May 1.	Brioc, B. C., disciple of St. Germanus.
490 Oct. 8.	Ceneu, or Keyna, V., sister-in-law of Gundleus.
492 Mar. 29.	Gundleus, Hermit, in Wales.
July 3.	Gunthiern, A., in Brittany.
453 Oct. 21.	Ursula, V.M. near Cologne.
bef. 500 Dec. 12.	Corentin, B.C. of Quimper.

FIFTH AND SIXTH CENTURIES
Welsh Schools

444–522 Nov. 14.	Dubricius, B.C., first Bishop of Llandaff.
520 Nov. 22.	Paulinus, A. of Whitland, tutor of St. David and St. Theliau.
445–544 Mar. 1.	David, Archb. of Menevia, afterwards called from him.
abt. 500 Dec. 26.	Tathai, C., master of St. Cadoc.
480 Jan. 24.	Cadoc, A., son of St. Gundleus, and nephew of St. Keyna.
abt. 513 Nov. 6.	Iltut, A., converted by St. Cadoc.
545 Nov. 23.	Daniel, B.C., first Bishop of Bangor.
aft. 559 Apr. 18.	Paternus, B.A., pupil of St. Iltut.
573 Mar. 12.	Paul, B.C. of Leon, pupil of St. Iltut.
Mar. 2.	Ioavan, B., pupil of St. Paul.
599 July 28.	Sampson, B., pupil of St. Iltut, cousin of St. Paul de Leon.
565 Nov. 15.	Malo, B., cousin of St. Sampson.
575 Oct. 24.	Magloire, B., cousin of St. Malo.
583 Jan. 29.	Gildas, A., pupil of St. Iltut.
July 1.	Leonorus, B., pupil of St. Iltut.
604 Feb. 9.	Theliau, B. of Llandaff, pupil of St. Dubricins.
560 July 2.	Oudoceus, B., nephew to St. Theliau.
500–580 Oct. 19.	Ethbin, A., pupil of St. Sampson.
516–601 Jan. 13.	Kentigern, B. of Glasgow, founder of Monastery of Elwy.

SIXTH CENTURY

529 Mar. 3.	Winwaloe, A., in Brittany.
564 June 4.	Petroc., A., in Cornwall.
July 16.	Helier, Hermit, M., in Jersey.
June 27.	John, C. of Moutier, in Tours.
590 May 1.	Asaph, B. of Elwy, afterwards called after him.
abt. 600 June 6.	Gudwall, B. of Aleth in Brittany.
Nov. 8.	Tyssilio, B. of St. Asaph.

398 Notes

SEVENTH CENTURY
Part I

600 June 10.	Ivo, or Ivia, B. from Persia.
596 Feb. 24.	Luidhard, B. of Senlis, in France.
616 Feb. 24.	Ethelbert, K. of Kent.
608 May 26.	Augustine, Archb. of Canterbury, Apostle of England.
624 Apr. 24.	Mellitus, Archb. of Canterbury, ⎫
619 Feb. 2.	Laurence, Archb. of Canterbury, ⎪
608 Jan. 6.	Peter, A. at Canterbury, ⎬ Companions of
627 Nov. 10.	Justus, Archb. of Canterbury, ⎪ St. Augustine.
653 Sept. 30.	Honorius, Archb. of Canterbury, ⎭
662 July 15.	Deus-dedit, Archb. of Canterbury.

SEVENTH CENTURY
Part II

642 Oct. 29.	Sigebert, K. of the East Angles.
646 Mar. 8.	Felix, B. of Dunwich, Apostle of the East Angles.
650 Jan. 16.	Fursey, A., preacher among the East Angles.
680 May 1.	Ultau, A., brother of St. Fursey.
655 Oct. 31.	Foillan, B.M., brother of St. Fursey, preacher in the Netherlands.
680 June 17.	Botulph, A., in Lincolnshire or Sussex.
671 June 10.	Ithamar, B. of Rochester.
650 Dec. 3.	Birinus, B. of Dorchester.
705 July 7.	Hedda, B. of Dorchester.
717 Jan. 11.	Egwin, B. of Worcester.

SEVENTH CENTURY
Part III

690 Sept. 19.	Theodore, Archb. of Canterbury.
709 Jan. 9.	Adrian, A. in Canterbury.
709 May 25.	Aldhelm, B. of Sherborne, pupil of St. Adrian.

SEVENTH CENTURY
Part IV

630 Nov. 3.	Winefred, V.M. in Wales.
642 Feb. 4.	Liephard, M.B., slain near Cambray.
660 Jan. 14.	Beuno, A., kinsman of St. Cadocus and St. Kentigern.

Note D. Series of Saints' Lives of 1843–4   399

673 Oct. 7.   Osgitha, Q.V.M., in East Anglia during a Danish inroad.
630 June 14.   Elerius, A. in Wales.
680 Jan. 27.   Bathildis, Q., wife of Clovis II., king of France.
687 July 24.   Lewinna, V.M., put to death by the Saxons.
700 July 18.   Edberga and Edgitha, VV. of Aylesbury.

SEVENTH CENTURY
Part V

644 Oct. 10.   Paulinus, Archb. of York, companion of St. Augustine.
633 Oct. 12.   Edwin, K. of Northumberland.
     Dec. 13. Ethelburga, Q., wife to St. Edwin.
642 Aug. 5.   Oswald, K.M., St. Edwin's nephew.
651 Aug. 20.   Oswin, K.M., cousin to St. Oswald.
683 Aug. 23.   Ebba, V.A. of Coldingham, half-sister to St. Oswin.
689 Jan. 31.   Adamnan, Mo. of Coldingham.

SEVENTH CENTURY
Part VI. — Whitby

650 Sept. 6.   Bega, V.A., foundress of St. Bee's, called after her.
681 Nov. 17.   Hilda, A. of Whitby, daughter of St. Edwin's nephew.
716 Dec. 11.   Elfleda, A. of Whitby, daughter of St. Oswin.
680 Feb. 12.   Cedmon, Mo. of Whitby.

SEVENTH AND EIGHTH CENTURIES
Part I

     Sept. 21. Hereswida, Q., sister of Hilda, wife of Annas, who succeeded Egric, Sigebert's cousin.
654 Jan. 10.   Sethrida, V.A. of Faremoutier, St. Hereswida's daughter by a former marriage.
693 Apr. 30.   Erconwald, A.B., son of Annas and St. Hereswida, Bishop of London, Abbot of Chertsey, founder of Barking.
677 Aug. 29.   Sebbus, K., converted by St. Erconwald.
     May 31.   Jurmin, C., son of Annas and St. Hereswida.
650 July 7.   Edelburga, V.A. of Faremoutier, natural daughter of Annas.
679 June 23.   Ethelreda, Etheldreds, Etheltrudis, or Awdry, V.A., daughter of Annas and St. Hereswida.

Mar. 17.	Withburga, V., daughter of Annas and St. Hereswida.
699 July 6.	Sexburga, A., daughter of Annas and St. Hereswida.
660 July 7.	Ercongota, or Ertongata, V.A. of Faremoutier, daughter of St. Sexburga.
699 Feb. 13.	Ermenilda, Q.A., daughter of St. Sexburga, wife of Wulfere.
aft. 675 Feb. 3.	Wereburga, V., daughter of St. Ermenilda and Wulfere, patron of Chester.
abt. 680 Feb. 27.	Alnoth, H.M., bailiff to St. Wereburga.
640 Aug. 31.	Eanswida, V.A., sister-in-law of St. Sexburga, granddaughter to St. Ethelbert.
668 Oct. 17.	Ethelred and Ethelbright, MM., nephews of St. Eanswida.
July 30.	Ermenigitha, V., niece of St. Eanswida.
676 Oct. 11.	Edilberga, V.A. of Barking, daughter of Annas and St. Hereswida.
678 Jan. 26.	Theoritgida, V., nun of Barking.
aft. 713 Aug. 31.	Cuthberga, Q.V., of Barking, sister of St. Ina.
700 Mar. 24.	Hildelitha, A. of Barking.
728 Feb. 6.	Ina, K. Mo. of the West Saxons.
740 May 24.	Ethelburga, Q., wife of St. Ina, nun at Barking.

SEVENTH AND EIGHTH CENTURIES
Part II

652 June 20.	Idaburga, V.	
696 Mar. 6.	Kineburga, Q.A.	
701 ———	Kinneswitha, V.	Daughters of King Penda.
———	Chidestre, V.	
692 Dec. 2.	Weeda, V.A.	
696 Mar. 6.	Tibba, V., their kinswoman.	
Nov. 3.	Rumwald, C., grandson of Penda.	
680 Nov. 19.	Ermenburga, Q., mother to the three following.	
Feb. 23.	Milburga, V.A. of Wenlock,	
July 13.	Mildreda, V.A. of Menstrey,	Grand-daughters of Penda.
676 Jan. 17.	Milwida, or Milgitha, V.	
750 Nov. 13.	Eadburga, A. of Monstrey.	

SEVENTH AND EIGHTH CENTURIES
Part III

670 July 24.	Wulfad and Ruffin, MM., sons of Wulfere, Penda's son, and of St. Erminilda.
672 Mar. 2.	Chad, B. of Lichfield.
664 Jan. 7.	Cedd, B. of London.
688 Mar. 4.	Owin, Mo. of Lichfield.
689 Apr. 20.	Cedwalla, K. of West Saxons.
690–725 Nov. 5.	Cungar, H. in Somersetshire.
700 Feb. 10.	Trumwin, B. of the Picts.
705 Mar. 9.	Bosa, Archb. of York.
709 Apr. 24.	Wilfrid, Archb. of York.
721 May 7.	John of Beverley, Archb. of York.
743 Apr. 29.	Wilfrid II., Archb. of York.
733 May 22.	Berethun, A. of Deirwood, disciple of St. John of Beverley.
751 May 22.	Winewald, A. of Deirwood.

SEVENTH AND EIGHTH CENTURIES
Part IV. — Missions

729 Apr. 24.	Egbert, C., master to Willebrord.
693 Oct. 3.	Ewalds (two), MM, in Westphalia.
690–736 Nov. 7.	Willebrord, B. of Utrecht, Apostle of Friesland.
717 Mar. 1.	Swibert, B., Apostle of Westphalia.
727 Mar. 2.	Willeik, C., successor to St. Swibert.
705 June 25.	Adelbert, C., grandson of St. Oswald, preacher in Holland.
705 Aug. 14.	Werenfrid, C., preacher in Friesland.
720 June 21.	Engelmund, A., preacher in Holland.
730 Sept. 10.	Otger, C. in Low Countries.
732 July 15.	Plechelm, B., preacher in Guelderland.
750 May 2.	Germanus, B.M. in the Netherlands.
760 Nov. 12.	Lebwin, C. in Overyssel, in Holland.
760 July 14.	Marchelm, C., companion of St. Lebwin, in Holland.
697–755 June 5.	Boniface, Archb., M. of Mentz, Apostle of Germany.
712 Feb. 7	Richard, K. of the West Saxons.

701–790 July 7.	Willibald, B. of Aichstadt, in Franconia,	} Children of St. Richard.
730–760 Dec. 18.	Winebald, A. of Heidenheim, in Suabia,	
779 Feb. 25.	Walburga, V.A. of Heidenheim,	
aft. 755 Sept. 28.	Lioba, V.A. of Bischorsheim,	
750 Oct. 15.	Tecla, V.A. of Kitzingen, in Franconia,	
788 Oct. 16.	Lullus, Archb. of Mentz,	} Companions of St. Boniface.
abt. 747 Aug. 13.	Wigbert, A. of Fritzlar and Ortdorf, in Germany,	
755 Apr. 20.	Adelhare, B.M. of Erford, in Franconia,	
780 Aug. 27.	Sturmius, A. of Fulda,	
786 Oct. 27.	Witta, or Albuinus, B. of Buraberg, in Germany,	
791 Nov. 8.	Willehad, B. of Bremen, and Apostle of Saxony,	
791 Oct. 14.	Burchard, B. of Wurtzburg, in Franconia,	
790 Dec. 3.	Sola, H., near Aichstadt, in Franconia,	
775 July 1.	Rumold, B., Patron of Mechlin.	
807 Apr. 30.	Suibert, B. of Verden in Westphalia.	

SEVENTH AND EIGHTH CENTURIES

Part V. — Lindisfarne and Hexham

670 Jan. 23.	Boisil, A. of Melros, in Scotland.
651 Aug. 31.	Aidan, A.B. of Lindisfarne.
664 Feb. 16.	Finan, B. of Lindisfarne.
676 Aug. 8.	Colman, B. of Lindisfarne.
685 Oct. 26.	Eata, B. of Hexham.
687 Mar. 20.	Cuthbert, B. of Lindisfarne.
Oct. 6.	Ywy, C. disciple of St. Cuthbert.
690 Mar. 20.	Herbert, H. disciple of St. Cuthbert.
698 May 6.	Eadbert, B. of Lindisfarne.
700 Mar. 23.	Ædelwald, H. successor of St. Cuthbert, in his hermitage.
740 Feb. 12.	Ethelwold, B. of Lindisfarne.
740 Nov. 20.	Acca, B. of Hexham.
764 Jan. 15.	Ceolulph, K. Mo. of Lindisfarne.
756 Mar. 6.	Balther, H. at Lindisfarne.
"	Bilfrid, H. Goldsmith at Lindisfarne.
781 Sept. 7.	Alchmund, B. of Hexham.
789 Sept. 7.	Tilhbert, B. of Hexham.

SEVENTH AND EIGHTH CENTURIES
Part VI. — Wearmouth and Yarrow

703 Jan. 12.	Benedict Biscop, A. of Wearmouth.
685 Mar. 7.	Easterwin, A. of Wearmouth.
689 Aug. 22.	Sigfrid, A. of Wearmouth.
716 Sept. 25.	Ceofrid, A. of Yarrow
734 May 27.	Bede, Doctor, Mo. of Yarrow.
804 May 19.	B. *Alcuin, A. in France.*

EIGHTH CENTURY

710 May 5.	Ethelred, K. Mo. King of Mercia, Monk of Bardney.
719 Jan. 8.	Pega, V., sister of St. Guthlake.
714 April 11.	Guthlake, H. of Croyland.
717 Nov. 6.	Winoc, A. in Brittany.
730 Jan. 9.	Bertwald, Archb. of Canterbury.
732 Dec. 27.	Gerald, A.B. in Mayo.
734 July 30.	Tatwin, Archb. of Canterbury.
750 Oct. 19.	Frideswide, V. patron of Oxford.
762 Aug. 26.	Bregwin, Archb. of Canterbury.
700–800 Feb. 8.	Cuthman, C. of Stening in Sussex.
bef. 800 Sept. 9.	Bertelin, H. patron of Stafford.

EIGHTH AND NINTH CENTURIES

793 May 20.	Ethelbert, K.M. of the East Angles.
834 Aug. 2.	Etheldritha, or Alfreda, V., daughter of Offa, king of Mercia, nun at Croyland.
819 July 17.	Kenelm, K.M. of Mercia.
849 June 1.	Wistan, K.M. of Mercia.
838 July 18.	Frederic, Archb. M. of Utrecht.
894 Nov. 4.	Clarus, M. in Normandy.

NINTH CENTURY
Part I. — Danish Slaughters, &c.

819 Mar. 19.	Alcmund, M., son of Eldred, king of Northumbria, Patron of Derby.
870 Nov. 20.	Edmund, K.M. of the East Angles.
862 May 11.	Fremund, H. M. nobleman of East Anglia.
870 Nov. 20.	Humbert, B.M of Elmon in East Anglia.
867 Aug. 25.	Ebba, V.A.M. of Coldingham.

NINTH CENTURY
Part II

862 July 2.	Swithun, B. of Winton.
870 July 5.	Modwenna, V.A. of Pollesworth in Warwickshire.
Oct. 9.	Lina, V. nun at Pollesworth.
871 Mar. 15.	Eadgith, V.A. of Pollesworth, sister of King Ethelwolf.
900 Dec. 21.	Eadburga, V.A. of Winton, daughter of King Ethelwolf.
880 Nov. 28.	Edwold, H., brother of St. Edmund.

NINTH AND TENTH CENTURIES

883 July 31.	Neot, H. in Cornwall.
903 July 8.	Grimbald, A. at Winton.
900 Oct. 28.	B. *Alfred*, K.
929 April 9.	Frithstan, B. of Winton.
934 Nov. 4.	Brinstan, B. of Winton.

TENTH CENTURY
Part I

960 June 15.	Edburga, V., nun at Winton, granddaughter of Alfred.
926 July 15.	Editha, Q.V., nun of Tamworth, sister to Edburga.
921 May 18.	Algyfa, or Elgiva, Q., mother of Edgar.
975 July 8.	Edgar, K.
978 Mar. 18.	Edward, K.M. at Corfe Castle.
984 Sept. 16.	Edith, V., daughter of St. Edgar and St. Wulfhilda.
990 Sept. 9.	Wulfhilda, or Vulfrida, A. of Wilton.
980 Mar. 30.	Merwenna, V.A. of Romsey.
990 Oct. 29.	Elfreda, A. of Romsey.
1016 Dec. 5.	Christina of Romsey, V., sister of St. Margaret of Scotland.

TENTH CENTURY
Part II

961 July 4.	Odo, Archb. of Canterbury, Benedictine Monk.
960–992 Feb. 28.	Oswald, Archb. of York, B. of Worcester, nephew to St. Odo.
951–1012 Mar. 12.	Elphege the Bald, B. of Winton.
988 May 19.	Dunstan, Archb. of Canterbury.
973 Jan. 8.	Wulsin, B. of Sherbourne.

984 Aug. 1.   Ethelwold, B. of Winton.
1015 Jan. 22.   Brithwold, B. of Winton.

TENTH AND ELEVENTH CENTURIES
Missions

950 Feb. 15.   Sigfride, B., apostle of Sweden.
1016 June 12.   Eskill, B.M. in Sweden, kinsman of St. Sigfride.
1028 Jan. 18.   Wolfred, M. in Sweden.
1050 July 15.   David, A., Cluniac in Sweden.

ELEVENTH CENTURY

1012 April 19.   Elphege, M. Archb. of Canterbury.
1016 May. 30.   Walston, C. near Norwich.
1053 Mar. 35.   Alfwold, B. of Sherborne.
1067 Sept. 2.   William, B. of Roschid in Denmark.
1066 Jan. 5.   Edward, K.C.
1099 Dec. 4.   Osmund, B. of Salisbury.

ELEVENTH AND TWELFTH CENTURIES

1095 Jan. 19.   Wulstan, B. of Worcester.
1089 May 28.   *Lanfranc, Archb. of Canterbury.*
1109 Apr. 21.   Anselm, Doctor, Archb. of Canterbury.
1170 Dec. 29.   Thomas, Archb. M. of Canterbury.
1200 Nov. 17.   Hugh, B. of Lincoln, Carthusian Monk.

TWELFTH CENTURY
Part I

1109   *Ingulphus, A. of Croyland.*
1117 Apr. 30.   B. Maud, *Q.* Wife of Henry I.
1124 Apr. 13.   Caradoc, H. in South Wales.
1127 Jan. 16.   Henry, H. in Northumberland.
1144 Mar. 25.   William, M. of Norwich.
1151 Jan. 19.   Henry, M.B. of Upsal.
1150 Aug. 13.   Walter, A. of Fontenelle, in France.
1154 June 8.   William, Archb. of York.
1170 May 21.   Godric, H. in Durham.
1180 Oct. 25.   *John of Salisbury, B. of Chartres.*
1182 June 24.   Bartholomew, C., monk at Durham.
1189 Feb. 4.   Gilbert, A. of Sempringham.
1190 Aug. 21.   Richard, B. of Andria.
1200   *Peter de Blois, Archd. of Bath.*

406 Notes

TWELFTH CENTURY
Part II. — Cistertian Order

1134 Apr. 17.	Stephen, A. of Citeaux.
1139 June 7.	Robert, A. of Newminster in Northumberland.
1154 Feb. 20.	Ulric, H. in Dorsetshire.
1160 Aug. 3.	Walthen, A. of Melrose.
1166 Jan. 12.	Aelred, A. of Rieval.

THIRTEENTH CENTURY
Part I

1228 July 9.	*Stephen Langton, Archb. of Canterbury.*
1242 Nov. 16.	Edmund, Archb. of Canterbury.
1253 Apr. 3.	Richard, B. of Chichester.
1282 Oct. 2.	Thomas, B. of Hereford.
1294 Dec. 3.	*John Peckham, Archb. of Canterbury.*

THIRTEENTH CENTURY
Part II. — Orders of Friars

1217 June 17.	John, Fr., Trinitarian.
1232 Mar. 7.	William, Fr., Franciscan.
1240 Jan. 31.	Serapion, Fr., M., Redemptionist.
1265 May 16.	Simon Stock, H., General of the Carmelites.
1279 Sept. 11.	*Robert Kilwardby, Archb. of Canterbury, Fr. Dominican.*

THIRTEENTH CENTURY
Part III

1239 Mar. 14.	Robert H. at Knaresboro'.
1241 Oct. 1.	Roger, B. of London.
1255 July 27.	Hugh, M. of Lincoln.
1295 Aug. 5.	Thomas, Mo., M. of Dover.
1254 Oct. 9.	*Robert Grossteste, B. of Lincoln.*
1270 July 14.	Boniface, Archb. of Canterbury.
1278 Oct. 18.	*Walter de Merton, B. of Rochester.*

FOURTEENTH CENTURY

1326 Oct. 5.	*Stapleton, B. of Exeter.*
1327 Sept. 21.	*Edward K.*
1349 Sept. 29.	*B. Richard, H. of Hampole.*
1345 Apr. 14.	*Richard of Bury, B. of Lincoln.*

Note D. Series of Saints' Lives of 1843–4   407

1349 Aug. 26.	*Bradwardine, Archb. of Canterbury, the Doctor Profundus.*
1358 Sept. 2.	*William, Fr., Servite.*
1379 Oct. 10.	*John, C. of Bridlington.*
1324–1404 Sept. 27.	*William of Wykeham, B. of Winton.*
	William, Fr. Austin.

FIFTEENTH CENTURY

1471 May 22.	*Henry, K. of England.*
1486 Aug. 11.	*William of Wanefleet, B. of Winton.*
1509 June 29.	*Margaret, Countess of Richmond.*
1528 Sept. 14.	*Richard Fox, B. of Winton.*

Note E. On Page 312

The Anglican Church[1]

I have been bringing out my mind in this Volume on every subject which has come before me; and therefore I am bound to state plainly what I feel and have felt, since I was a Catholic, about the Anglican Church. I said, in a former page, that, on my conversion, I was not conscious of any change in me of thought or feeling, as regards matters of doctrine; this, however, was not the case as regards some matters of fact, and, unwilling as I am to give offence to religious Anglicans, I am bound to confess that I felt a great change in my view of the Church of England. I cannot tell how soon there came on me, — but very soon, — an extreme astonishment that I had ever imagined it to be a portion of the Catholic Church. For the first time, I looked at it from without, and (as I should myself say) saw it as it was. Forthwith I could not get myself to see in it any thing else, than what I had so long fearfully suspected, from as far back as 1836, — a mere national institution. As if my eyes were suddenly opened, so I saw it — spontaneously, apart from any definite act of reason or any argument; and so I have seen it ever since. I suppose, the main cause of this lay in the contrast which was presented to me by the Catholic Church. Then I recognized at once a reality which was quite a new thing with me. Then I was

---

1. See the introduction to this volume and the preface to Newman's notes for the contemporary implications of this note.

sensible that I was not making for myself a Church by an effort of thought; I needed not to make an act of faith in her; I had not painfully to force myself into a position, but my mind fell back upon itself in relaxation and in peace, and I gazed at her almost passively as a great objective fact. I looked at her;— at her rites, her ceremonial, and her precepts; and I said, "This *is* a religion;" and then, when I looked back upon the poor Anglican Church, for which I had laboured so hard, and upon all that appertained to it, and thought of our various attempts to dress it up doctrinally and esthetically, it seemed to me to be the veriest of nonentities.

Vanity of vanities, all is vanity! How can I made a record of what passed within me, without seeming to be satirical? But I speak plain, serious words. As people call me credulous for acknowledging Catholic claims, so they call me satirical for disowning Anglican pretensions; to them it *is* credulity, to them it *is* satire; but it is not so in me. What they think exaggeration, I think truth. I am not speaking of the Anglican Church with any disdain, though to them I seem contemptuous. To them of course it is "Aut Cæsar aut nullus," but not to me. It may be a great creation, though it be not divine, and this is how I judge of it. Men, who abjure the divine right of kings, would be very indignant, if on that account they were considered disloyal. And so I recognize in the Anglican Church a time-honoured institution, of noble historical memories, a monument of ancient wisdom, a momentous arm of political strength, a great national organ, a source of vast popular advantage, and, to a certain point, a witness and teacher of religious truth. I do not think that, if what I have written about it since I have been a Catholic, be equitably considered as a whole, I shall be found to have taken any other view than this: but that it is something sacred, that it is an oracle of revealed doctrine, that it can claim a share in St. Ignatius or St. Cyprian, that it can take the rank, contest the teaching, and stop the path of the Church of St. Peter, that it can call itself "the Bride of the Lamb," this is the view of it which simply disappeared from my mind on my conversion, and which it would be almost a miracle to reproduce. "I went by, and lo! it was gone; I sought it, but its place could no where be found;" and nothing can bring it back to me. And, as to its possession of an episcopal succession from the time of the Apostles, well, it may have it, and, if the Holy See ever so decide, I will believe it, as being the decision of a higher judgment than my own;[2] but, for myself, I must have St. Philip's gift, who saw the sacerdotal character on the forehead of a gaily-attired youngster, before I

---

2. On the subsequent rejection of the validity of Anglican orders see John Jay Hughes, *Absolutely Null and Utterly Void: The Papal Condemnation of Anglican Orders, 1896* (Washington, D.C.: Corpus Books, 1968).

can by my own wit acquiesce in it, for antiquarian arguments are altogether unequal to the urgency of visible facts. Why is it that I must pain dear friends by saying so, and kindle a sort of resentment against me in the kindest of hearts? but I must, though to do it be not only a grief to me, but most impolitic at the moment. Any how, this is my mind; and, if to have it, if to have betrayed it, before now, involuntarily by my words or my deeds, if on a fitting occasion, as now, to have avowed it, if all this be a proof of the justice of the charge brought against me by my accuser of having "turned round upon my Mother-Church with contumely and slander," in this sense, but in no other sense, do I plead guilty to it without a word in extenuation.

In no other sense surely; the Church of England has been the instrument of Providence in conferring great benefits on me; — had I been born in Dissent, perhaps I should never have been baptized;[3] had I been born an English Presbyterian, perhaps I should never have known our Lord's divinity; had I not come to Oxford, perhaps I never should have heard of the visible Church, or of Tradition, or other Catholic doctrines. And as I have received so much good from the Anglican Establishment itself, can I have the heart or rather the want of charity, considering that it does for so many others, what it has done for me, to wish to see it overthrown? I have no such wish while it is what it is, and while we are so small a body. Not for its own sake, but for the sake of the many congregations to which it ministers, I will do nothing against it. While Catholics are so weak in England, it is doing our work; and, though it does us harm in a measure, at present the balance is in our favour. What our duty would be at another time and in other circumstances, supposing, for instance, the Establishment lost its dogmatic faith, or at least did not preach it, is another matter altogether. In secular history we read of hostile nations having long truces, and renewing them from time to time, and that seems to be the position which the Catholic Church may fairly take up at present in relation to the Anglican Establishment.

Doubtless the National Church has hitherto been a serviceable breakwater against doctrinal errors, more fundamental than its own.[4] How long this will last in the years now before us, it is impossible to say, for the Nation drags down its Church to its own level; but still the National Church has the same sort of influence over the Nation that a periodical has upon the party which it

---

3. It should be noted that at the time of his reception into the Roman Catholic Church in October 1845, Newman received a conditional baptism from Father Dominic. He does not report this event in the *Apologia*.

4. See remarks on this note in the editor's preface to Newman's notes above and note 47 of the introduction to this volume.

represents, and my own idea of a Catholic's fitting attitude towards the National Church in this its supreme hour, is that of assisting and sustaining it, if it be in our power, in the interest of dogmatic truth. I should wish to avoid every thing (except indeed under the direct call of duty, and this is a material exception,) which went to weaken its hold upon the public mind, or to unsettle its establishment, or to embarrass and lessen its maintenance of those great Christian and Catholic principles and doctrines which it has up to this time successfully preached.

Note F. On Page 343.

The Economy[1]

For the Economy, considered as a rule of practice, I shall refer to what I wrote upon it in 1830–32, in my History of the Arians.[2] I have shown above, pp. 163–164, that the doctrine in question had in the early Church a large signification, when applied to the divine ordinances: it also had a definite application to the duties of Christians, whether clergy or laity, in preaching, in instructing or catechizing, or in ordinary intercourse with the world around them; and in this aspect I have here to consider it.

As Almighty God did not all at once introduce the Gospel to the world, and thereby gradually prepared men for its profitable reception, so, according to

---

1. See the introduction to this volume for the broad issues discussed in this note.

2. Newman had first considered this topic in his *Arians of the Fourth Century, Their Doctrine, Temper, and Conduct, Chiefly as Exhibited in the Councils of the Church, between A.D. 325, & A.D. 381* (London: J. G. & F. Rivington, 1833). Because that volume appeared at the same time as the first of the *Tracts for the Times*, contemporaries regarded its contents as a commentary on the goals and tactics of the Tractarian Movement. In it Newman had discussed the concept and practice of a *Disciplina Arcani* whereby certain Christian truths were withheld from people young or inexperienced in the faith. The association of this idea with the Tractarians led many contemporaries to believe that they were less than honest and forthcoming in their public statements and publications.

the doctrine of the early Church, it was a duty, for the sake of the heathen among whom they lived, to observe a great reserve and caution in communicating to them the knowledge of "the whole counsel of God." This cautious dispensation of the truth, after the manner of a discreet and vigilant steward, is denoted by the word "economy." It is a mode of acting which comes under the head of Prudence, one of the four Cardinal Virtues.

The principle of the Economy is this; that out of various courses, in religious conduct or statement, all and each *allowable antecedently and in themselves,* that ought to be taken which is most expedient and most suitable at the time for the object in hand.

Instances of its application and exercise in Scripture are such as the following: — 1. Divine Providence did but gradually impart to the world in general, and to the Jews in particular, the knowledge of His will: — He is said to have "winked at the times of ignorance among the heathen;" and He suffered in the Jews divorce "because of the hardness of their hearts." 2. He has allowed Himself to be represented as having eyes, ears, and hands, as having wrath, jealousy, grief, and repentance. 3. In like manner, our Lord spoke harshly to the Syro-Phœnician woman, whose daughter He was about to heal, and made as if He would go further, when the two disciples had come to their journey's end. 4. Thus too Joseph "made himself strange to his brethren," and Elisha kept silence on request of Naaman to bow in the house of Rimmon. 5. Thus St. Paul circumcised Timothy, while he cried out "Circumcision availeth not."

It may be said that this principle, true in itself, yet is dangerous, because it admits of an easy abuse, and carries men away into what becomes insincerity and cunning. This is undeniable; to do evil that good may come, to consider that the means, whatever they are, justify the end, to sacrifice truth to expedience, unscrupulousness, recklessness, are grave offences. These are abuses of the Economy. But to call them *economical* is to give a fine name to what occurs every day, independent of any knowledge of the *doctrine* of the Economy. It is the abuse of a rule which nature suggests to every one. Every one looks out for the "mollia tempora fandi," and for "mollia verba" too.[3]

Having thus explained what is meant by the Economy as a rule of social intercourse between men of different religious, or, again, political, or social views, next I will go on to state what I said in the Arians.

I say in that Volume first, that our Lord has given us the *principle* in His own words, — "Cast not your pearls before swine;" and that He exemplified it in His teaching by parables; that St. Paul expressly distinguishes between the

---

3. "proper moment for speaking, and for proper words," Aeneid 4:293–294.

milk which is necessary to one set of men, and the strong meat which is allowed to others, and that, in two Epistles. I say, that the Apostles in the Acts observe the same rule in their speeches, for it is a fact, that they do not preach the high doctrines of Christianity, but only "Jesus and the Resurrection" or "repentance and faith." I also say, that this is the very reason that the Fathers assign for the silence of various writers in the first centuries on the subject of our Lord's divinity. I also speak of the catechetical system practised in the early Church, and the *disciplina arcani* as regards the doctrine of the Holy Trinity, to which Bingham bears witness;[4] also of the defence of this rule by Basil, Cyril of Jerusalem, Chrysostom, and Theodoret.

But next the question may be asked, whether I have said any thing in my Volume *to guard* the doctrine, thus laid down, from the abuse to which it is obviously exposed: and my answer is easy. Of course, had I had any idea that I should have been exposed to such hostile misrepresentations, as it has been my lot to undergo on the subject, I should have made more direct avowals than I have done of my sense of the gravity and the danger of that abuse. Since I could not foresee when I wrote, that I should have been wantonly slandered, I only wonder that I have anticipated the charge as fully as will be seen in the following extracts.

For instance, speaking of the Disciplina Arcani, I say: — (1) "The elementary information given to the heathen or catechumen was *in no sense undone* by the subsequent secret teaching, which was in fact but the *filling up of a bare but correct outline*," p. 58,[5] and I contrast this with the conduct of the Manichæns "who represented the initiatory discipline as founded on a *fiction* or hypothesis, which was to be forgotten by the learner as he made progress in the *real* doctrine of the Gospel." (2) As to allegorizing, I say that the Alexandrians erred, whenever and as far as they proceeded "to *obscure* the primary meaning of Scripture, and to *weaken the force of historical facts* and express declarations," p. 69. (3) And that they were "more open to *censure*," when, on being "*urged by objections* to various passages in the history of the Old Testament, as derogatory to the divine perfections or to the Jewish Saints, they had *recourse to an allegorical explanation by way of answer*," p. 71. (4) I add, "*It is impossible to defend such a procedure*, which seems to imply a *want of faith* in those who had recourse to it;" for "God has given us *rules of right and wrong*,"

---

4. Joseph Bingham (1668–1723) was the author of a ten-volume work titled *Origines Ecclesiasticae, or, the Antiquities of the Christian Church* published in the early eighteenth-century.

5. The source of these quotations as paginated in the text is Newman, *Arians of the Fourth Century*.

ibid. (5) Again, I say, — "The *abuse of the Economy* in *the hands of unscrupulous reasoners,* is obvious. *Even the honest* controversialist or teacher will find it very difficult to represent, *without misrepresenting,* what it is yet his duty to present to his hearers with caution or reserve. Here the obvious rule to guide our practice is, to be careful ever to maintain *substantial truth* in our use of the economical method," pp. 79, 80. (6) And so far from concurring at all hazards with Justin, Gregory, or Athanasius, I say, "It *is plain* [they] *were justified or not* in their Economy, *according* as they did or did not *practically mislead their opponents,*" p. 80. (7) I proceed, "It is so difficult to hit the mark in these perplexing cases, that it is not wonderful, should these or other Fathers have failed at times, and said more or less than was proper," *ibid.*

The Principle of the Economy is familiarly acted on among us every day. When we would persuade others, we do not begin by treading on their toes. Men would be thought rude who introduced their own religious notions into mixed society, and were devotional in a drawing-room. Have we never thought lawyers tiresome who did *not* observe this polite rule, who came down for the assizes and talked law all through dinner? Does the same argument tell in the House of Commons, on the hustings, and at Exeter Hall?[6] Is an educated gentleman never worsted at an election by the tone and arguments of some clever fellow, who, whatever his shortcomings in other respects, understands the common people?

As to the Catholic Religion in England at the present day, this only will I observe, — that the truest expedience is to answer right out, when you are asked; that the wisest economy is to have no management; that the best prudence is not to be a coward; that the most damaging folly is to be found out shuffling; and that the first of virtues is to "tell truth, and shame the devil."[7]

---

6. Exeter Hall was the structure in London where numerous evangelical gatherings took place.
7. Shakespeare, *Henry IV,* pt. I, III, i. 62.

Note G. On Page 350.

Lying and Equivocation[1]

Almost all authors, Catholic and Protestant, admit, that *when a just cause is present,* there is some kind or other of verbal misleading, which is not sin. Even silence is in certain cases virtually such a misleading, according to the Proverb, "Silence gives consent." Again, silence is absolutely forbidden to a Catholic, as a mortal sin, under certain circumstances, e. g. to keep silence, when it is a duty to make a profession of faith.

Another mode of verbal misleading, and the most direct, is actually saying the thing that is not; and it is defended on the principle that such words are not a lie, when there is a "justa causa," as killing is not murder in the case of an executioner.

Another ground of certain authors for saying that an untruth is not a lie where there is a just cause, is, that veracity is a kind of justice, and therefore, when we have no duty of justice to tell truth to another, it is no sin not to do so. Hence we may say the thing that is not, to children, to madmen, to men who ask impertinent questions, to those whom we hope to benefit by misleading.

Another ground, taken in defending certain untruths, *ex justâ causâ,* as if not lies, is, that veracity is for the sake of society, and that, if in no case

---

1. See the introduction to this volume for the broad issues discussed in this note.

whatever we might lawfully mislead others, we should actually be doing society great harm.

Another mode of verbal misleading is equivocation or a play upon words; and it is defended on the theory that to lie is to use words in a sense which they will not bear. But an equivocator uses them in a received sense, though there is another received sense, and therefore, according to this definition, he does not lie.

Others say that all equivocations are, after all, a kind of lying, — faint lies or awkward lies, but still lies; and some of these disputants infer, that therefore we must not equivocate, and others that equivocation is but a half-measure, and that it is better to say at once that in certain cases untruths are not lies.

Others will try to distinguish between evasions and equivocations; but though there are evasions which are clearly not equivocations, yet it is very difficult scientifically to draw the line between the one and the other.

To these must be added the unscientific way of dealing with lies: — viz. that on a great or cruel occasion a man cannot help telling a lie, and he would not be a man, did he not tell it, but still it is very wrong, and he ought not to do it, and he must trust that the sin will be forgiven him, though he goes about to commit it ever so deliberately, and is sure to commit it again under similar circumstances. It is a necessary frailty, and had better not be thought about before it is incurred, and not thought of again, after it is well over. This view cannot for a moment be defended, but, I suppose, it is very common.

I think the historical course of thought upon the matter has been this: the Greek Fathers thought that, when there was a *justa causa*, an untruth need not be a lie. St. Augustine took another view, though with great misgiving; and, whether he is rightly interpreted or not, is the doctor of the great and common view that all untruths are lies, and that there can be *no* just cause of untruth. In these later times, this doctrine has been found difficult to work, and it has been largely taught that, though all untruths are lies, yet that certain equivocations, when there is a just cause, are not untruths.

Further, there have been and all along through these later ages, other schools, running parallel with the above mentioned, one of which says that equivocations, &c. after all *are* lies, and another which says that there are untruths which are not lies.

And now as to the "just cause," which is the condition, *sine quâ non*. The Greek Fathers make it such as these, self-defence, charity, zeal for God's honour, and the like.

St. Augustine seems to deal with the same "just causes" as the Greek Fathers, even though he does not allow of their availableness as depriving untruths, spoken on such occasions, of their sinfulness. He mentions defence of life and of honour, and the safe custody of a secret. Also the great Anglican writers, who have followed the Greek Fathers, in defending untruths when there is the "just cause," consider that "just cause" to be such as the preservation of life and property, defence of law, the good of others. Moreover, their moral rights, e. g. defence against the inquisitive, &c.

St. Alfonso, I consider, would take the same view of the "justa causa" as the Anglican divines;[2] he speaks of it as "quicunque finis *honestus,* ad servanda bona spiritui vel corpori utilia;" which is very much the view which they take of it, judging by the instances which they give.

In all cases, however, and as contemplated by all authors, Clement of Alexandria, or Milton, or St. Alfonso, such a cause is, in fact, extreme, rare, great, or at least special. Thus the writer in the Mélanges Théologiques (Liège, 1852–3, p. 453) quotes Lessius:[3] "Si absque justa causa fiat, est abusio orationis contra virtutem veritatis, et civilem consuetudinem, etsi proprie non sit mendacium." That is, the virtue of truth, and the civil custom, are the *measure* of the just cause. And so Voit,[4] "If a man has used a reservation (restrictione non purè mentali) without a *grave* cause, he has sinned gravely." And so the author himself, from whom I quote, and who defends the Patristic and Anglican doctrine that there *are* untruths which are not lies, says, "Under the name of mental reservation theologians authorize many lies, *when there is for them a grave reason* and proportionate," i. e. to their character. —p. 459. And so St. Alfonso, in another Treatise, quotes St. Thomas to the effect, that if from one cause two immediate effects follow, and, if the good effect of that cause is *equal in value* to the bad effect (bonus *æquivalet* malo), then nothing hinders the speaker's intending the good and only permitting the evil. From which it will follow that, since the evil to society from lying is very great, the just cause which is to make it allowable, must be very great also. And so Kenrick:[5] "It is confessed by all Catholics that, in the common intercourse of life, all ambiguity of language is to be avoided; but it is debated whether such ambiguity is *ever* lawful. Most theologians answer in the affirmative, supposing a *grave*

2. See Josef L. Altholz, "Truth and Equivocation: Liguori's Moral Theology and Newman's *Apologia," Church History* 44 (1975): 73–84.

3. *Mélanges Théologiques* was a Belgian journal. Leonard Lessius (1554–1623) was a Jesuit professor at the University of Louvain.

4. Edmund Voit was a Jesuit writer of the eighteenth century.

5. Francis P. Kenrick (1797–1863) was an American Roman Catholic writer and prelate.

cause urges, and the [true] mind of the speaker can be collected from the adjuncts, though in fact it be not collected."

However, there are cases, I have already said, of another kind, in which Anglican authors would think a lie allowable; such as when a question is *impertinent*. Of such a case Walter Scott, if I mistake not, supplied a very distinct example, in his denying so long the authorship of his novels.

What I have been saying shows what different schools of opinion there are in the Church in the treatment of this difficult doctrine; and, by consequence, that a given individual, such as I am, *cannot* agree with all of them, and has a full right to follow which of them he will. The freedom of the Schools, indeed, is one of those rights of reason, which the Church is too wise really to interfere with. And this applies not to moral questions only, but to dogmatic also.

It is supposed by Protestants that, because St. Alfonso's writings have had such high commendation bestowed upon them by authority, therefore they have been invested with a quasi-infallibility. This has arisen in good measure from Protestants not knowing the force of theological terms. The words to which they refer are the authoritative decision that "nothing in his works has been found *worthy of censure*," "censurâ dignum;" but this does not lead to the conclusions which have been drawn from it. Those words occur in a legal document, and cannot be interpreted except in a legal sense. In the first place, the sentence is negative; nothing in St. Alfonso's writings is positively approved; and, secondly, it is not said that there are no faults in what he has written, but nothing which comes under the ecclesiastical *censura*, which is something very definite. To take and interpret them, in the way commonly adopted in England, is the same mistake, as if one were to take the word "Apologia" in the English sense of apology, or "Infant" in law to mean a little child.

1. Now first as to the meaning of the above form of words viewed as a proposition. When a question on the subject was asked of the fitting authorities at Rome by the Archbishop of Besançon, the answer returned to him contained this condition, viz. that those words were to be interpreted, "with due regard to the mind of the Holy See concerning the approbation of writings of the servants of God, ad effectum Canonizationis." This is intended to prevent any Catholic taking the words about St. Alfonso's works in too large a sense. Before a Saint is canonized, his works are examined, and a judgment pronounced upon them. Pope Benedict XIV. says, "The *end* or *scope* of this judgment is, that it may appear, whether the doctrine of the servant of God, which he has brought out in his writings, is free from any soever *theological censure*." And he remarks in addition, "It never can be said that the doctrine of

a servant of God is *approved* by the Holy See, but at most it can [only] be said that it is not disapproved (non reprobatam) in case that the Revisers had reported that there is nothing found by them in his works, which is adverse to the decrees of Urban VIII., and that the judgment of the Revisers has been approved by the sacred Congregation, and confirmed by the Supreme Pontiff." The Decree of Urban VIII. here referred to is, "Let works be examined, whether they contain errors against faith or good morals (bonos mores), or any new doctrine, or a doctrine foreign and alien to the common sense and custom of the Church." The author from whom I quote this (M. Vandenbroeck, of the diocese of Malines)[6] observes, "It is therefore clear, that the approbation of the works of the Holy Bishop touches not the truth of every proposition, adds nothing to them, nor even gives them by consequence a degree of intrinsic probability." He adds that it gives St. Alfonso's theology an extrinsic probability, from the fact that, in the judgment of the Holy See, no proposition deserves to receive a censure; but that "that probability will cease nevertheless in a particular case, for any one who should be convinced, whether by evident arguments, or by a decree of the Holy See, or otherwise, that the doctrine of the Saint deviates from the truth." He adds, "From the fact that the approbation of the works of St. Alfonso does not decide the truth of each proposition, it follows, as Benedict XIV. has remarked, that we may combat the doctrine which they contain; only, since a canonized saint is in question, who is honoured by a solemn *culte* in the Church, we ought not to speak except with respect, nor to attack his opinions except with temper and modesty."

2. Then, as to the meaning of the word *censura:* Benedict XIV. enumerates a number of "Notes" which come under that name; he says, "Out of propositions which are to be noted with theological censure, some are heretical, some erroneous, some close upon error, some savouring of heresy," and so on; and each of these terms has its own definite meaning. Thus by "erroneous" is meant, according to Viva,[7] a proposition which is not *immediately* opposed to a revealed proposition, but only to a theological *conclusion* drawn from premisses which are *de fide;* "savouring of heresy is" a proposition, which is opposed to a theological conclusion not evidently drawn from premisses which are *de fide,* but most probably and according to the common mode of theologizing; — and so with the rest. Therefore when it was said by the Re-

---

6. M. Vandenbroeck was a Roman Catholic priest and writer who lived in Malines, Belgium.
7. Dominico Viva (1648–1726) was an Italian Jesuit theologian.

visers of St. Alfonso's works that they were not "worthy of *censure*," it was only meant that they did not fall under these particular Notes.

But the answer from Rome to the Archbishop of Besançon went further than this; it actually took pains to declare that any one who pleased might follow other theologians instead of St. Alfonso. After saying that no Priest was to be interfered with who followed St. Alfonso in the Confessional, it added, "This is said, however, without on that account judging that they are reprehended who follow opinions handed down by other approved authors."

And this too I will observe, — that St. Alfonso made many changes of opinion himself in the course of his writings; and it could not for an instant be supposed that we were bound to every one of his opinions, when he did not feel himself bound to them in his own person. And, what is more to the purpose still, there are opinions, or some opinion, of his which actually have been proscribed by the Church since, and cannot now be put forward or used. I do not pretend to be a well-read theologian myself, but I say this on the authority of a theological professor of Breda, quoted in the Mélanges Théol. for 1850-1. He says: "It may happen, that, in the course of time, errors may be found in the works of St. Alfonso and be proscribed by the Church, *a thing which in fact has already occurred.*"

In not ranging myself then with those who consider that it is justifiable to use words in a double sense, that is, to equivocate, I put myself under the protection of such authors as Cardinal Gerdil, Natalis Alexander, Contenson, Concina, and others.[8] Under the protection of these authorities, I say as follows: —

Casuistry is a noble science, but it is one to which I am led, neither by my abilities nor my turn of mind. Independently, then, of the difficulties of the subject, and the necessity, before forming an opinion, of knowing more of the arguments of theologians upon it than I do, I am very unwilling to say a word here on the subject of Lying and Equivocation. But I consider myself bound to speak; and therefore, in this strait, I can do nothing better, even for my own relief, than submit myself, and what I shall say, to the judgment of the Church, and to the consent, so far as in this matter there be a consent, of the Schola Theologorum.

Now in the case of one of those special and rare exigencies or emergencies, which constitute the *justa causa* of dissembling or misleading, whether it be

---

8. Vincent Contenson (1641–1674) and Daniello Concina (1687–1756) were Dominican theologians.

extreme as the defence of life, or a duty as the custody of a secret, or of a personal nature as to repel an impertinent inquirer, or a matter too trivial to provoke question, as in dealing with children or madmen, there seem to be four courses: —

1. *To say the thing that is not.* Here I draw the reader's attention to the words *material* and *formal.* "Thou shalt not kill;" *murder* is the *formal* transgression of this commandment, but *accidental homicide* is the *material* transgression. The *matter* of the act is the same in both cases; but in the *homicide,* there is nothing more than the act, whereas in *murder* there must be the intention, &c., which constitutes the formal sin. So, again, an executioner commits the material act, but not that formal killing which is a breach of the commandment. So a man, who, simply to save himself from starving, takes a loaf which is not his own, commits only the material, not the formal act of stealing, that is, he does not commit a sin. And so a baptized Christian, external to the Church, who is in invincible ignorance, is a material heretic, and not a formal. And in like manner, if to say the thing which is not be in special cases lawful, it may be called a *material lie.*

The first mode then which has been suggested of meeting those special cases, in which to mislead by words has a sufficient occasion, or has a *just cause,* is by a material lie.

The second mode is by an *æquivocatio,* which is not equivalent to the English word "equivocation," but means sometimes a *play upon words,* sometimes an *evasion:* we must take these two modes of misleading separately.

2. *A play upon words.* St. Alfonso certainly says that a play upon words is allowable; and, speaking under correction, I should say that he does so on the ground that lying is *not* a sin against justice, that is, against our neighbour, but a sin against God. God has made words the signs of ideas, and therefore if a word denotes two ideas, we are at liberty to use it in either of its senses: but I think I must be incorrect in some respect in supposing that the Saint does not recognize a lie as an injustice, because the Catechism of the Council, as I have quoted it at p. 352, says, "Vanitate et mendacio fides ac veritas tolluntur, arctissima vincula *societatis humanæ;* quibus sublatis, sequitur summa vitæ confusio, ut *homines nihil a dæmonibus differre videantur.*"

3. *Evasion;* — when, for instance, the speaker diverts the attention of the hearer to another subject; suggests an irrelevant fact or makes a remark, which confuses him and gives him something to think about; throws dust into his eyes; states some truth, from which he is quite sure his hearer will draw an illogical and untrue conclusion, and the like.

The greatest school of evasion, I speak seriously, is the House of Commons; and necessarily so, from the nature of the case. And the hustings is another.

An instance is supplied in the history of St. Athanasius: he was in a boat on the Nile, flying persecution; and he found himself pursued. On this he ordered his men to turn his boat round, and ran right to meet the satellites of Julian. They asked him, "Have you seen Athanasius?" and he told his followers to answer, "Yes, he is close to you." *They* went on their course as if they were sure to come up to him, while *he* ran back into Alexandria, and there lay hid till the end of the persecution.

I gave another instance above, in reference to a doctrine of religion. The early Christians did their best to conceal their Creed on account of the misconceptions of the heathen about it. Were the question asked of them, "Do you worship a Trinity?" and did they answer, "We worship one God, and none else;" the inquirer might, or would, infer that they did not acknowledge the Trinity of Divine Persons.

It is very difficult to draw the line between these evasions and what are commonly called in English *equivocations;* and of this difficulty, again, I think, the scenes in the House of Commons supply us with illustrations.

4. The fourth method is *silence*. For instance, not giving the *whole* truth in a court of law. If St. Alban,[9] after dressing himself in the Priest's clothes, and being taken before the persecutor, had been able to pass off for his friend, and so gone to martyrdom without being discovered; and had he in the course of examination answered all questions truly, but not given the whole truth, the most important truth, that he was the wrong person, he would have come very near to telling a lie, for a half-truth is often a falsehood. And his defence must have been the *justa causa,* viz. either that he might in charity or for religion's sake save a priest, or again that the judge had no right to interrogate him on the subject.

Now, of these four modes of misleading others by the tongue, when there is a *justa causa* (supposing there can be such), — (1) a material lie, that is, an untruth which is not a lie, (2) an equivocation, (3) an evasion, and (4) silence, — First, I have no difficulty whatever in recognizing as allowable the method of *silence*.

Secondly, But, if I allow of *silence*, why not of the method of *material lying,* since half of a truth *is* often a lie? And, again, if all killing be not murder, nor all taking from another stealing, why must all untruths be lies? Now I will say freely that I think it difficult to answer this question, whether it be urged by St. Clement or by Milton; at the same time, I never have acted, and I think, when it came to the point, I never should act upon such a theory myself, except in one case, stated below. This I say for the benefit of those who speak hardly of

---

9. St. Alban (d. 304) was the first Christian martyr in the British Isles.

Catholic theologians, on the ground that they admit text-books which allow of equivocation. They are asked, how can we trust you, when such are your views? but such views, as I already have said, need not have any thing to do with their own practice, merely from the circumstance that they are contained in their text-books. A theologian draws out a system; he does it partly as a scientific speculation: but much more for the sake of others. He is lax for the sake of others, not of himself. His own standard of action is much higher than that which he imposes upon men in general. One special reason why religious men, after drawing out a theory, are unwilling to act upon it themselves, is this: that they practically acknowledge a broad distinction between their reason and their conscience; and that they feel the latter to be the safer guide, though the former may be the clearer, nay even though it be the truer. They would rather be in error with the sanction of their conscience, than be right with the mere judgment of their reason. And again here is this more tangible difficulty in the case of exceptions to the rule of Veracity, that so very little external help is given us in drawing the line, as to when untruths are allowable and when not; whereas that sort of killing which is not murder, is most definitely marked off by legal enactments, so that it cannot possibly be mistaken for such killing as *is* murder. On the other hand the cases of exemption from the rule of Veracity are left to the private judgment of the individual, and he may easily be led on from acts which are allowable to acts which are not. Now this remark does *not* apply to such acts as are related in Scripture, as being done by a particular inspiration, for in such cases there *is* a command. If I had my own way, I would oblige society, that is, its great men, its lawyers, its divines, its literature, publicly to acknowledge as such, those instances of untruth which are not lies, as for instance untruths in war; and then there could be no perplexity to the individual Catholic, for he would not be taking the law into his own hands.

Thirdly, as to playing upon words, or equivocation, I suppose it is from the English habit, but, without meaning any disrespect to a great Saint, or wishing to set myself up, or taking my conscience for more than it is worth, I can only say as a fact, that I admit it as little as the rest of my countrymen: and, without any reference to the right and the wrong of the matter, of this I am sure, that, if there is one thing more than another which prejudices Englishmen against the Catholic Church, it is the doctrine of great authorities on the subject of equivocation. For myself, I can fancy myself thinking it was allowable in extreme cases for me to lie, but never to equivocate. Luther said, "Pecca fortiter." I anathematize his formal sentiment, but there is a truth in it, when spoken of material acts.

Fourthly, I think *evasion*, as I have described it, to be perfectly allowable;

indeed, I do not know, who does not use it, under circumstances; but that a good deal of moral danger is attached to its use; and that, the cleverer a man is, the more likely he is to pass the line of Christian duty.

But it may be said, that such decisions do not meet the particular difficulties for which provision is required; let us then take some instances.

1. I do not think it right to tell lies to children, even on this account, that they are sharper than we think them, and will soon find out what we are doing; and our example will be a very bad training for them. And so of equivocation: it is easy of imitation, and we ourselves shall be sure to get the worst of it in the end.

2. If an early Father defends the patriarch Jacob in his mode of gaining his father's blessing, on the ground that the blessing was divinely pledged to him already, that it was his, and that his father and brother were acting at once against his own rights and the divine will, it does not follow from this that such conduct is a pattern to us, who have no supernatural means of determining *when* an untruth becomes a *material,* and not a *formal* lie. It seems to me very dangerous, be it ever allowable or not, to lie or equivocate in order to preserve some great temporal or spiritual benefit; nor does St. Alfonso here say any thing to the contrary, for he is not discussing the question of danger or expedience.

3. As to Johnson's case of a murderer asking you which way a man had gone, I should have anticipated that, had such a difficulty happened to him, his first act would have been to knock the man down, and to call out for the police; and next, if he was worsted in the conflict, he would not have given the ruffian the information he asked, at whatever risk to himself. I think he would have let himself be killed first. I do not think that he would have told a lie.

4. A secret is a more difficult case. Supposing something has been confided to me in the strictest secrecy, which could not be revealed without great disadvantage to another, what am I to do? If I am a lawyer, I am protected by my profession. I have a right to treat with extreme indignation any question which trenches on the inviolability of my position; but, supposing I was driven up into a corner, I think I should have a right to say an untruth, or that, under such circumstances, a lie would be *material,* but it is almost an impossible case, for the law would defend me. In like manner, as a priest, I should think it lawful to speak as if I knew nothing of what passed in confession. And I think in these cases, I do in fact possess that guarantee, that I am not going by private judgment, which just now I demanded; for society would bear me out, whether as a lawyer or as a priest, in holding that I had a duty to my client or penitent, such, that an untruth in the matter was not a lie. A common type of this permissible denial, be it *material lie* or *evasion,* is at the moment supplied

to me: — an artist asked a Prime Minister, who was sitting to him, "What news, my Lord, from France?" He answered, "*I do not know;* I have not read the Papers."

5. A more difficult question is, when to accept confidence has not been a duty. Supposing a man wishes to keep the secret that he is the author of a book, and he is plainly asked on the subject. Here I should ask the previous question, whether any one has a right to publish what he dare not avow. It requires to have traced the bearings and results of such a principle, before being sure of it; but certainly, for myself, I am no friend of strictly anonymous writing. Next, supposing another has confided to you the secret of his authorship: — there are persons who would have no scruple at all in giving a denial to impertinent questions asked them on the subject. I have heard a great man in his day at Oxford, warmly contend, as if he could not enter into any other view of the matter, that, if he had been trusted by a friend with the secret of his being author of a certain book, and he were asked by a third person, if his friend was not (as he really was) the author of it, he ought, without any scruple and distinctly, to answer that he did not know. He had an existing duty towards the author; he had none towards his inquirer. The author had a claim on him; an impertinent questioner had none at all. But here again I desiderate some leave, recognized by society, as in the case of the formulas "Not at home," and "Not guilty," in order to give me the right of saying what is a *material* untruth. And moreover, I should here also ask the previous question, Have I any right to accept such a confidence? have I any right to make such a promise? and, if it be an unlawful promise, is it binding when it cannot be kept without a lie? I am not attempting to solve these difficult questions, but they have to be carefully examined. And now I have said more than I had intended on a question of casuistry.

Editor's Preface to Newman's Supplemental Matter

In 1865 Newman included four items under the title "Supplemental Matter." The first two selections—a list of Newman's letters that he quoted in the course of his narrative and a list of his published works—provided necessary references for his readers. The letters may now be checked against the relevant volumes of *The Letters and Diaries of John Henry Newman*. The standard guide to his publications is Vincent Ferrer Blehl's *John Henry Newman: A Bibliographical Catalogue of His Writings* (Charlottesville: University Press of Virginia, 1978).

The other two parts of the "Supplemental Matter" require a brief comment. They are integral to Newman's goal of using his autobiographical narrative to establish his own theological and ecclesiastical position in the English Roman Catholic Church. As noted in the introduction to this volume, one of Newman's intentions in undertaking the *Apologia* was to reestablish his credentials for Catholic loyalty and faithfulness among English Roman Catholics and among critical circles in Rome. In particular, he had employed the final section of the *Apologia* to assert a broad spectrum for acceptable and tolerated theological opinion among Roman Catholics. He knew that ultramontanes, such as Henry Edward Manning and W. G. Ward, would reject his assertions, as might certain people in Rome.

First, Newman sought to protect himself against ultramontane criticism by publishing a letter of commendation from W. B. Ullathorne, his Roman Catholic bishop in Birmingham. That letter, dated June 2, 1864, functioned as an imprimatur for Newman's first, pamphlet edition of the *Apologia*. He received similar approval for his second edition. Newman attached much importance to this support. By publishing Ullathorne's letter in 1865 and then in every subsequent edition of the *Apologia*, Newman wrapped the book and its controversial opinions in the protection of Roman Catholic episcopal approval. For more information on Ullathorne's efforts to protect Newman, see note 71 of the introduction to this volume.

Second, the "Letters of Approbation and Encouragement from Clergy and Laity," which Newman had received in the course of 1864 during the direct conflict with Kingsley and the publication of the pamphlet edition of the *Apologia*, served a similar function. They originated overwhelmingly among groups of Old Catholics, with only a few from Anglican converts to the Roman Catholic Church. These English Roman Catholics generally resisted the goals of the ultramontanes and the movement toward ever-increasing papal authority in the Roman Church. By citing their confidence in the integrity of Newman's Roman Catholic faith, their admiration for his defense of the honesty of Roman Catholic clergy, and his enunciation of considerable freedom for Roman Catholics in theological matters, these letters demonstrated to other English Roman Catholics that Newman stood in what many in the church regarded as the mainstream. Such letters of confidence made it much more difficult for Newman's ultramontane critics and enemies to isolate him as an eccentric or unorthodox voice in the church when so many other clergy saw him as a powerful and effective defender of Roman Catholicism. Newman explained that he published these testimonials to refute the following internal Roman Catholic obloquy on his reputation: "The belief obtains extensively in the country at large, that Catholics, and especially the Priesthood, disavow the mode and form, in which I am accustomed to teach the Catholic faith, as if they were not generally recognized, but something special and peculiar to myself; as if, whether for the purposes of controversy, or from the traditions of an earlier period of my life, I did not exhibit Catholicism pure and simple, as the bulk of its professors manifest it" (436). Newman thus presented the testimony of more than five hundred priests as evidence to the contrary. These letters provided Newman with the same kind of credibility for honesty and faithfulness within the Roman Catholic communion as the generally warm Anglican response provided credibility within the Church of England.

Supplemental Matter

I.

Letters and Papers of the Author Used in the Course of This Work

		PAGE			PAGE
February	11, 1811	133	"	8, "	245
October	26, 1823	132	"	8, "	283
September	7, 1829	230	"	26, "	283
July	20, 1834	167	May	5, "	284
November	28, 1834	181	"	9, "	244
August	18, 1837	156	June	18, "	284
February	11, 1840	234	September	12, "	285
"	21, "	237	October	12, "	248
October	29(?)"	239	"	17, "	246
November	"	241	"	22, "	246
March	15, 1841	244	November	11, "	250
"	20, "	270	"	13, "	249
"	24, "	298	December	13, "	260
"	25, "	244	"	24, "	261
April	1, "	244	"	25, "	262
"	4, "	244	"	26, "	264

		PAGE			PAGE
March	6, 1842	276	April	3, "	296
April	14, "	273	"	8, "	312
October	16, "	271	July	14, "	290
November	22, "	287	September	16, "	322
Feb. 25, & 28, 1843		279	November	7, "	314
March	3, "	279	"	"	300
"	8, "	280	"	16, "	313
May	4, "	298	"	24, "	314
"	18, "	298	1844(?)		311
June	20, "	277	1844 or 1845		269
July	16, "	277	January	8, 1845	314
August	29, "	192	March	30, "	315
"	30, "	287	April	3, "	316
September	7, "	302	"	16, "	278
"	29, "	311	June	1, "	315
October	14, "	306	"	17, "	278
"	25, "	307	October	8, "	317
"	31, "	308	November	8, "	259
November	13, "	246	"	25, "	317
1843 or 1844		276	January	20, 1846	318
January	22, 1844	311	December	6, 1849	281
February	21, "	311			

Newman's references do not always exactly conform to the dates in *The Letters and Diaries of John Henry Newman*.

II.

List of the Author's Publications

The request has been made to me from various quarters for a list of my writings. This I now give, as follows: —

1. Life and Writings of Cicero. . . . . Griffin.
2. Life of Apollonius Tyanæus and Essay on Scripture Miracles . . . . Griffin.
3. Articles in the Christian Observer (excluding the footnotes)
    1821, p. 293, Mathematics, and 1822, p. 623, Religious Students; in British Review, May 1824, Duncan's Travels; in Theological Review, June 1825, Cooper's Crisis and Robinson's Acts; and in London Review, 1828, Greek Tragedy . . . . Out of print.
4. History of the Arians . . . . Lumley.
5–10. Parochial Sermons . . . . Vols. 1 and 4 out of print.
11. Plain Sermons (vol. 5th). . . . . Rivingtons.
12. In the British Magazine, 1833–1836, Home Thoughts Abroad, and 1834, On Convocation . . . . Out of print.
13. Tracts for the Times (smaller Tracts), Nos. 1, 2, 6, 7, 8, 10, 11, 19, 20, 21, 34, 38, 41, 45, 47 . . . . Rivingtons.
    Tracts for the Times (larger Tracts), Nos. 71, 73, 75, 79, 82, 83, 85, 88, 90 . . . . Rivingtons.

14. Pamphlets, 1830–1841. 1. Suggestions in behalf of the Church Missionary Society. 2. Suffragan Bishops. 3. Letter to Faussett. 4. Letters by Catholicus. 5. Letter to Jelf. 6. Letter to Bishop of Oxford.................................... Out of print.
                    Except Suffragan Bishops   Rivingtons.
15. Articles in British Critic, 1836–1842. 1. Apostolical Tradition. 2. Dr. Wiseman's Lectures. 3. De la Mennais. 4. Geraldine. 5. Memorials of Oxford. 6. Exeter Hall. 7. Palmer on the Church of Christ. 8. St. Ignatius of Antioch. 9. State of Religious Parties. 10. American Church. 11. Catholicity of the English Church. 12. Countess of Huntingdon. 13. Antichrist. 14. Milman's Christianity. 15. Bowden's Hildebrand. 16. Private Judgment. 17. Davison .... Out of print.
16. Church of the Fathers .... Duffy.
17. Prophetical Office of the Church .... Out of print.
18. Doctrine of Justification .... Rivingtons.
19. University Sermons....................................... Rivingtons.
20. Sermons on Subjects of the Day .... Rivingtons.
21. Annotated Translation of St. Athanasius................... Parker, Oxford.
22. Essay on Ecclesiastical Miracles .... Rivingtons.
23. Essay on Development of Doctrine .... Toovey.
24. Dissertatiunculæ Critico-Theologicæ .... Out of print.
25. Loss and Gain.. Burns and Lambert.
26. Sermons to Mixed Congregations .... Duffy.
27. Anglican Difficulties...................................... Duffy.
28. Catholicism in England .... Duffy.
29. Lectures on the Turks..................................... Duffy.
30. University Education .... Longman.
31. Office and Work of Universities .... Longman.
32. Lectures on University Subjects .... Longman.
33. Verses on Religious Subjects .... Out of print.
    (Vide also δ in Lyra Apostolica.)
34. Callista.. Burns and Lambert.
35. Occasional Sermons....................................... Burns and Lambert.
36. In the Rambler, 1859–1860, Ancient Saints, 1–5............ Burns and Lambert
37. In the Atlantis. 1. Benedictine Order. 2. Benedictine Centuries. 3. St. Cyril's Formula.................................. Longman.
38. Apologia pro Vitâ suâ .... Longman.

III.

Letter of Approbation and Encouragement from the Bishop of the Diocese of Birmingham, Dr. Ullathorne

"Bishop's House, June 2, 1864.

"My dear Dr. Newman,—

"It was with warm gratification that, after the close of the Synod yesterday, I listened to the Address presented to you by the clergy of the diocese, and to your impressive reply. But I should have been little satisfied with the part of the silent listener, except on the understanding with myself that I also might afterwards express to you my own sentiments in my own way.

"We have now been personally acquainted, and much more than acquainted, for nineteen years, during more than sixteen of which we have stood in special relation of duty towards each other. This has been one of the singular blessings which God has given me amongst the cares of the Episcopal office. What my feelings of respect, of confidence, and of affection have been towards you, you know well, nor should I think of expressing them in words. But there is one thing that has struck me in this day of explanations, which you could not, and would not, be disposed to do, and which no one could do so properly or so authentically as I could, and which it seems to me is not altogether uncalled for, if every kind of erroneous impression that some persons have entertained with no better evidence than conjecture is to be removed.

"It is difficult to comprehend how, in the face of facts, the notion should ever have arisen that during your Catholic life, you have been more occupied with your own thoughts than with the service of religion and the work of the Church. If we take no other work into consideration beyond the written productions which your Catholic pen has given to the world, they are enough for the life's labour of another. There are the Lectures on Anglican Difficulties, the Lectures on Catholicism in England, the great work on the Scope and End of University Education, that on the Office and Work of Universities, the Lectures and Essays on University Subjects, and the two Volumes of Sermons; not to speak of your contributions to the Atlantis, which you founded, and to other periodicals; then there are those beautiful offerings to Catholic literature, the Lectures on the Turks, Loss and Gain, and Callista, and though last, not least, the Apologia, which is destined to put many idle rumours to rest, and many unprofitable surmises; and yet all these productions represent but a portion of your labour, and that in the second half of your period of public life.

"These works have been written in the midst of labour and cares of another kind, and of which the world knows very little. I will specify four of these undertakings, each of a distinct character, and any one of which would have made a reputation for untiring energy in the practical order.

"The first of these undertakings was the establishment of the congregation of the Oratory of St. Philip Neri—that great ornament and accession to the force of English Catholicity. Both the London and the Birmingham Oratory must look to you as their founder and as the originator of their characteristic excellences; whilst that of Birmingham has never known any other presidency.

"No sooner was this work fairly on foot than you were called by the highest authority to commence another, and one of yet greater magnitude and difficulty, the founding of a University in Ireland. After the Universities had been lost to the Catholics of these kingdoms for three centuries, every thing had to be begun from the beginning: the idea of such an institution to be inculcated, the plan to be formed that would work, the resources to be gathered, and the staff of superiors and professors to be brought together. Your name was then the chief point of attraction which brought these elements together. You alone know what difficulties you had to conciliate and what to surmount, before the work reached that state of consistency and promise, which enabled you to return to those responsibilities in England which you had never laid aside or suspended. And here, excuse me if I give expression to a fancy which passed through my mind.

"I was lately reading a poem, not long published, from the MSS. De Rerum Natura, by Neckham, the foster-brother of Richard the Lion-hearted. He quotes an old prophecy, attributed to Merlin, and with a sort of wonder, as if recollecting that England owed so much of its literary learning to that country; and the prophecy says that after long years Oxford will pass into Ireland—'Vada boum suo tempore transibunt in Hiberniam.' When I read this, I could not but indulge the pleasant fancy that in the days when the Dublin University shall arise in material splendour, an allusion to this prophecy might form a poetic element in the inscription on the pedestal of the statue which commemorates its first Rector.

"The original plan of an Oratory did not contemplate any parochial work, but you could not contemplate so many souls in want of pastors without being prompt and ready at the beck of authority to strain all your efforts in coming to their help.

And this brings me to the third and the most continuous of those labours to which I have alluded. The mission in Alcester Street, its church and schools, were the first work of the Birmingham Oratory. After several years of close and hard work, and a considerable call upon the private resources of the Fathers who had established this congregation, it was delivered over to other hands, and the Fathers removed to the district of Edgbaston, where up to that time nothing Catholic had appeared. Then arose under your direction the large convent of the Oratory, the church expanded by degrees into its present capaciousness, a numerous congregation has gathered and grown in it; poor schools and other pious institutions have grown up in connexion with it, and, moreover, equally at your expense and that of your brethren, and, as I have reason to know, at much inconvenience, the Oratory has relieved the other clergy of Birmingham all this while by constantly doing the duty in the poor-house and gaol of Birmingham.

"More recently still, the mission and the poor school at Smethwick owe their existence to the Oratory. And all this while the founder and father of these religious works has added to his other solicitudes the toil of frequent preaching, of attendance in the confessional, and other parochial duties.

"I have read on this day of its publication the seventh part of the Apologia, and the touching allusion in it to the devotedness of the Catholic clergy to the poor in seasons of pestilence reminds me that when the cholera raged so dreadfully at Bilston, and the two priests of the town were no longer equal to the number of cases to which they were hurried day and night, I asked you to lend me two fathers to supply the place of other priests whom I wished to send as a further aid. But you and Father St. John preferred to take the place of danger which I had destined for others, and remained at Bilston till the worst was over.

"The fourth work which I would notice is one more widely known. I refer to the school for the education of the higher classes, which at the solicitation of many friends you have founded and attached to the Oratory. Surely after reading this bare enumeration of work done, no man will venture to say that Dr. Newman is leading a comparatively inactive life in the service of the Church.

"To spare, my dear Dr. Newman, any further pressure on those feelings with which I have already taken so large a liberty, I will only add one word more for my own satisfaction. During our long intercourse there is only one subject on which, after the first experience, I have measured my words with some caution, and that has been where questions bearing on ecclesiastical duty have arisen. I found some little caution necessary, because you were always so prompt and ready to go even beyond the slightest intimation of my wish or desires.

"That God may bless you with health, life, and all the spiritual good which you desire, you and your brethren of the Oratory, is the earnest prayer now and often of,
"My dear Dr. Newman,
"Your affectionate friend and faithful servant
in Christ,
"† W. B. ULLATHORNE."

IV.

Letters of Approbation and Encouragement from Clergy and Laity

It requires some words of explanation why I allow myself to sound my own praises so loudly, as I am doing by adding to my Volume the following Letters, written to me last year by large bodies of my Catholic brethren, Priests, and Laymen, in the course or on the conclusion of the publication of my Apologia. I have two reasons for doing so.

1. It seems hardly respectful to them, and hardly fair to myself, to practise self-denial in a matter, which after all belongs to others as well as to me. Bodies of men become authorities by the fact of being bodies, over and above the personal claims of the individuals who constitute them. To have received such unusual Testimonials in my favour, as I have to produce, and then to have suffered the honours conferred on me, and the generous feelings which dictated them, to be wasted, and to come to nought, would have been a rudeness of which I could not bear to be guilty. Far be it from me to show such ingratitude to those who were especially "friends in need." I am too proud of their approbation not to publish it to the world.

2. But I have a further reason. The belief obtains extensively in the country at large, that Catholics, and especially the Priesthood, disavow the mode and form, in which I am accustomed to teach the Catholic faith, as if they were not generally recognized, but something special and peculiar to myself; as if, whether for the purposes of controversy, or from the traditions of an earlier

period of my life, I did not exhibit Catholicism pure and simple, as the bulk of its professors manifest it. Such testimonials, then, as now follow, from as many as 558 priests, that is, not far from half of the clergy of England, secular and religious, from the Bishop and clergy of a diocese at the Antipodes, and from so great and authoritative a body as the German Congress assembled last year at Wurzburg, scatters to the winds a suspicion, which is not less painful, I am persuaded, to numbers of those Protestants who entertain it, than it is injurious to me who have to bear it.

I. *The Diocese of Westminster*

The following Address was signed by 110 of the Westminster clergy, including all the Canons, the Vicars-General, a great number of secular priests, and five Doctors in theology; Fathers of the Society of Jesus, Fathers of the Order of St. Dominic, of St. Francis, of the Oratory, of the Passion, of Charity, Oblates of St. Charles, and Marists.

"London, March 15, 1864.
"Very Reverend and Dear Sir,
    "We, the undersigned Priests of the Diocese of Westminster, tender to you our respectful thanks for the service you have done to religion, as well as to the interests of literary morality, by your Reply to the calumnies of [a popular writer of the day.]
"We cannot but regard it as a matter of congratulation that your assailant should have associated the cause of the Catholic Priesthood with the name of one so well fitted to represent its dignity, and to defend its honour, as yourself.
"We recognize in this latest effort of your literary power one further claim, besides the many you have already established, to the gratitude and veneration of Catholics, and trust that the reception which it has met with on all sides may be the omen of new successes which you are destined to achieve in the vindication of the teaching and principles of the Church.
    "We are,
        "Very Reverend and Dear Sir,
            "Your faithful and affectionate Servants in Christ."
                (*The Subscriptions follow.*)
"To the Very Rev.
    "John Henry Newman, D.D."

II. The Academia of Catholic Religion

"London, April 19, 1864.

"Very Rev. and Dear Sir,

"The Academia of Catholic Religion, at their meeting held to-day, under the Presidency of the Cardinal Archbishop, have instructed us to write to you in their behalf.

"As they have learned, with great satisfaction, that it is your intention to publish a defence of Catholic Veracity, which has been assailed in your person, they are precluded from asking you that that defence might be made by word of mouth, and in London, as they would otherwise have done.

"Composed, as the Academia is, mainly of Laymen, they feel that it is not out of their province to express their indignation that your opponent should have chosen, while praising the Catholic Laity, to do so at the expense of the Clergy, between whom and themselves, in this as in all other matters, there exists a perfect identity of principle and practice.

"It is because, in such a matter, your cause is the cause of all Catholics, that we congratulate ourselves on the rashness of the opponent that has thrown the defence of that cause into your hands.

"We remain,
"Very Reverend and Dear Sir,
"Your very faithful Servants,
"JAMES LAIRD PATTERSON, } Secretaries.
"EDW. LUCAS,

"To the Very Rev. John Henry Newman, D.D.,
"Provost of the Birmingham Oratory."

The above was moved at the meeting by Lord PETRE, and seconded by the Hon. CHARLES LANGDALE.

III. The Diocese of Birmingham

In this Diocese there were in 1864, according to the Directory of the year, 136 Priests.

"June 1, 1864.

"Very Reverend and Dear Sir,

"In availing ourselves of your presence at the Diocesan Synod to offer you our hearty thanks for your recent vindication of the honour of the Catholic Priesthood, We, the Provost and Chapter of the Cathedral, and the Clergy, Secular and Regular, of the Diocese of Birmingham, cannot forego the assertion of a special right, as your neighbours and colleagues, to express our veneration and affection for one whose fidelity to the dictates of conscience, in the use of the highest intellectual gifts, has won even from opponents unbounded admiration and respect.

"To most of us you are personally known. Of some, indeed, you were, in years long past, the trusted guide, to whom they owe more than can be expressed in words; and all are conscious that the ingenuous fulness of your answer to a false and unprovoked accusation, has intensified their interest in the labours and trials of your life. While, then, we resent the indignity to which you have been exposed, and lament the pain and annoyance which the manifestation of yourself must have cost you, we cannot but rejoice that, in the fulfilment of a duty, you have allowed neither the unworthiness of your assailant to shield him from rebuke, nor the sacredness of your inmost motives to deprive that rebuke of the only form which could at once complete his discomfiture, free your own name from the obloquy which prejudice had cast upon it, and afford invaluable aid to honest seekers after Truth.

"Great as is the work which you have already done, Very Reverend Sir, permit us to express a hope that a greater yet remains for you to accomplish. In an age and in a country in which the very foundations of religious faith are exposed to assault, we rejoice in numbering among our brethren one so well qualified by learning and experience to defend that priceless deposit of Truth, in obtaining which you have counted as gain the loss of all things most dear and precious. And we esteem ourselves happy in being able to offer you that support and encouragement which the assurance of our unfeigned admiration and regard may be able to give you under your present trials and future labours.

"That you may long have strength to labour for the Church of God and the glory of His Holy Name is, Very Reverend and Dear Sir, our heartfelt and united prayer."

(The Subscriptions follow.)

"To the Very Rev. John Henry Newman, D.D."

IV. The Diocese of Beverley

The following Address, as is stated in the first paragraph, comes from more than 70 Priests:—

"Hull, May 9, 1864.

"Very Rev. and Dear Dr. Newman,

"At a recent meeting of the clergy of the Diocese of Beverley, held in York, at which upwards of seventy priests were present, special attention was called to your correspondence with [a popular writer]; and such was the enthusiasm with which your name was received—such was the admiration expressed of the dignity with which you had asserted the claims of the Catholic Priesthood in England to be treated with becoming courtesy and respect—and such was the strong and all-pervading sense of the invaluable service which you had thus rendered, not only to faith and morals, but to good manners so far as regarded religious controversy in this country, that I was requested, as Chairman, to become the voice of the meeting, and to express to you as strongly and as earnestly as I could, how heartily the whole of the clergy of this diocese desire to thank you for services to religion as well-timed as they are in themselves above and beyond all commendation, services which the Catholics of England will never cease to hold in most grateful remembrance. God, in His infinite wisdom and great mercy, has raised you up to stand prominently forth in the glorious work of re-establishing in this country the holy faith which in good old times shed such lustre upon it. We all lament that, in the order of nature, you have so few years before you in which to fight against false teaching that good fight in which you have been so victoriously engaged of late. But our prayers are that you may long be spared, and may possess to the last all your vigour, and all that zeal for the advancement of our holy faith, which imparts such a charm to the productions of your pen.

I esteem it a great honour and a great privilege to have been deputed, as the representative of the clergy of the Diocese of Beverley, to tender you the fullest expression of our most grateful thanks, and the assurance of our prayers for your health and eternal happiness.

"I am,
"Very Rev. and Dear Sir,
"With sentiments of profound respect,
"Yours most faithfully in Christ,
"M. TRAPPES.

"The Very Rev. Dr. Newman."

V. and VI. *The Dioceses of Liverpool and Salford*

The Secular Clergy of Liverpool amounted in 1864 to 103, and of Salford to 76.

"Preston, July 27, 1864.

"Very Rev. and Dear Sir,
"It may seem, perhaps, that the Clergy of Lancashire have been slow to address you; but it would be incorrect to suppose that they have been indifferent spectators of the conflict in which you have been recently engaged. This is the first opportunity that has presented itself, and they gladly avail themselves of their annual meeting in Preston to tender to you the united expression of their heartfelt sympathy and gratitude.

"The atrocious imputation, out of which the late controversy arose, was felt as a personal affront by them, one and all, conscious as they were, that it was mainly owing to your position as a distinguished Catholic ecclesiastic, that the charge was connected with your name.

"While they regret the pain you must needs have suffered, they cannot help rejoicing that it has afforded you an opportunity of rendering a new and most important service to their holy religion. Writers, who are not overscrupulous about the truth themselves, have long used the charge of untruthfulness as an ever ready weapon against the Catholic Clergy. Partly from the frequent repetition of this charge, partly from a consciousness that, instead of undervaluing the truth, they have ever prized it above every earthly treasure, partly, too, from the difficulty of obtaining a hearing in their own defence, they have generally passed it by in silence. They thank you for coming forward as their champion: your own character required no vindication. It was their battle more than your own that you fought. They know and feel how much pain it has caused you to bring so prominently forward your own life and motives, but they now congratulate you on the completeness of your triumph, as admitted alike by friend and enemy.

"In addition to answering the original accusation, you have placed them under a new obligation, by giving to all, who read the English language, a work which, for literary ability and the lucid exposition of many difficult and abstruse points, forms an invaluable contribution to our literature.

"They fervently pray that God may give you health and length of days, and, if it please Him, some other cause in which to use for His glory the great powers bestowed upon you.

"Signed on behalf of the Meeting,
"THOS. PROVOST COOKSON.

"The Very Rev. J. H. Newman."

VII. *The Diocese of Hexham*

The Secular Priests on Mission in 1864 in this Diocese were 64.

"Durham, Sept. 22, 1864.

"My Dear Dr. Newman,

"At the annual meeting of the Clergy of the Diocese of Hexham and Newcastle, held a few days ago at Newcastle-upon-Tyne, I was commissioned by them to express to you their sincere sympathy, on account of the slanderous accusations, to which you have been so unjustly exposed. We are fully aware that these foul calumnies were intended to injure the character of the whole body of the Catholic Clergy, and that your distinguished name was singled out, in order that they might be more effectually propagated. It is well that these poisonous shafts were thus aimed, as no one could more triumphantly repel them. The 'Apologia pro Vitâ suâ' will, if possible, render still more illustrious the name of its gifted author, and be a lasting monument of the victory of truth, and the signal overthrow of an arrogant and reckless assailant.

"It may appear late for us now to ask to join in your triumph, but as the Annual Meeting of the Northern Clergy does not take place till this time, it is the first occasion offered us to present our united congratulations, and to declare to you, that by none of your brethren are you more esteemed and venerated, than by the Clergy of the Diocese of Hexham and Newcastle.

"Wishing that Almighty God may prolong your life many more years for the defence of our holy religion and the honour of your brethren,

"I am, dear Dr. Newman,
"Yours sincerely in Jesus Christ,
"RALPH PROVOST PLATT, V. G.

"The Very Rev. J. H. Newman."

VIII. The Congress of Würzburg

"September 15, 1864.

"Sir,

"The undersigned, President of the Catholic Congress of Germany assembled in Würzburg, has been commissioned to express to you, Very Rev. and Dear Sir, its deep-felt gratitude for your late able defence of the Catholic Clergy, not only of England, but of the whole world, against the attacks of its enemies.

"The Catholics of Germany unite with the Catholics of England in testifying to you their profound admiration and sympathy, and pray that the Almighty may long preserve your valuable life.

"The above Resolution was voted by the Congress with acclamation.

"Accept, very Rev. and Dear Sir, the expression of the high consideration with which I am

"Your most obedient servant,
"(Signed) ERNEST BARON MOIJ DE SONS.

"The Very Rev. J. H. Newman."

IX. The Diocese of Hobart Town

"Hobart Town, Tasmania, November 22, 1864.

"Very Rev. and Dear Sir,

"By the last month's post we at length received your admirable book, entitled, 'Apologia pro Vitâ suâ,' and the pamphlet, 'What then does Dr. Newman mean?'

"By this month's mail, we wish to express our heartfelt gratification and delight for being possessed of a work so triumphant in maintaining truth, and so overwhelming in confounding arrogance and error, as the 'Apologia.'

"No doubt, your adversary, resting on the deep-seated prejudice of our fellow-countrymen in the United Kingdom, calculated upon establishing his own fame as a keen-sighted polemic, as a shrewd and truth-loving man, upon the fallen reputation of one, who, as he would demonstrate, — yes, that he would, — set little or no value on truth, and who, therefore, would deservedly sink into obscurity, henceforward rejected and despised!

"Aman of old erected a gibbet at the gate of the city, on which an unsuspecting and an unoffending man, one marked as a victim, was to be exposed to the gaze and derision of the people, in order that his own dignity and fame might be exalted; but a divine Providence ordained otherwise. The history of the judgment that fell upon Aman, has been recorded in Holy Writ, it is to be presumed, as a warning to vain and unscrupulous men, even in our days. There can be no doubt, a moral gibbet, full 'fifty cubits high,' had been prepared some time, on which you were to be exposed, for the pity at least, if not for the scorn and derision of so many, who had loved and venerated you through life!

"But the effort made in the forty-eight pages of the redoubtable pamphlet, 'What then does Dr. Newman Mean?' — the production of a bold, unscrupulous man, with a coarse mind, and regardless of inflicting pain on the feelings of another, has failed, — marvellously failed, — and he himself is now exhibited not only in our fatherland, but even at the Antipodes, in fact wherever the English language is spoken or read, as a shallow pretender, one quite incompetent to treat of matters of such undying interest as those he presumed to interfere with.

"We fervently pray the Almighty, that you may be spared to His Church for many years to come, — that to Him alone the glory of this noble work may be given, — and to you the reward in eternal bliss!

"And from this distant land we beg to convey to you, Very Rev. and Dear Sir, the sentiments of our affectionate respect, and deep veneration."

(*The Subscriptions follow, of the Bishop Vicar-General and eighteen Clergy.*)

"The Very Rev. Dr. Newman,
&c. &c. &c."

Editor's Appendix
Six Sermons by John Henry Newman

During his years in the Church of England John Henry Newman was known as one of the most influential preachers of the age, a reputation gained as much from the publishing as the actual delivery of his sermons. He published ten volumes of sermons as an Anglican and wrote and preached many more. His immediate primary audience were members of the Oxford University community who came to hear him in St. Mary the Virgin Church and later in the church in Littlemore; his reading audience, however, stretched across the transatlantic world. Newman began printing his sermons in late 1833 just as the first of the *Tracts for the Times* appeared. He regarded his sermons, which were published and republished between 1833 and 1843, as fundamental contributions to the Tractarian Movement. When the eight volumes of his Anglican *Parochial and Plain Sermons* were reprinted in 1868, they achieved an audience throughout English-speaking Christian denominations.

Newman's voice as a preacher, just as his voice as a writer, provided a critical dissent from the evangelical religion and preaching that characterized so much British religious life during the first half of the nineteenth century. In pursuing his challenge to evangelical religion Newman determined that the message of Christian obedience and sanctification should have precedence over the preaching of justification and forgiveness through faith in the atonement. In other words, Newman found himself drawn to the preaching of the law over the gospel. His sermons, in contrast to those of evangelical preachers, were intended to draw listeners and readers to a meditation on their personal behavior and inner sanctity and not to produce a conversion experience.

The first four sermons included in this appendix—"Obedience to God the Way to Faith in Christ" (October 31, 1830), "Religious Emotion" (March 27, 1831), "The Religious Use of Excited Feelings" (June 3, 1831), and "Sudden Conversions" (January 25, 1832)—illustrate both the manner in which his preaching challenged evangelical preaching and doctrine and the kind of rigorous religious discipline to which he called his congregation. Each sermon criticizes the confusion Newman saw rampant in the British religious world between religious feeling and religious obedience. He believed his contemporaries, including his brother Francis, equated religious seriousness with the experience of intense religious feeling flowing from the experience of listening to a preacher of the gospel. Newman regarded such subjective religion as leading to the disintegration of real religion in the world. He thought evangelical preaching, with its emphasis on emotion and free grace through faith, promised a path of easy religion, whereas true religion involved spiritual obedience and rigor.

The two other sermons in this appendix relate to the close of the Tractarian Movement. Newman's sermon on "Wisdom and Innocence" (February 19, 1843), which he and Charles Kingsley so sharply debated, has never been published in the same volume with the *Apologia Pro Vita Sua*. For reasons outlined in the introduction to this volume, Newman, on the advice of a lawyer friend, refrained from publishing it as part of the controversy with Kingsley. From Newman's comments in the *Apologia* and its notes, it would appear that the sermon as published in *Sermons, Bearing on Subjects of the Day* (1843) differed somewhat from the sermon preached. Whatever the difference, Kingsley's accusations and Newman's response centered around the published sermon.

Newman delivered and published "Wisdom and Innocence" in the wake of the events after *Tract 90* when for months he and his fellow Tractarians had been berated in the press, journals, and episcopal charges for lack of honesty. In the sermon Newman presented Catholics in the English Church as a saving remnant of faithful Christians surrounded by forces of heresy. Under those conditions they, like beleaguered Christians of earlier eras, had the right to resort to extraordinary means of self-defense, including guile and craft, which Providence provided them. He presents Catholics in the Church of England as resisting an unbelieving world, some of whose voices inhabit the church itself. The persecution Catholics now encountered confirmed their standing as members of the true Christian Church and justified their use of what their opponents regarded as hypocrisy and duplicity. As noted in the introduction, this sermon represented an effort to carve out a safe position for a persecuted minority in the Church of England.

Newman preached "The Parting of Friends" (September 25, 1843) as his final sermon as a clergyman of the Church of England, although two more years would pass before his conversion. He delivered "The Parting of Friends" in the Littlemore church, which was filled with friends and admirers who understood that he was concluding his Anglican preaching ministry. The sermon was a self-conscious, angry valedictory. The friends from whom he saw himself departing were the Anglican high churchmen who had with greater and lesser degrees of intensity supported the Tractarian Movement at its inception and for several years thereafter. From 1838 and the publication of the first volumes of Froude's *Remains,* however, they had begun first to criticize the direction of the movement and after the appearance of *Tract 90* in early 1841 to set a distinct distance between the movement and themselves. By the autumn of 1843 they were publicly chastising the Tractarian Movement and its leadership. They are the people whom in the sermon Newman accuses of not knowing how to use their most loyal children.

What both sermons of 1843 demonstrate is not the sympathy for Rome of which first high churchmen and years later Kingsley accused Newman. Rather, they demonstrate Newman's determination to find a way to maintain space in the Church of England for a Catholic-minded minority who hoped to purge that institution of its evangelical Protestant excesses and to recapture certain pre-Reformation modes of Christian devotion.

The first four sermons are reprinted from John Henry Newman, *Parochial and Plain Sermons,* new ed. (London: Longmans, Green, and Co., 1891), vols. 1 and 8, and the last two from John Henry Newman, *Sermons, Bearing on Subjects of the Day* (London: J. G. F. & J. Rivington, 1843).

Obedience to God the Way to Faith in Christ

"When Jesus saw that he answered discreetly, He said unto him, Thou art not far from the kingdom of God." — MARK xii. 34.

The answer of the scribe, which our blessed Lord here commends, was occasioned by Christ's setting before him the two great commandments of the Law. When He had declared the love of God and of man to comprehend our whole duty, the scribe said, "Master, Thou hast said the truth: for there is one God; and there is none other but He: and to love Him with all the heart, and with all the understanding, and with all the soul, and with all the strength, and to love his neighbour as himself, is more than all whole burnt-offerings and sacrifices." Upon this acknowledgment of the duty of general religious obedience, Christ replied, in the words of the text, "Thou art not far from the kingdom of God," i. e. Thou art not far from being a Christian.

In these words, then, we are taught, first, that the Christian's faith and obedience are not the same religion as that of natural conscience, as being some way beyond it; secondly, that this way is "not far," not far in the case of those who try to act up to their conscience; in other words, that obedience to conscience leads to obedience to the Gospel, which, instead of being something different altogether, is but the completion and perfection of that religion which natural conscience teaches.

Indeed, it would have been strange if the God of nature had said one thing, and the God of grace another; if the truths which our conscience taught us without the information of Scripture, were contradicted by that information when obtained. But it is not so; there are not two ways of pleasing God; what conscience suggests, Christ has sanctioned and explained; to love God and our neighbour are the great duties of the Gospel as well as of the Law; he who endeavours to fulfil them by the light of nature is in the way towards, is, as our Lord said, "not far from Christ's kingdom;" for to him that hath more shall be given.

It is not in one or two places merely that this same doctrine is declared to us; indeed, all revelation is grounded on those simple truths which our own consciences teach us in a measure, though a poor measure, even without it. It is One God, and none other but He, who speaks first in our consciences, then in His Holy Word; and, lest we should be in any difficulty about the matter, He has most mercifully told us so in Scripture, wherein He refers again and again (as in the passage connected with the text) to the great Moral Law, as the foundation of the truth, which His Apostles and Prophets, and last of all His Son, have taught us: "Fear God, and keep His commandments; for this is the whole duty of man."[1]

Yet though this is so plain, both from our own moral sense, and the declarations of Scripture, still for many reasons it is necessary to insist upon it; chiefly, because, it being very hard to keep God's commandments, men would willingly persuade themselves, if they could, that strict obedience is not necessary under the Gospel, and that something else will be taken, for Christ's sake, in the stead of it. Instead of labouring, under God's grace, to change their wills, to purify their hearts, and so prepare themselves for the kingdom of God, they imagine that in that kingdom they may be saved by something short of this, by their baptism, or by their ceremonial observances (the burnt offerings and sacrifices which the scribe disparages), or by their correct knowledge of the truth, or by their knowledge of their own sinfulness, or by some past act of faith which is to last them during their lives, or by some strong habitual persuasion that they are safe; or, again, by the performance of some one part of their duty, though they neglect the rest, as if God said a thing to us in nature, and Christ unsaid it; and, when men wish a thing, it is not hard to find texts in Scripture which may be ingeniously perverted to suit their purpose. The error then being so common in practice, of believing that Christ came to gain for us easier terms of admittance into heaven than we had before (whereas, in fact, instead of making obedience less strict, He has enabled us to obey God more

---

1. Eccles. xii. 13.

strictly; and instead of gaining *easier* terms of *admittance,* He has gained us *altogether* our admittance into heaven, which before was closed against us); this error, I say, being so common, it may be right to insist on the opposite truth, however obvious, that obedience to God is the way to know and believe in Christ.

1. Now, first, let us consider how plainly we are taught in Scripture that perfect obedience is the standard of Gospel holiness. By St. Paul: "Be not conformed to this world: but be ye transformed by the renewing of your mind, that ye may prove what is that good, and acceptable, and perfect, will of God."[2] "Circumcision is nothing, and uncircumcision is nothing, but the keeping of the commandments of God."[3] "Whatsoever things are true . . honest . . just . . pure . . lovely . . of good report: if there be any virtue, and if there be any praise, think on these things."[4] By St. James: "Whosoever shall keep the whole law, and yet offend in one point, he is guilty of all."[5] By St. Peter: "Giving all diligence, add to your faith virtue . . knowledge . . temperance . . patience . . godliness . . brotherly kindness . . charity."[6] By St. John: "Hereby do we know that we know Him, if we keep His commandments." Lastly, by our Lord Himself: "He that hath My commandments, and keepeth them, he it is that loveth Me: and he that loveth Me, shall be loved of My Father, and I will love him, and will manifest Myself to him."[7] And, above all, the following clear declaration in the Sermon on the Mount: "Whosoever . . shall break one of these least commandments, and shall teach men so, he shall be called the least in the kingdom of heaven: but whosoever shall do and teach them, the same shall be called great in the kingdom of heaven."[8]

These texts, and a multitude of others, show that the Gospel leaves us just where it found us, as regards the necessity of our obedience to God; that Christ has not obeyed instead of us, but that obedience is quite as imperative as if Christ had never come; nay, is pressed upon us with additional sanctions; the difference being, not that He relaxes the strict rule of keeping His commandments, but that He gives us spiritual aids, which we have not except through Him, to enable us to keep them. Accordingly Christ's service is represented in Scripture, not as different from that religious obedience which conscience teaches us naturally, but as the perfection of it, as I have already said. We are

2. Rom. xii. 2.
3. 1 Cor. vii. 19.
4. Phil. iv. 8.
5. James ii. 10.
6. 2 Pet. i. 5–7.
7. John xiv. 21.
8. Matt. v. 19.

told again and again, that obedience to God leads on to faith in Christ; that it is the only recognized way to Christ; and that, therefore, to believe in Him, ordinarily implies that we are living in obedience to God. For instance: "Every man . . . that hath heard and hath learned of the Father, cometh unto Me;"[9] "He that doeth truth, cometh to the light,"[10] i. e. to Christ; "No man can come to Me, except the Father which hath sent Me, draw him;" "If any man will do the will of God, he shall know of the doctrine."[11] On the other hand: "He that hateth Me, hateth My Father also;"[12] "If ye had known Me, ye should have known My Father also;"[13] "Whosoever denieth the Son, the same hath not the Father;"[14] "Whosoever transgresseth, and abideth not in the doctrine of Christ, hath not God: he that abideth in the doctrine of Christ, he hath both the Father and the Son."[15]

In these and other passages of Scripture we learn, that though Christ came to be the light of the world, yet He is not and cannot be a light to all, but to those only who seek Him in the way of His commandments; and to all others He is hid, the god of this world "blinding the minds of them which believe not, lest the light of the glorious Gospel of Christ, who is the Image of God, should shine unto them."[16]

2. And if we look to the history of the first propagation of the Gospel, we find this view confirmed. As far as we can trace the history, we find the early Christian Church was principally composed of those who had long been in the habit of obeying their consciences carefully, and so preparing themselves for Christ's religion, that kingdom of God from which the text says they were not far. Zacharias and Elisabeth, to whom the approach of Christ's kingdom was first revealed, are described as "both righteous before God, walking in all the commandments and ordinances of the Lord, blameless."[17] Joseph, St. Mary's husband, is called "a just man;"[18] Simeon is spoken of as "a just and devout"[19] man; Nathaniel, as "an Israelite in whom was no guile;"[20] Joseph of Arimathea

---

9. John vi. 45.
10. John iii. 21.
11. John vii. 17.
12. John xv. 23.
13. John viii. 19.
14. John ii. 23.
15. 2 John 9.
16. 2 Cor. iv. 4.
17. Luke i. 6.
18. Matt. i. 19.
19. Luke ii. 25.
20. John i. 47.

was "a good man and a just;"[21] Cornelius, the centurion, was a "religious man, and one that feared God with all his house, who gave much alms to the people, and prayed to God alway."[22] And in the book of Acts generally, we shall find (as far as we are told any thing) that those chiefly were addressed and converted by St. Paul, who had previously trained themselves in a religious life:—At Perga, St. Paul addressed the Israelites and those who feared God, not the mere thoughtless heathen; and many of these followed him.[23] At Thessalonica a great multitude of religious Greeks believed;[24] and at Athens the Apostle still disputed with the Jews, and with the professedly religious persons, though he also addressed the educated heathens who lived there. Here then is much evidence that Christ and His Apostles chiefly sought and found their first followers, not among open sinners, but among those who were endeavouring, however imperfectly, to obey God.

But it may be asked, Did Christ hold out no hope for those who had lived in sin? Doubtless He did, if they determined to forsake their sin. He came to save all, whatever their former life, who gave themselves up to Him as their Lord and Saviour; and in His Church He gathered together of every kind, those who had departed from God, as well as those who had ever served Him well. Open sinners must have a beginning of repentance, if they are to repent; and on this first beginning Christ invites them to Him at once, without delay, for pardon and for aid. But this is not the question; of course all who come to Him will be received; none will be cast out.[25] But the question is, not this, but whether they are likely to come, to hear His voice, and to follow Him; again, whether they will, generally speaking, prove as consistent and deeply-taught Christians as those who, compared with them, have never departed from God at all; and here all the advantage, doubtless, is on the side of those who (in the words of Scripture) have walked in the ordinances of the Lord blameless.[26] When sinners truly repent, then, indeed, they are altogether brothers in Christ's kingdom with those who have not in the same sense "need of repentance;" but that they should repent at all is (alas!) so far from being likely, that when the unexpected event takes place it causes such joy in heaven (from the marvellousness of it) as is not even excited by the ninety and nine just persons who need no such change of mind.[27] Of such changes some instances are given us

21. Luke xxiii. 50.
22. Acts x. 2.
23. Acts xiii.
24. Acts xvii.
25. John iv. 3.7.
26. Luke i. 6.
27. Luke xv. 7.

in the Gospels for the encouragement of all penitents, such as that of the woman, mentioned by St. Luke, who "loved much." Christ most graciously went among sinners, if so be He might save them; and we know that even those open sinners, when they knew that they were sinners, were nearer salvation, and in a better state, than the covetous and irreligious Pharisees, who added to their other gross sins, hypocrisy, blindness, a contempt of others, and a haughty and superstitious reliance on the availing virtue of their religious privileges.

And, moreover, of these penitents of whom I speak — and whom, when they become penitents, we cannot love too dearly (after our Saviour's pattern), nay, or reverence too highly, and whom the Apostles, after Christ's departure, brought into the Church in such vast multitudes — none, as far as we know, had any sudden change of mind from bad to good wrought in them; nor do we hear of any of them honoured with any important station in the Church. Great as St. Paul's sin was in persecuting Christ's followers, before his conversion, that sin was of a different kind; he was not transgressing, but obeying his conscience (however blinded it was); he was doing what he thought his duty, when he was arrested by the heavenly vision, which, when presented to him, he at once "obeyed;" he was not sinning *against light,* but *in* darkness. We know nothing of the precise state of his mind immediately before his conversion; but we do know thus much, that years elapsed after his conversion before he was employed as an Apostle in the Church of God.

I have confined myself to the time of Christ's coming; but not only then, but at all times and under all circumstances, as all parts of the Bible inform us, obedience to the light we possess is the way to gain more light. In the words of Wisdom, in the book of Proverbs, "I love them that love Me; and those that seek Me early shall find Me. . . . I lead in the way of righteousness, in the midst of the paths of judgment."[28] Or, in the still more authoritative words of Christ Himself, "He that is faithful in that which is least, is faithful also in much;"[29] and, "He that hath, to him shall be given."[30]

Now let us see some of the consequences which follow from this great Scripture truth.

1. First of all, we see the hopelessness of waiting for any sudden change of heart, if we are at present living in sin. Far more persons deceive themselves by some such vain expectation than at first sight may appear. That there are even many irreligious men, who, from hearing the false doctrines now so common,

---

28. Prov. viii. 17. 20.
29. Luke xvi. 10.
30. Mark iv. 25.

and receiving general impressions from them, look forward for a possible day when God will change their hearts by His own mere power, in spite of themselves, and who thus get rid of the troublesome thought that now they are in a state of fearful peril; who say they can do nothing till His time comes, while still they acknowledge themselves to be far from Him; even this I believe to be a fact, strange and gross as the self-deception may appear to be. And others, too, many more, doubtless, are there who, not thinking themselves far from Him, but, on the contrary, high in His favour, still, by a dreadful deceit of Satan, are led to be indolent and languid in their obedience to His commandments, from a pretence that they can do nothing of themselves, and must wait for the successive motions of God's grace to excite them to action. The utmost these persons do is to talk of religion, when they ought to be up and active, and waiting for the Blessed Spirit of Christ by obeying God's will. "Awake thou that sleepest, and arise from the dead, and Christ shall give thee light."[31] This is the exhortation. And doubtless to all those who live a self-indulgent life, however they veil their self-indulgence from themselves by a notion of their superior religious knowledge, and by their faculty of speaking fluently in Scripture language, to all such the word of life says, "Be not deceived; God is not mocked;" He tries the heart, and disdains the mere worship of the lips. He acknowledges no man as a believer in His Son, who does not anxiously struggle to obey His commandments to the utmost; to none of those who seek without striving, and who consider themselves safe, to none of these does He give "power to become sons of God."[32] Be not deceived; such have fallen from that state in which their baptism placed them and are "far from the kingdom of God." "Whatsoever a man soweth, that shall he also reap."[33] And if any one says that St. Paul was converted suddenly, and without his exerting himself, it is sufficient to reply, that, guilty as St. Paul was, his guilt was not that of indolence, and self-indulgence, and indifference. His sin was that of *neglecting the study of Scripture;* and thus, missing the great truth that Jesus was the Christ, he persecuted the Christians; but though his conscience was ill-informed, and that by his own fault, yet he obeyed it such as it was. He did what he did ignorantly. If then the case really be that St. Paul *was* suddenly converted, hence, it is true, some kind of vague hope may be said to be held out to furious, intolerant bigots, and bloodthirsty persecutors, if they are acting in consequence of their own notions of duty; none to the slothful and negligent and lukewarm; none *but* to those who can say, with St. Paul, that they have

31. Eph. v. 14.
32. John i. 12.
33. Gal. vi. 7.

"lived in all good conscience before God until this day;"[34] and that not under an easy profession, but in a straitest religious sect, giving themselves up to their duty, and following the law of God, though in ignorance, yet with all their heart and soul.

2. But, after all, there are very many more than I have as yet mentioned, who wait for a time of repentance to come while at present they live in sin. For instance, the young, who consider it will be time enough to think of God when they grow old; that religion will then come as a matter of course, and that they will then like it naturally, just as they now like their follies and sins. Or those who are much engaged in worldly business, who confess they do not give that attention to religion which they ought to give; who neglect the ordinances of the Church; who desecrate the Lord's day; who give little or no time to the study of God's word; who allow themselves in various small transgressions of their conscience, and resolutely harden themselves against the remorse which such transgressions are calculated to cause them; and all this they do under the idea that at length a convenient season will come when they may give themselves to religious duties. They determine on retiring at length from the world, and of making up for lost time by greater diligence then. All such persons, and how many they are! think that they will be able to seek Christ when they please, though they have lived all their lives with no true love either of God or man; i. e. they do not, in their hearts, believe our Lord's doctrine contained in the text, that to obey God is to be near Christ, and that to disobey is to be far from Him.

How will this truth be plain to us in that day when the secrets of all hearts shall be revealed! *Now* we do not believe that strict obedience is as necessary as it is. I say we do *not* believe it, though we say we do. No one, of course, believes it in its fulness, but most of us are deceived by words, and say we accept and believe, when we hardly do more than profess it. We say, indeed, that obedience is absolutely necessary, and are surprised to have our real belief in what we say questioned; but we do not give the truth that place in the scheme of our religion which this profession requires, and thus we cheat our consciences. We put something *before* it, in our doctrinal system, as *more* necessary than it; one man puts faith, another outward devotion, a third attention to his temporal calling, another zeal for the Church; that is, we put a part for the whole of our duty, and so run the risk of losing our souls. These are the burnt-offerings and sacrifices which even the scribe put aside before the weightier matters of the Law. Or again, we fancy that the means of gaining heaven are something stranger and rarer than the mere obvious duty of

---

34. Acts xxiii. 1.

obedience to God; we are loth to seek Christ in the waters of Jordan rather than in Pharpar and Abana, rivers of Damascus; we prefer to seek Him in the height above, or to descend into the deep, rather than to believe that the word is nigh us, even in our mouth and in our heart.[35] Hence, in false religions some men have even tortured themselves and been cruel to their flesh, thereby to become as gods, and to mount aloft; and in our own, with a not less melancholy, though less self-denying, error, men fancy that certain strange effects on their minds — strong emotion, restlessness, and an unmanly excitement and extravagance of thought and feeling — are the tokens of that inscrutable Spirit, who is given us, not to make us something *other than* men, but to make us, what without His gracious aid we never shall be, upright, self-mastering men, humble and obedient children of our Lord and Saviour.

In that day of trial all these deceits will be laid aside; we shall stand in our own real form, whether it be of heaven or of earth, the wedding garment, or the old raiment of sin;[36] and then, how many (do we think) will be revealed as the heirs of light, who have followed Christ in His narrow way, and humbled themselves after His manner (though not in His perfection, and with nothing of His merit) to the daily duties of soberness, mercy, gentleness, self-denial, and the fear of God?

These, be they many or few, will then receive their prize from Him who died for them, who has made them what they are, and completes in heaven what first by conscience, then by His Spirit, He began here. Surely they were despised on the earth by the world; both by the open sinners, who thought their scrupulousness to be foolishness, and by such pretenders to God's favour as thought it ignorance. But, in reality, they had received from their Lord the treasures both of wisdom and of knowledge, though men knew it not; and they then will be acknowledged by Him before all creatures, as heirs of the glory prepared for them before the beginning of the world.

---

35. Rom. x. 8.
36. Zech. iii. 4.

Religious Emotion

> "But he spake the more vehemently, If I should die with Thee, I will not deny Thee in any wise." — MARK. xiv. 31.

It is not my intention to make St. Peter's fall the direct subject of our consideration to-day, though I have taken this text; but to suggest to you an important truth, which that fall, together with other events at the same season, especially enforces; viz. that violent impulse is not the same as a firm *determination*, — that men may have their religious feelings roused, without being on that account at all the more likely to obey God in practice, rather the less likely. This important truth is in various ways brought before our minds at the season sacred to the memory of Christ's betrayal and death. The contrast displayed in the Gospels between His behaviour on the one hand, as the time of His crucifixion drew near, and that both of His disciples and of the Jewish populace on the other, is full of instruction, if we will receive it; *He* steadily fixing His face to endure those sufferings which were the atonement for our sins, yet without aught of mental excitement or agitation; His disciples and the Jewish multitude first protesting their devotion to Him in vehement language, then, the one deserting Him, the other even clamouring for His crucifixion. He entered Jerusalem in triumph; the multitude cutting down branches of palm-trees, and strewing them in the way, as in honour of a king and conqueror.[1] He had lately raised Lazarus from the dead; and so great a miracle had given Him great temporary favour with the populace. Multitudes flocked to Bethany to see Him and Lazarus;[2] and when He set out for Jerusalem where He was to suffer, they, little thinking that they would soon cry "Crucify Him," went out to meet Him with the palm-branches, and hailing Him as their Messiah, led Him on into the holy city. Here was an instance of a *popular* excitement. The next instance of excited feeling is found in that melancholy self-confidence of St. Peter, contained in the text. When our Saviour foretold Peter's trial and fall, Peter at length "spake the more vehemently, If I should die with Thee, I will not deny Thee in any wise." Yet in a little while both the people and the Apostle abandoned their Messiah; the ardour of their devotion had run its course.

Now it may, perhaps, appear, as if the circumstance I am pointing out, remarkable as it is, still is one on which it is of little use to dwell, in addressing a mixed congregation, on the ground that most men feel too *little* about religion. And it may be thence argued, that the aim of Christian teaching rather should be to rouse them from insensibility, than to warn them against excess of religious feeling. I answer, that to mistake mere transient emotion, or mere good thoughts, for obedience, is a far commoner deceit than at first sight appears. How many a man is there, who, when his conscience upbraids him for neglect of duty, comforts himself with the reflection that he has never treated the subject of religion with open scorn, — that he has from time to time had serious thoughts, — that on certain solemn occasions he has been affected and awed, — that he has at times been moved to earnest prayer to God, — that he has had accidentally some serious conversation with a friend! This, I say, is a case of frequent occurrence among men called Christian. Again, there is a further reason for insisting upon this subject. No one (it is plain) can be religious without having his heart in his religion; his affections must be actively engaged in it; and it is the aim of all Christian instruction to promote this. But if so, doubtless there is great danger lest a perverse use should be made of the affections. In proportion as a religious duty is difficult, so is it open to abuse. For the very reason, then, that I desire to make you earnest in religion, must I also warn you against a counterfeit earnestness, which often misleads men from the plain path of obedience, and which most men are apt to fall into just on their first awakening to a serious consideration of their duty. It is not enough to bid you to serve Christ in faith, fear, love, and gratitude; care must be taken that it is the faith, fear, love, and gratitude of a sound mind. That

---

1. Matt. xxi. 8. John xii. 13.
2. John xii. 1–18.

vehement tumult of zeal which St. Peter felt before his trial failed him under it. That open-mouthed admiration of the populace at our Saviour's miracle was suddenly changed to blasphemy. This may happen now as then; and it often happens in a way distressing to the Christian teacher. He finds it is far easier to interest men in the subject of religion (hard though this be), than to rule the spirit which he has excited. His hearers, when their attention is gained, soon begin to think he does not go far enough; then they seek means which he will not supply, of encouraging and indulging their mere feelings to the neglect of humble practical efforts to serve God. After a time, like the multitude, they suddenly turn round to the world, abjuring Christ altogether, or denying Him with Peter, or gradually sinking into a mere form of obedience, while they still think themselves true Christians, and secure of the favour of Almighty God.

For these reasons I think it is as important to warn men against impetuous feelings in religion, as to urge them to give their heart to it. I proceed therefore to explain more fully what is the connexion between strong emotions and sound Christian principle, and how far they are consistent with it.

Now that perfect state of mind at which we must aim, and which the Holy Spirit imparts, is a deliberate preference of God's service to every thing else, a determined resolution to give up all for Him; and a love for Him, not tumultuous and passionate, but such love as a child bears towards his parents, calm, full, reverent, contemplative, obedient. Here, however, it may be objected, that this is not always possible: that we cannot help feeling emotion at times; that even to take the case of parents and children, a man is at certain times thrown out of that quiet affection which he bears towards his father and mother, and is agitated by various feelings; again, that zeal, for instance, though a Christian virtue, is almost inseparable from ardour and passion. To this I reply, that I am not describing the state of mind to which any one of us has *attained,* when I say it is altogether calm and meditative, but that which is the *perfect* state, that which we should aim at. I know it *is* often impossible, for various reasons, to avoid being agitated and excited; but the question before us is, whether we should *think highly* of violent emotion, whether we should encourage it. Doubtless it is no sin to feel at times passionately on the subject of religion; it is natural in some men, and under certain circumstances it is praiseworthy in others. But these are accidents. As a general rule, the more religious men become, the calmer they become; and at all times the religious principle, viewed by itself, is calm, sober, and deliberate.

Let us review some of the accidental circumstances I speak of.

1. The natural tempers of men vary very much. Some men have ardent imaginations and strong feelings; and adopt, as a matter of course, a vehement mode of expressing themselves. No doubt it is impossible to make all men

think and feel alike. Such men of course may possess deep-rooted principle. All I would maintain is, that their ardour does not of itself make their faith deeper and more genuine; that they must not think themselves better than others on account of it; that they must be aware of considering it a proof of their real earnestness, instead of narrowly searching into their conduct for the satisfactory *fruits* of faith.

2. Next, there are, besides, particular occasions on which excited feeling is natural, and even commendable; but not for its own sake, but *on account* of the peculiar circumstances under which it occurs. For instance, it is natural for a man to feel especial remorse at his sins when he first begins to think of religion; he *ought* to feel bitter sorrow and keen repentance. But all such emotion evidently is not the highest state of a Christian's mind; it is but the first stirring of grace in him. A sinner, indeed, can do no better; but in proportion as he learns more of the power of true religion, such agitation will wear away. What is this but saying, that change of mind is only the inchoate state of a Christian? Who doubts that sinners are bound to repent and turn to God? yet the Angels have no repentance; and who denies their peacefulness of soul to be a higher excellence than ours? The woman who had been a sinner, when she came behind our Lord wept much, and washed His feet with tears.[3] It was well done in her; she did what she could; and was honoured with our Saviour's praise. Yet it is clear this was not a permanent state of mind. It was but the first step in religion, and would doubtless wear away. It was but the accident of a season. Had her faith no deeper root than this emotion, it would soon have come to an end, as Peter's zeal.

In like manner, whenever we fall into sin, (and how often is this the case!) the truer our faith is, the more we shall for the time be distressed, perhaps agitated. No doubt; yet it would be a strange procedure to make much of this disquietude. Though it is a bad sign if we do not feel it (according to our mental temperament), yet if we do, what then? It argues no high Christian excellence; I repeat it, it is but the virtue of a very imperfect state. Bad is the best offering we can offer to God after sinning. On the other hand, the more consistent our habitual obedience, the less we shall be subject to such feelings.

3. And further, the accidents of life will occasionally agitate us: — affliction and pain; bad news; though here, too, the Psalmist describes the higher excellence of the mind, viz. the calm confidence of the believer, who "will not be afraid of any evil tidings, *for* his heart standeth fast, and believeth in the Lord."[4] Times of persecution will agitate the mind; circumstances of especial interest in the fortunes of the Church will cause anxiety and fear. We see the

3. Luke vii. 38.
4. Ps. cxii. 7.

influence of some of these causes in various parts of St. Paul's Epistles. Such emotion, however, is not the essence of true faith, though it accidentally accompanies it. In times of distress religious men will speak more openly on the subject of religion, and lay bare their feelings; at other times they will conceal them. They are neither better nor worse for so doing.

Now all this may be illustrated from Scripture. We find the same prayers offered, and the same resolutions expressed by good men, sometimes in a calm way, sometimes with more ardour. How quietly and simply does Agur offer his prayer to God! "Two things have I required of Thee; deny me them not before I die. Remove far from me vanity and lies; give me neither poverty nor riches; feed me with food convenient for me." St. Paul, on the other hand, with greater fervency, because he was in more distressing circumstances, but with not more acceptableness on that account in God's sight, says, "I have learned in whatsoever state I am, therewith to be content. I know both how to be abased, and I know how to abound;" and so he proceeds. Again, Joshua says, simply but firmly, "As for me and my house, we will serve the Lord." St. Paul says as firmly, but with more emotion, when his friends besought him to keep away from Jerusalem:—"What mean ye to weep and to break mine heart? for I am ready not to be bound only, but also to die at Jerusalem for the name of the Lord Jesus." Observe how calm Job is in his resignation: "The Lord gave, the Lord hath taken away; blessed be the name of the Lord." And on the other hand, how calmly that same Apostle expresses his assurance of salvation at the close of his life, who, during the struggle, was accidentally agitated:—"I am now ready to be offered. . . . . I have kept the faith. Henceforth there is laid up for me a crown of righteousness."[5]

These remarks may suffice to show the relation which excited feelings bear to true religious principle. They are sometimes natural, sometimes suitable; but they are not religion itself. They come and go. They are not to be counted on, or encouraged; for, as in St. Peter's case, they may supplant true faith, and lead to self-deception. They will gradually lose their place within us as our obedience becomes confirmed;—partly because those men are kept in perfect peace, and sheltered from all agitating feelings, whose minds are stayed on God;[6]—partly because these feelings themselves are fixed into habits by the power of faith, and instead of coming and going, and agitating the mind from their suddenness, they are permanently retained so far as there is any thing good in them, and give a deeper colour and a more energetic expression to the Christian character.

Now, it will be observed, that in these remarks I have taken for granted, as

---

5. Prov. xxx. 7, 8. Phil. iv. 11, 12. Josh. xxiv. 15. Acts xxi. 13. Job i. 21. 2 Tim. iv. 6–8.
6. Isa. xxvi. 3.

not needing proof, that the highest Christian temper is free from all vehement and tumultuous feeling. But, if we wish some evidence of this, let us turn to our Great Pattern, Jesus Christ, and examine what was the character of that perfect holiness which He alone of all men ever displayed.

And can we find any where such calmness and simplicity as marked His devotion and His obedience? When does He ever speak with fervour or vehemence? Or, if there be one or two words of His in His mysterious agony and death, characterized by an energy which we do not comprehend, and which sinners must silently adore, still how conspicuous and undeniable is His composure in the general tenour of His words and conduct! Consider the prayer He gave us; and this is the more to the purpose, for the very reason that He has given it as a model for our worship. How plain and unadorned is it! How few are the words of it! How grave and solemn the petitions! What an entire absence of tumult and feverish emotion! Surely our own feelings tell us, it could not be otherwise. To suppose it otherwise were an irreverence towards Him.—At another time when He is said to have "rejoiced in spirit," His thanksgiving is marked with the same undisturbed tranquility. "I thank Thee, O Father, Lord of heaven and earth, that Thou hast hid these things from the wise and prudent, and hast revealed them unto babes. Even so, Father, for so it seemed good in Thy sight."—Again, think of His prayer in the garden. He then was in distress of mind beyond our understanding. Something there was, we know not what, which weighed heavy upon Him. He prayed He might be spared the extreme bitterness of His trial. Yet how subdued and how concise is His petition! "Abba, Father, all things are possible unto Thee: take away this cup from Me; nevertheless, not what I will, but what Thou wilt."[7] And this is but one instance, though a chief one, of that deep tranquility of mind, which is conspicuous throughout the solemn history of the Atonement. Read the thirteenth chapter of St. John, in which He is described as washing His disciples' feet, Peter's in particular. Reflect upon His serious words addressed at several times to Judas who betrayed Him; and His conduct when seized by His enemies, when brought before Pilate, and lastly, when suffering on the cross. When does He set us an example of passionate devotion, of enthusiastic wishes, or of intemperate words?

Such is the lesson our Saviour's conduct teaches us. Now let me remind you how diligently we are taught the same by our own Church. Christ gave us a prayer to guide us in praying to the Father; and upon this model our own Liturgy is strictly formed. You will look in vain in the Prayer Book for long or vehement Prayers; for it is only upon occasions that agitation of mind is right,

---

7. Luke x. 21. Mark xiv. 36.

but there is ever a call upon us for seriousness, gravity, simplicity, deliberate trust, deep-seated humility. Many persons, doubtless, think the Church prayers, for this very reason, cold and formal. They do not discern their high perfection, and they think they could easily write better prayers. When such opinions are advanced, it is quite sufficient to turn our thoughts to our Saviour's precept and example. It cannot be denied that those who thus speak, ought to consider our Lord's prayer defective; and sometimes they are profane enough to think so, and to confess they think so. But I pass this by. Granting for argument's sake His *precepts* were intentionally defective, as delivered before the Holy Ghost descended, yet what will they say to His *example?* Can even the fullest light of the Gospel revealed after His resurrection, bring us His followers into the remotest resemblance to our Blessed Lord's holiness? yet how calm was He, who was perfect man, in His own obedience!

To conclude: — Let us take warning from St. Peter's fall. Let us not promise much; let us not talk much of ourselves; let us not be high-minded, nor encourage ourselves in impetuous bold language in religion. Let us take warning, too, from that fickle multitude who cried, first Hosanna, then Crucify. A miracle startled them into a sudden adoration of their Saviour; — its effect upon them soon died away. And thus the especial mercies of God sometimes excite us for a season. We feel Christ speaking to us through our consciences and hearts; and we fancy He is assuring us we are His true servants, when He is but calling on us to receive Him. Let us not be content with saying "Lord, Lord," without "doing the thing which He says." The husbandman's son who said, "I go, sir," yet went not to the vineyard, gained nothing by his fair words. One secret act of self-denial, one sacrifice of inclination to duty, is worth all the mere good thoughts, warm feelings, passionate prayers, in which idle people indulge themselves. It will give us more comfort on our death-bed to reflect on one deed of self-denying mercy, purity, or humility, than to recollect the shedding of many tears, and the recurrence of frequent transports, and much spiritual exultation. These latter feelings come and go; they may or may not accompany hearty obedience; they are never tests of it; but good actions are the fruits of faith, and assure us that we are Christ's; they comfort us as an evidence of the Spirit working in us. By them we shall be judged at the last day; and though they have no worth in themselves, by reason of that infection of sin which gives its character to every thing we do, yet they will be accepted for His sake, who bore the agony in the garden, and suffered as a sinner on the cross.

The Religious Use of Excited Feelings

"The man out of whom the devils were departed besought Him that he might be with Him; but Jesus sent him away, saying, Return to thine own house, and show how great things God hath done unto thee." — LUKE viii. 38, 39.

It was very natural in the man whom our Lord had set free from this dreadful visitation, to wish to continue with Him. Doubtless his mind was transported with joy and gratitude; whatever consciousness he might possess of his real wretchedness while the devils tormented him, now at least, on recovering his reason, he would understand that he had been in a very miserable state, and he would feel all the lightness of spirits and activity of mind, which attend any release from suffering or constraint. Under these circumstances he would imagine himself to be in a new world; he had found deliverance; and what was more, a Deliverer too, who stood before him. And whether from a wish to be ever in His Divine presence, ministering to Him, or from a fear lest Satan would return, nay, with sevenfold power, did he lose sight of Christ, or from an undefined notion that all his duties and hopes were now changed, that his former pursuits were unworthy of him, and that he must follow up some great undertakings with the new ardour he felt glowing within him; — from one or other, or all of these feelings combined, he besought our Lord that he might be with Him. Christ imposed this attendance as a command on others; He bade, for instance, the young ruler follow Him; but He gives opposite commands, according to our tempers and likings; He thwarts us, that He may try our faith. In the case before us He suffered not, what at other times He had bidden. "Return to thine own house," He said, or as it is in St. Mark's Gospel, "Go home to thy friends, and tell them how great things the Lord hath done for thee, and hath had compassion on thee."[1] He directed the current of his newly-awakened feelings into another channel; as if He said, "Lovest thou Me? this do; return home to your old occupations and pursuits. You did them ill before, you lived to the world; do them well now, live to Me. Do your duties, little as well as great, heartily for My sake; go among your friends; show them what God hath done for thee; be an example to them, and teach them."[2] And further, as He said on another occasion, "Show thyself to the priest, and offer the gift that Moses commanded, for a testimony unto them,"[3] — show forth that greater light and truer love which you now possess in a conscientious, consistent obedience to all the ordinances and rites of your religion.

Now from this account of the restored demoniac, his request, and our Lord's denial of it, a lesson may be drawn for the use of those who, having neglected religion in early youth, at length begin to have serious thoughts, try to repent, and wish to serve God better than hitherto, though they do not know how to set about it. We know that God's commandments are pleasant, and "rejoice the heart," if we accept them in the order and manner in which He puts them upon us; that Christ's yoke, as He has promised, is (on the whole) very easy, if we submit to it betimes; that the practice of religion is full of comfort to those who, being first baptized with the Spirit of grace, receive thankfully His influences as their minds open, inasmuch as they are gradually and almost without sensible effort on their part, imbued in all their heart, soul, and strength, with that true heavenly life which will last for ever.

But here the question meets us, "But what are those to do who *have* neglected to remember their Creator in the days of their youth, and so have lost all claim on Christ's promise, that His yoke shall be easy, and His commandments not grievous?" I answer, that of course they must not be surprised if obedience is with them a laborious up-hill work all their days; nay, as having been "once enlightened, and partaken of the Holy Ghost" in baptism, they would have no right to complain even though "it were impossible for them to renew themselves again unto repentance." But God is more merciful than this just severity; merciful not only above our deservings, but even above His own

1. Mark v. 19.
2. Col. iii. 17.
3. Matt. viii. 4.

promises. Even for those who have neglected Him when young, He has found (if they will avail themselves of it) some sort of remedy of the difficulties in the way of obedience which they have brought upon themselves by sinning; and what this remedy is, and how it is to be used, I proceed to describe in connexion with the account in the text.

The help I speak of is the excited feeling with which repentance is at first attended. True it is, that all the passionate emotion, or fine sensibility, which ever man displayed, will never by itself make us change our ways, and do our duty. Impassioned thoughts, high aspirations, sublime imaginings, have no strength in them. They can no more make a man obey consistently, than they can move mountains. If any man truly repent, it must be in consequence, not of these, but of a settled conviction of his guilt, and a deliberate resolution to leave his sins and serve God. Conscience, and Reason in subjection to Conscience, *these* are those powerful instruments (under grace) which change a man. But you will observe, that though Conscience and Reason lead us to resolve on and to attempt a new life, they cannot at once make us *love* it. It is long practice and habit which make us love religion; and in the beginning, obedience, doubtless, is very grievous to habitual sinners. Here then is the use of those earnest, ardent feelings of which I just now spoke, and which attend on the first exercise of Conscience and Reason, — to take away from the *beginnings* of obedience its *grievousness*, to give us an impulse which may carry us over the first obstacles, and send us on our way rejoicing. Not as if all this excitement of mind were to last (which cannot be), but it will do its office in thus setting us off; and then will leave us to the more sober and higher comfort resulting from that real *love* for religion, which obedience itself will have by that time begun to form in us, and will gradually go on to perfect.

Now it is well to understand this fully, for it is often mistaken. When sinners at length are led to think seriously, strong feelings generally precede or attend their reflections about themselves. Some book they have read, some conversation of a friend, some remarks they have heard made in church, or some occurrence or misfortune, rouses them. Or, on the other hand, if in any more calm and deliberate manner they have commenced their self-examination, yet in a little time the very view of their manifold sins, of their guilt, and of their heinous ingratitude to their God and Saviour, breaking upon them, and being new to them, strikes, and astonishes, and then agitates them. Here, then, let them know the *intention* of all this excitement of mind in the order of Divine providence. It will not continue; it arises from the novelty of the view presented to them. As they become accustomed to religious contemplations, it will wear away. It is not religion itself, though it is accidentally connected with it, and may be made a means of leading them into a sound religious course of life. It is graciously intended to be a set-off in their case against the first distastefulness and pain of doing their duty; it must be used as such, or it will be of no use at all, or worse than useless. My brethren, bear this in mind (and I may say this generally, — not confining myself to the excitement which attends repentance, — of all that natural emotion prompting us to do good, which we involuntarily feel on various occasions), it is given you in order that you may find it easy to obey at starting. Therefore obey *promptly;* make use of it whilst it lasts; it waits for no man. Do you feel natural pity towards some case which reasonably demands your charity? or the impulse of generosity in a case where you are called to act a manly self-denying part? Whatever the emotion may be, whether these or any other, do not imagine you will always feel it. Whether you avail yourselves of it or not, still any how you will feel it less and less, and, as life goes on, at last you will not feel such sudden vehement excitement at all. But this is the difference between seizing or letting slip these opportunities; — if you avail yourselves of them for acting, and yield to the impulse so far as conscience tells you to do, you have made a leap (so to say) across a gulf, to which your ordinary strength is not equal; you will have secured the beginning of obedience, and the further steps in the course are (generally speaking) far easier than those which first determine its direction. And so, to return to the case of those who feel any accidental remorse for their sins violently exerting itself in their hearts, I say to them, Do not loiter; go home to your friends, and repent in *deeds* of righteousness and love; hasten to commit yourselves to certain definite *acts* of obedience. Doing is at a far greater distance from intending to do than you at first sight imagine. Join them together while you can; you will be depositing your good feelings into your heart itself by thus making them influence your conduct; and they will "spring up into fruit." This was the conduct of the conscience-stricken Corinthians, as described by St. Paul; who rejoiced "not that they were made *sorry* (not that their feelings merely were moved), but that they sorrowed *to change of mind.* . . . For godly sorrow (he continues) worketh repentance to salvation not to be repented of; but the sorrow of the world worketh death."[4]

But now let us ask, how do men usually conduct themselves in matter of fact, when under visitings of conscience for their past sinful lives? They are far from thus acting. They look upon the turbid zeal and feverish devotion which attend their repentance, not as in part the corrupt offspring of their own previously corrupt state of mind, and partly a gracious natural provision, only temporary, to encourage them to set about their reformation, but as the substance and real excellence of religion. They think that to be thus agitated is to

---

4. 2 Cor. vii. 9, 10.

be religious; they indulge themselves in these warm feelings for their own sake, resting in them as if they were then engaged in a religious exercise, and boasting of them as if they were an evidence of their own exalted spiritual state; not *using them* (the one only thing they ought to do), using them as an incitement to *deeds* of love, mercy, truth, meekness, holiness. After they have indulged this luxury of feeling for some time, the excitement of course ceases; they do not feel as they did before. This (I have said) might have been anticipated, but they do not understand it so. See then their unsatisfactory state. They have lost an opportunity of overcoming the first difficulties of active obedience, and so of fixing their conduct and character, which may never occur again. This is one great misfortune; but more than this, what a perplexity they have involved themselves in! Their warmth of feeling is gradually dying away. Now they think that *in it* true religion consists; therefore they believe that they are losing their faith, and falling into sin again.

And this, alas! *is* too often the case; they *do* fall away, for they have no root in themselves. Having neglected to turn their feelings into principles by acting upon them, they have no inward strength to overcome the temptation to live as the world, which continually assails them. Their minds have been acted upon as water by the wind, which raises waves for a time, then ceasing, leaves the water to subside into its former stagnant state. The precious opportunity of improvement has been lost; "and the latter end is worse with them than the beginning."[5]

But let us suppose, that when they first detect this declension (as they consider it), they are alarmed, and look around for a means of recovering themselves. What do they do? Do they at once begin those practices of lowly obedience which alone can prove them to be Christ's at the last day? such as the government of their tempers, the regulation of their time, self-denying charity, truth-telling sobriety. Far from it; they despise this plain obedience to God as a mere unenlightened morality, as they call it, and they seek for potent stimulants to sustain their minds in that state of excitement which they have been taught to consider the essence of a religious life, and which they cannot produce by the means which before excited them. They have recourse to new doctrines, or follow strange teachers, in order that they may dream on in this their artificial devotion, and may avoid that conviction which is likely sooner or later to burst upon them, that emotion and passion are in our power indeed to repress, but not to *excite;* that there is a limit to the tumults and swellings of the heart, foster them as we will; and, when that time comes, the poor, misused soul is left exhausted and resourceless. Instances are not rare in the world

---

5. 2 Pet. ii. 20.

of that fearful, ultimate state of hard-heartedness which then succeeds; when the miserable sinner believes indeed as the devils may, yet not even with the devils' trembling, but sins on without fear.

Others, again, there are, who, when their feelings fall off in strength and fervency, are led to despond; and so are brought down to fear and bondage, when they might have been rejoicing in cheerful obedience. These are the better sort, who, having something of true religious principle in their hearts, still are misled in part, — so far, that is, as to rest in their feelings as tests of holiness; therefore they are distressed and alarmed at their own tranquillity, which they think a bad sign, and, being dispirited, lose time, others outstripping them in the race.

And others might be mentioned who are led by this same first eagerness and zeal into a different error. The restored sufferer in the text wished to be with Christ. Now it is plain, all those who indulge themselves in the false devotion I have been describing, may be said to be desirous of thus keeping themselves in Christ's immediate sight, instead of returning to their own home, as He would have them, that is, to the common duties of life: and they do this, some from weakness of faith, as if He could not bless them, and keep them in the way of grace, though they pursued their worldly callings; others from an ill-directed love of Him. But there are others, I say, who, when they are awakened to a sense of religion, forthwith despise their former condition altogether, as beneath them; and think that they are now called to some high and singular office in the Church. These mistake their duty as those already described neglect it; they do not waste their time in mere good thoughts and good words, as the others, but they are impetuously led on to *wrong acts,* and that from the influence of those same strong emotions which they have not learned to use aright or direct to their proper end. But to speak of these now at any length would be beside my subject.

To conclude; — let me repeat and urge upon you, my brethren, the lesson which I have deduced from the narrative of which the text forms part. Your Saviour calls you from infancy to serve Him, and has arranged all things well, so that His service shall be perfect freedom. Blessed above all men are they who heard His call then, and served Him day by day, as their strength to obey increased. But further, are you conscious that you have more or less neglected this gracious opportunity, and suffered yourselves to be tormented by Satan? See, He calls you a second time; He calls you by your roused affections and once again, ere He leave you finally. He brings you back for the time (as it were) to a second youth by the urgent persuasions of excited fear, gratitude, love, and hope. He again places you for an instant in that early, unformed state of nature when habit and character were not. He takes you out of yourselves, robbing sin for a season of its in-dwelling hold upon you. Let not those visitings pass away "as the morning cloud and the early dew."[6] Surely, you must still have occasional compunctions of conscience for your neglect of Him. Your sin stares you in the face; your ingratitude to God affects you. Follow on to know the Lord, and to secure His favour by *acting* upon these impulses; by them He pleads with you, as well as by your conscience; they are the instruments of His spirit, stirring you up to seek your true peace. Nor be surprised, though you obey them, that they die away; they have done their office, and if they die, it is but as blossom changes into the fruit, which is far better. They *must* die. Perhaps you will have to labour in darkness afterwards, out of your Saviour's sight, in the home of your own thoughts, surrounded by sights of this world, and showing forth His praise among those who are cold-hearted. Still be quite sure that resolute, consistent obedience, though unattended with high transport and warm emotion, is far more acceptable to Him than all those passionate longings to live in His sight, which look more like religion to the uninstructed. At the very best these latter are but the graceful beginnings of obedience, graceful and becoming in children, but in grown spiritual men indecorous, as the sports of boyhood would seem in advanced years. Learn to live by faith, which is a calm, deliberate, rational principle, full of peace and comfort, and sees Christ, and rejoices in Him, though sent away from His presence to labour in the world. You will have your reward. He will "see you again, and your heart shall rejoice, and your joy no man taketh from you."

---

6. Hosea vi. 4.

Sudden Conversions

"By the grace of God I am what I am: and His grace which was bestowed upon me was not in vain." — 1 COR. xv. 10.

We can hardly conceive that grace, such as that given to the great Apostle who speaks in the text, would have been given in vain; that is, we should not expect that it would have been given, had it been foreseen and designed by the Almighty Giver that it would have been in vain. By which I do not mean, of course, to deny that God's gifts are oftentimes abused and wasted by man, which they are; but, when we consider the wonderful mode of St. Paul's conversion, and the singular privilege granted him, the only one of men of whom is clearly recorded the privilege of seeing Christ with his bodily eyes after His ascension, as is alluded to shortly before the text; I say, considering these high and extraordinary favours vouchsafed to the Apostle, we should naturally suppose that some great objects in the history of the Church were contemplated by means of them, such as in the event were fulfilled. We cannot tell, indeed, why God works, or by what rule He chooses; we must always be sober and humble in our thoughts about His ways, which are infinitely above our ways; but what would be speculation, perhaps venturous speculation, before the event, at least becomes a profitable meditation after it. At least, now, when we read and dwell on St. Paul's history, we may discern and insist upon the suitableness of his character, before his conversion, for that display of free grace which was made in him. Not that he could merit such a great mercy — the idea is absurd as well as wicked; but that such a one as he was before God's grace, naturally grew by the aid of it into what he was afterwards as a Christian.

His, indeed, was a "wonderful conversion," as our Church in one place calls it, because it was so unexpected, and (as far as the appearance went) so sudden. Who of the suffering Christians, against whom he was raging so furiously, could have conceived that their enemy was to be the great preacher and champion of the despised Cross? Does God work miracles to reclaim His open malevolent adversaries, and not rather to encourage and lead forward those who timidly seek Him?

It may be useful, then, to mention one or two kinds of what may be called sudden conversions, to give some opinion on the character of each of them, and to inquire which of them really took place in St. Paul's case.

1. First; some men turn to religion all at once from some sudden impulse of mind, some powerful excitement, or some strong persuasion. It is a sudden resolve that comes upon them. Now such cases occur very frequently where religion has nothing to do with the matter, and then we think little about it, merely calling the persons who thus change all at once volatile and light-minded. Thus there are persons who all of a sudden give up some pursuit which they have been eagerly set upon, or change from one trade or calling to another, or change their opinions as regards the world's affairs. Every one knows the impression left upon the mind by such instances. The persons thus changing may be, and often are, amiable, kind, and pleasant, as companions; but we cannot depend on them; and we pity them, as believing they are doing harm both to their temporal interests and to their own minds. Others there are who almost profess to love change for change-sake; they think the pleasure of life consists in seeing first one thing, then another; variety is their chief good; and it is a sufficient objection in their minds to any pursuit or recreation, that it is old. These, too, pass suddenly and capriciously from one subject to another. So far in matters of daily life; — but when such a person exhibits a similar changeableness in his religious views, then men begin to be astonished, and look out with curiosity or anxiety to see what is the meaning of it; and particularly if the individual who thus suddenly changed, was very decided before in the particular course of life which he then followed. For instance, supposing he not merely professed no deep religious impressions, but actually was unbelieving or profligate; or, again, supposing he not merely professed himself of this creed or that, but was very warm, and even bitter in the enforcement of it;

then, I say, men wonder, though they do not wonder at similar infirmities in matters of this world.

Nor can I say that they are wrong in being alive to such changes; we *ought* to feel differently with reference to religious subjects, and not be as unconcerned about them as we are about the events of time. Did a man suddenly inform us, with great appearance of earnestness, that he had seen an accident in the street, or did he say that he had seen a miracle, I confess it is natural, nay, in the case of most men, certainly in the case of the uneducated, far more religious, to feel differently towards these two accounts; to feel shocked, indeed, but not awed, at the first—to feel a certain solemn astonishment and pious reverence at the news of the miracle. For a religious mind is ever looking towards God, and seeking His traces; referring all events to Him, and desirous of His explanation of them; and when to such a one information is brought that God has in some extraordinary way showed Himself, he *will* at first sight be tempted to believe it, and it is only the experience of the number of deceits and false prophecies which are in the world, his confidence in the Catholic Church which he sees before him, and which is his guide into the truth, and (if he be educated) his enlightened views concerning the course and laws of God's providence, which keep him steady and make him hard to believe such stories. On the other hand, men destitute of religion altogether, of course from the first ridicule such accounts, and, as the event shows, rightly; and yet, in spite of this, they are not so worthy our regard as those who at first were credulous, from having some religious principle without enough religious knowledge. Therefore, I am not surprised that such sudden conversions as I have been describing deceive for a time even the better sort of people—whom I should blame, if I were called on to do so, not so much for the mere fact of their believing readily, but for their not believing the Church; for believing private individuals who have no authority more than the Church, and for not recollecting St. Paul's words, "If any man . . . though we, or an Angel from heaven, preach any other Gospel unto you than that ye have received, let him be accursed."[1]

2. In the cases of sudden conversion I have been speaking of, when men change at once either from open sin, or again from the zealous partizanship of a certain creed, to some novel form of faith or worship, their light-mindedness is detected by their frequent changing—their changing again and again, so that one can never be certain of them. This is the test of their unsoundness;—having no root in themselves, their convictions and earnestness quickly wither

1. Gal. i. 8, 9.

away. But there is another kind of sudden conversion, which I proceed to mention, in which a man perseveres to the end, consistent in the new form he adopts, and which may be right or wrong, as it happens, but which *he* cannot be said to recommend or confirm to us by his own change. I mean when a man, for some reason or other, whether in religion or not, takes a great disgust to his present course of life, and suddenly abandons it for another. This is the case of those who rush from one to the other extreme, and it generally arises from strong and painful feeling, unsettling and, as it were, revolutionizing the mind. A story is told of a spendthrift who, having ruined himself by his extravagances, went out of doors to meditate on his own folly and misery, and in the course of a few hours returned home a determined miser, and was for the rest of his life remarkable for covetousness and penuriousness. This is not more extraordinary than the fickleness of mind just now described. In like manner, men sometimes will change suddenly from love to hatred, from over-daring to cowardice. These are no amiable changes, whether arising or not from bodily malady, as is sometimes the case; nor do they impart any credit or sanction to the particular secular course or habit of mind adopted on the change: neither do they in religion therefore. A man who suddenly professes religion after a profligate life, merely because he is sick of his vices, or tormented by the thought of God's anger, which is the consequence of them, and without the love of God, does no honour to religion, for he might, if it so chanced, turn a miser or a misanthrope; and, therefore, though religion is not at all the less holy and true because he submits himself to it, and though doubtless it is a much better thing for *him* that he turns to religion than that he should become a miser or a misanthrope, still, when he acts on such motives as I have described, he cannot be said to do any honour to the cause of religion by his conversion. Yet it is such persons who at various times have been thought great saints, and been reckoned to recommend and prove the truth of the Gospel to the world!

Now if any one asks what test there is that this kind of sudden conversion is not from God, as instability and frequent change are the test, on the other hand, in disproof of the divinity of the conversions just now mentioned, I answer, — its moroseness, inhumanity, and unfitness for this world. Men who change through strong passion and anguish become as hard and as rigid as stone or iron; they are not fit for life; they are only fit for the solitudes in which they sometimes bury themselves; they can only do one or two of their duties, and that only in one way; they do not indeed change their principles, as the fickle convert, but, on the other hand, they cannot apply, adapt, accommodate, modify, diversify their principles to the existing state of things, which is the opposite fault. They do not aim at a perfect obedience in little things as well as great; and a most serious fault it is, looking at it merely as a matter of practice, and without any reference to the views and motives from which it proceeds; most opposed is it to the spirit of true religion, which is intended to fit us for all circumstances of life as they come, in order that we may be humble, docile, ready, patient, and cheerful, — in order that we may really show ourselves God's servants, who do all things for Him, coming when He calleth, going when He sendeth, doing this or that at His bidding. So much for the practice of such men; and when we go higher, and ask *why* they are thus formal and unbending in their mode of life, what are the principles that make them thus harsh and unserviceable, I fear we must trace it to some form of selfishness and pride; the same principles which, under other circumstances, would change the profligate into the covetous and parsimonious.

I think it will appear at once that St. Paul's conversion, however it was effected, and whatever was the process of it, resembled neither the one nor the other of these. That it was not the change of a fickle mind is shown by his firmness in keeping to his new faith — by his constancy unto death, a death of martyrdom. That it was not the change of a proud and disappointed mind, quitting with disgust what he once loved too well, is evidenced by the variety of his labours, his active services, and continued presence in the busy thoroughfares of the world; by the cheerfulness, alacrity, energy, dexterity, and perseverance, with which he pleaded the cause of God among sinners. He reminds us of his firmness, as well as gentleness, when he declares, "What mean ye to weep, and break my heart? for I am ready not to be bound only, but also to die at Jerusalem for the Name of the Lord Jesus;" and of his ready accommodation of himself to the will of God, in all its forms, when he says, "I am made all things to all men, that I might by all means save some."[2]

3. But there is another kind of sudden conversion, or rather what appears to be such, not uncommonly found, and which may be that to which St. Paul's conversion is to be referred, and which I proceed to describe.

When men change their religious opinions really and truly, it is not merely their opinions that they change, but their hearts; and this evidently is not done in a moment — it is a slow work; nevertheless, though gradual, the change is often not uniform, but proceeds, so to say, by fits and starts, being influenced by external events, and other circumstances. This we see in the growth of plants, for instance; it is slow, gradual, continual; yet one day by chance they grow more than another, they make a shoot, or at least we are attracted to their growth on that day by some accidental circumstance, and it remains on our memory. So with our souls: we all, by nature, are far from God; nay, and

2. Acts xxi. 13. 1 Cor. ix. 22.

we have all characters to form, which is a work of time. All this must have a beginning; and those who are now leading religious lives have begun at different times. Baptism, indeed, is God's time, when He first gives us grace; but alas! through the perverseness of our will, we do not follow Him. There must be a time then for beginning. Many men do not at all recollect any one marked and definite time *when* they began to seek God. Others recollect a time, not, properly speaking, when they began, but when they made what may be called a shoot forward, the fact either being so, in consequence of external events, or at least for some reason or other their attention being called to it. Others, again, continue forming a religious character and religious opinions as the result of it, though holding at the same time some outward profession of faith inconsistent with them; as, for instance, suppose it has been their unhappy condition to be brought up as heathens, Jews, infidels, or heretics. They hold the notions they have been taught for a long while, not perceiving that the character forming within them is at variance with these, till at length the inward growth forces itself forward, forces on the opinions accompanying it, and the dead outward surface of error, which has no root in their minds, from some accidental occurrence, suddenly falls off; suddenly, — just as a building might suddenly fall, which had been going many years, and which falls at this moment rather than that, in consequence of some chance cause, as it is called, which we cannot detect.

Now in all these cases one point of time is often taken by religious men, as if the very time of conversion, and as if it were sudden, though really, as is plain, in none of them is there any suddenness in the matter. In the last of these instances, which might be in a measure, if we dare say it, St. Paul's case, the time when the formal outward profession of error fell off, is taken as the time of conversion. Others recollect the first occasion when any deep serious thought came into their minds, and reckon this as the date of their inward change. Others, again, recollect some intermediate point of time when they first openly professed their faith, or dared do some noble deed for Christ's sake.

I might go on to show more particularly how what I have said applies to St. Paul; but as this would take too much time I will only observe generally, that there was much in St. Paul's character which was not changed on his conversion, but merely directed to other and higher objects, and purified; it was his creed that was changed, and his soul by regeneration; and though he was sinning most grievously and awfully when Christ appeared to him from heaven, he evidenced then, as afterwards, a most burning energetic zeal for God, a most scrupulous strictness of life, an abstinence from all self-indulgence, much more from all approach to sensuality or sloth, and an implicit obedience to what he considered God's will. It was pride which was his inward enemy — pride which needed an overthrow. He acted rather as a defender and protector, than a minister of what he considered the truth; he relied on his own views; he was positive and obstinate; he did not seek for light as a little child; he did not look out for a Saviour who was to come, and he missed Him when He came.

But how great was the change in these respects when he became a servant of Him whom he had persecuted! As he had been conspicuous for a proud confidence in self, on his privileges, on his knowledge, on his birth, on his observances, so he became conspicuous for his humility. What self-abasement, when he says, "I am the least of the Apostles, that am not meet to be called an Apostle, because I persecuted the Church of God; but by the grace of God I am what I am." What keen and bitter remembrance of the past, when he says, "Who was before a blasphemer, and a persecutor, and injurious; but I obtained mercy, because I did it ignorantly in unbelief."[3] Ah! what utter self-abandonment, what scorn and hatred of self, when he, who had been so pleased to be a Hebrew of Hebrews, and a Pharisee, bore to be called, nay gloried for Christ's sake in being called, an apostate, the most odious and miserable of titles! — bore to be spurned and spit upon as a renegade, a traitor, a false-hearted and perfidious, a fallen, a lost son of his Church; a shame to his mother, and a curse to his countrymen. Such was the light in which those furious zealots looked on the great Apostle, who bound themselves together by an oath that they would neither eat nor drink till they had killed him. It was their justification in their own eyes, that he was a "pestilent fellow," a "stirrer of seditions," and an abomination amid sacred institutions which God had given.

And, lastly, what supported him in this great trial? that special mercy which converted him, which he, and he only, saw — the Face of Jesus Christ. That all-pitying, all-holy eye, which turned in love upon St. Peter when he denied Him, and thereby roused him to repentance, looked on St. Paul also, while he persecuted Him, and wrought in him a sudden conversion. "Last of all," he says, "He was seen of me also, as of one born out of due time." One sight of that Divine Countenance, so tender, so loving, so majestic, so calm, was enough, first to convert him, then to support him on his way amid the bitter hatred and fury which he was to excite in those who hitherto had loved him.

And if such be the effect of a momentary vision of the glorious Presence of Christ, what think you, my brethren, will be their bliss, to whom it shall be given, this life ended, to see that Face eternally?

---

3. 1 Tim. i. 13.

Wisdom and Innocence

> *"Behold, I send you forth as sheep in the midst of wolves; be ye therefore wise as serpents, and harmless as doves."* — MATTHEW x. 16.

Sheep are defenceless, wolves are strong and fierce. How prompt, how frightful, how resistless, how decisive, would be the attack of a troop of wolves on a few straggling sheep which fell in with them! and how lively, then, is the image which our Lord uses, to express the treatment which His followers were to receive from the world! He Himself was the great Exemplar of all such sufferings. When He was in the hands of His enemies, surrounded by a mad multitude, gazed on by relentless enemies, jeered at, struck, hurried along, tormented by rude soldiers, and at length nailed to the cross, what was He emphatically but a sheep among wolves? "He is brought as a lamb to the slaughter, and as a sheep before her shearers is dumb, so He openeth not His mouth." And what He foretold of His followers, that the Psalmist had declared of them at an earlier time, and His Apostle applies it to them on its fulfilment. "As it is written," says St. Paul, "For Thy sake we are killed all the day long; we are accounted as sheep for the slaughter."[1] Such was the Church of Christ in its beginnings, and such has it been in every age in proportion to its

---

1. Rom. viii. 36.

purity. The purer it has been, the more defenceless; whenever it has been pure, it has, in one way or another, been defenceless. The less worldly it has been, and the more it has cultivated its proper gifts, and the less it has relied upon sword and bow, chariots and horses, and arm of man, the more it has been exposed to ill-usage; the more it has invited oppression, the more it has irritated the proud and powerful. This, I say, is exemplified in every age. Seasons of peace, indeed, have been vouchsafed to it from the first, and in the most fearful times; but not an age of peace. A reign of temporal peace it can hardly enjoy, except under the reign of corruption, and in an age of faithlessness. Peace and rest are future.

Now then, what is it natural to suppose will be the conduct of those who are helpless and persecuted, as the Holy Spouse of Christ? Pain and hardship and disrepute are pleasant to no man; and, though they are to be gloried in when they are undergone, yet they will rather, if possible, be shunned or averted. Such avoidance is sanctioned, nay, commanded, by our Lord. When trials are inevitable, we must cheerfully bear them; but when they can be avoided without sin, we ought to prevent them. But how were Christians to prevent them when they might not fight? I answer, they were allowed the arms, that is, the arts, of the defenceless. Even the inferior animals will teach us how wonderfully the Creator has compensated to the weak their want of strength, by giving them other qualities which may avail in their struggle with the strong. They have the gift of fleetness; or they have a certain make and colour; or certain habits of living; or some natural cunning, which enables them either to elude or even to destroy their enemies. Brute force is countervailed by flight, brute passion by prudence and artifice. Instances of a similar kind occur in our own race. Those nations which are destitute of material force, have recourse to the arts of the unwarlike; they are fraudulent and crafty; they dissemble, negotiate, procrastinate, evading what they cannot resist, and wearing out what they cannot crush. Thus is it with a captive effeminate race, under the rule of the strong and haughty. So is it with slaves; so is it with ill-used and oppressed children; who learn to be cowardly and deceitful towards their tyrants. So is it with the subjects of a despot, who encounter his axe or bowstring with the secret influence of intrigue and conspiracy, the dagger and the poisoned cup. They exercise the unalienable right of self-defence in such methods as they best may; only, since human nature is unscrupulous, guilt or innocence is all the same to them, if it works their purpose.

Now, our Lord and Saviour did not forbid us the exercise of that instinct of self-defence which is born with us. He did not forbid us to defend ourselves, but He forbad certain *modes* of defence. All sinful means, of course, He forbad, as is plain without mentioning. But, besides these, He forbad us what is not sinful, but allowable by nature, though not in that more excellent and perfect way which He taught, — He forbad us to defend ourselves by force, to return blow for blow. "Ye have heard," He says, "that it hath been said, An eye for an eye, and a tooth for a tooth; but I say unto you, that ye resist not evil, but whosoever shall smite thee on thy right cheek, turn to him the other also. And if any man will sue thee at the law, and take away thy coat, let him have thy cloke also. And whosoever shall compel thee to go a mile, go with him twain." Thus the servants of Christ are forbidden to defend themselves by violence; but they are not forbidden other means; direct means are not allowed them, but others are even commanded. For instance, *foresight;* "beware of men:"[2] *avoidance,* "when they persecute you in this city, flee ye into another:" *prudence and skill,* as in the text, "Be ye wise as serpents."

Here we are reminded of the awful history with which the Sacred Volume opens. In the beginning, "the serpent was more subtle than any beast of the field which the Lord God had made." First, observe then, our Lord in the text sanctions that very reference which I have been making, to the instincts and powers of the inferior animals, and puts them forth as our example. As we are to learn industry from the ant, and reliance on Him from the ravens, so the dove is our pattern of innocence, and the serpent of wisdom. But moreover, considering that the serpent was chosen by the Enemy of mankind, as the instrument of his temptations in Paradise, it is very remarkable that Christ should choose it as the pattern of wisdom for His followers. It is as if He appealed to the whole world of sin, and to the bad arts by which the feeble gain advantages here over the strong. It is as if He set before us the craft, the treachery, the perfidy of the captive and the slave, and bade us extract a lesson even from so great an evil. It is as if the more we are forbidden violence, the more we are exhorted to prudence; as if it were our bounden duty to rival the wicked in endowments of mind, and to excel them in their exercise. And He makes a reference of this very kind in one of His parables, where "the lord commended the unjust steward, because he had done wisely; for the children of this world are in their generation wiser than the children of light." "Be ye wise as serpents," He said; then, knowing how dangerous such wisdom is, especially in times of temptation, if a severe conscientiousness is not awake, He added, "and harmless as doves." "Behold, I send you forth as sheep in the midst of wolves; be ye therefore wise as serpents, and harmless as doves."

It needs very little knowledge of the history of the Church, to understand how remarkably this exhortation to wisdom has been fulfilled in it. If there be one reproach more than another which has been cast upon it, it is that of fraud

---

2. Matt. x. 17.

and cunning,—cast upon it even from St. Paul's day, whose word was accused of being "yea and nay;"[3] and himself of "walking in craftiness, and handling the word of God deceitfully;"[4] of being a "deceiver" though he was "true;"[5] of "terrifying by letters;"[6] and of "being crafty," and "catching" his converts "with guile."[7] Nay, cast upon it in the person of our Lord, who was called "a deceiver," and said to "deceive the people." Priestcraft has ever been considered the badge, and its imputation is a kind of note of the Church; and in part, indeed, truly, because the presence of powerful enemies, and the sense of their own weakness, has sometimes tempted Christians to the abuse, instead of the use of Christian wisdom, to be wise without being harmless; but partly, nay, for the most part, not truly, but slanderously, and merely because the world called their wisdom craft, when it was found to be a match for its own numbers and power. Christians were called crafty, because they were so strong, though professing to be weak. And next, in mere consistency, they were called hypocritical, because they were, forsooth, so crafty, professing to be innocent. And thus whereas they have ever, in accordance with our Lord's words, been wise and harmless, they have ever been called instead crafty and hypocritical. The words "craft" and "hypocrisy," are but the version of "wisdom" and "harmlessness," in the language of the world.

It is remarkable, however, that not only is harmlessness the corrective of wisdom, securing it against the corruption of craft and deceit, as stated in the text; but innocence, simplicity, implicit obedience to God, tranquillity of mind, contentment, these and the like virtues are themselves a sort of wisdom;—I mean, they produce the same results as wisdom, because God works for those who do not work for themselves; and thus they especially incur the charge of craft at the hands of the world, because they pretend to so little, yet effect so much. This circumstance admits dwelling on.

By innocence, or harmlessness, is meant simplicity in act, purity in motive, honesty in aim; acting conscientiously and religiously, according to the matter in hand, without caring for consequences or appearances; doing what appears one's duty, and being obedient for obedience-sake, and leaving the event to God. This is to be innocent as the dove; yet this conduct is the truest wisdom; and this conduct accordingly has pre-eminently the appearance of craft.

It appears to be craft, and is wisdom, in many ways.

3. 2 Cor. i. 17.
4. 2 Cor. iv. 2.
5. 2 Cor. vi. 8.
6. 2 Cor. x. 9.
7. 2 Cor. xii. 16.

1. First: sobriety, self-restraint, control of word and feeling, which religious men exercise, have about them an appearance of being artificial, because they are not natural; and of being artful, because artificial. I do not deny there is something very engaging in a frank and unpremeditating manner; some persons have it more than others; in some persons it is a great grace. But it must be recollected that I am speaking of times of persecution and oppression to Christians, such as the text foretels; and then surely frankness will become nothing else than indignation at the oppressor, and vehemence of speech, if it is permitted. Accordingly, as persons have deep feelings, so they will find the necessity of self-controul, lest they should say what they ought not. All this stands to reason, without enlarging upon it. And to this must be added, that those who would be holy and blameless, the sons of God, find so much in the world to unsettle and defile them, that they are necessarily forced upon a strict self-restraint, lest they should receive injury from such intercourse with it as is unavoidable; and this self-restraint is the first thing which makes holy persons seem wanting in openness and manliness.

2. Next let it be considered that the world, the gross, carnal, unbelieving world, is blind to the peculiar feelings, objects, hopes, fears, affections of religious people. It cannot understand them. Religious men are a mystery to it; and, being a mystery, they will in mere self-defence be called by the world mysterious, dark, subtle, designing; and that the more, because, as living to God, they are at no pains to justify themselves to the world, or to open their hearts, or account to it for their conduct. The world will impute motives, either because it cannot find any, or because it simply will not believe those motives to be the real ones, which are such, and are avowed as such. It cannot believe that men will deliberately sacrifice this world to the next; and where they profess to do so, it thinks that of necessity there must be something behind, which they do not divulge. And again; all the reasons which religious men allege, seem to it unreal, and all the feelings fantastical and strained; and this strengthens it in its idea that it has not fathomed them, and that there is some secret to be found out. And indeed it has not fathomed them, and there is a secret; but it is the power of Divine grace, the state of heart, which is the secret; not their motives or their ends, which it is told to the full. Here is a second reason why the dove seems but a serpent. Christians give up worldly advantages; they sacrifice rank or wealth; they prefer obscurity to station; they do penance rather than live delicately; and the world says, "Here are effects without causes sufficient for them; here is craft."

3. Further, let this be considered. The precept given us is, that "we resist not evil;" that we yield to worldly authority, and "give place unto wrath." This the early Christians did in an especial way. But it is very difficult to make the world

understand the difference between an outward obedience, and an interior assent. When the Christians obeyed the heathen magistrate in all things not sinful, it was not that they thought the heathen right; they knew them to be idolaters. There are a multitude of cases, and very various, where it is our duty to obey those who nevertheless have no power over our belief or conviction. When, however, religious men outwardly conform, on the score of duty, to "the powers that be," the world is easily led into the mistake, that they have renounced their opinions as well as submitted their actions; and it feels or affects surprise, to learn that their opinions remain; and it considers, or calls, this an inconsistency, or a duplicity. It argues that they are breaking promise, cherishing what they disown, or resuming what they professed to abandon. And thus the very fact that they are so harmless, so inoffensive, that they do so much in the way of compliance, becomes a ground of complaint against them, that they do not more, — that they do not more than they have a right to do. They yield outwardly; to assent inwardly would be to betray the faith; yet they are called deceitful and double-dealing, because they do as much as they can, and not more than they may.

4. Again: the cheerfulness, contentment, and readiness with which religious men resign their cause into God's hands, and are well-pleased that the world should seem to triumph over them, have still further an appearance of craft and deceit. For why should they be so satisfied to give up their wishes, unless they knew something which others did not know, or were really gaining while they seemed to lose? Other men make a great clamour and lamentation over their idols; there is no mistaking that they have lost them, and that they have no hope. But Christians resign themselves. They are silent; silence itself is suspicious, — even silence is mystery. Why do they not speak out? why do they not show a natural, an honest indignation? The submitting to calumny is a proof that it is too true. They would set themselves right, if they could. Still more strange and suspicious is the confidence which religious men show, in spite of apparent weakness, that their cause will triumph. The boldness, decisiveness, calmness of speech, which are necessarily the result of Christian faith and hope, lead the world to the surmise of some hidden reliance, some secret support, to account for them; as if God's word, when received and dwelt on, were not a greater encouragement to the lonely combatant, than any word of man, however powerful, or any conspiracy, however far-spreading.

5. And still stronger is this delusion on the part of the world, when the event justifies the confidence of religious men. The truest wisdom is to stand still and trust in God, and to the world it is also the strongest evidence of craft. God fights for those who do not fight for themselves; such is the great truth, such is the gracious rule, which is declared and exemplified in the Gospel; "Dearly

beloved, avenge not yourselves," says St. Paul, "but rather give place unto wrath, for it is written, Vengeance is Mine, I will repay, saith the Lord."[8] Do nothing, and you have done every thing. The less you do, the more God will do for you. The more you submit to the violence of the world, the more powerfully will He rise against the world, who is irresistible. The less you ward off the world's blows from you, the more heavy will be His blows upon the world, if not in your cause, at least in His own. When then the world at length becomes sensible that it is faring ill, and receiving more harm than it inflicts, yet is unwilling to humble itself under the mighty hand of God, what is left but to attribute it to the power of those who seem to be weak? that is, to their craft, who pretend to be weak when really they are strong.

6. To this must be added, that the truth has in itself the gift of spreading, without instruments; it makes its way in the world, under God's blessing, by its own persuasiveness and excellence; "So is the kingdom of God," says our Lord, "as if a man should cast seed into the ground, and should sleep, and rise night and day, and the seed should spring and grow up, he *knoweth not* how."[9] The Word, when once uttered, runs its course. He who speaks it has done his work in uttering it, and cannot recall it if he would. It runs its course; it prospers in the thing whereunto God sends it. It seizes many souls at once, and subdues them to the obedience of faith. Now when by-standers see these effects and see no cause, for they will not believe that the Word itself is the cause, which is to them a dead letter; when it sees many minds moved in one way in many places, it imputes to secret management that uniformity, which is nothing but the echo of the One Living and True Word.

7. And of course all this happens to the surprise of Christians as well as of the world; they can but marvel and praise God, but cannot account for it more than the world. "When the Lord turned again the captivity of Sion," says the Psalmist, "then were we like unto them that dream."[10] Or as the Prophet says of the Church, "Thine heart shall fear and be enlarged; because the abundance of the sea shall be converted unto thee, the forces of the Gentiles shall come unto thee,"[11] and here again the Christian's true wisdom looks like craft. It is true wisdom to leave the event to God; but when they are prospered, it looks like deceit to show surprise and to disclaim the work themselves. Moreover, meekness, gentleness, patience, and love, have in themselves a strong power to melt the heart of those who witness them. Cheerful suffering, too, leads spec-

8. Rom. xii. 19.
9. Mark iv. 26, 27.
10. Psalm cxxvi. 1.
11. Is. lx. 5.

tators to sympathy, till, perhaps, a re-action takes place in the minds of men, and they are converted by the sight, and glorify their Father which is in heaven. But it is easy to insinuate, when men are malevolent, that those who triumph through meekness, have affected the meekness to secure the triumph.

8. Here a very large subject opens upon us, to which I shall but allude. Those who surrender themselves to Christ in implicit faith, are graciously taken into His service; and, "as men under authority," they do great things without knowing it, by the Wisdom of their Divine Master. They act on conscience, perhaps in despondency, and without foresight; but what is obedience in them, has a purpose with God, and they are successful, when they do but mean to be dutiful. But what duplicity does the world think it, to speak of conscience, or honour, or propriety, or delicacy, or to give other tokens of personal motives, when the event seems to show, that a calculation of results has been the actuating principle at bottom! It is God who designs, but His servants seem designing; and that the more, should it so happen that they really do themselves catch glimpses of their own position in His providential course. For then what they do from the heart, approves itself to their reason, and they are able to recognize the expedience of obedience.

How frequently is this remark in point in the history, nay in the very constitution of the Church! Moses, for instance, is sometimes called skilful in his measures or his laws, as if wise acts might not come from the Source of wisdom, and provisions were proved to be human, when they could be shown to be advisable. And so, again, in the Christian Church, bishops have been called hypocritical in submitting and yet opposing themselves to the civil power, in a matter of plain duty, if a popular movement was the consequence; and then hypocritical again, if they did their best to repress it. And in like manner, theological doctrines or ecclesiastical usages are styled politic if they are but salutary; as if the Lord of the Church, who has willed her sovereignty, might not effect it by secondary causes. What, for instance, though we grant that sacramental confession and the celibacy of the clergy do tend to consolidate the body politic in the relation of rulers and subjects, or, in other words, to aggrandize the priesthood? for how can the Church be one body without such relation, and why should not He, who has decreed that there should be unity, take measures to secure it? Marks of design are not elsewhere assumed as disproofs of His interference. Why should not the Creator, who has given us the feeling of hunger that we may eat and not die, and sentiments of compassion and benevolence for the welfare of our brethren, when He would form a more integral power than mankind had yet seen, adopt adequate means, and use His old world to create a new one? and why must His human instruments set out with a purpose, because they accomplish one? Nothing is safe in revelation on such an interpretation. As the expedience of its provisions is made an objection to their honesty, so the beauty of its facts becomes an argument against their truth. The narratives in the Gospels have lately been viewed as mythical representations from their very perfection; as if a Divine work could not be most beautiful on the one hand, and most expedient on the other.

The reason is this; men do not like to hear of the interposition of Providence in the affairs of the world; and they invidiously ascribe ability and skill to His agents, to escape the thought of an Infinite Wisdom and an Almighty Power. They will be unjust to their brethren, lest they must be just to Him; they will be wanton in their imputations, rather than humble themselves to a confession.

But for us, let us glory in what they disown; let us beg of our Divine Lord to take to Him His great power, and manifest Himself more and more, and reign both in our hearts and in the world. Let us beg of Him to stand by us in trouble, and guide us on our dangerous way. May He, as of old, choose "the foolish things of the world to confound the wise, and the weak things of the world to confound the things which are mighty!" May He support us all the day long, till the shades lengthen, and the evening comes, and the busy world is hushed, and the fever of life is over, and our work is done! Then in His mercy may He give us a safe lodging, and a holy rest, and peace at the last!

The Parting of Friends
Preached on the Anniversary of the
Consecration of a Chapel

"Man goeth forth to his work and to his labour until the evening."
—Psalm civ. 23.

When the Son of Man, the First-born of the creation of God, came to the evening of His mortal life, He parted with His disciples at a feast. He had borne "the burden and heat of the day;" yet, when "wearied with His journey," He had but stopped at the well's side, and asked a draught of water for His thirst; for He had "meat to eat which" others "knew not of." His meat was "to do the will of Him that sent Him, and to finish His work;" "I must work the works of Him that sent Me," said He, "while it is day; the night cometh, when no man can work."[1] Thus passed the season of His ministry; and if at any time He feasted with Pharisee or Publican, it was that He might do the work of God more strenuously. But "when the even was come, He sat down with the Twelve." "And He said unto them, With desire have I desired to eat this Passover with you, before I suffer."[2] He was about to suffer more than man had ever suffered or shall suffer. But there is nothing gloomy, churlish, violent, or selfish in His grief; it is tender, affectionate, social. He calls His

1. John iv. 6, 34; ix. 4.
2. Matt. xxvi. 20. Luke xxii. 15.

friends around Him, though He was as Job among the ashes; He bids them stay by Him, and see Him suffer; He desires their sympathy; He takes refuge in their love. He first feasted them, and sung a hymn with them, and washed their feet; and when His long trial began, He beheld them and kept them in His Presence, till they in terror shrank from it. Yet, on St. Mary and St. John, His Virgin Mother and His Virgin Disciple, who remained, His eyes still rested; and in St. Peter, who was denying Him in the distance, His sudden glance wrought a deep repentance. O wonderful pattern, the type of all trial and of all duty under it, while the Church endures!

We indeed to-day have no need of so high a lesson and so august a comfort. We have no pain, no grief which calls for it; yet, considering it has been brought before us in this morning's service,[3] we are naturally drawn to think of it, though it be infinitely above us, under certain circumstances of this season and the present time. For now are the shades of evening falling upon the earth, and the year's labour is coming to its end. In Septuagesima the labourers were sent into the vineyard; in Sexagesima the sower went forth to sow;—that time is over; "the harvest is passed, the summer is ended,"[4] the vintage is gathered. We have kept the Ember days for the fruits of the earth, in self-abasement, as being unworthy even of the least of God's mercies; and now we are offering up of its corn and wine as a propitiation, and eating and drinking of them with thanksgiving.

"All things come of Thee, and of Thine own have we given Thee."[5] If we have had the rain in its season, and the sun shining in its strength, and the fertile ground, it is of Thee. We give back to Thee what came from Thee. "When Thou givest it them, they gather it, and when Thou openest Thy hand, they are filled with good. When Thou hidest Thy face, they are troubled; when Thou takest away their breath, they die, and are turned again to their dust. When Thou lettest Thy breath go forth, they shall be made, and Thou shalt renew the face of the earth."[6] He gives, He takes away. "Shall we receive good at the hand of God, and shall we not receive evil?"[7] May He not "do what He will with His own?"[8] May not His sun set as it has risen? and must it not set, if it is to rise again? and must not darkness come first, if there is ever to be morning? and must not the sky be blacker, before it can be brighter? And cannot He, who can

3. Sept. 25.
4. Jer. viii. 20.
5. 1 Chron. xxix. 14.
6. Ps. civ. 28–30.
7. Job ii. 10.
8. Matt. xx. 15.

do all things, cause a light to arise even in the darkness? "I have thought upon Thy Name, O Lord, in the night season, and have kept Thy Law;" "Thou also shalt light my candle, the Lord my God shall make my darkness to be light;" or as the Prophet speaks, "At the evening time it shall be light."[9]

"All things come of Thee," says holy David, "for we are strangers before Thee and sojourners, as were all our fathers; our days on the earth are as a shadow, and there is none abiding."[10] All is vanity, vanity of vanities, and vexation of spirit. "What profit hath a man of all his labour which he taketh under the sun? One generation passeth away, and another generation cometh; but the earth abideth for ever; the sun also ariseth, and the sun goeth down; . . . all things are full of labour, man cannot utter it; . . . that which is crooked cannot be made straight, and that which is wanting cannot be numbered."[11] "To every thing there is a season, and a time to every purpose under the heaven; a time to be born and a time to die; a time to plant and a time to pluck up that which is planted; a time to kill and a time to heal; a time to break down and a time to build up; . . . a time to get and a time to lose; a time to keep and a time to cast away."[12] And time, and matter, and motion, and force, and the will of man, how vain are they all, except as instruments of the grace of God, blessing them and working with them! How vain are all our pains, our thought, our care, unless God uses them, unless God has inspired them! how worse than fruitless are they, unless directed to His glory, and given back to the Giver!

"Of Thine own have we given Thee," says the royal Psalmist, after he had collected materials for the Temple. Because "the work was great," and "the palace, not for man, but for the Lord God," therefore he "prepared with all his might for the house of his God," gold, and silver, and brass, and iron, and wood, "onyx stones, and stones to be set, glistering stones, and of diverse colours, and all manner of precious stones, and marble stones in abundance."[13] And "the people rejoiced, for that they offered willingly; . . . and David the king also rejoiced with great joy." We too, at this season, year by year, have been allowed in our measure, according to our work and our faith, to rejoice in God's Presence, for this sacred building which He has given us to worship Him in. It was a glad time when we first met here, — many of us now present recollect it; nor did our rejoicing cease, but was renewed every

9. Zech. xiv. 7.
10. 1 Chron. xxix. 15.
11. Eccles. i. 3–15.
12. Eccles. iii. 1–6.
13. 1 Chron. xxix. 1, 2, 9.

autumn, as the day came round. It has been "a day of gladness and feasting, and a good day, and of sending portions one to another."[14] We have kept the feast heretofore with merry hearts; we have kept it seven full years unto "a perfect end;" now let us keep it, even though in haste, and with bitter herbs, and with loins girded, and with a staff in our hand, as they who have "no continuing city, but seek one to come."[15]

So was it with Jacob, when with his staff he passed over that Jordan. He too kept feast before he set out upon his dreary way. He received a father's blessing, and then was sent afar; he left his mother, never to see her face or hear her voice again. He parted with all that his heart loved, and turned his face towards the strange land. He went with the doubt, whether he should have bread to eat, or raiment to put on. He came to "the people of the East," and served a hard master twenty years. "In the day the drought consumed him, and the frost by night; and his sleep departed from his eyes."[16] O little did he think, when father and mother had forsaken him, and at Bethel he laid down to sleep on the desolate ground, because the sun was set and even had come, that there was the house of God and the gate of heaven, that the Lord was in that place, and would thence go forward with him whithersoever he went, till He brought him back to that river in "two bands," who was then crossing it forlorn and solitary!

So had it been with Ishmael; though the feast was not to him a blessing, yet he feasted in his father's tent, and then was sent away. That tender father, who, when a son was promised him of Sarah, cried out to his Almighty Protector, "O that Ishmael might live before Thee!"[17] — he it was, who, under a divine direction, the day after the feast, "rose up early in the morning, and took bread, and a bottle of water, and gave it unto Hagar, putting it on her shoulder, and the child, and sent her away. And she departed, and wandered in the wilderness of Beersheba."[18] And little thought that fierce child, when for feasting came thirst and weariness and wandering in the desert, that this was not the end of Ishmael, but the beginning. And little did Hagar read his coming fortunes, when "the water was spent in the bottle, and she cast the child under one of the shrubs, and she went and sat her down over against him a good way off; . . . for she said, Let me not see the death of the child. And she sat over against him, and lift up her voice, and wept."

14. Esth. ix. 19.
15. Heb. xiii. 14.
16. Gen. xxxi. 40.
17. Gen. xvii. 18.
18. Gen. xxi. 14.

So had it been with Naomi, though she was not quitting, but returning to her home, and going, not to a land of famine, but of plenty. In a time of distress, she had left her country, and found friends and made relatives among the enemies of her people. And when her husband and her children died, Moabitish women, who had once been the stumbling-block of Israel, became the support and comfort of her widowhood. Time had been when, at the call of the daughters of Moab, the chosen people had partaken their sacrifices, and "bowed down to their gods. And Israel joined himself unto Baal-peor, and the anger of the Lord was kindled against Israel." Centuries had since passed away, and now of Moabites was Naomi mother; and to their land had she given her heart, when the call of duty summoned her back to Bethlehem. "She had heard in the country of Moab, how that the Lord had visited His people in giving them bread. Wherefore she went forth out of the place where she was, and her two daughters-in-law with her, and they went on the way to return unto the land of Judah."[19] Forlorn widow, great was the struggle in her bosom, whether shall she do? — leave behind her the two heathen women, in widowhood and weakness like herself, her sole stay, the shadows of departed blessings? or shall she selfishly take them as fellow-sufferers, who could not be protectors? Shall she seek sympathy where she cannot gain help? shall she deprive them of a home, when she has none to supply? So she said, "Go, return each to her mother's house: the Lord deal kindly with you, as ye have dealt with the dead and with me!" Perplexed Naomi, torn with contrary feelings; which tried her the more, — Orpah who left her, or Ruth who remained? Orpah who was a pain, or Ruth who was a charge? "They lifted up their voice and wept again; and Orpah kissed her mother-in-law, but Ruth clave unto her. And she said, Behold, thy sister-in-law is gone back unto her people and unto her gods; return thou after thy sister-in-law. And Ruth said, Entreat me not to leave thee, or to return from following after thee: for whither thou goest, I will go; and where thou lodgest, I will lodge: thy people shall be my people, and thy God my God. Where thou diest, will I die, and there will I be buried; the Lord do so to me, and more also, if aught but death part thee and me."[20]

Orpah kissed Naomi, and went back to the world. There was sorrow in the parting, but Naomi's sorrow was more for Orpah's sake than for her own. Pain there would be, but it was the pain of a wound, not the yearning regret of love. It was the pain we feel when friends disappoint us, and fall in our esteem. That kiss of Orpah was no loving token; it was but the hollow profession of those who use smooth words, that they may part company with us with least

---

19. Ruth i. 6–8, 14, 15.
20 Ruth i. 14–17.

trouble and discomfort to themselves. Orpah's tears were but the dregs of affection; she clasped her mother-in-law once for all, that she might not cleave to her. Far different were the tears, far different the embrace, which passed between those two religious friends recorded in the book which follows, who loved each other with a true love unfeigned, but whose lives ran in different courses. If Naomi's grief was great when Orpah kissed her, what was David's when he saw the last of him, whose "soul had from the first been knit with his soul," so that "he loved him as his own soul?"[21] "I am distressed for thee, my brother Jonathan," he says; "very pleasant hast thou been unto me; thy love to me was wonderful, passing the love of women."[22] What woe was upon that "young man," "of a beautiful countenance and goodly to look to," and "cunning in playing, and a mighty valiant man, and a man of war, and prudent in matters;"[23] when his devoted affectionate loyal friend, whom these good gifts have gained, looked upon him for the last time! O hard destiny, except that the All-merciful so willed it, that such companions might not walk in the house of God as friends! David must flee to the wilderness, Jonathan must pine in his father's hall; Jonathan must share that stern father's death in battle, and David must ascend the vacant throne. Yet they made a covenant on parting: "Thou shalt not only," said Jonathan, "while yet I live, show me the kindness of the Lord, that I die not; but also thou shalt not cut off thy kindness from my house for ever; no, not when the Lord hath cut off the enemies of David, every one from the face of the earth. . . . And Jonathan caused David to swear again, because he loved him, for he loved him as he loved his own soul." And then, while David hid himself, Jonathan made trial of Saul, how he felt disposed to David; and when he found that "it was determined of his father to slay David," he "arose from the table in fierce anger, and did eat no meat the second day of the month; for he was grieved for David, because his father had done him shame." Then in the morning he went out into the field, where David lay, and the last meeting took place between the two. "David arose out of a place toward the south, and fell on his face to the ground, and bowed himself three times; and they kissed one another, and wept one with another, till David exceeded. And Jonathan said to David, Go in peace, forasmuch as we have sworn both of us in the Name of the Lord, saying, The Lord be between me and thee, and between my seed and thy seed for ever. And he arose and departed; and Jonathan went into the city."[24]

21. 1 Sam. xviii. 1–3.
22. 2 Sam. i. 26.
23. 1 Sam. xvi. 12, 18.
24. 1 Sam. xx. 14–42.

David's affection was given to a single heart; but there is another spoken of in Scripture, who had a thousand friends, and loved each as his own soul, and seemed to live a thousand lives in them, and died a thousand deaths when he must quit them: that great Apostle, whose very heart was broken when his brethren wept; who "lived if they stood fast in the Lord;" who "was glad when he was weak and they were strong;" and who was "willing to have imparted unto them his own soul, because they were dear unto him."[25] Yet we read of his bidding farewell to whole Churches, never to see them again. At one time, to the little ones of the flock; "When we had accomplished those days," says the Evangelist, "we departed, and went our way, . . . with wives and children, till we were out of the city; and we kneeled down on the shore and prayed. And when we had taken our leave one of another, we took ship, and they returned home again." At another time, to the rulers of the Church: "And now behold," he says to them, "I know that ye all, among whom I have gone preaching the kingdom of God, shall see my face no more. Wherefore, I take you to record this day, that I am pure from the blood of all men, for I have not shunned to declare unto you all the counsel of God. . . . I have coveted no man's silver, or gold, or apparel; . . . I have showed you all things, how that so labouring ye ought to support the weak; and to remember the words of the Lord Jesus, how he said, It is more blessed to give than to receive." And then, when he had finished, "he kneeled down, and prayed with them all. And they all wept sore, and fell on Paul's neck, and kissed him; sorrowing most of all for the words which he spake, that they should see his face no more. And they accompanied him unto the ship."[26]

There was another time, when he took leave of his "own son in the faith," Timothy, in words more calm, and still more impressive, when his end was nigh: "I am now ready to be offered," he says, "and the time of my departure is at hand. I have fought a good fight, I have finished my course, I have kept the faith. Henceforth there is laid up for me a crown of righteousness, which the Lord, the Righteous Judge, shall give me at that day."[27]

And what are all these instances but memorials and tokens of the Son of Man, when His work and His labour were coming to an end? Like Jacob, like Ishmael, like Elisha, like the Evangelist whose day is just passed, He kept feast before His departure; and, like David, He was persecuted by the rulers in Israel; and, like Naomi, He was deserted by His friends; and, like Ishmael, He cried out, "I thirst" in a barren and dry land; and at length, like Jacob, He went

---

25. Acts xxi. 21, 22. 1 Thess ii. 8; iii. 8. 2 Cor. xiii. 9.
26. Acts xxi. 5, 6; xx. 25–27, 33, 35, 36–38.
27. 2 Tim. iv. 6–8.

to sleep with a stone for His pillow, in the evening. And, like St. Paul, He had "finished the work which God gave Him to do," and had "witnessed a good confession;" and, beyond St. Paul, "the Prince of this world had come, and had nothing in Him."[28] "He was in the world, and the world was made by Him, and the world knew Him not. He came unto His own, and His own received Him not."[29] Heavily did He leave, tenderly did He mourn over the country and city which rejected Him. "When He was come near, He beheld the city, and wept over it, saying, If thou hadst known, even thou, at least in this thy day, the things which belong unto thy peace! but now they are hid from thine eyes." And again: "O Jerusalem, Jerusalem, which killest the prophets, and stonest them that are sent unto thee, how often would I have gathered thy children together, as a hen doth gather her brood under her wings, and ye would not! Behold, your house is left unto you desolate."[30]

A lesson surely, and a warning to us all, in every place where He puts His Name, to the end of time; lest we be cold towards His gifts, or unbelieving towards His word, or jealous of His workings, or heartless towards His mercies.... O mother of saints! O school of the wise! O nurse of the heroic! of whom went forth, in whom have dwelt, memorable names of old, to spread the truth abroad, or to cherish and illustrate it at home! O thou, from whom surrounding nations lit their lamps! O virgin of Israel! wherefore dost thou now sit on the ground and keep silence, like one of those foolish women who were without oil on the coming of the Bridegroom? Where is now the ruler in Sion, and the doctor in the Temple, and the ascetic on Carmel, and the herald in the wilderness, and the preacher in the market-place? where are thy "effectual fervent prayers," offered in secret, and thy alms and good works coming up as a memorial before God? How is it, O once holy place, that "the land mourneth, for the corn is wasted, the new wine is dried up, the oil languisheth, . . . because joy is withered away from the sons of men?" "Alas for the day! . . . how do the beasts groan! the herds of cattle are perplexed, because they have no pasture, yea, the flocks of sheep are made desolate." "Lebanon is ashamed and hewn down; Sharon is like a wilderness, and Bashan and Carmel shake off their fruits."[31] O my mother, whence is this unto thee, that thou hast good things poured upon thee and canst not keep them, and bearest children, yet darest not own them? why hast thou not the skill to use their services, nor

28. 1 Tim. vi. 13. John xiv. 30.
29 John i. 10, 11.
30 Luke xix. 41, 42; xiii. 34, 35.
31 Joel i. 10–18. Isa. xxxiii. 9.

the heart to rejoice in their love? how is it that whatever is generous in purpose, and tender or deep in devotion, thy flower and thy promise, falls from thy bosom and finds no home within thine arms? Who hath put this note upon thee, to have "a miscarrying womb, and dry breasts," to be strange to thine own flesh, and thine eye cruel towards thy little ones? Thine own offspring, the fruit of thy womb, who love thee and would toil for thee, thou dost gaze upon with fear, as though a portent, or thou dost loath as an offence; — at best thou dost but endure, as if they had no claim but on thy patience, self-possession, and vigilance, to be rid of them as easily as thou mayest. Thou makest them "stand all the day idle," as the very condition of thy bearing with them; or thou biddest them be gone, where they will be more welcome; or thou sellest them for nought to the stranger that passes by. And what wilt thou do in the end thereof? . . . Scripture is a refuge in any trouble; only let us be on our guard against seeming to use it further than is fitting, or doing more than sheltering ourselves under its shadow. Let us use it according to our measure. It is far higher and wider than our need; and it conceals our feelings while it gives expression to them. It is sacred and heavenly; and it restrains and purifies, while it sanctions them.

And now, my brethren, "bless God, praise Him and magnify Him, and praise Him for the things which He hath done unto you in the sight of all that live. It is good to praise God, and exalt His Name, and honourably to show forth the works of God; therefore be not slack to praise Him." "All the works of the Lord are good; and He will give every needful thing in due season; so that a man cannot say, This is worse than that; for in time they shall all be well approved. And therefore praise ye the Lord with the whole heart and mouth, and bless the Name of the Lord."[32]

"Leave off from wrath, and let go displeasure; flee from evil, and do the thing that is good." "Do that which is good, and no evil shall touch you." "Go your way; eat your bread with joy, and drink your wine with a merry heart, for God now accepteth your works; let your garments be always white, and let your head lack no ointment."[33]

And O, my brethren, O kind and affectionate hearts, O loving friends, should you know any one whose lot it has been, by writing or by word of mouth, in some degree to help you thus to act; if he has ever told you what you knew about yourselves, or what you did not know; has read to you your wants or feelings, and comforted you by the very reading: has made you feel that

32 Tob. xii. 6. Eccles. xxxix. 33–35.
33. Ps. xxxvii. 8. 27. Tob. xii. 7. Eccles. ix. 7, 8.

there was a higher life than this daily one, and a brighter world than that you see; or encouraged you, or sobered you, or opened a way to the inquiring, or soothed the perplexed; if what he has said or done has ever made you take interest in him, and feel well inclined towards him; remember such a one in time to come, though you hear him not, and pray for him, that in all things he may know God's will, and at all times he may be ready to fulfil it.

Index

absolution, 184, 204n, 381
Academia of Catholic Religion, 438
Achilli, G. G., 29
Acton, Lord, 40n62
Aeneas, 161n64, 377
African Church, 228, 340
Alban, Saint, 423, 423n9
Alcester Street mission, 435
Aldhelm, Saint, 301
Alexander, Natalis, 350, 350n, 421
Altholz, Josef L., 4, 5
Ambrose, Saint, 136, 156, 201, 270, 340
American Episcopal Church, 263n20
Analogy (theological and philosophical), 140, 151, 155, 194, 290
Andrewes, Lancelot, 189, 210, 238
angels, 132, 155–156, 178, 289, 344, 460
Anglican Church, 2, 47, 55, 80, 72, 92, 94, 110, 120, 126, 133, 173, 174, 175, 191, 192, 194, 209, 210, 216, 216n14, 218, 220–222, 224, 228, 231, 232, 233, 234, 236–239, 242, 248, 252–255, 258, 260, 266, 268, 269, 281, 292, 293, 295, 302, 304, 309n63, 310, 312, 312n, 313, 315, 357, 365, 409; Note on, 32, 312n, 357, 408–411
Anglican divines, 18, 135n13, 169, 174, 175, 179, 185, 185n34, 186, 189n42, 192, 218, 220, 232, 238n44, 294, 418. *See also* Caroline Divines
Anglican Prayer Book, 174. *See also* Prayer Book
Anselm, Saint, 340, 341n
anti-Catholicism, 16, 39–40, 189. *See also* anti-Roman sentiments and statements
Antichrist: Council of Trent and, 171n12, 177; papacy as, 136, 137n18, 176, 178, 178n20; Rome as, 176n17, 223n10, 231; Liberalism and, 286
Anti-dogmatic Principle, 56, 89, 173, 294, 359
antinomianism, 135, 135n15

Antiquity, 16, 17, 17n22, 47, 144, 154, 170n10, 177, 196n49, 211, 216, 220, 221, 225, 226, 228, 254, 259, 269, 280, 290, 296, 363. *See also* Primitive Church and Christians

anti-Roman sentiments and statements by Newman, 16, 16n21, 45, 46, 187n38, 190, 231, 306n61

Apologia Pro Vita Sua: A History of His Religious Opinions (Newman): breaking distrust between Protestants and Roman Catholics, 44; circumstances of composition, 32–38, generating support from Bishop W. B. Ullathorne and contemporary Roman Catholic clergy, 433–443; historically privileged status, 1–6, situated in larger context of Victorian religious transformations, 106–115; transforming Newman's position in the English Roman Catholic Church, 37–38; ultramontane criticisms of, 45–46

Apostolicity, 21, 208, 220, 220n22. *See also* Apostolic(al) succession

Apostolic(al) succession, 9, 13, 21, 91, 110, 135n13, 140, 140n26, 191n43, 157, 169, 170, 190, 220, 231, 232, 248, 259, 290

Aquinas, Saint Thomas, 330, 333, 333n, 418

Arianism, 143, 143n31, 144n34, 154, 245, 331

Arius, 143n31, 172, 227, 376, 376n10

Arnold, Matthew, 56, 64, 64n90

Arnold, Thomas, 3, 38, 65, 67, 68, 77, 82, 160–161, 160n62, 299, 364

Arnold, Thomas, Jr., 11, 76n107

asceticism, 22, 25, 47, 98, 105–106, 108, 146n41, 194n48, 253n1. *See also* celibacy; monasticism

assizes, 162n68

Assize Sermon (John Keble), 81, 162

Athanasian Creed, 135, 135n14, 143–144, 281, 333, 366

Athanasius, Saint, 135n14, 143n31, 154, 194, 227, 228, 245, 273, 330, 340, 415, 423

atheism, 291, 295, 324

Athenaeum (magazine), 40

Athenagoras, 156

atonement, 7, 12, 13, 22, 22n29, 61, 68, 190, 215n12, 343n31, 366, 455, 457, 462

Augustine, Saint, 91n129, 136, 180n23, 201, 216, 223, 228–229, 238, 301, 330, 338, 340, 350, 351, 417–418

autobiography, 1, 3, 5–6, 32, 36, 37n56, 44, 44n65, 54, 85, 106, 107n153, 110, 119n1, 215n12,

Bacon, Francis, 363
Badeley, Edward, 50–51, 316
Bagot, Richard, 48, 102–103, 175, 175n16, 195n49, 206n56, 206n57, 236n42, 249n57, 275n30
Baptism, 9n11, 10n12, 12, 29, 56, 58, 78, 87, 89, 139n22, 174, 201, 204, 212n8, 239, 248, 261n15, 449, 464, 465, 476. *See also* Gorham Judgment; Baptismal Regeneration
Baptism: conditional, 10, 410n3
Baptism: Pusey on, 8n10, 184, 185
Baptismal Regeneration, 10n12, 87, 89, 138, 138n22, 146n41, 183, 249. *See also* Gorham Judgment; regeneration
Baptists, 88
Baradaeus, Jacob, 247n56
Barberi, Dominic, 101–103, 317, 317n69, 410n3
Barrow, Isaac, 227, 227n30, 295
Barter, William Brudenell, 262, 262n16
Basnage, Jacques, 373, 373n6
Bellarmine, Robert, 218, 218n19, 237
Benedict XIV, 419–420
Bentham, Jeremy, 51–52
Berengarius, 342, 342n
Berkeley, George, 148, 148n46
Berkeleyism, 148, 148n46
Bernard of Clairvaux, 333, 333n
Beveridge, William, 238, 238n44

Beverley, Diocese of, 439–440
Bible, 17, 18, 56, 59, 63, 66, 67, 77, 88, 89, 110, 131, 139n24, 140n25, 152, 160n62, 170n10, 262n18, 290n44, 325, 325n6, 354, 355, 363, 367, 453
Bickerstaffe, Isaac, 386n2
Bill for the Suppression of the Irish Sees, 160, 160n61. *See also* Church of Ireland
Bingham, Joseph, 414, 414n4
Birmingham, Diocese of, 438–439
Birmingham Oratory, 3, 49n, 106, 353, 434, 435
Bittleston, Henry, 353
Blehl, Vincent Ferrer, *John Henry Newman: A Bibliographical Catalogue of His Writings*, 427
Blessed Virgin. *See* Virgin Mary
Blomfield, Charles, 99–100, 157, 157n52, 206n57, 263n21
Bloxam, J. R., 236n42
Bollandists, 389, 389n1
Bonaventure, Saint, 341, 341n28
Boniface, Saint, 301, 389
Book of Homilies, 200–202, 200n54, 210
Borromeo, Carlo, 235, 235n41
Bowden, John William, 24, 104, 147, 147n42, 193, 237, 243, 248, 301, 369
Bramhall, John, 174, 174n15, 195, 210, 227, 227n30
branch theory of the church, 191n43
breviary, 20, 47, 194, 194n47, 275n30
Brilioth, Yngve, 24
British and Foreign Bible Society, 12, 59, 140, 140n25, 191
British Critic (journal), 13–14, 14n19, 26–28, 66, 113, 183, 183n29, 194–195, 210, 224, 237, 241n48, 248, 255, 266n24
British Magazine, 13, 60, 105, 159n59, 161, 164, 193, 221, 368–369
Brougham, Henry, 57
Brown, Dan, *The Da Vinci Code*, 113

Buckle, George, 318, 319n71
Bull, George, 143, 154, 210, 242, 259, 265
Bunsen, C. J. K., 161, 161n63, 222, 247
Burnet, Gilbert, 347, 347n41
Butler, Joseph, 149, 189; *Analogy of Religion*, 140, 140n27, 194
Byron, George Gordon, Lord, 337

Calvin, John, 134, 134n9
Calvinism, Calvinists, 18, 77–78, 134n10, 134n11, 135–136, 138, 203, 204, 231, 247, 247n55, 249n57, 250
Canons of Councils, 333–334
Carlisle, Richard, 51
Carlyle, Thomas, 38; *Sartor Resartus*, 107
Carnival, 177
Caroline Divines, Caroline Church, 27, 135n13, 153n32, 383. *See also* Anglican Divines
casuistry, 350, 421, 426
Caswall, Edward, 353
Catechism of the Council of Trent, 350–352
Catenas of Anglican divines, 185, 185n
Catholic Apostolic Church (Irvingites), 109n156
Catholic Emancipation, 7, 57, 79, 144n37, 145, 173, 219n20, 233n38, 363–364
Catholic Teaching, 197, 198, 202, 291, 371
Catholicism (Anglo), 189
Catholicism, Roman. *See* Roman Catholicism
Catholicism (Tractarian), 48, 66, 105, 186n36, 215, 253n1, 277, 292
Catholicity, 21, 25, 42, 91, 93, 95, 96, 217, 220, 220n22, 221, 222, 237, 242, 242, 248, 254, 283, 291, 298, 307, 310n66, 343, 434
Catholic University, Dublin, Ireland, 30, 434

celibacy: clerical, 47, 80, 101, 142n29, 381–82; Froude and, 142n29; Kingsley and, 35; monastic, 27; Newman and, 86, 105–106, 137. *See also* asceticism, monasticism
censura, 419–421
certitude, 149–151, 257n7, 291, 292, 302, 303
Chadwick, Owen, 57
Charles I, King of England, 174n15
Christ, Jesus, 7, 9n11, 10, 11, 17, 21, 50, 61, 66, 68, 79, 81, 82, 87, 89, 110, 135, 143, 151, 156, 171n11, 174, 175, 180, 201, 203, 204n, 210, 213, 215, 223, 225n27, 229, 231, 260, 262n18, 287, 296, 317, 345, 354, 414, 448–459, 462–465, 468–471, 475–480, 485, 493
Christian Observer (journal), 15, 238n45, 259, 259n9
Christian Remembrancer (journal), 32
Chrysostom, John, 335, 335n19
Church, Richard, 64–65, 260, 260n12, 318, 319n71
Church Discipline Act, 100
Church Fathers, 14, 18, 79, 105, 136, 136n17, 144, 153–154, 174, 179–180
Churchill (colonel), 377
Church Missionary Society, 80, 87
Church of Alexandria, 154–155
Church of England, as mentioned by Newman, 139, 179, 192, 193, 218, 224, 238, 241, 242, 250, 253, 255, 269, 282, 297, 303, 307, 310, 315, 316. *See also* Anglican Church
Church of England, reform of, 7–9
Church of Ireland, 7, 110, 160n61, 162n68, 163n. *See also* Anglican Church; Church of England, reform of; church-state relations; Erastianism
Church of Scotland, 47
church-state relations, 7–9, 29n, 58, 142n30, 143, 165. *See also* Church of Ireland, Erastianism
Churton, Edward, 213, 213n9, 276n

Clement, 154, 156, 344
Coelestius, 342, 342n
Colenso, John William, 52, 66; *The Pentateuch and Book of Joshua Critically Examined*, 66
Coleridge, Samuel Taylor, 212
Comte, Auguste, 52, 109
concealment: Newman and, 46–53; in Victorian society, 51–52
Concina, Daniello, 421, 421n8
conditional baptism, 10
confessional manuals, 41n
Congress of Würzburg, 442
Conservative Party, 263n21. *See also* Toryism
Contenson, Vincent, 421, 421n8
Conversion(s): evangelicalism and, 7, 9; fickleness in, 472–473; gradual, 475–476; Newman as instigator of Roman Cathoic, 235, 246, 276n31, 304–306; Newman's, Roman Catholic, 28–29, 86, 91–106, 259, 287–288, 292, 313–321; Newman's evangelical, 6, 86, 133–37, Protestant attitude toward Roman Catholic, 106–107; rigidity in, 474–475; and salvation, 134n9; St. Paul's, 471–472, 475–477; sudden, 471–477
Convocation of 1571, 96, 202
Cookson, Thomas, 441
Copeland, W. J., 318, 318n71
Copleston, Edward, 77, 146, 146n39, 167
Coulson, John, 31
Council of Antioch, 340
Council of Chalcedon, 225n27
Council of Nicea, 143n31, 154, 340
Council of Trent, 100, 171, 171n12, 177, 197, 197n51, 202, 261, 333, 341, 350
Court of Arches, 99–101
Cox, George William, 66, 71
Cranmer, Thomas, 227, 227n29, 309n63
Cranmer Memorial, 309, 309n63
Creed of Pope Pius IV, 197, 197n51
Cullen, Paul, 30

Index 501

cultural apostasy, 63, 112, 127
Cyprian, Saint, 223
Cyril, Saint, 223

daimónia, 156
Dalgairns, John Dobrée, 30, 101, 103, 108n154, 300n53, 357
Daniel, Book of, 136, 156, 231
Darby, John Nelson, 87, 109–111
Darwin, Charles, 32–33, 52, 56
Da Vinci Code, The (Brown), 113
Davison, John, 77
Decree of Urban VIII, 420
demoniac, story of restored, 464–465
Denison, George Anthony (archdeacon), 72
development of doctrine (doctrinal development), 30, 92, 198, 289–291, 290n44, 313, 340
diocesan rights, 254, 254n3
Dionysius, 154
Disciplina Arcani, 344, 344n33, 412n2, 414
Dissent and Dissenters: 7, 8, 9, 12, 13, 55–60, 63, 80–82, 89, 160n61, 177n5, 180n25, 219n 21
doctrine, development of. *See* development of doctrine
Dodsworth, William, 213, 213n10, 310, 310n64
Dogma(s), 23, 42, 59, 69, 80, 83, 114, 114n164, 133, 136, 173–174, 176, 180, 190, 197–199, 202, 219, 231, 232, 295, 330, 336, 340, 341
Döllinger, J. J. I. von, 359n2
Dominic, Father. *See* Barberi, Dominic
Donatists, 223, 223n25, 227–228, 307
Dornford, John, 79, 141n28
Dublin Review, 2, 21, 39, 43, 45, 45n67, 48, 49n71, 56–57, 72, 76, 90. *See also* ultramontanes
Dulles, Avery Cardinal, 57

Ealing School, 6, 78, 86, 132n3
Ecclesiastical Commission, 7, 263, 263n21

ecclesiastical miracles, 124, 150n48, 355, 370–378
economy, principle of, 34, 40–41, 155, 157, 171, 172n13, 343–344, 358, 412–415. *See also* reserve, principle of
Ecumenical Councils, 153, 197, 333, 340, 342
Edinburgh Review, 167, 321n2
Edward II, King of England, 389
Effusions of grace, 151
Elijah, 25, 91, 253n2, 257n7, 260
Eliot, George. *See* Evans, Marianne
Eliseus, 372
Elizabeth, Queen of England, 199
emotion, religion and, 457–463, 466–470
Encyclopædia Metropolitana, 144
English Calvinists, 134n9
English Reformation, 22–23, 178n20, 194n48, 196n50, 227n29 309n63
English Roman Catholics, 42–46, 49, 71–75, 90, 241, 343, 343n30, 358, 427–428
Episcopal system, 91, 175
Episcopal tradition, 17
equivocation, 50, 41, 122, 346–347, 350, 358, 379, 387; Note G on Lying and, 416–426
Erastianism, 29, 58–59, 90, 142, 142n29, 165, 165n4, 167, 217, 263n21
errors of Rome in Newman's anti-Roman polemics, 197, 198, 202, 205, 230, 233, 268, 284
Essays and Reviews, 29n42, 55, 56, 58, 83, 319n71
eternal happiness, 136
eternal punishment, 136
Eucharist, 10, 170, 262, 262n18, 273, 289, 290, 310n64
Eusebius, 340
Eutyches, 225n27, 226
Eutychianism, 331
Evangelicalism, 12–13, Tractarians opposed to, 14–15, 219n21; New-

Evangelicalism (*continued*)
 man's critique of, 58–63, 158, 158n55, 179n21, 187n38, 210n5, 216–217, 260n11, 261n15, 445–446; critique as related to concept of Liberalism, 59–63, 65, 87; confrontation with Francis Newman over, 86–89. *See also* atonement; low church; popular Protestantism; rationalism; reserve; ultra-Protestantism
Evans, Marianne (pseudonym George Eliot), 109
evasion, 41, 52–53, 244, 279, 417, 422–425
Exeter Hall, London, 241, 241n, 415n6
Existence of God, 323–324

Faber, Frederick, 29, 30
faith: certitude and, 149; reason and, 141, 193. *See also* justification: by faith
Fathers of the Church. *See* Church Fathers
Feuerbach, Ludwig, 109
First Vatican Council, 329n
Fleury, Claude, *Histoire Ecclésiastique*, 183, 183n30, 193
formal lie, 41, 425
Frazer, James, 52
French Revolution, 133n6, 360; of l830, 157
Froude, Catherine, 16, 95, 296n50
Froude, James Anthony, 69
Froude, Richard Hurrell, 8, 22–23, 26, 58, 78–79, 80, 141n28, 142, 142n29, 143, 145, 147–148, 152–153, 159, 161, 163, 165, 165n3, 166, 167, 171, 176–179, 193, 194, 213n11, 233, 296n50, 233, 363, 369
Froude, William, 94–95, 296, 296n50
Fust, Herbert Jenner, 100–101

Galileo Galilei, 339, 339n25
George IV, King of England, 164n2
Gerdil, Hyacinthe, 350, 350n42, 421
German historical criticism, 243n50, 355
Giberne, Maria R., 61

Gilpin, Bernard, 178, 178n20
Gladstone, William, 19, 26, 26n37, 95, 97, 182n27, 306n61, 356
Goldsmid, Nathaniel, 302, 302n57
Gorham Judgment, 29, 29n42, 56, 58, 147n42, 213n10, 265n23
Gospel, Newman's preference for preaching Law over, 61, 445
Gradus ad Parnassum, 231, 231n
grazie, 371, 375
Great Disruption in Church of Scotland (1843), 47
Greek Church, 342
Greek Fathers, 417–18
Gregory I, 176, 340
Gregory VII, 193, 217n17, 342, 342n29
Gregory XVI, 74
Gregory, Saint, 377
Gregory in Pontus, Saint, 370, 371n3
Grote, George, 6, 52

Hammond, Henry, 189, 210
Hampden, R. D., 59–60, 65, 69, 77, 70, 77, 80–85, 89, 90, 167, 167n5, 173, 180n25, 181n26, 182n27, 186n35, 188n41, 205n55; *Observations on Religious Dissent*, 180n25
happiness, eternal, 136
Harding, Stephen, 300–301, 357
Harrison, Benjamin, 249n57
Hawkins, Edward, 77–80, 82, 85, 138–39, 138n21, 141n28, 167n5; *A Dissertation upon the Use and Importance of Unauthoritative Tradition*, 139n24
Hebdomadal Board, 244n53, 365
Henry VIII, King of England, 199
heresiarchs, 172
heresy, 15, 21, 31, 63, 92, 95, 97, 153n31, 164n50, 172, 221n23, 232, 247n55, 248, 249n57, 250, 255n5, 261, 261n15, 264n22, 284, 331n13, 335, 363, 376n10, 420, 446
Hexham, Diocese of, 441–42
Hey, John, 347, 347n41
high church and high churchmen, 8, 9,

11n13, 16, 17, 17n22, 19, 20, 22, 23, 26, 26n37, 27, 28, 53, 55, 58, 66, 70, 71, 72, 74, 75, 77, 78, 80, 81, 94, 95, 96, 99, 107, 143n31, 154n49, 164n2, 165n3, 168, 170, 170n10, 192, 194n48, 204n, 213, 213n9, 245, 247n55, 252n1, 261n13,15, 264, 276n31, 282n35, 300n52, 300n54, 356, 357, 362, 366, 447
Hilary, Saint, 340
Hinds, Samuel, 77
Hobart Town, Diocese of, 442–43
Holy Catholic and Apostolic Church, 10, 21, 23, 190–191, 191n43
Holy Trinity. *See* Trinity, Holy
Home and Foreign Review,, 42, 48
Homilies, Books of, 200–202, 200n54, 210
Hook, Walter Farquhar, 182n27, 205, 205n55, 213, 262n18
Hooker, Richard, 210, 210n4, 242–243
Hope, James Robert, 27, 104–105, 311, 311n67
Hope-Scott, James Robert. *See* Hope, James Robert
Horace, 366
Howley, William, 191, 191n44
Hume, David, 133, 133n7, 348
Hunt, Leigh, 337
Hurrell Froude, Richard. *See* Froude, Richard Hurrell
Hussey, Robert, 365, 365n8
Hutton, R. H., 12, 44, 54–55, 67n94, 75
Huxley, T. H., 13, 113

idolatry, 177, 223, 224
Ignatius, Saint. *See* Loyola, Ignatius
Immaculate Conception, 44, 49n71, 332–333, 332n14
infallibility of Roman Catholic Church, 42, 44, 325–339
Inge, William Ralph, 20
Inglis, Robert, 164n33, 184
Inquisition, 172
intellectual excellence, 144

invisible church, 12, 82, 174n14
Irenaeus, 156
Irish Temporalities Act, 7, 57, 81, 162n68, 191n44
Irons, William Joseph, 2n1
Irving, Edward, 109n156

Jacobites, 247, 247n56
James, Saint, 203, 450
James, William, 140, 140n26
James II, King of England, 157n53
Jansen, Cornelius, 331n13
Jansenism, 331, 331n13
Jelf, Richard, 206n56, 206n57, 239, 239n46, 275n30
Jerome, Saint, 340
Jerusalem bishopric, 92, 95, 161n63, 222, 246–51, 246n55, 249n57, 254, 254n3, 256, 257–58, 263, 303, 308,
Jesus. *See* Christ, Jesus
Jewel, John, 227, 227n29
John, Saint, 136, 176, 450
Johnson, Manuel, 301, 301n55, 318, 318n71
Johnson, Samuel, 346, 347, 364, 425
Jones, William, 135, 135n13
Judicial Committee of the Privy Council, 29, 55, 56, 58
just cause for lying, 347, 416–418, 421–424
justification: by faith, 13, 61, 199, 212n8; degrees of, 136; Newman on, 183, 192–193
Justin, Saint, 153, 156
Justinian, 377

Kaye, John, 279
Keble, John, 8, 22, 25, 26, 48, 72, 78–79, 81, 83, 93, 97–98, 103, 143n31, 145, 145n38, 147–149, 152, 162, 162n68, 163, 164n2, 166–167, 170n11, 194, 206, 209n3, 213, 215, 215n12, 232n36, 238n43, 243n50, 249n57, 279, 362–364, 369; *Christian Year*, 148, 148n45, 155, 176

Keble, Thomas, 215, 215n12
Ken, Thomas, 263, 263n19
Kenrick, Francis P., 418, 418n5
Kingsley, Charles, vii–viii, 2–3, 27, 32–40, 45n67, 50–51, 53–55, 65, 83, 109, 112, 113, 119n1, 120n3, 121–128, 242n49, 260n12, 328n9, 354–357, 428, 446, 447; *Hypatia,* 35; "What, Then, Does Dr. Newman Mean?", vii, 33–36, 53, 122, 328n9, 354,
Knox, Alexander, 212, 212n8

Lacordaire, Jean-Baptiste, 359–360, 359n2
Lactantius, 156
Langdale, Charles, 438
Latimer, Hugh, 227, 227n29, 309n63
latitudinarianism, 79, 85, 86, 88, 90, 108
Laud, William, 174, 174n15, 189, 296
Law, Newman's preference for preaching over the Gospel, 61, 445
Law, William, *A Serious Call to a Devout and Holy Life,* 136, 136n16
lay communion, 242, 253, 281, 303
Leo I, 230–232, 254, 259, 269, 340
Leo XIII, 1
Lessius, Leonard, 418, 418n3
Levine, George, 4
Lewis, David, 318, 319n71
liberalism, 78, 82, 83, 85, 86, 87, 90, 108, 114n164, 144, 145, 148n44, 153, 158, 157n62, 165, 166, 168, 173, 181, 216, 216n15, 217, 218, 267, 286, 294, 295, 337; discussion of Newman's concept of, 54–76; Note A on, 14, 124, 144n36, 67, 71, 72, 354, 359–369; pre-Tractarian comments on, 59–61; Newman's poem entitled, 60, 369; difficulties encountered in understanding Newman's concept of, 57. 74–75; as related to in Newman's thought: Antichrist, 286; evangelicalism, 59–63, 65, 87; Francis Newman, 87–90; Oxford University, 360–368; private judgment, 62–63, 67–68, 73; rationalism, 68–69, 337, 361–362; R. D. Hampden, 59–60, 81–84; response to Syllabus of Errors and *Quanta Cura,* 71–76. *See also* Erastianism; Liberal Party, Liberals

Liberal (journal), 337, 337n
Liberal Party, 56, 57, 209, 235, 365
Liberals, 45, 53–57, 59, 65, 70, 71, 74, 81, 99, 158, 160, 232, 294, 302, 337, 359, 364, 365
liberty, 74
Library of the Fathers of the Holy Catholic Church, 180, 180n23, 184, 192
life, note of, 255, 258–259, 287
Liguori, Alfonso Maria de, 33, 34, 39–41, 122, 288–289, 346–350, 357n40, 418–421
Littlemore, 25–26, 93, 101–102, 104–106, 132, 132n4, 239, 253n1, 261n14, 271–277, 273n, 275n30, 281, 304, 446
Liverpool, Diocese of, 440–441
Lives of the English Saints. See Newman, John Henry; saints
Lloyd, Charles, 219, 219n20
Lockhardt, William, 26, 48, 276n31, 277–278, 277n32, 301–302
London Oratory, 434
Longman publishing house, 36
Lovejoy, Arthur, 54
low church, 29, 53, 71, 77, 168, 170, 170n10, 192, 361. *See also* Evangelicalism; ultra-Protestantism
Loyola, Ignatius, 153, 174, 175, 217, 217n17, 221, 289, 289n43
Lucas, Edward, 438
Luther, Martin, 192, 217
Lutheran and Lutheranism, 192, 198, 203, 219n21, 231, 247, 247n55, 249n57, 250, 331, 334
Lyall, William Rowe, 80, 153, 154n49
Lyell, Charles, 52
lying, 38–54, 157, 343–352, 358, 379; Note G on, 416–426. *See also* economy, truthfulness

Mabillon, Jean, 373, 373n7
Macaulay, Thomas Babington, 321, 321n2
Macmillan, Alexander, 33, 39–40, 55
Macmillan's Magazine, 32
Malchion, 340, 341n28
Malcom, John, 377–378
Manichæism, 331
Manning, Henry Edward, 3, 19, 20, 29, 43, 45–46, 48, 58n83, 72, 76, 95–97, 306–9, 306n61, 309n62, 357–358, 427; *The Workings of the Holy Spirit in the Church of England*, 358
Marcellinus, 377
Marcus Aurelius, 375n9
Marian devotion, 49n71, 288n41
Marriott, Charles, 261, 261n14, 312, 316, 317
Martin, Saint, 370, 371n3
Martineau, James, 15
Martyrs' Memorial, 309n63
Mary. *See* Virgin Mary
material lie, 422, 423, 425
Matthew, H. C. G., 78
Mawworm (character), 385–386, 386n2
Mayers, Walter, 6, 18, 78, 86, 87, 133–134
McNeill, John, 378
meekness, 255, 383–384, 468, 494, 495
Melanchthon, Philip, 192
Mélanges Théologiques (journal), 418, 418n3, 421
Melbourne, Lord, 83, 84
Meletius, Saint, 255, 255n5
Merrigan, Terrence, 57
Metaphysical Society, 112, 112n162
Methodism and Methodists, 8, 12n16, 15, 63, 212n8, 260n11
Meyrick, Thomas, 372n5
Middleton, Conyers, 144, 144n35, 377
Mill, John Stuart, 15, 52, 53; *On Liberty*, 52–53
Miller, John, 149, 149n, 362
Mills, Henry Austin, 353
Milman, Henry Hart, 147, 148n44, 243; *History of Christianity to the Abolition of Paganism in the Roman Empire*, 243n51
Milner, Joseph, 136, 136n17, 151–152, 158
Milton, John, 346–47, 350, 418, 423
miracles, 78, 133, 151, 287, 300, 324, 472; argument from analogy and, 151–152; ecclesiastical, 124, 144, 150, 150n48, 151, 152, 355–356; Note B on ecclesiastical, 354, 370–378; general principles regarding, 371–72; Newman and, 27, 34, 144, 355–356, 370n2; popular concept of, 376; Protestants versus Catholics on, 44, 354–355; providence versus, 371; reason and, 324; science and, 374; scripture, 144; St. Walburga and medicinal oil, 372–374
mission work, 435
Moberly, George, 261, 261n13, 262
Moij de Sons, Ernest, 442
monasticism, 15, 21, 25, 27, 35, 47, 81, 101, 105–106, 108, 132n4, 226, 228, 231, 239, 268, 272–275, 273n19, 275n30, 276n31, 282n35, 300n52, 307, 357. *See also* asceticism; celibacy
Monophysites, 21–22, 25, 29, 92–97, 225–228, 225, 225n27, 229n34, 231–232, 236, 245, 247, 247n56, 248, 265, 266, 307
Monsell, William, 72
Montalembert, Charles Forbes René, Comte de, 359–360, 359n2
More, Thomas, 321
Morris, John B., 236n42
Mozley, James, 365
Mozley, J. B., 95, 97
Mozley, Thomas, 14, 26, 28, 48, 183n29
muscular Christianity, 113, 383
mysteries of the faith, 148, 155

natural theology, 56, 150, 323n5
Nazianzen, Gregory, 156, 182, 182n28
Neri, Philip, 177, 177n19, 351

Nestorians, 225n, 247
Neville, William Paine, 353
Newman, Charles, 63n88, 86–87
Newman, Francis, 63n88, 86–91, 98, 104, 109–113, 131n3, 158n55, 162n67, 263n20, 446; *Phases of Faith*, 110–112
Newman, Jemima, 36, 84, 87, 94, 187n38
Newman, John (father), 6, 77, 86
Newman, John Henry Cardinal: academic work of, 30, 434; and Anglican tradition, 18, 26; and asceticism, 25, 98, 105–106, 253n1; on biblical interpretation, 66–67, 88–89; biographical study of, 2–5; birth of, 6; burial of, 353n44; Catholicism of, 15–17, 23–27, 47–48, 81, 95–96, 104, 158, 209n3, 238–39, 283, 283n, 291–292, 447; and celibacy, 86, 105–106, 137; childhood of, 131–133; and Church Fathers, 14, 18, 79, 105, 136, 136n17, 144, 153–154, 174, 179–180; on Church of England, 32n47, 47, 55–56, 179, 209–210, 216, 216n14, 300n54, 307, 357–358, 408–411; clothing of, 108, 108n154; and concealment, 46–53; evangelical conversion as youth of, 6, 86, 133–137 (*see also* Roman Catholic conversion of); and conversion of others, 235, 246, 276n31, 304–306; departure of, from Church of England, 21, 25–26, 91–104, 226–265, 302–319; and devotional freedom, 42–43; and dogma, 114, 114n, 133, 173–174; evangelical influences on, 18, 77, 86; evangelicalism criticized by, viii, 7, 13–15, 59–63, 63n88, 65, 68–69, 87–88, 158, 158n55, 179n21, 187n38, 210n5, 216–217, 260n11, 261n15, 445–446; family of, 6, 77, 84, 85–91; friendships of, 78–79, 101–102, 104, 145–147, 267; illnesses of, 76, 81, 87, 144, 144n36, 161–162, 161n66, 169n7; income of, 26, 47, 77, 78, 79, 84, 86, 281n; influence of, 181–182, 305 (see also *Apologia Pro Vita Sua* [Newman]); and Kingsley dispute, 32–38, 50–51, 53–55, 112, 120n3, 121–128; and lay communion, 253, 281, 303; letters of, to Catholic acquaintances, 283–287; letters of approbation for, 43, 433–443; and liberalism, 44–46, 48, 54–76, 87, 144, 160, 173, 216, 266n, 294–295, 337, 359–369; and Littlemore, 25–26, 93, 101–102, 104–106, 132, 132n4, 239, 253n1, 261n14, 271–277, 273n, 275n30, 281, 304, 446; Mediterranean tour of, 80–81, 159–62, 177; minority positions of, 44, 46, 47, 446; and miracles, 27, 34, 144, 355–356, 370n2; and monasticism, 21, 27, 47, 105–106, 272–275, 273n, 275n30, 276n; and Oriel fellowship, 76–85, 137n19, 141n, 146, 281n; and proposed Oxford Roman Catholic house, 43, 49n, 55, 74, 105; and prophetical tradition, 17, 30, 137n18; Protestantism criticized by, 29, 179n21, 187n38, 189, 231; reputation of, 1–2, 31, 35–37, 120, 123, 125–128, 445; resignation from St. Mary's, 26, 239–243, 253–254, 275–276, 278, 292, 297–302, 307, 356; retractions of anti-Roman statements made by, 292–297, 292n, 304; as Roman Catholic, 1, 28–32, 37, 90–91, 320–322, 326; Roman Catholic Church attractive to, 20–21, 132–133, 177–178, 267; Roman Catholic Church criticized by, 15–17, 176–179, 178n21, 232–236, 232n, 256, 297n; Roman Catholic conversion of, 28–29, 92–93, 101–104, 120, 259, 287–288, 292, 302, 313–321; and science, 374n; self-defense of, as Englishman, 44, 63, 106–7, 127n; sermons of, vii–viii, 6–7, 445; on state of the world, 322–323, 323n5, 327; superstition of, 132; and Tractarian Movement, 8–15, 22–29,

55–56, 163–207, 253; and tradition, 139–140, 139n24; and truthfulness, 39–43, 121–25, 128, 267–270, 343–44, 356, 379, 385–387; as tutor, 6, 78, 80, 84–85, 85, 141n; ultramontanes and, 45–46, 45n, 49n, 105, 107, 266n, 288n41, 320, 358, 427–428; and via media, 14, 18–20, 101, 186n37, 189–190, 216, 254, 260, 268–269, 295; and Victorian religious world, 106–115

Newman, John Henry Cardinal, works by: *Advent Sermons on Antichrist (Tract 83),* 65, 176n17; *Against Romanism,* 19; *Apologia Pro Vita Sua* (see separate entry); *The Arians of the Fourth Century,* 80, 143n31, 154, 154n49, 344n33, 412; Bilietto speech, 63; *Callista,* 35; "The Catholicity of the English Church," 224, 224n26, 237, 255, 255n4, 307; *Certain Difficulties Felt by Anglicans in Catholic Teaching Considered,* 29, 34, 55–56, 58; *The Church of the Fathers,* 14, 105, 193; "Elijah the Prophet of the Latter Days," 257n7; *Elucidations of Dr. Hampden's Theological Statements,* 83, 182n27; *An Essay on Ecclesiastical Miracles,* 150–151, 150n, 355, 370, 375; *An Essay on the Development of Christian Doctrine,* 28, 66, 92–93, 150, 198, 198n53, 282, 282n, 289, 290n, 313, 317, 325n; "Grounds for Steadfastness in Our Religious Profession," 257n7; *History of My Religious Opinions,* 36, see *Apologia Pro Vita Sua,* "Home Thoughts Abroad," 221–25; *The Idea of a University,* 30; *On the Introduction of Rationalistic Principles into Religion (Tract 73),* 68; "Invisible Presence of Christ," 257n7; *Lectures on Justification,* 13, 192-193; *Lectures on the Present Position of Catholics in England,* 29–30, 34; *Lectures on the Prophetical Office of the Church, Viewed Relatively to Romanism and Popular Protestantism,* 13, 18–19; *Lectures on the Scripture Proof of the Doctrines of the Church (Tract 85),* 13, 66, 113, 325n; *Letter Addressed to the Rev. E. B. Pusey,* 44, 45; *Letter to the Duke of Norfolk,* 75; list of, in *Apologia,* 431–432; *The Lives of the English Saints,* 27, 34, 193–194, 260n12, 299–301, 300n52, 356–357, 370, 389–407; *Loss and Gain,* 106n; *Lyra Apostolica,* 60, 159, 159n59, 161, 172, 230, 368–369; *Mr. Kingsley and Dr. Newman: A Correspondence on the Question Whether Dr. Newman Teaches That Truth Is No Virtue,* vii, 33; "Obedience to God the Way to Faith in Christ," 61, 448–456; "On Consulting the Faithful in Matters of Doctrine," 30, 31, 320; "On Divine Calls," 229; "Outward and Inward Notes of the Church," 257n7; *Parochial and Plain Sermons,* 445; "The Parting of Friends," viii, 26, 356, 446, 487–496; "Private Judgement," 224, 224n26 *The Prophetical Office of the Church,* 16, 62, 186–190, 186n37, 187n38, 225, 230; "Religious Emotion," 457–463; "The Religious Use of Excited Feelings," 464–70; *Remarks on Certain Passages in the Thirty-Nine Articles (see Tract 90); Sermons, Bearing on Subjects of the Day,* 257–258, 257n7, 356, 381; *Sermons, Chiefly on the Theory of Religious Belief,* 64n; "State of Religious Parties," 210–218; "Sudden Conversions," 471–477; Tract 7, 62, 62n, 70; Tract 8, 149–150; Tract 10, 10, 171n11; Tract 11, 174; Tract 15, 10, 171, 171n12; Tract 73, 68; Tract 83, 65, 176n17; Tract 85, 13, 66, 113, 325n; Tract 90, 19, 23–25, 23n, 27, 47–49, 52–54, 69–71, 76, 85, 92, 95–97, 99–101, 164n, 188,

Newman, works by: (*continued*)
  196–206, 198n53, 200n, 206n56,
  206n57, 210n3, 233, 238–239, 243,
  245n, 246, 257, 260, 264n, 265, 266n,
  268, 270–271, 294, 297–298, 306,
  365, 365n7, 385–386; *Translation of
  the Treatises of St. Athanasius*, 194;
  University Sermons, 150; *The Via
  Media of the Anglican Church,*, 19;
  "Wisdom and Innocence," vii–viii, 33,
  49–51, 379–388, 446, 478–486
Newman, Mary, 78, 87, 144n36
Newmania, 20, 105
New Test, 365, 365n7
Newton, Thomas, 136, 136n18
Nicene Creed, 144, 144n34
Nockles, Peter, 71
Noetics, 77–78, 167n5
Nonjurors, 157n53, 228
North British Review (journal), 71
Notes of the Church, 231, 237, 255–256, 287, 343, 383

Oakeley, Frederick, 2n2, 27–28, 99–101, 105, 124, 213, 213n11, 266, 266n24, 275n30
Oakeley decision in Court of Arches, 99–102, 104
obedience: Christ and, 450–451; consequences of, 453–456, 485; difficulties in, 465–468; early Church and, 451–52; necessity of, 449–450, 455, 470; Newman on, 6–7, 135n15, 448–456; to political authorities, 50, 482–483.
O'Connell, Daniel, 57, 233, 233n38, 235, 241
œquivocatio, 422
O'Faolain, Sean, 5
Ogle, James Adey, 318, 319n71
Oratory of St. Philip Neri, 28–29, 352-353, 434
Oriel College and fellowship, 6, 18, 26, 76–87, 90, 137n19, 270; influence of personalities on Newman, 137–149, 146, 167, 270, 281n34

Oriel College Tutorial Reform, 79–80, 141n28, 84, 85, 167n5a
Origen, 140, 154, 156, 335, 340
original sin, 144, 100, 324, 328; Virgin Mary conceived without, 332, 332n14; of Roman Catholicism 332
Osberga, Saint, 389
Oxford Convocation, 28, 28n40, 53, 71, 83, 94n132, 99, 144, 167n5, 180n25, 182n27, 186, 205, 260n12, 362, 365
Oxford election of 1829, 79, 144–145, 144n37, 164n33
Oxford Heads of Houses, 24, 70, 71, 82, 85, 99, 145n37, 240, 244, 244n53, 272, 310n64, 365
Oxford Movement. *See* Tractarian Movement
Oxford University, and liberalism, 360–368. *See also* Oxford Convocation; Oxford Heads of Houses

Paine, Thomas, 133, 133n6
Paley, William, 347–348, 350,
Palmer, Roundell, 182n27
Palmer, William (Magdalen), 164, 164n, 234
Palmer, William (Worcester), 26n37, 81, 95, 163, 164n2, 165n3, 166–167, 187, 205, 213, 261, 263, 356; *A Narrative of Events Connected with the Publication of the Tracts for the Times*, 26, 164n2
papacy: as Antichrist, 136, 137n18, 176, 178, 178n20; authority of, 31, 44, 342, 342n19; decisions made by, 333–334; infallibility of, 329n12; sympathy for, 27, 177. *See also* ultramontanes
Pascal, Blaise, 235, 235n41
Patterson, James Laird, 438
Pattison, Mark, 318, 319n71
Paul, Saint, 136, 173, 178, 203–204, 331, 372, 382, 413, 450, 453, 454, 471–472, 475–477, 484
Pearson, John, 210, 210n4

Peel, Robert, 57, 79, 102–103, 144–145, 144n37, 164n33, 219n20
Pelagianism, 331
Pelagius, 342
Perceval, Arthur, 9n, 164, 164n2, 165n3, 166–67, 205, 213
Perrone, Giovanni, 187, 187n40
perseverance, 134, 136
Petavius, Dionysius, 226, 226n28
Peter, Saint, 450, 457–459, 463
Petre, Lord, 438
Philip, Saint. *See* Neri, Philip
Pitt, Valerie, 98
Pius IV, 197, 197n51, 202. *See also* Creed of Pope Pius IV
Pius IX, 42, 45, 71–76, 332, 343, 343n30
Platt, Ralph, 442
play upon words, 346, 417, 422, 424
Plymouth Brethren, 87–88, 109, 162n67
Pope. *See* papacy
Pope, Simeon Lloyd, 59, 87
Popery, 27, 127, 178–179, 186, 189, 198, 199, 217, 219, 232, 263n18
popular Protestantism, 14, 19, 62, 63, 65, 190, 219n21. *See also* Evangelicalism; ultra-Protestantism
Porter, Jane and Anna Maria, 133, 133n5
Powell, Baden, 77
Prayer Book, 23, 143, 174, 175, 191, 204n, 219n20, 372
predestination, 134
priests, devotion of, 344–346
Primitive Church and Christians, 136, 153, 169, 188, 200, 201, 215, 220, 221, 223, 231, 241, 291, 298, 389n2. *See also* Antiquity
private judgment, 25, 42, 62–63, 67–70, 73, 89n124, 109, 113, 151, 209n3, 219, 225, 242, 283, 284, 296, 330–331, 336, 339, 367, 424
probability, 140n27, 141, 149–151, 200, 291–292, 291n46, 303, 420,
Procopius, 377

Prophecy, 23, 68, 128, 137n18, 158n55, 176n17, 213,
prophetical tradition, 17, 30
Protestantism, 1, 13, 14, 16n21, 19, 20, 21, 29, 31, 47, 51, 53, 62, 63, 64, 64n90, 65, 70, 81, 90, 98, 110, 112, 126, 176n17, 179n21,n22, 186, 187n38, 189, 190, 200, 208, 209, 216n15, 217, 218n19, 219, 219n21, 230, 231, 247, 284, 294, 298n40, 306n61. *See also* Evangelicalism, low church, popular Protestantism, ultra-Protestantism
Protestant Reformation. *See* Reformation
Protestants, 13, 14, 20, 35, 37, 38, 39, 40, 41n63, 55, 60, 62, 66, 70, 72, 106, 150n48, 152, 176n17, 188, 197, 203, 225, 226, 227, 235, 247n55, 249, 284, 286, 321, 332, 350, 354, 355, 370, 383, 419, 437
Providence, 4, 5, 13, 23, 84, 212, 216, 230, 261, 263, 271, 274, 283, 330, 371, 375, 376, 410, 413, 443, 446, 466, 486
providences, 230, 263, 371, 375
Prussia, 95, 161n63, 247–249, 247n55
punishment, eternal or future, 136, 190, 328, 329, 361
purgatory, 197, 199, 219, 233
Pusey, E. B., 8, 8n10, 24, 24n32, 44, 45, 45n67, 49n71, 78, 83, 93, 95, 97, 146, 146n41, 176n17, 180n23, 183–185, 184n32, 192, 206n57, 213, 225, 271, 271n26, 279, 280, 298, 299, 309–311, 309n62, 310n64, 310n65, 318, 386
Pusey, E. B., wife of, 10
Puseyite Movement (Puseyism), 8n10, 146n41, 173, 240. *See also* Tractarian Movement

Quanta Cura (Pius IX), 71–73, 76

Radcliffe, Ann, 133, 133n5
Rambler (journal), 30, 31n45, 39, 42, 44, 48, 320n1

Ramsey, Michael, 18
rationalism, 15, 60, 65, 68–69, 217, 243, 243n50. *See also* Reason
Real Presence, 153, 193
Reason, reasoning, reasoners, 41, 42, 62, 64, 64n90, 68, 73, 82, 88, 114, 122, 127, 137, 141, 142, 177, 178, 184, 188, 193, 226, 230, 231, 238, 259, 284, 291, 292, 306, 314, 315, 323, 324, 330, 331, 332, 335, 337, 339, 340, 341, 353, 361, 362, 363, 366, 367, 381, 384, 408, 415, 429, 464, 466, 485. *See also* rationalism; Unbelief
Record (newspaper), 15, 168, 168n
Reform Act, 20, 191n44
Reformation, 21, 22, 24, 47, 58, 62, 62n87, 125, 153, 158, 171n12, 178n20, 194n48, 196n50, 199, 211, 227n29, 286, 309n63, 331n13
regeneration, 9, 10, 10n12, 12, 68, 87, 89, 107, 138n22, 146n41, 183, 476. *See also* Baptism; Baptismal Regeneration
René, Charles Forbes, Comte de Montalembert, 359–360, 359n2
repentance, 34, 266, 316, 413, 414, 452–455, 460, 465–467, 477, 488
reserve, principle of, 22, 215n12, 343, 343n31, 387 413, 415. See also *Disciplina Arcani*; economy
revelation, 65, 66, 73, 78, 140, 150, 291, 301n46, 320, 321, 326, 328, 332, 336, 361, 375, 449, 486
Richard, Saint, 301
Ridley, Nicholas, 227, 227n29, 309n63
Rivington publishing firm, 26, 356
Rogers, Frederic (Lord Blachford), 75, 76, 94, 241–242, 242n, 265, 365
Romaine, William, 134, 134n10
Roman Catholicism, 1, 11, 14, 15, 16, 19, 26, 29, 30, 35, 43, 45, 46, 54, 72, 73, 76, 93, 94, 96, 106, 110, 113, 136, 149, 154, 156, 186, 186n36, 194, 212, 213, 214, 233, 234, 242n49, 253n1, 275n23, 288, 291, 291n45, 297n51, 310n64, 311n67, 322, 356, 385, 428, 437
Romanism, Romanish 10, 16, 16n21, 23, 27, 28n40, 187, 190, 222, 236n42, 241–243, 276, 293, 297n51, 310n64
Rose, Hugh James, 80, 81, 153, 153n, 164–166, 164n, 165n3, 193
Ruskin, John, 38
Russell, Charles, 104, 287–289, 287n39
Ryder, Henry, 158, 158n54, 353

sacramental clericalism, 9–12, 9n11
sacramental confession, 379, 380, 381, 485
sacramental principle, system, 148, 154–155, 190, 231
sacraments. *See individual sacraments*
sacrifice (relating to eucharist), 170, 170n11, 262,
saints: *The Lives of the English Saints*, 27, 34, 102, 124, 183, 193–194, 260n12, 299–301, 300n52, 319n71, 355–357, 370n1, 372n5, 379n2, 389–407; calendar of English, 391–396; Blessed Virgin and, 177, 223, 233, 253, 269, 281
Salford, Diocese of, 440–441
Salmeron, Alphonsus, 341, 341n28
salvation, 7, 9, 73, 82, 87, 134, 134n9, 145n15m, 190, 289, 313, 366, 387, 453, 461, 467
Samaria, 257n6
sanctification, 43, 61, 343, 445
sanctity, note of, 255–256
Santini, Abbate, 159
Satan, 156
Saturday Review, 31, 74, 108–109
Scavini, Petro, 347–348, 347n40
Schism, schismatic, 12n16, 21, 25, 59, 79, 81, 90, 96, 102, 104, 107, 114, 196n49, 216, 223n25, 226n27, 228, 242, 248, 255, 258, 263, 298, 313, 342, 377; Note of, 224

Scott, Thomas, 134–135, 134n11, 158
Scott, Walter, 212, 302, 419
Scottish Episcopal Church, 263n20
scripture. *See* Bible
Second Reformation, 23, 158, 169, 169n8
Second Vatican Council, 113
sectarianism and sectarian, 13, 89, 90, 91. *See also* Schism, schismatic
secular lay culture, 64, 64n90
Shaftsbury, Lord, 95
Shelley, Percy Bysshe, 337
Smethwick mission, 435
Smiles, Samuel, 38
Smith, Robertson, 52
Socinianism, Socinian, Socinianizing, 8, 60, 69, 82–83, 85, 88, 134n11, 143n31, 181n26, 262, 262n18, 263, 263n18
sola scriptura, 13
Southey, Robert, 212; *Thalaba the Destroyer*, 161, 161n65
Sozzini, Fausto, 262n18
Sozzini, Lelio, 262n18
Spectator (journal), 54, 108
Spencer, George, 233–235, 234n39
Stanley, Arthur, 53, 67, 71
Stephen, Fitzjames, 74–75
Stillingfleet, Edward, 174, 174n15, 227, 227n30
St. John, Ambrose, 101–102, 353, 353n44, 435
St. Mary the Virgin Church, Oxford, 6, 26, 78, 80, 88, 239–243, 254, 261n14, 275–276, 278, 292, 297–302, 307, 356
Strachey, Lytton, 3
Strauss, David Friedrich, 66, 109
Subscription to the Thirty-Nine Articles, 25, 53, 54, 54n77, 81, 82, 99, 100, 105, 197, 197n50, 201, 281, 365n7, 367. *See also* New Test; *Tract 90*
Sulpicius, 156
Sumner, Charles, 138n22

Sumner, John Bird, 138, 138n22, 245n54, 264n22
superstition, superstitious, 132, 150, 196n49, 322, 340, 355, 367
supremacy of scripture, 296
Supremacy of the Holy See, 199, 280, 290
Syllabus of Errors (Pius IX), 71–73, 76
Symons, Benjamin, 103, 366, 366n9

Tablet (journal), 70
Talbot, George, 43, 45
Taylor, Jeremy, 227, 227n30, 242, 295, 346, 350
Tertullian, 156, 340
theism, 291
Theophilus, bishop of Alexandria, 335, 335n19
Thirlwall, Connop, 67
Thirty-Nine Articles, 23–28, 31, 53–54, 69–71, 81, 82, 87, 89, 98–100, 134n9, 191, 196–203, 196n50, 204n, 205, 210, 210n3, 237–239, 239n46, 244, 253, 266n14, 281, 284, 286, 299, 307, 347, 347n41, 365n7, 366. *See also* Subscription to the Thirty-Nine Articles; *Tract 90*
Thomas, Saint. *See* Aquinas, Thomas
Thomas the Martyr, 191n44
Thorndike, Herbert, 210, 210n4
Thornton, Henry, 38
Thundering Legion, 375, 375n9
toleration, 59, 89
tongue, miracle concerning, 377–378
Toovey, James, 300n54, 356
Torres Vedras, 25, 253, 253n2
Toryism, 153, 360, 362, 363, 364. *See also* Conservative Party
Tractarian Movement: *Apologia* as furnishing inadequate account of, 2–3; origins and position among parties in Church of England, 7–9; sacramental clericalism of, 9–13; later radicalism of 22–28; collapse of, 98–102; see also *Tracts for the Times* and individual tracts

Tracts for the Times, 5, 8, 10n12, 11, 15, 25, 81, 87, 105, 149, 167, 168n6, 174, 185, 195–196, 214, 215, 239n46, 244–246, 276, 343, 412n2, 445. *See also individual tracts by number*
Tract 4, 170n11
Tract 10, 10, 171n11
Tract 11, 174
Tract 15, 11, 171, 171n12
Tract 35, 9n11
Tract 41, 13, 158n58
Tract 71, 62, 70 186, 192
Tract 73, 68
Tract 80, 215n12, 343n31
Tract 81, 149–150
Tract 83, 65, 176n17
Tract 85, 13, 66, 113, 325n6
Tract 87, 215n12, 343n31
Tract 90, 19, 23–25, 23n, 27, 47–49, 52–54, 69–71, 76, 85, 92, 95–97, 99–101, 164n, 188, 196–206, 198n53, 200n, 206n56, 206n57, 210n3, 233, 238–239, 243, 245n54, 246, 257, 260, 264n22, 265, 266n24, 268, 270–271, 294, 297–298, 306, 365, 365n7, 385–386
Tradition Unauthoritative, 139–140, 139n24
Transubstantiation, 210, 243, 261, 286, 321
Trappes, M., 440
Tridentine Council, 199, 333. *See also* Council of Trent
Trinity, Holy, 135, 143–144, 144n34, 190, 233, 322, 344, 414, 423
Trinity College Oxford, 6, 86, 318-319
truthfulness: evangelicalism and, 38; judicial proceedings and, 38–39; Newman and, 39–43, 121–125, 128, 267–270, 343–344, 356, 379, 385–387; Roman Catholicism and, 39–43, 344–353; Victorian concern with, 38–39. *See also* lying; equivocation
two-bottle orthodoxy, 71, 144

Ullathorne, William Bernard, 43, 48, 49n71, 288n41, 345, 345n36, 428, 433–435
ultramontanes, 31, 42–46, 45n, 49n71, 52, 72, 90, 105, 107, 266n24, 288n41, 320, 342n19, 358, 427–28. *See also* Manning, Henry Edward; Ward, William George
ultra-Protestantism, ultra-Protestants, 13, 15, 53, 70, 88, 96, 169n8, 219, 219n21. *See also* popular Protestantism; Evangelicalism
Unbelief, 106, 324, 358, 477
Unitarianism, 12n16, 82, 135, 139n23, 262n18
Urban VIII, 420
Ussher, James, 227, 227n30, 295

Vandenbroeck, M., 420, 420n6
Vaughn, Herbert, 43, 45
Venn, Henry, 38
Véron, François, 288, 288n40
via media, 14, 18–21, 101, 186n37, 189–190, 197, 199, 211, 216, 217, 218, 220, 223, 225, 226, 229–230, 245, 254, 260, 266, 268–269, 295
Victor, Bishop of Vito, 377
Victoria, Queen of England, 164n2
Vincentius of Lerins, 221, 221n23, 290
Virgilius, 335, 335n20
Virgin Mary, 49n, 153, 177, 233, 253, 267, 281, 288–289, 332, 332n14
visible Church, 13, 140, 151, 174, 174n14, 176, 410
Viva, Dominco, 420, 420n7
Voit, Edmund, 418, 418n4
Voltaire, 133, 133n8
Von Wallenburgh, Adrian and Peter, 288, 288n40

Walburga, Saint, 355, 370, 372–74, 372n5
Walker, John, 74
Wallace, Alfred, 33
Walrond, Theodore, 69, 71

Ward, William George, 27–28, 30, 43, 45, 45n67, 48–49, 57, 72, 76, 76n107, 98, 99, 101–102, 105–106, 205n55, 213n11, 266n24, 271n26, 283n36, 310n65, 427; *The Ideal of a Christian Church*, 28, 98–99. *See also Dublin Review*; ultramontanes

Watson, Joshua, 53

Watts, Isaac, 132, 132n2

Wellington, Duke, 57, 145, 219n20

Westminster, Diocese of, 437

Westminster Review, 71

Whately, Richard, 21n14, 69, 70n99, 77, 78, 82, 85, 99, 124, 137, 137n20, 138, 140, 141–147, 142n30, 167, 174; *Letters on the Church by an Episcopalian*, 142–143, 142n30, 214

Whigs, 56, 57, 81, 83, 157, 164, 169, 180n25, 188, 188n, 263n21, 364

White, Joseph Blanco, 77, 139, 139n23, 141, 173

Wilberforce, Henry, 82–85, 94, 96–98, 101, 265, 265n23, 275n30, 277, 310n66

Wilberforce, Robert, 79, 94, 95, 141n28, 147, 147n42, 265, 369

Wilberforce, Samuel, 61, 182n27

Wilberforce, William, 66

Wilkes (editor), 259

William III, King of England, 157n53

William IV, King of England, 164n2

Williams, Isaac, 215, 215n12, 369; *On Reserve in Communicating Religious Knowledge*, 22, 215n12, 245n54, 343n31

Wilson, Daniel, 134, 135n12

Wilson, Thomas, 189

Wiseman, Nicholas, 21, 30, 31, 92–93, 103–104, 159–161, 159n60, 175, 186, 186n36, 227, 278, 318, 343n30

Wood, Samuel Francis, 156, 156n51, 260

Woodgate, H. A., 96

Wordsworth, William, 212

Ximenes de Cisneros, Francisco, 235, 235n41

Zosimus, 342, 342n29

www.ingramcontent.com/pod-product-compliance
Lightning Source LLC
Chambersburg PA
CBHW021229300426
44111CB00007B/485